Teaching Representations
of the Spanish Civil War

Modern Language Association of America
Options for Teaching
Joseph Gibaldi, Series Editor

For a complete listing of titles,
see the last pages of this book.

Teaching Representations of the Spanish Civil War

Edited by
Noël Valis

The Modern Language Association of America
New York 2007

For information about obtaining permission to reprint material from MLA
book publications, send your request by mail (see address below), e-mail
(permissions@mla.org), or fax (646 458-0030).

CREDITS

Demonic Roland. By David Salle. 1987. Acrylic and oil on canvas, 94 × 136
 inches. The Eli and Ethyl L. Broad Collection, Los Angeles. © David Salle /
 VAGA, New York / DACS, London 2005.
Franco at the moment of his consecration before the Christ of Lepanto, 20 May
 1939. Daniel Sueiro and Bernardo Díaz Nosty, *Historia del franquismo.*
 Madrid: Ediciones Sedmay, 1997. Vol. 1, p. 18.
Propaganda. Photograph by Hans Namuth. 1936. Posthumous reproduction
 from original negative. © 1991 Hans Namuth Estate.
Ejército victorioso. Franco, Caudillo del Ejército, Caudillo de España.
 (Victorious Army: Franco, Caudillo of the Army, Caudillo of Spain.)
 Photograph by Pascual Marín. Ministerio de Educación, Cultura y Deporte,
 Archivo General de la Administración, Spain.
"How to Look at the Picasso *Guernica* Mural." By Ad Reinhardt. *PM* 5 Jan.
 1947: 6. © Estate of Ad Reinhardt / Artists Rights Society (ARS) New York.
 © Estate of Pablo Picasso / Artists Rights Society (ARS) New York.
View of exterior of Spanish Pavilion, 1937 Exposition Internationale des
 Arts et Techniques dans la Vie Moderne, Paris. Photograph by François
 Kollar. © Ministère de la Culture, France.

LIBRARY OF CONGRESS CATALOGING-IN-PUBLICATION DATA

Teaching representations of the Spanish Civil War / edited by Noël Valis.
    p. cm.
  Includes bibliographical references and index.
  ISBN-13: 978-0-87352-823-8 (hardcover : alk. paper)
  ISBN-13: 978-0-87352-824-5 (pbk. : alk. paper)
  1. Spain—History—Civil War, 1936-1939—Study and teaching
(Secondary—United States.   I. Valis, Noël Maureen, 1945–
DP269.A555T43 2006
946.081'071273—dc22
ISSN 1079-2562   2006030537

Cover illustration of the paperback edition: Manuel Monleón,
C.N.T. Comité Nacional A.I.T., Oficina de Información y Propaganda, 1936.
Poster from the Southworth Spanish Civil War Collection, Mandeville Special
Collections Library, University of California, San Diego.

Published by The Modern Language Association of America
26 Broadway, New York, NY 10004–1789   www.mla.org

Contents

Acknowledgments

For their help and suggestions, my thanks go to Cal Walker, Eva Teba Fernández, Andrés Fuentes, Carolyn Richmond, Antonio Cazorla-Sánchez, William Hinrichs, Stephanie Sieburth, Jeffry Larson, Wayne Valis, Roberto González Echevarría, Dorota Heneghan, Isabel Jaén-Portillo, Regina Sloan, María Crocetti, and Eleonora Crocetti. I am grateful to Curtis Wasson for his expert technical assistance in pulling this project together and to the staff of the MLA, especially Sonia Kane, Joseph Gibaldi, Michael Kandel, and Sara Pastel for their support, advice, and expert editing. My deepest appreciation goes to all the contributors of this volume, for their patience, good humor, and unflagging enthusiasm during the preparation of this project.

Spain and the Spanish Civil War:
Timeline of Events

1873–74	First Spanish Republic.
1875	Restoration of monarchy under Alfonso XII.
1879	Spanish Socialist Party founded.
1882	UGT (Unión General de Trabajadores), Socialist trade union, founded.
1898	Spanish-American War. Loss of Cuba, Puerto Rico, Guam, and Philippines.
1902–31	Constitutional monarchy of Alfonso XIII.
1909 (26 July)	Barcelona Tragic Week of antimilitarist, anticlerical violence and government repression.
1910	CNT (Confederación Nacional del Trabajo), anarcho-syndicalist trade union, founded.
1914	Spain declares neutrality in WWI.
1917	Russian Revolution.
1917–23	Social unrest, anarchist terrorism, and government repression in Barcelona and Andalusia.
1921	Moroccan War. Slaughter of Spanish troops at Annual.
1922	Mussolini's March on Rome. Fascists take power in Italy.
1923–30	Dictatorship of General Miguel Primo de Rivera.
1926	General strike in Great Britain. Stalin takes over in USSR.
1929 (Oct.)	Wall Street crashes. Great Depression begins.
1930	Nazis emerge as a major party in Germany.
1931 (14 Apr.)	The Second Spanish Republic is proclaimed. Alfonso XIII goes into exile.
1931 (May)	Church burnings.
1932	Nazis emerge as largest party in Germany but without a majority.
1932 (Jan.)	Anarchist uprisings.
1932 (Sept.)	Catalan Statute of self-government and agrarian reform legislation.
1933	Hitler becomes chancellor in Germany.

1933 (Jan.)	Anarchist revolts in Barcelona. Massacre of anarchists in Casas Viejas.
1933 (Mar.)	Religious reform bill passed. Engelbert Dollfuss becomes dictator in Austria.
1933 (29 Oct.)	José Antonio Primo de Rivera founds the Falange Española.
1933 (Nov.)	Center-right coalition wins Spanish elections.
1934 (11 Feb.)	Falange merges with the Juntas de Ofensiva Nacional-Sindicalista.
1934 (Mar.)	General strike.
1934 (July)	Dollfuss murdered in Austria.
1934 (6 Oct.)	Uprisings in Asturias and Madrid and declaration of Catalan independence. Army intervenes, with severe repression.
1936 (16 Feb.)	Popular Front wins elections.
1936 (Feb.–July)	Street violence increases. Strikes.
1936 (Mar.)	José Antonio Primo de Rivera arrested. Falange banned. Church burnings. Land seizures in the south.
1936 (12–13 July)	Leftist José Castillo assassinated. Rightist José Calvo Sotelo assassinated in revenge.
1936 (17–18 July)	Military uprising by Franco's forces. Spanish Civil War begins.
1936 (July)	Siege of the Alcázar in Toledo.
1936 (July–Aug.)	Massive anticlerical killings.
1936 (8 Aug.)	France closes its border with Spain.
1936 (12 Aug.)	First International Brigade volunteers arrive.
1936 (14 Aug.)	Nationalist capture of Badajoz and massacre of Republicans.
1936 (19 Aug.)	Murder of the poet Federico García Lorca by Nationalists.
1936 (28 Aug.)	First aerial bombardment of Madrid.
1936 (Sept.)	Stalin purge trials begin. Robert Capa takes *Falling Militiaman* photograph. Non-intervention Committee established in London.
1936 (7 Oct.)	Basque government of Euzkadi formed.
1936 (6 Nov.)	Republican government leaves Madrid for Valencia.
1936 (20 Nov.)	José Antonio Primo de Rivera executed.
1936 (23 Nov.)	Battle for Madrid ends in stalemate, which continues for next two years.

1937	Joris Ivens: *The Spanish Earth* (film). André Malraux: *L'espoir* (novel). Franz Borkenau: *The Spanish Cockpit* (memoir). Miguel Hernández: *Viento del pueblo* (poetry). Bertolt Brecht: *Die Gewehre der Frau Carrar* (drama). Pablo Neruda: *España en el corazón* (poetry). *Poetas en la España leal.*
1937 (Feb.)	Battle of Jarama.
1937 (26 Apr.)	German Condor Legion destroys Basque market town of Guernica.
1937 (May)	Street battles pitting Communists and Catalan separatists against anarchists and the POUM (Partido Obrero de Unificación Marxista) in Barcelona.
1937 (May–June)	Picasso completes *Guernica*, exhibited at Spanish Pavilion in the Paris World's Fair.
1937 (July–Aug.)	Battles of Brunete and Belchite. Failed Republican offensive. Second International Congress of Anti-fascist Writers convenes in Valencia.
1937 (15 Dec.)	Republican offensive at Teruel, Aragón.
1938	Agustín de Foxá: *Madrid de corte a checa* (novel). George Orwell: *Homage to Catalonia* (memoir). Robert Capa and Gerda Taro: *Death in the Making* (photography). José María Pemán: *Poema de la bestia y el ángel* (poetry).
1938 (22 Feb.)	Nationalists recapture Teruel.
1938 (10 Mar.)	Hitler invades Austria.
1938 (14 Apr.)	Nationalists reach Mediterranean, splitting the Republican zone in two.
1938 (25 July)	Republican offensive at the River Ebro.
1938 (15 Nov.)	Farewell parade of International Brigades in Barcelona. Republicans beaten back across the Ebro.
1939	Roy Campbell: *Flowering Rifle* (poetry). Stephen Spender and John Lehmann, eds.: *Poems for Spain.* Jean-Paul Sartre: *Le mur* (stories). Constancia de la Mora: *In Place of Splendor* (memoir). Carmen Conde: *Mientras los hombres mueren* (poetry).
1939 (26 Jan.)	Barcelona falls. Mass exodus of refugees to French border.
1939 (15 Mar.)	Hitler invades Czechoslovakia.
1939 (28 Mar.)	Nationalist forces enter Madrid.

1939 (1 Apr.)	End of Spanish Civil War. Five months later, WWII begins. Franco declares neutrality. Nazi-Soviet Pact.
1939–43	Franco's repression of Republicans. Mass executions and imprisonment.
1940	Ernest Hemingway: *For Whom the Bell Tolls* (novel). César Vallejo: *España, aparta de mí este cáliz* (poetry). Gustav Regler: *The Great Crusade* (novel). Concha Méndez: *Lluvias enlazadas* (poetry). Construction of the Nationalist war memorial, El Valle de los Caídos, begun.
1941	Franco sends Blue Division to fight with Germany at Russian front. *Raza* (film), with script by Franco.
1943	Film version, *For Whom the Bell Tolls*, released. Rafael García Serrano: *La fiel infantería* (novel). Gonzalo Torrente Ballester: *Javier Mariño* (novel). Max Aub: *Campo cerrado*, first of the series *El laberinto mágico* (novel).
1944	Carmen Laforet: *Nada* (novel). Paulino Masip: *El diario de Hamlet García* (novel).
1945	WWII ends. André Malraux's film, *L'espoir / Sierra de Teruel*, released.
1949	Francisco Ayala: *La cabeza del cordero* (stories).
1953	United States–Spain agreement, establishing American bases in Spain. Concordat signed with the Vatican. Ramón Sender: *Mosén Millán* (*Réquiem por un campesino español*; novel).
1955	Spain admitted to the United Nations.
1959	Completion of El Valle de los Caídos.
1962	Mercè Rodoreda: *La plaça del Diamant* (novel). Frédéric Rossif: *Mourir à Madrid* (documentary).
1965	Carlos Saura: *La caza* (film).
1966	Miguel Delibes: *Cinco horas con Mario* (novel).
1969	Franco names Juan Carlos de Borbón as heir to throne.
1973	Víctor Erice: *El espíritu de la colmena* (film).
1975 (20 Nov.)	Death of Franco.
1975 (22 Nov.)	Juan Carlos crowned.
1977 (June)	First democratic elections in Spain since February 1936. Catalan Statute of Autonomy reinstated.
1978	Carmen Martín Gaite: *El cuarto de atrás* (novel).
1978 (Dec.)	Constitution proclaimed.

1979	Basque Statute of Autonomy. Carlota O'Neill: *Una mujer en la guerra de España* (memoir).
1981	Picasso's *Guernica* returns to Spain.
1981 (23 Feb.)	Attempted military coup.
1984	Noel Buckner, Mary Dore, and Sam Sills: *The Good Fight* (documentary).
1985	Julio Llamazares: *Luna de lobos* (novel). Tomasa Cuevas: *Cárcel de mujeres* (memoir).
1986	Dolors Genovès: *In Memoriam* (documentary). Antonio Muñoz Molina: *Beatus ille* (novel).
1986 (Jan.)	Spain joins the European Economic Community.
1990	Carlos Saura: *¡Ay, Carmela!* (film).
1994	Dolors Genovès: *Sumaríssim 477* (documentary).
1995	Ken Loach's film, *Land and Freedom*, released.
1996	Lucía Sánchez Saornil: *Poesía*.
1998	Manuel Rivas: *O lapis do carpinteiro* (novel).
2001	Javier Cercas: *Soldados de Salamina* (novel).

Noël Valis

Introduction

Why does the Spanish Civil War continue to haunt us? A national conflict with wide-ranging international significance, the war (1936–39) has often been seen (and contested) as both the military and ideological testing ground and precursor of World War II. Fascists and Communists, liberals and conservatives fought bitterly over the future of the Spanish territory. The Second Spanish Republic (1931–36), which began with extraordinarily and perhaps unrealistically high hopes, degenerated in the last two years into factionalism and bloody street reprisals from both extremes. Many people in Europe and the Americas saw the civil war as the "last great cause" or the "good war," which was worth fighting and had to be fought, because the alternative—fascism or, for others, Communism—was unthinkable. And indeed, despite the official policy of nonintervention of many governments, Germany and Italy allied themselves with Francisco Franco's forces, whereas the Soviet Union aided Republican Spain.

The war had its origins in a complex array of causes, although the immediate provocation for Franco's rebellion against the legitimate Republican government was the Popular Front victory in the February 1936 elections. The army had played a dominant role in Spanish society since the nineteenth century. In that sense, the Francoist revolt could be seen as yet one more *pronunciamiento,* or military coup, in a string of such events, except that this uprising occurred within two special contexts.

First, Spain became a republic in 1931, a progressive modernizing move that had to contend with entrenched political, social, and religious opposition. The conflicts that ruled Spain from 1931 to 1936 reflected unresolved, historically embedded tensions between highly stratified social classes, violent anticlericalism and ultra Catholicism, centralism and regionalism, liberalism (and other isms of the left) and conservatism (ranging from traditionalists to monarchists to Falangists, or fascists). Second, the republic and the war itself played out against the growing polarization between the extreme right and the extreme left occurring elsewhere. Hitler and Mussolini had established fascist dictatorships in Germany and Italy, and Stalin had begun to purge the ranks of the Communist Party in the Soviet Union. Mass unemployment everywhere exacerbated social and economic tensions. There were strikes and a miners' uprising in Asturias in 1934. Stymied efforts at agrarian reforms to alleviate rural poverty also provoked violence, such as the government's brutal quashing of an anarchist rising at Casas Viejas. By 1936, politically motivated assassinations were bloodying the streets of Spanish society.

The passion that people brought to this war created, even in the midst of the conflict, enduring myths that arose from both sides. The passage of time has only intensified these myths and, in some cases, fixed them in stone. Franco's supporters saw the Republicans and the left in general as Reds, or *rojos,* and believed that Communists would ultimately win if the *franquistas* did not prevail. Later, this view of the war served cold-war aims as well. The left idealized the Second Republic and, as losing sides sometimes do, encased the war in an aura of bittersweet nostalgia. This was, for them, a just war; they were on the right side, and they had lost. The thousands of international volunteers felt the same but saw the defeat in a larger context than the national one, as important as it was to Spain.

In that larger context, the Spanish Civil War produced a remarkable array of international and national responses. Millions of words—in fiction, histories, essays, poems, journalism, and plays—have dwelled on it. Films, paintings, posters, drawings, and photographs have etched in memory scenes like the bombing of the Basque town Guernica, the assassination of the poet Federico García Lorca, the battle of the Ebro River, the defense of Madrid, and the terrible exodus of thousands of defeated Republicans into France at the end of the war. The Spanish Civil War has become a defining myth and reality of the twentieth century. Courses dealing with the war are given regularly in literature, culture, and history departments worldwide. But, to my knowledge, no volume yet exists that attempts to guide teachers in the different ways the richly diverse cornucopia of materials and issues might be presented in the classroom. This volume is intended to fill that gap.

Any discussion of the Spanish Civil War must come to grips with the multifaceted nature of, and response to, the war. The historical, ideological, and cultural aspects of the war are ultimately inseparable. Its complexities—which cannot be divorced from consideration of the Second Spanish Republic, the exile of Spanish Republicans, World War II, and the Franco and post-Franco periods in Spain—can be daunting. Debate over the war continues to this day. Why did the Republicans lose? What role did the Germans and Russians really play in the outcome? What is a good war? What is a just war? The Spanish conflict was considered a holy war for Franco's side. Is it possible to conduct a holy war? How does one reconcile such a notion with the moral ambiguities and loss of innocence that all wars bring?

These historical and ethical questions may not seem related to representations of the war in literature and the arts. Yet perhaps the largest difficulty in giving a course on the Spanish Civil War is to distinguish between what happened during (and after) the war and how what happened was represented in words and images. Take, for example, the now iconic *Life* magazine photograph by Robert Capa of the Republican soldier falling backward as he died. This extraordinary image quickly became a symbol of the Republican cause. But accusations that the photograph was staged surfaced. Capa himself said that "[n]o tricks are necessary to take pictures in Spain. You don't have to pose your camera [i.e., pose your subjects]. The pictures are there, and you just take them. The truth is the best picture, the best propaganda" (qtd. in Whelan, *Robert Capa: A Biography* 97). Capa shot his pictures as opportunities arose, but his artist's eye is present in the selection, framing, and composition of his work. His comment that "the truth is the best picture, the best propaganda" also reveals how blurry the distinctions were between truth and propaganda. For Capa and for many others, propaganda served the truth. The power and intensity of the photograph can also communicate a historical reality and an ethical-moral vision that transcend (but do not obviate) questions of aesthetic and ideological import. Moreover, as Valentine Cunningham has observed, photographs, like writing and art in general, "are textual, but they are also turned towards and tuned into history, they capture and preserve traces of the past, they testify to the inerasable presence of the real for all that they have textualised it." The war, Cunningham continues, is "that border at which fact overlaps fiction, and vice versa" (Introduction xxviii).

From Capa to Ernest Hemingway, Pablo Picasso to André Malraux, Roy Campbell to W. H. Auden, no one could remain on the fence about the Spanish Civil War. By the same token, those who give courses on the war usually have definite views on its nature and on the victors and losers. Most instructors (and I include myself) unsurprisingly sympathize with the Republican cause. Instructors need to be open and aboveboard in stating not only any sympathies and allegiances but also any ambivalence about the war. Complete objectivity is impossible and perhaps undesirable. What is being studied are representations of the war, that is, often subjective and ambiguously mediated understandings of how events, participants, and circumstances of the Spanish Civil War were, and are, interpreted and experienced through the filter of literature and the arts.

Representation is a loaded concept, difficult to grasp, especially when we are dealing with history and the arts together, given the gap between mimesis and historical events. The origins of representation are complex and put multiple meanings in play. *To represent* has long meant "to make present," but it also has the symbolizing function of standing for something or someone. The stage, as Raymond Williams points out (and from whom I take this discussion of the term's multivalence), coalesces both meanings (267). In addition, *representation* has political connotations, in which a representative stands (in) for and speaks for others in order to make present their views. By mid–nineteenth century, representation was also associated with realism and, later, with naturalism. The sense of the typical (the representative) and of accurate reproduction (representational art) were realist tenets. Williams observes:

> The degree of possible overlap between representative and representation in their political and artistic senses is very difficult to estimate. In the sense of the typical, which then stands for ("as" or "in place of ") others or other things, in either context, there is probably a deep common cultural assumption. (269)

Edward Said notes that "there is no such thing as a delivered presence, but a re-presence, or a representation" in culture (*Orientalism* 21). But this statement slides over the complex, contradictory relation between representation in art and literature and representation in history. Representation may be inescapable, but so is history. There will always be a gap in meaning and accessibility between historical events, such as the Spanish Civil War, and their representation, but we cannot forget that history, both directly and indirectly, has produced these representations. Representation, as W. J. T. Mitchell observes, is "always of something or someone, by something or someone, to someone" (12). Its dialogic character immediately contextualizes any instance of it. Therefore we have to ask, Who created these representations and why? Who viewed them? Students need to grasp, above all, how to distinguish between history and the historicizing effect of its representations. For example, Picasso's *Guernica* offers "no visual evidence of the war itself, only symbolization," as Simon Gikandi remarks. In that sense, it is "an artistic translation of the bombing of Guernica, not an image of the original event" (240). How students understand the history of the civil war depends to a significant degree on the various ways it has been represented (see also Gikandi 242).

One thing that makes understanding the Spanish Civil War and its representations particularly fraught with contradiction and ambiguity is their political complexity. Any contemporary texts on the war are also immersed in this complexity and, in this sense, are a part of history too. One could construe them as representational or "narrowly documentary," as Dominick LaCapra terms them (*History and Criticism* 38). LaCapra also says that one cannot read texts without examining the rhetoric that shapes them. The rhetoric of the Spanish Civil War is often inescapably highly politicized, for what was at stake in this war was the very identity of a nation and a people. The war was a battle over the future history of Spain and who would represent that history. In this very real and radical sense, as Williams contends, representation in art, literature, and other media cannot be divorced from its political roots.

Belief systems shape the tropes and structures—the very colors of painting, the metaphors and characters of novels and poems—of the multiple representations of the war.[1] The political meanings of representation that Williams associates with democratic governance can be seen in nearly all the literary and visual representations of the conflict: most artists, writers, and filmmakers felt strongly that they stood or spoke for someone or something else when presenting their views. Such passionately held convictions can readily be reduced to a black-and-white, Manichaean universe, and often were, at some risk to a fuller, more nuanced understanding of the events and texts that came out of this period of history.

If history is a body of knowledge, it is often contested knowledge. Elizabeth Fox-Genovese emphasizes that history consists "in the sum of reliable information about the past that historians have discovered and assembled. . . . History cannot simply be reduced—or elevated—to a collection, theory, and practice of reading texts" (216). What is up for grabs, however, is the interpretation of history. The essays in this collection indicate how history has been variously interpreted in the texts under discussion and in the interpretations contributors have made about texts that have already been worked over, or inscribed into history.

The historicity of these texts does not make it easier for today's students to enter into them. The very passion with which participants on both sides of the conflict made and lived history, a passion that can be seen as a kind of history itself, may seem remote, belonging to an era quite different from ours. Ours is an age of uncertainty, an age lacking conviction. To hold—and act on—convictions speaks of larger-than-life dreams, even of utopianism. The 1930s, of course, had no more certainty than our era has, but events like the Spanish Civil War, when viewed from the distance of nostalgia, appear more firmly settled than they are. In writing on Picasso's *Guernica*, the art historian Frank Russell has observed that the artist "was the illustrator of an unsure age. One of his difficulties, in particular, was that the present age is not one in which artists are born to illustration, especially illustration of passion and of large occurrence" (311).

Significantly, Picasso's *Guernica*, like the war itself, is an unsettling picture. As Russell remarks, there is "an uneasiness" in viewing the painting,

> an uncomfortable rattling as of stray pebbles slipping from the summit. Why, for instance, must the picture be eternally argued, searched? Why is there not . . . that unquestioned, that unquestionable quality we find in some earlier tragic expressions . . . [such as the] Bach Passions, Giotto? (311)

Similarly, why is the war still argued, searched? I suggest that what causes such uneasiness is not only the rhetoric of the painting or the way it is represented—its form, structure, color, and imagery—but also what lies beneath and within it: the war itself. The presumably black-and-white representations of the war reveal a profound lack of agreement that centered on opposing political beliefs and opposing understandings of what the Second Republic and the war meant and of what actually happened.

To take a vivid example from more recent headlines: when terrorists bombed trains at Madrid's Atocha Station on 11 March 2004, before the national elections, the event immediately evoked the civil war's bitter divisions between right and left. Some people, like the film director Pedro Almodóvar, accused Aznar, the leader of the center-right party then in power, of trying to sabotage the elections to prevent a socialist victory. Both sides tend to see their political roots planted in the trauma of the civil war. The right accuses the left of co-opting the civil war tragedy to discredit the center-right Popular Party. What happened on 11 March reopened old memories and old wounds (see Feros). "The divide in Spain," Carlta Vitzthum and John Carreyrou observe, "pits the nation's right, a democratic descendant of the Franco movement that ruled for nearly 40 years, against its left, which sees itself as heir to the Spanish Republic that Franco overthrew" (1).

A 2003 book by Pío Moa—*Los mitos de la guerra civil* ("The Myths of the Civil War")—also dramatizes to what extent the interpretation of the war is still in play. He argues that Franco "saved Spain from the trauma of revolution and territorial fragmentation" (qtd. in Feros). That this perspective is another version of the Francoist view of the republic and the war and an attempt to rewrite both the past and the present does not obviate the fact that the meaning of the war is not settled. If people in 2004 still cannot agree on what actually happened or what it signified, one can imagine how these highly charged contemporary accounts and other representations are fraught with interpretive difficulties. Belief systems constitute a rhetorical and ideological context for the multiple representations of the Spanish Civil War.

It becomes particularly important, then, that both sides of the conflict are put forward as fairly and completely as possible. The histories and the representations of both the *franquistas* and the *republicanos*, as well as those of their supporters, should be studied and discussed together in class. Yet how often is a tendentious and even appalling work like *Flowering Rifle: A Poem from the Battlefield of Spain* (1939), written by the Francoist Campbell, read? The likelihood that Campbell was far from the battlefield when he wrote the poem cries out for discussion. Or the novel by A. R. McGratty, SJ, *Face to the Sun* (1942), which according to the dust jacket blurb is about "Franco and his intrepid army as they beat their way from Africa through the defiant ranks of the Reds"? Or what about pro-Franco accounts like William Foss and Cecil Gerahty's *The Spanish Arena* (1938), with a foreword by His Grace the Duke of Alba and Berwick, for whom "[t]he Rising started as a protest against a ruthless tyranny [the Second Spanish Republic], and Franco's soldiers, as they marched up from the sea to the Tagus and on to Toledo, were hailed as deliverers" (8)? And what about the pro-Franco novels produced in Spain, such as Concha Espina's *Retaguardia: Imágenes de vivos y de muertos* (1937; "Rearguard: Images of the Living and the Dead"); Agustín de Foxá's *Madrid de corte a checa*

(1938; "Madrid, from Court to Cheka"); and Rafael García Serrano's *La fiel infantería* (1943; "The Loyal Infantry")? Or more-difficult-to-categorize, ambiguous works like Gonzalo Torrente Ballester's *Javier Mariño: Historia de una conversión* (1943; "Javier Mariño: The Story of a Conversion")? Surely we should be able to include texts like these, alongside Pablo Neruda and César Vallejo, Hemingway and Malraux, without running the risk of appearing to present the "official version" of the war. (I must confess that the first time I designed a course around the Spanish Civil War, not one pro-Franco text was on my syllabus.)

Offering texts from both sides does not, however, exempt us from considering the question of aesthetic value and the frequent artistic disparity between works produced by Republican Spain and those produced by Francoist Spain. A significant part of the richness of pro-Republican works like Picasso's *Guernica*, Malraux's *Man's Hope*, and George Orwell's *Homage to Catalonia* concerns their ambiguities and nuanced complexity, in contrast with the more uniform, homogenized view of the world in Nationalist texts. Such complexity in part reflects divisiveness on the Republican side. What could be viewed artistically as a strength was politically and militarily a weakness in the long run.

The pedagogical issue of how to present both sides of the conflict is also an ethical and ideological one. The distance of time and cultural differences add more layers of complexity to the issue. Undergraduate courses on the Spanish Civil War are sometimes given in English, with texts translated, and sometimes in Spanish, depending on the kind of students enrolled (Spanish majors versus non-Spanish majors) and the departments offering these courses. But even for those students with some knowledge of the Spanish language, history, and culture, this historical event can often seem confusing and overwhelming in its complexities. For the instructor it is tempting to simplify the war to a black-and-white struggle between fascism and Communism, because the war was often perceived this way in the 1930s and afterward. There is, of course, some truth to this viewpoint, but a dichotomized presentation of the war does not allow students to distinguish clearly between propaganda and historical reality, between mediated representations and historical events, nor does it allow them to see how much representations of the war have colored our understanding and perception of it. Thus when I refer above to giving both sides of the conflict, each side is a multilayered series of responses of mixed ideological, cultural, and aesthetic character that cannot be explained away with the simple use of terms like *fascist* or *antifascist*.

For the same reason, it is also appealing to introduce texts like Hemingway's *For Whom the Bell Tolls* (1940) into a course on the war. The novel centers on an American volunteer for the Republican cause, thus enabling an easy identification and sympathy not only with the protagonist but also with Republican Spain. The film version works in the same way. Both the novel and the film romanticize Spaniards and the Loyalists (or pro-Republicans) in particular. Hemingway idealizes Spaniards by simplifying them as elemental symbols of the primitive. They possess an "extra sacrament," the "old one that they had before the new religion came from the far end of the Mediterranean. . . . They are the people of the Auto de Fé; the act of faith" (309). In some respects, as Francisco Ayala observed, Hemingway's Spanish characters seem to be an oddly sympathetic reincarnation of the "black legend" of Spain ("La excentricidad" 1183–84). The one truly intricate mind in the novel is Robert Jordan's. Jordan at one point says to himself:

> You believe in Liberty, Equality and Fraternity. You believe in Life, Liberty and the Pursuit of Happiness. Don't ever kid yourself with too much dialectics. They are for some but not for you. You have to know them in order not to be a sucker. You have put many things in abeyance to win a war. If this war is lost all of those things are lost. (328)

Using Hemingway's novel in class can be very instructive when students realize how much this novel on the Spanish Civil War is about American values and perceptions.

This observation leads me to the issue of non-Spanish participation in, and interpretation of, the conflict. Despite many Western nations' official policy of nonintervention, individual foreigners came by the thousands to fight in the war, especially for the Republican side. Many others observed and wrote about it. The war in Spain did not necessarily mean to foreigners what it did to Spaniards. For Jay Allen, who wrote the preface to Capa and Gerda Taro's book of Spanish Civil War photographs, *Death in the Making* (1938), "Spain was the last terra incognita on the map of the civilized world," a "pueblo race" of uncommon qualities ([1–2]). Like Hemingway's vision of Spain, Allen's participates in the mythmaking propensities of many Loyalist supporters. In the opening of *Homage to Catalonia*, Orwell gestures toward myth—the myth of universal man and universal comradeship—when he describes his chance meeting with an Italian militiaman in Barcelona. He says:

> It was as though his spirit and mine had momentarily succeeded in bridging the gulf of language and tradition and meeting in utter

intimacy. I hoped he liked me as well as I liked him. But I also knew that to retain my first impression of him I must not see him again; and needless to say I never did see him again. One was always making contacts of that kind in Spain. (3–4 [1966])

Spain as myth becomes for Hemingway, Orwell, and Allen the last originary space. Elsewhere, I have suggested that the chance to fight in the Spanish Civil War and in Spain

> symbolized, among other things, a kind of "home" in both the political and existential senses of the word. Losing the war meant losing that vision of a mythologized polis which also represented "home." Losing the war meant an affective exile from a home that was not theirs, but that they wished was. (128)

This internationalization of the war and of Spain is a fundamental issue, then, that goes well beyond its external political dimensions and demonstrates both the power of mythmaking and the inseparability of myth and history in this particular instance. Ferreting out and examining these distinctions are key in both the scholarship and pedagogy of the multiple representations of the Spanish Civil War.

It could also be asked, To what extent did the internationalization of the Spanish Civil War help Spain define what *Spain* meant? In other words, the international dimensions of the conflict also became a national issue of identity, an identity both forged and problematized not only through internal trauma but also through the presence and perceptions of outsiders. Franco's defensively nationalistic posture after the war can be attributed in part to his movement's need to distinguish itself from the Second Republic as well as from the image of a new Spain of universal comradeship and open-ended democracy propagated by non-Spanish supporters of the Republican cause. The impact of the war reverberates in multiple ways decades after 1939, both in and outside Spain.

The organization and contents of this volume follow the dual objective of viewing representations of the war as both an inside and an outside experience, as seen by Spaniards and non-Spaniards. Most of the essays negotiate a delicate balance between theoretical issues and practical concerns. In a subject as broad, complex, and exhaustively treated as the Spanish Civil War, it is not possible to cover everything in one volume. Although there is no single essay devoted to Orwell's *Homage to Catalonia*, for example, discussion of Orwell comes up in many essays. Key representations of the war, like Franco's *Raza* ("Race"), Capa's

"Falling Militiaman," Joris Ivens's *The Spanish Earth*, and Hemingway's *For Whom the Bell Tolls*, reappear in this volume, offering different perspectives, insights, and emphases, as well as linkages among essays.

This volume is divided into seven parts: "Representations of Historical Contexts"; "Rhetoric, Ideology, and the War"; "Writing the War"; "The Arts and the War"; "Memory, Displacement, and the War"; "Resources"; and "Course Syllabi," followed by a glossary. "Resources" provides a representative selection of primary and secondary materials in the following categories: cinematography (documentaries and feature films), music, photography, posters, poetry, prose (novels, short stories, plays, dialogues, biography, memoirs, and testimonies), and secondary sources (history, literature and the arts, and Web sites).

In the first five sections, the volume addresses these questions:

1. Representations of Historical Contexts. How can the complex historical antecedents of the war be presented clearly yet not reductively to students? How can instructors contextualize the war as both a national and an international historical event? How did micronationalisms—in particular, those of the Basque Country, Galicia, and Catalonia—define the war's trajectory? Can the war also be understood as a religious conflict? How is the war presented, and its meanings understood or contested, historiographically?

2. Rhetoric, Ideology, and the War. How are the uses of rhetoric and ideology to be taught? What kinds of classroom materials would be helpful in analyzing the role and significance of ideology and rhetoric during the Spanish Civil War? How do such issues as race and identity, gender and class, become part of the rhetoric and ideology of the war and postwar periods? Race comes into play during the war in Franco's deployment of Moroccan troops, which evoked the ghosts of the Arab conquest of Spain and stereotypical images of the racialized *moro* (Moor) poised to pillage Republican homes and rape Republican women, and in the participation of African Americans in the Abraham Lincoln Brigade, which lent itself to reconsidering the question of racial equality and to seeing parallels between the Republican ideals and those of blacks in America.

One of the most significant aspects of the war was the visible presence of women both on and off the battlefield. Women, Spanish and non-Spanish alike, wrote on the war, as essays in part 5 ("Memory, Displacement, and the War") demonstrate. Some women were volunteers in the International Brigades. The participation of female soldiers (the Republican *milicianas*) became so controversial that they were soon removed from action, though their symbolic value proved useful to the cause. The *franquistas* also exploited the propagandist worth of women in the more traditional roles of caretakers and guardians of the hearth.

Class differences, of course, lay at the core of the conflict. Many of the social reforms of the Second Republic struck terror in the minds and hearts of the large landowners, the church, and the military. Films like Ken Loach's *Land and Freedom* (1995) and novels like Ramón Sender's *Requiem for a Spanish Peasant* (1953) illustrate the complexities of the social conflict in 1930s Spain. How do instructors approach this material, keeping in mind both the historical-ideological specificity of the moment and the aesthetic questions of how gender and social differences were represented?

3. *Writing the War.* What kinds of text selection should be made? On what basis are texts to be selected? How do instructors approach aesthetically and theoretically the texts chosen? What issues should be emphasized in selecting and analyzing them? How do instructors deal with the question of translation and translated texts? Additionally, the status of outsider to the Spanish arena should be addressed. What are the aims of writings by outsiders? What sorts of perspectives on Spain and the war do they give? Texts by Abraham Lincoln Brigade volunteers offer examples of an outsider view. How do texts by outsiders illuminate non-Spanish issues, such as the political problems of the United States in the instance of some American-authored texts, or other problems, such as those of class and gender?

4. *The Arts and the War.* How do instructors use nonliterary materials effectively in class? What kinds of selection should be made? What kinds of approaches should be used in dealing with such materials as posters and photographs, films and documentaries? The wealth of materials is impressive, ranging from Picasso's *Guernica* to the striking propaganda posters, from war photojournalism to children's drawings to films like *¡Ay, Carmela!* and *The Spanish Earth.* When does propaganda become art and art, propaganda? What kinds of differences and similarities are there in the presentation of Republican and Nationalist propaganda? How are international propaganda responses to the war expressed?

5. *Memory, Displacement, and the War.* The heartbreaking exodus of thousands of Republicans in 1939, many of whom were greeted by French concentration camps, was one of the immediate consequences of the war. For decades exile was both a place and a state of mind for many Spaniards, and it stimulated the production of memoirs, novels, essays, and histories. What is the relation between the war and exile? How is exile to be under-

stood: as merely a state of mind, as a historical-cultural phenomenon, or as both? What is the relation between exile and national identity?

How has the memory of the war been represented in literature, memoirs, histories, and other media? What kinds of memories have been singled out more than others? What impact does gender have on such memories? To what extent has the memory of the Spanish Civil War been repressed or smoothed over during the Franco regime and after the dictator's death, in 1975? The ghosts of the war were literally and figuratively entombed in Nationalist monuments like the Valley of the Fallen, in which the real history of Francoist repression and Republican sacrifice was airbrushed out. More recently, exhumations of executed Republican victims at mass grave sites have reopened old wounds and renewed debate over the war. A citizens group, the Association for the Recovery of Historic Memory, has spearheaded the recovery and reburial of as many of the over thirty thousand bodies as possible. The Popular Party, then in power, refused to fund the project, saying, "This issue is closed for us. We don't have to look at the past" (qtd. in Goodman; see also Silva and Macías; Thibaud; Armengou and Belis). One of those victims is the poet Federico García Lorca, whose family prefers not to disturb his remains. "There are some people who believe that being in a mass grave is something degrading, which we do not believe," Manuel Fernández-Montesinos García, the son of Lorca's sister Concha, has said (qtd. in Kolbert 70). Such events and reactions tell us that the memory of the war in Spain also serves present-day ends and that the past continues to be seen through the present.

To what extent have explanations and memories of the war also been used to reconcile post-Franco Spain's left and right? It is useful to recall here, for example, that the socialist PSOE (Partido Socialista Obrero Español) government refused to "sanction any official commemoration of the 50th anniversary of the Civil War in 1986," as Paul Preston notes (*Politics* 34). Yet the March 2004 national elections, in which the political and ideological divisions of the conflict once more surfaced in bitter recriminations, suggest that the war is very much a living presence in Spain. Are there still international reverberations of the war? The memories of the survivors of the International Brigades come immediately to mind. How can such resources as the Abraham Lincoln Brigade Archives be used to explore these memories? How do instructors frame the issue of memory in historical, cultural, and aesthetic terms? How do they deal with the intricate relation between memory and history?

Finally, if we want to instill in students the enduring significance of this extraordinarily international civil war, which for many continues to be seen as the "good war" and the "last great cause," we will need to deal with the issue of memory in the form of nostalgia. Susan Suleiman has observed:

> We may look with a certain nostalgia at the urgency and passion of the texts inspired by that war. But we should not let the nostalgia for "committed art" blind us to the horror of the events that art converted into words, or images. (941)

In this regard, it is instructive to consider one of the finest stories to come out of the conflict, Ayala's "El Tajo" ("The Cleft"). Ayala, a supporter of the republic, explores "the Civil War in the hearts of men" (*Cabeza* 67). The main character of "El Tajo," Santolalla, a Nationalist soldier, stumbles on Anastasio, a Republican *miliciano*, who like him is foraging for food. Santolalla kills Anastasio in an unthinking panic. Afterward, he is tormented by guilt and an unnamed anguish. He holds on to the dead soldier's identity card, and the memory of the soldier's death haunts him, invading his mind like the smell of decay coming from the *miliciano*'s corpse and the olfactory memory of his dog Chispa's rotting body. Neither death, ultimately, has a rational explanation.

After the war, Santolalla tries to make restitution to the family of the dead Republican, who comes from the same hometown, but, in a sharp reversal, the mother refuses to take back her son's identity card. She remains fearful and hostile, suspecting Santolalla's motives because Santolalla is unable to tell her the true circumstances of her son's death. Ayala seems to suggest a certain reversibility in the roles of victim and killer. One could argue that Santolalla in his own way is as much a victim of the war as Anastasio. After all, the Republican could have shot him instead. But would an ex-Republican soldier have gone to the family of a dead Nationalist and offered restitution? It seems unlikely. Only the winners have that privilege. There is no catharsis in "El Tajo," no forgiveness and no forgetting, but rather a deep and cutting divide in the before and after of the Spanish Civil War.

Note

1. Belief systems also shaped, needless to say, the very actions of artists. The cellist and conductor Pau Casals would not play in Spain while Franco was still in power, and the Chilean writer Gabriela Mistral published her 1938 book of poetry, *Tala*, for the benefit of Spanish, and especially Basque, children orphaned by the war. The best-known example is Picasso's refusal to allow *Guernica* to return to Spain until democracy was reestablished there.

Part I

Representations of Historical Contexts

Sandie Holguín

Navigating the Historical Labyrinth of the Spanish Civil War

When Gerald Brenan tried in 1943 to explain the conditions in Spain that led to the civil war, he aptly named his book *The Spanish Labyrinth*. Over sixty years later, teachers are still trying to navigate interested students through the complexities of this war. In the United States, the difficulty of the task is compounded by Spain's virtual disappearance from European history textbooks after the defeat of the Spanish Armada in 1588. Generally the books do not mention Spain again until they reach 1936, and only then by speaking of the war as a prelude to the "real" European war of 1939–45. While professors already bemoan college students' lack of historical training, the problem is more severe when it comes to Spain. How does one talk about Carlists and socialists and anarchists and Alfonsine monarchists—to name but a few of the war's protagonists—when American students do not know the broad outlines of European history, let alone the rudiments of Spanish history? How does one evoke and make relevant the passions of that war to a student body whose general experience of war comes from sanitized, disengaged television broadcasts that make war look like a video game? Finally, how does one persuade students to take seriously the participants' ideas about social revolution in a post-cold-war and consumerist age? The task is daunting. One way to approach the Spanish conflict is to see it as a series of intense culture wars that reached their height during the Second Republic. The failure to resolve these culture wars meant that they were carried over to the battlefields of the civil war.

These culture wars, often represented by the oversimplified but sometimes useful notion of the two Spains, proved very real and ultimately insurmountable to their participants. The people of one Spain, whose representatives included the Catholic Church, landed and industrial elites, the aristocracy, and elements of the military, viewed themselves as upholders of Spanish tradition. They sought to preserve monarchical and clerical privileges; hierarchical social order; and a strong, unified Spain bolstered by empire. They balked at ideas derived from the Enlightenment. The people of the other Spain included workers, progressive liberals and Republicans, secularists, and regional nationalists. Tracing their intellectual heritage back to the Enlightenment, they sought to catch up with the rest of industrialized Europe. They called for greater secularization, a multinational state, industrialization, and a social safety net.

Each camp oversimplified the complexities of social alliances and denigrated the opposition through metonymic insults. Thus each group elicited a variety of negative responses by tarring the other with labels such as "bourgeois," "reactionary," and "fascist" or "Reds" and "atheists." By the eve of the civil war, these labels hardened and became a shorthand for understanding competing visions about Spain's national identity. By using the culture wars framework, American students, who are themselves living in the midst of culture wars, should be able to grasp some of the conflict's complexities. This framework also helps students analyze both the national and international dimensions of the war and provides a transition for discussing cultural representations of the war.

To illustrate the constant tension and dialogue between the domestic and international dimensions of the war, one needs to examine long-term trends in both European and Spanish history. The ideological, political, and economic challenges posed by the French Revolution and the Enlightenment, followed by more contemporary developments such as the Great Depression and the rise of fascism and Communism, form the backdrop to how Spaniards adapted domestic issues in larger historical contexts. By the time students learn about the Second Republic, they should be able to see how the different cultural battle lines were drawn and how these representations were often used to obfuscate complex issues. Any exploration of the various fault lines would have to begin with

the Enlightenment and the French Revolution, because the cultural fallout from these historical periods continued to influence many Europeans
throughout the nineteenth century and confronted Spaniards through the
Francoist period.

The Enlightenment emphasized thinking for oneself, individual liberty, and human equality; it challenged the authority of all social and political institutions, especially the Catholic Church and the monarchy, and
therefore butted against royal and religious prerogatives. This ideology,
along with the effects of the French Revolution, utterly transformed the
world in the eyes of the power holders of the Old Regime. The changes
included the legal end of feudalism in many parts of Europe, the temporary overthrow of the European monarchies, the establishment of state
constitutions, the subordination of church to state, the development of
equality under the law, and the beginnings of nationalism. While many of
the traditional authorities regained their positions in Europe and Spain
after the French Revolution, their status and power had certainly lessened.
Thereafter, the great powers of Europe pledged to stop any group that
hinted at revolution. Reactionary politics ensued in Europe in the nineteenth century, punctuated by periods of revolution and attempted revolution. Here Spain followed European trends closely. In this period some
of the cultural and political fissures began to emerge, namely, between secularists and the Catholic Church and between absolute monarchists and
constitutional monarchists or republicans.

Liberalism was another important trend in nineteenth-century
Europe, one that developed out of Enlightenment ideology and the slow
destruction of feudalism. Although most scholars associate liberalism with
Britain, the term came from Spain in 1812. During the revolutionary
wars, representatives calling themselves liberals gathered at the Cortes of
Cádiz to write a constitution for a soon-to-be-liberated Spain. European
liberalism exalted individual liberties; a constitutional representational
government; and, in the name of efficiency, laissez-faire economics and
the centralization of the state.

Spanish liberals struggled for two-thirds of the nineteenth century to
bring their vision to Spain. By 1840 they had achieved much of their program, especially the creation of private property. Much of what they created, however, was a superficial liberalism: a centralized state in name but
one with very little infrastructure; the semblance of a representational government but one elected through ingeniously corrupt methods and representing few people's interests. A highly contested liberal reform of the

nineteenth century was the disentailment of church lands, that is, the confiscation and selling off of church lands to buyers who then converted the land to private property. Obviously, the church objected to this act because it lost property and income. Similarly, secular entail was eliminated by 1836. Noble property became private property, although it remained in the same hands (Shubert 59). Originally, many peasants backed the liberals' disentailment plans because they were led to believe that they might benefit from the redistribution of land. They did not share the spoils of disentailment, however. Instead, they began to lose their customary rights to land their families had inhabited and farmed for generations. Disentailment transferred around thirty percent of national land to different hands, but the structure of land ownership changed little (Shubert 60). In fact, the failure of Spanish elites to solve the land distribution problem contributed to some of the greatest conflicts of the Second Republic. Additionally, the liberal policy of centralizing the state and its laws offended people like the Basques, who had had centuries-old traditions of local rule, known as *fueros*. By outlining the development of liberalism, we can point students to a number of fault lines that would continue until the civil war began: liberals versus the church, liberals versus authoritarian monarchs, liberals versus the peasantry, and centralizers versus regional nationalists.

Liberal reforms worked symbiotically with yet another great movement of the nineteenth century, the Industrial Revolution. Although the Industrial Revolution did not sink roots in all of Spain as it did in England, it did take hold in Barcelona and Bilbao. The problems associated with industrialization colored Spaniards' lives in profound ways. The people of Barcelona and Bilbao lived in conditions characteristic of other industrializing nations: a rapid increase of immigrants from other parts of the country who lived in overcrowded slums of unspeakable squalor; extreme pollution; poverty; increased disparity of wealth between the worker majority and the bourgeois minority; urban renewal and expansion, which allowed the bourgeoisie to display their wealth and which consigned workers to the worst parts of the city; and, finally, class warfare.

Given these conditions and given that the political and economic underpinnings of liberal ideology prohibited government intervention, two major European ideologies—socialism and anarchism—emerged as rivals for the hearts and minds of the European working classes. Both ideologies gave workers a language to understand and articulate their discontent. For nineteenth-century Marxist socialists, revolution was both a scientific fact and a product of historical determinism. Once urban workers reached a critical mass, they would overthrow the bourgeoisie in a bloody revolution, abolish bourgeois institutions such as the church, found a dictatorship of the proletariat, and move toward a proletarian state in which all classes would disappear. Eventually the state would wither away. In contrast, Mikhail Bakunin's anarchism stipulated that the revolution would come from the most dispossessed members of society, the landless agricultural laborers. This anarchism was libertarian at its core: individual rights superseded all others, and any institutional infringement on those rights by the state and religion had to be abolished through violent revolution. Finally, land and resources would be locally controlled.

By the end of the nineteenth century, workers in most European countries chose socialism over anarchism. In Spain, however, workers chose both, and unlike any other European country, Spain had a strong anarchist presence until 1939. Despite Bakunin's pronouncements about the rural foundations of anarchism, anarchists were strong in both rural and urban Spain, dominating places as disparate as Andalusia and Barcelona. From the end of the nineteenth century until the civil war, tensions flared periodically between urban workers and industrialists and between rural laborers and large landowners. This tense atmosphere was especially prevalent in Barcelona and Andalusia, where workers and management fomented the greatest unrest and violence during the Bolshevik Triennium of 1917–19. Some Spaniards perceived anarchist workers as the most dangerous, for the anarchists sometimes resorted to terrorist violence. They attacked sacred bourgeois places, like the Barcelona opera, and sacred people, like the king and queen and numerous government leaders. They thought that such "propaganda by the deed" would alert the world to the crimes of the bourgeoisie and to the justice of their cause. Anarchist anticlericalism was also the most strident. Anarchists were unjustly but wholly blamed for such disasters as Tragic Week, the 1909 burning of hundreds of convents in Barcelona. Socialists and especially anarchists represented social disorder to Spain's ruling classes. Therefore, elites used all means possible to keep workers out of the political process and did little to ameliorate laborers' poor working and living conditions.

It is important to stress to students both the truly violent nature of these confrontations between laborers and owners and the depths to which the Spanish state sanctioned and facilitated the violent suppression of workers. Most American students do not believe that class conflict exists. Once they understand how profound the antagonism was between these groups and how people suffered, the problems and alliances of the Second Republic and the civil war begin to make sense. Students also need to know that socialists and anarchists did not generally ally with each other in worker solidarity. In fact, much of the time they were ideologically opposed to each other.

Nationalism was the last European trend to affect Spain, and it did so in more diverse ways than in many other European nations. From the mid–nineteenth century on, tensions between those who wanted to centralize the Spanish state and those who wanted to nourish regional nationalisms escalated (see the essays by Cazorla-Sánchez and Ucelay-Da Cal in this volume). In their attempts to unify Spain, liberals alienated people in the Basque Country and Catalonia.

A form of right-wing Basque nationalism emerged in the nineteenth century under the guise of Carlism. Although the nineteenth-century Carlist wars were really attacks on Spanish liberalism, the Carlist battle cry to institute a decentralized monarchy and to regain the *fueros* the Basques had lost could be seen as a form of nationalism. Most scholars, however, see Basque nationalism's beginning in the late nineteenth century, with the tireless efforts of Sabino de Arana y Goiri, who founded the Basque Nationalist Party (PNV). Basque nationalism did not become a mass movement until the Second Republic. The primary goal for Basque nationalists during the Second Republic was regional autonomy, but unlike the leftist Catalan nationalists of the 1930s, many Basques were conservative nationalists who wished to retain their Catholic confessional ties.

Catalan nationalism began as a form of cultural nationalism in the mid–nineteenth century but transformed into political nationalism by the late nineteenth century. Spain's defeat in 1898 proved pivotal since Catalonia, the most productive region in Spain, suffered great economic setbacks with the loss of Spain's colonies. Catalan industrialists, upset that the central government was not protecting their interests, began lobbying to form their own political parties and institutions. Left-wing Catalan nationalism did not gain strength until the late 1920s and 1930s. Instead, a conservative nationalism emerged in the late nineteenth century, dominated by industrialists wedded to the Catholic Church. These nationalists opposed the working classes in Catalonia. In fact, when workers' strikes and riots threatened public order and Catalan industry, Catalan nationalists chose to let the central government use its military might to suppress worker discontent in exchange for relinquishing their claims to autonomy. In 1914, Catalans gained a modicum of regional governance with the establishment of the *Mancomunitat.* But when the right-wing General Miguel Primo de Rivera became dictator in 1923, he soon eliminated the political institutions of Catalan nationalism, which he felt threatened the unity of Spain. Only after Primo de Rivera made these institutions illegal did a left-wing version of Catalan nationalism emerge that incorporated the working classes.

While the unity of Spain was being challenged by regional nationalists, other nationalists of varying political leanings pushed for a unified Spain under the cultural and political hegemony of Castile. Scholars often identify the army, the Catholic Church, and eventually the Falange as the true upholders of Spanish nationalism, but many Republicans and socialists also believed that national interests were best served by having a united Spain dominated by one culture (Holguín). With the establishment of the Second Republic, the left's ambivalence toward a pluralistic state would come out clearly in the debates over regional nationalisms. For the right, there was no ambivalence, of course: Spain was an indivisible country.

At least one more piece of the puzzle is needed to contextualize the republic and the civil war: the Spanish army. During the preceding two centuries the military intervened in politics when generals believed that politicians were on the wrong track or that public order needed to be restored. The *pronunciamiento* (or coup d'état) became a favored tool of political change in 1820, when Rafael de Riego led one to reinstate the Spanish constitution. There were numerous *pronunciamientos* in the nineteenth century, some conservative, some liberal. Primo de Rivera's rule began with a coup in 1923. The Nationalist generals in July 1936 saw their own revolt as a traditional *pronunciamiento* that would restore order to Spain after the chaos of the Second Republic. Looking at all these pieces, students should be able to see that the causes of the civil war and the players in it were far more complex than they imagined. After outlining these broad trends, one could concentrate on the Second Republic and its relation to particular historical problems and to the general European trends of the interwar period.

It is imperative for students to know that the emergence of the Second Republic cannot be separated from European-wide developments of the interwar period. To many Europeans, liberalism failed to stave off the economic crises and workers' unrest of the early 1920s. The Great Depression, it seemed, hammered the last nail on liberalism's coffin. Alternatives to liberalism appeared in the forms of Communism in the Soviet Union and fascism in Italy and Germany. In the early 1930s dictatorships emerged in Portugal and Austria, conservatives ruled England, and France came close to civil war between an ever-polarizing left and right. In the midst of this reconfiguration of European politics, economy, and society, Spain bucked European trends by ushering in a (relatively) democratically elected republic in 1931. Although indigenous conditions enabled Spaniards to take a different path from other European powers in 1931, the political course of events during the republic were reactions to developments both in Spain and in the rest of Europe.

The provisional government and the first official government of the republic contained an assortment of revolutionary and reformist socialists and Republicans of the left, center, and right. A host of unresolved problems from the nineteenth century awaited the coalition, including inequitable land distribution and religious, class, and regional conflicts. Given the fractious state they inherited, the members of the new government hoped to consolidate their rule as quickly as possible. They therefore instituted a series of cultural programs, which included transforming the educational system and passing anticlerical measures to reflect the values of the new secular, Republican-socialist state. But their reforms would prove to be difficult. The heterogeneous nature of the coalition and the intransigence of conservative members of Spanish society resisted efforts at reform. Would the coalition institute a reformist or a revolutionary program? How could one or the other be achieved without alienating its more conservative or leftist members? In the end, the coalition's worldview would antagonize both the right and the far left.

The republic lost any credibility it might have had with the right almost from the outset. First, Francesc Macià prematurely declared a Catalan state and republic on 14 April 1931, presaging tensions that would occur between centralizing and regional nationalists. Later, after the Catalan autonomy statute was passed and attempts were made to enact a Basque autonomy statute, the right would accuse the left of being unpatriotic by contributing to the breakup of Spain. Even more damaging to the republic's cause, the right felt, was the speed with which anticlerical acts were carried out. The convent burnings in Madrid in May 1931 and the refusal of Republican officials to stop them immediately guaranteed the republic the full enmity of members of the Catholic Church and other traditionalists. The May and June decrees that enshrined freedom of religion and limited the church's influence over education cemented Catholic antagonism toward the republic. The constitution reined in the Catholic Church even more: Spain would have no official religion; the government would no longer support the church financially; religious orders were closely regulated and some, like the Jesuits, were disbanded, and their property was to be sold off. The Law of Congregations (June 1933) prohibited religious orders from teaching in the Spanish educational system.

Agrarian reform also proved troublesome for the architects of the republic, because it went too slowly for revolutionary anarchists and socialists and too quickly for traditionalists. Although members of the left recommended radical changes as early as April 1931, it took until September 1932 for the Cortes to pass a watered-down and convoluted agrarian reform bill. Large landowners in the south viewed land reform as the invasion of foreign Marxism into Spain, and they did everything possible to obstruct land reform efforts. In contrast, leftist landless laborers became disenchanted with the slow pace of reform and began in some places to occupy the land. With the election of a center-right coalition in November 1933, any transformation of the agrarian system halted or was reversed. After the election of the Popular Front in February 1936, however, agrarian reform resurfaced, mostly because of a large "wave of land seizures" and a series of strikes (Esenwein and Shubert 98). The necessary attempts at agrarian reform polarized the different strata of Spanish society more than ever.

The year 1934 proved to be a watershed that would harden ideological positions, so much so that civil war seemed inevitable. Events in Europe in 1934 would also color events in Spain. Austrian Nazis assassinated Chancellor Engelbert Dollfuss, Germany began rearming, and France barely averted a civil war between its left and far right in February. The Soviet-backed Comintern called on workers in European nations to unify in socialist-Communist coalitions to fight fascism. Social tensions grew in Spain, but the radical Alejandro Lerroux responded by appointing members of the conservative CEDA (Confederación Española de Derechas Autónomas) to his cabinet. Socialists, knowing that fascists had gained ground in much of Europe and fearing fascist rule in Spain, called for a revolution. It failed in most parts of Spain, except in Asturias, and was put down brutally by Francisco Franco and his African troops. The numerous deaths and the imprisonment of at least thirty thousand people demoralized the left, but the trauma also led to the fragile unification of leftist forces in the Popular Front victory of February 1936.

The numerous reforms initiated by the first Republican-socialist coalition of the republic started, stuttered, and stopped between April 1931 and February 1936, depending on which way the political winds blew.

With the return of the left in February 1936, reform began anew. But it was too late for changes or conciliation. Street violence increased: "According to the best estimates, there were 269 political killings from February to mid-July 1936" (Esenwein and Shubert 32). Finally, the right gave up on politics and used the *pronunciamiento* to restore order and to save Spain from its current turmoil. The military leaders of the July revolt believed that the republic represented all that was wrong with Spain: the Enlightenment, atheism, and Marxism. Similarly, given their perspective of Spanish history and contemporary European events, the left viewed the right as an enemy of social change and as an incubator for fascism in Spain. Once the war began, domestic and international propaganda machines worked in full force, simplifying the complexities of the war for foreign and domestic consumption. The diversity of Spain's problems had been reduced to two: Communism and fascism. Now, through their studies of cultural representations, educators must recover that complexity and give students a more nuanced understanding of the Spanish Civil War.

Enric Ucelay-Da Cal

The Spanish Civil War
as a National Conflict

The Spanish Civil War remains the outstanding example of a highly ideolo-
gized and symbolic conflict in modern Europe. All the leading ideologies
of the twentieth century—socialism, anarchism (plus anarcho-syndical-
ism), Communism (Stalinist and anti-Stalinist), liberal democracy, fascism,
Catholic traditionalism, Christian democracy, and minority nationalisms—
played significant roles, proffering their formulas for utopia. As such, the
war seemed to sum up—from numerous and discordant perspectives—the
contradictions of the interwar period in Europe, if not in the world, and as
such it has been evaluated by both international and Spanish historiography. As research and scholarship accumulate, however, the standard perceptions of Spanish events and their international implications can be seen in
radically different ways. The experience of later civil wars in the Mediterranean area can also be used to reinterpret the Spanish revolution and
counterrevolution in a less grandiose and less Eurocentric manner, one less
subject to the ideological preconceptions of left, right, and center. In particular, any reevaluation of the conflict from outside the country would
have to incorporate a deeper understanding of the underlying trends in
Spanish politics and society, trends that have been all too easily dismissed
and replaced with pat ideological explanations.

The significance of the Spanish Civil War has depended on simple questions: Which revolution? Urban or rural? Anarchist-inspired or Stalinist-led? Was there a spontaneous social revolution that dominated the Republican zone up to the crushed May revolt in 1937 in Barcelona? Was there a Stalinist dictatorship or a popular democracy in 1937–39? One could even ask if the counterrevolution was a national revolution (as the *falangistas* claimed) or a repressive conservative fraud. This political discussion of wartime goals and assessments has conditioned all later historiography, to the extent that the conflict has not been able to become a historical event but instead remains an ongoing ideological confrontation, despite the democratization of Spain after 1975.

Spaniards saw the political and social background of events in their country with a passionate clarity of detail since their past was marked by sustained internal strife and stable partisan attitudes, little given to compromise or power sharing. Since the beginning of the nineteenth century, no Spanish regime has lasted successfully for fifty years. Parliamentary monarchy, military dictatorship, and democratic republic have all failed. By 1936, after a sequence of revolts from all reaches of the political spectrum, Spanish society was visibly polarized by the Popular Front. Thus an unsuccessful coup d'état (a common enough event in Spain for both the left and the right) exploded into a civil war that promptly involved all the major European powers and their corresponding ideological alignments. In the strictest terms, nobody, on one or the other side of the growing ideological polarization, was expecting a war, much less a long one.

But Spanish internal logic could often be hard to follow for foreigners. Some Spaniards (such as Catalan or Basque nationalists) even denied that there was such a thing as Spain. Accordingly, Spaniards on both sides used religious traditions (including anticlericalism) as a means to condition the external evaluation of Spanish events. Soon, both sides and their diverse contingents were selling their respective causes as products of cultural and religious perspectives: Protestants and Jews worldwide were inspired by the democratic struggle against a "New Inquisition"; while Catholics were similarly stirred by Franco's "crusade" (see Ucelay-Da Cal, "Ideas"). The controversy abroad had little to do with what people in Spain thought they were fighting for and against: local ideals derived from local knowledge, examples, affinities, and antagonisms. The experience of war, however, tended to merge nationalist themes with international clichés, as Spaniards clung to the relevance of their struggle to the world at large.

After the defeat of the Republicans, the Spanish Civil War became a recognized antecedent of World War II and endured as a frozen political example during the cold war, even for Spaniards. The long life of the Franco dictatorship ensured that Spanish political memory, closely linked to Spain's turbulent history leading up to the civil war, became homogenized by the simplifying ideological models imposed by outside supporters of the differing factions.

Civil War, Civil Society, and Civic Culture

Nineteenth-century Spain was marked by semicontinuous civil war, in both the Iberian Peninsula and the overseas colonies. The French invasion in 1808 set off a vicious internal conflict between the partisans of Napoleonic reform and the defenders of the patriot cause, both liberals and traditionalists. The six-year-long struggle against the French in the peninsula stimulated revolts and then civil wars in Spain's American colonies. The ongoing battles for independence in the Americas then provoked a liberal revolution in metropolitan Spain, which was stifled by another French invasion and an occupation that lasted several years. By the mid-1820s, Spain had lost all its possessions on the American mainland, retaining only Cuba and Puerto Rico in the Antilles and the Philippines in Asia. Bitter ideological confrontation between liberals and traditionalists escalated to armed conflict between rival wings of the reigning Bourbon dynasty (1833–40, 1846–49), an antagonism that dominated Spanish politics for the next several decades. The traditionalists, better known as Carlists for their dynastic option, lost repeatedly, until they were seen as subscribing to a chronically lost cause. The liberals split into moderates and progressives, a division that gave the military the decisive role of arbiter. In 1868, a democratic revolution with strong military backing attempted to systematize an up-to-date monarchical system, but sought-after stability proved elusive as rebellion broke out in Cuba, and then a new Carlist uprising disrupted the peninsula (1872–76). The experiment of a Republican regime (1873–74) descended into chaos as diverse towns proclaimed their independence. Meanwhile the army continued to combat the Carlists. In Cuba, there were close to thirty years of sustained shooting, which began with full-scale civil war in 1868, was followed by a period of guerrilla skirmishing in 1878 (the so-called *Guerra chiquita* or Little War), then broke out again into open combat in 1895. The restoration of the liberal branch of the Bourbons in 1874, which stabilized under the

Constitution of 1876 as a working parliamentary system vaguely based on the English model, was hailed as a peaceful solution that would relegate the army to the background.

Defeat in a brief war with the United States over Cuba in 1898 left Spain as less than a second-rate power, no longer an empire but not quite a nation. After 1815, Spain escaped from the general trend of European warfare (the conflicts of 1864–71 to World War I) but internal dissension and uneasy colonial fighting more than made up for the absence of international entanglement. Remaining outside major European conflicts had both evident short-term benefits and hidden long-term costs for Spain, whose preoccupations, overly self-absorbed, were never quite tuned to general continental trends. At home and abroad, the conviction grew, and was endlessly repeated, that Spain was somehow exceptional, somehow different.

In short, what characterized Spain from 1808 to 1939 (or perhaps even until Franco's death in 1975) was the easy recourse to devastating civil war. This pattern was certainly noted by foreign observers and also provoked a good deal of internal commentary. The problem, however, was not Spain's inclination toward civil war—after all, the unifications of Germany and especially Italy produced a spate of repeated conflicts that were in some sense internal. The problem was that the Spanish conflicts seemed indecisive, never reaching a settlement, never giving a sense of finality. Even though the forty-seven-odd years of parliamentary monarchy between the end of the Carlist wars in 1876 and the establishment of military dictatorship in 1923 represent the longest period of government uninterrupted by major violence, at no time during the last two centuries has Spanish politics been free of the threat of revolt. There has always been (right up to present-day Basque nationalist terrorism) a sector of opinion ready to manifest its dissension through armed action. One might compare Spain with Latin American societies, such as Colombia, which have never successfully stabilized a civil society and peaceful politics, or with the successive Muslim states of the Mediterranean basin, which in different ways have remained submerged in the conflict between religion and secularization (an influence of the West) since the late nineteenth century.

The true opposite of civil war, civil peace, was never a consensus, accepted only partially under the parliamentary monarchy and the present democratic system instituted in 1977. Since its inception in seventeenth-century England, parliamentary life, the basis of representative government, has been a sublimation of civil war: the rival sides agree to disagree, engage in stylized verbal confrontation instead of physical combat, and build parallel mythologies of left and right. The rest of what we call democracy has less to do with state formation than with civil society, the complex of associative networks that exchange information, goods, and services and require enough freedom to instill and acquire the habits that encourage yet greater interactions. In practical terms, economy and politics are abstractions, and the marketplace for products or ideas can be experienced only through the manifold entities of civil society, be they small family firms, midsize companies, large business combinations, local political clubs, like-minded civic networks, or mass parties. This expansive and varied welter of private associations gives life to the limited scale of public institutions. The problem, however, is that civil society is always incomplete; its spontaneity is subject to gaps, produced by factors such as resistance to participation or lack of trust. So the state and civil society are locked in a somewhat uncomfortable commensal relation, whereby the failings of civil society justify the widening of the state's regulation and intervention and the offer of public services always lags behind private initiative. Together, the state and civil society are not unlike the relation between hardware (the state) and software (civil society).

The liberal revolution in nineteenth-century meridional Europe loosened the restrictions on civil society of the old regime, at the expense of the authority of the Catholic Church, but it legally imposed a doctrinal model of individualist activity that did not reflect the collective style of Mediterranean social life. Much of the redefinition of liberal institutions at the end of the nineteenth century and the beginning of the twentieth accordingly forced the recognition of corporative associations, from labor unions to management syndicates or professional bodies, led by working-class spokespeople—or even Catholics—who represented those who felt excluded from the existing political networks. At the same time, the growing demand for better public services (such as education or health) put pressure on the state to fund social promotion (e.g., recognition of schoolteachers as functionaries).

In idealistic terms, the interface between a state's democratic development and a healthy civil society should produce an effective, working civic culture. "Civic culture," a term developed by two American political scientists in the mid–twentieth century, is a pluralist framework of consensus and diversity, based on communication and persuasion, that permits change but also moderates its potentially disruptive impact (Almond and Verba, ch.1). In less idealistic terms, civic culture is a certain set of rules shared by all participants in the political process, which establishes the groundwork for institutional life. In Spain the constant presence of civil war made a functional civic culture more an aspiration than a reality. Each party believed that its solution would achieve a civic culture, as opposed to the false pretensions and useless factionalism of its adversaries. As control of the state could only generate partial patriotism, civil society could not fix a common basis of sociopolitical values; there were not enough shared criteria.

Spanish civil society, aside from its systemic incompleteness, its gaps, had the structural difficulty of being very unevenly extended. Some areas, like Catalonia, with its old merchant and artisan tradition and early experience of industrial revolution, had a rich associative tissue, but the people in other parts of Spain lacked the habits, such as punctuality and a recognized work ethic, that facilitated the takeoff of industrialization. The liberal assault on the church and the breakup of its extensive landholdings after 1837 directed investment toward the always prestigious ownership of agrarian property rather than toward commerce or manufacturing. This focus, in turn, involved new landholders in liberal politics and factional strife but without the backup of a healthy civil society. The consistent trend toward urbanization, the push to get off the land, had two focal points: Madrid and Barcelona. The focus for agrarian interests and most especially for social promotion through politics became Madrid, the state capital and parliamentary and administrative center of Spain, while Barcelona became the economic center of the country, a second city that developed into an anticapital and the hub of all dissent against politics as usual. Madrid was a large city, but its habits reflected traditional rural values and a taste for stateliness; Barcelona was characterized by the modern push and shove of business (see Salcedo; also M. Rivière). Promising different kinds of personal success and having clearly dissimilar cultural markets, Madrid and Barcelona attracted different immigrants. Both cities grew extensively in the second half of the nineteenth century and engaged in a kind of race for size and rank. By the 1930s they had become metropolitan centers with million-plus populations. The rest of Spain was equally driven by the pressure of urbanization, but no other Spanish city came close to the twin rivals (see, for a more complete explanation, Ucelay-Da Cal, "Llegar a capital").

A War of Cities

Late-nineteenth-century Spanish society was marked by deep cleavages— religious, regional, social—that reflected the uneven spread of economic growth, as well as the bitter memory of accumulated civil wars. While representative government had been successfully imposed, many Spaniards felt that politics was superficial, a pretense, and that liberal institutions were false unless they became fully participative. The rejection of participation colored most aspirations to radical change, from the diverse nationalisms opposed to liberal centralization to the revolutionary appeal of anarchism. Much of the change effected in the nineteenth century was made law but not put into practice for decades. By the early twentieth century, the implications of conflict born of socioeconomic disparity could best be seen by the overall pattern of city growth and the resulting urban system (see Jacobs, *Cities* and *Quebec*). The continuous driving force of urbanization led to what has been called a revolution of rising expectations (Lerner), which determined the politics of the Second Republic after 1931. Accordingly, urban studies of Spanish politics are an increasingly productive line of investigation (Radcliffe).

The steady pressure of urbanization was invisible to many observers, especially foreigners, who tended to identify backwardness with widespread inefficient grain production and therefore with the dead weight of an overwhelming agrarian question (see the British testimony gathered by Cunningham [*Spanish Front*]). But the secret to Spain's future lay in its cities. Civil peace, civil society, and civic culture all met in the reality of urbanization, and all presupposed the triumph of urban values over the traditional verities of the agrarian way of life, which outsiders found so attractive. Even combat in the Spanish Civil War reflected the contemporary implications of urban development. From its inception, the struggle was waged for the control of cities, and the defense or fall of urban centers decided campaigns and, ultimately, the conflict itself. Spain is a very mountainous country, with a high central plateau and transversal ranges, which did nothing to facilitate transport. Offensive and defensive movement was made largely possible by the roads (*carreteras nacionales*) built during Miguel Primo de Rivera's dictatorship in the 1920s, and battles were often planned with road maps in hand.

The underlying urban logic that marked the war derived largely from the immediate cause of its outbreak, a failed army coup that deepened the political divide between left and right. As the uprising spread along the lines of confrontation among cities and across provinces, some garrisons held to their word and successfully rebelled, whereas others wavered in their decision, faltered, and were overcome. The moderate president of the parliament, Diego Martínez Barrio, who became premier of the short-lived cabinet on 18–19 July, manned the phones all night and talked numerous military authorities out of their commitment, but the coup organizer, General Emilio Mola, refused to yield, and the left-wing socialists forced President Manuel Azaña to withdraw the government (see Alonso Baño). The negotiations succeeded in determining the territorial configuration of the revolt. Over the next couple of days, the plotters attempted to seize control of all provincial capitals and other, lesser towns—garrison towns—and the coup turned into a generalized conflict. Enthusiastic rebels found the political backing that encouraged them to arrest superior officers willing to contemporize, or else they were unnerved by the resistance that confronted them.

The borders between territory held by the Nationalists and the Loyalists—the Republicans and the revolutionaries—marked the physical and moral distance between inner, agrarian Spain and the two major metropolitan centers united with the export-oriented periphery. The Republicans held Madrid, Barcelona, Valencia, Bilbao, and Málaga. The only important cities (those with over two hundred thousand inhabitants) that the military rebels held were Sevilla, Zaragoza, and Granada, all agrarian. Significantly, those towns that voted for monarchical candidates in the municipal elections that acted as a plebiscite in April 1931 and brought on the proclamation of the republic were also the main support points of the July 1936 revolt. Places such as Lugo, Burgos, Soria, Ávila, Vitoria, Pamplona, Cádiz, Palme de Mallorca, and Las Palmas de Gran Canaria proved of outstanding importance to the rebels in the first couple weeks of war. The junta of generals established its center in Burgos in July, and Franco, on being proclaimed *generalíssimo* in October, fixed his high command in Salamanca. Both headquarters were located in interior towns that had not held political significance for centuries. Catholic partisans of the Glorious National Uprising compared the conflict to Saint Augustine's confrontation between the City of God and the venal City of Man (see Sánchez Recio).

For both sides the strategically decisive factor was control of Madrid. From July 1936 until March of the following year, the rebels sought to take the capital, the ultimate symbol of authority. What saved Madrid was Republican control of the railroad (the Madrid-Zaragoza-Alicante, or MZA), which ran from the Mediterranean (Cartagena and Alicante) and connected the capital with Valencia, Barcelona, and the French border. Foreign military assistance—Soviet ships at the ports and railheads—was accordingly able to reach the beleaguered capital in the fall of 1936 and stave off the assault at the right moment. The International Brigades were headquartered in Albacete, in what would seem an unlikely choice but for its location just above the juncture of the Alicante and Cartagena rail lines leading to the capital. Similarly, the Republican government moved out of besieged Madrid, first to Valencia (under Francisco Largo Caballero) and then along the MZA to Barcelona in October 1937 (under Juan Negrín). After Italian pirate submarines sank Soviet vessels, the French Communist Party set up a line of freighters to sustain the maritime lifeline of the Republican cause.

Seen from a kind of macroeconomic perspective, the war thus became a long-drawn-out struggle between the less-developed agrocities of the interior and the metropolitan network of major cities open to foreign influences. Well-fed and unimaginative in the face of sharp imbalances of wealth, the agrocities were marked by religious fundamentalism and rural folkways. While the cities of the agrarian interior remained focused on the national market, the major cities sought business with outsiders. The metropolitan network, based on the major railway, included Madrid, the traditional hub of the transport system; Barcelona, the industrial capital of the Spanish economy; and Málaga, Cartagena, Alicante, and Valencia, the export centers of the Mediterranean coast. Also in Republican hands was the north coast of Spain, from Gijón to Bilbao, separated from Madrid and the urban arc of the Mediterranean by a wide band of insurgent territory. The population in the urban network was angry with the drag of cultural backwardness and filled with egalitarian ardor for citizenship as something inherent to cities. This aggressive sense of modernity even imbued the lifestyle of pro-Republican areas defined by market-oriented agriculture: Valencian agrocities, for example, which shipped citrus fruits to London, were particularly virulent centers of anticlerical fury (see Bosch). In sum, though there may have been no common civic culture, there was a confrontation of modern civil society, which itself was divided between moderate Republicans and *obrerista* partisans of working-class revolution, with traditional premodern civil society, which was centered on the church.

As the war dragged on, the agrocities of the Nationalist cause basked in their abundance of food production, although they lacked the manufactured goods that came out of the factories of the metropolitan network, especially textiles. The Republican zone, in contrast, went hungry, particularly when the loss of Andalusia cut back on olive oil. The urban workers had taken for granted that the countryside would feed them while they went about their self-important ideological missions. Tired of revolutionary interference, the peasantry in Republican-held territory withdrew produce from controlled markets, stimulating inflation. Refugees fleeing besieged Madrid and the advancing Nationalist armies flooded the major Republican cities on the coast: Barcelona's population grew from a little over a million at the beginning of the struggle to some three million by the end. Such a pressure of hungry mouths only made the problems of urban consumption worse, even as the Republican government won control of the system of distribution after the spring of 1937. Starting with Alicante in late 1936, the swollen cities were submitted to aerial bombardment along the main transport route (the MZA and *carreteras nacionales*), until 1938, when such attacks became systematic and were aimed at the urban centers themselves. This scale of civilian victimization was new in warfare and fixed the reputation of the Spanish conflict as the rehearsal for the next world war (see Lindqvist).

Under Franco's leadership as *generalísimo* after October 1936, Nationalist forces conquered the Basque provinces, Santander, and Asturias in 1937, then pressed down along the Ebro River, cutting the link between Valencia and Barcelona in April 1938. Control of the Lérida Pyrenees at the same time also meant that Barcelona's electricity—the power that drove the factories came from dams in the mountains—could be shut off, adding to the urban misery. The failure of the Republican counteroffensive to reestablish the connection between Catalonia and the central zone in the summer of 1938 sealed the fate of the republic. Franco's forces conquered Barcelona at the end of January 1939, sweeping half a million soldiers and refugees before them, and took over the border with France in early February. The Republican holdings were reduced to the railroad backbone from Madrid to Cartagena, Alicante, and Valencia, which succumbed a few weeks later.

The Franco dictatorship was not generous with the agrocities of the interior that gave it victory. Rumors spread of punishing Madrid for her betrayal and sinfulness (see Giménez Caballero) by making Sevilla the capital of the "New Spain," but nothing came of the idea (Girón de Velasco 61). The new regime preferred not to experiment and kept the traditional capital. With no significant support for Burgos, Salamanca, or any other similar city, the payback for the undeveloped interior did not involve increased public investment in the conservative heartland but rather produced a perverse kind of cultural promotion. The values and agenda of the rural interior were imposed on the more sophisticated metropolitan system, and political immigrants from minor agrocities were allowed to lord it over the conquered city dwellers, whose proud values of modernity were quashed by the consistent advocacy of traditional customs and religiosity. Nevertheless, over time, and somewhat paradoxically, postwar repression marked the trends by which definitive urbanization triumphed in Spain after the 1960s, when a strong tendency toward abandonment of historic agrarian areas and a clear majority of urban inhabitants held sway. These same trends and the resulting change in attitudes guaranteed the eventual end of the Franco regime and everything it stood for (see Miguel).

David K. Herzberger

Representations of the
Civil War in Historiography

One of the earliest histories of the civil war published in Spain is entitled *La guerra de reconquista española y el criminal comunismo: El glorioso ejército nacional. Mártires y héroes* ("The War of Spanish Reconquest and Criminal Communism: The Glorious National Army: Martyrs and Heroes"). The book appeared in 1940 and was written during and immediately after the war by Enrique Esperabé de Arteaga, a well-known historian and member of the Spanish Royal Academy of History. Manuel García de Prieto, Marqués de Alhucemas, wrote the prologue to the book and praised the author for his "objectivity," "pureness of intention," and "love of truth"[1] in representing the events and meaning of the conflict (ix).

Both the title and prologue of Esperabé's book (as well as the nearly 650 pages that follow) hardly point to objectivity. But the work does illustrate the perspective that official historiography in Spain would take over the next few decades and underscores several problems of historical inquiry related to the official version of the Spanish Civil War. These problems are especially relevant for students who have not been trained in historical methodology or who may be studying the civil war for the first time; they involve matters of fact as well as of narration. For example, who is speaking about the war in Spain and who is not permitted to speak?

What information is made available for public consumption and what information is suppressed? Who is portrayed as bearing the mantle of virtue in the war and who as embodying the forces of destruction? How do language and narration shape the meaning of history and seek to define truth in the context of the stories that are told? Certainly, these problems are not uncommon in the writing and reading of history in general, but they have particular resonance in Francoist Spain, where control over history became largely the private enterprise of the state.

Even a cursory look at Esperabé's book shows how these issues immediately move to the fore. For example, what is viewed as a civil war by the rest of the world is labeled the Spanish Reconquest in the author's title; thus the conflict is linked to the popular mythology of the Christian victory over the Arabs in medieval Spain. Further, the Republican side is framed by the evils of Communism, portrayed now as the devil incarnate. For the fallen heroes of the Nationalist army, martyrdom sanctions their glory in service to God and country. In the work of Esperabé and other Francoist historians, the entire history of the war—from the strategies of combat to the intrigue of international politics—is depicted as a clash between the true, authentic Spain (the Nationalists) and the false, traitorous Spain (the Republicans). Thanks to the righteous hand of God and the courageous spirit of the victors, Spain may now turn, in 1940, to the restoration of its essential character that once lifted it to moral and imperial majesty.

Most Spanish historians who wrote about the civil war during the nearly four decades of Francoist rule did so from the perspective of the victors. For students studying the conflict, this approach may not be unexpected. They probably understand that the winners of a war gain a power and authority to which the losers can only aspire. But students in the United States generally believe that both losers and dissenters will have the opportunity to enter the fray and give voice to their perceptions of the past, even if these perceptions are unpopular among most of the population. Students might also assume that historians are working from a common body of archival material available to all who wish to study it, which was clearly not the case in Spain during the Franco years; historians sympathetic to the defeated republic were denied not only access to materials but also a voice.

The exclusion of Republican sympathizers is not surprising, since the Nationalist regime set out not only to control all forms of publishing, including textbooks and scholarly writing, but also to exert authority over the teaching of history throughout the country and to oversee faculty appointments in university history departments. Such controls were critical for implementing the larger Francoist agenda related to history, which, as Paul Preston has noted, was the "continuation of the war by other means" (*Politics* 30). For the regime and its historians, all that took place in the war, as well as the political instability that had overwhelmed earlier Republican attempts to govern the nation, confirmed the need for the military uprising in 1936, justified the bloodshed of the conflict, and legitimized the repression carried out by the Franco government. In other words, students need to understand from the beginning that, although all historiography conveys a certain perspective, during Francoist rule this perspective was single-voiced and narrowly focused to give historical substance to the regime.

Most students in the American classroom will probably have little detailed knowledge of the Spanish Civil War. They may have heard of Guernica, for example, but are unlikely to know what actually took place there. A good encyclopedic overview of the war, with general reference to the political conflicts and military encounters, would provide the necessary context. An overview is all the more pressing when Spanish historiography is being taught, since the military aspects of the conflict were generally consigned to a secondary status by Spanish historians during the Franco years. There were a number of reasons for this downplaying, some linked to the desire to portray the conflict solely in a way that validated the political standing of the regime and some born of practicality: archives were not well maintained, documents were lost, and papers were purposely destroyed by the military and police to eliminate evidence of atrocities, executions, and other abuses. From within Spain, it was thus virtually impossible to confirm the facts of the military conflict, including casualties in any given battle, tactics of the officers in war planning, the range of weapons used, and the number and type of soldiers who participated (e.g., mercenaries, foreigners, conscripts, or militia). After Franco's death in 1975, military archives were gradually opened and many "lost" materials were finally examined. Nonetheless, historians did not gain access to a number of political and military documents from the war until well into the 1990s.

Given both the inaccessibility of data and the reluctance to explore details of the military side of the conflict, Francoist historians sought primarily to explain the necessity and virtue of the war in the broad context of Spanish history. Because of the significance that Francoists attached to the distant past, it is important for students to have a general grasp of Spanish history, from the medieval and imperialist periods through the sixteenth century. Knowing the crucial facts about the past that were the basis for Francoist historiography, they will see how historians used these facts to their advantage. Students need to grasp how events of the distant and recent past are connected in the story of Spain told by historians of the regime so that the Franco victory becomes a central part of that story.

Two dominant approaches to the civil war emerged under the umbrella of Francoist history, both closely linked to the study of medieval and imperial Spain. For the Falange, whose influence immediately after the war was especially important for solidifying the regime's political base, history showed that the Spanish character was formed by the nobility of struggle and conflict. In this way of thinking, the Spanish people revealed from the beginning of their existence a propensity for aggression and exaltation; they were a religious, Christian people whose struggles led them to explore and conquer the world. The Falange could therefore extol the civil war as an integral component of tradition whereby violence served as a creative force that had fostered many accomplishments in the past (see also Moreiras-Menor in this volume). Further, as Michael Richards has pointed out ("Civil War"), once violence underpinned the ideological framework of Spanish historiography, it could more easily be implemented as policy, allowing the regime to purify the nation by ridding it of elements incompatible with its authentic history.

The idea of purifying the nation finds resonance in the second approach to the war that dominates Spanish historiography—that of the church. For the most part, the Vatican supported the Nationalist forces throughout the war, viewing the republic as a dangerous enemy of the church and its long tradition of influence in Spanish society. Following Franco's victory in April 1939 the pope sent a congratulatory telegram to the Spanish leader thanking him for "the desired Catholic victory in Spain" and urging the Spanish people to "return with renewed vigor to the ancient and Christian traditions" that had guided them for centuries (Preston, *Politics* 32). With the church's blessing firmly in hand, the metaphor of crusade soon gained prominence in Spanish historiography as a way of linking the Nationalist victory to a noble, religious undertaking rooted in Christian conquest in general and the Reconquest in Spain in particular (see also Richards in this volume). In fact, the first biography of Franco published after the war located the Nationalist leader squarely in the tradition of the legendary El Cid and was titled *Franco, el reconquistador* ("Franco, the Reconqueror"; Herce Vales and Sanz Nogués).

Spanish historians thus set about portraying the Nationalist victory as a return to the true and authentic values of Spain. They demanded from historiography "a militant commitment" (Pasamar Alzuria 191) aimed at rooting out the nineteenth-century traditions of liberalism and positivism that had not only misinterpreted the essential character of the past but also led the nation astray in the present. Liberalism, which had promoted diversity, progress, and democratic values linked to political and industrial transformations in Europe, was demonized as anticlericalism. Historians characterized the war as primarily an attack on the church, emphasizing the burning of convents and monasteries and the execution of priests and nuns.

Students will most likely grasp the general principle that Spanish historians tell a story in which Franco is a hero, but it is important to have them see examples. A particularly good one is the representation of the church during what the Francoists portrayed as the Republican tyranny that caused the war. In his 1940 book on the Spanish church entitled *La gran víctima* ("The Great Victim"), Aniceto de Castro Albarrán offers text and photos to illustrate how the church was targeted for destruction by Republicans before and during the war. The book is filled with pictures of the bombing and burning of churches during the 1930s, with an accompanying commentary on the church's heroic contributions to what the book assures the reader is the authentic Christian Spain. In the context of Spanish historiography, the photographs are meant to show the danger of allowing the national core, the eternal Spain, to be undermined by internal dissent. The conclusion to be drawn from the book is that the poor physical condition of churches in many towns throughout Spain, and the lack of priests in these towns, was due to the looting, burning, and general violence of the Communists, anarchists, and other godless groups from which the Franco regime saved Spain. In this way, Spanish historians condemned a large segment of the past by tying Republican atrocities during the civil war to misguided liberalism of the previous century. What is more, they contended that liberalism continued to vitiate the national character in the early decades of the twentieth century. In contrast, the Nationalists were seen to embody the values of the church and thus of traditional Spain, giving both a preeminent role in the nation's history. Again, if students are well versed in the Spanish past and how the church helped shape Spanish history (especially during the fifteenth and sixteenth centuries), the strategies of Francoist historians come into sharper focus (see also Vincent in this volume).

During the first decade after the war, both the Falange and the church helped create a narrow view of the conflict as a fight for the authentic character of the nation linked primarily to the past rather than as a progression toward a new and vital future. Such a vision of the war, and of Spanish history as a whole, continued to be taught in the schools and promoted in historical research well into the 1960s. By the late 1940s, historians began to write a revised version of the civil war aimed at linking Spain more closely to the victorious Western allies of World War II, then fully immersed in the cold war. The intention of the regime thus shifted to reinventing the civil war as a prescient revolution against the imperialistic evils of Communism. As Preston notes, Franco's consistent opposition to the liberal democratic traditions of the Western allies mattered far less than his "defence against the Soviet threat" (Introduction 3). Francoist historiography thus moved from the religious crusade metaphor to portrayals of the war as an early struggle against the onslaught of Soviet aggression. This shift does not mean that the crusade mentality disappeared entirely from Spanish historiography on the civil war; rather, the changing political realities of a polarized world required a different use of history. The myths of national unity and social harmony in Spain, firmly established as outgrowths of the authentic Spanish past, still held sway in historiography. Attaching itself solidly to the anti-Communist values of the West, the regime thus quelled the once-strong aversion among the allies to Franco's ties to Hitler and Mussolini.

It is important for students to understand that while Francoist historians sought to justify the civil war as a religious crusade, as a fight against Communism, and as a means of restoring the true Spain to prominence, they generally excluded from study the long-simmering principal reasons for the war: the divisive economic structures of Spanish society and the class struggle over wealth held by a small number of landowners. The regime had relied heavily during the war on the backing of upper-class Spaniards and industrialists, who continued to play a pivotal role in the government's stability after the Nationalist victory. In the postwar period historians therefore avoided drawing links between the economic reforms sought by the Republicans in the 1930s—reforms intended largely to redistribute wealth—and the conservative rejection of these reforms as a major cause of the war. The past was more usable when depicted in terms of good versus evil, the spiritual versus the material, and traditionalism versus modernization, with the outcome of the civil war affirming the righteousness of the good, the spiritual, and the traditional. It was only after

Franco's death that a more nuanced and socioeconomic perspective found its way into Spanish historiography and into the teaching of the civil war.

When students see how Francoist historians dominated the representation of the Spanish past, they are ready to consider voices of dissent from Francoist historiography. It is important, however, that they not think of this dissent as an expression of unsullied truths told by those with a noble cause, in contrast to perfidious lies of the Franco regime. Rather, these writings of dissent locate the civil war in a context that creates different meanings. In general, non-Francoist historians set out not to create a new body of facts that would set the record straight but to establish the foundation for a different political agenda: to show the illegitimacy of all that Franco represented. For this reason, it is more useful to have students first read the Francoist historians and then turn to dissident writers whose works can be read against the official historiography of the regime.

Republican historians who wished to write about the civil war—its causes, battles, and meaning—faced nearly insurmountable obstacles. A large number of liberal historians chose exile after the war; those who remained in Spain were severely restricted by censorship, limited access to historical documents, and sometimes fear for their personal safety. Many found it more feasible to explore less contemporary periods of the Spanish past, hoping to avoid controversy by examining materials generally of scant interest to censors and other government caretakers of history. The ability of Republican historians to give meaning to the war and its aftermath through study of the past was also restricted by lack of funding for their research projects and by their exclusion from academic positions in universities and institutes.

Many historians sympathetic to the republic fled Spain after the war and accepted university positions in other countries (e.g., Manuel Tuñón de Lara in France, Américo Castro in the United States, and Claudio Sánchez Albornoz in Argentina). In general, for these historians the war served less as a focal point for military analysis than as an impetus for reflection on what had produced such a tragic conflict. To a large extent, the exiled historians pursued an explanation within what they vaguely defined as the Spanish character or the Spanish mind. Hence they constructed a rhetorical history (as opposed to a more science-based, analytic study of the facts) that paralleled in style and technique the very history of the Francoists that they had set out to oppose. Rather than use data to locate the root causes of the war in a social and economic system that kept wealth in the hands of a few, retarded social and economic equality, and hindered modernization, Republican historians most often pursued the abstract concept of Spanish history as a manifestation of the nation's soul. They then represented the civil war as a conflict deeply embedded in this soul. Only the Catalan historian Jaume Vicens i Vives pursued a more objective, data-oriented historiography during this period. Although he opposed the essentialist tradition of Spanish historians and opened the past to statistical analysis, he and his small cohort of colleagues in Barcelona were marginalized by the powerful historical establishment sympathetic to the regime and thus had little impact on Spanish historiography until late in the Franco years.

Of the Spaniards living in exile, the two most prominent historians to gain broad recognition were Américo Castro and Claudio Sánchez Albornoz. Both embraced historiography in the rhetorical, essentialist mode and both sought to explain the past and present by identifying a series of salient national traits. Castro writes in *España en su historia* (1948; "Spain in Its History") that it is important to understand Spain as a nation that simultaneously affirms and rejects life and therefore lives in a permanent state of conflicting desires. For Castro, the principal trait of Spanish history is its "Spanishness," defined as all that makes Spain non-European (e.g., the unique confluence of Muslims, Jews, and Christians beginning in 711) and therefore different from other countries. In a similar rhetorical vein, Sánchez Albornoz claims in *España, un enigma histórico* (1956; "Spain, a Historical Enigma") that the Spanish character is enigmatic, even mysterious, and thus defies complete comprehension. In contrast to Castro, Sánchez Albornoz views the Arab invasion of Spain as a destructive force that inhibited development and modernization and kept Spain removed from progressive European influences. Yet for both Castro and Sánchez Albornoz, the civil war was an inevitable conflict related to the nation's unique character flaws that could be detected early in its history.

Republicans writing in exile produced no significant work of historical scholarship on the civil war or its causes during the Franco years. Nonetheless, students need to understand that many Republican intellectuals undertook activities to help shed light on the conflict, even if the impetus for their work was overtly political. In 1965, José Martínez, who had founded in Paris the publishing house Ruedo Ibérico to promote leftist causes in Spain, began to publish *Cuadernos del Ruedo Ibérico*. The journal quickly gained intellectual prestige both in and outside Spain as a strong voice of opposition to the regime, often focusing on Spanish historiography. As Preston has pointed out, its goal was to "[dismantle] the lies and distortions of the regime concerning both its present and its past" (Introduction 4). Further, while many exiled Republican groups carried on a small-scale version of the polemics and often petty disputes that had plagued the Republican ranks during the war, Ruedo Ibérico promoted serious scholarship with the publication of two key books on the conflict. First, Ruedo Ibérico published the Spanish translation in 1961 of Hugh Thomas's *The Spanish Civil War*, which was smuggled into Spain by the thousands of copies and soon became a prominent counterpoint to the regime's historiography among left-leaning Spaniards. Second, in 1963 Ruedo Ibérico published Herbert Southworth's *El mito de la cruzada de Franco* ("The Myth of Franco's Crusade"), which derided the crusade mentality of Spanish histories of the war and undermined their credibility. The book drew irate condemnation from historians in Franco's Center for Civil War Studies but was embraced by the international community as a rigorous debunking of Franco's mythification of the war. Both the journal and publishing house of Ruedo Ibérico gave voice to Republican dissent in the exiled community but had a far smaller impact in Spain itself, where its publications were often blocked for political reasons.

Claude Lévi-Strauss once noted that "History is . . . never history, but history for" (*Savage Mind* 257). Republican historians, intellectuals, and political figures certainly sought to use history to their advantage, and they did so in ways not unlike the Francoist regime's use of the past to build a solid foundation for the legitimacy of their position. In the years before the civil war, Manuel Azaña (who served as war minister and premier of the Second Republic) attempted to promulgate a Republican history of Spain. In a series of speeches in 1932 (*Obras*), he legitimized the republic by affirming that the only authentic Spain of the past was one of diversity and change—hence the future lay in innovation and progress that embraced pluralism. Francoist historians would later define authenticity in the Spanish past in opposition to Azaña's way of thinking, but in both instances history was perceived as a means of legitimizing one position over another. Of course, Azaña's pronouncements fell far short of defining a national history standard on the scale of Francoist historiography. His influence was also short-lived, as the republic slipped into chaos and chaos soon led to civil war.

Students might focus on how Republican and exile historiography generally imitates the style and technique of Francoist writing, though it does so to set forth a different understanding of the civil war and the regime. They might read one historiography against the other and look for points of contrast (e.g., in myth, metaphor, storytelling, or the essence of national character). Comparing the two is critical, for it is difficult to exaggerate the overbearing weight of Francoist representations of the war and the role that history played in giving legitimacy to the dictatorship from 1939 until 1975. As Franco himself put it, his regime represented "the coronation of a historical process" (*Franco* 20). Consonance of historical writing became paramount as the regime sought to gain ownership of the past rather than awaken it to unfettered scrutiny. If the purpose of official historiography was a "continuation of the war by other means," the desired end was easily achieved (Preston, *Politics* 30). As the Spanish historian and ardent Franco supporter Rafael Calvo Serer wrote in 1949, "We must maintain now at all costs the homogeneity achieved in 1939" (167). While brute force and oppression were used by the Franco government to secure this homogeneity, historiography served as a less violent but potent means of shaping and defining the government's authority. Students may start out thinking about the military victory of Franco as the key to his control over Spain, but if they come to understand that brute force was only the beginning phase of a domination of Spanish culture and society deeply rooted in control over Spanish history, they will also come to understand the role of words as a social and political determinant of power.

Note

1. All translations from the Spanish are mine unless otherwise noted.

Mary Vincent

The Spanish Civil War
as a Religious Conflict

No subject lends itself more to contested representations than religion does. Two thousand years of Christian history make it impossible to present events as simple occurrences: they will be understood and represented in an eschatological framework that both imputes divine purpose to the way in which events unfold and endows some of these events—most dramatically religious killing, or martyrdom—with a specific theological significance. In this framework the individual sacrifice of a life for Christ becomes the central fact of the Spanish Civil War; the martyrs' assured place in heaven puts them in a transcendental drama that is enacted throughout and outside historical time. The Spanish Civil War is understood ahistorically as a venue for an eternal symbolic struggle.

Religious violence is thus a difficult subject to address. The events of 11 September have made the subject more resonant but not necessarily more understandable to students from essentially secular Western societies. Current media depictions of Islamic notions of martyrdom play on its exoticism, positing a profound opposition between fundamentalism and democracy. Herein lies the crux of the difficulty. Our students perceive religion as a private affair, a matter of individual conscience. Accommodating different religious beliefs in the classroom is governed by our shared, secular value of tolerance and so is not a problem, though it may be a source of debate. Such coexistence is not foreign to democratic, pluralist societies, but the ambition to determine the religious and moral beliefs (or at least behavior) of others definitely is. The aspiration that all citizens of a particular country either should or should not practice a particular religious faith is thus a means of confronting students with the otherness of the past. For, as such an aspiration was fundamental to the conflict that tore Spain asunder between 1936 and 1939, it is fundamental to any historical representation of the Spanish Civil War.

While the main fault line running through Spain in the 1930s was that between pro- and anti-Republicans, embedded in this struggle was a myriad of other, overlapping conflicts. The Republican constitution of 1931 inaugurated a bitter legislative battle to make Spain a secular state along the French model, with an independent church, devoid of state support or official function, and religious practice confined to the private sphere. Only civil marriages were recognized in law, cemeteries were secularized, and in many areas processions and church bells were banned. Despite a fiercely intransigent response by much of the Spanish church, including the cardinal primate, Isidro Gomá y Tomás, some sectors were willing to accede to at least part of this program, as the French church had eventually done (Lannon, "Church's Crusade").

The 1931 constitution instituted freedom of worship for only the second time in Spain's history. Yet there was some distance between the intellectual secularism of many parliamentary deputies and the popular anticlericalism demonstrated on the streets. In May 1931, urban crowds attacked and torched churches and convents in several Spanish cities. There was considerable destruction, but no one was killed and only in Málaga was every church in the city damaged. Classroom discussion of the various forms taken by anticlerical violence often benefits from diachronic comparisons. Why were priests killed in the violence that accompanied the Asturias uprising of October 1934 but not during the church burnings of May 1931? Students might also look further back, to the Barcelona Tragic Week of 1909, which cost only three lives but many churches, or even to the Paris Commune of 1871.

People and buildings were not the only objects of anticlerical attack. During the Tragic Week, bodies were disinterred from convent burial grounds and exposed to public view, as they were again in 1936 (Lincoln). As photographic evidence reveals, these actions were (and are) profoundly shocking, but oral history suggests that at least some observers reacted with amusement (Fraser, *Blood of Spain: The Experience* 152). Though Ronald Fraser's informant refers specially to children finding the corpses funny, these children were part of a society in which the grotesque provoked ridicule and physical deformity was comic. This combination of violence, ridicule, and transgression—so reminiscent of carnival—reminds us that the form of antireligious violence was as important as its occurrence (Delgado Ruiz). Despoiling corpses was a form of street violence, embarrassing to the Republican authorities and far removed from the secularism of Republican intellectuals.

Desecrating graves was distressing, yet it was not an attack on sentient beings. During the Spanish Civil War some 6,832 priests, monks, and nuns were killed by the Republican militias (Montero Moreno). While very few of these deaths were authorized by the government, this statistic is still unpalatable, particularly for many seminar teachers who, like me, sympathize instinctively with the Republican side. The raw shock of the numbers can inspire a confrontation with the past for students who may interpret the Second Republic as a modernizing and even as a progressive regime. The atrocious ways in which many priests were killed serves as another reminder of this contradiction. Beatings, torture, humiliation, sexual taunting, and mutilation (both ante- and postmortem) were all common (Montero Moreno; Cueva Merino, "Religious Persecution" and "'Si los curas'"). There were cases of postmortem castration in which the severed genitals were inserted in the victims' mouths—a gesture recorded both in the early modern wars of religion and in medieval warfare. There is no straight line from, for example, twelfth-century Europe to 1930s Spain, but that does not negate the usefulness of comparison. Students may also profitably explore anthropological work on ritual violence, particularly in a Spanish context (T. Mitchell; Gilmore).

Priests' status, both as men and as celibates, was clearly implicated in these ritualized forms of violence. The clergy's self-perception as a "caste apart" (Vincent, *Catholicism* 26), their distinctive dress and social distinction, made them an object of sexual and scatological fascination in popular culture (Álvarez Junco). Both perpetrators and victims of the killings were overwhelmingly men. According to Antonio Montero Moreno, only 283 of the victims were nuns, even though there were many more religious sisters in Spain in 1936 than there were priests or monks. This statistic is not reflected in contemporary representations of the killings: tales of raped nuns were a propaganda staple. Though these were intended as atrocity stories, sexual violation also served as a metaphor for the violation of sacred space—churches, shrines, cemeteries—that accompanied the killings. No nuns were actually raped (Sánchez, *Spanish Civil War* 57–58), though convents and nuns' bodies were, if anything, even more popular sites for pornographic fantasy than their male equivalents were. The respect accorded to female virginity in contemporary popular culture may have protected these women, whereas the contempt for male virginity sealed the fate of many priests.

Most of the anticlerical killings took place in July and August 1936. Many were carried out extralegally, usually by groups of militiamen. Churches were set alight, religious artifacts and parish archives were burnt in the streets, and images were removed from churches and shrines and often mutilated or burned. Arturo Barea struggled to make sense of what he saw:

> Bit by bit, I recognized the pieces of scenery in the despoiled church before me. Here were the ladders of worm-eaten pinewood, which had been blazing with votive candles. Here was the shrine, open and void. (*Clash* 168)

As Barea indicates, such violence involves catharsis. Space is re-created or redefined and the old is destroyed to make way for the new. An interesting way into this subject might be David Salle's 1987 painting *Demonic Roland*. Salle has repainted a photograph of militiamen holding the

Demonic Roland, by David Salle. 1987.

severed heads of religious statues as the central part of his composition, which re-creates not only space but also time. Among contemporary records, photographs of confessionals placed in the streets attest to this re-creation, or even inversion, of sacred space.

Photographs appear to capture the past, presenting historic moments as they occurred. They are thus some of the best texts to use in the classroom, for in reading the images students have to consider how the photographs may have been falsified (see also Wasson in this volume). The posed propaganda pictures produced in quantity by both sides offer straightforward examples of manipulation; the subtler influences of angle, composition, and aesthetic judgment in the works of photographers such as Robert Capa and "Chim" Seymour may be harder to discern. A parallel may be found in eyewitness accounts and memoirs of the civil war, which suggest differing perceptions of the violence. Franz Borkenau commented that church-burning "seemed an administrative business" (74), whereas Barea reported gunfire coming from churches, which were then stormed in an outburst of popular anger (*Clash* 121–25). Both texts are prime examples of Valentine Cunningham's "border at which fact overlaps fiction" (Introduction xxviii).

Of all the representations of the religious violence of the civil war, the image of priests firing from bell towers is among the most tenacious. It featured heavily in the process of claim and counterclaim that served as propaganda during the war and has been vividly dramatized more recently in Ken Loach's film *Land and Freedom* (1995). Yet this image is fictional, unsubstantiated by historical evidence (Cueva Merino, "'Si los curas'"). Its endorsement by the Republican authorities reveals their profound discomfort with the killings, with the brutality and vulgarity of popular anticlerical violence, and with the government's complete inability to stop it. Official Republican discourse used the clichéd image of rifle-wielding clerics as a means both of denying and of justifying anticlerical violence. Such representations also endorsed the church's identification as a class enemy, which lay behind much of the proletarian violence.

Andreu Nin's claim that "the working class has solved the problem of the Church, simply by not leaving one standing" (Delgado Ruiz 154; my trans.) disguises a profound difference between bourgeois and proletarian anticlericalism, even while it acknowledges that virtually all Republican groups perceived the church as a problem. Paradoxically, Nin's analysis finds an echo among the victors of the civil war, for whom the anticlerical massacres simply confirmed a persecuting trajectory directed against the church under the Second Republic. For some, not least of them General Franco, this persecution was the result of a shadowy conspiracy between the occult forces of atheistic Communism, Freemasonry, and international Jewry. Neither the inherent absurdity of such a combination nor the paucity of these groups in Spain—where the Communist Party only gained a mass membership during the civil war, the Freemasons had as strong a following among army generals as among Republican intellectuals, and there was no Jewish population—seems to have dented this belief among its subscribers. An interesting topic for classroom discussion is thus the issue of conspiracy theories, when they become prevalent, who believes them, and why (Girard).

It is not only conspiracy theorists who posit a trajectory of persecution from the beginning of the Second Republic. Some clerical commentators, notably the historian Vicente Cárcel Ortí (*La persecución*), argue strongly that the bloodletting of the civil war was the violent culmination of an anticlerical persecution that began much earlier. As the Benedictine historian Hilari Raguer has pointed out, Cárcel Ortí's work is directly related to the campaigns to have the clerical martyrs of the civil war recognized as saints by the Catholic Church. These efforts came to fruition on 11 March 2001 when Pope John Paul II beatified 233 priests and religious killed during the Spanish Civil War, the greatest single number of beatifications in the church's history. They were presented in the context of twentieth-century persecutions of the Christian faith, but there was still a continuity with the crusade ideology that had characterized the Nationalists' war effort. Cárcel Ortí's work is part of what might be termed an official church historiography, one that sees popular and intellectual anticlericalism as two sides of the same coin, draws a causal link between secularizing legislation and antireligious violence, and assigns an essentially passive role to the Spanish church (Pérez Ledesma).

Such an approach raises the question not only of different representations of the past but also of the use of these representations, or what we might call the purpose of the past. Cárcel Ortí's work is written for the historical record and edification of the public, but the intended audience for his research is first and foremost the Vatican. While no scholar today would dispute that priests, monks, and brothers were killed because of their office and not because of their actions, denying the church any political role is not convincing. As the history of Spanish anticlericalism shows, the church was identified as a class enemy by sectors of the Spanish proletariat well before 1931. The reasons that anticlericalism took such violent forms in 1936 lie in the Second Republic, a period characterized by radicalism at both ends of the political spectrum in which the great majority of Spanish Catholics was aligned with the right.

The process of beatification changed the church from victim and protagonist to simple victim. Nuns, for example, are statistically overrepresented among the sainted, reflecting a gendered perception of innocence. Presenting candidates for beatification—who must have died for their faith, not for their political beliefs—resurrected the literary form of the martyrology (e.g., Cárcel Ortí, *Mártires españoles*), which had been prevalent during and after the civil war. Martyrologies identify the victims, offer an account of their lives, describe their deaths, and make a claim for their sanctity. This process is done through literary formulas and tropes: the biographies dwell on the martyrs' vocations and pastoral or spiritual work, the descriptions of physical suffering emphasize the Christian virtues of fortitude and acceptance of the will of God, and the account of the moment of death makes much of the victims' stoicism and how they forgave their killers. Their suffering was redemptive, echoing that of other saints and martyrs and, ultimately, the passion of Christ. Such representations of martyrdom thus both contribute to and reflect an eschatology of Christian redemption. The focus on the victims makes the perpetrators curiously redundant: they are anonymous agents of evil, whose actions and cruelties are recounted as a catalog of barbarity that highlights the suffering of the victims. No attempt is made to understand or interpret their actions, and the killers are the unwitting tools of Providence, for a martyr's crown is a great spiritual reward.

This lack of interest in the motives of the killers is also reflected in the main source for the martyrologies, the *Causa General*, though here the killers are identified. This extraordinary archive—established by decree in 1940—contains what is in effect evidence for a prosecution of the Second Republic for crimes against Spain (Sánchez, Ortiz, and Ruiz). Public prosecutors were appointed to each province to collect and deposit this evidence, although standards of proof varied considerably. By 1940, Francoist Spain already had its own image of the Republican rearguard, a violent shadowy place dominated by *checas* (kangaroo courts) and *paseos* (politically motivated assassinations), depicted in novels such as Concha Espina's *Retaguardia* (1937; "Rearguard") or Tomás Borrás's *Checas de Madrid* (1940; "Checas of Madrid"). This image is reinforced by the representation of the war in the *Causa*, itself part of the general process of purging and repression that marked the early years of Francoism. Evidence for religious persecution was provided by the diocese, usually as statements from the bishop's office and religious communities. Clerical martyrs, desecrated churches, and broken images were presented as scapegoats for the satanic fury of the "Reds." The suffering of the church thus justified the retribution meted out to the Reds, who were themselves scapegoats disguised as villains (T. Mitchell 65; Girard).

The great bulk of the sources for the study of anticlerical violence in the civil war has been mediated by the church, which again raises the difficult question of how to approach this material. The *Causa General* is ample evidence of the Francoist regime's ambition to control history. Though the *Causa* is more obviously an artifact than most archives, it is still the best source we have for a historical phenomenon that, almost by definition, leaves few traces. Extralegal violence leaves few records, particularly when, as in this case, it is embarrassing to the official regime. In contrast, of course, the Franco regime made much of the anticlerical violence, both to justify the military coup of July 1936 and to give real content to the crusade by avenging the church.

The *Causa* is part of the institutionalized, bureaucratic, and lifeless crusade that suffocated dissidence and independence in the early Franco years. Yet the question of the crusade is a complex one. For Republican apologists it was easily—and crudely—dismissed as a post hoc attempt to legitimize the Franco regime. But for the Nationalists, particularly for young men at the front, the crusade represented a cause or quest for which many were willing to lay down their lives. Before Franco's final victory, the crusade exerted a real moral force, not least because it was waged in part to avenge the priests and religious killed by Republican militiamen (Vincent, "Martyrs"). These men and women died because the church was perceived as a political and class enemy, but during the war, this reasoning did not detract from the myth-making power of their deaths.

This power is clearly revealed in the international responses to the civil war. Catholics shared a sense of community that transcended national boundaries. News of anticlerical atrocities thus had a profound effect on international opinion (Sánchez, *Spanish Civil War*). The anticlerical massacres were the Nationalists' most potent weapon in the search for support and validation outside Spain. Paul Claudel's "Aux martyrs espagnols" (1937; "To the Spanish Martyrs") and Roy Campbell's poems—not only the vigorous, vicious doggerel of *Flowering Rifle* but also the Toledo sonnets in *Mithraic Emblems*—are the most famous paeans to the Spanish church. Most Catholics in most countries were convinced by Franco's crusade, precisely because of the savage cruelty meted out to the Spanish church. The church's suffering fixed Catholics' anti-Republican feeling, which could not be shaken by stories of Nationalist repression (particularly the aerial bombardment of the Basque towns Guernica and Durango) or by the dissenting voices of Thomist philosophers such as Jacques Maritain and independent Catholic writers such as Graham Greene.

The question at issue was whether the civil war was a just war. The claim of crusade sacralized the war effort, turning what was, in military terms at least, a war of conquest into a holy war. Whether or how war may be justified is a moral and philosophical debate separate from the question of why some of those fighting in the Spanish Civil War genuinely believed it to be a holy war. This distinction shows the claim to holy war as a claim for legitimacy; fighting must be accepted as a rightful activity, or, at the very least, the arguments in favor of war must outweigh those against it. Historians are concerned with legitimacy in a practical sense; they refer to representations of the experience of those who lived at the time and try to ascribe meaning from within. In contrast, a moral debate uses legitimacy in a normative sense, from an observer's standpoint. Understanding the difference between the two positions is important for any student of history and vital to any historical representation of the Spanish Civil War.

Antonio Cazorla-Sánchez

At Peace with the Past: Explaining the Spanish Civil War in the Basque Country, Catalonia, and Galicia

Civil wars not only ravage a nation's social tissue but also threaten the survival of the nation itself. They undermine the idea of national community and open the door for external intervention. In this sense, the Spanish Civil War was complex because of Spain's competing national identities. Thus the conflict has been explained in very different and even opposing ways: from the peripheral nationalist view, as an aggression against the three historical nationalities of Spain (Catalonia, the Basque Country, and Galicia), to a centralist view, as a threat to the Spanish nation. This dichotomy between nationalisms was in reality even more misleading because the main causes of the war were not so much about national loyalties as about social conflicts.

When looking at the civil war, those who embrace an ahistorical, eternal, essential view of the nation have to acknowledge their uncomfortable position as members of a supposedly timeless community that has been torn apart by murder, theft, destruction, and rape and has resorted to the aid of foreign, nonnational allies. This harrowing reality scarcely fits the victimized approach to history so dear to Nationalists: that of a country always at risk of being obliterated, always fighting together with nobility against an external enemy. Nearly the same could be said for those who

63

embrace a rigid view of how social classes are constructed and how they function in history. For these people, mostly but not exclusively orthodox Marxist historians who believe that there are objective interests and right ways of asserting them, it must be disconcerting to see "oppressed" social groups siding with the "oppressors" against the forces fighting for their "liberation."

Any serious analysis of the war has to consider the links between national and social identities, how those identities have changed since the end of the conflict, and, consequently, how the war has been explained at different times. This essay summarizes the main interpretations of the problematic crossroads of four nationalities (Spain, Catalonia, the Basque Country, and Galicia), ideologies, and social conflicts. My objective is to contrast the complexity and diversity of both Spanish society and the civil war from a historical point of view with the almost seamless moral discourses developed from ahistorical nationalist interpretations of the past, which are more concerned with preserving the past's ideals of community than with acknowledging the contradictions and opposite interests at stake inside each "nation."

When explaining the war, peripheral and Spanish (both Francoist-conservative and democratic-progressive) nationalist movements resort to a similar device to preserve the imaginary, essential unity of the community: otherness. This discourse places outside its boundaries the roots of the major conflicts. Thus the other becomes a device used to obliterate the reality of diversity in the nation. The war appears as the result of the intervention of external elements, physical or ideological, that first penetrated and then disestablished the community, provoking an unwanted, spurious civil war, an outcome that almost destroyed "the" nation. By stressing external factors, the discourse minimizes internal differences, making the relations with the other—not with the national community—the source of the confrontation. Disconnected from reality, the other becomes malleable, changes faces; such discourse works in a Manichaean way to preserve the idea of nation. The imagined community, to use Benedict Anderson's concept, needs an imagined, ductile, opposite other to exorcise any difficulties that may threaten the community's stability and even existence.

History implies diversity, and diversity does not endorse a two-sided rhetorical discourse. No ideological interpretation of the Spanish Civil War can deny that the social and political landscapes of all four competing national identities were very diverse in 1936 and that the diversity ran along lines very different from national boundaries. Both Catalonia and the Basque Country were clearly divided between heavily (by Spanish parameters) industrialized areas, usually near the urban centers, and the countryside, where small farms dominated. Most towns and other minor urban centers of the interior were predominantly agrarian. The polarization between urban and rural areas was less marked in Galicia, where industrialization and urbanization were far less advanced. In socioeconomic terms, these three areas cannot be differentiated from the broad, diverse context of northern Spain, although Catalonia also resembles other Spanish areas along the Mediterranean coast.

The socioeconomic diversity of the three historical nationalities translated into political diversity. Political diversity was the norm in Spain, but there was even more diversity in Catalonia and the Basque Country (see García de Cortázar and Fusi 20). In the wider Spanish context, parties and unions occupied the classic ideological spectrum from right to left; in Catalonia and the Basque Country, this spectrum included nationalist organizations. There were significant differences between the nationalist movements in these two regions. Catalonian nationalism was dominated by the progressive Catalonian Left Republican party (ERC), a lay organization that in principle was not hostile to immigrants from other parts of Spain. Basque nationalism was led by the National Basque Party (PNV), a conservative force, heavily clerical, born from an ethnoxenophobic interpretation of nation. In many ways the PNV was closer in its outlook to the *Lliga Regionalista*, the conservative, Catholic organization that was Catalonia's second most important autonomist party. Galicia, however, did not have a nationalist party comparable to those in Catalonia and the Basque Country, where all the major political parties, like those in other parts of urbanized Spain, had achieved significant success in mobilizing their potential political constituencies. In Galicia, as in the rest of rural Spain, the old political habits of client-patron relations and political apathy dominated.

It is striking, then, that in the last years of the Second Republic before the start of the war (1931–36) the political trends in these regions were similar to those in the rest of Spain. Polarization in the last years of the republic was increasingly between Republican and anti-Republican parties. In the 1933 general elections, the center right, led by the center-right Radical Party and the Catholic CEDA, a conservative party not committed to Republican legality, achieved a resounding victory over the governing leftist Republicans and socialists. This swing to the right was not as evident in

Catalonia. In the Basque Country, however, the shift to the right was very marked. In the neighboring, partially Basque province of Navarre, the leading force was the Traditionalist Communion (also called Carlists), an antiliberal, monarchist, antinationalist, and ultra-Catholic party that two and a half years later would provide tens of thousand of volunteers for the Francoist army. Finally, in Galicia, the right had an absolute majority (two to three times more votes than the left, depending on the province) over the Republicans, including the few nationalists among them.[1]

The three regions again followed the political trend of the rest of Spain, swinging to the left during the crucial elections of February 1936, which led to the July military rising. In Catalonia, the nationalist Republicans and the nonnationalist left clearly triumphed, though the conservative *Lliga* still had a strong showing. The situation in the Basque Country was more complicated. The votes were divided among the socialists, the PNV, and the Carlists. In Galicia, the vote was fairly distributed among the right, center, and left. Thus on the eve of the civil war, all three regions were politically diverse.

Without taking into account the ideological diversity of Spain, we cannot understand the events at the start of the war or the attempts to explain the conflict. According to the official version offered by Franco's regime for nearly forty years, the conflict was the product, and the dramatic turning point, of the long decline of the nation, which began in the eighteenth century with the introduction of foreign Enlightenment ideas. The situation worsened in the nineteenth century with the arrival of liberalism (another notorious product of foreign lands); anticlericalism; and the three modern ills, capitalism (which destroyed the ancestral social harmony of the nation), Marxism (foreign, antinational, and Jewish), and peripheral nationalism (the supreme betrayal of the motherland). Under these foreign influences, Spain abandoned both its imperial tradition and Catholicism, which were not just the pillars of its greatness but the essence of the nation (see Boyd 232–72). The war was thus a rebellion of the national spirit against the spurious forces that threatened to annihilate Spain.

The official Francoist vision of the war was formed at the beginning of the conflict and was promoted by, among others, propaganda posters created by Carlos Sáenz de Tejada. His posters, by far the best in the Nationalist zone, featured modern Spanish hidalgos (most of them Basque traditionalists), austere and devout, taking up arms once again for an eternal, Catholic Spain (see Miravitlles et al. 345–46). The anticlerical violence of the first months of the war, which resulted in the assassination of almost seven thousand clerics and the destruction of thousands of churches, sanctioned this image that fused Spanish nationalism with Catholicism.[2] Furthermore, the massive support of the godless Soviet Union—the quintessential example of the danger of foreign influences—for the republic permitted Franco to portray the Spanish tragedy as a fight against external forces rather than as an internal dispute.

The problem with this interpretation of the past is that millions of Spaniards had freely endorsed the policies of the "anti-Spanish" left. The ideologues of the new state countered this fact by presenting the Red population as intoxicated by demagogues. Rooted in a pessimistic and paternalistic view of the masses, which saw them as both brutish and innocent, the Francoists blamed ambitious, antipatriotic elites for corrupting and misleading simple Spaniards. Eradicate the corrupting, foreign-influenced elite, and both the people and the nation would be saved. The dictatorship presented the past in religious terms of sin and redemption, of fallen saint-heroes and defeated villains, of true Spain against anti-Spain (see also the essay by Richards in this volume). This concept informs the most significant monument that the regime erected, the huge Cross of the Valley of the Fallen (see Sueiro).[3] Buried under it are the corpses of (many) Nationalist and (far fewer) Republican soldiers from all over Spain, including the historical nationalities. Those soldiers were supposed to represent the supreme sacrifice of Spaniards in the war, brothers again thanks to Franco and the church in a new Spain at peace. Those soldiers are the good, simple soldiers, the true Christians who redeemed Spain with their blood.

A second set of views about the war can be defined as democratic-progressive or left-wing Spanish nationalist. According to this view, the conflict took place not between Spain and anti-Spain but between progress and reaction, or between the true Spanish people and the old corrupt elites.[4] In this explanation, as in its Francoist alternative, the other plays a crucial role: the Republicans saw foreign hands aiding the enemy's troops. Also in this argument, as in the Francoist argument, there is a real and eternal Spain. This Spain refused to succumb to decadence and foreign intervention. The vanguard of this proud, simple Spain, which confronted the assault of fascists and feudal forces, is the people. If the Francoists had hidalgos rescuing their true nation from Moscow, the Republicans and democratic-progressives had the brave Spanish militiamen fighting the foreign agents of oppression: ruthless fascists and barbarian Moors. This characterization can be seen clearly in one of the most celebrated war posters of Republican propaganda, which represents the Nationalists (*Los Nacionales*) as a boat in which an Italian general, a German banker, and a Spanish bishop sail escorted by two armed Moroccan soldiers who represent the rebel colonial army (see Miravitlles et al. 331). The imperial eagle is perched atop the boat's mast, from which hangs a rope that strangles the map of Spain. This map is the people celebrated in Republican war songs, such as the epic "They Shall Not Pass" of the battle in Madrid in November 1936 when the Republican forces unexpectedly stopped the rebels' advance. The people were militiamen (and some militiawomen) dressed in the blue of the industrial worker or in the white shirt of the peasant, as in Robert Capa's well-known picture of the dying Republican soldier or in the equally famous film *The Spanish Earth* (see Miravitlles et al., cover).

This version of events is problematic at best, for the Spanish people did not seek to follow the path of liberation with universal enthusiasm and very often fought against its cause of progress and political, social, and national freedom. Two of the most notable examples of armed dissension happened in Galicia and in the Basque Country. In Galicia, the military rebellion triumphed almost unopposed, and the region immediately became one of the main sources of soldiers for Franco's armies (Fernández). The poor peasants of Galicia became the backbone of the army that conquered neighboring Asturias after defeating the local, mostly miners' militias. In the Basque Country, a huge number of volunteers flocked to join the ranks of the Carlist militias in July 1936. Like their Galician comrades, most of these militiamen were poor farmers (Ugarte Tellería). The Basque traditionalists almost took Madrid in the first weeks of the war, and in 1937 they were the main force that conquered the Basque Country for Franco. Nations, ideologies, and the past are never one-sided. One of the great myths of the Republican cause, Pasionaria (Dolores Ibárruri), had an elder brother who fought in a Carlist unit in the rebel army (Cruz 30–31). The father of the future leader of the post-Franco PNV, Xabier Arzallus, fought in another Carlist unit.

The vision of the people resisting to the end is equally flawed. In Catalonia (in Republican hands until January 1939), as in the rest of Republican Spain, workers' and peasants' commitment to the Loyalist cause faded as self-interest and survival came to prevail. Most of the people lost their faith and desire to fight well before the war was lost in the battlefield (Seidman).

A third view of the war is that of the peripheral nationalists. Since Galicia had a weak nationalist movement and was taken over immediately by the Francoist troops, it was in the Basque Country and in Catalonia where the nationalist discourse on the causes and development of the conflict became more complex. To different degrees, both nationalist movements claimed not to be responsible for the war. Spain had imposed the war on them, and it was the "Spanish" (i.e., the working-class immigrants who were the bulk of the socialist, anarchist, and Communist militias that initially controlled the periphery) who were to blame for the worst aspects of the Republican side, such as the first killings. This belief was more prevalent among the PNV, where, in the first days of the war, some leaders toyed with the idea of requesting neutrality in the conflict (Fusi, *País* 217). Neutrality was not a feasible option since the PNV had split at the beginning of the war. The provinces of Álava and Navarra supported the military rising; Vizcaya and Guipúzcoa opposed it. As a result of this initial ambivalence among Basque nationalists, until October 1936 it would be the Spanish left, not the Basque nationalists, who defended both the republic and the future autonomy of the region, which the Francoists had made clear they would not tolerate. Moreover, when the Basque Country was finally overrun, the Basque nationalist battalions surrendered in August 1937, disobeying orders from the central government and leaving the rest of the Republican army in the north in an even more precarious situation. Before surrendering, they negotiated with the Italian generals commanding the troops sent by Mussolini to support Franco and offered to switch sides in exchange for Basque autonomy.

Basque ambivalence toward the democratic republic sharply contrasted with the Catalonian attitude. Here the nationalist forces also split: the conservative, Catholic *Lliga* supported the rebellion, and the progressive ERC supported the Loyalist cause. Unlike the PNV, the ERC lent reliable support to the republic. There was tension, however, between its middle-class old Catalan constituency and the armed militias who had held the real power in the streets for several months, particularly the anarcho-syndicalists described by George Orwell (*Homage to Catalonia*) and others. There was also tension between the left- and Republican-leaning cities and the more conservative countryside. When Catalonia was conquered by the Nationalist forces in early 1939, many sectors of the middle classes and the peasantry were relieved, since in the last months of the war the region had suffered a new bout of violence inflicted by the retreating Republican troops (Juliá 259–64). Franco immediately suppressed

Catalonia's political autonomy, local language, and culture, but for many it was a price worth paying to have their idea of law and order restored.

The final defeat of the republic in March 1939 meant death, imprisonment, and exile for hundreds of thousands of Spaniards. The dictatorship officially forgot the vital assistance from Hitler and Mussolini and the use of Muslim colonial troops to reconquer Catholic Spain. More important, the imposition of official truth prevented the development of an open debate about the war, especially about the role of the historical nationalities in the war. Archives were closed to historians or purged, and independent or progressive historians were dismissed. Thus the images, myths, and explanations minted during the war endured practically unchallenged during the next thirty-six years. The relatively quick democratization of Spain after 1976 permitted the rediscovery (and the reinvention) of the national identities suppressed by the dictatorship and opened the reassessment of the role of the nationalities in the civil war.

During the immediate post-Franco period, most scholars, particularly historians, gave a balanced account of the events and worked hard to debunk many of the myths surrounding the civil war. Politicians in the central government, meanwhile, were busy forgetting the war and the dictatorship for the sake of the stability of the newborn democracy. The agenda of their nationalist colleagues in the periphery was different; rather than accept forgetfulness, they embraced the politics of national victimhood. Using their control of school curricula and local public television, they tried to re-create national histories that suited their political needs (A. Rivière 161–219). The civil war and the subsequent dictatorship were fertile territory for this remarkable exercise in rewriting history. The worst aspects of the period in the periphery began to be presented as a consequence not of fascist aggression or internal disputes but of the regions' links to Spain. The dictatorship appeared to be less the product of a complex historical process that affected all of Spain than an unwanted import that assaulted the otherwise pacific Catalonia and Basque Country.

While it is not surprising that peripheral nationalist politicians operated mostly in terms of eternal versus external national identities, it is remarkable that the left uncritically accepted this distortion of the past and came to identify Spain with the Francoist dictatorship. In the early eighties, using the word *Spain* became politically incorrect; the acceptable term was *the Spanish State*, a term that was, ironically, a Francoist invention. This confusion between a regime and a national identity derived from the

Francoists' appropriation of the idea of Spain, which the dictatorship claimed to represent exclusively and consequently discredited Spanish nationalism. It was an unfortunate superimposition of concept and reality. The civil war was separated from its true causes—a conflict of interests, classes, identities, and ideologies—and became a war between Spain and its historical nationalities (for a critique see I. Riera; Morán).

As a result of the dynamic reconstruction of national identities in democratic Spain, Spanish citizens still have not been offered a critical account of the past. Such an account (or accounts) is necessary because the civil war has become a blatant political tool, often used and abused (though not by the left, who continue to embrace a sort of historical amnesia). While an open defense of the Francoist past is not yet acceptable, the recent best-selling pseudohistorical books by Pío Moa have been cheered by the conservative media. The peripheral nationalist forces have been especially keen on resorting to the past to support their political objectives. For example, one of the most enduring images of the Spanish Civil War, the bombing of the Basque village Guernica, has been appropriated by the PNV. When the German Condor Legion razed the town in April 1937, the world was not yet accustomed to such a level of horror. Confronted with international condemnation, the Francoists denied any role in the crime and cynically blamed the Republicans (see Southworth, *Guernica!*). The tragedy was immortalized in Pablo Picasso's painting (see also the essay by Mendelson in this volume). Picasso, an Andalusian raised in Barcelona but long established in Paris, did the painting under commission of the Republican government. His work was not a cry for Basque national freedom but a denunciation of fascist aggression. Leading politicians of the PNV, however, have claimed for years that the painting should hang in the Basque Country and not in Madrid. "We got the bombs, and they get the painting," said Arzallus, the PNV party leader who was also the son of a Carlist volunteer (M. Aguilar).

Bereft of context, however, we cannot explain the particularities of historical content. When Republican Basque Guernica was bombed, other parts of Spain had already been ravaged for nine months. Republican Castilian Madrid, for example, was shelled daily for two and a half years, from November 1936 to March 1939. The first bombs that fell on the capital came from the northern front, manned for the most part by Basque, Galician, and Castilian soldiers. These same soldiers took Barcelona in early 1939. In late 2004, however, the present leader of the ERC, J. L. Carod-Rovira, demanded "an apology from Spain to Catalonia" for the civil war (Azúa, " ¿Será?"). The sad irony in this request for historical justice is not that Carod-Rovira is the son of a Francoist Civil Guardsman but that the real experiences and expectations of those who suffered in the war are absent. In the ideal past and the ideal future (which are the same) of national history, there is no room for people; ideas take their place.

Notes

1. All the data come from Tusell 2: 261–401.

2. This was the image that Francoism wanted to present abroad. Ireland offers a good example of the intense Catholic uproar over real and alleged crimes committed against the clergy. See McGarry.

3. See also in this volume Valis's essay "Civil War Ghosts Entombed."

4. The classic exponent of this historical interpretation can be found in the enormously influential work of the late Manuel Tuñón de Lara.

Part II

Rhetoric, Ideology,
and the War

Cary Nelson

Advocacy and Undecidability: The Pedagogy of the Spanish Civil War

The Spanish Civil War offers an extraordinary opportunity to test and apply some of recent theory's most ambitious claims, particularly key elements of cultural studies and poststructuralism. In this war, art and politics came together with exceptional force. In such circumstances cultural studies arguments about the necessity of contextualizing cultural production become not merely useful but essential. The war was also a decisive instance of common purpose across cultural domains; music, painting, photography, literature, reportage, political intrigue, and military planning interacted and fed off one another. Thus the slogan "No Pasarán" ("They Shall Not Pass") occurs in political speeches, military broadsides, newspaper editorials, poems, songs, and letters and appears on posters and public banners. Cultural studies and poststructuralism have both pressed the relationality and interdependence of cultural domains; here is an opportunity to test that claim.

Cultural studies rejects belief in the ultimate autonomy of cultural products, including works of art. Faith in the autonomy of works of art is notably difficult to sustain when many political forces are at work to shape and give meaning to aesthetic production. Though the Spanish Civil War is a natural subject for cultural studies, working entirely within the confines of one nation-state is fundamentally disabling in cultural studies. You cannot know what is distinctive about any one country without comparative analyses. Yet literary studies is mostly organized by national traditions. The Spanish Civil War, however, illustrates both politically and artistically a mix of international influences and so lends itself well to a comparative perspective. Cultural studies also typically promotes multidisciplinary analysis: the diverse nature of the Spanish Civil War archive encourages scholars to draw on multiple disciplinary traditions.

As images and discourses recur across different cultural domains, the effect is one not simply of rich, celebratory plurality but also of epistemological instability and undecidability. There are multiple theoretical tropes to describe this slippage and transferability, which also complicates the interpretive challenge. Indeed, it is often unclear what cultural category a given artifact belongs in and thus what disciplinary discourse should possess it. Are the vivid posters from the fall of 1936 depicting civilian deaths during the bombardment of Madrid part of the history of art or politics? There is no shortage of art historical discourse treating paintings with unmistakable political or social content in purely formal and aesthetic terms, but how should these posters, mass-produced and perhaps lacking singular aesthetic aura, be treated? Moreover, their political use is unmistakable, so any effort to sever their relation to history is patently fraudulent. On the other hand, the posters often borrow simultaneously from high art and advertising; their cultural reversibility is thus embedded in the images.

It would be possible to confine such issues to Spain itself, yet the war rapidly became a political and cultural event with international implications and explicit international participation. Not only did Hitler and Mussolini immediately supply the rebel generals with arms, but a significant number of volunteers arrived from Western democracies to fight on the other side. The international circulation of graphic images and literary texts meant that artists and writers from many countries saw and read one another's work, responded to and imitated one another, and contributed to an unusually concentrated international phenomenon of interactive artistic production.

Nevertheless, the fundamental historical meaning (and legacy) of the war has remained exceptionally unresolved. Indeed, the passionate political and interpretive struggles that raged during the war have continued unabated ever since. It is not unheard of for a major conflict to reach a military resolution without reaching a universal cultural resolution. Thus in the southern United States the meaning of the American Civil War remains culturally contested (though it was hardly a subject of intense international debate for very long). The circumstances surrounding the defeat of the Spanish Republic were in many ways unique.

First, a critical portion of the defeated population went into exile, reconstituting itself spiritually and ideologically. Yet even this signal and influential diaspora would not alone account for the war's remaining such a volatile topic. Although few recognized it at the time, the Spanish Civil War was becoming a crucible for the major political and cultural conflict of the second half of the twentieth century, namely, the cold-war struggle between capitalism and Communism. The Soviet aid to the republic helped give the fairly small Spanish Communist Party much more influence than it could ever have wielded had, say, Britain and France sold arms to Spain as well (see Esenwein in this volume). The Spanish Communist Party won the hearts of many Spaniards after its Fifth Regiment played a key role in the defense of Madrid. These factors, combined with the Comintern responsibility for organizing the Internationals, gave Franco (and the church) the opportunity to recast the war as a conflict between Christianity and Communism. Red-baiting ensued in Spain and elsewhere, notably during the McCarthy era.

For some, Spain would come to be the site of international Communism's finest hour. For others, it was yet one more example of Stalinist perfidy. George Orwell, renowned for his anti-Communism, wrote in *Homage to Catalonia* one of the most powerful accounts of the events of May 1937, when the Communist Party actively suppressed the anti-Stalinist left in Barcelona. (Ken Loach's film *Land and Freedom* covers the same ground.) Yet Orwell considered the Comintern-organized International Brigades a genuine antifascist force. He was thus capable of differentiating Communist Party initiatives in Spain, which were by no means unitary and consistent. Many since then have not wished to make distinctions of this kind. There has consequently been a sixty-year struggle over the fundamental moral and political character of much that happened in Spain.

In effect, the war continued to be fought throughout the world long after it was over and remains a passionately disputed cultural battleground today. People continue to use the war to test and define both their own identities and their sense of twentieth-century world history. Until Franco's death in 1975, in Spain the only permitted version of the war was the victors' story of Christian knights triumphing over the Red menace. Franco won on the peninsula (and among his fascist allies), but he had no definitive victory anywhere else, despite America's willingness to make him a cold-war ally in the 1950s. The victors in the Spanish Civil War did not absorb their enemies and erase their memories, cultural identities, and capacity to dispute the character of events, though Franco did his best to exterminate the surviving opposition in Spain.

Everything about the Spanish Civil War retains a political and moral reversibility that is relatively unusual for a war fought seventy years ago. Whether in comparison with other modern wars this war differs in degree or kind may be debated, but it surely is a case of particularly fraught historical undecidability. Every fact about Spain is fundamentally unstable, and each fact's relation to another is in significant ways undecided. Nor has the historical record been steadily corrected and clarified in the intervening years. Most witnesses to the events of the war have had continuing interests to pursue in their evolving accounts, which is one reason there are no facts available to settle these debates, to resolve the story of the war and decide its moral force once and for all. A death is a "murder," an "execution," an "assassination," or a "casualty" depending on which value system we use. The body of a POUMist, an International Brigader, a Russian adviser, a German aviator, or a Spanish priest is never simply there for any informed observer: it is a destination for convictions and identities.

As with many events both major and minor, the historical archive of the Spanish Civil War has continued to grow, and this growth has simultaneously provided answers to old questions and raised new questions. Access to Spanish archives increased after Franco died and Spain once again became a democracy. Yet the most dramatic change in the historical record did not come until after the fall of the Soviet Union in 1991, when the vast archives of the Comintern and the International Brigades became available (see also essays by Esenwein and Coale in this volume). Work on these archives has barely begun, but the archives will clearly provide evidence for competing interpretive positions.

Finally, it has often proved impossible to settle basic questions about significant events in the war. The infamous fog of war alone makes battlefield details difficult to reconstruct reliably, and the continuing struggles over meaning have exacerbated the problem, since many accounts of the war are inflected by current political needs. Thus students of the Spanish Civil War must tolerate a great deal of uncertainty and cultivate a kind of negative capability about the terrain. They proceed through a mix of powerful narratives, telling events, and fundamental irresolution. Of course, such a mixture of doubt and certainty is typical of all historical inquiry, where constructing a narrative is often a matter of discovering the possibilities and limits of interpretive confidence. What is unusual about Spain, beyond the arguments mustered so far, is the radical multidisciplinarity of this problem. Yet the historical character of the war's cultural production is inescapable. Everything about the war, as I suggest at the outset, is embedded in overdetermined contextuality.

Moreover, there is a long-standing tendency in disciplines like art history and literary studies to project interpretive plurality and irresolution against relative historic, even epistemic, stability. In Spain that sort of study is impossible except through a willed act of political commitment, for both figure and ground are indeterminate. Thus scholars of the literature and graphic arts of the war must abandon the disciplinary traditions of single-minded aestheticization. Painting, sculpture, fiction, and music are all embedded in the vicissitudes of life. Is Picasso's *Guernica* (1937) art or propaganda? Should the contemporary political debates about Hemingway's *For Whom the Bell Tolls* (1940) be part of the way we read the novel? Does poetry written to be read in wartime trenches carry that performative history with it decades later? What commercial and aesthetic traditions did Spanish Civil War poster artists rearticulate to fit wartime necessities? What audiences did they have in mind for their work? What status does such cultural bricolage have? How do the events of May 1937 color work that seeks to evoke political solidarity resolving or suppressing ideological differences? How do we negotiate the contradictory terrain of representation and self-representation that characterizes wartime images of women, images that sometimes shatter traditional conceptions of gender and sometimes relentlessly reinforce them? Robert Capa's 1936 photograph *Falling Militiaman* has been both accused of being faked and defended as being authentic. Does it matter? Are images of childhood innocence and vulnerability corrupted when they are mustered for political advocacy? The most widely circulated photograph of a dead child, which appears on the 1936 poster "Madrid—The 'Military' Practice of the Rebels" and in dozens of newspapers, pamphlets, and other media worldwide, for years remained an anonymous image. Now we can cite the little girl's name (María Santiago Robert), address (number 6, Calle de Paloma, Madrid), and date of death (30 Oct. 1936). She was killed in an aerial bombardment, and the famous photograph was taken the following day. What difference does the knowledge of her name make in the long history of her afterlife? Is a comparative aesthetics traversing both Loyalist and Nationalist art possible without a comparative politics? What role should critics' political investments play in the interpretive process? Is political neutrality with regard to the war possible or desirable?

These questions map the rich, difficult, and endlessly fascinating terrain traversed by a course in the Spanish Civil War. There follow several sample course modules that take advantage of some of the conflicted topics listed above. I am assuming a course taught in English, though I have listed some Spanish publications that offer materials of particular interest. As in most areas of study, there is an increasing problem of books going out of print.

Sample Course Modules

Frances Lannon's *The Spanish Civil War, 1936–1939* and Gabriele Ranzato's *The Spanish Civil War* offer concise overviews of the war. For a more detailed overview, I recommend George Esenwein and Adrian Shubert's *Spain at War*, Helen Graham's *The Spanish Republic at War*, or Hugh Thomas's *The Spanish Civil War*.

Women, Gender, and the War

Brothers, Caroline. "Women at Arms"
Bruzzichezi, Ave. Letters
Carulla, Jordi, and Arnau Carulla. *La guerra civil en 2000 carteles: República, guerra civil, posguerra*
Cleminson, Richard. "Beyond Tradition and 'Modernity': The Cultural and Sexual Politics of Spanish Anarchism"
Graham, Helen. "Women and Social Change"
Jackson, Angela. "The Aftermath: Women and the Memory of War"
Lannon, Frances. "Women"
———. "Women and War: Two Memoirs"
Millet, Martha. "Women of Spain"
Nash, Mary. "The Battle Lost"
———. "Heroines, Combative Mothers, and Mythmakers"
———. "Liberate the Prostitutes"
———. "'Milicianas' or Homefront Heroines"
Pla y Beltrán, Pascual. "Girl Fighter of Spain"
Preston, Paul. "Nan Green"
———. "La Pasionaria"
Sim. *Estampas de la revolución española 19 julio de 1936*

Americans in the International Brigades

Carroll, Peter. *The Odyssey of the Abraham Lincoln Brigade*
Courtois, Stéphane, and Jean-Louis Panné. "The Shadow of the NKVD
　　in Spain"
Eby, Cecil. *Between the Bullet and the Lie: American Volunteers in the
　　Spanish Civil War*
Klehr, Harvey, et al. "Fighting Deviationists and Bad Elements in the
　　Spanish Civil War"
Knox, Bernard. "Premature Anti-fascist"
Nelson, Cary, and Jefferson Hendricks. *Madrid 1937: Letters of the
　　Abraham Lincoln Brigade from the Spanish Civil War*
Wolff, Milton. *Another Hill: An Autobiographical Novel*

The Events of May 1937

Carr, Raymond. "Spain and the Communists"
Graham, Helen. "The Barcelona May Days and Their Consequences"
Orwell, George. *Homage to Catalonia*
———. "Spilling the Spanish Beans"
Rous, Jean. "Spain 1936–39: The Murdered Revolution"

Robert Capa's Falling Militiaman

Brothers, Caroline. *War and Photography: A Cultural History* 178–85
Nelson, Cary. *The Aura of the Cause: A Photo Album for North American
　　Volunteers in the Spanish Civil War* 28–33
Whelan, Richard. "Robert Capa's *Falling Soldier* : A Detective Story"

Film, Memory, and Representation

Land and Freedom. Dir. Ken Loach
Reviews of *Land and Freedom*: Anonymous, Andy Durgan, Martha
　　Gellhorn, Kevin Morgan, Richard Porton, Paul Preston, Roy
　　Quickenden, Jonathan Steele, Hugh Thomas, Martine Vidal

Hemingway and Spain

Baker, Carlos. *Ernest Hemingway* 299–357
Fleming, Robert. "Communism vs. Community in *For Whom the Bell
　　Tolls* "

Hemingway, Ernest. *The Fifth Column and Four Stories of the Spanish Civil War*
———. *For Whom the Bell Tolls*
———. *The Sun Also Rises*
Lynn, Kenneth S. *Hemingway* 475–97
Malraux, André. *Man's Hope* (*L'espoir*)
Rudat, Wolfgang E. H. "Hamlet in Spain: Oedipal Dilemmas in *For Whom the Bell Tolls*"
San Juan, E., Jr. "Ideological Form, Symbolic Exchange, Textual Production: A Symptomatic Reading of *For Whom the Bell Tolls*"
Watson, William Branch. "Hemingway's Attacks on the Soviets and the Communists in *For Whom the Bell Tolls*"

Poetry and the Spanish Civil War

Bauer, Carlos. *Cries from a Wounded Madrid: The Poetry of the Spanish Civil War*
Cunningham, Valentine. *The Penguin Book of Spanish Civil War Verse*
Genoways, Ted. *The Selected Poems of Miguel Hernández*
Monteath, Peter. "Anarchist Poetry"
———. "Literature and the Popular Front"
Nelson, Cary. *The Wound and the Dream: Sixty Years of American Poems about the Spanish Civil War*

    This brief list gives several modules of flexible units for a general course on the war. Some orientation to the history of the war is essential to any course. A number of the compact standard introductory overviews, like Paul Preston's *A Concise History of the Spanish Civil War* (1996), are out of print, but still more concise overviews, by Frances Lannon and Gabriele Ranzato, are available. Among the few more-ambitious general histories in print as I write are a 2003 revision of Hugh Thomas's redoubtable *The Spanish Civil War* and *Spain at War* by George Esenwein and Adrian Shubert, the latter of interest in part because of its sympathies with the radical left in Spain and its attention to a wider range of cultural issues. The wondrously and maddeningly complex wartime political history of the republic is given its most reliable and up-to-date treatment in Helen Graham's *The Spanish Republic at War* (2002), an essential book for faculty members and advanced students. It is inadvisable to assay one of these full-length books without first mastering some basic information about the war. Materials should include some simple maps of the republic's gradual loss of territory, such as those available in the histories by Thomas and by Esenwein and Shubert. Numerous brief but helpful accounts of the military history of the war are available on the Internet, and they are a good place to start. An undergraduate course might limit the required introduction to one of the concise summaries. Most Spanish Civil War courses would benefit from an extensive library reserve list, since many relevant art and photography books are either out of print or too expensive for use as assigned texts.

I placed the unit Women, Gender, and the War first, both because it is one of the most starkly contradictory arenas of wartime representation and because it makes for pointed comparisons across cultural domains. Nowhere is this distinction more evident than in Republican posters and graphic work, which include gritty images of armed women in battle and idealized images of women as nurses and mothers. In Sim's *Estampas*, a collection of watercolors, this fundamental dichotomy is apparent. From there one may branch out to other posters, either in Jordi Carulla and Arnau Carulla's massive volumes or online (see "Resources," "Posters" in this volume), and to the critical commentary on women's roles and representations in the war. Detailed biographical studies of individual women, both Republican and fascist, are available in Preston's work; Lannon offers brief biographies. Mary Nash offers wartime broadsides by revolutionary women. The scholarly literature focuses on images of women rather than men, in part because women's roles were intensely debated during the war and in part because the images of women in battle have retained their capacity to shock, but the archive includes more than enough representations of masculinity for comparison and contrast.

The unit on the Americans in the International Brigades includes the best history of their political role (Carroll), the major collection of their letters home (Nelson and Hendricks), an autobiographical novel by their last commander (Wolff), and passages from conservative critiques (Courtois et al.; Klehr et al.; and Eby). The literature about May 1937 is vast, but this brief selection embodies some of the divergent positions, beginning with Orwell's classic 1938 memoir and Jean Rous's 1939 analysis, and includes the most recent scholarly research. The small unit on Capa's *Falling Militiaman* focuses on what may be the single most famous photograph of modern war. This unit might well be expanded into a larger unit on Spanish Civil War photography. Ken Loach's *Land and Freedom* is perhaps the most controversial narrative film about the war, combining astonishingly persuasive re-creations of typical wartime events with implausible invented scenes. The unit on Hemingway can easily be expanded or contracted. *The Sun Also Rises* is listed to provide evidence of Hemingway's prewar commitment to Spain and to suggest the status of Spain in his fiction, but a Spanish Civil War course might focus only on *For Whom the Bell Tolls*, in which case the novel's Hollywood film adaptation offers a supplementary route of study. A favorite alternative is to compare Hemingway's and André Malraux's Spanish Civil War novels (see also the essays by Valis ["Hemingway's War"] and Boak in this volume). Teaching Spanish Civil War poetry is made more difficult than it need be by books' going out of print. Whether in course packets or on reserve lists, the titles listed offer a range of poems from Spain, Britain, and the United States. Several have substantial critical introductions.

Many of these topics benefit from collaborative student work, for the cultural output of the war traverses not only multiple domains—from photography to poetry to reportage—but also many disciplines. Students trained in art history, literary studies, history, and political science can work together to interpret a poster, photograph, novel, or political document and then share the results with the rest of the class. I assigned graduate students to four-person groups to analyze their choice of two Spanish Civil War posters in a jointly authored written report. Each group had at least one person fluent in Spanish, a distinct advantage. Advanced research can also involve research in multiple languages. The diplomatic and military history involves numerous countries, as does the history of volunteers who came to the aid of the Spanish republic. Not only a compelling topic in its own right, the war is also ideal terrain on which to study the relations between art and politics and to confront the problematics of interpretation.

If appropriate archival resources are available, one further topic dramatically highlights both the relevance of a comparative cultural studies approach and the overdetermination of interpretive strategies—the study of Spanish Civil War magazines as integrated, coherent collage forms. The materials in a magazine are traditionally divvied up and handed out to scholars of various disciplines to interpret: the illustrations to historians of photography, art, or design; the poems and stories to literature professors; the advertisements to advertising professionals; the editorials to historians or political scientists; the news stories to journalists; and so forth. Few scholars are ready to take on all these sorts of materials, yet readers of magazines cross these disciplinary boundaries without permission and without fear. The cultural work that magazines do is fundamentally multidisciplinary, and thus the disciplinary specialist can substantially distort the lived experience of the time.

Substantial as this disciplinary barrier to understanding is, there are still more intractable theoretical barriers before us. In describing these magazines as collage forms, I have in mind several rather different forms of collage. The most obvious, of which Spanish Civil War magazines offer scores of striking examples, are literal collages produced by a single artist on single pages or on two-page spreads. But magazines also create a serial collage effect as one reads, whether turning the pages sequentially or nonsequentially. Some of these collage effects are produced by magazines' art directors and designers; others are arguably effects of readerly behavior, as juxtapositions and connections are produced by accidents of consumption. There is, alas, no hard-and-fast distinction between intent and effect here. In a single text, we may comfortably attribute effect to intent, as do many readers of literature, but when discussing interrelations among multiple contributions to a magazine, confidence about semiotic cause is less warranted.

An argument about these interrelations is necessary, however, because of the extreme degree of political and ideological coherence in particular magazines. During the Spanish Civil War, individual magazines had a historical coherence that was evident to all readers. These magazines were part and parcel of the culture of the war, and thus a sense of unified political intent was part of the production, individually and collectively. Once you compare the politically coherent products of different political parties, conflict and difference are foregrounded. Asking about the relation between the parts of a magazine was a natural outgrowth of the historical context and arguably part of the general production gestalt even when this relation was not worked out in detail for each contribution to each issue. A Spanish Civil War magazine is something like a city. To open one is to enter a metropolis with elements at once designed and accidental. It is a mix of urban planning and entrepreneurial initiative. As you walk through the magazine metropolis—a movement that makes collage partly cinematic and thereby adds montage to the discourse of magazine reception—continuities and contiguities assemble out of the sequence of steps you take, the route you choose. Only by a hypothetical and whimsical gesture does such a metropolis become a world separate from its historical context, for referentiality to that other wartime world in which metropolitan residents die in the streets every day is an insistent dimension of every page.

Yet these magazines have their own vision, for they are pronouncers and levelers, agents of monumentality and deconstruction. Some magazine covers are every bit as graphically striking, colorful, and effective as posters. Indeed Sim, José Bardasano, and Josep Renau designed magazine covers that have all the monumentality of posters, making larger-than-life creative declarations about the titanic struggle between democracy and fascism. Yet the same artists sometimes abandoned monumentality for ephemerality, producing marginal illustrations that recycled the same graphic motifs. Sim created posters and lithographs as well as secondary decorative borders of articles. Bardasano did hundreds of drawings at every level of significance. In the churning blizzard of wartime magazine pages, every graphic signature is decomposed and reassigned to the general cause. There are no masters, only foot soldiers of the arts.

At the same time, the rarity of most of the magazines means that several of the most ordinary categories of cultural production now merit examination. There is no catalogue raisonné for the artists who worked in ephemera, and though Jordana Mendelson is assembling a catalog of the magazines, we cannot expect that a comprehensive one could ever be assembled. We can describe the kinds of work Sim, Ramón Puyol, Renau, or Bardasano did, but we cannot evaluate the corpus of any of them.

Yet this paper blizzard was central to the wartime climate. The military struggle was reflected, represented, and conducted in the blizzard of ephemera, a source of meaning and inspiration for the war. It still eddies around us in awesome drifts, uncontrollable, mobile, rediscovered, forgotten, fundamentally and eternally unquantifiable. And in that phenomenal excess, the magazines have a special charm, for they march through history as battalions of pages, embodiments of the republic's plurality of disputes and alliances. I refer again to the metropolitan metaphor, for nothing else among the legacies of the paper war suggests the complex, multilayered, conflictive, and collaborative social spaces of wartime Spain so fully as these plural texts. Exploding into consciousness, imploded in a historical conjuncture, the magazines of Spain are a privileged terrain of witness.

Yet even to speak of magazines relies on a material category that feels somewhat insufficient in this context. What about illustrated calendars with different political texts on each page? Are they really a wholly distinct form of production? What about portfolios combining text and illustration? Newspapers during the war often included powerful graphics of broadside size, along with poems, manifestos, and a range of visual and textual material that might as well have been published in magazines. Does the use of color, glossy paper, and staples really qualify magazines as a category for analysis and understanding? Once again, concern with thematic categories destabilizes these forms of material production. The magazines draw attention to some of the theoretical and methodological problems we face in a cultural environment of intense cross-fertilization and conflict. Nothing in the cauldron of this war stands alone, everything burns together. Everything is related, everything is bound to everything else.

Among the central theoretical and methodological problems is reflexivity. Many students, whether progressive or conservative, find themselves drawn to one of the political positions on the war, so that even belated recruits to the last great cause will be implicated in its dynamic. Students on the left may identify with one of the infamously competing leftist constituencies. Anti-Communist students may be drawn to the appropriate revisionist historians. Catholic students may be challenged by the local and international role of the church during the war. Students thus reenact the problematic contexts of Spanish Civil War history and scholarship, and from the elusive, contaminated character of Spanish facts, they may be led to rethink the nature of all historical knowledge.

Michael Richards

Doctrine and Politics
in Nationalist Spain

Classroom debates about the Nationalist side during the Spanish Civil War and the origins of the Franco regime should aim to distinguish the doctrine propounded in the Franco zone from the process of gaining and consolidating support for the rebel cause. Of course, the intimate relation of these two things can leave students with the impression that the ideology and symbolism successfully determined the relation between the nascent Francoist state and society, that the relation was a straightforward reflection of the doctrine. However, the sacralization of political discourse in the Nationalist zone has to be contextualized. Taking into consideration the conditions and moral ethos of wartime and debating the differences among rhetoric, representation, and reality usefully complicates the picture and encourages historical thinking. This issue of the relation between doctrine and political power also impinges directly on what is currently the most urgent problem in the historiography of the Franco years: the status and usefulness of the ambiguous notion of consensus, or *consenso*, in what has rightly been seen as a coercive political context.

It is logical to address the question of distinguishing between doctrine and politics by exploring the two areas. A brief survey of the doctrine of the Catholic right and some of its key representations forms the first area. Some suggestions for interpreting or decoding these representations will lead to the second area of discussion: the political activities of the embryonic Francoist state and their relation to wartime society. It is worth noting, however, that considerations of culture and cultural practice are essential to an understanding of the relation between doctrine and the Nationalist political project of the authorities. Though there is insufficient space here to develop the point fully, assessing the reception of doctrine and subsequent political mobilization (based on nationalism, for example) depends also on analysis of group sentiments, identities, and consciousness.

Discourse and Symbolism

The simplest symbols in the Nationalist zone were restorative: reversion to the red and gold Spanish national flag in August 1936 and later the declaration of the "Marcha Real" as the national anthem. Certainly the flag was a powerful symbol, but the messages of Nationalist symbols were more complex than a simple return to the pre-Republican past.

The Catholic version of the nation drew on the conservatism of Spanish historical philosophy concerned with the "psychological problem" of Spain's "way of being," exemplified by the late-nineteenth-century high priest of Spanish nationalist doctrine, Marcelino Menéndez Pelayo (1856–1912), famously author of the multivolume history of heterodoxies in Spain (1880–82). In this "Hispanic culture," the nation was personified and incarnated, emphasizing its "organic continuity," a factor that played on the Spanish Catholic Church's traditional emphasis on the organic or natural society based on the Christian family (Gomá y Tomás, *La familia*).

History was recycled, not least in school textbooks of the 1940s and 1950s, which may have operated as comforting symbols of consensus in the exhausted postwar period, even if they contained much that was antimodern and factually questionable, highly partial or incorrect. These textbooks drew analogies, partly through graphic imagery, with the Reconquest, or *Reconquista*, culminating in the Moorish and Jewish "purifications" of the fifteenth century (Cámara Villar; Martínez Tórtola; Sopeña Monsalve; "Manuales"). Spanish nationality was forged over centuries, it was claimed, through war, propagation of the Catholic faith, and the purging of enemies (Richards, *Time*). Contesting this version of history in the 1940s and 1950s created much controversy. It is useful to introduce to students an example of "exile" history to illustrate how the sense of history was central to the struggle during the civil war era. When in Argentina in 1948 the liberal historian of medieval Spain Américo Castro published his account of the flourishing melting-pot culture of Christians, Moors, and Jews in pre-Reconquest Spain, copies had to be smuggled into Spain, where they were circulated enthusiastically among students and intellectuals (Castro, *España*; see also Herzberger in this volume).

Doctrinally, the emergent Nationalist authority absorbed the counter-revolutionary discourse of Hispanidad and Hispanic culture that had been developed during the prewar 1930s by anti-Republican Catholic intellectuals, bishops, ideologues, and military officers through the journal *Acción Española* (González Cuevas; Maeztu; Gomá y Tomás, "Apología"). The 1930s works of Ramiro de Maeztu, the editor of *Acción Española*; Víctor Pradera; and José Calvo Sotelo, for example, represented a notably Catholic and fascistized "updating" of turn-of-the-century regenerationism that rejected democracy (Richards, "Constructing"). The style and message can be sampled in a number of English-language collections, which, however, tend to concentrate on literary examples (Kenwood; G. Thomas; Fraser, *Blood of Spain: The Experience*). This use of history contributed to the myth of the civil war as a religious crusade—a struggle of eternal Spain against the anti-Spain—one of the most effective examples of the conscription of the past during the war.

An important section of the governing elite denied (and continued to deny into the 1960s) that the conflict was a civil war. Rather, it was a war of liberation against foreigners, in defense of the Catholic faith. Spanish Nationalist soldiers were assured in wartime devotional booklets that they were enlisted in "the army of Christ," fighting against "today's anti-Christs." The spirit of 1936 depended on perpetuating the story of the unvarying constants of Spain's "being": her sense and direction. Any veracity accorded to the black legend, associated with Spain's inquisitorial past, was roundly condemned, although such condemnation tended to conflict with the glorious vision of the Reconquest. According to the Francoist view, there never had been a traditional Spain (bad) and progressive Spain (good), as liberals claimed; there had only been eternal Spain and anti-Spain. The crusade representation signified an irreducible opposition that, by definition, canceled out the relativism of the two-Spains thesis.

The crusade myth was used to legitimize, in the eyes of those with power after 1 April 1939, an effective purge of state institutions, public offices, schools, universities, and the professions, and it rigidly controlled the flow of information in the public sphere. A rich vein of relatively short declarations from the early weeks of the war can form the basis of classes on primary source interpretation. On 15 August 1936, the Fiesta of the Assumption of the Virgin, General Emilio Mola broadcast one of many speeches made by leading rebels on that day, calling on all Spaniards to support the "Holy Crusade to save the Patria." He also took the opportunity to promise punishment for the leaders of the Popular Front coalition and described President Manuel Azaña as a "mental degenerate."[1]

The hierarchy of the Catholic Church obviously sanctioned the crusade theme. The collective letter of Spanish bishops published on 1 July 1937, following the fall of the profoundly Catholic Basque Country to the insurgents and endorsing Franco, is a valuable and substantial source for debating many aspects of church-state relations during the war.

The crusade discourse implicitly invited Nationalist authorities and supporters to revel in the glorious and epic aspects of military conflict. Students can consider the relative attributes of symbolism, metaphor, and propaganda in this Nationalist grand narrative. One approach explores the several meanings attached to the fall of Toledo in September 1936. The propagandistic elements of the city's "liberation" and Franco's diversion from the central—and more rational—target of Madrid to free the Nationalist supporters holding out in the citadel of the Alcázar are of obvious interest. But the mythic significance of Toledo and the sense of the Alcázar, even in its architectural style, as a metaphor for austerity, steadfastness, virility, and warrior values can also be developed. The triumphal parade in Madrid in May 1939, in which two hundred thousand troops marched down the Avenue of the Castellana in a sixteen-mile procession to salute the Caudillo, was a conscious replaying of history that reinforced the same ideas. The ceremony was a restaging of the ritual performed when Alfonso VI recaptured Toledo from the Moors in 1085, an event that made the city the capital and the focal point of the church in Spain for almost five centuries (Miranda Calvo). The pennant adorning the tomb of El Cid Campeador was once more held high at Franco's parade. The standard of Tenerife, embroidered by Queen Isabella herself, was also prominent, as were the pennants of Columbus and the Alcázar of Toledo. As the culmination of the ceremony, Franco was awarded Spain's highest honor for heroism, the Gran Cruz Laureada de San Fernando, becoming one of a "privileged caste" representing an indispensable Spanish essence.

The performative element of doctrinal representations can also be discussed through visual images. In a highly theatrical performance the day after the Madrid victory parade, the doctrine of the Francoist state was effectively sacralized in consecration of Franco's victory. The focus of this consecration in the royal basilica of Santa Bárbara in Madrid was the figure of the Caudillo and his symbolic sword of victory, as the photograph below shows. Cardinal Isidro Gomá, primate of Spain, performed the blessing surrounded by several of the military relics of Spain's crusading past, including the Cristo de Lepanto, representing the 1571 Catholic victory over the Islamic infidel. The moment of consecration represents a powerful synthesis of the religio-nationalist doctrine accompanying the war, its material and spiritual sacrifices, and the divinely sanctioned charisma of the Caudillo. This was typical of images that adorned the front pages of the Spanish newspapers illustrating the providential associations of Franco's victory and his monarchical pretensions.

Heroism and martyrdom were intrinsic to the imagination of the crusade. For the Spanish church, the origin of the theocratic new state was the blood tribute of martyrs, nearly seven thousand religious killed during the

Franco at the moment of his consecration before the Christ of Lepanto, 20 May 1939.

war. Upholding the notion of a sacred conflict required very public sacrifice, which would not be politically effective if focused on religious martyrs; the primary consecrated hero had to be General Franco. Chief among the secular martyrs were José Antonio Primo de Rivera and José Calvo Sotelo, but each locality supportive of the cause had its own martyrs, and the relatively discrete communities of memory in the immediate aftermath—Falangist veterans, Carlist Requetés, or *mandos* of the Sección Femenina—favored particular "witnesses to the glory." In November 1939, the third anniversary of the execution of Primo de Rivera was commemorated by the ceremonial transferal of his mortal remains from Alicante to Philip II's palace near Madrid, the Escorial.

Public holidays in Franco's Spain cemented this process of consecration. The most important days dedicated to individuals were the Día del Caudillo (1 October), José Antonio Day (20 November), and Victory Day, which featured a military parade in Madrid and other cities every 1 April until 1976 (Aguilar Fernández). Victory Day fell conveniently close to the public commemoration of the Passion of Christ. The temporal association of Holy Week with the Nationalist triumph both recalled the war and linked the outcome with providence, inserting its commemoration into a timeless, mythical cycle. The official commemoration days were appreciated for the time off work but seem never to have been as genuinely popular as the saints' days. The religious director of the Francoist youth movement declared in 1940 that the nature and purpose of the Frente de Juventudes was to perpetuate the example of martyrdom and to shape youngsters' morality in order to redeem the sacrifice of the war. The gulf between the rhetoric and the reality of life in the Frente has, however, been exposed by the historian of the organization, Juan Sáez Marín.

It is worth considering further this use of history and the attempt to control and represent time in a particular way. Whereas Marxist revolutionaries construct a teleological, overtly political vision of the future, counterrevolutionaries visualize a cyclical traditional-spiritual temporal structure. They attempted to control time and to shape social groups in the moral and ethical image of what they saw as the principal agent of history. In revolutionary situations this agent would be a particular social class, but in the counterrevolution the engine of history was the (Spanish) nation.

In 1937 a Nationalist decree proclaimed 18 July a national holiday. For years this was the occasion for a summation by the dictator of the condition of Spain. In his 1937 speech, Franco addressed the background to the movement of salvation; he railed against the treason of the Freemasons and

94   Doctrine and Politics

outlined the transcendental aims of the Reconquest and the planned social
program of the new state (Díaz-Plaja, *La guerra de España* 250–53). In his
1938 speech, Franco acknowledged the debt that Spain owed to the
Falangist leader Primo de Rivera. He reiterated that the war was a crusade
against atheistic Communism as well as a monastic crusade for religion. He
attacked the international sectarianism against Spain and denounced the
horrendous crimes of Red Spain. Finally, he characterized the nascent Francoist state as a missionary and totalitarian state, echoing the ideas of both
Maeztu and Mussolini (338–44).

The sources of ideological justification, represented in the rituals,
were reflected in the official normative standards of morality and conscience, though they were received in a complex way. The behavior values
of the Catholic-military Counter-Reformation—honor, austerity, disciplined hierarchies—were part of reconstruction and repression. The
Franco state was depicted as a recovery of the austere, ascetic, sixteenth-
century missionary state of Philip II (see, e.g., Pemartín). The Spanish
mystics were invoked as exemplary images; Santa Teresa and San Ignacio
de Loyola were particular favorites. The images of saints and heroes from
the past were redrawn in vulgar terms in postwar Spain. Theoretically they
would stiffen wartime and postwar discipline and also, perhaps, contribute
to redeeming the sacrifice of the war, giving it some sense or meaning. At
the time these idealized images were repressive, though now they tend to
be looked on with a sense of nostalgia (see, e.g., "La Educación"). Masses
of educational books and pamphlets were produced by the Falangist
Movimiento, and courses were offered on *formación política* (political
education) and *formación familiar y social* (family and social education—
for women and girls), which included sections about Franco and the war,
religion, etiquette, and manners (see, e.g., Sección Femenina).

The State and Politics

Thus, at the doctrinal level, an imagined community coalesced around the
triumphal narrative. The aim of this community was the inoculation of
Spanish society against forgetfulness or deviations. This aim struck with
particular force in the denial of regional-national identity. In May 1937, as
the Nationalist forces penetrated deeper into the Basque Country, the
authorities prohibited use of any language other than Castilian in Basque
shops and businesses. A similar decree, in March 1938, prohibited the
public use of Catalan.

Some twenty years after the war, in May 1958, the newly formulated Fundamental Principles of the Movement, one of the quasi-sacred texts of the regime, continued to base authority on the "communion of Spaniards in the ideals that gave life to the Crusade." According to article 1, the unity of Spain and Spaniards was a "sacred duty" (García-Nieto and Donézar 414–16). This constitutional reform, as the regime liked to depict it, was of course compromised by the doubtful proposition that Francoist political evolution amounted to the formation of a nation. In truth, this national community had been relatively precarious and even relatively limited in size at the height of Francoist triumphalism in 1939. Its ideas tended to be self-referential, backward looking, and not very effective in the sense of political mobilization.

One of the first things that the new state does in civil wars is demonstrate the illegitimacy of the old state—in this war, the government and institutions (both local and national) of the Spanish Second Republic of 1931, which had brusquely altered the course of Spain's history. At the height of the war, in December 1938, the Franco authorities established a commission of notables to demonstrate the illegitimacy of the powers of the republic. This commission was composed of academics, judges, ex-ministers—all representatives of the new state, several of whom had been prominent during the Primo de Rivera years in the 1920s and contributors to *Acción Española* in the 1930s. They claimed that the republic was illegitimate because of its origin (falsified elections, as they argued) and its exercise of powers (descent into revolutionary anarchy). These predictable conclusions served as a template for much of the policy that followed. The new power subsequently dedicated much of its activity to effacing the republic and its effects.

The organization of the state, based on this negation of the reforms introduced since April 1931, was made concrete through institutions, sacred texts, and repressive activities against enemies. In December 1936 the purging of all state and local functionaries contrary to the Movimiento Nacional was announced. The objective was to investigate the antecedents of all public employees in what amounted to a thorough cleansing of the public authorities. Political parties, as formally free intermediaries between state and society, were banned. They were replaced officially in April 1937 with the well-known Decree of Unification, which forcibly united all of the political forces of Nationalist Spain under the control of a new state organization, Falange Española Tradicionalista y de las JONS, headed by Franco. The program of the Movimiento—formalized in the so-called twenty-six points of the Falange, first announced in 1934—officially became the basis of the new state, rather in the way that state party programs became the primordial, quasi-sacred texts of the regimes of Hitler and Mussolini. As in Germany and Italy, the activities of the state had a tenuous link to the official text. It was probably the militarization of society in Spain that was felt most repressively in daily life. The power of state instruments was thus more symbolic than tangible. Another Francoist statute worthy of decoding is the corporativist Fuero del Trabajo (Labor Charter) of March 1938, which reveals the compromise reached by the monarchist, Catholic, and fascist elements of the new power at the expense of the social groups previously represented by free trade unions.

A battery of legislation established the framework for the punishment of Republicans. Military jurisdiction was declared over all those persons found to be contrary to the rebellion, only weeks after it began, in July 1936. The infamous Law of Political Responsibilities, decreed in February 1939 against those who had supported the Popular Front government, was the most elaborate repressive statute of the war. The detailed categories of crime suggest much about the mentality of the victors. The law initiated a huge endeavor by the state to establish special tribunals all over the country that would hear thousands of cases and would impose pecuniary sanctions against Republicans in Spain or confirm the banishment and denationalization of those already in exile. As well as setting this punishment process in motion, these instruments of repression carried a heavy symbolic weight. The 1939 law implied that the war had been the responsibility of the left and reduced to the same criminal category both the legal reforms of the Republican governments and the direct action of the revolution.

The Nationalist authorities also established particular state-run bodies to control cultural production and dissemination and to censor information. A revealing link was made in the decree of December 1936 prohibiting the circulation of pornographic, socialist, and Communist books. A number of official publications gave long lists of recommended works of literature. Similarly restrictive measures were applied to scientific endeavor. In 1939 the new state established the Consejo Superior de Investigaciones Científicas (the Higher Council of Scientific Research) within the Ministry of National Education with the aim of creating "a Catholic science." A substantial part of the activities and funds of the new institution would be devoted to the life of the spirit, with subinstitutes of theology, canonic law, ecclesiastical history, and so on (Brugarola

8–9). In 1940, the government also sponsored the creatio͏
sejo de Hispanidad (the Council of Spanishness) to glorif͏
legacy, to bring Spaniards and other Hispanic peoples together, and to
strengthen the ties between them.

In setting forth its fundamental objectives for education, the
Nationalist authorities reached an unmatched hyperbole that possibly
reflected their belief in the way the republic perverted the minds of children. This belief was also reflected in the violence of the purge of teachers,
decreed in December 1936 (Álvarez Oblanca). Liberal teachers had
sinned particularly in confusing the traditional sense of gender roles, the
foundation of an ordered world. Coeducation was outlawed as early as
September 1936, and female teachers were only permitted to teach in
girls' schools. Religious subjects and patriotism would take priority. The
law of reform of secondary education, pronounced in the middle of the
war, in September 1938, called for "the definitive extirpation of the anti-
Spanish, foreign pessimism, which is the child of apostasy and of the hate-
ful and lying black legend" (Martínez Tórtola 34). This demand was
hardly a reasoned basis for a modernizing or consensual nationalization of
the masses. Inevitably, the image of the past imposed onto children had
some effect. One testimony in 1970 from a witness born in 1937 recalled
how "gradually it was instilled in me and I always believed that Spain had
won the war against foreigners, enemies of our historic greatness" (Borràs
Betriu 481).

The obsession with gender and the family in education, largely
imposed by the Catholic Church, was part of a broader project. In March
1938 civil marriage, which had been introduced in the 1931 constitution
of the republic, was declared illegal, and all civil arrangements made under
Republican authority became null and void in territory occupied by
Nationalist forces. Similarly, in September 1939 the divorce law introduced by the republic was annulled. In October 1937 the Nationalists
established the system of obligatory social service for women (see also
López de Martínez in this volume). The contradictions between the idealized image of woman restricted to the private sphere and the call for
women to be active in society, albeit along lines formally set by the state,
are evident, as recent research has shown (Blasco Herranz).

A comparative methodology, which is often effective in seminar work,
requires some kind of theoretical model. We could reduce the essential
activities of civil war cultures—as a generic type—to three areas: doctrine,

politics and sentiments, consciousness or identity. First, like revolutions, civil wars are inherently more ideological than interstate wars, a characteristic reflected in the doctrinal output and representations of civil wars. The rhetorical exigencies of war heighten the human tendency to impose a sense of simple opposition on complex situations. Establishing or strengthening group identities (such as national identity), often defined explicitly in opposition to the adversary, widens divisions and deepens repression. Second, civil wars become central to founding myths of modern states, based initially on an irreducible opposition between images of winners and losers. The myth is essential to constructing coherent political power through state organs and institutions. Images produced during the war reinforce the myth, and the representation of these images becomes the aim of cultural politics in each competing zone. The political project is built, however, on the basis of nationalism, which requires a coherent, effective state authority representing the interests of the most dynamic forces in society. Third, reconciling other priorities (Catholic faith or identity, proletarian revolution and class consciousness) that potentially conflict with nationalist activities is problematic. In the Nationalist heartland of Castile and large parts of northern Spain, the nation's "destiny" was complicated by the precedence of religious identity over national identity.

The doctrine of the Nationalist side during the civil war (and in the first years thereafter) was more internally coherent than the composition of state institutions and the articulation of political strategy to organize the power of the new state. The remembered or reconstructed experience of war, in the peculiar moral and spiritual climate of the aftermath, gave meaning to the war. In Spain, as in other sites of civil war, the state granted an exclusive right to patriotic sentiments, public self-justification, and a sense of community (articulated in the public sphere) and sacrifice to the victors, especially during the 1940s and most of the 1950s. The Republican war effort was denied expression, representation, and public ritualization. This repression was essentially a continuation of the war through symbolic violence.

Note

1. Mola 1180, 1178. All translations from the Spanish are mine unless otherwise noted.

Adrian Shubert

Between Documentary and Propaganda: Teaching *The Spanish Earth*

The Spanish Earth was made and released in 1937. The list of people responsible for its creation reads like a roll call of the United States cultural world at the time: script by Ernest Hemingway; music by Virgil Thompson and Marc Blitzstein; narration by Orson Welles and Hemingway; on location work by John Dos Passos; and financial support from Lillian Hellman, Dorothy Parker, Clifford Odets, and Archibald MacLeish. It was immediately—and rightfully—recognized as a brilliant achievement and one of the seminal cultural creations of the Spanish Civil War, an assessment that has not changed over the subsequent seven decades. This almost legendary status, combined with the film's wide availability[1] and accessibility to students who know no Spanish, makes it an obligatory resource for courses on the war.

The Spanish Earth raises numerous questions. On the one hand, it is a historical document and a primary source, and, as with any such source, it needs to be interrogated. What does it say? Who made it? For whom? And for what purpose? That it is a film, and not a written document, raises additional questions: What type of film is it? How does it use the conventions and techniques of film to convey its message? On the other hand, it is a work of art. It takes us into the field of representations, of creations we need to understand as "artistic translation[s]" of particular events (Gikandi

99

242), not as the actual events it purports to portray. And these representations pose questions of authorship, audience, and intent (W. Mitchell 12).

Its creators described *The Spanish Earth* as a documentary, and it was received as such at the time of its release. The *New York Herald Tribune* praised it as a documentary,[2] and the film has been called a documentary ever since.[3] Documentary, both in film and photography, was a new category of cultural production in the 1930s (see also Pingree in this volume). The term was first used by the British filmmaker John Grierson in 1926, when he defined it as "a creative treatment of actuality" (Barsam 2). It has not been an entirely fixed category since then, and Grierson's definition, which he himself described as "clumsy," was only the first of many. These numerous and varied definitions fit between two poles, which we can describe as the objective and the engaged. The former was proposed by John Cawston: "the totally objective type of program, which is what I have made more of myself. . . . [I]ts job is to reflect society, not influence it" (qtd. in Edmonds 12). He contrasted the objective documentary to "the fully subjective committed documentary which is made by a man who wants to use it to say something himself."[4] Most documentary filmmakers who have written on the subject fall into the engaged camp. Joris Ivens, the Dutch director of *The Spanish Earth*, was himself very much part of, indeed one of the pioneers of, the politically engaged documentary. In his autobiography, he noted:

> I was often asked, why we had not gone to the other side too, to make an *objective* film? My only answer was that a documentary filmmaker has to have an opinion on such vital issues as fascism or anti-fascism— he *has* to have feelings about these issues if his work is to have any dramatic, emotional or artistic value. . . . If anyone wanted that objectivity of "both sides of the question," he would have to show two films, *The Spanish Earth* and a film by a fascist filmmaker, if he could find one. (*Camera* 136–37)

Ivens made a similar point in a lecture given in New York in 1939:

> Of course, you find a great problem here, and that is the objectivity and subjectivity of the director. Would you rather see both sides of the Civil War in Spain, or would you rather see it from the loyalist side and the fascist side in separate films? Do you prefer to see a man handling both sides of it, trying to give an objective point of view? . . . I think that in such great problems as life and death and democracy and fascism, there is no objectivity for an artist.[5] ("Documentary" 251–52)

Perhaps because of the predominance of commercial television, with its particular kind of documentary, in general usage the word *documentary* has lost this charge of engagement and come to imply a naive veracity that what is on screen is somehow objectively true. Lindsay Anderson said that makers of documentary, himself included, "photograph the natural life, but you also, by your juxtaposition of detail, create an interpretation of life" (qtd. in Edmonds 13). He suggested:

[O]ne of the things that has fouled up the discussion of documentaries, I think, in recent years, has been the identification of documentary with information or even instruction. Maybe it's a word that has out-lived its usefulness because I think that it no longer has a very clear significance. (11)

For Ivens, *The Spanish Earth* was a "militant documentary"; its task was to inform and move the audience in order to "agitate-mobilize them to become active in connection with the problems shown in the film" (*Camera* 137). His film presents in a powerful manner a definite interpretation of the nature of the Spanish Civil War. In his memoirs, Ivens described Spain as the place "where ideas of Right and Wrong were clashing in such clear conflict, where fascism was preparing a second world war" (qtd. in Edmonds 103). Moreover, the film was made by Americans for Americans and for a specific purpose: to convince them that their country should end its nonintervention and support the republic against Franco and his German and Italian allies. Ivens's "militant documentary" can thus be considered as propaganda, which Terence Qualter defines as "the deliberate attempt by the few to influence the attitudes and behavior of the many by the manipulation of symbolic communication" (124). He explains:

Any act of promotion can be propaganda only if and when it becomes part of a deliberate campaign to induce action through influencing attitudes. Once it is established that any statement, book, poster or rumour, any parade or exhibition, any statue or historic monument, any scientific achievement or abstract of statistics, whether true or false, rational or irrational in appeal or presentation, originates as the deliberate policy of someone trying to control or alter attitudes, then that thing or activity becomes part of a propaganda process. (122)

When Ivens directed *The Spanish Earth*, he was already well known as a documentary filmmaker with left-wing political opinions. All those who had a significant role in creating the film were from the United States, and

they undertook the project with the specific aim of trying to generate support for the Republican cause in their country.

The financial backing for *The Spanish Earth* came from a company called
Contemporary Historians, which had been formed by a number of well-
known literary figures in New York, among them Lillian Hellman, Dorothy
Parker, and Archibald MacLeish, for the specific purpose of funding the film.
Ivens had been in the United States since early 1936, working on a project
for the Rockefeller Foundation. When MacLeish approached him about
making a film about the civil war, Ivens quickly accepted the offer. He arrived
in Spain with a script idea prepared by one of the New York group, but once
there he decided that it was impractical. In Madrid, John Dos Passos helped
him canvass ideas, and in the end they settled on the irrigation project in
Fuentedueña as the focus. After a month of filming, Ivens went to Paris,
where he met Hemingway, who offered to help with the script. Hemingway
joined Ivens when he returned to Spain and spent several weeks working with
him. Hemingway also recruited Sidney Franklin, "the Brooklyn bullfighter,"
to work on the film "as a sort of Liaison Officer" (Ivens, *Camera* 113).

Once the filming was complete, Ivens returned to New York. There,
Helen van Dongen did the editing while the composers Marc Blitzstein
and Virgil Thompson were putting together the sound track, "combing
through dozens of records of Spanish music" (Ivens, *Camera* 128). Orson
Welles read the narration, but Ivens and some of his American backers felt
that the effect was not what they wanted:

> [T]here was something in the quality of his voice that separated it from
> the film. It is possible that Welles' voice, coming directly from the rich,
> rounded periods of Marlowe and Shakespeare, hadn't made the neces-
> sary adaptation to the "stripped" sentences of Hemingway. (128)

Hemingway himself replaced Welles as narrator, and in Ivens's view "the
lack of a professional commentator's smoothness helped you to believe
intensely in the experiences on the screen" (129).[6]

The film was first screened at the White House for President and Mrs.
Roosevelt. This premiere was followed by a series of screenings in Los
Angeles, including one at the house of the actor Frederic March, where
Ivens asked for money to help buy ambulances for the Republican forces.
The seventeen guests each gave $1,000, and a later screening at a Los
Angeles cinema raised a further $2,000. However, despite strong support
from "creative people in Hollywood," *The Spanish Earth* was not picked
up for general release in the United States (132).[7]

How does *The Spanish Earth* work as propaganda? The essence of propaganda is simplification, the reduction of a conflict to the starkness of good versus evil. It has no room for nuance or for the complexity that inevitably accompanies historical events, such as the Spanish Civil War.

The Spanish Earth is constructed around a simple narrative. Julián, a young Republican militiaman, returns from the front to Fuentedueña, his village of fifteen hundred people on the main highway to Valencia near Madrid. The villagers are building an irrigation system. The rest of the film shows the defense of Madrid, including scenes of aerial bombardment, which was then still a novelty. The juxtaposition of these two elements conveys the message of the film: the struggle of simple villagers to irrigate their land is the metaphor for the struggle in Spain as a whole. Julián serves as the human connection between the two elements. We first see him as a soldier engaged in the defense of Madrid, writing to tell his parents that he will soon be coming home for a short leave.

This connection is further reinforced by Ivens's cutting between one story and the other:

> You get a kind of daring cutting, I would venture to say. . . . There is no longer an elementary, visual editing. Psychological elements are coming into the editing. . . . In one sequence there is a long canal flowing toward the screen and then, immediately after that, you see the trucks going to Madrid. In editing, it is important to have three or four links. One very elementary link is that the water comes down, and the main attention of the audience is at the front part of the water. Then, when I cut to the truck, I did so in such a manner that the truck starts where the water left off. . . . You see the water and you have a feeling of contentment. You feel how wonderful it is that the Spanish earth is receiving this water. And that is why I show the trucks going to Madrid, to bring happiness to the audience, in the knowledge that the people were going to receive food. . . . This kind of cutting is not just symbolic, because it goes much deeper than that. It is part of the theme of the film. It is optimism. (Ivens, "Documentary" 255–56)

Two other sets of cuts connect the two stories. One moves from Julián drilling the village boys to new recruits drilling in Madrid; the other cuts from the president of the republic, Manuel Azaña, giving a speech in which he mentions the villages of Spain to a shot of the men of Fuentedueña. Ivens later described three "levels of editing" he used in the film (*Camera* 125). The first was "simple visual editing . . . where the continuity is based on the direct visual sensation of shot after shot." The second level included "psychological factors . . . the editing treatment of Julián's homecoming aimed at overall emotional warmth, rather than a story point that could be isolated and identified" (125–26). The third level was "taking the emotional aim up to a point of view—the personal, social and political point of view of the film maker." Ivens explains:

> This might be called emphatic cutting, pulling the spectator by his emotions from stage to stage of an idea's development. In the fourteen shots that compose the core of the sequence of the bombing of the village, the editing follows an emotion-idea line: tension before the bombing; the threat; the fright; the explosion; the destruction; the horror of not knowing what it's all about; the running around of the women; the start of activity, searching for victims; the slight happiness of a baby; then the horror of corpses and the accusation against the enemy—ending on a feeling of young life, a preparation for the counterblow, and then that blow itself. (127–28)

For Ivens the third level distinguished his endeavor from that of the newsreel; it came "mostly from a wish to deepen the relation of real things—to show what is below the surface." For someone producing a newsreel, "an editor interested in giving information alone," many of the shots in this sequence would have been superfluous (127).

Ivens's interweaving of the irrigation of the land of Fuentedueña and the struggle for the Spanish capital is highly effective. By using Fuentedueña as the metaphor for the republic, the film implies that the Republican side was as united in its struggle against the enemy as the villagers are shown to be in their struggle to irrigate the land. This interweaving, however, is not the only, or even the most significant, way in which the film works to convince its audience to support the Republican cause; the deliberate decision to leave the description of the two contending sides as vague as possible is the most successful method of persuasion. The film definitely has its own politics, but it achieves them by obliterating the politics of the Spaniards themselves.

The most striking example of this obliteration occurs in the scenes featuring the announcement of the fusion of the various party and union militias into a single Republican army. Ivens describes the event in his autobiography:

> We filmed the meeting at which the People's Army was officially founded. All the different regiments fighting in their own way on the Loyalist side—the communist, socialist, anarchist, regiments—were fused into *one* Republican Army at a meeting attended by delegates from all fronts. (122)

In the film, however, this lengthy scene goes by without a single mention that there were different political affiliations, let alone politically based fighting units, on the Republican side. Nor is the political affiliation of all the speakers who are shown, all leading figures in the Communist Party, mentioned. Enrique Líster, commander of the Communist Fifth Regiment, is described as a "brilliant young soldier"; José Díaz, the leader of the Communist Party, is merely a member of parliament; and Dolores Ibárruri (La Pasionaria), another leading Communist, is simply "the most famous woman in Spain." There is no hint that there was opposition to the elimination of the militias, especially from anarchists, Trotskyists, and some socialists.

A similar political omission happens earlier in the film. As we are introduced to the village of Fuentedueña and shown how the villagers are working together for the "common good" and to grow food for the defenders of Madrid, at no point are we told how this situation had come about. We are told that for fifty years, an unspecified "they" had prevented the villagers from carrying out the irrigation project. We are not told how the villagers overcame that opposition, that there had been a widespread agrarian revolution in the Republican zone, that in many places land had been collectivized and villages were being governed by party or union committees. There is a scene in which women appear to be buying bread, and even though we are shown a loaf stamped with the initials of the socialist trade union confederation, UGT (Unión General de Trabajadores), the only comment in the narration, one that would be acceptable to an audience in the United States, is that this loaf is "good bread, stamped with the union label."

The film reduces the issues behind the Spanish Civil War to the struggle for land, the metaphor for the Republican cause, which means that other fundamental issues are absent. At no point during *The Spanish Earth* is the church mentioned. Again, Ivens certainly knew better. When he and his crew arrived in Fuentedueña, they were put up in a room attached to the apothecary's shop.

> The villagers who came there in their brief free time to talk to us about the film told us, "You know, you are living in the room where we paid for our lives, all our lives.". . . We learned that the village priest had used this room as an office, where payments were made to the church for every child born, every couple married, every person who wore out and died. These were not real, but "spiritual" taxes—and I think the people hated the force exerted over their spiritual life more than any physical hardship. (*Camera* 110)

How was this hatred manifested once the war broke out and the village was collectivized? Was the church used for other purposes? Were its statues taken out and burned? And what happened to the priest? Did he flee or was he among the almost seven thousand clergy who were killed? In a country that, like the United States, had a large Catholic population, much of which was inclined to oppose the republic, those were uncomfortable questions to ask.

The enemy is more clearly defined than the politics are, and the film emphasizes those aspects to which its American audience would be most likely to respond. The first mention of the enemy is the unspecified "they" who had prevented the villagers from irrigating the land. We are then told that the Republicans are fighting to defend their country, the implication being that the enemy is primarily foreign. The Spanish enemy is mentioned only once: in the scenes of the struggle in Madrid's University City, we are told that the enemy soldiers are Civil Guards and Moors, brave fighters but professional soldiers who enjoyed aid from Italy and Germany.

The only time the enemy actually appears on screen, they are exclusively Germans and Italians. We are shown an aerial bombardment by what we are told are Junker planes. Then, in one of the most famous scenes in the film, we are shown a German plane that had been shot down, and, as the camera lingers on some German writing, Hemingway says, "I can't read German either." In a 1939 article, Ivens referred to this scene as "straight propaganda":

> I knew there would be people who would not understand the long German words, so I held the scene a little longer, to get them annoyed, and then I had the commentator say, "I can't read German either." In other words, I think sometimes you have to anticipate the feelings of your audience. ("Documentary" 258)

Finally, the camera lingers over the corpses of soldiers from Italy, while Hemingway says that the letters found on them were all "very sad."

The Spanish Earth is a rich resource for classroom use. Made by non-Spaniards, in this case Americans, who intended to persuade their fellow Americans to support the republic, the film is an outstanding example of how the war was presented outside Spain. Comparing the film's interpretation of the war and the issues behind it with the historians' interpretations will make clear the extent of simplification used and how this technique enables the film to achieve its goal more convincingly. The effectiveness of this technique can be made even clearer if we look at how *The Spanish Earth* works as a film. *The Spanish Earth* is an important primary source, a representation of the Spanish Civil War that speaks to the internationalization of the Spanish conflict.

Notes

1. *The Spanish Earth* was released in 2000 on DVD, along with another film by the same director, Joris Ivens, *The 400 Million* (SlingShot Entertainment, Sherman Oaks, CA).

2. Not all the reviews were laudatory. See Ivens, *Camera* 133–35.

3. The abstract of the DVD edition, however, describes it as a "docudrama."

4. Edmonds and Barsam both have longer discussions of various definitions of the documentary film.

5. Much of the controversy aroused by Michael Moore's popular film *Fahrenheit 9/11* has centered on precisely this question of objectivity versus engagement.

6. This switch helps explain the animosity between Welles and Hemingway that led to an all-out brawl between the two men at a Paris showing of the film.

7. The speech Ivens gave after the screening in March's house is published in Bakker 247–49.

Michael Ugarte

The Question of Race
in the Spanish Civil War

> Listen, Moorish prisoner, hell!
> Here, shake hands with me!
>
> (qtd. in Mullen 157)

So speaks the poetic voice of a North American black man fighting on the
Republican side of the Spanish Civil War as rendered by the celebrated
African American poet Langston Hughes. This voice is unique among the
many heard in the 1930s describing, lamenting, and talking excitedly
about the war because its dramatic force depends almost exclusively on
the race, in the most conventional sense, of the speaker. Indeed, racial
and ethnic conflicts and tensions have received little attention in the otherwise multilayered social and literary historiography of the Spanish Civil
War.

Race in all its complexity, both as a real marker of human existence
and as a construction, played an immensely important role in the war. Historians' attempts to assess the causes and development of the conflict have
understandably focused on class disparities, demands for social improvements, strikes and uprisings in the face of glaring poverty, and the virulent
reactions against those demands on the part of powerful institutions such as

the Spanish state, the Catholic Church, and the land-owning oligarchies. But racial factors are central to the understanding of how class dimensions manifested themselves in 1930s Spain.

When one adds the issue of representation to the complexities of race—How is race represented? Who constructs those representations? How are those representations communicated?—the labyrinthine ideological issues surrounding the Spanish Civil War become even more convoluted. In this essay, I argue that the presence of the black other on both sides of the conflict made for inconsistency on both sides of the ideological divide.

For those of us studying and working in the English-speaking world, especially in the United States, a country whose national identity has been defined in part by race relations, it is important to distinguish what we mean by race. In Spain racial tensions have developed in a very different way and are often linked to other indications of identity such as religion (e.g., the Sephardic Jews and Muslims in the Middle Ages through the sixteenth and seventeenth centuries) and the effects of colonialism. I refer especially to the indigenous peoples of Latin America and Africa. The latter area played a crucial, albeit underacknowledged, role in the war.

Francisco Franco began his military career in northern Africa, specifically Spanish Morocco. His participation in the colonial war in that region in the late nineteenth and early twentieth centuries would later determine his leadership of an insurgency that ended in his dictatorial leadership of the country, a period that came to a close only after his death in 1975. But it was not only Franco who came of age as a military leader in Morocco in the first third of the twentieth century. Equally important was a group of high-ranking military officers (Generals Sanjurjo, Mola, Yagüe, Millán-Astray, Queipo de Llano, and others) known as the *africanomilitaristas* (Africa-based militarists), all of whom had formative experiences in Africa. All were major participants in the rebellion against the Second Republic, and all were representatives of the most fervent of Spanish Nationalist ideals. These officers learned from their wartime experience quelling northern Moroccan movements for self-determination and used this experience, as well as conscripted indigenous soldiers, to topple the Second Republic. The use of these conscripts, both as cannon fodder and as symbols of Nationalist strength, may be seen as a paradox, an inconsistency in the right-wing line of argumentation: the grandiosity of the Spanish nation is predicated on its victory over Islam, not its incorporation or assimilation of it.

However, the use of Moroccans as allies may not seem as paradoxical when we consider that one of the ideological underpinnings of the right-wing rebellion was the perceived disaster of the colonial collapse of Spain, the loss of the last of its New World possessions at the dawn of the twentieth century. By then, European colonialism had turned away from this less than new world and fixed its eyes on Africa. We need only recall Mussolini's invasion of Ethiopia in 1935 for a model of comparison on which we can gauge the importance of the resurrection of a dead empire. Spanish Nationalist and fascist ideology was imbued with similar visions of the need for a resurgence of Spanish domination over the colonial subaltern.

In *Los moros que trajo Franco*, an informative (and in many ways pioneering) work on the Moroccan troops' participation in the Spanish Civil War, María Rosa de Madariaga argues compellingly that the origins of Francoism and all that it entailed ideologically and politically can be traced to Spanish Morocco. The Moroccan presence in the war could be seen as something like the Spanish race card, the historical dimension of the conflict that brought into play all the infamous practices and thought patterns that deem race the determining factor of behavior and station in life. The white man's burden of colonization and civilization was used constantly as a justification for war.

In the 1920s Moroccans, or *moros amigos* ("Moorish friends") as they were called by the Spanish militarists, were used as soldiers to put down rebellions against Spanish domination, the most notable of which was led by Abd el Krim, a highly educated journalist and teacher from the Rif (the Spanish protectorate in northern Morocco) who sought not only self-government but also democracy for the area (see Woolman, ch. 5). The *africanomilitaristas* were determined to undermine Krim's efforts and were largely successful. On 17 July 1936, Franco rose against the republic from Morocco with a strong contingent of *moros amigos*. The Moroccans joined him to escape poverty through the realization of promises of the spoils of battle, soldiers' wages, uniforms, and the advantages of fighting on the side of the valiant saviors of Spain in the face of a godless onslaught of Reds. Franco's Moorish soldiers were seen by people on both sides of the conflict as one of the insurgents' most terrifying weapons, soldiers with little or nothing to lose, savages whose prime motivation was to kill and rape. The *africanomilitaristas* perpetuated this image to terrify the enemy, although the Moors to them were loyal servants who knew their low status as subalterns and were grateful to the Spanish colonizers for bringing them civilization.

More complex (and revealing) is how those who were loyal to the republic perceived the invading Moors. It is one of the many glaring ironies (and in this instance an ideological inconsistency) of the history of the civil war that the Spanish left used the rhetoric of reactionary nationalism to discredit Franco's insurgency. The Moorish soldiers who obeyed the rebellious generals were projected as a renewal of the Muslim conquest of Spain. In this scheme the defense of the republic was seen as a reenactment of the Christian Reconquest. Posters picturing rabid blacks with turbans, thirsty for Republican blood and eager to rape Spanish women, were prominent. Much of the antifascist lore surrounding the Moors was imbedded with racist images depicting the defenders of the republic as white victims of black barbarians in the service of militarists and despots (M. Madariaga 296–318). Moreover, the leaders of the republic with few exceptions were reluctant to grant its Moroccan protectorate independence because to do so would have alienated the French government, which was waging its own colonial battles in that area, and the Spanish left was depending on France as a potential ally against Franco, despite the Non-intervention Pact. It is important to add that some Moroccan nationalists urged the republic not to give up the protectorate for fear that it would be swallowed up by France. But while some Republicans argued that autonomy, which had been granted to Catalonia, was a possibility for Morocco, the idea was not pursued aggressively.

Indeed, the Spanish left's discourse on race during the civil war had many facets. Coupled with the common association of Franco's Moroccan troops as African invaders was a recognition by some Republicans, particularly in the Spanish Communist Party, that Moroccans were also victims of right-wing politics and practices. The Spanish Communist Party's journal, *Mundo Obrero*, argued that Franco's Moroccan soldiers were potential allies for the Republican cause and should be persuaded to defect (M. Madariaga 323–24). The anarchists occasionally had similar arguments, but there were also instances in anarchist publications of impassioned cries to defend the motherland, *madre España, la santa*, against Germans, Italians, and *moros* (M. Madariaga 367–68). Not even Pablo Neruda was free of this stereotype: he cries out in his famous poem about the Spanish Civil War, "Explico algunas cosas" ("I Explain Some Things"), against the "bandits with planes and with Moors"(Neruda, *Antología* 100). Relatively few cultural artifacts of the period (songs, poems, drawings, letters, and articles) dealt with the Moor as a conflicted human being skeptical about any European colonizer as an ally in the struggle for freedom.

W. E. B. DuBois's thoughts about the inherent "double consciousness" of blacks would have been an inroad to the Spanish left's understanding of the Moroccan presence in Spain, but few Spaniards were aware of them.

Perusing the many *romances* written during or about the Spanish Civil War that dealt with race (see Salaün, *Romancero libertario*; Ramos-Gascón; López Aranda; Vicente Hernando; Santonja, *Romancero*), I have found one that stands out for its incarnation of the contradictions and tensions surrounding the presence of Africans in Spain at a crucial moment of Spanish history. It was composed by none other than Emilio Prados, well known in Spain as a member of the illustrious group of poets of the so-called Generation of 1927, the most prominent of which was Federico García Lorca. Prados's "El moro engañado" ("The Deceived Moor") is a poem based on an apostrophe in which the poetic voice speaks to a Moor (the Moor incarnate) who has been duped by the Francoist forces into coming to Spain to fight for a cause in which he has no interest. It is a long poem filled with what may be read at first as invectives against the deceived Moroccan. The poetic voice cries to him to get out of Spain and return to Africa: "Go back, Spain has nothing for you," "the money that buys you is money that sells you." As the speaker continues in this vein, he appeals to what seems like a natural order that mitigates against the very presence of the Moor on Spanish soil: "leave our peaks, you don't understand their winds, there [in Africa] the sun awaits you, here the snow spits at you" (my trans.). Thus the geography of Spain cooperates in yet another historical expulsion of the Moor. One wonders what Prados would have said about a poor lad from sunny Alicante shivering in the front line of battle on the banks of the Jarama in February 1937.

However, the poem is composed of more than a series of patronizing remarks to the deceived Moor; the speaker also offers him advice. The poetic voice tells the Moor not to leave his rifle behind on his way back to Africa and to nurture the ardor with which he is fighting, because there is a battle waiting for him back home. "Look, they're fighting in your land . . . fighting for liberty, for your children and your women, to liberate a land suffering in captivity." The speaker again invokes nature and insists that the Moor is unwelcome: "the tree that was born in the lowlands dies in the high mountains." Thus the Moor is to go back to his natural and familiar habitat and turn his weapons against those who keep him in bondage, "those who bite with black deception." In the final verses, the speaker suggests not difference between himself and the Moor but common ground in their struggle for freedom. The Moorish other is converted into a man with desires all too human, like those of the speaker himself. "If we fight [together] for liberty, we will know how to defend you," which I read as an acknowledgment (albeit with a note of paternalism) of a common struggle, perhaps the most dominant leitmotif of the Republican discourse on the war.

The participation of the indigenous Moroccan troops in the toppling of the republic is not the only chapter in the history of the war that contains a racial dimension. It is equally important to consider the contributions made by African Americans in the defense of the republic. North American blacks volunteered to fight in Spain against the fascists as members of the Abraham Lincoln Brigade and as such were connected to the American Communist Party (CPUSA), although not all the volunteers were Communists (see also Coale in this volume). The CPUSA had recruited in the black community in the 1920s and 1930s. After the Italian fascist invasion of Ethiopia (considered as a spiritual homeland by many American blacks), interest in defending Spain rose because of Mussolini's ideological proximity to Franco. In fact the CPUSA was the only American labor organization in the 1930s that addressed African American concerns.

There are testimonies of the one hundred or so blacks who went to Spain with the Lincoln Brigade, an example of which is *A Negro Nurse in Republican Spain*, a pamphlet detailing Salaria Kee's experience as a field nurse for the republic. Similarly, the documentary film *The Good Fight* is a revealing and powerful portrayal of the North American labor activists, black and white, who went to great sacrifice—many died—for the Spanish Popular Front's cause against fascism. Among African American intellectuals, both Richard Wright and Langston Hughes were close to the CPUSA and thus vitally interested in Spanish politics. Hughes was in Spain during the war as a correspondent for the *Baltimore Afro-American* (see Mullen 34–38, 93–148).

Indeed, Hughes's connection to the Spanish Civil War is most intimate, and his experience in and writings on Spain are crucial to the understanding of the racial underpinnings of the war. While Hughes changed his political views on his return to the United States, in the 1930s he was an ardent supporter of the antifascist cause. According to his foremost biographer, Arnold Rampersad, Hughes spoke with passion and singularity of purpose on the injustice blacks were suffering as well as the tyranny of fascism on a world scale. "We negroes," he affirmed at a speech he gave in Paris in the presence of Alejo Carpentier, W. H. Auden, Louis Aragon, and Bertolt Brecht, "are tired of a world divided superficially in the basis of blood and color. . . . And we see in the tragedy in Spain how far the world-oppressors will go to retain their power" (qtd. in Rampersad 1: 346).

Yet at the same time, Hughes's portrayal of the conflict was imbued with a hidden ambivalence on the racial aspects of the war that was not always clear in his correspondence, with the exception of "Letter from Spain Addressed to Alabama," a poem wrenching in its pathos and insightful in its deceptive simplicity:

Lincoln Battalion
International Brigades
November Something, 1937.

Dear Brother at home:
We captured a wounded Moor today.
He was just as dark as me.
I said, Boy, what you been doin' here
Fightin' against the free?
He answered something in a language
I couldn't understand.
But somebody told me he was sayin'
They nabbed him in his land
And made him join the fascist army
And come across to Spain.
And he said he had a feelin'
He'd never get back home again.
He said he had a feelin'
This whole thing wasn't right.
He said he didn't know
The folks he had to fight.
And as he lay there dying
In a village we had taken,
I looked across to Africa
And seed foundations shakin'.
Cause if a free Spain wins this war,
The colonies, too, are free—
Then something wonderful'll happen
To them Moors as dark as me.
I said, I guess that's why Old England
An I reckon Italy, too,
Is afraid to let a workers' Spain
Be too good to me and you—
Cause they got slaves in Africa—

And they don't want 'em to be free.
Listen, Moorish prisoner, hell!
Here, shake hands with me!
I knelt down there beside him,
And I took his hand —
But the wounded Moor was dyin'
And he didn't understand.
Salud,
Johnny

(qtd. in Mullen 156–57)

Although Rampersad finds this poem "maudlin" (1: 351) in comparison with others Hughes wrote about the civil war, I prefer to call it pathetic, especially in the light of the historical context at the time Hughes wrote the poem and of the outcome of the war. The voice of Johnny as an African American fighting in Spain, committed to a workers' revolution that would extend to Africa, is clearly ingenuous. But its simplicity is dismantled by both historical circumstances and by the readers' (or listeners') possible responses.

Cary Nelson, in the introduction to his compilation of North American poetry about the Spanish conflict, also disagrees with Rampersad (*Wound* 18–21). Nelson sees Hughes's poetic letter as a synthesis of a complex series of issues and interests: workers' rights, colonialism, African American progress, the threat of fascism. Indeed, this poem is anything but propaganda and in my opinion not the least bit maudlin. It questions the very assumptions made by the Communist Party. The Moorish prisoner does not understand the language or the political lesson offered to him. The gesture of a black worker's solidarity with the invitation "hell, here, shake hands with me" is replete with pathos. He offers to shake hands with a man about to die, a man who has no idea who is kneeling down beside him, a man duped by the fascists, a man whose death will never be used as a rallying cry for world revolution.

If there is any political message that can be extracted from this poem, it is a resounding cry against war, even the one fought nobly by Johnny and his comrades, black and white. Moreover, it is a poem that asks questions about the social interests and political authenticity of those like Johnny and the Moorish prisoner: What did the Communist Party offer blacks if the leadership, in alliance with the proponents of the republic, was unable to deliver on the promise of the liberation of Africa? Indeed, it is questionable if the leaders of the Communist-liberal alliance were seriously interested in Africa at all.[1]

For those of us looking back at the Spanish Civil War with political nostalgia for a just cause, for a commitment to an egalitarian future based on socialist and Marxist principles, perhaps a close look at that war will question that nostalgia. Moreover, for those in the English-speaking first world who are both experientially and intellectually cognizant of racism, the war in Spain offers many lessons on the ubiquity of race despite the most recent and compelling indications of its biological artificiality. Indeed, it is another striking indication that, as Cornel West asserts, "race matters."

Note
1. Domingo Manfredi, a prolific Spanish writer of the mid–twentieth century, published his novel *Juan, el negro* in the mid-1970s in Spain. The protagonist is an African American from Louisiana who chooses to fight in Spain with the Lincoln Brigade partly to avoid a jail sentence for murder, a crime that is portrayed as (somewhat) justifiable. The novel is something of an epic of the black man's adventures and exploits during the civil war and is highly revealing of racial attitudes and injustices among the Republican ranks. It is a fascinating rendering of these issues, although its literary merit leaves much to be desired. I would like to thank Noël Valis for the reference.

Cristina Moreiras-Menor

War, Postwar, and the Fascist Fabrication of Identity

An important albeit brief part of any seminar on the Spanish Civil War should be spent on fascist literary texts produced during this period and shortly thereafter. The novels, stories, and poems of authors like Concha Espina, Agustín de Foxá, Wenceslao Fernández Flores, Rafael García Serrano, Dionisio Ridruejo, Víctor de la Serna, and Gonzalo Torrente Ballester are fundamental to understanding the cultural foundations of identity that not only led Franco's military and his allies to rise up against the republic but also contributed to the making of the Francoist subject who would, in effect, become the ideal Spanish subject. Perhaps the biggest classroom problem is to convince students of the historical and cultural importance of texts that for the most part possess a low aesthetic quotient. These texts are, nevertheless, essential reading in a historical, cultural, and social analysis of a conflict that, by opposing two radically different conceptions of national life, changed the course of history.

I would begin the class with a brief discussion of the ideological context in which these writings were produced.[1] An explanation of European social, political, and ideological movements should consider Italian fascism, German Nazism, and the main Spanish movements that informed Franco's ideology, such as Carlism (a politicized form of Catholic traditionalism) and the Falange.[2] Indeed, the Nationalist ideology that led to the military uprising in 1936 was profoundly connected to historical and political events in the rest of Europe (see Holguín in this volume). While *franquismo* maintains important differences with respect to Italian fascism or German Nazism, it responds to the same political and social uncertainties: the decomposition of nineteenth-century liberalism, the failure of the ideals of the Enlightenment, and the threat of Communism since its triumph in Russia.[3] Like Mussolini and Hitler, Franco made the fight against both individualism and Communism one of the state's main priorities. Spanish fascism is a counterrevolutionary movement born, like Italian fascism and German Nazism, from the desire to establish an ideological alternative to the Enlightenment, liberalism, and parliamentarism and to impose a new social order. The nostalgia for empire; the return to tradition as the fountain of goodness; antiliberalism; the utopian desire for a "new man"; the cult of leadership, or *caudillismo*; the mass demonstrations; the distinctive style and paraphernalia that defined collective events (dress, ceremonies, symbols, etc.); propaganda; and a fascination with youth are all elements shared by fascist ideology across Europe. As in other countries, Spanish fascism developed, as Juan Linz comments, "new forms of political organization. . . . It was the type of organization that, like the communist counterpart, offered an opportunity for action, involvement, participation, breaking with the monotony of everyday life" (67).

Thus students should be encouraged to contextualize a broad spectrum of right-wing ideologies within and beyond Spain. Fascism should also be discussed as a concept, as Stanley Payne proposes in an attempt to articulate both the peculiarities of Spanish fascism and its common roots with a wider ideology and political system ("Fascism").[4] In this vein, it is obvious that Spanish fascists share with their European counterparts the taste for violence, authoritarianism, aggressive nationalism, and racism.[5] All those features are expressed and worked out in the literature and culture of the Spanish Civil War. The aim here is to see how culture represents the ideals of fascist writers.

The literary and film texts I focus on function as a cultural model of identity that was the basis for the new Spanish identity officially imposed by the triumphant Franco regime. This approach to the teaching of the war is built on texts in which an imaginary national subjectivity is articulated out of the ashes of conflict: specifically in "Elogio de la alegre retaguardia" ("In Praise of the Happy Rearguard"), by de la Serna; *La fiel infantería* ("The Loyal Infantry"), by García Serrano; "Umbral de la madurez" ("The

Threshold of Wisdom"), by Ridruejo; and *Raza* ("Race"), by Francisco Franco (published under the pseudonym Jaime de Andrade). These texts serve as a counterpoint to those of an opposite ideological stripe. Keeping in mind the ideological premises aestheticized by these writers, one would examine *franquismo*, less as an ideological apparatus of power dominating social and political life for nearly forty years, than as a literary language explicitly loaded with an ideological content that preceded the formation of the Francoist state (1939–75). This literary language played a fundamental role in the fabrication of a specific fascist imaginary during the immediate postwar period. I would center class discussion on how reactionary thought—such as we find in the speeches and discourse of intellectuals and politicos like José Antonio Primo de Rivera, Onésimo Redondo, and Franco himself—produces culture (understood as literature, pedagogical systems, images, cultural practices, belief systems, interpretations) and struggles to equate the state with culture.

Crisis and Identity

In his 1933 founding speech of the Falange, Primo de Rivera affirmed a form of Spanish fascism:

> But our movement would be misunderstood if it is thought of as only a way of thinking. No: it is a way of being. We ought not simply to propose a structure, a political architecture. We need to adopt, for the whole of life, and in every one of our acts, an attitude that is human, profound and total. This attitude is the *spirit of service and sacrifice, the ascetic and military sense of life.* (107)

This idea, expressed by the founder of the Falange, is not new to Spanish thought. Two years before the Spanish disaster of 1898, Ángel Ganivet wrote *Idearium español* ("Spain, an Interpretation"), a response not only to the idea of history and his experience and rationalization of a sociopolitical crisis in Spain (the "spiritual ruin of Spain") but also to the socioeconomic, historical, and cultural conflicts of modernity (162). Inserting himself into a long tradition of antimodern thinkers, Ganivet posits a new system of being for Western societies, based fundamentally on his concept of the Spanish race and spirit. Of the nation he says, "Spain is a peninsular territory; territory creates spirit." Of history he says, "the greatness of Spain can be attributed to its lasting effects on History" and, "History constitutes the character, the expression of a nation's personality" (71, 53, 109). Tradition itself as the foundation of national character aspires to a new national religion out of which the Spanish Christ springs, as José María Beneyto observes. Ganivet begins with the fundamental notion that Spain is sick—that Spain has lost its spirit, its national soul, which is indissolubly linked to tradition and to the land—an idea that will be taken up again and again not only by members of the generations of 1898 and 1914 such as Antonio Machado and José Ortega y Gasset but also by Primo de Rivera and Franco himself. Indeed, for Ganivet this crisis, which is symptomatically rooted in illness, finds regeneration in the restoration of the spiritual life of Spain.

Thus the context for the fascist uprising against the legitimate Republican government, the war, and the decades-long ideological hegemony of *franquismo* arises out of a tradition of thought in which the idea of a national sociopolitical and historical crisis reigns supreme. A new national identity develops from within the ambiguities and contradictions of crisis. Through this notion, students will be able to trace the origins of the war politically (right versus left, fascism versus Communism), socially, and symbolically.

Though not a fascist text, Ganivet's *Idearium* uncovers a kind of thought that is constitutive of the ideology and practices of fascism as encountered in the Spanish Falange and later in the Francoist state proper. Ganivet conceives of history as sacrifice and establishes violence as the basic principle for preserving the imperative desire of filial-national unity. He tells the story of a father who must sacrifice his youngest son to a pack of wolves to save the rest of the family. This sacrifice for the community's salvation is achieved through the exemplary conduct of an exemplary citizen. The violence that such a sacrifice entails is justified by its ends. Ganivet concludes:

> Spain must behave like that savage but extraordinarily loving father. Not for nothing is this the country of Guzmán el Bueno, who permitted his son's beheading before the walls of Tarifa. Some sentimental souls will surely say that this is far too brutal a response, but in the presence of Spain's spiritual ruin, one needs a stone where the heart is, one needs to throw as many as a million Spaniards to the wolves, or we will all end up thrown to the swine. (64–65)

In this prophetic passage, the violence of the surrender of the weakest son, of those million citizens, is rationally and morally justified because it maintains national unity; it preserves the group identity of individuals who share common bonds, blood, and spirit, exemplified in this case as a family willing to sacrifice one of its own members for the benefit of the collective good. In the same vein Primo de Rivera affirms in his 1933 inaugural speech at the Teatro de la Comedia:

> If this [national revolution] sometimes has to be achieved through violence, let us not be stopped by violence. . . . Dialectic is all well and good as the first means of communication. But there is no dialectic more suitable than the dialectic of fists and pistols when justice or the nation is insulted. (qtd. in J. Thomas 31)

He also maintains that "violence is lawful when it is employed for an ideal that justifies it" (J. Thomas 37). We find the literary counterpart to these words in García Serrano's *La fiel infantería* and his character Ramón, who wants nothing better than to read Georges Sorel's *Reflections on Violence*: "Ramón insisted dogmatically that solitary thinkers are not geniuses, but neurasthenics, and that only someone capable of inspiring men willing to die for their world is worth saving" (Mainer 126). García Serrano again addresses this theme in *Eugenio o la proclamación de la primavera* ("Eugenio, or the Proclamation of Spring"), where characters weigh in on the "pedagogy of the pistol" (Rodríguez-Puértolas 2: 271).

Violence and sacrifice are built into these characters, whose actions are rooted in the intertwining of reason and faith, of will and desire. They are the foundation that sustains the nation. For fascism and the Falange, violence grounds the political action destined to construct a new order, in which the individual is the last sacrificial link in a chain that originates with the state. Thus Primo de Rivera, the founder of the Falange, declares:

> We have to begin with man himself, with the individual who is Western, Spanish and Christian, we have to go beyond his organic unity, and thus pass from man to the family, and from the family to the town, and to the syndicate as well, culminating in the State, which represents complete harmony. This is the political, historical, and moral conception with which we contemplate the world. (qtd. in J. Thomas 55)

The 1941 film *Raza*, based on a script by Franco, illustrates this fabrication of a reactionary subject who is part of a larger, transcendent community. In this unapologetic work Franco and the director José Luis Sáenz de Heredia (first cousin to Primo de Rivera) offer, through the vehicle of the Churruca family, the image of the family-nation and subject that would overwhelmingly prevail for the next four decades.

Raza (together with its later version, *Espíritu de una raza* ["Spirit of a Race"], in which the fascism and anti–United States criticism are toned down) exemplifies the marriage of faith and reason that underlies the thinking of Ganivet and Primo de Rivera. This way of thinking is taken up again in the *franquista* state's promotion of its citizenry's most desirable qualities (for another perspective of the film, see Deveny in this volume). In the film the father fights and dies for his country and, indeed, for history itself in the Cuban war of 1898. His three sons struggle to find the right path. The mother and sister represent that sublime goodness of women who, above all, support their menfolk. In all these characters, as in those of Espina, Foxá, García Serrano, and Rafael Sánchez Mazas, reason and faith are welded into a relation of intimacy that is articulated as the foundation of both Nationalist political thought and individual experience. This relation between reason and faith founds and justifies rationally and morally all violent action carried out by either the individual or the state and, most important, turns the subject into part of a collective whole that constitutes his being. Thus Ramón in *La fiel infantería* declares, "On a night like this was born my God in the midst of Empire" (139). Later he reasons:

> He remembered his comrades wandering through the city and the countryside, bringing the nation to life with their blood, waking the nation to the dead, amid the bitter laughter of cowards, the sons of those who went to the bullfight on Saint James's day in '98, and the wicked aggression of traitors. They alone with their flag and their Caesar demonstrate the truth with the supreme reasoning of their own veins, baptizing assassins with their pardon; these sacred madmen, these children of God, these Falangists. (139–40)

People who find their sole reason for being, their signs of identity, in the uniquely homogeneous community of the state must also embrace violence and faith, the capstones of their essence as national subjects. Primo de Rivera explained this qualification when he defended himself against the journalist Torcuato Luca de Tena's accusation in *ABC*, a leading daily paper in Spain, that fascism was totalitarian and violent:

> Fascism is not a tactic—It is an idea—unity. In a fascist state victory does not go to the strongest class or to the more numerous party. . . . What triumphs is the orderly principle common to all, consistent national thought, of which the state is the expression. (Payne, *Fascism in Spain* 79)

He continues:

> Fascism was born to light a faith, neither of the right (which at bottom aspires to preserve everything, even the unjust) nor of the left (which at

bottom aspires to destroy everything, even the just), but a collective, integral, national faith. Its fruitfulness lies in this faith, against which all persecution is unavailing. (Payne, *Fascism in Spain* 79)

We can draw several important conclusions about fascism from Primo de Rivera's words and from its representation in the fascist literature of the period. On the one hand, the original impulse behind fascism and *franquismo* is as much political and ideological as it is spiritual. On the other hand, this founding spirituality is intimately related to a national vision based on the establishment of a single will and a common faith. Individuals are subsumed into the group and disappear as singular identities; their greatest virtue is to belong to the group and to sacrifice their will, through violence if necessary, for that of the group (in this case, the nation). Mark Neocleous observes:

> Two of the central features of fascism follow from the rejection of reason and intellect and their replacement by the will and spirit, though they are both rooted in the same fascist mentality. The first is the rejection of theory, and the second is the conceptualization of politics and society as a realm of permanent struggle and war. (13)

Of course, this all-justifying, national "spirit," which constitutes the praxis, ideology, and aesthetics of fascism and *franquismo*, was already present in the work of Ganivet.

The relation between reason (which is really the will) and faith—a relation that supposedly defines the Spanish subject—is perhaps one of the most obvious lines of continuity between Spanish reactionary thinking in the nineteenth and early twentieth centuries (the Carlist wars, the political-cultural tensions between modernity and tradition and between science and religion) and Spanish fascism, *franquismo*, and the Falange. The literature and culture of the right during the war and postwar are firmly rooted in a national intellectual imaginary that existed well before 1933. For example, *franquismo* could be read as a foundational desire, perfectly represented in *Raza*, to complete the unfinished history of the Spanish empire. In this version of history, the Spaniard is always a warrior and a believer, symbolically incarnated in the figure of the Almodarave, the model soldier, who appears in the stories the father tells his sons in *Raza*. The literature that ideologically supports the Nationalist rebellion and the institutionalization of the Franco regime and imaginary can be understood as the recuperation and reinstallation of a lost history.

Subject and Race

In effect, beginning with the relation between reason (or will) and faith in turn-of-the-century thought (a relation that was later secularized for the Falange but not necessarily for the *franquistas*), students can trace affective and ideological ties between the intellectuals and writers of the prewar and postwar periods. In the works of Ganivet, Ramiro de Maeztu, and Ortega y Gasset (in his *España invertebrada* ["Spain Invertebrate"]), as well as in Ernesto Giménez Caballero, Redondo, Ramiro Ledesma, Sánchez Mazas, or Franco, the notion of *raza* becomes particularly important for defining the notion of national spirit (for further discussion of race, see Ugarte in this volume). These authors do not use a biological concept of race. Instead they refer to a cultural race from which the national community creates racial myths founded in the idea of a "racism without a race," as Étienne Balibar observes (23). In his "Is There a 'Neo-Racism'?" Balibar affirms:

> A racism which does not have the pseudo-biological concept of race as its main driving force has always existed, and it has existed at exactly this level of secondary theoretical elaborations. Its prototype is anti-Semitism. Modern anti-Semitism—the form which begins to crystallize in the Europe of the Enlightenment, if not indeed from the period in which the Spain of the *Reconquista* and the Inquisition gave a statist, nationalistic inflexion to theological anti-Judaism—is *already* a "culturalist" racism. Admittedly, bodily stigmata play a great role in its phantasmatic, but they do so more as signs of a deep psychology, as a sign of spiritual inheritance rather than a biological heredity. . . . His [the Jew's] essence is that of a cultural tradition, a ferment of moral disintegration. (23–24)

The thinkers and writers of this period refer to this concept of race when they meditate on the Spanish *raza*, the national spirit, or the notion of *hispanidad*. They express a profound nostalgia for the Spain of the Reconquest and for a Spanish empire.

The idea of race understood not in biological but in cultural terms produces two ideological positions that are shared, willingly or not, by turn-of-the-century intellectuals and Spanish fascists. These two positions also influenced the literature and cinema of the 1930s and 1940s. First, the absolute acceptance of violence to further the restoration of a politics of empire (expansion of national territory as well as preservation of a threatened peninsular unity) and, second, the practice of personal and collective sacrifice as a way to revive Spanish imperial grandeur. Violence and sacrifice are the two paths through which these thinkers and fascist ideologues transform the Spanish subject into a people and a race, thereby substituting for the individual and society a homogeneous cultural ethnicity (or race) over which the Castilian language and Catholicism exercise absolute control. Fascism, Neocleous observes, "posits human beings as individual only in so far as they coincide with the state, which, in turn, is rooted in the concept of life and rests on an intuition of an organic vision" (12).

The themes of race and spirit (which are often interchangeable elements) are the structuring and organizing principles of the idea of Spain and its national history. Race permits the selection and conservation of the best, of the good Spaniards, who in turn are one and indivisible, that is, the nation. The individuals become part of a project that swallows them up as subjects and converts them into minimal particles of an organism, meaningless in their minuteness. To speak of race is to speak of spirit, of a collective soul grounded in struggle. Race, as a category of thought and the principal sign of identity, opens itself up in this way to history, conceptualizing a particular notion of history that is directed at once toward the past and the future. As Linz suggests, "While linking with the real or imagined historical national tradition, it [fascism] is not committed to a conservative continuity with the recent past or a purely reactionary return to it but is future-oriented" (64). Out of this conception of race emerges the way of life envisaged as the spirit of the race and embodied in the final moments of *Raza*.

The final scene of the film is one of its most complex moments. A montage is projected over the Victory Parade that synthesizes the film's entire story: Pedro Churruca speaking to his sons about the exemplary soldier, the Almodarave; the conversion and salvation of the Republican son, Pedro; the death of the priestly son; and so on. The scene of the first Victory Parade (later institutionalized as an annual televised event in Franco's Spain) is organized around the images of soldiers, in particular the enhanced image of the chosen soldier, José, a kind of resurrected Christ figure, and the history of sacrifice and valor that led to the victory. At this moment Isabel pronounces the film's final words to her son: "This is called Race, my son."

In the film race presupposes military violence as a means of forging a superior national subject. Race is a form of so-called natural selection produced on the basis of historical evidence (the Spanish race has been in existence since the Reconquest, as is "proven" in *Raza*). Race would also guarantee a future national renaissance. That is, in my view, the reading that Franco wishes to impose on history in his film script, which, in a class on the civil war, gives us a fascinating glimpse into the way ideology is articulated as the aesthetics of an experience. It also permits us to trace a line of continuity between the thinking of the prewar, the war, and the postwar. Well before Franco, and from a different ideological perspective, Ortega y Gasset, in the closing words to *España invertebrada*, condensed exceptionally well the idea of race as a historical mission and forceful selection:

> If Spain wishes to resurrect herself, she will need to grasp an enormous appetite for perfection of all kinds. The great misfortune of Spanish history has been the absence of elite formations and the pervasive, indifferent domination of the masses. Therefore from now on, one imperative ought to govern the spirit and orient the will: the imperative of selection. There is no better means of ethnic purification and improvement than that eternal instrument of a will operating selectively. Using it like a chisel, we must begin to forge a new kind of Spaniard. Political reforms are insufficient: what is essential is a much more profound mission to produce the fine tuning of a race. (116)

Are those not the very ideas behind Franco's *Raza*? The *franquista* project to regenerate the race is racist in that it believed blindly in the spiritual superiority of the Spanish race. It is violent in that, in accordance with that faith, any colonizing or imperial action that tended toward the greatness of Spain is justified. As seen in the opening scenes of Franco's film, "the American colonization, that marvelous event, represents the only true, substantively great thing that Spain has achieved" (Ortega y Gasset 107). Ortega y Gasset characterizes the Crusades as "*marvelous examples* of riotous luxury, of superabundant energy, of sublime historic sport" (103; my emphasis). This vision of a "new man" is converted into the José of Franco's film, into the ideas and marks of identity that would sustain the political, ethical, and aesthetic bases of the Falange and later *franquismo*. Ridruejo aestheticizes this "new man" in his 1944 poem "Umbral de la madurez," in which he exalts and celebrates war and country, praising the patriotic and religious virtues of the young warrior, who will achieve undying fame, bearing within him the spiritual essence of the nation:

> And so you passed, carrying your banner, with the people,
> but no company could deter you,
> because every soul was with you.
> Remember this only:

your senses were like little honeycombs;
every taste, every light, every sound,
every hardness, every length, every scent
found room to your measure
and everything was pure geometric rapture
distilling honey into your heart.

(186)

The subject created out of this ideology, based on race and spirit, sacrifice and violence, is reflected in practically all the literary texts of fascist orientation from the 1930s and 1940s, especially during the war years. This is the subject of mystical reason, the product of the tradition of Christian faith and imperial will that shaped Spain as a nation and as an empire. The Spanish male subject of the 1930s and 1940s represented in fascist, Falangist, and *franquista* literature is a mystical-rational subject who always places his life in the service of the ideological cause. Female subjects behave similarly. In *Raza*, Isabel and José's fiancée represent the pure woman (the Virgin Mary), ready at any moment to sacrifice herself for the cause and for her man.

It is interesting to note that this subject of mystical reason (José in *Raza*, Ramón in *La fiel infantería*, Eugenio in *Eugenio o la proclamación de la primavera*) produces long, overly charged moral discourses justifying the phantom presence of imperial-colonial violence. Indeed, these exemplary subjects always construct themselves on a foundation of violence. This violence is conceived, along Darwinian lines, as something natural, as a variation of the survival of the fittest (or the superior). It is also represented as a gift to the community that keeps the nation whole and without fissures, a sacrifice of the individual for national history and the nation. History, therefore, is sacrifice, an idea that is not uniquely Spanish. Mussolini has proclaimed, "Fascism does not, generally speaking, believe in the possibility or utility of perpetual peace. It therefore discards pacifism as a cloak for cowardly supine renunciation in contra-distinction to self-sacrifice" (19).

Ideologically the Falange, whether represented in the political arena or in literature, makes violence a lifestyle for the benefit of a national revolution designed to save Spain from the Communist hordes, maintain her "predestined, universal unity," and reconstitute it as an expansionist empire (J. Primo de Rivera, "España" 114). *Franquismo*, as expressed in the literature and cinema of the 1940s, comes across as an ethical and ethnic system of violence in favor of the people. Reason and faith appear, as they did in the fascist ideology of the 1920s and 1930s, ominously and closely united. Violence is sublimated as sacrifice for a just cause, as the regeneration and preservation of a superior race and the recuperation of a lost history through a racial, aesthetic, and political mystique that repeats and reproduces in the very act of aggression the violence of the glorious past.

These ideas about race, spirit, and sacrifice allow us to trace a certain continuity of thought between reason as will and the faith that founded the Falangist movement and the reason-faith tenet on which the literary and cultural system of the 1930s and 1940s based its narrative and poetic representations of Spain and history. These representations produced the regime's exemplary and obligatory identity. The Spanish subjects are always chained to a history that nourishes them and integrates them into a national space of belonging.

This rational mysticism of Spanish fascism and *franquismo*, this idea of sacrifice, is converted into a program that annihilates individuality, that collectively cannibalizes the individual. The national project emerges, among intellectuals of the right, out of decadence and loss and, among Spanish fascists and Falangists, out of the idea of the reconstruction of empire. Nevertheless, this idea of reconstruction is not a melancholy position that preserves the past as a corpse (see Ganivet) but a manic position recalling Ortega y Gasset's "superabundant energy" and inciting action to imitate the glorious past of empire. In emphasizing that manic necessity, Falangist literature of the 1930s—Foxá, Ridruejo, Espina, García Serrano, Edgar Neville, José María Pemán—leads to the creation of characters brimming over with energy, joy, and youth who are always ready to sacrifice, kill, and be killed for the nation of which they are but a minuscule part.

Notes

Essay and quotations translated from the Spanish by Cristina Moreiras-Menor, Noël Valis, and Anne McGee.

1. I highly recommend for this contextualization of both European and Spanish fascist and reactionary thought Payne's *The Franco Regime, 1936–1975*, Preston's *The Politics of Revenge: Fascism and the Military in Twentieth-Century Spain*, Kallis's *The Fascism Reader*, Herrero's *Los orígenes del pensamiento reaccionario español*, and Rodríguez-Puértolas's *Literatura fascista española*.

2. For a brilliant discussion of Carlism and its relation to right-wing European movements, see Enric Ucelay-Da Cal's essay "Lost Causes as a Historical Typology of Reaction."

3. *Franquismo* is also rooted in the particularities of Spanish history. As Preston observes, the military uprising, the war, and the dictatorship "share a socially and

politically partisan function. The function . . . was, in addition to rooting out regionalism and reasserting the hegemony of institutionalized Catholicism, the protection of the interests of the agrarian-financial-industrial élites. In particular, that meant shielding the reactionary landed oligarchy from the challenge to Spain's antiquated economic structures embodied in the reforms of the Second Republic." Preston also explores the idea that "the Franco regime was not strictly fascist" (*Politics* 3, 8).

4. Payne's article should be part of the bibliography of the class since it not only offers a definition of fascism but also discusses different types of fascism, pointing out both similarities and discontinuities between the right-wing ideologies of this period.

5. There is a significant difference between the racism of Nazi Germany and that of Italian and Spanish fascisms. While the first is largely a biological racism based on the superiority of the Aryan race, the other two share a cultural racism based on tradition and national imaginaries. This cultural racism is the subject of my essay.

Adelaida López de Martínez

Class and Gender Representation in Post–Civil War Spanish Narrative

The Spanish Civil War officially ended on 31 March 1939. Triumphant, General Francisco Franco, who had succeeded in overthrowing the Republican government elected in 1936, did what all dictators do: he expurgated, exiled, imprisoned, censored, suppressed individual freedoms, and abused human rights. He who had succeeded in war failed at building peace. Not only was he unable to unify the nation, but he instituted policies that kept alive the ideological confrontations that had instigated the war. Although ostensibly silenced during the thirty-nine-year Francoist regime, the struggle for power that preceded the war continued in the postwar collective imaginary and symbolic order of discourse. High and popular art found ways to subvert repression and register countless and disparate views of the war and postwar years.

During the postwar period, after the vanguard experimentation of the 1920s and early 1930s, the Spanish canonical novel underwent a dramatic change. Camilo José Cela's *La familia de Pascual Duarte* (1942; *The Family of Pascual Duarte*) epitomized a new neorealist trend. Traumatized by civil war, uncertain about Spain's future after World War II, and threatened by censorship, Spanish novelists of the 1940s drew nonheroic characters, imitated everyday language, and set their plots in contemporary Spain. By the mid-1950s, neorealism had acquired a social dimension and a thinly disguised political agenda, becoming what is now referred to as social realism. Novelists produced stories written in transparent, almost colloquial language, with collective rather than individual main characters, and denounced the suffering, isolation, and deprivation experienced by much of Spanish society, particularly the underprivileged working classes (see Sobejano).

Two outstanding novels of the initial postwar period—Cela's novel and Ramón José Sender's *Réquiem por un campesino español* (1953; *Requiem for a Spanish Peasant*)—illustrate and reflect back on the earlier structures of power that kindled the demand for social changes and eventually led to civil war. Two later, equally superb novels, Miguel Delibes's *Cinco horas con Mario* (1966; *Five Hours with Mario*) and Carmen Martín Gaite's *El cuarto de atrás* (1978; *The Back Room*)—the double centerpiece of my analysis—further explore the ramifications of the civil war, subverting Francoism through internalization of the authoritarian regime's own discourse.

La familia de Pascual Duarte presents class and gender as determined by cultural convictions rather than by explicit political mandates, whereas Sender's *Réquiem* uses the issues of class and gender to pinpoint how the war polarized the civilian population. Narrative action in *La familia* has been coded as taking place at the outbreak of the Spanish Civil War, although this event is never mentioned. The primitive way of life depicted in the novel points to an ancestral Spain still ruled by traditional values. The setting is rural and isolated; the characters are illiterate and politically unaware. Thus the protagonist-narrator, Pascual, does not challenge the status quo. He accepts the distribution of wealth according to birthrights as predestined and understands that people's homes are signs of their social class. He finds it natural that, in accordance with his low standing in society, his house is small and dark and located at the outskirts of town. Similarly, it seems appropriate to him that Don Jesús González de la Riba, as Count of Torremejía, has a two-story house with a well-attended flower garden, located on the main square. The description of Pascual's environment, which at first glance appears to be unbiased, is filled with subtle ironies, leading readers to question the justice system of a class society and to keep thinking about the possible reasons behind Pascual's eventual assassination of the count.

Gender roles and attitudes in *La familia* also reveal centuries-old popular beliefs. Men's and women's occupations are well defined: men work outside the home, and women must confine themselves to domestic chores. Women socialize separately from men and only in one another's homes, never at the tavern or other public place. The traditional sense of personal honor popularized by the Spanish drama of the Golden Age and passed on culturally from generation to generation looms fatally over Pascual. Transgression of gender norms, of which all the female characters in the novel are guilty, takes the form of sex outside marriage and triggers some of the protagonist's violent reactions. He feels bound by social expectations to act decisively and unequivocally. When his wife, Lola, teases him for kissing the parish priest's hand, he stops immediately lest his masculinity come into question, and when she begs him to let her carry to term her pregnancy by another man, El Estirado, Pascual's world order leaves him no choice:

> I didn't want to be hard—God knows that—but the truth is that one is bound to convention like an ass to its halter. [I]f my position as a man would have allowed me to forgive, I would have forgiven her. But the world is the way it is, and to go against the current is useless. (119–20)

His attempt to legitimize the killing of El Estirado as a gendered social obligation underlines the degree of violence characteristic of "tremendism," the extreme form of twentieth-century neorealism exemplified in *La familia*. This is the social and gender-inflected environment that by implication metaphorically sets the stage for the eruption of violence in 1936.

Written in exile and safe from censorship, *Réquiem por un campesino español* is a partisan, pro-Republican account of the outbreak of civil war. The narrative action is set in an isolated small village between Madrid and Barcelona, which remains anonymous by authorial design to bestow it with paradigmatic value and indicate that the war disrupted the lives of all Spaniards. The town's population is divided into two basic social classes that can be described as the haves and the have-nots. The have-nots challenge the status quo; the haves want to preserve it. The characters are very much aware that they belong to one class or the other, and when the conflict erupts, they instinctively know which side they are on. Willingly or not they are pushed into one of two ideological domains. In the text, the ideological divide is further underscored by a series of structural tensions sustained on two axes: that of Paco and Don Valeriano (in the political confrontation) and that of Mosén Millán and La Jerónima (in the sociospiritual realm).

Paco is a farmer who takes on local leadership in support of the Republic, which has been recently voted into power. He moves quickly (perhaps too quickly) to right what he perceives to be a centuries-old wrong against the rural working classes, the burdensome fees peasants must pay to an absentee, aristocratic landlord. Paco heads a revolt, refusing to pay these taxes. His quest for social justice makes him the number one target for assassination by the Nationalists. The unsettled argument between Paco and Don Valeriano, the duke's estate manager, represents the clash between the uncompromising forces of reform and the reaction of the status quo, which in historical reality led Spain to the war.

Set against the backdrop of a conflict over the very soul of the town, class and gender come into play in the character of La Jerónima, carrier of the ancestral beliefs of a female lineage, who emerges as a natural leader in competition with the canonical ideals of the priest Mosén Millán. La Jerónima claims the priest dislikes her, and she ignores his attempts to keep her quiet. Mosén Millán fears that his sermons and sacramental practices will be neutralized by her superstitious chants and spells.

The most telling structural and social binary opposition in the text is set up between fictional public and private spaces. Thus physical ground becomes a political metaphor and metonymy in the novel: a metaphor for the national territory over which the war was fought and a metonymy for the two factions. The story ends with an image of the church—represented by the village's three wealthiest men—standing in direct contrast to the women's *carasol* (a sunny place under a curtain of rock on the outskirts of town). Here the voices of the peasant women that used to chronicle village life have been suppressed by the winners of the war. The attendance of only Don Valeriano, Don Gumersindo, and Cástulo Pérez at the requiem for their political enemy Paco—the mass at which Mosén Millán, full of guilt, prefers to officiate without payment—leaves no doubt that Sender wants to register the unholy alliance of church and fascism during the Spanish Civil War. In the eyes of the fascists, the most egregious offense of the *carasol* women is the sin of gossip. The women's *dijendas* ("tattlings") function as a popular daily broadcast and represent a form of free speech. Fascism uses death to silence them. Yet communal discourse is as resilient in Sender's fiction as it is in real life: La Jerónima talks and even shouts again in the *carasol* when she thinks she cannot be heard, and the story of Paco ends with his deeds retold in the popular ballad that the new altar boy admiringly recites.

Réquiem leaves the reader with the impression that the war broke out because verbal communications among social classes had ceased. For instance, the villagers have no idea that the young outsiders are Falangists and find their harangues baffling:

That same afternoon the *señoritos* from the city herded the people into the square and made speeches which nobody understood, speaking of Empire and Immortal Destiny, of Law and Order and the Holy Faith. Then they sang a hymn with arms raised and hands outstretched, whereupon everyone was ordered to go home and forbidden, under serious penalty, to go out again until the following day. (115)

The most poignant example of the breakdown of communications is the last encounter between Mosén Millán and Paco, right before Paco is dragged away to be shot by the Nationalists. The two men have shared a loving relationship for years, and the priest claims to be a spiritual father to Paco. Yet when the moment of truth arrives they cannot make sense of each other's words:

> Confused and stammering, Mosén Millán talked about the designs of God and after a long lamentation, asked the final question.
> "Do you repent your sins?"
> Paco did not understand him. It was the first of the priest's expressions he did not understand. (118)

Réquiem aims at exposing the stigma of an entrenched class society, implicit in the title of the novel (which speaks of the death not just of any Spanish citizen but of a peasant) and is thus an emblematic novel of the social realism that characterized Spanish narrative in the 1950s.

The 1960s saw a general rebellion against authority at all levels of the social order, initiating a new era, now termed postmodernism. In the novel, this crisis of values took the form of experimentation with language, structure, time-space relations, and author-text-reader associations. In the experimentalist novel, language reigns supreme: plot and structure are kept to a minimum and subjectivism becomes paramount, making infinite, changeable points of view possible while demonstrating the unstable nature of reality. It was within this context that novelists Delibes and Martín Gaite registered their accounts of the war and the postwar period.

New and peculiar categories of class and gender—dictated by the ideology of the winners of the war—determined the social status of every Spaniard alive after 1939. For students to appreciate how the art of narrative transforms reality into fiction, as in the representation of the Spanish Civil War in literature, it is helpful to review the historical conditions that inform the texts under discussion. In 1933 José Antonio Primo de Rivera founded the Spanish Falangist Party. The Falange condemned socialism, Marxism, republicanism, and capitalism and proposed that Spain become a fascist state similar to that established by Benito Mussolini in Italy. At the request of the party's female supporters, in June 1934 the Sección Femenina (Women's Section) was created, and Primo de Rivera's sister, Pilar Primo de Rivera, was appointed its national leader. Over time the party became just another component among many in the regime's power base known as the National Movement. By contrast, the Women's Section grew stronger and survived as long as the regime.

The Women's Section maintained its presence in all fifty Spanish provinces through a local and provincial hierarchy of leaders who followed directives from national headquarters. Its overriding mission was to return Spanish women to the traditional moral and social values of pre–Second Republic Spain. During the republic, women had attained the same voting rights as men; a divorce law was also passed (Richmond 5). By reestablishing the Civil Code of 1889, under which women were legally subordinate to men, Franco sought to undo Republican reforms. In a "natural" order, women's destiny was "to serve as the perfect complement of man" (Richmond 107). Marriage was the noblest goal for a woman. The 1938 Labor Law claimed to "liberate the married woman from the workshop and the factory" (Richmond 100).

The Women's Section was an important and efficient agent of indoctrination and social control for the Francoist regime. While mandating the return to a patriarchal society and the restoration of traditional gender roles, its nationwide network of leaders also ensured the civil obedience of the female population. Unmarried women between the ages of seventeen and thirty-five were required to enroll in a domestic education program run by the Women's Section while completing six months of compulsory social service. On completion of the program, women earned a certificate of service that was "necessary for entry to the professions, government employment, and even to obtain a passport or driving license" (Richmond 17). In *El cuarto de atrás*, the narrator's aversion to the excessive zeal with which her grandmother's maids hound even the tiniest trace of dust speaks to the quasi-domestic metaphor used by the Francoist regime in charging postwar Spaniards with cleansing the nation. This cleansing alluded to political as well as physical decontamination, as documented in the 23 May 1939 headline in the Falangist newspaper *Arriba*: "Campaign to Disinfect Madrid from the Misery Left by Marxism" (Richmond). As Kathleen Richmond reports:

> The women of the SF were to be frontline workers in the cleansing of Spain, their brooms and disinfectant the external embodiment of a

moral and spiritual campaign. Falangist nurses would be "immuniz-
ing" the spirit of Spaniards from unhealthy doctrines. (15)

Both Delibes in *Cinco horas con Mario* and Martín Gaite in *El cuarto
de atrás* incorporated this postwar state of affairs as the theme and background of their stories. Their novels are uniquely suited to study class and
gender representation in the Spanish narrative of the period and can be
read as politically subversive texts. By integrating the discursive practices
of an authoritarian regime into their rhetoric, they manage to tell and
simultaneously challenge the official story of the Spanish Civil War. In so
doing they provide a double take on issues and events, leaving readers free
to decide what to infer from the texts.

Cinco horas con Mario

Born in 1920, Delibes became a social realist in the 1950s. *Cinco horas con
Mario* combines social realism with experimental concerns. While character and setting are rooted in a representation of recognizable reality, the
discursive elements storyline, time, and space are fragmented by the
chaotic pattern of a foolish woman's anxious monologue. Free from
authorial restraints, the protagonist reminisces about her life, indulging
her obsessions in a stream of complaints.

The novel can be read on four different planes. First, at the *narrative*
level, *Cinco horas* tells the story of an estranged married couple for whom
meaningful communication has become impossible. The novel opens with
Mario Díez Collado's obituary, dated 4 March 1966, followed by a short
chapter in which an anonymous narrator describes the wake at his house; it
continues with a 244-page monologue in which Mario's wife, Carmen,
addresses his corpse for five hours; and it closes with the return of the
anonymous narrator, after Mario's body has been taken away for burial on
5 March.

Second, at the level of *discourse*, the novel adheres to a disjointed pattern in which recurrent flashbacks of past incidents send Carmen's mind
into a spontaneous repetition of speech habits, through which she renders
a personal assessment of her life and times.

Third, at the *metaphorical* level, *Cinco horas* presents a society torn by
the ideological differences that the civil war thirty years earlier had not settled. Mario and Carmen have ceased to communicate because both cling
to their incompatible ideologies, which she calls social classes. They dis-

agree about nearly everything. Their failure to communicate functions as a synecdoche for the population at large, in conflict with itself, still divided by the opposing views of the warring parties.

Fourth, at the *archetypal* level, the novel reenacts the lust for power exposed in the Cain-Abel struggle, where the blood shed on either side is one's own.

Mario's adult life runs parallel to the postwar years and is covered in the form of memories of the war and accounts of its consequences on the lives of people and on institutions. As the novel opens, Mario's body has been laid out in his study, where his colleagues, acquaintances, and Carmen's friends come to pay their final respects. Together, they represent a wide sampling of the contemporary social and ideological spectrum and a microcosm of the national sphere where the two Spains continue at each other's throats.

Cinco horas is an incisive criticism of Franco's regime, yet it easily escaped censorship. Delibes conceals his indictment of Carmen and her social class—and, by extension, Franco's government—through a skillful use of irony. By characterizing the protagonist-narrator as a staunch supporter of the government and letting Carmen do all the talking, Delibes appears neutral and nonjudgmental. In giving her the self-sufficient arrogance and intolerance of the war's winners, however, he exposes their fraudulent invention of history.

Carmen has assimilated the official rhetoric and keeps repeating the political clichés with which the regime and its advocates justified their positions. She also mimics their belittling of dissidents as Reds, Freemasons, and unpatriotic. For Carmen there are still two Spains at play: "them" (those who hold any ideology other than that sanctioned by Francoism) and "us" (supporters and proponents of the official version of history). In the process, however, she inserts into her monologue the views of the opposition. Although she establishes a contrast between the two linguistic registers as dividers of social classes, she also acts as a conduit for the entire community. She becomes the voice of her generation, turning her speech into an ironic, unintentional example of heteroglossia, as well as an indicator of political confrontation at the level of discourse.

Carmen cannot understand why Mario wrote books with strange titles about old people and dispossessed, starving children instead of simple melodramas. Mario never made enough money from his writing to buy her a SEAT Seiscientos car. Carmen's obsession with the Seiscientos symbolizes the consumerism that, spurred by tourism and the emigration of

Spanish workers, took off in the early 1960s. In developing nations, ownership of an automobile is seen as a rite of passage to a higher social class. Of all the status symbols denied her, this is the hardest for Carmen to accept because it signals publicly that her husband was a failure. By depriving her of a car, Mario pushed her into a social category lower than that of manual workers. Failed professionals were usually dissidents who opposed the regime. The reverse side of the coin is Paco, a Nationalist war veteran who has profited from the business opportunities created by government investments in industrial parks. Carmen, a childhood schoolmate of his, remembers him as the son of manual laborers, a boy who frequently confused similar-sounding words. Nonetheless, when they run into each other after so many years, his current financial success transforms him into the image of a dashing cinema leading man. If the Seiscientos is the outward sign that defines Carmen's beliefs and aspirations, it stands in contrast to the books that define Mario's values. For Mario, as his son observes, "the books were him." Carmen, on the other hand, thinks books are good only "to collect dirt" (16).

As a woman growing up under Franco's dictatorship, Carmen is indoctrinated by the Falangist Women's Section's beliefs in patriarchal conventions, including pre–Vatican II Catholic ideals, traditional gender roles, family customs, and obedience to authority. Because of her gender, Carmen is discouraged from thinking on her own. In contrast, Mario, a university graduate, takes advantage of the Vatican II resolutions, which allowed individual examination of the Bible, and reads it daily. Unlike Carmen, Mario is a thinking man who knows that all is not well in Spain in the 1960s. Yet he is just as deaf to her side as she is to his: "[T]hose men were speaking in code and she couldn't understand them nor had Mario, when he was alive, ever taken the trouble to explain their language to her" (14). Carmen reads and rereads everything Mario has written. But she is simply unable to understand concepts such as "structures," "symbols," "theses," and "amnesties." Mario never explains his ideological thinking to "his other half" and dismisses her, "What a little reactionary you are" (98). She has trouble grasping the meanings of words until those in positions of authority have digested them first. Mario, in contrast, is aware of the power of language. After only one contribution, he stops collaborating with a Madrid newspaper because the editor changes the words "civil war" to "crusade" (73).

Silenced by death—in a symbolic representation of the nation under the Francoist dictatorship—Mario cannot respond to Carmen's diatribe.

A case could be made that he articulates his side of the issues through the Bible passages he has underlined, which in turn underscores that postwar Spain is one reality, susceptible to diverse readings from different ideological perspectives. It is up to the new generation of Spaniards, free from the scars of the war, to reconcile the two sides. Carmen's lack of sophistication leads her to a Manichaean vision of the world, divided into good and evil halves. Her son, Mario, Jr., knows better:

> For God's sake, Mother! There's our savage Spanish Manicheanism, the good and the bad. The good ones on the right and the bad ones on the left! That's what they taught you, didn't they? But you people prefer to accept it without question, rather than taking the trouble to look inside yourselves. We're all both good and bad, Mother. Both things at the same time. (255–56)

Distanced from the war itself, Mario, Jr., anticipates a more peaceful coexistence through dialogue and democratic participation, which Spain has achieved at the dawn of the twenty-first century.

El cuarto de atrás

By the time Martín Gaite (1925–2000) published her award-winning novel *El cuarto de atrás* in 1978, Spain had undergone a profound transformation. A constitutional monarchy had replaced Franco's dictatorship. The constitution signed into law that year established equal rights for women. Censorship was abolished in 1977. Following Franco's death, Spaniards flooded the book market with personal memories of the war and postwar years. They realized they were witnessing the end of an era and saw a national future overflowing with possibilities. Generally conceived for sentimental reasons, most of these stories hardly qualify as art.

Like these writings, *El cuarto* is partly a retrospective of the war and postwar years in Spain. As the narrator says, she began to write the novel on 23 November 1975, the day Franco was buried. The book is above all a work of fiction, however, in which language creates meaning in symbolic ways and stands as a paradigm of the self-referential, experimentalist, and open-ended narrative of the 1970s.

El cuarto can be read on the same four levels as *Cinco horas* can.

At the *narrative* level, it is the account of a female writer, Carmen, fighting insomnia and the blank page. She receives an unexpected visit from a man dressed in black, whom she takes to be a reporter wanting to interview her. She tells the story of her writing, which is inseparable from the story of her life. She is fifty-three years old, which indicates that she went from childhood to womanhood during the postwar years.

At the *discourse* level, the novel emerges as a dialogue between the female writer and the man in black. Spurred by his pointed questions and comments, her thoughts follow the random design of a relaxed conversation, zigzagging in boundless flashbacks that fragment and rearrange traditional conceptions of narrative time and space.

At the *metaphorical* level, a theory postulating literature as freedom is formulated. Focusing mostly on narrative, the protagonist and her visitor discuss literature's manifestations, rhetoric, purposes, contexts, relation to other art forms, and reason for being.

At the *archetypal* level, *El cuarto* articulates both a process of female self-discovery toward individuation and a foundational theory of knowledge, posing the question: on what is knowledge—including self-knowledge—to be based? Perception? Sensation? Memory? Introspection? And what evidence is required to substantiate the reliability of such a basis?

El cuarto has an evident autobiographical dimension. The text also provides quotable instances that support seeing the novel as a sort of generational autobiography, or "unique *Bildungsroman* for a whole generation of Spanish women" (Levine 168). Appropriately, then, the narrator observes that she and Carmen Franco (the dictator's daughter), although political opposites, are the same age: "We have been victims of the same manners and mores, we've read the same magazines and seen the same movies. Our children may be different, but our dreams have surely been much the same" (133 [1983]). Martín Gaite thereby creates a testimonial subtext that spans forty years of history, intertwined with the rhetoric of fantastic fiction.

I concentrate on Martín Gaite's eyewitness account of growing up female in Spain during those years, focusing on the interaction of time and space as the narrator evokes her experiences, free from chronological sequence, in chronotopic images. Thus the ideological struggle that followed the civil war is textualized as a process of invasion of (and concurrent resistance to) personal and national space. The most significant chronotope at the individual level is contained in the metaphor of the title, and the most striking one at the public level literally equates Franco with time:

[Franco] had been the devious and secret force of that block of time, the chief engineer and the inspector and the manufacturer of the transmission gears, and *time itself*, whose flow he had damped, damned, and directed, with the result that one barely felt either time or him move, and the imperceptible variations that inevitably came about, merely because of the passage of time, in language, in dress, in music, in human relations, in public entertainment, in places, seemed to have simply fallen from heaven. (134; my emphasis)

Franco's chronotope expands through his ubiquitous presence on the national scene, his image reproduced ad infinitum in the press and the newsreels, on TV and postage stamps, and in schoolrooms and government offices (129–30).

As the novel unfolds, Franco's invasion of the cultural and private spheres escalates through his surrogates: censors, secret police, personally appointed editors and bureaucrats, and the Women's Section. When the narrator is threatened with the denial of a passport because she has not yet fulfilled the Social Service office's requirement, she realizes that the true aim of the Women's Section is to turn back the clock and confine women to a domestic environment in support of men. Reproducing almost verbatim the utterances of the Women's Section's lectures, thus bordering on free indirect style, she exposes the fallacy of their rhetoric as propaganda. The narrator does not succumb to the regime's agenda as Carmen Franco has. The TV image of Franco's daughter as a middle-aged woman, captured the day her father died, "with that bitter, empty expression her face has been set in for years now" (133), is a chronotopic image of submissiveness. Publicly recognized only because of her father's fame, she has accomplished nothing on her own. She resembles those leaders in the Women's Section who preached with cheerless faces the joy of domestic work.

Carmen the narrator, on the other hand, has followed a path of development exemplified by women like her mother, her friend Sofía Bermejo, and the folksinger Conchita Piquer. As counterbalancing role models, these three women enable her to defy patriarchy by finding a voice—her own—to register Spanish contemporary history from a female perspective. Martín Gaite defines the postwar years in terms of lack, elaborating a veritable essay on war-induced deprivation within the novel (184–86), which underscores the general perception of the times through such words as *amortize, requisition, ration, hoard,* and *camouflage* (184).

Carmen's first liberating space, supplied by her mother, is a back room (thus the book's title), where Carmen and her sister play, free from social restrictions and adult supervision. As Franco's forces gain hold, the girls lose control of the back room when it becomes a pantry for extra food. This transformation coincides with the years of the narrator's painful rites of adolescence and loss. This triple transition of nation, room, and self is a crucial experience in her life and the pivotal motive in her narrative: "I've come to the most important point, I would really have to tell this part well" (184). The dual function of the back room as an area of freedom and resistance to oppression transforms a domestic space into a metaphor for fifty years of Spanish social history.

The resourceful attitude of the narrator's mother toward socially imposed gender roles endows Carmen with the self-confidence to counterbalance patriarchal pressures. These pressures are embodied in the paternal grandmother's residence, where the womenfolk spend all their time performing housekeeping chores, viciously persecuting even the tiniest specks of dust, always on guard against the slightest defiance of established order. When this grandmother objects to Carmen's habit of reading and a friend warns that so much studying will hinder her chances to marry, Carmen's mother's response offers freedom of choice: "A clever person learns even such a thing as how to sew a button on better than a stupid one" (87). Both types of endeavors, domestic and intellectual, have survived into the narrator's adulthood.

The second positive female influence in the narrator's development comes from her high school friend, Sofía Bermejo. Sofía's parents, who were teachers, are in prison for their Red ideology, but Sofía is proud, not afraid, to support them publicly, in contrast with the adult population, which is silenced by fear. She has learned to cope with material and emotional hardship by creating a space of her own, ruled by her needs and desires, an escape from reality to the freedom of her imagination, a domain where neither Franco nor patriarchy can penetrate uninvited. Safer for a child than political exile, Sofía's place is the wonderland of fiction. Sofía and Carmen merge their budding identities into one space by combining syllables of their last names and calling their sanctuary "Bergai." Naming is creating—such is the power of words. The island of Bergai compensates for the deprivations of the war and postwar years: "'Bergai was invented with exactly that—scarcity—as a point of departure, like all fantasies, like all true affairs of the heart that deserve such a name,' I say" (181). The narrator equates Bergai with literary invention: both are attempts to survive and to overcome time. To her, this function of literature is its sole reason for being (193–95).

Conchita Piquer (1908–90), a popular singer during the Franco dictatorship, offers a third, different perspective on life outside the regime's model. Her songs escaped censorship because of their apparent sentimentality.

> Nobody wanted to speak of the cataclysm that had just torn the country apart, but the bandaged wounds still throbbed, though no moans or shots could be heard. It was an artificial silence, *an emptiness that there was an urgent need to fill with anything whatsoever*. (151; my emphasis)

As a public storyteller, Piquer contributed to the discourse of postwar resistance to political brainwashing. She sang about women characterized as "the rubble left by the war," waiting without hope: "Waiting was the key word, patient waiting was the trump suit. And we learned to wait, not thinking that the wait would turn out to be such a long one" (150, 151).

Piquer's melodramatic songs contrast ironically with the haughty images of Queen Isabella (turned into an icon and a role model by the regime), thus subverting the regime's efforts to exploit the putative connection between itself and the monarch who had given birth to an empire. In promulgating the queen's likeness (most notably in school textbooks), Francoism contended that sometimes history demands austerity, intolerance, and unquestioned authority to preserve the conquests of the past and lead the country to a glorious future. Franco's ideals of national unity were made to appear as the basis for his sociopolitical measures, just as Queen Isabella's goals had shaped hers:

> We were given talks about her iron will and her spirit of sacrifice, we were told how she had held the ambition of the nobles in check, how she had created the Holy Office, expelled the traitorous Jews, given up her jewels to finance the most glorious undertaking in our history. Yet even so there had been those who had slandered her because of her fidelity to her ideals, those who had called her abnegation cruelty. (89)

The brief appearance of the narrator's daughter at the end of the novel is structurally important, because she symbolizes a new generation of Spaniards whose lives are developing at a healthy distance from the Francoist regime. Unlike Mario, Jr., in Delibes's novel—still anguishing over the postwar's Manichaean rhetoric—the daughter in *El cuarto* is a university student just back from a party, preoccupied only with her forthcoming final exams. The narrator herself no longer has to worry about official censorship. She can—and does—write her novel in the way she deems most appropriate to satisfy both her desire to create fantastic fiction and her need to bear personal witness to the social history of postwar Spain. As she remarks on the day Franco was buried, "It was then that I realized I knew all about that period" (135).

In a classroom setting the preceding analysis may be developed to demonstrate in the broadest sense how a text can be read at various levels and how different critical emphases require distinct critical praxes. Students discover how necessary it is to examine class and gender representations in a political context, since both concepts are social constructs derived from the distribution of power as well as categories that share a common origin in political ideology. Students can also see that when a society engages in war against itself, a clash of ideologies in political discourse usually precedes—and follows—the battleground confrontation. The winning side structures the sociopolitical order according to its own ideological agenda, driving resistance and opposition into silence, exile, death, or the underground. Yet dissenting views always find their way into the symbolic order of discourse. Finally, classroom discussions should also prompt questions about the role of the writer in a modern mass society. Students may well conclude that, in chronicling the dynamics at work in the Spanish Civil War and its aftermath, these writers hoped that future generations would be compelled to prevent the devastating impact of totalitarianism and war on civilized societies.

Part III

Writing the War

Part III

Winning the War

George Esenwein

Seeing the Spanish Civil War through Foreign Eyes

The eruption of civil war and revolution in Spain in July 1936 raised questions in the international community. Foremost among these was what attitude foreign governments should adopt toward Spain's domestic crisis. After it became apparent that both Italy and Germany were providing military and economic assistance to the insurgent forces, the great powers France and Great Britain agreed that a policy of nonintervention was the best way to contain the Spanish conflict. This decision led to the August 1936 signing of a series of nonintervention agreements by twenty-seven countries. But despite the diplomatic will demonstrated by this collective act, the ongoing intervention of Germany, Italy, Portugal, and (after October) the Soviet Union—all of whom were signatories to the 1936 pacts—underscored the fact that Spain's troubles could not be easily divorced from events in the wider world (see Alpert).

In fact, the internationalization of the Spanish Civil War greatly contributed to the notion that what was happening in Spain was a reflection of the wider ideological tensions that were coming to a head elsewhere in Europe and around the globe. As a result, most contemporary interpretations of the war ignored the fact that it had sprung from deeply rooted domestic issues. The outbreak of World War II, in 1939, reinforced the tendency among writers and historians to emphasize the international aspects of the civil war, a practice that persisted many years after the conflict had ended.

It is ever more difficult today to find serious studies that view the Spanish Civil War as the harbinger of World War II, though some scholars still insist on giving primacy to its international dimensions. It remains to be seen whether this trend is largely due to the current popularity of memory literature (which constructs the past around personal viewpoints and experiences that tend to run counter to shifting historiographical paradigms) or to the pressures on scholars and writers to make their subject matter relevant to a wider audience. In any event, the coexistence of these competing interpretive models presents a number of vexing pedagogical problems. Perhaps the most important challenge facing today's teachers of the civil war is how to provide their students with a coherent and compelling explanation that takes into account both the domestic and international dimensions of the war.

One way of grappling with this problem is to examine how the perceptions of foreigners, both at the time of the conflict and ever since, have shaped and colored our interpretations of the war. The framework for such an analysis is broad. On one level, it would be necessary to take into account the various meanings that foreign governments attached to the war. This approach would require a thoroughgoing review of the diplomatic responses to the conflict. Because of the significant ideological and moral issues it raised, the war also attracted the attention of ordinary people and celebrities throughout Europe and the Americas. In the United States, the war stirred the political passions of movie stars, artists, writers, and the average citizen alike. Joan Crawford, Shirley Temple, Paul Robeson, Ben Shawn, Langston Hughes, Josephine Herbst, Upton Sinclair, John Dos Passos, and Ernest Hemingway were among the notable personalities who publicly took a stand on the war. Political activists from all social groups and classes also responded to Spain's crisis. The most committed of these joined the much celebrated International Brigades. The differing and often conflicting perspectives of the conflict held by this disparate group of individuals contributed to the foreign image of Spain's war.

Another dimension of the war, and the focus of this essay, concerns the perceptions of it that were promoted by the pro-Republican members of the international literary community. News of the rebellion began to filter through the European presses and prompted a swift reaction from foreign novelists, journalists, and poets. Some came to Spain to witness the fighting as writer tourists, while others—André Malraux, Ralph Bates, Jef Last, Gustav Regler, and George Orwell to name only a few—took up arms for the side they supported. For them, the war became a testing ground for political and moral convictions. Because most outsiders were either ignorant of or unconcerned with the complex underlying social, economic, and political circumstances that had given rise to the conflict, they were predisposed to see the war in black-and-white terms. Thus the war was depicted in the fictional and reportorial accounts of left-wing writers as a showdown between the international forces of fascism and antifascism. Projecting the war as moral allegory made political choices much easier. Indeed, this highly politicized group of writers hoped that presenting the conflict in this way would help convince others that the cause in Spain mattered and that it was necessary for everyone, but especially for governments, to take a stand.

Intellectuals, Writers, and the Allegory of Spain's War

United by their sense of outrage toward both the fascist powers that were supporting the Nationalist cause and the Western democracies that seemed ready to abandon the republic to its fate, politically conscious writers of the era refused to close their eyes to what was happening in Spain (see Wilkinson; Romeiser, *Red Flags*). Given the obvious relevance and topical urgency of the Spanish War, it was fitting that the Communist-sponsored Second International Congress of Anti-fascist Writers selected Republican Spain as the venue for its gathering on 4 July 1937. By the time the congress convened in Valencia, the civil war was already weighing heavily on the world's conscience. Fresh in the minds of all the participants was the April bombing of the undefended Basque town Guernica, a scandalous episode that testified to the cruel consequences of the Nationalists' total war tactics.[1] The antifascist congress attracted some of the most talented and well-regarded leftist writers, political essayists, journalists, and poets, including Pablo Neruda, César Vallejo, Malraux, Hemingway, Stephen Spender, Mikhail Kolstov, Alexis Tolstoi, Antonio Machado, Miguel Hernández, and Anna Seghers. The central theme of the congress was the defense of a democratic culture against its enemies on the right and anti-Stalinist left.

It is essential to note in this connection that the meaning of *democracy* was not easy for the casual observer to decipher. For the liberal-minded

Popular Front intellectuals, the term suggested a pluralistic and open society ruled by representative government institutions that were then operating under Western parliamentary systems. Indeed, it was this sense of the word that was being promoted by Communists in their effort to broaden the base of their antifascist alliance. Thus American units of the Communist-directed International Brigades were named Lincoln and Washington rather than Lenin and Marx. But for Comintern insiders *democratic* did not refer to the kind of liberal democracy that was associated with Western capitalist countries. Rather, they believed that a true people's or mass democracy could only come about when class privileges, rights, prejudices, and other barriers to establishing a truly proletarian society had been swept away. Although they were understandably contemptuous of the elitist and abstract notion of culture that they identified with bourgeois capitalism, both liberal and Communist Popular Front intellectuals reserved their greatest scorn for fascism, which they saw as the main threat to the progressive cultural values they were striving to uphold during the Popular Front period.

Since this broad group of writers felt that the Soviet Union was the only major power willing to engage in the global *kulturkampf*, they also felt that it was their duty to defend Stalin and Stalinism against their left-wing detractors. For this reason "Trotskyites"—a term that was applied to both devotees of Leon Trotsky and left-wing critics of the Soviet regime—were especially reviled. By the late 1930s Trotsky had become in the eyes of orthodox Communists the world's leading representative of reaction and an agent of fascism. In consequence, Communist propaganda stirred up such a profound hatred of its ideological opponents that few of those who supported the Communist movement as represented by the Soviet Union objected to an all-out assault against Trotskyites and other targeted enemies of the people. In Spain this life-and-death struggle involved the forces of the Popular Front on the one side and those of the revolutionary left on the other. The anti-Stalinist POUM (Partido Obrero de Unificación Marxista) was branded a Trotskyist organization and was thus declared the most dangerous force among the fifth columnists. Although the POUM was neither Trotskyist nor affiliated with the Fourth International movement, it was relentlessly and ruthlessly persecuted by the Communists during the war.

The hypocrisy of taking such a dogmatic stance, which violated the principles of the open and democratic culture that the writers' congress professed to be defending, did not seem to matter to most participants. First and foremost, the Popular Front group assumed that antifascist writers and intellectuals everywhere were at that moment in history locked in a mortal struggle against a common enemy. It was thus made clear at the congress that the right to criticism, particularly if it were aimed at the Soviet Union, could not be tolerated. That was the unequivocal message delivered by the president of the congress, the prominent Spanish Catholic writer José Bergamín, when he joined the chorus denouncing the French writer André Gide for publicizing his disillusionments with the Soviet state.[2] Gide, who had been one of the most celebrated speakers at the First Congress for the Defense of Culture held in Paris in 1935, was accused of stabbing the Spanish republic in the back.

While Bergamín probably spoke for most of his fellow intellectuals at the congress, not everyone attending the meetings at Valencia and Madrid was convinced that critical thinking posed a danger to the antifascist cause. The Dutch Communist writer and activist Jef Last believed that Gide's criticism of the Soviet Union was "morally brave and objectively necessary" (*Tragedy* 198). Despite this fair assessment, Last objected to the publication of *Retour de l'U.R.S.S.* at a time when the Soviet Union was the only major country that was lending support to Spain's antifascist struggle. Still, in the face of enormous pressure from both Soviet and French Communists attending the congress, Last refused to make a statement condemning his close friend's book. Another silent supporter of Gide attending the congress was the celebrated French writer and defender of the Republican cause André Malraux. Like Last, Malraux saw Gide's attacks on the Soviet Union as undermining the unity of the left in its hour of crisis.[3] But perhaps because Malraux shared Gide's fear that the spirit of dissent was being increasingly repressed by the Communists' strident call for unconditional subservience to the party's line, he did not follow the example set by Bergamín, Mikhail Kolstov, and other pro-Communist delegates, who felt impelled to use a public meeting held in the midst of Spain's civil war to denounce Gide's critical views on the Soviet experiment.

For the most part, however, those who may have felt personally offended by an ideologically motivated assault against a fellow writer refused to defend Gide. No doubt they sensed that, by speaking out, they too would be branded enemies of the "good fight." Looking back on this event some fifty years later, the Mexican poet and writer Octavio Paz expressed regret for having kept his silence. For him, those who chose not to defend the freedom of expression against the partisans of ideological conformity contributed to the "petrification" of beliefs that lay at the heart of their revolutionary idealism (26).

That the leading literary talents at the congress promoted ideological censorship to combat intolerant regimes reveals their views on the political realities of the 1930s. Above all, they were consumed with the idea of defeating their principal enemy, fascism. Because they believed it was a war without borders, in which the lines separating the actors on and off the battlefield were blurred, they argued that circumstances demanded the subordination of personal freedoms and self-expression to the martial virtues of sacrifice, loyalty, and solidarity.

The beliefs and opinions expressed at the congress formed part of a larger ideological perspective that would shape the future historiography of the civil war in various ways. According to the pro–Popular Front delegates, Spain's war should be understood primarily as an antifascist struggle rather than as a conflict rooted in domestic issues unrelated to fascism. Though some critics of this interpretation argued that it merely mirrored the political slogans and clichéd ideas that informed the Soviets' explanation of world events, the view that the civil war was causally connected to the wider political crisis developing on the international stage seemed to be validated by the outbreak of World War II, in September 1939, only five months after Franco had declared victory for the Nationalist cause. That the European war was ignited by fascist aggression made it possible for left-wing political pundits to place Spain's war in the overall sequence of events that were rapidly unfolding. In those circumstances, it made sense to see the civil war as the first phase of World War II. For those who saw the war as a global conflict against fascism, the Spanish Civil War was elevated to a topic worthy of historical study and, as such, was rescued from the oblivion to which it would most likely have been consigned had it been interpreted as an exclusively Spanish affair.[4]

There is a further reason why the Communists' (and fellow-travelers') ideological frame of reference for understanding the civil war dominated, at least outside Spain, both during the war and for many years afterward. Both the anti-Stalinist left and the right were largely unsuccessful in presenting their respective views on the significance of the Spanish conflict. The left failed in this aspect in part because its understanding of the war contrasted sharply with the one promoted by the Communists and their supporters. Writers and intellectuals who were sympathetic to the revolutionaries in the Republican camp saw a political, social, and economic reality that was much different from the one publicized in Communist and pro-Communist literature. Astute observers like George Orwell and Franz Borkenau tried to find a receptive audience for their eyewitness accounts of what was happening in the Republican camp during the war but largely failed because their testimonies forcefully challenged the validity of the Communists' official version of events. Although the viewpoints expressed by Orwell and other anti-Stalinist writers were relegated to obscurity during the war, they would form one of the cornerstones of the war's historiography produced in the cold-war era, 1948–89.

Interpretations of the Spanish Civil War offered by the right also failed to have a lasting impact on the war's historiography since the right, more so than the left, tended to present the war in terms that were aimed at provoking moral outrage rather than effecting an intellectual understanding of the conflict.[5] Those who supported the Nationalists, like the British authors Florence Farmborough and Harold Cardozo, tended to depict the war as a contest between the barbarian Reds (Communists and anarchists), who were seeking to plunge Spain into a state of insurrection and disorder, and the moderate members of the right, who were trying to save their country from the ravages of these lawless (and mostly foreign) forces. The wave of politically motivated killings that swept through Republican territory during the early phases of the war—particularly the ferocious attacks against the Catholic Church—only underscored the alleged validity of these assumptions. Over time, however, the force and fundamental simplicity of these viewpoints became increasingly difficult to sustain. In the aftermath of Badajoz, Guernica, and other highly publicized examples of Nationalist atrocities, it was no longer possible for right-wing writers to argue convincingly that the Nationalists were occupying the higher moral ground.

Franco's victory in April 1939 allowed the right to impose its historical views of the war inside Spain. Nationalist historical discourse on the war reflected a highly selective memory of the causes and consequences of the conflict and made no effort to present the complexities and multiple political realities of the two Spains. Moreover, because it was being used exclusively as an instrument of ideological persuasion, the Francoist narrative had little or no explanatory power beyond Spain's national frontiers.[6] This limited influence was especially evident in the aftermath of World War II. The fascist overtones of Franco's government as well as Spain's return to a period of acute isolationism meant that the Nationalists' attempt to present a simplified and sanitized view of the civil war was increasingly at odds with the prevailing views of the international community.

Although the Francoist narrative of the civil war suffered in comparison with the pro-Communist one in the years immediately after World War II, the debate over the civil war was far from over. In the democratic West the onset of the cold war produced yet another shift in the historiography of the Spanish conflict. What follows is a brief review of how the theme of anti-Communism challenged the dominant antifascist narrative.

Interpreting the "Good Fight"

Most pro-Republican non-Spanish writers identified the war as a pivotal episode in the left's global struggle against fascism. Constructing their understanding of the war around this assumption, these writers were remarkably successful in presenting the various anti-Nationalist factions as a unified (Popular Front) cause that was fighting to preserve the progressive and democratic values embodied in the prewar Republican regime. As powerful and effective as this image was in advancing the political agenda of the Communists, its value as an explanatory model of wartime Republican Spain was open to question. In fact, it was eyewitnesses like Orwell who first revealed how misleading it was to portray the Republican government as a united front of antifascist forces.

The accuracy of Orwell's reading of events during the war has been the subject of numerous debates, and it is not my intention to resolve these here.[7] It is necessary, however, to explain how Orwell's writings have been used to construct an anti-Communist paradigm of the war. His reputation as a sharp-eyed observer of Republican politics in Catalonia was established during the cold-war era, and he is still seen by many, in the words of Robert Stradling, as "the brightest star in a galaxy of foreign writers who participated in the Spanish Civil War" (*History* 48).

It is not surprising that interest in the Spanish Civil War was revived during the cold-war period, when the ideological struggle between East (Communism) and West (liberal democracy) took center stage. After all, it was well known that the Soviet Union had played a major role in a conflict that was still regarded by many on both sides of the cold-war ideological divide as a pivotal event in the political world of the 1930s. It was against this background that Orwell's major contribution to Spanish Civil War literature, *Homage to Catalonia*, was embraced by anti-Soviet Western writers and intellectuals on both the left and right. It particularly appealed to this diverse group that Orwell's eyewitness account of Republican Spain was seriously at odds with the pro-Communist views that had greatly influenced

Western historiography of the war since the 1930s. Above all, Orwell's account made it clear that, contrary to what the Communists and the supporters of the Popular Front program were arguing, the Spanish left-wing parties were divided over fundamental issues. His riveting description of the controversial events of May 1937, for example, highlights the bitter struggle that had been raging for some months inside Republican Spain between those who supported a revolutionary conception of the civil war and those who opposed it.[8] By documenting how the anti-Stalinist POUM—the party with which Orwell was affiliated—fell victim to the government's efforts to suppress the revolutionary movement, Orwell exposes the nefarious role that the Communists played in this murky process. Yet, as mentioned earlier, his efforts to publicize the Communists' counterrevolutionary role in the war fell mostly on deaf ears. Few foreigners at the time were concerned about the fate of a party or revolutionary movement about which they knew very little and for which they had no sympathy. These same blinkered left-wing observers believed that anyone who criticized the Popular Front policies of the Republican government while it was in the throes of a life-and-death struggle was betraying the antifascist cause.

To the anti-Soviet writers and intellectuals of the cold-war era, however, Orwell's revelations about Communist wrongdoings provided further proof of the subversive character of their ideological enemies. While Orwell's writings were, in this sense, being put to a specific political use, they were at the same time providing a powerful impetus for academics and scholars to revise their understanding of the Spanish Civil War. It is important to note in this connection that, though Orwell was widely credited for having exposed the crimes of the Communists during the war, many other writers and historians, quite independently of Orwell, had accomplished the same thing. During the war, a number of nonaligned leftists wrote accounts of their experiences in Republican Spain that echoed the anti-Communist views found in *Homage*. Borkenau's *The Spanish Cockpit*, perhaps the most politically sophisticated and objective analysis of events in Republican Spain written from firsthand observations, bears witness to the duplicitous and heavy-handed methods the Communists employed in their attempt to establish hegemonic control over the government and armed forces. It was therefore no accident that, along with Orwell's *Homage*, Borkenau's study enjoyed a certain popularity during peak periods of the cold-war debates in the 1960s and 1970s.

Because the works of authors like Orwell and Borkenau criticized Communist behavior during the Spanish Civil War, they were often characterized by both the right and the Communists as books about breaking with the left. In fact, many of the political beliefs held by this anti-Communist group were as repugnant to the cold-war right as they were to the Stalinist left. This dislike was aimed particularly at Orwell, whose *Homage* demonstrated a certain degree of sympathy and respect for the revolutionary aspirations of the POUM and the anarchists of the CNT–FAI (Confederación Nacional del Trabajo–Federación Anarquista Ibérica).[9] In this sense, it was Orwell's reputation as a morally scrupulous witness rather than his personal politics that was being celebrated by the anti-Soviet school of intellectuals and writers.

Given the popularity Orwell was enjoying in cold-war reading circles, it is ironic that his writings did not seriously undermine the dominant paradigm of Spanish Civil War historiography. Perhaps because of the book's politically charged associations with right-wing ideologues, well-regarded and widely read Spanish Civil War historians like Hugh Thomas and Gabriel Jackson saw no reason to revise their pro–Popular Front perspectives in the light of the information in *Homage*.[10] Thomas himself dismissed it as "a better book about war itself than about the Spanish war" (*Spanish Civil War* 653n2). Nevertheless, the perceptions that informed *Homage* mirrored those found in a small but growing body of historical literature that was increasingly challenging the assumptions that underlay the standard liberal and Communist interpretations of the war. Burnett Bolloten's groundbreaking *The Grand Camouflage* (1961) was the first major scholarly work in English to document both the significance of the popular revolution and the degree to which internecine squabbling among Republican factions had been concealed by the Communists' Popular Front narrative. Notwithstanding the prodigious scholarship that was brought to bear in supporting these viewpoints, *The Grand Camouflage* was treated more as an anti-Communist diatribe than as a serious historical work. It was perhaps a sign of the polarized political climate of the era that it took over twenty years for the iconoclastic views expressed in this and similar so-called anti-Communist works to be incorporated into the mainstream of the war's historiography.[11]

The icy reception that *Homage* and other books critical of the Communists received from most Soviet and Western-based Spanish Civil War scholars in the 1960s testifies to the staying power of the Popular Front historiographical paradigm. Its durability was again made clear during the last years of the cold war. During the mid-1980s, a school of revisionist left-oriented scholars based primarily in Spain and the United Kingdom set out to reverse the inroads that *Homage, The Grand Camouflage*, and similar books had made in challenging the validity of the Popular Front interpretation of the war. Their efforts were substantially reinforced by a spate of autobiographical studies and oral testimonies produced by a group of surviving veterans of the International Brigades who had strong ties to the academic community.[12] In this group's memoir and commemorative literature, Orwell and anyone else critical of the Soviets' role in the war were, at best, irrelevant or, at worst, traitors to the Republican cause. In passing such harsh judgments on those who disagreed with their personal (and highly politicized) views, these veterans were merely resurrecting the language and political practices of the 1930s. Yet although their attempts to refute the arguments of the anti-Communists leaned heavily on the rhetorical force of outdated polemics, they succeeded in mounting a formidable war of words. Their success was due in part to the tendency among political observers to understand the cold-war conflicts of the 1980s—especially in Central America—in terms of the ideological struggles of the 1930s and in part to the scholarly endorsements the veterans received from the aforementioned circle of left-wing academics. With few exceptions, the academics privileged in this debate the oral testimonies of activists who had not only made great personal sacrifices to join a worthy cause but also suffered the hardships of political persecution during the cold-war era.[13]

The collapse of Communism in Eastern Europe and the Soviet Union, in the last years of the twentieth century, seems to have had little impact on revisionist efforts to discredit Orwell and the so-called cold-war historians of the Spanish Civil War. Some members of this newer generation of historians attempt to justify their continued offensive on the grounds that Western Spanish Civil War historiography has been dominated by cold-war perceptions for too long (see Preston and Mackenzie).[14] Others argue that because Orwell and other foreign eyewitnesses often failed to take into account the Spanish dimensions of the political and social realities they recorded, the scholarly value of their writings can no longer be taken for granted.

On the other hand, those who belong to the Orwellian tradition are equally convinced that the doctrinaire views of pro-Soviet scholars have exercised a disproportionate influence over our understanding of the war. They are also convinced that overcoming the ideological obstacles of the past cannot be achieved by ignoring the uncomfortable truths that emerge in the process of reevaluating the assumptions of the war's historiography.

The foregoing discussion should make it clear to students of modern Spanish history that, after many years of politically charged argument, a consensus about the Spanish Civil War is as far away as ever. Judging from past experiences, a resolution to this controversy will no doubt depend less on the factual record than on a thoroughgoing revision of the presuppositions that have long informed our interpretations of this conflict. By confronting such a dichotomous and contentious historiography, students will no doubt gain a greater appreciation of the degree to which foreign perceptions continue to dominate the literature on the war.

Notes

1. Its impact on left-wing public opinion outside Spain was refracted through Pablo Picasso's provocative monochromatic mural simply titled *Guernica*, which was exhibited at the Paris World Exhibition in June 1937. See also Mendelson in this volume.

2. Gide, once a fellow traveler, summarized his impressions of the culturally oppressive nature of the Soviet Union in his pamphlet *Retour de l'U.R.S.S* (1936). The work provoked a furor, and Gide was excommunicated from the Communist community. See Furet; Sheridan.

3. *L'espoir* (1937; *Man's Hope*) was Malraux's literary tribute to the Spanish Civil War.

4. While it was true that the historical significance of the civil war had been secured on the left, there was nothing immutable about the way in which it was to be interpreted. Given that Stalin had entered into a friendly alliance with the Axis powers, Popular Front intellectuals and writers who were still loyal to the Soviet Union were no longer permitted to identify the Spanish struggle as an antifascist crusade. But this line of interpretation was short-lived. Less than two years after the war began, the Soviet Union joined the Allies, and, as a result, the civil war was thereafter seen as the opening battle in the war against Hitler.

5. This is not to deny that the left appealed to the public's emotions in an effort to rally support for the Republican cause nor that its propaganda was any less tendentious than that of its opponents. Because they insisted on seeing Franco and his forces as tools of Mussolini and Hitler, left-wing observers rarely presented in their writings an accurate picture of the diverse (and mostly nonfascist) factions fighting on the Nationalist side.

6. For a discussion of how the dictatorship used history as an instrument of cultural control, see Boyd 232–72.

7. See, for example, Christopher Norris's relentlessly anti-Orwellian anthology, *Inside the Myth* (1984). The essays relating to Orwell's Spanish Civil War writings are flawed above all because they do not take into account the numerous other eyewitness testimonies that corroborate Orwell's overall impressions of Republican politics, such as Souchy's *The Tragic Week in May* (1937) and McNair's *Spanish Diary* (1937). Equally hostile to the view that Orwell should be regarded as a standard-bearer of intellectual honesty and decency is the more recent *The Betrayal of Dissent: Beyond Orwell, Hitchens, and the New American Century*, by Scott Lucas.

8. A fictionalized reconstruction of this ideological battle can be found in Ken Loach's film *Land and Freedom* (1995).

9. It is noteworthy in this regard that several of the anti-Communist studies that were aimed at revising the antifascist narrative of the civil war in the cold-war period were written by authors, like Burnett Bolloten, who were or had been close to the left.

10. Liberals and Marxists alike dismissed revelations regarding subversive Communist activities during the civil war found in the writings of prominent ex-Communists like Walter Krivitsky and Alexander Orlov. Documents that, until recently, have been buried in the Comintern and Soviet military archives, however, tend to confirm at least some of the more substantial accusations against the Communists made by Krivitsky et al. See Radosh, Habeck, and Sevostianov.

11. Noam Chomsky's critical analysis of so-called liberal scholarship in the late 1960s drew attention to Bolloten's hitherto overlooked contributions to Spanish Civil War historiography. See Chomsky 23–158.

12. Even those who had broken ranks with the Communists were exceedingly hostile to anyone who dared to tarnish the mostly positive memories they conserved of the Soviets' and Communists' contributions to the Republican war effort.

13. See, for example, the oral history of North American volunteers compiled by John Gerassi.

14. A major difficulty with using the cold-war label routinely invoked by this group is its selective application. Only those on the political right (or writers whose views are embraced by those on the right) are guilty of having a cold-war mentality. Thus the pro-Soviet viewpoints of Western writers and scholars are not examined with the same critical eye that is used to evaluate anti-Communist perspectives.

Robert S. Coale

The Abraham Lincoln Brigade Volunteers: Historical Contexts and Writings

Between 1936 and 1938, 2,800 Americans ignored the interdiction of the United States government and found their way across the Atlantic Ocean, over the Pyrenees, and into the ranks of the International Brigades. Their motivations, actions, and historic legacy have been the subject of study and debate for close to seventy years. Volumes have been written about them from different political and emotional perspectives, and yet their history remains unknown to most students and teachers alike. This essay does not pretend to resolve the political debate surrounding the International Brigades. It is up to students to draw their own conclusions on the validity of the differing interpretations. In the following pages I outline briefly the International Brigades, offer a portrait of the American men and women who volunteered in Republican Spain, and identify sources readily available for personal study or classroom use to present the men and women commonly, although somewhat inaccurately, referred to as the Abraham Lincoln Brigade.

In the fight between a democratic government and a military rebellion in Spain, most of the more creative and successful poets, writers, and artists sided with the Loyalists. Inevitably the Republican struggle for survival has been portrayed more romantically than the fascist coup. Rafael Alberti's poem "A las Brigadas internacionales" ("To the International Brigades"), for example, mentions the blood of international volunteers as "singing without borders," words that reinforce the image of a spontaneous solidarity across the globe (*Poeta* 72; all translations are mine). Dolores Ibárruri, in her farewell speech to *brigadista* survivors in Barcelona, set the tone of future idealistic interpretations of the volunteers' heroism by proclaiming, "You are history, you are legend" (*En la lucha* 355). The first history of the Lincoln Battalion, by Edwin Rolfe, although noting that most volunteers were Communists, makes no mention of the Communist International (Comintern) organization of the brigades. The most celebrated American novel to come out of the war, Ernest Hemingway's *For Whom the Bell Tolls,* intertwines guerrilla warfare with a love story between the American Robert Jordan and the young Maria, thus perpetuating the romantic aura of the Internationals.

The political and diplomatic dynamics of Western democracies soon sealed the fate of the Second Spanish Republic. The Non-intervention Committee was established, and Spain's legal government was hampered in its attempts to purchase weapons abroad to defend itself. Republican Spain was forced to turn to the Soviet Union of Joseph Stalin for arms at inflated prices. The die was cast for ideological interpretations for decades to come. Conservative historians seize on the privileged position of the Soviet Union to attack the Loyalist cause. Given the popularity of the USSR in sectors of Republican Spain, Francoist historians as well as conservative Western writers influenced by cold-war politics, such as Ronald Radosh, Mary Habeck, Ricardo de la Cierva, and Pío Moa, repeatedly attempt to expose the myth that the International Brigades were not fighting for democracy in Spain but were merely a front for the spread of Stalinist totalitarian Communism to the Iberian Peninsula. Research in Moscow archives has failed to produce material to support this claim. Furthermore, in their haste to attack, these critics fail to realize that the antiquated weapons, high casualty rates, and poor military leadership they denounce belie the thesis they put forward. If the International Brigades were a veritable Comintern army slated for Stalinist designs in postwar Spain, why were these choice battalions allowed to be decimated on the battlefields, underarmed, and constantly in the hottest of the fighting? Why were up to thirty percent of non-Communists accepted into the ranks? As Antonio Elorza, Marta Bizcarrondo, and Daniel Kowlasky point out, Stalin's activities in Spain were directly linked to foreign policy issues, not to sinister plans for the postwar period. The situation in 1936 should not be interpreted from a 1945 perspective.

Sympathy for the Popular Front government of Spain in its fight for survival was widespread among progressives from the outbreak of the civil war. The considerable outpouring of support from around the world took many forms, including attempts to pressure Western democracies to aid the constitutional government and campaigns among the working classes to collect funds, clothing, and humanitarian aid for Republican Spain. For some, sending money, food, or hospital supplies was simply not enough. Foreigners living in Spain and some international athletes present in Barcelona for the Popular Olympiad, a workers' alternative to the official Olympic Games held in Berlin, spontaneously joined militia units in July 1936. As the eyes of the world remained fixed on the unfolding tragedy, more volunteers trickled into Spain and enrolled in existing units or created small "international columns" (Lefebvre and Skoutelsky 22–35). It was not until mid-September 1936, however, that the Comintern decided to harness the popular momentum in defense of the republic and actively recruit volunteers from around the world to form the International Brigades (Elorza and Bizcarrondo 459–60). This move took place at the same moment that the Soviet Union, having seen Germany and Italy supply Franco with considerable aid, shifted from a policy of nonintervention to one of outright military aid to the Loyalist forces (Kowalsky 196–98).

Albacete, midway between Madrid and Valencia on the plain of La Mancha, became the site of the training camp and the command center for the International Brigades. Volunteers began arriving in mid-October. The Frenchman André Marty was in overall political command of the operation. Exact totals of how many men and women served in the International Brigades have been subject to considerable conjecture since the war. Francoist historians tend to inflate totals so that they equal or surpass the Italian contingent with which Mussolini aided the rebels. In a recent publication, Cierva gives estimates ranging from 70,000 to 120,000 men (385). The French historian Rémi Skoutelsky has put an end to such exaggerated numbers. After researching original documents in the Comintern archives in Moscow, he confirms that the total number of volunteers, of all nationalities, was approximately 35,000 (Skoutelsky, *Novedad* 168). Of those, 2,800 were from the United States (Carroll 204).

The American volunteers hailed from every state of the union except Wyoming and Delaware; urban and industrialized centers provided the main stock. They were overwhelmingly blue-collar workers of all trades (Rosenstone 368–69). There was a sizable representation of seamen and dockworkers, who were at the forefront of many contemporary labor struggles

(Rosenstone 102–03). Statistics in one study indicate that Hemingway's Robert Jordan, reputedly inspired in part by Major Robert Merriman of the Lincoln Battalion, was the exception rather than the rule: teachers and students composed only two and five percent, respectively, of total volunteers (Levenson 27). Hemingway made his character even more exceptional by portraying him as a guerrilla fighter rather than a common infantryman.

According to Peter Carroll, the youngest volunteers were eighteen years old, the eldest volunteer was sixty, and the median age was slightly over twenty-seven (15–16). Some volunteers were World War I veterans, and others had served in the armed forces at one time or another, although military knowledge of any sort was not the norm (Rosenstone 111). Despite what the age statistics suggest, the proportion of married volunteers was low. Most were single, probably because of the difficult economic situation of the Great Depression years.

The economic troubles of the times—periods of joblessness, meager salaries, abusive bosses, and homelessness—not only kept the American volunteers single but also shaped their political consciousness. This strife of the 1930s set the tone for their future struggles. Choosing to go to Spain was not their first political commitment: for many it was the logical continuation of a political, social, or student activism that predated the war and the plea for volunteers. Milt Felsen, for example, had worked a variety of odd jobs in New York. In his memoirs he describes how he was exposed at the age of eighteen to radical views in the streets of the city:

> When people could not pay their rent, their furniture was thrown out into the street. But then other people came with signs and leaflets of protest and fought to put it back. I began to meet these people, the Communists, socialists and anarchists. They knew so much and had so much to say: the capitalist system was breaking down. (27)

Felsen later rode the rails and ended up at the University of Iowa, where he became a student organizer. There he heard a plea for volunteers from Isabel de Palencia and, with a friend, decided to return to New York, join other volunteers, and head to Spain. Harry Fisher, also of New York, had a similar experience. He became politically active on learning that it was Young Communist League (YCL) members who were helping move evicted families back into their apartments. Joining the YCL gave him a sense of fighting social injustices (Fisher 2). This history of activism, in the trade union movement or in leftist political parties, was common among those who headed to Spain.

Statistical breakdowns using existing records shed some light on the party adherences of the American volunteers. One of the first studies notes that fifty-one percent were members of the Communist Party of the United States of America (CPUSA) and an additional twelve percent were members of the YCL (Levenson 26). The remaining thirty-seven percent either belonged to other parties or had no affiliation. In another study, the participation of non-Communist volunteers is given as twenty-eight percent (Carroll 71). This proportion of non-Communist volunteers, ranging from one-quarter to one-third, underscores the appeal to defend the Popular Front government and strike out against fascism that was felt across the left, beyond the boundaries of a single party. Indeed, some veterans claimed that they joined the CPUSA solely to improve their chances of getting to Spain (Carroll). In many ways the rank and filers were a cross section of America, socially and professionally, and pains were taken to emphasize this diversity in International Brigades literature during the war. Nonetheless, radicals who had experience in the labor and social struggles of the day dominated the ranks (Rosenstone 97–98).

The American contingent was racially and ethnically mixed. The largest ethnic group, approximately thirty percent of the volunteers, consisted of those who claimed Jewish ancestry. Many were from recent immigrant families, a background that gave them closer emotional ties to, and a clearer awareness of, European politics (Carroll). They were among the first to appreciate fully the threat posed by Hitler, much as the recent Italian immigrants were more aware of the dangers of Mussolini's fascism. The Lincoln Battalion was the first racially integrated fighting unit in United States history, and African American volunteers made up approximately two and a half percent of the Americans in Spain. Oliver Law, a former Army sergeant from Chicago and a political radical, became the first black person to command a racially integrated American fighting force. Another first occurred in 1997, when President Bill Clinton awarded posthumous Medals of Honor to several African American servicemen from World War II. One of these men was Sergeant Edward Carter, a Lincoln veteran who, despite heroic exploits in Germany, had been forced out of the United States Army in 1947 because of his service in Spain (Galloway 43). Carter thus became the first Lincoln veteran to earn the nation's highest military honor. The African American volunteers saw their struggle against fascism in Spain as a parallel to their struggle in America for civil rights, for an end to lynchings and segregation (see also Ugarte in this volume).

The Americans did not operate in a vacuum; they were an integral part of the structure of the International Brigades as a whole, though they made up less than ten percent of the total number of volunteers. In turn the International Brigades operated as part of the regular People's Army of the Republic. During the spring and summer of 1937, once the urgency of the battle for Madrid had passed, the brigades were reorganized to facilitate communication and better incorporate the increasing number of Spanish recruits. In general the brigades were regrouped as much as possible along linguistic lines as follows: Eleventh, Germanic; Twelfth, Italian; Thirteenth, Slavic and central European languages; Fourteenth, francophone; and Fifteenth, anglophone. The Fifteenth Brigade included eventually the British Battalion, the Lincoln Battalion, the Washington Battalion, the Mackenzie-Papineau Battalion—which contained a large percentage of Canadians—and the Spanish Battalion (Johnstone 83–88). Following the heavy casualties at the battle of Brunete in July, the two battalions named for American presidents were amalgamated into one, officially named the Lincoln-Washington Battalion but often simply known as the Lincoln Battalion. (See the works of Castells Peig, Delperrié de Bayac, and Skoutelsky for details on the composition of different brigades over the course of the war.) During the war the brigade in which most Americans served was commonly referred to as La Quince Brigada (The Fifteenth Brigade), and one version of the lyrics to the popular wartime song "El Paso del Ebro" is known alternatively as "Viva la Quinta (or Quince) Brigada" (*Spain in My Heart*). Apart from the infantry battalions mentioned above, Americans served in units such as the John Brown Artillery Battery, the transportation unit Regiment de Tren, the International Brigades motor pool, and in the American Hospital Group as ambulance drivers, doctors, and nurses; there were also at least three guerrilla fighters. Nationality was not the only factor that decided where one served. A combination of elements, such as special technical training, military experience, linguistic aptitude, and date of arrival in Spain also determined placement.

Given the diversity of organizations that contained Americans, the name Abraham Lincoln Brigade sprang up on the home front largely through confusion of the different military terms. Although no military unit in Spain was known as the Abraham Lincoln Brigade, the name caught on and was used to encompass all the American volunteers for the Loyalist cause, regardless of where they served. Two often cited examples of this misnomer are Veterans of the Abraham Lincoln Brigade and Friends of the Abraham Lincoln Brigade, the organization that, among other endeavors, sent packages of tobacco, soap, candy, and socks to the soldiers in Spain.

Throughout the conflict the five International Brigades maintained their role as special troops slated for difficult tasks. They fought in every major engagement, from the battle of Madrid to the later stages of the battle of the Ebro. By 1937 an increasing percentage of Spaniards entered their ranks, and as the war progressed foreign soldiers became a minority. In fact, in September 1938, when the foreigners were withdrawn, the brigades were able to maintain their respective positions in the line.

There is no shortage of sources, both new and old, on the International Brigades. Historical texts; fiction; contemporary writings; and collections of photography, artwork, poetry, and letters offer a wealth of perspectives to study all aspects of the brigades' legacy.

Classic histories of the war, such as Hugh Thomas's *The Spanish Civil War*, cover the brigades briefly, but there are also many works specific to the brigades from which to choose, such as Verle B. Johnstone's *Legions of Babel: The International Brigades in the Spanish Civil War*. In Spanish, the monumental *Las Brigadas Internacionales*, by Andreu Castells Peig, is a complete although outdated text. Jacques Delperrié de Bayac's *Les Brigades Internationales* is an early and solid text in French. These fundamental books remain valuable sources, although the production of texts by authors who have had access to previously restricted archives disproves some of the information presented in them.

As Carroll notes, one can identify several generations of writings on the Lincolns (ix). The first generation is by the veterans themselves, who wrote about their experiences in the immediate postwar period. *The Lincoln Battalion*, by the poet and soldier Rolfe, is the first history of the Americans in Spain and, contrary to the title, does not limit itself to the first American battalion. In the same year, 1939, Alvah Bessie, novelist, veteran, and future member of the Hollywood Ten, published *Men in Battle*, an autobiographical account of his journey to Spain, his training, and his participation in the battles of 1938. This straightforward description of daily life in the Lincoln Battalion, from the perspective of a thirty-four-year-old company adjutant, is full of details that are absent from general histories of the brigades. Bessie does not avoid describing the difficulties and shortcomings he encountered in Spain, thus contradicting the assertion that early books on the International Brigades were simply romantic or propagandistic.

In the late 1960s a second generation of books began to come to light. These were mostly written by historians who had limited access to original source material or who conducted series of personal interviews with veterans. In 1967 the Lincoln veteran Arthur Landis published *The Abraham Lincoln Brigade*. Much lauded by veterans, this volume goes to great lengths to discuss the participation of a wide array of volunteers. The book is based largely on personal interviews and includes a considerable number of firsthand accounts that are not found elsewhere. Soon afterward, in 1969, Robert A. Rosenstone's *Crusade of the Left* appeared. The most balanced history up to that time, it is the first general work on the American Internationals written from an outside though sympathetic perspective. Cecil Eby's *Between the Bullet and the Lie* appeared in the same period. His book is less a history than a series of narrated anecdotes, many of which are erroneous. The political slant of the work is evident from the title, which reflects the author's thesis that many volunteers were coaxed into heading to Spain for the wrong reasons and, once there, were trapped.

Over the past twenty years, there has been a fairly constant flow of veterans' memoirs. The veterans narrate their difficulties growing up as a way to explain their political beliefs and subsequent decision to volunteer. James Yates's *Mississippi to Madrid*, Hank Rubin's *Spain's Cause Was Mine*, Felsen's *The Anti-warrior*, and Fisher's *Comrades* are a few excellent and readily available examples of more recent memoirs. Carl Geiser's *Prisoners of the Good Fight* is a first-person account of a lesser-known aspect of the war: the Internationals who were taken prisoner and survived to tell about their experiences. Geiser also provides insight into the often criticized role of the political commissar. This position is often paralleled with that of chaplains in traditional armies. The commissar's job was multifaceted. He saw to the morale of the troops and provided political interpretations of the war's progress from local, national, or international perspectives. In addition to personal narratives, there are contributions from family members of deceased veterans. *Alvah Bessie's Spanish Civil War Notebooks*, edited by Bessie's son, is an important firsthand account of the war by this novelist turned soldier. *American Commander in Spain* (Merriman and Lerude) is the story of Robert H. Merriman, written, in part, by his widow, who consulted his surviving war diaries. There are still other memoirs, which were published in the years before this outpouring of personal narratives: *American Commissar*, by the former brigade historian Sandor Voros, is an often critical work of a disgruntled former commissar. John Gates, by contrast, although he had left the CPUSA by the time he wrote his memoir, did not use his autobiography, *The Story of an American Communist*, to attack his former convictions. The abundance and diversity of these memoirs suggest a possible approach to understanding the experience of the Lincolns: to compare those who distanced themselves drastically from their wartime political convictions with those who remained faithful to their beliefs and actions in Spain.

Because of the political changes of the last fifteen years, International Brigades source material, once jealously guarded in official archives in Moscow, is now more readily accessible. This availability has spawned yet another generation of texts. Several historians have used these sources to write updated histories and present new perspectives on the conflict. Three works on the brigades stand out. The first, *L'espoir guidait leurs pas*, by the French historian Skoutelsky, is a solid study of the volunteers from France, who made up one-fourth of the total number of *brigadistas*. Although the book does not mention the Americans in detail, it does offer important interpretations on several subjects—in particular, Marty and his reported reign of terror—which are often mentioned by authors critical of the International Brigades. Well known for his role in the 1919 Black Sea mutiny, Marty, a member of the French parliament and one of the seven secretaries of the Comintern, was not a judicious choice for political head of the brigades. Hotheaded and constantly suspicious of fifth columnists and defeatists, he often threatened subordinates with the firing squad, a characteristic that gained posterity through Hemingway's novel. This image of Marty, fueled partly by his personal enemies and partly by rebel propaganda, has survived to this day. Both Carlos Serrano (*L'enjeu*) and Skoutelsky have demonstrated, however, that the legend of Marty as the Butcher of Albacete is unfounded.

Skoutelsky has published a Spanish version of his original study of the French volunteers, expanded to cover the history of the International Brigades. *Novedad en el frente* is remarkable and recommendable as the most serious general study to date.

Carroll's *Odyssey of the Abraham Lincoln Brigade* is the definitive work on the Americans, not only of their experiences in Spain but also of their postwar lives of activism. Based on research gathered from the archives in Moscow, the Abraham Lincoln Brigade holdings in the United States, and numerous personal interviews, the work tells the story of the men and women in Spain, presents their motivations for choosing Spain, and shows how commitment to progressive ideals followed them throughout their lives. Many Lincoln veterans served in World War II, despite the United States Army's reluctance to accept them for combat or for positions of command. Later, key members of the Veterans of the Abraham Lincoln

Brigade suffered criminal prosecution and jail during the McCarthy witch hunts. Still, the veterans' organization survived and became active in the movement against the Vietnam War and against the Reagan administration's involvement in Nicaragua.

Spain Betrayed, by Radosh, Habeck, and Grigory Sevostianov, presents views from a different political perspective. Radosh, whose uncle was killed in Spain fighting in the Lincoln ranks, has long espoused a harsh interpretation of the Soviet policy in Spain and of the International Brigades in general. The volume presents an interesting selection of documents culled from the various archives in Moscow and translated into English. While the documents undoubtedly provide material for further study of the Soviet involvement in the Spanish Civil War, they do not corroborate the authors' denunciations of Stalin's supposed intentions.

There is enough material offering differing interpretations on the Abraham Lincoln Brigade to provide for rich discussion and debates in class. Rosenstone gives a detailed description of many sources (*Crusade* 376–84). Although many of the pamphlets and articles published during the war or shortly afterward are often inaccessible, studying available contemporary texts—rather than writings that view the war through the filter of over half a century of world politics—provides insight into how the war was interpreted as it progressed. Articles written during the war by newspaper correspondents such as Vincent Sheenan and Herbert L. Matthews offer moving descriptions from friendly yet outsider eyes. The Veterans of the Abraham Lincoln Brigade have published two collections of writings: *The Heart of Spain* (Bessie) and *Our Fight: Writings by Veterans of the Abraham Lincoln Brigade, Spain, 1936–1939* (Bessie and Prago). *Madrid 1937*, edited by Cary Nelson and Jefferson Hendricks, is an extraordinary collection of letters sent to the United States from Spain that touches on virtually every aspect of the struggle in the words of those who participated in the war.

Fiction pieces that refer to the International Brigades experience offer another avenue for understanding the period and the men and women who lived in it. Because there are already volumes, in Spanish and English, devoted to works of fiction, I limit my comments to several titles most directly related to the American experience. *For Whom the Bell Tolls*, Hemingway's most popular novel, is an easily accessible work to begin classroom discussion, although it is less effective as a portrayal of a typical American volunteer. His lesser-known short stories and the play *The Fifth Column* present moving sketches of Internationals. Upton Sinclair contributed his less than successful, tendentious novel *No Pasarán,* which he published at his own expense in 1937. Scholars rarely mention or include it in discussions of his works. Two Lincoln Brigade veterans have also written fiction. Milton Wolff, last commander of the Lincoln Battalion, tells of his experiences in the autobiographical novel *Another Hill*. William Herrick, who testified against his former comrades before the House Un-American Activities Committee, wrote *Hermanos!* as a much more critical presentation of the war and the brigades. Veterans have questioned many of the scenes he describes. There are also several volumes of poetry. Nelson, for example, has published an anthology of American poetry, *The Wound and the Dream*, which includes works from several veterans, as well as that of other renowned poets.

For all its power, the written word is not the only venue to project images of Spain and the International Brigades. Photographs and artwork give a more immediate perception of the war. *Heart of Spain*, the collection of Robert Capa's photographs, includes several pictures of Lincolns as well as non-American International Brigaders. The collection of rarely seen photographs from the Abraham Lincoln Brigade Archives, *Aura of the Cause* (edited by Nelson), as both an exhibit and a catalog, gives an impressive view of life in Spain at the time and the activities of volunteers both on and off the battlefield. Collections of wartime propaganda posters, such as those by John Tisa or Jordi Carulla and Arnau Carulla, include examples of International Brigade posters produced by their own Commissariat of Propaganda.

Several documentaries have been produced on the Lincoln Brigade and are available on video. *The Good Fight* contains poignant interviews with veterans, including two women, the nurse Salaria Kee and the truck driver Evelyn Hutchins. *Forever Activists,* the 1991 Academy Award nominee for Best Documentary, was filmed when a sizable group of veterans returned to Spain for the fiftieth anniversary commemoration of the civil war. "*You Are History, You Are Legend*" retraces the return of the *brigadistas* to Spain for the sixtieth anniversary celebrations and documents the overwhelming welcome the Spanish people gave them. The veteran and indefatigable activist and educator Abe Osheroff has produced two documentaries. *Dreams and Nightmares* is a personal narrative, and *Art in the Struggle for Freedom: The Posters, Poetry, and Music of the Spanish Civil War* is an overview of the artistic expressions that accompanied the republic in its fight for survival. These productions are unambiguous in their support of the veterans' cause and postwar careers. Not so *Extranjeros de sí mismos*, a Spanish documentary centered on those who fought in other countries' wars. It features interviews with Italians who fought for Franco; Spanish volunteers in the Blue Division, which Franco sent to Hitler to use on the Eastern Front; as well as several *brigadistas*. There is a brief interview with Wolff, but other brigaders who were interviewed, Americans and Europeans, offer a less complimentary view of the elder veterans. They are presented as inconsolable nostalgics, unable to overcome the loss of the cause they chose to defend.

Feature films can also furnish insight. Magí Crusells makes note of many full-length feature films that include references to Americans fighting in Spain. Filmgoers may remember that Rick, Humphrey Bogart's character in *Casablanca*, admits to having fought for the republic. To date, there are no feature films centered on the Americans in Spain; however, there are films that include International Brigaders in general. Carlos Saura's *¡Ay, Carmela!* contains a climactic scene, constructed around a group of Polish *brigadistas* taken prisoner, that pays homage to the spirit of all Internationals. The East German film *Five Cartridges*, readily available on video, features a group of five men of different nationalities who must remain together under difficult circumstances to complete a special mission. Finally, Ken Loach's *Land and Freedom* must be noted. The main character and many secondary ones are foreign volunteers, but they serve in a POUMist militia unit on the Aragón front and not in the International Brigades. For many this detail goes unnoticed. Confusing all foreigners who fought for the Spanish Republic with members of the International Brigades is a common mistake that should be avoided.

One last source of information and materials on the Abraham Lincoln Brigade is the Web site of the Abraham Lincoln Brigade Archives, www.alba-valb.org, which was established in the mid-1990s. This everexpanding site allows visitors access to issues of the bulletin of the Veterans of the Abraham Lincoln Brigade, the *Volunteer*, dating from 1938 to the present. Educational modules on several subjects, the first two of which deal with the Jewish and African American participation in the brigades, are now online, and others are scheduled to appear in the near future. There is also an Internet discussion list where scholars and students from around the world exchange an average of forty messages each month on a wide variety of topics related to the Spanish Civil War.

Interpretations of the American participation in the International Brigades are varied, but one thing can be said unequivocally: the average volunteer was neither a Robert Jordan nor a dyed-in-the-wool revolutionary but was somewhere in between. All texts and sources bring understanding to a subject that remains controversial. The diversity of views of the brigaders offers a challenge to teachers and students of the conflict and of the American volunteers dedicated to the Republican cause.

Janet Pérez

Teaching Allegory and Concealment: Covert Dissent from within the Franco Camp

Historical, Political, and Cultural Context

Neither of Spain's brief, abortive experiments at democratic self-governance before the death of Francisco Franco in 1975 were popularly elected, united, democratic regimes. Neither grew out of a popular revolution or enjoyed the widespread support of an effective majority. Both the First Republic (1873–74) and the Second Republic (1931–36) came into being thanks to the monarchy's failure to cope with the country's socioeconomic problems and deteriorating political situation. The new governments inherited problems unsolved for centuries, such as quasi-feudal divisions of land and serious injustices in the distribution of wealth and power. In 1931, the church owned nearly one-third of the land in Spain, and almost one-third of Spaniards were in religious orders or the military (i.e., not engaged in production); three to four percent of the population controlled ninety-six percent of the country's capital, and ninety-six percent of the population shared the remaining four percent of the wealth. An emerging urban proletariat, increasingly radicalized by socialist, Marxist, and anarchist organizers active in Spain from the 1880s onward, continued living in poverty and ignorance, as did the peasant majority. The Second Republic never achieved internal unity and struggled for survival as a coalition of disparate—and increasingly contentious—ideologies. During the initial biennium (1931–33), the Republican-socialist government attempted most of the reforms historically associated with the republic (military, education, and land distribution), contributing to the onset of the Spanish Civil War. The military, the church, and wealthy landowners supported the status quo, backing Franco during the war and subsequent dictatorship.

Another attempted reform sought to address long-standing problems of ethnic minorities, periodic sources of separatist conflict in the nearly five centuries since the peninsula was forcibly united (see also Cazorla-Sánchez in this volume). In *España invertebrada* (1921; *Invertebrate Spain* [1937]), José Ortega y Gasset (1883–1955) focuses on Spain's perennial separatist movements (Basque and Catalan, most visibly), correctly perceiving that Spain's resurgent national divisiveness originated in the late Middle Ages. Ferdinand and Isabella, having unified the country in 1492, made the Castilian dialect Spain's official language and suppressed the languages of former kingdoms, such as Galician, Catalan, and Aragonese. Discouraged, ridiculed, marginalized, outlawed, and silenced for hundreds of years, vernacular languages and cultures nonetheless survived. They experienced a diverse cultural revival in the late nineteenth and early twentieth centuries but were crushed after the civil war. The ethnic minorities' continuing desire for autonomy underlay Franco's outlawing of Spain's minority languages and his persecution of those associated with regional nationalist movements. Franco's policy is one origin of the current Basque conflict. Perhaps the best analogy from recent European history for today's students involves the tribulations of ethnic communities in the former Yugoslavia. Contending political ideologies, divisive and repressed minorities, and perennial socioeconomic injustice constitute the relevant *circunstancia*, or context, for the Second Republic, the Spanish Civil War, and the Franco dictatorship (1939–75).

This context illuminates the explosive outbursts promoting heretofore outlawed regional autonomy movements after Franco's death (1975), the proliferation of pent-up linguistic and cultural pluralism characterizing Spain's transition to democracy. The minority cultural context provides indispensable background for understanding and teaching many of the texts by Spain's opposition writers, a body of literature epitomized by one of the most extraordinary best sellers of the Franco era, Gonzalo Torrente Ballester's *La Saga/fuga de J. B.* (1972; "J. B.'s Saga and Fugue"), which satirizes the central government's "elimination" of Galicia—and implicitly other regional-language areas—from national maps. The author, a former *galleguista* (member of the outlawed Galician independence movement), followed the example of other minority activists and joined the Falange—the only legal party under Franco—to protect his family, but he consistently wrote works that demythologize war, militarism, invasion, and the victors' manipulation of the historical record. Many of his works portray military revolts against the legitimate government that are followed by invasion, civil war, and a totalitarian dictatorship; however, Torrente often camouflaged his works as myth, fairy tale, or "history somewhere else," to suggest that his daring literary abstraction of recent Spanish history was harmless fiction unrelated to reality. Torrente used the covert rhetoric of opposition employed by many dissenters of varying ideologies who wrote under Franco, notably Galicians and Catalans prohibited from using their own languages but also Castilian writers of Republican leanings and disaffected Falangists. Many writers who were children or adolescents during the war (the "mid-century generation") reacted against the dictatorship's orgy of self-glorification and attempted to express implicit dissent by portraying alternative views of the conflict, especially from the perspective of women and children, to emphasize the war's innumerable negative effects rather than its heroics. Examples include the slightly older Dolores Medio, the brothers Juan and Luis Goytisolo, and Ana María Matute. Some writers who were young men of draft age at the war's outbreak (e.g., Camilo José Cela, Miguel Delibes, and José Luis Sampedro) served in Franco's Nationalist armies because of their families' beliefs that Franco represented law and order, as opposed to the anarchy and terrorism preceding and during the war. While these men were not Falange members, they initially supported Franco but became increasingly disenchanted with him. Protest in their works was incidental and thus more subtle than in the mid-century generation writings, in which protest was a prime fictional motive. Torrente is among the writers of concealed or muted protest who belonged to the Falange during the war, as is the idealistic poet Dionisio Ridruejo, a founding Falangist whose outspoken criticisms of the dictator resulted in a regime sentence of internal exile in Catalonia.

Teaching Literary Context: Censorship and Covert Protest

One important rule for reading Spanish works from or about the civil war or the Franco era is to remember *las Españas,* or the (many) Spains, and to recall that the former kingdoms differ not only in language, culture, and geography but also in economies, individual histories, values, aspirations, and treatment by the central government. Writers outside the majority culture (or the controlling ideology) joined the vanquished and disaffected supporters of the dictator in seeking to express covert dissent. Because the Franco regime prohibited all writing about the war other than glorification of the victors, any portrayal of a different version had to be covert, even—or especially—if authors had ties to the regime. It is equally important in the teaching and understanding of writers of dissent to remember that reading literally is insufficient and usually produces confusion and error. Many writings have allegorical dimensions, as understood in the broadest and simplest sense that allegory, as Angus Fletcher argues, "says one thing and means another" (2). Etymologically *allegory* means "other than speaking openly" (2). Expressing covert dissent, like allegory, requires saying one thing and meaning another, or not speaking openly. Objects and characters in allegorical narrative implicitly have meanings that lie outside the narrative and represent one thing in the guise of another. Because writing does not occur in a vacuum, especially writing that seeks to express covert dissent, awareness of the sociopolitical context—the locus of those meanings that lie outside the narrative itself for such writings—is indispensable. Ortega y Gasset's oft cited dictum "Yo soy yo y mi circunstancia" ("I am myself plus my circumstances") enunciates a fundamental human existential reality that also applies to literature, likewise the product of a human self and that self's particular context or circumstances. Francoist censorship varied from language to language and writer to writer and also fluctuated in its treatment of given writers at different times. Censorship's effect on writers can be very direct, as when works are banned, cut, or rewritten, or more subtle, as when writers censor themselves hoping to avoid official intervention. José M. Martínez Cachero in *La novela española entre 1939 y 1969* provides fascinating exchanges between censors and writers together with documents attesting the sometimes absurd reasons for prohibiting a work.

At the war's end, 1 April 1939, Franco sealed Spain's borders and initiated systematic purges to eliminate all those who had served the republic, including hundreds of thousands of low-level functionaries (postal employees, village schoolmasters, librarians, archivists, etc.) who had begun government service under the monarchy and merely continued during the republic. Also purged were higher-level bureaucrats, from national ministers to provincial governors, and numerous university officials and professors, especially from the fields of law and history. Associating with *rojos*

(Reds, or Communists—the regime's blanket term for all Republican supporters) and showing interest in exiles or the outlawed minority vernacular cultures (their art, music, architecture, literature, archaeology, etc.) could provoke purging and exacted penalties ranging from loss of employment or property to imprisonment or execution. Not content with criminalizing regional autonomy movements and public use of minority languages, the regime began to erase the minority cultures' existence—along with much concerning the republic—from Spain's history, destroying archival collections, purging specialized scholars, prohibiting study of regional cultures and Republican artists, and discouraging preservation of art and work on writers loyal to the republic (Miguel de Unamuno, Antonio Machado, Federico García Lorca, among many others). As the regime expunged prior history and those familiar with it, it created its own official historiography. Torrente—a history teacher—observed and reacted to all these repressive activities, allegorizing, satirizing, demythologizing, and appropriating official discourse to subvert the regime. These were among the standard techniques deployed by Torrente and nonaligned writers obliquely treating the civil war in postwar Spain.

Many writers such as Torrente and Ridruejo, often grouped by critics and literary historians with the fascists, harbored multiple motives for dissent. They wrote narratives superficially seen as pro-Falangist that nevertheless covertly subverted the movement, its ideology, and its paradigmatic figures.[1] Nonaligned writers and others sympathetic to the vanquished Republican cause also sought to express opposition without drawing censorial attention, sometimes by a red herring technique—by beginning one narrative to abandon it for a subplot, a distraction that kept the censors, as well as many readers, preoccupied with the initial narrative instead of the second. Another common ploy involved "long ago and far away" settings, which evoked fairy tale and myth and insinuated a lack of relevance for contemporary Spain. Still another device was to interrupt a subversive conversation at its most crucial point and leave a key sentence unfinished. When the sentence was resumed many pages later, most readers, censors included, failed to associate the sentence fragment with the interrupted conversation. Numerous Franco-era writings published in Spain contain multiple layers of meaning and prove on close examination to utilize baroque techniques, indirect or obscure allusions, complications of vocabulary and syntax, or omissions to mystify censors. Teachers and students might list such techniques and watch for them while reading, to facilitate understanding of the texts. Spain's threefold censorship—political, religious, and moral—was undertaken mostly by bureaucrats, military officers, and priests. Few were trained literary scholars, historians, or critics skilled in spotting such devices or identifying subtle irony, parody, and demythologization or veiled political satire and allegory. Officially nonexistent, the censors scrutinized everything printed in Spain—including not only all texts but also maps, playing cards, matchbooks, even magazine covers. Of the three censorial entities, the most powerful and dangerous was political censorship: political offenders could be jailed or even executed, and their writings and belongings were confiscated. Because the dictatorship denied censoring, writers learned by trial and error, not by government guidelines, not to criticize the government, its functionaries, or the Falange (Spanish fascist party); to refrain from negative portrayal of the church, police, or military; to avoid sympathetic depiction of the republic or its supporters; and not to present the losers' view of the war. The recent internecine conflict, mythologized and idealized by the regime, could not even be called a civil war: official rhetoric demanded the use of the term "our glorious Nationalist uprising" or "our glorious National crusade." Given the obligatory terminology, only rabid Franco supporters referred directly to the conflict. Regime propagandists unceasingly proclaimed Franco the sole alternative to Communism, the "Savior of Spain," and Radio Nacional (the only nationwide radio network) began every broadcast hour for over a quarter-century with "Gloriosos caídos por Dios y la Patria" ("Glorious heroes fallen for God and the Fatherland"), a litany of the names of those—exclusively Nationalists—fallen on that date. The mythologization of Franco and the Falange excluded positive treatment of their adversaries or of differing views.

Also prohibited were promotions of divorce, birth control, and euthanasia and depictions of adultery, premarital eroticism, and deviant sexuality. Writers were limited to glorifying the Franco rebellion and the Falange (and vilifying the legally instituted republic), evasion (as treating topics totally unrelated to Spain's contemporary political situation came to be called), and covert expression of dissent. Because the regime officially and assiduously glorified Spain's imperial past, especially the reign of Philip II (1527–98, promulgated as an official model), literature of his reign, the sixteenth-century golden age, was imitated by some, anachronisms notwithstanding. Franco's idealization of the age of empire explains movements such as postwar *garcilasismo*, the imitation of early Renaissance pastoral poetry by Garcilaso de la Vega (1501–36), whose primary attraction was its irrelevance, which rendered it safe to cultivate. Writers who refused to glorify Franco and the Falange or retreat to the

Renaissance risked problems with censorship, and those, like Torrente, with anything to hide—be it a politically unacceptable past or critical intent—exercised additional care, which made their works difficult to interpret (a direct response to *circunstancia*).

The war years and immediate postwar period, dubbed the era of *triunfalismo* ("triumphalism"), witnessed an orgy of self-glorification by the fascists, who exalted Franco, José Antonio Primo de Rivera (the Falange founder executed by Republicans early in the war), militarism, the Nationalist triumph, and Falangist and fascist values: patriotism, heroism, duty, honor, the cult of machismo and virility, courage, youth, force, discipline, violence, and brutality. These values were the essentials of the myth of fascism, and there was zero tolerance for shadings. Their totalitarian credo—"Those who are not with us are against us"—was buttressed by fear and horror of non-Catholics, Masons, Jews, homosexuals, intellectuals, drug addiction, perversion, pacifism, Communism, separatism, local autonomy, regional cultures, and dissent. The absolutist and extremist official (pro-regime) discourse lent itself to subversion: totalitarian, traditional, reactionary, patriarchal, and puritanical values provided apt models for demythologization. Many female writers—both in wartime and postwar Spain—covertly protested the Franco regime's abolition of hard-won advances for women.[2] Falangist values were better suited to propaganda than to the production of serious literature, and an enormous aesthetic gap existed between staunchly pro-Franco, Falangist writers, such as Rafael García Serrano (Pamplona, 1917–88), and nonaligned or covertly opposed writers, grouped with the Falangist writers by later critics, such as the Nobel laureate Cela (1916–2001) and the Cervantes prizewinners Delibes (1920—) and Torrente (1910–2000), among other highly respected names.[3] These three who joined Franco during the war became progressively more disillusioned. Most disaffected was Torrente, who, as a former *galleguista*, was most at risk and yet was the most daring in targeting and subverting regime ideology. Although he was long deemed pro-Franco, careful analysis of his writing demonstrates the error of such attribution.

Teachers and students alike can better appreciate writings of covert dissent as demythologization, a response to regime historiography. The intense period of mythmaking during the war and first postwar decade was part of the regime's information management and rewriting of history (see also Herzberger in this volume). Roland Barthes (*Mythologies*) remarks that "myth is a language" and "a mode of signification, a form. Myth is not defined by the object of its message, but by the way in which it utters this message" (11, 109). Myth obviously involves rhetoric but transcends speech, comprising "modes of writing or of representations, not only written discourse, but also photography, reporting, sport, shows, publicity" (110); it is well suited for use in the media. In a totalitarian state with controlled media, regime myth is a customized product of propagandistic slants (be they far right or far left), selectivity, hype, and censorship. Barthes recognizes such myth as politically conservative: "myth is on the right. . . . It takes hold of all aspects of the law, of morality, of aesthetics, of diplomacy, of household equipment, of literature, of entertainment" (148). Amplifying the truism that victors (re)write the history books, Barthes observes that the winners in historical conflicts replace the myths of the vanquished with their own, and that "it is precisely because they are historical that history can very easily suppress them" (120). Myths are intended, however, to outlast the human subject; they present an idealized, retouched portrait from which imperfections have been erased. The leader of a successful revolt or coup cannot be depicted as an average, flawed human being but must appear as a national hero, with defects and shortcomings deleted: George Washington, as "Father of His Country," cannot be portrayed as the notorious womanizer he was—an aspect silenced in favor of the perhaps apocryphal myth of the brave, truthful little boy who confessed to chopping down his father's cherry tree. Francoist propaganda created a mythic hero—austere, ascetic, Spartan, almost a monk or hermit—downplaying and omitting Franco's betrayal of the legitimate government and the atrocities countenanced in the process of his becoming Spain's "savior." Logical shortcomings that all human beings possess vanish in the myth, and the public prefers the retouched mythic portrait to imperfect reality. In response to regime mythmaking, Torrente—as a historian and teacher of history—chronicles the relation between mythmaking and historiography and Franco's transformation from rebel general to savior of Spain.[4]

Teaching Texts in Context: Patterns, Structures, and Examples of Covert Dissent

Torrente's entire career evinces his deep, abiding preoccupation with the relation between man and myth. Teacher and student identification of demythologization and its strategies facilitates and enhances the reading of works of covert opposition and dissent, becoming a sine qua non for proper interpretation, study, and teaching. Torrente employed variations of two basic techniques: first, what he termed *destripar el mito* ("disemboweling the myth" or other classic models) and, second, allegorically abstracting and recontextualizing essentials of the civil war (i.e., rebellion by an ambitious, self-promoting officer who overthrows the legally constituted government and becomes a tyrannical dictator), transferring the core plot to another time, another place. Disemboweling the myth involved preserving the skeleton of well-known mythic events (or structure of classic models) and developing characters (mere outlines in the original model) whose vile motivations for epic actions tarnish their heroism. Circumstances vary, but Torrente replicated this pattern numerous times, beginning during the war from inside the Falange communications center in Burgos. Already repeatedly chastised for journalistically defending liberal positions, Torrente published *Javier Mariño* (1943), his first novel. The censors had previously rejected the novel because of its unsatisfactory resolution; they felt it should have a happy ending, politically and religiously. Torrente rewrote the novel, conforming (with deliberate ideological vagueness) to the censorial requirements by adding a new ending, but *Javier Mariño* was nonetheless banned—for other reasons—and sequestered from bookstores by police raids. Spoiled, self-indulgent, pedantic, and naive Javier, a dissolute, hedonistic, egotistical, socially conservative, prejudiced, macho, upper-class playboy and pseudointellectual, symbolizes the (preconversion) Falangist. Too self-centered and superficial to commit himself fully either to a woman or to a cause, Javier seduces and later abandons Magdalena, escaping the pending war by moving to Latin America and leaving her to commit suicide. In the rewritten ending Javier converts to Franco's crusade and decides to marry Magdalena, return to Spain, and join the Falange in defending the radical right. Unnoticed was the fact that Javier is a most unattractive poster child for any party, a parody of the hero of fascist and Falangist novels who, living a bohemian existence, experiences an epiphany, embraces the Franco cause, and thereby resolves all religious and other quandaries. Torrente's hero is so unappealing—Javier is a real jerk—that his joining the fascist cause actually argues against it.

Torrente wrote more works lampooning regime myths during the 1940s that demonstrate his other techniques and illustrate the range of his skill and daring.[5] In *La princesa durmiente va a la escuela* ("Sleeping Beauty Goes to School"), a continuation of the fairy tale, Beauty has been sleeping for five centuries instead of one, awaiting the prince's kiss.

Employing the mock-heroic mode, Torrente targets the pomp and circumstance of state ceremonials in "Minimuslandia" (a mask for Spain, the term deliberately opposes Spain's lost international territory and power to the regime's dream of recovering the age of empire). He parodies the regime's vulgarization of traditions and exaggerated protocol (highly visible in Franco's official appearances) and takes aim at speculation and profiteering by highly placed government officials (many Franco minions were becoming millionaires in the black market). In this ferocious political satire, Torrente exploits the premise that the princess, who fell asleep before Luther or the Reformation, will awaken in the twentieth century with the mentality of the fifteenth and therefore need to be given elaborately staged history lessons re-creating significant events of the past five hundred years. The novel satirizes both regime historiography and the conflicting interest groups vying to control its texts: the princess's education is hotly disputed by rival groups, and the whole affair turns into a Hollywood extravaganza. Beauty's education goes awry after she views the spectacle of the French Revolution and joins the proletariat's march on the palace. Beauty and the Prince (who dies trying to protect her) are machine-gunned by professional agitators hired by the ruling party to prevent the king from establishing contact with the populace—an allusion to the fascist doctrine justifying excessive force.

Torrente's little-known tale "Gerineldo," first published in 1944 in a long-defunct periodical, exemplifies the aesthetics and subversive charge of works by certain reputedly pro-Franco authors whose sympathies inclined to opposition. "Gerineldo" subverts another classical model, the chivalric tale or epic, and alludes explicitly to Charlemagne, Roland, the Carolingian empire, and the twelve peers of France (who represent Spain's powerful aristocracy). The emperor and his secretary fret over the probability of a popular revolution in a deliberately anachronistic spoof of the Franco regime's terror of Reds and social revolution. The emperor, torn between paternal love and outraged honor after discovering the love between his daughter Berta and the page Gerineldo, turns for advice to his secretary, Eginardo (who typifies the intellectual villains invented by Torrente to function as red herrings and distract censors imbued with fascist contempt for the intelligentsia). Concealing his personal desire for revenge—Berta spurned him—Eginardo advises Charlemagne to marry the pair and make Gerineldo a peer of the realm, thereby rescuing the emperor's honor. Before the marriage takes place, a "messenger" from the empire's eastern-most extremes arrives beseeching aid against invading barbarians, and

Eginardo suggests that Gerineldo command the defending army—a convenient, honorable way to eliminate the page. News of the conflict is sparse, and rumors of Gerineldo's fabulous victories proliferate; "spontaneous" popular ballads commemorating his heroic deeds are composed, suspiciously, in "good university Latin" (168; my trans.). Eventually returning as an arrogant, victorious hero, Gerineldo recounts his search for a phantom enemy and his accidental and enraging discovery that all was a ruse to discredit him in Berta's eyes. He tells how he slew the herald who inadvertently revealed the plot, struggled against desire to burn Paris to the ground in vengeance, and convinced his men to "plunge into the frozen steppes and seek out the enemy in their homes" (172; my trans.), slaughtering a peaceful populace in their beds. Gerineldo is proclaimed a count and a peer of the realm and marries the princess.

The obvious, superficial resemblances of the story to the quest pattern model of the chivalric romance and fairy tale insinuate its lack of relevance to postwar Spain. The unappealing hero incorporates many Falangist values, as did Javier Mariño. One obvious ideological target is the control of information (censorship), including Eginardo's management of news and use of disinformation to create the image of a false superhero and render Gerineldo an impostor if he lived to return. More significant, the putative savior and heroic defender of the fatherland murdered another country's (or regime's) peaceful citizenry with no motive other than personal aggrandizement (a probable allusion to Hitler and World War II). Seemingly sanctified by formulaic presentation, Gerineldo's story is but one more tale of slaughter, rape, and pillage. Oblique allusions to medieval glorification of war and militarism (e.g., "Blessed be the Lord of Hosts, who has sent to us an enemy" [168; my trans.]) parallel fascist and Falangist values and suggest that those espousing similar beliefs in the present are modern barbarians.[6] A full appreciation of Torrente's skill and daring would require juxtaposing "Gerineldo" with *triunfalismo* models, but an understanding of his works—as well as the works of other authors writing in Spain during the 1940s who sought to express covert dissent—can be enhanced by reading against the grain to tease out the covert targeting and satire of the Falange and the regime.

Notes

1. Ironically, exiled Republican writers (Francisco Ayala, Ramón Sender, and Max Aub, among many others) who hoped their works would reach the Spanish public likewise resorted to allegory, seeking to hoodwink the censors. Prime exam-

ples are Ayala's short story collections *La cabeza del cordero* and *Los usurpadores*. This ploy failed, despite Ayala's masterfully executed and camouflaged subversion of Falangist myths, because exiled authors' political ties to the republic automatically disqualified them from publishing in Spain.

2. This topic requires a book, but a brief listing of such writers includes Rosa Chacel, Carmen Conde, Mercè Rodoreda, Ana María Matute, Dolores Medio, and—from the earliest postwar period—Carmen Martín Gaite, as well as supposedly pro-regime writers such as Elena Quiroga, and Carmen Laforet.

3. Adequate treatment of this topic likewise deserves a book, perhaps a multivolume set. Significant voices of opposition include Antonio Buero Vallejo, Alfonso Sastre, and Carlos Muñiz (to mention only some first-rate dramatists successfully employing allegory) and the poets Gabriel Celaya, Blas de Otero, Ángela Figuera, Gloria Fuertes, and the Nobel laureate Vicente Aleixandre. Most of these writers began writing before or during the war but did not become well known until later.

4. Although Torrente's daring brought repeated fines and sanctions (including the loss of several positions and a prohibition from publishing under his name so that he was obliged to spend a number of years in the United States), the author eventually garnered numerous literary prizes, nearly all of them after the passing of Franco and his regime. In addition to receiving two or three national prizes for literature and two prestigious critics' prizes, Torrente was awarded the significant Cervantes Prize, which is given by consensus of the national language academies of the twenty-three countries where Spanish is spoken. The Premio Cervantes recognizes lifetime achievement and is comparable to a Nobel Prize in Literature in the Spanish language.

5. *El golpe de estado de Guadalupe Limón*, Torrente's second novel (1945) and first major incursion into humor, satire, and burlesque, portrays revolution in a fictitious South American country. Investigating the formation, culmination, decay, and destruction of a historical myth (and paralleling official mythologization of Franco), Torrente incorporates numerous caricatures and downplays plot similarities with 1930s events in Spain. Other demythologizing works include his drama *El retorno de Ulises* (1946) and the novelette *Ifigenia* (1949). *Ifigenia* deflates such Falangist values as exalted nationalism, close ties between religion and the state, glorification of war, exaltation of violence and militarization, idealization of the homeland, and sacrifice of the individual to the interests of the state.

6. Gerineldo is a reductive parody of characters created by "triumphalist" writers, such as in García Serrano's *La fiel infantería* and *Eugenio, o la proclamación de la primavera*, two texts that unabashedly glorify militarism, violence, and slaughter. For a full comparison of "Gerineldo" and a "triumphalist" Falangist text, see my "Fascist Models and Literary Subversion."

Michael Iarocci

War and the Work of Poetry: Issues in Teaching Spanish Poetry of the Civil War

In the closing lines of a well-known poem from his *España en el corazón* (*Spain in My Heart*), the Chilean poet Pablo Neruda bears witness to the profound transformation that poetic discourse in Spain underwent with the advent of the civil war. "You must be asking," he writes from Spain to a distant, imagined reader, "why does his poetry / not speak to us of dreaming, of the leaves, / of the great volcanoes of his native country?" (Morales 194; all translations are my own). Neruda's answer is formulated as a simple but powerful exhortation to this hypothetical reader, an imperative that is repeated three times as it spills over the last five lines of the poem:

> Come see the blood in the streets,
> come see
> the blood in the streets,
> come see the blood
> in the streets!

> (Morales 194)

In a similar vein, the Peruvian César Vallejo closes the series of poems he dedicated to the war—*España, aparta de mí este cáliz* ("Spain, Let This Cup Pass from Me")—with expressions of a foreboding sense that the future of all peoples was at stake in the Spanish conflagration: "If mother Spain falls . . . / Go out, children of the world; go find her!" (482).

Together, Neruda and Vallejo—the best-known Spanish American poets to respond to the crisis—offer a rich body of work that testifies to the symbolism of the war for artists of the Spanish-speaking world. For both poets the conflict represented a clear clash of political principles, fascism versus democracy and social revolution, but as part of the literary culture of Republican Spain—Neruda had lived in Madrid, Vallejo was in frequent dialogue with Spanish poets—their work also conveys a very personal sense of their commitment to the cause. *España en el corazón* and *España, aparta de mí este cáliz* register a pain informed not only by each poet's political solidarity with the republic but also by the deep linguistic and cultural affinities they felt with a symbolic motherland that had exploded into fratricidal violence. In poems such as "Madrid (1936)," "Canto a las madres de los milicianos muertos" ("I Sing to the Mothers of Dead Militiamen"), and "Madrid (1937)," Neruda expresses solidarity with his Spanish comrades and inveighs against Franco's uprising as a brutal act of treason. For his part, Vallejo's fifteen-poem series, first published by Republican soldiers in 1937, ranges from hymns ("Himno a los voluntarios de la República" ["Hymn to the Volunteers of the Republic"]) to commentary on specific battles ("Invierno en la batalla de Teruel" ["Winter at the Battle of Teruel"]) to elegies to the fallen ("Pequeño responso a un héroe de la república" ["Small Prayer to a Hero of the Republic"]).

As examples of the urgent, violent, and unavoidable *hic et nunc* that the war became for writers, these poems speak to a series of fundamental issues that students inevitably confront as they approach the poetry written between 1936 and 1939. What was poetry's role in the bloodstained streets of Spain? What purposes did poetry serve as the Spanish polity tore itself apart until dictatorship finally put an end to war? In the midst of the most harrowing of conditions, what did poetry mean and how did it matter? That these questions tend to be posed and answered primarily in a sociohistorical register gestures to the centrality of the war itself as the overarching referent of the poetry of these years. The war demanded a kind of engagement that put an end to the waning *vanguardista* aesthetics of the years leading up to the conflagration. Already by the early 1930s the need to rehumanize poetry through a more explicitly social focus had become a topic of frequent debate among Spanish-language poets (Lechner 120–38; Cano Ballesta 201–12; García de la Concha 13–103). The outbreak of war put the question to rest definitively, and for Spanish poets, the kind of explanation Neruda and Vallejo offered international readers was not necessary; the fact of the war was all too painfully obvious. To appreciate fully the significance of the wartime shift toward a poetics of "direct" social engagement (Puccini 70), it is useful for students to recall the numerous projects—*modernismo, poesía pura, gongorismo, creacionismo, ultraísmo, surrealismo, superrealismo*, and so on—that from the *fin de siglo* to the early 1930s had left their imprint on Spanish and Spanish American poetry. Against such a backdrop, the simple but profound meaning of the return of historical reference, that function of language that had so often been suspended, eschewed, or subverted by the modernist pursuit of aesthetic autonomy, might begin to be understood more deeply. To be sure, poetry did not simply turn to a facile realist idiom— the tropological life of lyric discourse remained—but its object was no longer in question. The poetry of the Spanish Civil War written by Spaniards was unabashedly and urgently about the world, a world in violent conflict, and such historical context thoroughly conditions the meaning and teaching of this poetry.

Precisely because the poetry of the war is so intimately bound to its historical moment, the reprinting of civil war poetry in modern editions poses a number of challenges for contemporary readers. Students often encounter this material in a form that symbolically excises poetry from the war. Carefully prepared texts, anthologies, and translations preserve this body of work, but modern editions also inadvertently cleanse the poems of context. The poetry of the war did not appear solely in journals: it was shouted across trench lines; printed on postcards, leaflets, and posters; painted on walls; sung at battles; and declaimed on loudspeakers at political rallies. It was part of the conflagration it sought to address, and its context of enunciation and reception was more often than not public and popular (G. Díaz-Plaja 2–12). The poems of the civil war were symbolic acts within the war, a dimension of the work that can easily be overlooked in twenty-first-century university classrooms. Where time permits, a reconstruction of context, such as the video documentary *Art in the Struggle for Freedom*, directed by Abe Osheroff, can be especially useful to students.

At the same time, it is worth recalling the degree to which Spanish Civil War poetry is largely an ex post facto construct. From 1936 to 1939, poetry, like most Spanish cultural production, was Republican or Nationalist before it was of the civil war. As almost all scholarship on the subject notes, the field of poetic writing was split along the same basic ideological lines that divided the nation. The attempt to gather this poetry together today as part of a unified field of inquiry is consequently not without its historical ironies, and teachers of the poetry of the Spanish Civil War will face a number of difficult questions as they approach this material: To what degree should both sides be represented? How far should one's own ideological commitments bear on the selection of materials? What are the ethical and political implications of a neutral approach to the poetry of the war? What kind of interpretive contract does war poetry hold out for readers who were not a part of the war? A productive way of dealing with such questions is to transform them into objects of reflection in the classroom; that is, to invite students to struggle with the issues themselves. Students may then begin to appreciate the degree to which reading the poetry of the Spanish Civil War, for all its historical distance, is a dynamic and disquieting contemporary activity.

Simply determining the corpus of poetry to be considered presents a significant challenge. While the work of some fifty Spanish poets has over the years come to make up the pool that is most frequently scrutinized, poetry was a massive, popular phenomenon during the war. On the Republican side, there were close to five thousand poets writing in the war years. The first year of the war witnessed the creation of over five hundred publications attached to the militias that had organized to resist the Nationalist military uprising. Many militias often had their own journals, along with their own poet-combatants. Of the poetry that appeared in the more than thirteen hundred wartime publications, only fifteen percent was penned by poets of prior renown. Fully half of the poems in the Republican zone were written by anarchists, many of whom rejected the very notion of authorship in the name of a more radically democratic, communal conception of cultural production. One-fifth of the poetry of the war was either anonymous, initialed, or published under a pseudonym (Salaün, "Poetas" 182–83).

There is thus an unavoidable tension between, on the one hand, the pedagogical imperative to select individual, representative Spanish poets and, on the other, the fact that such a selection often runs counter to the communal conception of poetry that informed a considerable portion of the poetic production of the war years. Echoing this tension are the competing values that often coexist in wartime poetry. That most of the poetry of the civil war was openly political, ideologically committed, and often propagandistic raises the question of the relation between the aesthetic and the ideological, between art and politics. While for some, "from today's perspective, the turn to social and political poetry before and during the Civil War [has] an impoverishing effect" (Debicki 53), for others, a fundamental effect of the poetry of the civil war is precisely to problematize "today's perspective"—and the putative independence of aesthetic appreciation—by recognizing there are times when other values might legitimately make stronger claims. Indeed, this problem—the role of aesthetic judgment in the reception of war poetry—might be a useful topic for classroom discussion. To what extent ought the question, Is it a good poem? guide inquiry into poetry of war? Can a poem about war be beautiful? Should one even ask? What kinds of knowledge do these questions enable? What do they disregard?

Such tensions mirror divisions within the cultural production of the war years themselves, as reflected in the two most renowned Republican journals of the time, *Hora de España* ("Spain's Hour") and *El Mono Azul* ("The Blue Overall"). The first gathered some of the most established poets of the day and published work that tended toward a high cultural aesthetic, even as it contemplated the war. In the statement of purpose that accompanied its first issue, it was clear that *Hora de España* meant to bear witness to the continuity of culture in the republic, despite the conflagration. Its aim was thus to publish writings that,

> moving beyond the national area, might be understood by comrades or sympathizers spread throughout the world, people who do not understand by shouting, the way household relatives do; in short, Hispanophiles who will find great happiness upon seeing that Spain continues its intellectual life or the life of its artistic creation in the midst of the gigantic conflict in which it is fighting. ("Propósito" 5)

In contrast, *El Mono Azul*, founded by the Asociación de Intelectuales Antifascistas, tended to publish poetry that was more decidedly populist. Although the journal also gathered established poets, at the prompting of Rafael Alberti the center pages of *El Mono Azul* were dedicated exclusively to ballads written from the battlefronts.

The publication of ballads in *El Mono Azul* was symptomatic of a broader poetic tendency, for, overwhelmingly, most of the poetry of the war was written in the *romance*, or ballad, form. The *romance*, students should be reminded, had been the traditional mode of narrative poetry in Spain from the time of the medieval epic. This history, along with the ballad's open-ended structure and flexible, assonant rhyme scheme, made it a natural narrative vehicle for poets who aimed to record and comment on deeds of battle. Several collections appeared during the war years, such as the *Romancero de la guerra civil, Serie I* (1936), the *Romancero popular de la revolución* (1937), and the *Romancero general de la guerra de España* (1937). These texts readily display the ethically dichotomous discourse traditionally associated with the mythologizing potential of epic. Indeed, among the more predictable discursive features of this corpus is the Manichaean universe it postulates:

> [G]ood and evil, without the slightest possible nuance, without the slightest mediation. Good must triumph because that is its nature, its destiny. . . . In this titanic struggle between two irreducible forces, poetry is not merely song, or chronicle or subjective impression. It is above all a decisive weapon in determining the end results of battles. It maintains the morale of the rearguard and it stimulates the combatants. (Salaün, "La poesía" 807)

In their encounters with the poetry of the civil war, students can reflect more broadly on a defining feature of the rhetoric of organized violence, the invocation of moral absolutes to authorize wartime agendas. Its power to galvanize stems largely from its capacity to simplify, and as political complexity is effaced, the ethical imperative to act seems to trump all else. As Víctor García de la Concha concludes, the poetry of the wartime *romancero* "served as a weapon of combat, facilitating the spread of exemplary events, clarifying the ideological motives of the war, haranguing, disqualifying the enemy" (136). A rich compendium of some of the most popular poems of the war years, the wartime *romanceros* offer students an intriguing and often understudied point of entry into the subject.

For instructors who choose to focus on the more canonical poets, several modern anthologies are available (Bauer; Cunningham; Hernando; Morales). The commonly anthologized poets of the republic include Alberti, Vicente Aleixandre, Manuel Altolaguirre, José Bergamín, Luis Cernuda, León Felipe, Juan Gil-Albert, Miguel Hernández, Antonio Machado, José Moreno Villa, and Emilio Prados. The Nationalist poets most often evoked are Agustín de Foxá, Manuel Machado, Eduardo Marquina, José María Pemán, Dionisio Ridruejo, and Luis Rosales. Despite considerable variations from poet to poet, the poetics of each side of the conflagration tend to echo the rhetorical and ideological features that defined Nationalist and Republican cultural politics more generally. (See part 2 in this volume.) On the Nationalist side, it is not difficult to identify a cohesive poetic program that reflects a monolithic vision of Spanish culture, a vision centered largely on the exaltation of Spain's imperial, Catholic past and the anticipated return of its splendor. Many Spanish fascists conceived of their movement in decidedly poetic terms and explicitly opposed their conception of poetry to a vilified Marxist-anarchist materialism (García de la Concha 114). For many Nationalists, the very concept of poetry was coterminous with the imagined grandeur of an essentialized national Catholic tradition.

José María Pemán's long allegorical epic *Poema de la bestia y el ángel* (1938; "Poem of the Beast and the Angel") is among the more iconic examples of such poetics and as such functions well in the classroom. Divided into three extensive *cantos*, the poem charts the struggle between the angelic forces of an eternal, glorious, traditional Spain and the dark powers of a Red, Judeo-Masonic beast that threatens to destroy Spanish authenticity. The work ends with the promise of a new, Nationalist Spain triumphantly sailing into its providential historical destiny: "Golden pilots of the New Spain / Raise your oars! / To the sight of God!" (Pemán 201). The poem's anti-Semitism, evocation of the iconography of empire, and figuration of the war as the latest instantiation of Spanish *reconquista* make it an intriguing case study in Nationalist poetics. Working with this text, students should be able to chart some of the key features of Nationalist rhetoric.

Indeed, the poetry of Nationalist Spain offers clear articulations of an iconography that students may have encountered in other media. To cite one example, Manuel Machado's sonnet of praise "Francisco Franco" succinctly couples the trope of the Reconquest with quasi-messianic imagery that figures the soon-to-be dictator as a force of national redemption and regeneration. As a symbolic inversion of common wartime images of battlefields strewn with the bodies of the dead, Machado's sonnet is a good example of how the epic, myth-making functions of the poetry of the war often erased the very essence of combat: injury, death, and destruction. The poem offers instructors the occasion to reflect with their students on how representations of war often sanitize the defining feature of armed conflagration—organized killing—by recoding material conflict as a symbolic struggle of values. (For more extensive commentary on this poem, see Whiston in this volume.) For teachers interested in linking such inquiry to the present, examples taken from recent discourses of war—such as post-9/11, antiterrorist discourse; the rhetoric of the 2001 Afghan war; the various framings of the United States–Iraqi conflict—demonstrate the continuity of this rhetorical strategy. Nationalist poetry is replete with such examples, and several collections were published in the later stages of the war. Among them are Jorge Villén's *Antología poética del alzamiento* (1939) and the *Corona de sonetos en honor de José Antonio Primo de Rivera* (1939). If instructors prefer a narrower selection of poems, in addition to the poems cited above, the following is a recommended cross section from Andrés Morales's *España reunida: Antología poética de la guerra civil española*: "Trincheras del frente de Madrid" (Foxá; "Trenches on the Madrid Front"); "La niña de Talavera" (Pemán; "The Little Girl of Talavera"); "Soneto a José Antonio que descubrió, expresó y defendió la verdad de España. Murió por ella" (Rosales; "Sonnet to José Antonio, Who Discovered, Expressed, and Defended Spain's Truth: He Died for It"); "Al 18 de Julio" (Ridruejo; "To the 18th of July").

The poetics of Republican writers were much less cohesive than those of Nationalist writers. Critics have nevertheless tended to organize this material into two basic divisions. The first corresponds roughly to the divide between high cultural notions of poetry and populist-revolutionary conceptions. This division is normally framed as a contrast between amateur and professional poets, between the ballad tradition and more expressly lyric poetic forms, or between "direct" and more "reflexive" poetry (Lechner 153). The second common division is diachronic, for Republican poets tended to move from a poetics of urgent engagement in the first years of the war to a more meditative and even nostalgic mode as the republic's defeat began to loom large. Regardless of how one conceptualizes such differences, it is clear that the very idea of poetry and of art more generally came under profound scrutiny in the social revolutions of Republican Spain. As anarchists, Communists, and other trade unionists dreamed of (and sometimes briefly established) an entirely new social order, it stood to reason that the role of poetry and the poet would be thoroughly reshaped as well.

Whether Republican poetry met this challenge is a much debated question. For Serge Salaün, one of the most assiduous researchers of the Republican *romancero* tradition, virtually all the canonical poets of the republic fell short of translating revolutionary politics into a new poetic idiom. Salaün notes that, in the republic, as the war progresses, "an apolitical conception of art, the supremacy of the individual and of instinct over conscience, the vision of the artist as a seat of divine inspiration, dominate once again." This turn, he concludes, together with the aesthetic elitism of the intellectuals of *Hora de España*, limited most of the republic's famous poets to "a traditional and bourgeois conception of culture and of art" (*Poesía* 365). Regardless of one's position on such matters,

Salaün's critique raises an important point that is fruitful to discuss with students, for it is a reminder that the expressive self—so central to the traditional idea of lyric—sat in uneasy tension with revolutionary programs that saw individualism as part of an oppressive social order they aimed to transform. As students read the poets of the republic, they might focus on the various selves constituted by the poems to begin to apprehend some of the political valences of poetic subjectivity. More broadly still, students might reflect on the ways in which selfhood can be thought of as a political category. Instructors who choose to teach Pemán's *Poema de la bestia y el ángel* as an example of Nationalist poetics will find Miguel Hernández's *Viento del pueblo: Poesía en la guerra* (1937; "Wind of the People: Poetry in War") an illuminating Republican counterpoint. Among the most celebrated books of poems written by a Spaniard during the war years, *Viento del pueblo* gathers together the poetry that Hernández wrote during the initial stages of the war. The anthology includes a wide range of poetic subgenres—elegies, satires, and calls to combat. Some of his most popular poems, also in Morales—"El niño yuntero" ("The Ploughboy"), "Madrid," and "Canción del esposo soldado" ("Song of the Soldier Husband")—were broadcast as part of Radio Valencia's wartime programming. The opening of Hernández's title poem, "Vientos del pueblo," provides a useful contrast with the poetic universe of Pemán, and students gain from juxtaposing the two projects explicitly. Hernández's first verses underscore the themes of solidarity and collective struggle that characterize much of the poetry of the republic. Distinctions between the individual and the communal are suggestively blurred; indeed, the figures of the poet and the people are almost fused:

> Winds of the people take me,
> winds of the people pull me along,
> they spread my heart out in pieces
> and they fan my throat on the winds.

> (Morales 79)

Appealing to the various regional peoples of Spain, the poem is a call to resistance against those who would enslave:

> They want to put yokes on you
> . . . .
> yokes that you should leave
> broken on their backs.

> (Morales 81)

Labor, the land, and the rural world are the more common features of the poet's lexicon, and as the poem closes, Hernández proclaims his willingness to die for the Republican cause, making clear that for him poetry itself is part of the struggle:

> Singing, I await death,
> for there are nightingales that sing
> on top of rifles
> and in the middle of battles.

> (Morales 81)

Set against Pemán's triumphal ending, Hernández's closing offers an instructive and historically poignant contrast, particularly in the light of the death in Franco's prisons that awaited the poet after the war.

In addition to the *romancero* verses and the Republican journals, several poetic anthologies were published in the republic during the war years. Of particular note are *Poetas en la España leal* (1937; "Poets in Loyal Spain"), which commemorated the Second International Congress of Anti-fascist Writers, and *Homenaje a las Brigadas Internacionales* (1938; "Homage to the International Brigades"). Although brief (fourteen poems), the latter publication gathers poems of appreciation for the departing International Brigades. It is a rich resource for those who wish to focus on how Spaniards of the republic responded to the international solidarity movement. For instructors who, again, prefer to focus on fewer representative poems, the following texts in Morales's anthology will provide a good initial overview of some of the better-known poems from the republic. They are poems that exhort (Claudio Rodríguez's "Llamo a la juventud" ["I Call the Young"]); denounce (José Bergamín's "El Traidor Franco" ["Franco the Traitor"]); mythologize (Alberti's "Romance a la defensa de Madrid" ["Ballad of the Defense of Madrid"]); dream of agrarian, proletarian utopias (Serrano Plaja's "Federación de Trabajadores de la Tierra" ["Federation of Workers of the Earth"]); and bear witness to loss, as in Antonio Machado's meditation on the assassination of Federico García Lorca, "El crimen fue en Granada" ("The Crime Was in Granada"). These are poems in which testimony—the need to tell the story—remains a central value. Given that the republic was crushed and symbolically erased from Spanish national life for much of the twentieth century, the testimonial dimension of Republican poetry is difficult to overstate. Moreover, as the number of surviving participants on both sides of the civil war diminishes each year (see Herrmann in this volume), the importance of such poetic witness seems destined to grow.

In courses that take up the gender politics of Republican Spain, it is worth noting that despite high profile female political leaders (e.g., Dolores Ibárruri, or La Pasionaria; Federica Montseny; Dolores Bargalló) and early, iconic images of the revolutionary *miliciana* (e.g., Lina Odena), the poetry of the war that has been canonized remains overwhelmingly male-authored. The published work of the female poets of the so-called Generation of 1927—Concha Méndez, Rosa Chacel, Ernestina de Champourcín, Carmen Conde—has only recently begun to receive critical attention (see Miró; Pérez, "Voces"), and within this body of work poems dedicated to the conflagration have rarely made it into anthologies of war poetry. A fascinating series of prose poems by Conde, for example, decries the war from a pacifist perspective that emphasizes grieving mothers, widows, and orphaned children. Entitled *Mientras los hombres mueren* ("While Men Die"), the collection conceives of reproduction and motherhood as the very antitheses of war:

> You women who wander in mourning because hatred brought death to your lap, refuse to conceive children so long as men do not efface war from the world! Refuse to birth the man who tomorrow will kill the man who is the son of your sister, the woman who will birth another man to kill your brother! (210)

Much of the work that appeared in the publications of women's revolutionary organizations—such as the Agrupación de Mujeres Antifascistas, the Unió de Dones de Catalunya, and Mujeres Libres—is still unavailable in modern editions. A recent exception is the poetry of Lucía Sánchez Saornil, a major feminist thinker in the anarchist movement who was responsible for editing the *Romancero de Mujeres Libres* (1937; "Ballads of Free Women"). Her poems were republished in 1996. Where library holdings include firsthand material such as Saornil's *Romancero*, students can find a rich and relatively uncommented-on body of work by revolutionary women. An excellent introduction to the subject is Mary Nash's *Defying Male Civilization: Women in the Spanish Civil War* (see also "Resources," "Poetry," in this volume).

Independent of the particular path instructors choose to pursue through this material, it is clear that the poetry of the Spanish Civil War can productively be linked to many of the questions that inform literary and cultural studies today: questions of canon and of aesthetic judgment, questions regarding art and politics, the enigma of poetic subjectivity and its meanings, the workings of myth and memory, and so on. Such is, in part, the critical reflection that Spanish poetry of the civil war calls for today, and as teachers of this material, we must invite our students first to hear and then perhaps to heed such a call. In doing so, students may realize the relevance today of reading Spanish poetry of the civil war, not only because the poetry of the war continues to pose compelling moral, political, and aesthetic questions but also because armed conflagration remains very much a part of our present. As the opening years of the twenty-first century have shown in no uncertain terms, the work of critically mediating between poetry—or culture more generally—and the collective violence we call war is timely indeed.

James Whiston

"Committed"(?) Writing in the Spanish Civil War

Studying the literature of the Spanish Civil War offers a useful benchmark by which to judge how specialists generally teach literary criticism. Whereas in most works of literature we search for such qualities as complexity, subtlety, and depth of resonance, in the literature of the Spanish Civil War we are more often drawn to the striking encapsulation of a position or situation, a richly suggestive and effective expression that has been sloganized by the genius of the artist for the purposes of the war. Miguel Hernández's line from his "Song of the Married Soldier," in his 1937 collection *Viento del pueblo* ("Wind of the People") is just such an instance: "It is needful to kill to continue with living" (*Obra completa* 1: 602).[1] This line, probably a reflection of Hernández's view of the war, cuts through all debate about the rights and wrongs of taking life, whether offensively or defensively. It also dramatizes the soldier's battlefront song to his wife, telling her why he is fighting in the war. The poem celebrates married sexuality, its ensuing procreation, the strength and delicacy of feminine nurture, the exhuberance of youth, the disdain of death, and the exaltation of heroism. It advertises the youthful vigor of the six-year-old republic. The personal experience and example of the young soldier capture the republic's defense of the rights to life, liberty, and happiness. The poem is thus a complete lyrical expression of the political ideal of the republic.

So far so good. It is still clear to students, however, that the poem presents a very personal account of the war. This subjectivity is probably due to the very circumstances of the conflict, the separation, deprivation, and imagined closeness of death that fostered fear, frustration, and loneliness. Given such uncertainties and fear; the lack of the established, ordered civilities of society; and the absence of even basic creature comforts, it is astonishing that writers like Antonio Machado and Hernández wrote with such expressiveness throughout the war. One thing that kept them writing was the sense of continuity with their cultural and intellectual past, that is, a determination not to allow fascism to disrupt their culture. These two Republican writers offer a fascinating contrast in their responses to the crisis. The creative, personal immersion of Hernández in the conflict is offset by the perspectivist, removed stance Machado adopted to see the issues more clearly and to reject the attitude of ivory-tower intellectuals, those who placed themselves above the fray.

The republic's ethos depended on pluralism for its identity. Simply being oneself, and remaining loyal to the republic, was a guarantee to both the artist and the republic of the kind of freedom of expression that underpinned the different existences and identities of the poet and the state. This espousal of liberal humanist freedom became more of a necessity for the republic once Franco's threat to the state became manifest, since, for both civic and political reasons, the republic was aligned with the parliamentary democracies of Britain and France, against the Axis powers who supported Franco. Any conflicts that emerged in Nationalist Spain during the civil war concerned differences in strategy and temperament: Franco's command was broadly accepted as the necessary means of victory. This unity is evident in the two Nationalist poems by Manuel Machado and Dionisio Ridruejo that I discuss later. The republic, on the other hand, was riven by faction—geographical, political, and ideological—and could never sustain the single command that it needed to overcome Franco. This pluralism in the wartime republic strengthened artistic activity, but the gain from such activities could only make a distant contribution to the war effort. The value was long-term and in the image of the artist's freedom of expression in a pluralist republic rather than in the expressions of pro-Republican sentiment. Even in the poetic wartime work of the militant Hernández, the creative impulse still takes precedence over direct political rhetoric.

The republic itself was a kind of creative experiment that tuned in well with artistic endeavor. Utopianism rather than republicanism was probably a better description of the official Spanish state from 1931 to 1939. Antonio Machado's witty comment on the dangers of rote learning, on the need not just to know but to reflect on knowledge, appeared in the second item in his contribution to *Hora de España*'s first issue: "He learned so many things—my teacher wrote, on the death of an erudite friend of his—that he had no time to think about any of them" (*Poesía* 4: 2312). While this anecdote might bring a smile of satisfaction to the lips of any liberal humanist, it requires a substantial leap to extract from it the conclusion that not to reflect on and examine one's knowledge leaves one open to the messianic claims of those in political authority, including the dictators. Liberal humanist writing at its most characteristic, this anecdote leaves it to the reader to derive conclusions other than the one that is immediately available in the text.

As this brief extract shows, the writer's agenda is only tangentially relevant to the defense of the republic: what is even more striking is that *Hora de España* was funded by the Ministry of Propaganda. Any attempt, therefore, to understand "representations" of the Spanish Civil War has to come to terms with Republican writings that did not always or even usually work directly in singleminded pursuit of military victory.

Antonio Machado's sonnet to Colonel Enrique Líster (*Poesía* 2: 826) is a good litmus test to consider the balance between poetic expressiveness and the demands of the war effort. Along with Machado's poem on the death of Federico García Lorca, the sonnet has become one of the best-known pieces of writing in Spanish to emerge from the civil war. When Machado wrote the sonnet, Líster was the principal military officer in the Republican army: the poem refers to the river Ebro because of its strategic importance in what was to be the last great battle of the Spanish Civil War, during the summer of 1938. The sonnet's subject matter—the poet's reply to a letter he received from the military man—illustrates the republic's desired alliance among artists, intellectuals, and those who pursued the war at the strategic and military level.

First, one notices how Machado integrates the personal note into his poem with the use of the opening possessive adjective "Tu," in the original Spanish, thereby expressing an easy intimacy (lost in translation unfortunately) with the person to whom the poem is dedicated and giving the poem a warmth that balances its more public, political points. Given the disruptions of communication occasioned by the war, it is not surprising that Machado repeats the phrase "your letter" three times in the first five lines. The military man Líster's letter ably communicated to Machado, the professional writer, the decisive importance of what was happening in the war at that juncture: the mention of the letter is not the last time in the poem that descriptive writing is prized over physical action. The letter revives the poet from a deathlike inertia and spurs him on to proclaim along the length of the river Ebro—emblematic of Spain—his own words of commitment at the end.

The reference in the poem to the captain's pistol is especially relevant to our discussion. As a weapon suited to the conduct of a battle in which aviation, tanks, and heavy artillery were the order of the day, the pistol is of scant import, but as an emblem of a chivalrous, romantic captain of a former age, it is an effective evocation. Although Machado does, at least, modernize the classical pen and sword analogy with the pen-pistol parallel at the end, he is still a long way from creating an imaginative engagement with modern warfare. Toward the war's end and facing the republic's certain defeat, Machado in an interview conceded that, militarily, the republic had lost the war but added that, "humanly, I am not so sure. . . . Perhaps we have won it" (*Poesía* 4: 2300). As exemplified in the Líster sonnet, the poet seems interested more in the value of personal example than in military victory. He leapfrogs the issue of winning the war and turns the poem inward, toward those values of integrity and inner strength that subsist after military victories have been consigned to history.

In the creative fiction at the end of the poem, Machado regains his strength in two imaginative conceits, not devoid of wit and humor. The question for any student of what on the surface appears to be a directly political poem—the exaltation of Líster's heroic example for the civilian population—is whether these conceits add to or detract from the poet's message. The conceits are organized around the flow of the river Ebro from Cantabria to the Mediterranean. In the first one, Machado imagines the arrival of the river to the sea, in a quasi-regal manner, being announced by the blowing of a conch shell. The poet then imagines his own "word" being given volume and authority by this sonorous instrument (*Poesía* 2: 826). In the second conceit, the meandering course of the river is the flourish of the pen, beloved of Spaniards, that appends their signature to a document. The document in question is the Iberian Peninsula itself, and the signature of the river Ebro, the eponymous river of Iberia, attests to the sovereignty and natural freedom of Spain to forge its own direction and destiny. The conceits draw attention to themselves, for both the elaborate conceptualization that underpins them and their implicit humor (the image of the ailing Machado using the conch shell as a kind of megaphone to project his voice or of the meandering course of the river as a series of lines on a page).

The baroque configuration of the language seems more a product of the poet's creative need, brought about perhaps by the use of the sonnet form, than a means of expressing an urgent view of the war at this perilous point in the republic's history. Once again, historians, scholars, and teachers will have to come to terms with writing that does not offer an immediate message. The temptation has been to quote the famous last two lines of the poem, with their pithy linguistic balancing of "pen" and "pistol," and pass over the much more distancing, aesthetic effects produced by the conceptual elaboration of the metaphor of the river.

Hernández's poem "Rosario, Dynamite Girl" (*Obra completa* 1: 579–80) gives us another interesting insight into how poetic effect and political message found it hard, if not impossible, to bed down together in the wartime republic. The poem's subject, the young *miliciana* Rosario Sánchez Mora, had her hand blown off in a munitions accident, and Hernández strives to raise her disfiguring disability, acquired in the service of the republic, to a level of mythical, exemplary heroism. The poet pulls out all the stops of conceit and fantasy, moving between heroic eulogy and chivalric compliment: he envisages Rosario's beauty as having been raised to mythical status while reminding us that she sacrificed her comeliness to further the Republican cause.

In the poem to Rosario, Hernández's artistic instinct is to move the theater of the conflict away from the realities of inadequacy (the disfigurement) toward a higher reality, and the poet does not allow us to return to the everyday reality of the war until the end of the poem, when he calls our attention to the "traitors" who deserve to have Rosario's bombs hurled at them. This forty-line poem becomes a jeu d'esprit and a celebration of writing. It is addressed to Rosario's nonexistent hand, which is conceived of as still existing on another plane of reality because of its past deeds of righteous valor. The exploding dynamite that destroyed her hand is cast in the role of dangerous, jealous lover; its fuse is the desire for Rosario's hand. Rosario then becomes the "spume" of the trenches and the "cream" of the women taming the dynamite and using its fury against the enemy. Next, mythologized as a bearer of lightning bolts, Rosario's hand is etherealized by the Spanish pun on the verb "to explode" (*estrellarse*, "to be scattered like the stars") and so, in another play on words, is transformed into a star. In the last stanza Rosario has been transformed into the emblem of a proudly waving flag of resplendent triumph, the fluttering of the flag analogous to her breathless efforts for the cause, and she serves as an example to the men to rally for what both the flag and its female emblem represent.

The baroque elements in this poem (the strict requirements of the form, its wit, humor even) and the origin of the subject (Rosario's destroyed hand) pull the poem in two directions at once. The setting is cosmic and mythological rather than political, and yet some of the poetic diction—the way in which the vocabulary of munitions, bombs, explosions, shrapnel, dynamite, and fuses is incorporated into the text—places the poem unmistakably in the arena of the war. This blending of myth and reality makes it impossible to extract only those elements that refer to the violence of the war and to leave the poem intact. In this poem, Hernández has added enormously to the history and aesthetic impact of the diction of Spanish poetry by using a classic strophic and metrical form (the *décima*) in a modern way. The impact of the poem comes from his playful manipulation of this form, the carefree but precise control in walking the tightrope between the air of metaphor and the ground of realism. It is impossible to read this poem and not be aware that it concerns more than the praises of a young, unfortunate militia woman: it is Hernández the poet who is at the center of the poem, showing us, or attempting to show us, his mastery of this traditional Renaissance form in a contemporary context.

The dominant impression afforded by these Republican writers is that their personal artistic sensibilities intruded heavily into the political concerns of the day. As we turn to two sonnets dedicated to Franco by two of the best poets in the Nationalist zone, Manuel Machado and Dionisio Ridruejo, we immediately discern that any personal element is omitted; instead, the business of panegyric and propaganda is single-mindedly pursued.

The first poem to be considered, by Antonio Machado's brother, Manuel, achieved instant popularity, and it is not hard to imagine its vacuous penultimate line, "for a Spain even more than ever Spain" ("para una España más y más España" [*Poesía* 171]), becoming a Nationalist slogan. Throughout the sonnet, one can detect the same sort of empty panegyric, devoid of the patent personal stamp observable in the work of the two Republican writers. The sonnet's theme—that Franco is a humane, beloved leader who through his genius can turn swords into ploughshares while still excelling in the military arts—is negated by the triumphalist tone throughout, as is the corresponding assertion that Franco's humane responsibility takes precedence over his desire for military glory. For example, the assertion that Franco "inspires faith and love" is negated by the sonnet's next lines, "the triumphal prestige that accompanies him reaches everywhere" (*Poesía* 171). Manuel Machado's recital of Franco's triumphal march through Spain has the thin, cold air of distant adulation that leaves the reader gasping for the oxygen of his brother Antonio's intricate and delicate flow of communication with the republic's military leader in his sonnet written some fifteen months later. Of a poet renowned for the wit and warmth of his prewar and even postwar work, we can only assume that Manuel Machado was writing here to a preestablished pattern deemed most suitable for promoting the cause of Franco.

Ridruejo's sonnet to Franco (Calamai 220–21), published at the beginning of 1939, when the war was effectively won, is analogously astonishing for the coldness and distance of its tone, even though this sonnet uses the familiar "you" form in each quartet and tercet and Manuel Machado's used third-person description. The diction is stereotyped and abstract, making it difficult to find any image or phrase that one can take from the poem as a meaningful contribution to the literature of the civil war. In a note in his collection *Poesía en armas* ("Poetry in Arms"; in *Primer libro*), published in the year following his and Franco's death, Ridruejo mentions that he has excluded the sonnet but gives no explanation (167). The omission must have been as much for aesthetic as for political reasons.

The sonnet attempts to chart Franco's progress through the four corners of Spain, his victories on land and sea during the course of the war, and hints at a future call to the world's stage. Such a broad scheme in such a brief format, a kind of whistle-stop tour, in which west, east, south, and north; the North Atlantic, the Mediterranean, Castille, Spanish Morocco, and the Pyrenees; and the world itself all compete for space, leaves little room for any consideration of the supposed subject of the sonnet in personal or human terms, except as something tagged on to these geographical entities in the most general way.

As a piece of Nationalist writing inspired by the civil war, Ridruejo's sonnet fails to convince us, not only because we may disagree with the political sentiments expressed but also because there is a poverty of expression, a predictability in the diction and metaphor. The bleak, general utterances about Franco's victory and the hope it may bring leave us cold. The totalitarian image of Franco has hijacked the poet's sensibility, and the image of Spain and its inhabitants is expressed by pallid, repetitious abstraction. The reader need only turn to Hernández's poem on the married soldier to register the abyss of passion and dramatic sensibility that separates the Republican poem from these two Francoist poems on the soldier as hero.

Both Nationalist poems examined here might be called monumental sonnets because of their predictable, exteriorized tone in the grand fascist manner; the Republican poems we examined are certainly public poems. Antonio Machado and Hernández are poets at play, engaged with the serious, ludic business of their art, whereas the Nationalist propagandists Ridruejo and Manuel Machado are in thrall to the didactic requirements of dictatorship, in which the free play of metaphorical art is subordinated to the solemn certainties of victory and military glory. Of course it is not possible to extrapolate from just two poems from either side an assumption that all others will bear the same stamp. In Manuel Machado's second poem to Franco at the end of the war, "Salute to Franco" (*Poesía* 307), when the poet urges the general to unite brother with brother in a common enterprise, Machado must surely have been remembering his own visit to his brother Antonio's grave in exile two months earlier, thereby excising, at least from the end of that poem, any triumphalist notions. Similarly, for Antonio Machado and Hernández, as evidenced in the poems on the young militia woman, the married soldier, and the colonel-in-chief of the Republican army, the only certainty is death, whether of a fascist or Republican. The remaining time is to be spent experiencing the present drama of life, praising examples of vigilant and active human beings through gestures of personal affection and love, and attempting to express the whole in language that will outlive its subjects and authors. In the Nationalist sonnets discussed, there is no death, just an eternal icon, frozen in time. Teachers and students of the Spanish Civil War must ask themselves whether the aesthetic writings produced during it, on either side, may truly be called committed in the political sense.

Note

1. All translations are mine. The English prose versions of the five poems discussed in this essay are in the appendix.

Appendix

Antonio Machado, "To Líster, Chief of the Armies of the Ebro"

Your letter—oh noble, watchful heart, untamable Spaniard, strong of fist—your letter, heroic Líster, consoles me for this flesh of death that weighs me down. The noise of holy battle for the Iberian countryside has come to me in your letter; my heart, too, has woken to the smell of gunpowder and rosemary. Where the sea conch announces that the Ebro has arrived, and at the cold summit whence springs that flourish of Spain, from hill to sea, this word of mine: "If my pen were worthy of your captain's pistol, I should die content."

Miguel Hernández, "Rosario, Dynamite Girl"

Rosario, dynamite girl, the dynamite kept a fierce and jealous eye on your pretty hand. Nobody on looking at it could believe that in its heart there was a desperation of glass, of shrapnel, anxious for the fray, thirsty for an explosion. It was your right hand that could melt lions, the flower of munitions and the desire of the fuse. Rosario, good harvest, tall as a belltower, you sowed the enemy with furious dynamite and your hand, Rosario, was a wrathful rose. Buitrago has witnessed the lightning-like deeds of valor that I pass over, of the hand in question. Well did the enemy know this girl's hand, that today is not a hand, because without its even wagging a single finger, the dynamite fell in love with it and turned it into a star! Rosario, dynamite girl, you can be a man and you are the cream of women and the spume of the trenches. Look at her, dynamiting herdsmen, as worthy as a victorious, shining flag, her breath fluttering, and send your bombs to the wind of the souls of traitors.

Miguel Hernández, "Song of the Married Soldier"

I have peopled and ploughed your womb with love and seed, I have prolonged the echo of blood to which I respond, and I await above the ploughed line as the plough waits: I have reached the depth. Brown-skinned, of tall towers, light and eyes, spouse of my skin, long gulp of my life, your wild breasts grow toward me with the leaps of a newborn deer. It now seems to me that you are a delicate crystal: I fear that you will break at the least fall, and I wish I were a cherry tree to reinforce your veins with my soldier's skin. Mirror of my flesh, sustainer of my wings, I give you life in the death that they give me and that I will not take. Wife, wife, I love you surrounded by bullets, desired by lead. I love you above the fierce coffins that lie in wait, above the very dead without remedy or grave, and I would wish to kiss you, with my whole breast even in the dust, my spouse. When beside the fields of combat you are in my head, that your image does not relieve or cool, you come close to me like an immense mouth of hungry teeth. Write to me at the conflict, feel me in the trench: here with rifle I evoke and fix your name, and I defend your womb of the poor that awaits me, and I defend your child. Our child will be born with clenched fist, wrapped in a clamor of victory and guitars, and I will leave at your door my soldier's life without fangs or claws. It is needful to kill to continue with living. One day I will go under the shade of your faraway hair, and I will sleep in the starched and clamorous sheet sewn by your hand. Your determined feet and your determined mouth of untameable lips go straight to give birth, and faced with my loneliness of explosions and fractures you follow a path of unstoppable kissses. The peace that I am forging will be for our child. And finally in an ocean of bones lost forever, your heart and mine will shipwreck, leaving a man and a woman wasted by kisses.

Manuel Machado, "Francisco Franco"

Leader of the new Reconquest, Lord of Spain, that is reborn in its faith, he knows how to win and smile, and he makes the conquered land a field of bread. He knows how to win and smile . . . his military ingenuity, sure and firm, excels in warlike glory. And to make history, God willed to give much more: genius. He inspires faith and love. The triumphal prestige that accompanies him reaches everywhere, while the Fatherland grows before his thrust. On a tomorrow, that does not dismiss the past, on a Spain that is even more than ever Spain, the smile of Franco shines!

Dionisio Ridruejo, "Sonnet to Franco"

From El Hacho[1] to the Pyrenees you have ascended plain of swords with fleet foot, and first from your Galician sea you contemplate Ulysses's sea redeemed. Raised to the rank of fortress, to tough encampment, warlike sun, your land of Castille defended, the Orb sounds to take the path again. Father of arms and peace, by your promise West reveals its enterprise anew and East expands its beauty, with the South to the fore and the North assured and you in quarters, accompanied by the people who need in you their youthful undertaking.

[1]A military fortress in Ceuta, Spanish Morocco.

Kevin Foster

"Your Country Does Not Matter": British and Irish Writers on the Spanish Civil War

Once the focus of bitter social division in Britain and the object and occasion of class, gender, and regional rancor, World War I (1914–18) has, over time and through a concerted effort of cultural repackaging, been promoted as a key ceremony in the articulation and affirmation of British national unity, a central component of what Patrick Wright terms "the National Past." In this context,

> far from being somehow "behind" the present, the past exists as an accomplished presence in public understanding. In this sense it is written into present social reality, not just implicitly as residue, precedent or custom and practice, but explicitly as itself—as History, National Heritage and Tradition. Any attempt to develop and assert a critical historical consciousness will find itself in negotiation if not open conflict with this established public understanding of "the past." (142)[1]

At a literary and cultural level, this struggle over the remains of World War I between the frail protestations of "historical consciousness" and the irresistible juggernaut of "the past" has been conducted in newspaper and television production offices, publishing houses, critical journals, lecture theaters, and classrooms. In these venues, World War I has come to be seen less as a narrative of catastrophic waste than as a celebration of how the nation was augmented by the trauma of war, as an account not of what was lost but of what was gained—namely, a common code of veneration for those who played a part in the war, tinged with righteous reproach for those who led them so poorly. The war and its multitudinous dead have thereby furnished a new focus for moral unanimity and so bequeathed the British a stronger sense of what they share and who they are.

> In this sense the national past can be thought of as a controlling attribute of citizenship: something that at a generalised level enables citizens . . . to find a unity . . . between themselves and to override unresolved socio-political contradictions and differences. (Wright 146)

The refashioning of World War I as a locus for the celebration of national unity has been achieved at the cost of any widespread contemporary recognition of the bitter moral and ideological divisions it occasioned at the time. The staggering complexity of a conflict conducted over three continents in jungles, deserts, and sodden pastures; beneath the oceans; in the air; on and under the ground; by uniformed technocrats and painted tribesmen, passionate crusaders and ambivalent conscripts in pursuit or defense of a vast array of conflicting causes has been all but anthologized into extinction. The assumption of World War I's central place in the British national past and its promotion of national unity has stripped the war of its political and social divisiveness and transformed it into a moral progression from innocence to experience, from acclamation through protest to pity and the quasisacramental art it breeds. Thus is the World War I soldier transformed from contested ideological subject to national Christ figure. Stoically rising from the trench, he takes his place on the barbed wire cross, embracing his fate as a sacrifice to the nation: "happy are those who are called to his supper" (Bouley 292).[2]

The Spanish Civil War, it seems, is going the same way as World War I. Despite the efforts of an isolated few, writers, poets, editors, anthologists, and critics have, over the past half century and with varying degrees of culpability and compunction, radically redrafted what Stephen Spender called "the map of pain" (*Collected Poems* 108–09). The complicated landscape of the war has been stripped down to its most elemental, topographical forms, to the bold compass points of moral outrage and ideological fervor. Thus, at least in the world of British and Irish literature, the baffling experience of the war has been reduced to an array of decorative postures—clenched fists and fascist salutes. This synoptic account of the war has been conveyed through a handful of poems and memoirs produced by a select group of writers whose social origins, education, and espoused political positions seem uncannily uniform. Though not necessarily unrepresentative of their time or their societies, the voices of W. H. Auden, Spender, C. Day-Lewis, Louis MacNeice, Sylvia Townsend Warner, Laurie Lee, and Tom Wintringham were the voice of the age rebroadcast in the well-modulated inflections of Received Pronunciation—the voice of history as experienced by literary London's educated elite.[3] Our first task then is to encourage students to identify and examine the breadth of the war's representation, to straddle in their reading the gender, class, and ideological divides that characterized the conflict. That said, in what follows I concern myself, very broadly, with the works of these leftist literati. This focus is driven by curricular concerns as well as by pedagogical and scholarly principles. As for curricular concerns, anybody teaching the English literature of the Spanish Civil War will find that the key anthologies are overwhelmingly populated by the work of the writers noted above and their left establishment friends and contemporaries. Valentine Cunningham's two edited collections (1980 and 1986) offer the best and broadest range of writing on the conflict, but these are avowedly literary collections as opposed to more broadly cultural or historical collections. The work of the establishment leftists is heavily represented, and room is found for a few distinguished bluestockings and the odd crusty right-winger, but there is scarcely a contribution from the working classes and far too little from the fascists and their sympathizers.

For more detail on the otherwise marginalized voices from the Spanish Civil War, Judith Keene offers a judicious analysis of the memoirs and literature produced by British, Irish, and other volunteers to the Nationalist (Francoist) cause. Her text also furnishes an excellent list of sources for further reading in the field.[4] Jim Fyrth and Sally Alexander offer a vital source of testimony of women from Britain, the United States, Australia, and New Zealand who fought in Spain and an invaluable means of setting these "ordinary" women's responses against the literary constructions of the war. They also provide a fascinating point of contrast and comparison with Shirley Mangini's 1995 collection of Spanish women's oral testimonies, diaries, autobiographies, and letters from the conflict. Another source, the International Brigade Memorial Trust (www.international-brigades.org.uk), was set up to "educate the public in the history of the men and women who fought in the International Brigades . . . by preserving and cataloguing valuable historical material . . . [and] by making such material available to the public." Its focus is predominantly on the memoirs and accounts of the thousands of predominantly working-class men and women who fought with the brigades.[5] The Marx Memorial Library (www.marxlibrary.net) in London contains, "arguably, the most comprehensive collection in the world on the Spanish Civil War," a collection that is slowly being included in, and made available through, the library's database.[6] Foremost among published sources detailing the experiences and accounts of working-class volunteers in Spain is Bill Alexander's *British Volunteers for Liberty*. A comprehensive list of both unpublished and published sources can be accessed at www.international-brigades.org.uk/ british_volunteers/memoirs.html. Drawing on this and other related material it would no doubt be possible—and an excellent project—to compile a dedicated course reader reflecting the breadth of writing on the war. But time and resource restrictions often force lecturers back to the few established anthologies that are in print, available, and affordable, and these overwhelmingly feature the left establishment writers whose work I look at here. Compelled by the brutal economies of publishing to revisit many of the most well-known commentators on the war, it behoves us, at least, to offer a fresh perspective on their perceptions of the conflict. Accordingly, I sketch out here alternative approaches to these writers to offer a means of exploring the forces that shaped their responses to the war and thereby a better grasp of how our own understandings of the war have been framed and formed.

The uniformity of World War I's modern representation reflects a complex process of historical revisionism in which once-substantial ideological discordances are sublimated in the heat of national reimagining. In representations of the Spanish Civil War, ideology is explicitly to the fore. Yet the social and political differences that ostensibly animated the warring parties underpin a radically simplified map of the conflict's moral topography, subsequently reaffirmed in the wake of World War II by the moral fallout from the Holocaust and the simple dichotomies of the cold war. This comfortable binarism not only misrepresents the complexity of the political landscape in Spain but also fails to account for the discursive complexities that informed and framed the conflict. It does not recognize the argument that representations of the war were determined less by the writers' responses to events in Spain, their experiences or convictions, than by the representational forms at their disposal, the illustrative armory that they drew on to imagine and organize their responses.

From the outset students need to grasp the fundamental concept that the war and its representation are not one and the same. They need to recognize that just as the Spanish Civil War was not fought in a social or political vacuum, so the responses of the war's contemporary writers did not emerge from a cultural, literary, or representational void. Students might consider how the writers' experiences and representations of the war were informed by their responses to the prevailing concerns, crises, and hopes. That is not to say that the literature class should be prefaced by a history lesson. Students can, however, be encouraged to identify and explore the events and experiences—World War I, the Irish Civil War, the Great Depression, the rise of fascism—that shaped the men and women whose responses defined our understanding of the Spanish Civil War. Students might then be better prepared to consider whether the British and Irish responses to the Spanish Civil War are concerned with Spain at all or whether Spain served these writers as motivation for their treatment of what were essentially local issues. I focus here on the discursive influence that World War I, and to a lesser extent the Irish Civil War, exercised over representations of the Spanish Civil War. World War I is significant in this context not merely as an instructive precedent for the cultural remapping of the Spanish Civil War but also—and this applies equally to the Irish Civil War— through its provision of a vital cultural and semiotic framework within which the struggle in Spain might be understood and experienced.

Throughout the late 1920s, as Britain and Europe were still struggling to assess the damage done by World War I, many of the economic, social, and theological ideals that ostensibly inspired the conflict were buckling under the strain of twin crises—the "crisis of culture" (Leavis 5), which found its most concentrated expression in the modernist disillusionment of the early mid-1920s,[7] and a crisis of faith in capitalism. Surveying the wreckage of Britain's industrial regions, ravaged by the barrage of collapses and closures attendant on the Great Depression, Auden portrayed the nation's productive heartland in terms drawn directly from World War I. The mines and railways, power stations and factories, like the once prosperous farms and villages of northern France, were now a desolate and depopulated no man's land, shattered by the bomb damage of a global economy in retreat:

> Get there if you can and see the land you once were proud to own
> Though the roads have almost vanished and the expresses never run:
>
> Smokeless chimneys, damaged bridges, rotting wharves and choked canals,
> Tramlines buckled, smashed trucks lying on their side across the rails;
>
> Power stations locked, deserted, since they drew the boiler fires;
> Pylons fallen or subsiding, trailing dead high-tension wires;

Head gears gaunt on grass grown pit-bank, seams abandoned years ago;
Drop a stone and listen for its splash in flooded dark below.

Squeeze into the works through broken windows or damp-sprung doors;
See the rotted shafting, see holes gaping in the upper floors.

(qtd. in Cunningham, *British Writers* 37)

Britain's foremost Marxist theorist of the day, Christopher Caudwell, argued that the industrial wastelands of northern Britain and Ireland's stagnant rural sector were harbingers of "the final economic crisis of capitalism" in which "all bourgeois culture" entered "the throes of its final crisis" (qtd. in Cunningham, *British Writers* 37).[8] Unfortunately, for Caudwell at least, the mid-1930s turned out to be a period of relative prosperity in Britain. Though the industrial regions of the north remained depressed and millions languished in unemployment and poverty, the south of the country enjoyed a boom as light industries relocated to the outskirts of London and new towns flourished. But creeping suburbanization did not please everybody. That John Betjeman's disdain for the tinned civilization of "Slough" (1937) should find expression in images of bombardment amply demonstrates the extent to which World War I had saturated ordinary life and discourse in the 1930s:

Come friendly bombs and fall on Slough
It isn't fit for humans now,
There isn't grass to graze a cow
Swarm over, Death!

(Betjeman 22)

In Britain throughout the mid-1930s the focus of the crisis shifted from the economic hardships of home to the political instability on the Continent, from Jarrow's flat-capped hunger marchers through Oswald Moseley's East End provocations to the black-shirted legions in the new empires of fascist Europe. In Ireland, the crisis was closer to home. The early 1930s saw violent clashes on the streets and in the countryside. The left, organized by the Irish Republican Army (IRA) and the Communist Party of Ireland, often fought daily battles against the Blueshirts, who represented the interests of big agriculture, the banks, big business, and slum landlords. By 1933–34, with over forty-eight thousand members, the Blueshirts had "mushroomed into what was—in relative terms—the largest non-governing fascist organisation in the world" (Stradling,

Irish 1).[9] As the crisis neared its critical point, there was a widespread sense of fear and vulnerability neatly captured by Auden:

> O what is that sound that so thrills the ear
> Down in the valley drumming, drumming?
> Only the scarlet soldiers, dear,
> The soldiers coming.
>
> O what is that light I see flashing so clear
> Over the distance brightly, brightly?
> Only the sun on their weapons, dear,
> As they step lightly.
>
> (*Collected Poems* 120)

According to Paul Fussell, British literature of the 1930s was shot through by this sort of foreboding, haunted by an atmosphere of anxiety, danger, and conflict directly traceable to World War I and the literary responses to it that poured out in ever-greater profusion through the late 1920s and early 1930s.[10] The events of July 1936 thus found a literary community, steeped in the blood of Flanders and the vocabulary it spawned, whose fears of political Armageddon seemed to have found their focus and enactment in Spain. It is little wonder then that so much of the writing from the Spanish Civil War uncannily echoes the literature of World War I.[11]

For Irish writers, Ireland's civil war and its uneasy legacy of class and sectarian conflict significantly framed their experience of Spain. Indeed, Frank Ryan, who eventually led the pro-Republican Irish contingent in Spain, observed that the Spaniards' endeavors to throw off the yoke of class and foreign tyranny made their struggle an extension of the Irish people's quest for liberty and national unity: "the Spanish trenches are right here in Ireland" (qtd. in S. Cronin 79). This observation found an unexpected echo on the right. When the former Blueshirt commander General Eoin O'Duffy was raising an Irish Brigade to fight for Franco and the church, a Galway town councillor, Mr. Healey, suggested that "word be sent to O'Duffy stating that if he is going to form a brigade, the brigade is needed in Belfast more than in Spain" (qtd. in Stradling, *Irish* 11).

In Britain, World War I did far more than provide the writers of the 1930s with a ready-made vocabulary for their responses to Spain. For many it framed the personal context in which they experienced the war and furnished the epistemological structures by which they understood it. Most of the 1930s writers for whom Spain was such a passionate cause were, as Orwell noted, "just too young" to have served in World War I.

Though initially disdainful of the conflict and dismissive of those who had fought and died in it, "the dead men," Orwell reflected,

> had their revenge after all. As the war fell back into the past, my particular generation . . . became conscious of the vastness of the experience they had missed. You felt yourself a little less than a man, because you had missed it. (*Penguin Essays* 141)

According to Cunningham:

> When the Spanish Civil War broke out many of the young . . . seized on it as the chance to catch up with their fathers, their older brothers and the dead Old Boys to wipe out their guilt over having missed the First War. There was a lot of catching up to do, and that the young should wish to is a tribute to the immense potency of First War images that the 20s and then the 30s carried in their heads. With a terrible kind of naturalness the writings of the period fell into war language, into a semiotic supplied by what had been learned from the war time fronts. The war was in almost every writer's mental luggage. (*British Writers* 49–50)

One of the most persistent and prevalent forms of this World War I semiotic was what Fussell has called "gross dichotomizing," a habit traceable, in his view,

> to the actualities of the Great War. . . . Prolonged trench warfare, with its collective isolation, its "defensiveness," and its nervous obsession with what "the other side" is up to, establishes a model of modern political, social, artistic and psychological polarization. (75–76)

World War I and the habit of gross dichotomizing it engendered decisively shaped the contemporary understanding and experience of the Spanish Civil War, as is made plain in "the question" directed by, among others, Auden, Nancy Cunard, Pablo Neruda, Spender, and Tristan Tzara, "To the Writers and Poets of England, Scotland, Ireland and Wales":

> It is clear to many of us throughout the whole world that now, as certainly never before, we are determined or compelled to take sides. The equivocal attitude, the Ivory Tower, the paradoxical, the ironic detachment, will no longer do. . . . To-day the struggle is in Spain. Tomorrow it may be in other countries—our own. But there are some who, despite the martyrdom of Durango and Guernica, the enduring agony of Madrid . . . , are still in doubt, or who aver that it is possible that Fascism may be what it proclaims it is: "the saviour of civilisation."

> This is the question we are asking you:
> Are you for, or against, the legal Government and the People of
> Republican Spain?
> Are you for, or against, Franco and Fascism?
> For it is impossible any longer to take no side.
>
> (qtd. in Cunningham, *Spanish Front* 51)

Entrenched adversarialism of the kind bred by World War I was, it seems, the only basis on which the events in Spain could be conceptualized. The replies were published in a sixpenny pamphlet, *Authors Take Sides on the Spanish War* (1937), and of the 149 authors who responded to the question, most declared themselves "for" the Spanish republic.[12] As Cunningham has noted, the editors fudged the results, drafting numerous equivocators into the "for" camp or refusing to publish the responses of others—perhaps most notably Orwell's angry dismissal of the questionnaire as "bloody rot" (Orwell, *Collected Essays* 312). Yet despite his evident hostility to the question's bland polarities, Orwell's own endeavors in *Homage to Catalonia* (1938) to organize and so understand his experience of the fighting in Spain were structured by an identical system of radical oppositions drawn explicitly from World War I. That war permeated every aspect of Orwell's expectations about, and experience of, Spain. It provided a framework for his discursive construction of the Spanish Civil War and was a ready tool for visualizing the war's moral, political, and physical topography and for mapping his place and purpose in it. It also furnished an experiential model through which his personal insecurities might be confronted and resolved. Spain was his test, his opportunity to prove that he was not less of a man than those who had fought in World War I:

> On and off, I have been toting a rifle ever since I was ten, in preparation not only for war but for a particular kind of war, a war in which the guns rise to a frantic orgasm of sound, and at the appointed moment you clamber out of the trench, breaking your nails on the sandbags, and stumble across mud and wire into the machine-gun barrage. I am convinced that part of the reason for the fascination that the Spanish Civil War had for people of about my age was that it was so like the Great War. (*Penguin Essays* 142).

Yet the basic structuring principle of *Homage to Catalonia* centers on the categorical disappointment of these expected similarities through a recurring pattern of anticipation succeeded by often comic deflation. Orwell discovered that Spain was fundamentally unlike World War I and, through his experience of the May fighting in Barcelona, comes to see that the conceptual framework through which he endeavored to make sense of the conflict, the easy binaries he brought with him from World War I, was simply inadequate, unable either to illustrate or explain the complex web of antagonisms that characterized Republican Spain.[13]

For Irish volunteers the apparently simple binaries of class and politics were hopelessly complicated by religion. Religion for the pro-Franco forces occupied a roughly analogous place to that of socialism and class solidarity for the left, proving itself equally illusory in its capacity to unite otherwise disparate groups and ultimately serving as a focus for division and fratricidal antipathy on both sides. Volunteers on the right found that the Catholic solidarity that had brought them to Spain allied them with Moors; Nazis; Freemasons; their natural class enemies, the manufacturers and landholders who exploited them at home; as well as more deadly foes from the near past. Soon after their arrival in Spain, O'Duffys's Brigade, the Fifteenth *Bandera*, was issued brand new Mausers and surplus German military clothing from World War I. For those ex-Tommies who had fought in World War I, here, at last, was the clear view of the enemy they had longed for in the trenches! For the Irish left there was no possibility of maintaining a united front when so many of its natural constituency, working-class Catholics, were hostile to the Republican cause on religious grounds.[14] Once these volunteers got to Spain they found that the fight against fascism was no less bitter than the internecine struggles in the Republican movement. Ironically then, if the left front foundered on issues of secular theology (doctrinal disputes over the true meaning of socialism), the Irish right splintered over the growing recognition among the would-be crusaders that they were merely political cannon fodder: "We were not long in Spain until [sic] we were convinced that it was a political campaign" (qtd. in Stradling 105).

Orwell was not alone in identifying in Spain an opportunity to resolve essentially personal dilemmas while serving a larger, political cause. Yet the question is, What was that larger cause? For many among the bourgeois left literati who defended the republic with rifle or pen, Spain was less their ultimate cause than an emblem of or an ideal context in which that true cause might be found. The war offered the card-carrying party member, the admirer of Soviet industry and its muscular Stakhanovism, the left intellectual, the liberal socialist, and the ambivalent fellow traveler what birth, education, geography, and even their accents had denied them—genuine contact with the workers:

> [A]ctual contact with the masses was [for bourgeois writers of the 1930s] exceedingly difficult to contrive. Going over, even in its loosest sense of a cross-border reconnaissance, a spying sortie to see what the proletarian regions beyond the social frontier were like, was a tricky undertaking. For almost as rigidly as in the nineteenth century, Britain was still divided into what Disraeli had labelled the Two Nations, the rich and the poor. And they lived apart: the rich in pastoral rurality, as in the more prosperous Midlands and South, or in the smart quarters of cities; the poor shoved away in slum ghettoes in London and other great cities, or, more crucially distanced still from the political and cultural centre around which the writers and publishers congregated, in the depressed industrial provinces. . . . To get there bourgeois writers had to make special journeys, across town or across country. (Cunningham, *British Writers* 224–25)

Those who were prepared to make the journey found that once they got there they could only get close to the workers by erasing every sign of their own class origins, by roughing up their clothes and scuffing their accents, in short by resorting to disguise and deception. Yet even then, as Orwell bitterly reflected in *The Road to Wigan Pier,* they were no closer to that mythical, authentic contact with the workers:

> For some months, I lived entirely in coal-miners' houses. I ate my meals with the family, I washed at the kitchen sink, I shared bedrooms with miners, drank beer with them, played darts with them, talked to them by the hour together. But though I was among them, and I hope and trust they did not find me a nuisance, I was not one of them, and they knew it even better than I did. (145)

Spain provided the bourgeois British writer with the perfect camouflage. Fighting alongside Spaniards, Frenchmen, Italians, Germans, and Americans, the British writers found that their accents were bleached of the caste marks of class and education and that they were accepted for what they were—fellow soldiers in the cause of freedom. It is little wonder then that Orwell so fondly remembered his time in the hills around Aragón or that his most intimate and hagiographic memories of Spain are moments of speechless brotherhood with his comrades.[15] For the British bourgeois writer, the Irish worker, the Italian Communist, and the German antifascist, the fight for Spain was the first battle for the liberation of their own homelands. One Irish volunteer expressed the wish that "every bullet I fired in Spain would be a bullet against the Dublin landlords" (Stradling, *Irish* 139). If for the British, Spain was symbolic of the struggle to come, for Irish volunteers and writers, Spain was the continuation of past battles, a new front in a civil conflict that in many ways had never ended: "the Spanish Civil War offered (amongst other things) a chance to reverse the decision of the war of 1922–3, to vindicate a cause which had been tragically overthrown" (Stradling, *Irish* 140). Indeed, many volunteers, from the left and the right, went to Spain explicitly to fight for Ireland, seeing in the struggle of the Spanish people an opportunity to right the wrongs visited on the Irish; they sought justice in Spain for Ireland: "it seems that for people all over the British empire who identified with the oppressed, 'Ireland' and 1916 had become a symbolic talisman of freedom which somehow melded, in 1936, into 'Spain'" (Stradling, *Irish* 142). Thus for many of the volunteers who passed across it, the Spanish frontier symbolized the gateway to a vision of their own land as it once was and as it might soon be again, the threshold of universal fraternity:

The Volunteer

Tell them in England, if they ask
What brought us to these wars,
To this plateau beneath the night's
Grave manifold of stars—

It was not fraud or foolishness,
Glory, revenge, or pay:
We came because our open eyes
Could see no other way.

There was no other way to keep
Man's flickering truth alight:
These stars will witness that our course
Burned briefer, not less bright.

Beyond the wasted olive-groves,
The furthest lift of land,
There calls a country that was ours
And here shall be regained.

Shine to us, memoried and real,
Green-water-silken meads:
Rivers of home refresh our path
Whom here your influence leads.

Here in a parched and stranger place
We fight for England free,
The good our fathers won for her,
The land they hoped to see.

(Day-Lewis 190–91)

Contrary to Luis Pérez Infante's insistence that, for those who took up arms to fight in Spain, "[y]our country does not matter" (20–21), it seems that few things mattered more.

Notes

1. For a more recent appraisal of the divisiveness of World War I, see Ferguson 174–247. In Australia, the debate over conscription brought deep social and religious divisions to the surface (see Clark 209–12). Wright identifies Remembrance Day as one of the key, public ceremonies celebrating national unity. Yet Wal Hannington recalls the 1922 commemoration, when twenty-five thousand unemployed ex-servicemen marched past the cenotaph with their medals attached to red banners and pawn tickets pinned to their lapels (see Hannington 77–78).

2. See Parsons, Silkin, and Stallworthy for this sacramental response to the war and the Christlike soldier.

3. Robin Skelton's collection, *Poetry of the Thirties*, offers one striking embodiment of this trend.

4. Of particular interest in this regard are Jerrold; Kemp; Lunn; and Frank Thomas.

5. Its Web site hosts an array of useful links to other sites that feature and examine the lives and experiences of Republican volunteers from, among others, the Irish Volunteers, the Abraham Lincoln Brigade, and Canada's Mackenzie-Papineau Battalion.

6. The Working Class Movement Library (www.wcml.org.uk) in Salford also houses an extensive collection on the Spanish Civil War with particularly good holdings of unpublished memoirs from local (northwestern English) volunteers.

7. Leavis's "crisis of culture" has been exhaustively documented and examined. For a useful synopsis see Bradbury and McFarlane.

8. Students might be encouraged to identify and examine the works of other critical thinkers of the day—economic, political, social, and cultural—and to consider their influence on writers' responses to and experiences of the events in Spain.

9. For more on the history and influence of the Blueshirts see Manning; Cullingford; and M. Cronin.

10. You can find evidence of this trend all over British literature of the 1930s: Auden's 1932 poem, quoted here, is just one example. Students might be encouraged to seek out others. The years 1929–30 famously saw the publication of Richard Aldington's *Death of a Hero*, Robert Graves's *Goodbye to All That*, Edmund Blunden's *Undertones of War*, Frederic Manning's *The Middle Parts of*

Fortune, Ernst Jünger's *Storm of Steel*, and Ernest Hemingway's *A Farewell to Arms*: an impressive catalog of horrors by any measure.

11. Striking examples include Miles Tomalin's poem "Christmas Eve 1937" (Cunningham, *Penguin Book* 227) and Spender's "Two Armies" (97–98).

12. For more on this question see Cunningham, *British Writers* 438–39.

13. For more on Orwell's experience in Spain see Foster 19–32.

14. For more on this tension see Stradling, *Irish* 133–34.

15. See Orwell, *Homage to Catalonia* 1–2, 176–78.

Denis Boak

The French Literary Response to the War: Malraux and Others

Before 1936 Spain did not much preoccupy the twentieth-century French mind. Whatever Spain's glorious past, as a nation it was now considered a has-been, a political, economic, and cultural backwater. Spain had not, some might think wisely, taken part in World War I, and few French people knew the country firsthand. Myth and stereotypes replaced any real knowledge and experience: Spain was the colorful, violent country of *Carmen*, of bullfighters and gypsy dancers. Those French writers who did write about Spain tended to do so in terms of a personal, exotic, and aesthetic adventure, typified by the striking title of Maurice Barrès's book *Du sang, de la volupté et de la mort* ("Blood, Sensuality, and Death"), which perfectly fits the stereotype of violence and sexual passion. Henry de Montherlant followed the Barrès pattern with his novel *Les bestiaires* (1926; "The Gladiators"), in which the hero, his alter ego, pursues the art of bullfighting, aestheticized as "tauromachy," in a personal, almost mystical test of asexual virility as much as courage. Despite the Spanish settings, *Les bestiaires* has more to do with the hero's own French preoccupations and fantasies than with any realities of Spanish life.

Nor were French intellectual circles much interested in Spanish culture: their inspiration came from elsewhere, mainly from east of the Rhine.

Translations from the Spanish were sporadic and arbitrary; even the novels of Benito Pérez Galdós, "the Spanish Zola," were little known in France. Although Miguel de Unamuno, who had an international reputation as Spain's leading thinker and writer, went into exile in Paris in the late 1920s, he rates not a single mention in André Gide's voluminous journal for those years. Yet Gide considered himself at the hub of French intellectual life and had, indeed, been involved in publishing a translation of one of Unamuno's books in 1916.

By 1936, though, political sensibilities had been sharpened. Idealist French hopes of the 1920s had rapidly dissolved with the rise of dictatorships of left and right; in February 1934 Paris itself had been shaken by rioting, which might easily have led to a right-wing coup. In October of that year, in a Spain torn by political instability ever since the republic had been proclaimed in 1931, there was an insurrection by miners in the north, only put down with heavy bloodshed. (This uprising led the youthful Albert Camus, in his Communist phase, to collaborate with three Algiers fellow students in writing a short drama, *Révolte dans les Asturies* [1936; "Revolt in the Asturias"]. The play, an immature and derivative work, was never staged but was published in a small edition, with little impact.) The elections of May 1936 were the most bitterly fought of any in interwar France. The Front Populaire, a loose coalition of the left partly inspired by the Frente Popular, which had won the Spanish elections in February that year, gained a similarly narrow majority. Polarization was keen, passions ran high, and opinions hardened into prejudice. When the military insurgency in Spain occurred, with success only partial and the arming of workers making a general conflict inevitable, the French of both the right and the left were equipped with a set of ready-made ideological attitudes, passions, and prejudices that could be, and were, switched directly to Spanish affairs.

Once it became obvious that the intended coup had turned into civil war, Spain generated enormous interest in the French press, and articles and maps concerning the war appeared daily. Graphic war photography came of age during the Spanish Civil War, after the tightly controlled censorship on both sides during World War I. French newspaper opinion was split, and there was little pretense at objectivity: correspondents, who rarely had profound knowledge of the background to the struggle, were sent to the favored side, with a simplistic identification of Frente Popular and Front Populaire and little distinction between reporting and political commentary. Thus the workers' militias were heroic idealists to one side and *canaille* ("scum") to the other, and the Nationalists were either murderous fascists or necessary restorers of order, Christian crusaders even. French writers were polarized along the same lines. They had their political opinions already, and not many changed their stance as the war went on. The poet Paul Claudel, recently retired from a career as one of France's leading diplomats, took an orthodox Catholic position, reviling the Spanish republic and all its works while writing an ode to "the Spanish martyrs" ("Aux martyrs"). An exception was the novelist François Mauriac, who started with his sympathies going out to the insurgents but, on further knowledge of events, came to change his views. Mauriac did not, however, use Spain in his literary works. The theologian Jacques Maritain was another public supporter of the Republican cause.

Georges Bernanos, the novelist and polemical journalist who had been living in Majorca since 1934, was another Catholic writer who grew to detest the Nationalists. Initially all Bernanos's instincts and opinions led him to support the insurgents, who rapidly took over in Majorca, but the brutal repression before his eyes—in a place where, since there had been little fighting, the repression was therefore for their ideas, not their actions—soon led him to change his mind, and in 1937 he left Spain. Back in France that year he published *Les grands cimetières sous la lune* (1938; "The Moonlit Cemeteries"), a highly successful work in which, with all the bitterness of the deceived, he expressed his loathing, especially of the established Spanish church for backing the repression. Bernanos is in fact a rather special case, unleashing a passionate all-around diatribe, but above all obsessed with his own relation with the Catholic religion and his detestation of aspects of the church as an institution and of the right-thinking, churchgoing bourgeoisie in France as much as in Spain. In doing so, he assimilates what he saw in Spain to his own preoccupations as a Frenchman, seeing the Spanish Civil War much in terms of the 1871 Paris Commune.

The Front Populaire government in Paris, which did not command a majority in the French upper house of parliament—the Senate—feared defeat if it took bold action to aid the Republican government in Spain and was in any case primarily concerned with internal social reform. Soon the French joined the British in a policy of nonintervention, which effectively blocked the legal Spanish government from purchasing arms with which to defend itself, forcing it to rely on the Soviet Union for concrete assistance. The many French who feared Communism more than fascism deepened their opposition to the Front Populaire. At the same time, volunteers of the International Brigades, many of them French, made their way to Spain. The French volunteers were mainly committed Communists, and there were fewer idealists of the George Orwell or Robert Jordan type among them than among the British and American contingents.

Jean-Paul Sartre first became widely known in the literary world in July 1937 with his story "Le mur" ("The Wall"). Sartre uses the Spanish Civil War as the setting for a situation symbolizing what would come to be known as the absurd. Pablo is one of three men arrested and condemned to summary execution, and the men's conversation during their last night forms much of the narrative, as Pablo is forced to confront the horrified realization (existential anguish) of the emptiness and pointlessness (the absurdity) of human existence. Pablo is offered his life if he will reveal the whereabouts of a Republican comrade. Although he has actually no idea of the man's whereabouts, in an *acte gratuit* ("gratuitous action"), which is completely unmotivated, Pablo finds himself saying that his comrade is hiding in the village cemetery. Through a savage irony this statement turns out to be true, and soldiers sent to investigate do indeed find the man in the gravedigger's hut, where he is killed in the resulting shoot-out. The Nationalist officer keeps his word, and Pablo survives. This is a powerful tale, though one may suspect that Sartre's interest was as much in the existential problem as in the war. (Although both he and Simone de Beauvoir would later claim that the war was at the forefront of their preoccupations throughout this period, when the insurgency began, they were on the point of setting out on their summer vacation to fascist Italy. They did not cancel their trip.) Except for occasional indirect allusions, Sartre did not use Spain again in his work, and "Le mur," at fewer than thirty pages, remains a brilliant one-off, entirely different from Sartre's other stories.

Although "Le mur" has held its place in literary history, another Spanish Civil War story of 1937 has been completely eclipsed, no doubt because its author took what would become the unfashionable line of supporting the Nationalist cause. This novel is *El requeté* ("The Carlist Volunteer"), by Lucien Maulvault, a minor novelist now largely forgotten. The Carlists were originally dissident monarchists from the northern province of Navarra and the Basque Country during the dynastic struggles of the early nineteenth century. In 1936 their group, wearing distinctive red berets with their uniforms, immediately threw its support behind the Nationalists and played a leading part in defeating the Republicans in the north during the early months of the war. Juan, the principal character in the novel, although living in France and not immediately involved in

Spain, volunteers for Carlist service, taking part in bloody fighting—and repression—only to discover that his father, a man of some standing, has been arrested and is being held prisoner by the Republicans in San Sebastián. In what he believes is the only way to save his father from execution, Juan pretends to desert and makes his way to the city, where a former friend is supposed to have a high position in Republican councils. The friend, a leading anarchist portrayed as morally deformed by his beliefs and now largely cynical, is indeed in a position to obtain Juan's father's release but will only do so if Juan agrees to join the anarchist militia and fight on their side. Juan is obliged to join, and the narrative begins when he has deserted for a second time and succeeded in returning to the Carlist lines, where he is put on trial for his life as a traitor. When the full story comes out, Juan is released back into the Carlist army, and all earlier events are narrated as flashbacks.

El requete is by no means negligible as a novel, and Maurice Rieuneau is right to devote several pages to a close analysis in his monumental survey (533–37). Here, the idealism is on the insurgents' side: the Carlists are dedicated idealists with their own heroic solidarity, unassailably in the right, and their opponents bloodthirsty savages. Maulvault pulls no punches. There are two scenes of brutal rape, and combatants on both sides engage in savage street fighting where no quarter is given. The narrator is especially contemptuous of the revolutionaries who have taken over San Sebastián and set up a reign of drunken terror; at least the anarchist militia in the field are fighting. As in "Le mur," the plot turns on an existential dilemma, a vital personal choice: is Juan justified in deserting, even to save his father? In fact he has no hesitation, just as he has had no hesitation in crossing back from France to join the Carlists, a deployment of will and energy just as impressive as any on the Republican side. Maulvault's novel is set against the backdrop of the early fighting in the north, which lends plausibility to the basic personal dilemma.

Events in Spain produced one outstanding French novel, André Malraux's *L'espoir* (*Man's Hope*), which came out in late 1937, while the conflict was still at its height. The novel was an immediate success and has become both a twentieth-century classic and a widely translated best seller. Malraux, then a leading left-wing and antifascist activist who had gained an international reputation with his two "revolutionary" novels set in contemporary China, *Les conquérants* (*The Conquerors*) and *La condition humaine* (*Man's Fate*), wasted no time when the uprising occurred, plunging himself into efforts to secure planes and aircrew for the Republicans, then traveling to Spain to set up an international squadron of volunteers and mercenaries, flying makeshift sorties against the insurgents. When, in early 1937, the remnants of this squadron were incorporated into the regular Republican Air Force, Malraux devoted his efforts to a propaganda campaign, including a two-month speaking tour across North America. His presence in Spain, like Ernest Hemingway's, stood out as a symbol of literary anti-fascism, but Malraux was not just an observer and commentator. As a colonel in command of his squadron, he took part in bombing raids and, at one point, was lucky to escape with his life from a crash. At the same time he was composing his new novel, which was completed and brought out with great speed. Malraux took no more part in fighting in Spain, but at the war's end he was back in Barcelona, filming a version of his novel. He was obliged to flee back to France with his film unfinished, but, postwar, it would become a minor film club classic.

L'espoir, at six hundred pages in the most accessible edition, easily the longest of Malraux's novels, is a panoramic work, spanning a wide range of events, characters, and settings over the first six months of the war. As such it is at the other extreme from *For Whom the Bell Tolls* (the only other Spanish Civil War novel to have gained, and kept, an international reputation), which, though sizable itself, deals with a limited group of characters and the events of a few days only (see the essay by Valis ["Hemingway's War"] in this volume). Malraux's structure is extremely loose, and though the novel is linear, in that events are treated more or less chronologically, the author has no hesitation in rapidly switching settings and characters, as well as narrative register. Interspersed with scenes of fighting on the ground are episodes based on his own aviation experiences, though he himself does not appear as a character.

In the first section of the novel, "L'illusion lyrique" ("The Lyrical Illusion"), which covers the beginning and early weeks of the struggle, the scene moves from Madrid to Barcelona, the two key cities in which the insurgency failed, then back to Madrid, then on, at extended length, to events in Toledo. Here the uprising was equally unsuccessful, and the insurgents took refuge in the Alcázar, the fortified citadel. The Republican militia, disorganized and leaderless, failed to dislodge them in over two months and then, faced with General Franco's troops moving up from the southwest, took to their heels down the railway. This is the lyrical illusion: the belief that the Spanish workers who had defeated the insurgents in Madrid and Barcelona in an initial burst of fraternal heroism and enthusiasm could go on to win the whole war in the same way. Malraux insists that an illusion it is and that being morally in the right is not enough, nor is enthusiasm not backed up by military skill. Winning is what matters; noble principles and moral purity may be more admirable, more aesthetically impressive, but they are no use to losers on the ground. And since both sides shot many prisoners from the start, losers stood a good chance of being dead. Military efficiency is the essential factor, and it requires disciplined action and proper leadership—the deployment of energy in action. Not surprisingly Malraux makes no pretense of being neutral. The insurgency has to be fought, and disciplined military effort is needed to defeat it. A secondary thesis is that only the Communists already possess the dedication and discipline to succeed in this mission.

The second, much shorter section is entitled "Le Manzanarès," after the river in Madrid, and deals largely with the capital bearing up under siege and bombardment. Franco's troops had by late 1936 reached the western suburbs, but the Republicans succeeded in holding out for over two more years. This section of the novel contains powerful and memorable passages that depict what is perhaps the first ever fictional account of a city under wholesale air bombing (although soon it would be overtaken by the numerous accounts of World War II blitzes). At the time, these scenes, and the scenes of violent insurrection, were something new in fiction, a literature of "extreme situations" that had much in common with dramatic war journalism. Then, in the third and final section, much shorter again and also called "L'espoir," Malraux moves his narrative to the south of Spain and the fall of Málaga, where once again the Republican militia flees without a fight; then back north to what has been called "the descent from the mountain," where local peasants bring down the survivors of a Republican plane crash; then finally to the battle of Guadalajara, a victory in March 1937 that prevented the total encirclement of Madrid. At this point the final outcome of the struggle was still open, and the novel can conclude on an upbeat note, but one very different from the wild hope and enthusiasm of the opening chapters.

Malraux was indignant at suggestions that *L'espoir* was intended in any way as reportage. He did not see himself as a novelist in the realist tradition but as a poet in the widest sense, going beyond any notion of simply transcribing or reproducing real events on paper and thus transcending realism in the banal, day-to-day sense by presenting a memorable fictional account, the unfolding of human destiny against a background of violent struggle, which would somehow contain both the essence of the events of the war and reflections on their intellectual implications. Presentation of events is thus perhaps a better term than representation, a slippery metaphor that covers too many different, sometimes conflicting senses. Malraux's basic compositional method is the creation of important dramatic scenes, some brief, others extended, alternating with intellectual dialogues; passages of description that can only be termed lyrical, even elegiac; crisp fragments of conversation; memorable brief formulations; and a wealth of imagery of various kinds, which perhaps best illustrates the essentially poetic nature of his talent. These scenes do not form a seamless whole and are not linked by any continuous narrative; there are leaps from setting to setting and unbridged time gaps. Malraux attempts to eliminate the redundant and give all his scenes dramatic or intellectual significance, gripping both the imagination and the intellectual attention of the reader. He wastes little time expounding historical background and avoids transitional passages. His impressive range of technique demonstrates his versatility, using pragmatically whatever narrative device might suit his immediate purpose. The result is an elliptical, fragmentary narrative, which makes for difficult but exhilarating reading. Some brilliant scenes, such as a Barcelona anarchist ramming a field gun in a commandeered car or Republicans captured by the Nationalists at Toledo facing the firing squad, have become anthology pieces in their own right.

The guiding principle behind Malraux's scenes is dramatic impact, aesthetic "resonance." Though generally the scenes Malraux writes are factually verifiable, he does not hesitate to deviate from strict accuracy to increase dramatic effect by telescoping events and simplifying. His work can in no way be looked on as a primary historical source, although the unwitting have sometimes done so. The events covered in *L'espoir* end in March 1937, long before the victors could be predicted and before the bombing of Guernica or the "mini–civil war" between Communists and anarchists in Barcelona. In modern days of general literacy, most war narratives, including the most admired, have not been fiction at all but memoirs by participants. These accounts necessarily reflect the authors' viewpoint: participants have no choice about which side they are on, which does not in any way make their accounts hopelessly prejudiced. And though memories grow fainter and may become deliberately distorted or exaggerated, they still bear some definite relation to actual events. As a genre the memoir provides a more accurate representation of war than fiction does, since fiction uses war primarily for aesthetic rather than recording purposes. Most memoirs contain not only accounts of the war as experienced but also the authors' later reflections on events and their significance. War novelists are under enormous disadvantages if they have not also been participants: documentation comes a poor second to lived experience. In compensation, though, novelists are not confined to a single narrative viewpoint and can comment on events without relying on simple authorial intervention, which so easily comes across as preaching and in any case lacks dramatic tension.

Malraux understood this flexibility perfectly. From his own reading of Dostoyevsky, he had developed a technique of intellectual dialogues as a means of bringing out intellectual significance. In these dialogues, the significance of ideas could be expressed through speech rather than reported thought, showing rather than telling. This technique corresponds closely to Mikhail Bakhtin's "monological" and "dialogical" forms of the novel, though at the time Malraux wrote, Bakhtin's work—equally developed from a reading of Dostoyevsky—was unknown in the West and for that matter scarcely heard of even in the Soviet Union (Bakhtin). The weight of ideas in *L'espoir* is carried by fifteen dialogues, at different points in the novel, divided among seventeen characters, and a long conversation one might call a symposium, shared by a number of participants before the fall of Toledo. In these dialogues, events are placed in intellectual relief, ideas can be dramatized at a level above the partisan, and deeper questions about the ultimate significance of the war can be aired. The focus is not so much on the political—Malraux's commitment to the war was practical more than ideological—as on the general ethical implications of war in the first place. These questions are not necessarily answered or answerable: much of the effect of the novel relies on unresolved tensions. In the West the left at the time was deeply divided between active antifascists and idealist pacifists, still very powerful. The latter, drawing their beliefs from their view of World War I, largely based on protest novels such as Erich Maria Remarque's *All Quiet on the Western Front* (1929), had come to believe that general war was so horrible that anything else whatever was better, even a Nazi-dominated world. They were utterly wrong, instead helping bring on the new, even more appalling war they so much feared by convincing Hitler that the democracies would never offer him serious resistance. In the Spain of 1936, however, such absolute pacifism was a position impossible to sustain, as reflected in some of Malraux's dialogues, where characters find themselves forced by events to abandon earlier pacifist views and, in the face of the insurgency, actively commit themselves to war. Violence now became a tragic necessity, just as it does for Maulvault's Carlist.

Intellectual dialogues are one technique deployed by Malraux to enable his novel to transcend the topical. Another is his creation of what has generally come to be known as a subtext, a convenient term to denote reading between the lines. This subtext implicitly pulls against the message of the surface text; its key is Malraux's choice of terminology and imagery. Thus beyond the use of concepts on the political level, such as revolution, others belong more to the existential and metaphysical levels: the nature of humanity, death, the eternal, and destiny. This last term cannot easily be defined, being not only the individual's confrontation with death but also his struggle with the elements, which are unmoved by human feelings or heroism. Events of the war are set against the backdrop of Spanish and European history generally through the use of colorful imagery: an anarchist is compared with one of Emperor Charles V's officers; off-duty airmen rattle knucklebones, a game played by Roman legionaries. These images often move into a timeless dimension: an aviator has a sensation of absolute cosmic peace high above the fighting and the passions of humanity on the ground below. The inevitable result is that events of the war, even defeats, tend to lose their immediate significance against this timeless perspective. Other terms add to this effect, such as the repeated use of the adjective *dérisoire*, meaning both ridiculous and contemptible: a Republican intelligence officer, an art historian in civilian life, walks in the Toledo cemetery and senses that in the presence of these whitened stones all armed struggle is derisory. Again, the impression is created of a deeper level of meaning in the novel, and this level is far from optimistic in its implications: vanity, all is vanity. The tension created by this discordance between surface text and subtext is one of the key features of the novel.[1]

L'espoir in its entirety is too long to be conveniently taught in undergraduate courses and, as a text for graduate classes, is perhaps best studied with Hemingway's *For Whom the Bell Tolls* and Orwell's *Homage to Catalonia*. All three texts convey, in different degrees, this ultimate impression of disillusionment, not surprisingly most poignant in *For Whom the Bell Tolls*, written after the military and political defeat of the Republicans, when hope had indeed been snuffed out, with eventual tragic failure built into the whole fictional structure. If history can scarcely be taught through works of imagination alone, requiring far more analytical background than can be supplied by fiction, which inevitably, and often deliberately, distorts, novels can nevertheless be invaluable in firing the historical imagination. So can memoirs, which, unlike fiction, can be genuine historical sources if treated with caution. At the same time, *L'espoir* can be examined as a fictional treatment of a historical topic, a seminal work, exemplary in the most literal sense in that it can be studied in relation to critical notions, some of which, like the dialogical, came to the fore years after the book's publication. Thus in most of its fifty-nine chapters, covering well over fifty characters and a wide variety of events, a narrative viewpoint is rapidly identifiable, as Malraux puts himself in the place of his different characters, narrating events as supposedly perceived by them and reducing the need for direct authorial intervention. This multiple viewpoint is what has more recently been called focalization; as a technique it is of course not particularly new, being more or less obligatory in the sprawling Dickens-type novel switching among simultaneous events, not to speak of the epistolary novel in the eighteenth century. Other critical notions illustrated include reader-response theory: the critical reception of the novel in France has been studied, with, it must be said, not very surprising results. Antifascists gave the book high praise, whereas enemies of the left criticized it severely, making perhaps an exception of scenes that portrayed the Republicans disfavorably, such as the final fall of Toledo, where they collapse into a near rabble.

What *L'espoir* certainly does not convey is any kind of feminist message or sympathy. Although Malraux was capable of creating strong female characters, there is little in the way of female presence here, in sharp contrast to Hemingway's novel, where Jordan's affair with the girl Maria seems implausible and intrusive. In any case, all the evidence indicates that women played little active role in the Spanish fighting: none at all on the Nationalist side, and those in the Republican ranks rapidly relegated to their traditional roles, cooks and nurses. Nor do we see much of the sexual side of the male characters, since they devote themselves almost asexually to the struggle. Malraux uses the term *fraternité virile* to describe the elated idealism of the Republicans, but in English "heroic comradeship" fits better, since the virility he presents excludes the sexual. Women are seen in his novel mainly as obstacles to the exercise of the male will, and they are absent from the intellectual dialogues. The impression gained is not that Malraux's male characters are macho—far from it—but that they move on a higher plane of heroic activity and intellectual interrogation than do women.

Nor can the novel be treated as that mythical creature, the self-referential work. If ever any novel was palpably about something, this is it. For Malraux, as for his characters, the Spanish Civil War was a serious matter: the terms *comédie* and *carnaval*, which occasionally appear, are marks of contempt, not the half-amused self-indulgence of postmodernism. War narratives, indeed, have run counter to the trends of twentieth-century fiction. Because many such narratives have been memoirs, not novels, realism, not any kind of modernism, has been the dominant mode of both genres, and only with the American experience in Vietnam have wide-scale fictional attempts been made to treat war nonrealistically. (Malraux's elliptical technique, one should note, is, if fragmentary, far from chaotic.) Even then, many writers, in their attempts to convey the perceived chaos of an unpopular war through a similarly chaotic narrative (what may be called the chaotic fallacy), are in fact engaged in an extreme form of mimeticism if they are attempting to transcribe lived experience rather than project fantasy. Authors of memoirs, however, have generally had as a primary aim the "mimetic imperative," the desire to bear witness, with often a subsidiary eye on making sense of lived experience through later reflection. (This is particularly true of the many memoirs by Holocaust survivors, who have frequently described themselves as driven to express their experiences.) Both objectives are difficult to achieve if authors spurn the realistic; they may distort and exaggerate, but only in a general perspective of what they are presenting as genuine, factual experience.

L'espoir shows Malraux at the height of his powers as a novelist, and many critics have regretted that he did not go on to use this fictional ability to write a similar panoramic novel of World War II. The novel is an amazing tour de force for a writer who scarcely knew Spain before 1936 and did not speak the language. His greatest gift is perhaps his swift apprehension and assimilation of ideas and images and his lyrical presentation of them. This gift is probably the key factor in ensuring that his novel is still widely read and admired as a modern epic, long after the political theses have lost their relevance. Here we may once again speak of the notion of transcendence. Yes, *L'espoir* is a thesis novel, but unlike most thesis novels it has aesthetic and intellectual qualities that take it far beyond the purely topical. Again, it is a novel of commitment, commitment to a cause dead within a few years but here raised to a metaphysical level.

One crucial point must be made about the reception of *L'espoir*. The novel is a presentation of the Spanish Civil War by an outsider, not a Spaniard, and its success, like that of Hemingway's novel, lay essentially outside Spain. For years, in any case, translations of *L'espoir* were banned in Spain, but those Spanish readers who obtained access to the book failed to identify with Malraux's narrative. They found the novel overintellectualized and in a sense overidealized, while its cultural background is not so much Spain as the preoccupations of the French intellectual. Malraux's fundamental romanticism, reinforced by his Nietzschean belief in will and energy, leads him as well to present events in Spain as an exotic adventure, against the same picturesque backdrop used by Barrès. For Spaniards, the civil war was a bloodthirsty reality, with untold misery and hundreds of thousands of dead. For them, any notion of lyrical heroism and comradeship had evaporated in a sordid nightmare. Above all it was their own war, not an optional, temporary commitment for outsiders. Nor, for them, was it the first battle of World War II, but the last gasp of an unhappy phase of Spain's own history. A parallel point is that whereas most of Malraux's leading characters in *L'espoir* are Spanish—unlike in *La condition humaine*, where the Shanghai revolutionaries are mostly non-Chinese—his target or implied reader is really a culture-oriented non-Spanish intellectual like himself.

One more French novel needs to be mentioned here, since it is sometimes referred to as if a major theme in it was the Spanish Civil War, though in fact only its epilogue, little more than a tenth of its seven hundred pages, deals with the war. This novel is *Gilles* (1939), by Pierre Drieu la Rochelle, a long-standing colleague and friend of Malraux, who had a considerable reputation as a novelist and essayist between the two world wars. Drieu too was imbued with Nietzschean values; a few years older than Malraux, he had served with distinction in World War I (he was wounded several times), and this experience led him to despise pacific democracy as a kind of decadence. His values, without depending on hereditary aristocracy, were the traditional ones of the warrior: courage, leadership, nobility, contempt for death, willingness to accept violence, above all energy, which is of course as a quality politically and morally neutral. He admired Lenin as an energetic achiever, but by the mid-1930s he admired Hitler more, having been dazzled by a Nuremberg rally.

Gilles was intended as Drieu's major fictional work. The eponymous hero, an obvious mixture of autobiography and wish fulfillment, is a problematic character, a confused combination of the superior individual he considers himself to be and the moral weakling he actually is. The novel covers his life from World War I, from which he returns a wounded hero, through a failed marriage and episodes in politics and journalism to his final throw, when he volunteers in Spain on the Nationalist side. (During World War II Drieu backed the Nazis; then, in early 1945, under threat of trial for his life, he committed suicide, his life ultimately the same wasteful failure as that of Gilles.)

Drieu uses events in Spain less as a subject for informed commentary than as a springboard for Gilles in his personal existential situation. The novel contains two episodes in Spain, tacked onto the main body of the novel in a somewhat clumsy way, almost as an afterthought. In the first episode, Gilles, now calling himself Walter, attempts to flee Barcelona, where he is engaged in mysterious business, to return to France, but he finds himself on the wrong plane, landing on Ibiza in the Balearics, temporarily under Republican control. He is lucky to escape and join up with local Nationalists, who regain control of the island. A later, unconnected episode has him in Burgos as a French journalist, until he moves to a small town somewhere in Extremadura, which is under heavy attack from Republicans. He claims to be neutral but once again insists on joining in the fight, though this time his chances of survival appear minimal, and the novel ends as he fires at the enemy from the bullring being used as a defensive strongpoint.

There is something unsatisfactory about both these scenes. The first is plausible enough, but the second simply does not ring true. Burgos is nowhere near Extremadura, which anyway rapidly fell to Franco's troops, who were in no way outnumbered and outgunned. It is as if Drieu simply wanted to use the Spanish Civil War to end his novel, so that his hero could make an unnecessary, probably suicidal, gesture of commitment, fighting courageously against enormous odds. As such the episode has less to do with Spain than with Gilles's unstable personality. All around, it would be laughable to compare *Gilles* with Malraux's achievement in *L'espoir*, while Maulvault's novel too, in treating similar themes of commitment to the right, comes across as much more powerful.

In assessing the total impact of the Spanish Civil War on French writers, one is immediately struck by how limited it was beyond the handful of authors discussed here. The established generation of literary figures, if they had ever been tempted to write about Spain, would have been discouraged by the fact that Malraux, whose personal experience gave him incomparable authority and prestige, had preempted them with *L'espoir*. Gide's attentions were no doubt fully occupied with his disillusionment after a trip to the Soviet Union, embodied in his influential *Retour de l'U.R.S.S.* (1936; *Return from the U.S.S.R.*), but we look in vain in his journal for any interest in the Spanish war. When he mentions meeting Malraux, just back from Spain, Gide writes not about the events in Spain but about the disintegration of Malraux's marriage, in which Spain acted as a catalyst, and includes some admiring comments about *L'espoir*

(1253–54, 1292). Montherlant also greatly admired Malraux's novel, describing one scene as the ultimate in the art of writing, but avoided writing on Spain himself despite his earlier experience in the country ("Comble").

Nor did the surrealists take much literary interest in events in Spain. André Breton, who regarded himself as their leader, had, it is true, broken with Communism in 1935, but others, such as Louis Aragon and Paul Éluard, who had put their faith in the Soviet Union neglected Spain equally in their writings. It is perhaps unfair to say that surrealists were by definition not living in the real world, since Aragon, Éluard, and René Char would later gain a reputation as war poets for their work written during the German occupation of France. On the other side of politics, Louis-Ferdinand Céline, who exerted a great influence on Sartre in the 1930s, took a brief interest in Spain in 1938, but only to consider it, along with Canada and the United States, as a possible refuge from a France he had come to loathe. Nor, for that matter, did François Mitterand, at that stage in his career deeply involved in the virulent extreme right of politics, take any particular interest in the Spanish war.

Among the next generation of writers, Sartre made one outstanding contribution, "Le mur," but then left Spain alone. Though Camus set his ambitious but flawed drama, *L'état de siège* (1948; *The State of Siege*), in Francoist Cádiz, its theme is not the civil war but an epidemic of plague, presented in an abstract and symbolical manner. Since his mother was Spanish, Camus was unlikely to forget Spain, and continued in a number of postwar pieces to denounce the Franco regime, deploring the fact that the dictator had not been removed in 1945 and indeed had been readmitted to international respectability in the 1950s under the umbrella of anti-Communism. These pieces, however, belong to the prolific output of Camus the political journalist, not Camus the creative writer.

It was the disastrous course of politics at home, rather than the dismal result of the civil war, that drove Spain from the preoccupations of the French. In May 1940 war ceased being a spectator sport for the French, becoming instead for the next few years the very texture of their lives. By that time they had too much to think about on their own doorsteps to take much further interest in Spain, which had paled not so much into insignificance as irrelevance. And whereas the Republicans in Spain held out tenaciously for two and a half years, the Third Republic in France collapsed ignominiously in a matter of weeks. With the signing of the Nazi-Soviet Pact, the notion of the Communists being the linchpin of the

European antifascist movement became laughable. Most of the survivors of the civil war, whether Spanish or not, who made their way to the Soviet Union in 1939 were rapidly purged. Large numbers of Republican refugees, including women and children, crossed the French border in early 1939 only to be interned as undesirables in sickness-ridden camps, where many died. Then, from 1940 on, new groups of Frenchmen crossed the Pyrenees into Spain, this time as would-be volunteers for the Allies in Britain or later in North Africa. These volunteers were eventually allowed to proceed on their way after a period of internment in a camp at Miranda de Ebro; they could just as easily have been imprisoned for the duration of the war or even sent straight back to Vichy France or handed over to the Germans. Imprisonment at Miranda led the young Lucien Bodard, who later became a leading journalist and novelist, to write his first book, a memoir, *La mésaventure espagnole* (1946; "The Spanish Misadventure").

Malraux, for his part, was sadly disillusioned by the final Republican defeat, and no doubt even more so by the Nazi-Soviet Pact that led immediately to the invasion of Poland and World War II. His novel had not in the end helped the Spanish Republicans, and June 1940 in France was more like the shameful collapses he had described at Toledo and Málaga than the heroic defense of Madrid. Nevertheless he preserved his loyalty to the Republican cause, refusing for the rest of his life to set foot in Franco's Spain. His Spanish experiences are notable for being entirely overlooked in his autobiography, *Antimémoires* (1967; *Antimemoirs*). However, *L'espoir* remained one of his three favorites among his own works, though he felt it was too long. One may surmise that it was the political material that he later considered largely superfluous: after World War II, having long broken with the Communist movement and become a minister under De Gaulle, he became irritated that *L'espoir* was still encouraging young people, out of heroic idealism, in their own lyrical illusion, to commit themselves to the extreme left.

Interest in Spain among French intellectuals relapsed to 1920s levels after World War II. By then the orthodoxy was the left, and Spain was a political outcast. In France the very word *fasciste* had been watered down to become an indiscriminate term of abuse for political moderates and conservatives. Apart from the occasional memoir from a participant, few French writers were tempted to write about the Spanish Civil War. One child refugee from Republican Spain, Jorge Semprún, indeed gained an impressive reputation as a French writer, but for his works on deportation as a member of the French Resistance.

Taking a broad view, therefore, one has to say that the Spanish Civil War, with the few exceptions noted here, produced less lasting resonance in the French than in the British or American literary world. Whereas the Spanish experience remained a beacon for many writers in the Anglo-Saxon world, the crushing experience of the Nazi occupation and then the exhilaration of liberation would overshadow the memory of Spain as, post–World War II, French literature took a new turn. Yet those exceptions include one of the finest war novels ever written, *L'espoir*, and a minor masterpiece, "Le mur," two brilliant works that will surely survive.

Note

1. I have discussed this discordance and other topics at greater length in my monograph *Malraux: L'espoir*.

Peter Monteath

German Literary Responses
to the War

Above all else the Spanish Civil War was a bitter conflict of Spaniard
against Spaniard. Some families were torn apart by the divisions in Spanish
politics and society even before the conflagration of 1936. But with the
open outbreak of war in July of that year, a peculiarly Spanish affair, stemming from distinctively Spanish tribulations, soon graduated to a full-
fledged international issue. This development was true in a military sense,
since in a short time troops, "advisers," and matériel arrived on the peninsula from various parts of the world, and in a nonmilitary sense—the
Spanish Civil War was an event that engaged the world's attention. It filled
headlines, fueled passionate debate, and pricked the moral and political
consciences of people everywhere, because for a time at least it seemed
that events in Spain might determine the fate of the world.

In the summer of 1936, even in the grip of the Nazi regime, Germany
could not remain immune to events in Spain. Many Germans, including
members of the Condor Legion, reported on events in Spain and the
apparently irresistible crushing of the "Reds." But Germans of an antifascist bent, too, were persuaded to take up arms, and many gave their
lives to defend the Spanish republic and its ideals. Those who did not find
their way to the fields of battle found other ways to support the cause.

Many followed the adage that the pen is mightier than the sword; they wrote about the war in the firm belief that they could influence its outcome.

Thus the Spanish Civil War was in small part a battle of German against German, and both sides produced a body of literature that testifies to the strength of their commitment to their causes. For these writers Spain was a kind of surrogate war, the civil war that Germany had avoided because of Hitler's spectacular success in 1933. From their perspectives, to conquer or to save Madrid was tantamount to winning the war against the enemy at home.

Nazi Involvement and Literature

In the light of the militarily highly effective role played by the Condor Legion, it seems surprising in retrospect that there was some initial reluctance in Germany's commitment of forces to Spain. In the middle of 1936 Berlin was basking in the glory of hosting the Olympics, a wonderful opportunity to showcase the "new" Germany and its purported rebirth under a regime in power for not much more than three years. When the foreign ministry received the initial request from General Franco to provide support for a *pronunciamiento* threatened with the ignominy of rapid defeat, its response was a polite but firm no. It was not until Franco directed his request to Hitler personally, while the führer was attending his beloved annual Wagner festival in Bayreuth, that the Spanish general secured the response he so desperately needed. Hitler, like the public servants in the foreign ministry, was eager that Germany should do nothing to damage its image as a nation devoted to the cause of international peace. At the same time, he had already indicated—above all through the remilitarization of the Rhineland in March 1936—that in matters of foreign policy he was prepared to take some risks. Acknowledging what he interpreted as the impending threat of Bolshevism in Spain, Hitler dispatched some Junker transport aircraft to Spanish Morocco (Monteath, "Hitler").

Over the course of the war German commitment increased from that initial contingent, but it never grew to the scale of Franco's other major international ally, the Italians. Altogether some eighteen thousand Germans saw military service on Franco's side, though not as ground troops, and because of the rotation system in place there were never more than about sixty-five hundred of them in Spain at one time. They were taken to

Spain in clandestine circumstances and were even referred to as volunteers, though they were following official orders. Many years later one of them, Adolf Galland, who rose to prominence during World War II as a fighter ace, recalled the hushed circumstances of these Spanish tours of duty:

> No one knew anything in detail about the strength and the type of the commitment. It only became evident that one or the other comrade disappeared, without anyone's knowing anything about his transfer or deployment. And after about half a year he came back in good spirits and with a suntan; he bought himself a new car and told his most intimate friends in the greatest confidentiality remarkable things about Spain, where the later world conflict was being, so to speak, carried out within the parameters of a sandpit. (27–28; my trans.)

The relatively small number of "volunteers" and the practice of avoiding any use of the notorious swastika on German military equipment allowed the Germans to continue with the farce of retaining their representation on the multinational Non-intervention Committee, which continued to meet in London. In this hypocrisy they were by no means alone, but frequent reports of German military activity underlined their brazen dishonesty.

The policy of nonintervention meant that the Germans who were sent to Spain could not write about their experiences there, at least not during the war. This is not to say that the German public remained unaware that a major conflict was being fought in a not-so-distant part of Europe. On the contrary, German newspapers reported the war, drawing attention to the danger of the Reds and the atrocities attributed to them, as well as the heroic actions performed on behalf of God and country by the "Nationals." In particular the defense of the Alcázar of Toledo received expansive treatment for its model of collective martyrdom. But these newspapers, like the German newsreels of the day, said not a word about the Condor Legion, even in the wake of the notorious bombing of Guernica in April 1937; following the conventional propaganda line of Franco's forces, the destruction of the ancient Basque town and the deaths of an indeterminate number of its civilians were attributed to retreating Reds, who allegedly resorted to dynamiting towns like Guernica to block the Nationalist advance. If German servicemen could not yet report their contribution to the war, other means were nonetheless still available to exploit the war's propaganda potential. German publishers brought to an eager reading public the works of German noncombatants, as well as books by non-German combatants. An example of the first of these categories is Edwin Erich Dwinger's book *Spanische Silhouetten: Tagebuch einer Frontreise* (1937; "Spanish Silhouettes: Diary of a Journey to the Front"). Dwinger was already well known in Germany for a trilogy set during World War I. With his extensive experience of that war behind him, Dwinger traveled to Spain in September 1936. In *Spanische Silhouetten* he describes his predictably favorable impressions of developments in Nationalist Spain; at the same time he is unsparingly virulent toward the Reds.

The second group of works, those by non-Germans, might be represented by Conrad Everard's curious book, *Luftkampf über Spanien: Kriegserlebnisse eines freiwilligen englischen Kampffliegers bei der nationalen Armee* ("Air Battle over Spain: The War Experiences of a Volunteer English Fighter Pilot with the National Army"). As the title suggests, Everard was allegedly an Englishman on Franco's side, a scenario not outside the realm of possibility, though oddly there appears to be no English original of the book, which was first published in German in 1937. As a fighter pilot the possibly pseudonymous Everard gathered the same sort of experience as many Condor Legion pilots; he certainly shares their political views unreservedly and conveys the sense of enthusiasm for battle that typifies the later writings by Condor Legion pilots.

By the end of the war in 1939 there was no reason to continue to cloak the activities of the Condor Legion in secrecy. On the contrary, from a propaganda viewpoint much was to be gained from highlighting Germany's military contribution. After all, Germany had been on the winning side, and the war had demonstrated that German forces were technologically and strategically cutting-edge. From this point onward books appeared in which German combatants wrote with great enthusiasm about their Spanish experience. Typically, given the nature of the German commitment, many of these books were by pilots. The literature they produced is marked by the self-confidence of those who could by then count themselves among the victors, but it is also distinguished by the bird's-eye view of the pilot sitting comfortably above the destruction and suffering to which he contributed.

An example of this kind of literature is Hannes Trautloft's book *Als Jagdflieger in Spanien: Aus dem Tagebuch eines deutschen Legionärs* ("As a Fighter Pilot in Spain: From the Diary of a German Legionnaire"). Published in 1940, it recounts the period from 28 July 1936, when the author received the news of his mission in Spain, to March 1937, the end of his tour of duty. At every stage Trautloft's account conveys his eagerness to do battle; he is anxious to depart Hamburg in case he should arrive too late in Spain, and he expresses annoyance at any bad weather that prohibits action or at the failure of the enemy to appear. As he puts it, "to live only in a state of preparedness for action is boring for us in the long term. We want to fly, to fight; that's the reason we came here" (31). The order to return to Germany before the war is won is greeted with an almost bitter sense of lost opportunity:

> Leaving the war is so difficult for you, I murmur to myself. How strange. I am supposed to fly toward home as if the war were not continuing here, as if it were at an end. The soldier in me is rebelling, a bitter feeling arises inside me. (243; my trans.)

For Trautloft the war is above all an adventure; its tragic dimension appears alien to him. He is at his most satisfied when he is seated in his cockpit, far removed from the war being waged far below. As the work of Dieter Kühn has shown, Trautloft's perspective is typical of pilots, whether in this war or others. The experience of flying high above events on the ground acts, Kühn argues, something like a drug. The pilot forgets his problems and comes to terms with himself, but in the process he also forgets the conditions under which the civilian population has to suffer during and after the war (192). Trautloft illustrates this mentality when he describes a bombing raid over Madrid:

> One after another the bombs drop; this time their effect is immense. There where the positions of the Reds are, I see complete blocks of houses collapse. Everything in the area, we assume, which is still puffing and panting and has not been crushed to death, must be fleeing in a state of terrified panic. (139–40; my trans.)

In a similar vein, another pilot writes:

> Remarkable how little one notices the bloody battles that are raging down there at this moment: we know it, we know how fiercely the war is being waged, but we don't see it; it is as if we are freed in our lonely heights from all events on earth. (Bley 192; my trans.)

The pilot's detachment from the horrors of war, reinforced by an ideologically driven callousness toward the Reds, provided a portrayal of the Spanish Civil War that was not only popular but also officially sanctioned. The accounts reminded their readers of the superiority of German forces—both technologically and morally—while highlighting the depravity and military inadequacies of the enemy. War, in these accounts at least, was not to be feared; indeed from a height of several thousand feet it could almost be savored.

Writing for the Republic

The German pro-Republican literature of the Spanish Civil War offers a striking contrast to the pro-Franco literature. The circumstances in which it was written and published were quite different. Numerous renowned German literary figures, among them the brothers Heinrich and Thomas Mann and the playwright Bertolt Brecht, had gone into voluntary exile after the Nazi seizure of power; in their adoptive countries many would struggle to find publishers and readerships. For those who had no literary background but had fought in Spain and wanted to convey to their fellow Germans their experiences, the opportunities were even more limited. The Nazis' political opponents, above all socialists and Communists, supported their cause with an underground press that sought to inform Germans of events in Spain and of the ignominious role of the Condor Legion. But this press had to contend with an apparatus of oppression that was both efficient and ruthless.

There were many Germans who made their way to Spain to continue their struggle against fascism. According to Hugh Thomas there were about five thousand volunteers from Germany and Austria who served in the International Brigades, of whom about two thousand gave their lives for the cause (*Spanish Civil War* 983). They were the second largest foreign contingent; the French were the largest. One battalion of the International Brigades, the Ernst Thälmann Battalion, was named for the German Communist Party leader who had been incarcerated by the Nazis in 1933 and was ultimately murdered in Buchenwald in 1944.

Unlike the members of the Condor Legion, the German volunteers for the republic really were volunteers, and unlike their fellow Germans on Franco's side, they were not supplied with the most modern technology. They fought their war alongside Spaniards and multinational forces, often in lice-infested trenches and often with the aid of equipment supplied by the Soviet Union. Theirs was not the bird's-eye perspective of the Condor Legion pilots but rather the so-called *Froschperspektive* ("frog's perspective") made famous in German literature by Erich Maria Remarque's World War I literary classic, *Im Western nichts Neues* (*All Quiet on the Western Front*).

The ideological divide aside, there is a distinct tone in the pro-Republican literature that separates it from the Nazi literature. These are not the enthusiastic adventure stories of the Condor Legion pilots, which sanitize and even glorify war. Rather the works by German combatants in the International Brigades convey a moral earnestness that does not affirm the war experience but accepts it as a necessary evil. These Germans remembered the lesson of World War I and of such writers as Remarque; nonetheless they understood the struggle in Spain to be a just and necessary one, since it was directed against a vicious and inhumane ideology. Ludwig Renn, a veteran of World War I and a prominent literary figure, summarized this view in an impassioned speech he delivered at a writers' conference in Madrid:

> Everything for ideas that are hostile to war! Inimical to war, we say, men of war, we soldiers! Because the war, in which we are helping, is no pleasure for us, no end in itself, but rather something that has to be overcome. (qtd. in Kreuzer 34)

Illustrative of the problems confronted by those Germans who sided with the republic, Renn's account of his experiences in Spain, like the works of many pro-Republican German writers, was not published until after the war. In the wake of the republic's defeat, Renn went to Mexico, where he remained until 1947. In that year he returned to Germany, though by his own choice not to West but to East Germany. When the German Democratic Republic was founded in 1949, he held a chair at the Technical University in Dresden, and it was in his adoptive state that his account of the Spanish Civil War, titled *Im Spanischen Krieg* ("In the Spanish War"), was finally published in 1955.

That kind of personal and literary experience was repeated by other Germans who backed the republic and who, faced with its defeat, were forced into another stage of exile and continued difficulties in pursuing any kind of literary career. They had limited opportunity to make their views on what they perceived as the Spanish tragedy more widely known, at least until World War II finally sealed fascism's fate. Bodo Uhse, like Renn, made his way to Mexico after Spain. His novel set in the war, *Leutnant Bertram* ("Lieutenant Bertram"), was published in 1948 and is of particular interest because its German protagonist personifies the struggle of the two sides. The protagonist's decision to abandon Nazism in favor of the Spanish republic was firmly grounded in the author's life experience: Uhse had for a time supported the radical right as a journalist in the late 1920s, only to throw in his lot with the German Communist Party. Not surprisingly therefore, he also chose the German Democratic Republic as his favored abode when he returned to post–World War II Germany. There he found that veterans of the Republican cause in the Spanish Civil War were regarded as antifascist heroes in a state constructed on a tradition—if not a myth—of antifascism, and their works were keenly promoted and read. It served the German Democratic Republic's interests well to locate a tradition of German antifascism that could be traced back years before the state's foundation.

Other German writer-veterans of the Republican cause opted to live in West Germany, though they did not necessarily find an eager readership for their accounts of the war in a country keen to put the horrors of Nazism behind it. Not only did the Nazi literature of the war cease to be published after 1945, but often pro-Republican works did not find a readership willing and eager to absorb them until the 1970s. Gustav Regler's novel *Das große Beispiel* did not appear in German until 1978, though it was published in English as early as 1940, under the title *The Great Crusade*. Regler was a Communist when he went to Spain to fight for the republic, but he became disillusioned with the party and chose the Federal Republic over the German Democratic Republic. His journey from Communist commitment at the height of the war to apolitical concerns after the war is recorded in his autobiographical *Das Ohr des Malchus* (*The Owl of Minerva*), published in West Germany in 1958.

Compared with their Nazi compatriots, pro-Republican German writers found it difficult to publish their works during the war and to influence a mass readership, especially if their favored genre was the novel or book-length reportage. There were occasional exceptions, such as Willi Bredel, whose book *Begegnung am Ebro* ("Encounter at the Ebro") was published in Paris in 1939, and the Hungarian-born, German-speaking writer Arthur Koestler, who published his *Ein spanisches Testament* (*Spanish Testament*) in Switzerland.[1] An earlier version of Koestler's text appeared in the British newspaper *News Chronicle*, for which Koestler had been working as a journalist when he was arrested by insurgents. His report details his arrest, his prolonged period of incarceration in a Sevilla jail in the first half of 1937, and his coming to terms with the very real possibility that he would soon be executed as a spy. But Bredel and Koestler were exceptions; because most pro-Republican writers' literary activity was subordinated to their military roles or restricted to genres best suited to the exigencies of the day. In practice that might mean working for radio or writing reportage and poetry, which could be published in brigade and company newspapers or in the International Brigades' multilingual organ *El voluntario de la libertad*.

Others offered their literary services for the cause from outside Spain. The playwright Brecht was just one who, though he did not make the journey to Spain, took up the pen in defense of the Republican cause. Like many German intellectuals and writers, Brecht wisely chose to go into exile; despite his strong Communist sympathies, he picked Scandinavia over the Soviet Union. Living in Skovbostrand in Denmark at the outbreak of the war, Brecht relied on newspaper reports and correspondence from friends in Spain to follow the course of events there. He wrote a contribution to the Second International Congress of Anti-fascist Writers in Madrid in 1937, along with a poem and a number of shorter pieces on the war. Above all he was moved to write a one-act play, *Die Gewehre der Frau Carrar* ("Frau Carrar's Rifles"), dealing with the war.

Although it is not widely studied, *Die Gewehre der Frau Carrar* is one of the most performed of Brecht's works, and during the Spanish Civil War it was staged in Paris, Copenhagen, Prague, Stockholm, New York, London, Västerås, Odessa, San Francisco, and Sydney. As the title suggests, at the center of the play is a woman, Teresa Carrar, whose husband was killed defending the rights of the oppressed during the 1934 Asturian uprising. Hoping that her sons might avoid the same fate, she becomes an advocate of neutrality during the Spanish Civil War and will not allow her sons to take up arms. The opposing view is put forth by her brother Pedro Jaqueras, who returns from the front to retrieve a cache of rifles hidden in Frau Carrar's house. He argues the folly of neutrality, and his stance is soon vindicated by the course of events. The elder son, Juan, is murdered in his fishing boat by fascists. When his corpse is delivered to his mother, she recognizes the justice and the necessity of the fight; she retrieves the rifles herself and sets off to the front with her younger son, José.

The play's setting is realistic and historically specific. The action takes place in an Andalusian fishing village; there are specific references to the massacre at Badajoz, to Generals Mola and Franco, and to the role of the International Brigades. Brecht even inserts extracts from the Sevilla radio addresses of General Gonzalo Queipo de Llano, the "Radio General."

This kind of realism suggests that *Die Gewehre der Frau Carrar* is in many respects a traditional play. It follows a typically Aristotelian structure, working from the exposition to the buildup to a point of crisis, followed by the denouement. The play openly invites emotional engagement and empathy with its protagonist. Moreover, the three unities are strictly observed—the entire action takes place in a single house in the time that it takes Frau Carrar's loaf of bread to bake. The play is not regarded as an example of the so-called theater of illusion, in which some of the principles of Aristotelian drama are turned on their head and for which Brecht became renowned in the following years.

Brecht argued that this play and his other work from his exile years can be regarded as works of realism. That does not mean that they faithfully regarded actual events or circumstances; rather it means that as works of literature they were designed and intended to intervene in the real world. *Die Gewehre der Frau Carrar* was written and performed to make a difference to the war and its outcome, to persuade everyone who would listen that pacifism had to be overcome, that fascism had to be overcome on the field of battle, and that it was a moral duty for everyone to take sides.

With the benefit of hindsight it might well seem that the literature of the pro-Franco Germans was more effective than that of Brecht and other pro-Republican writers. Though one might seek in vain for a work of enduring quality among German Franco sympathizers, their literature played its part in the propaganda tasks it was assigned. It demonstrated to Germans living under Hitler their führer's determination to meet the Bolshevik threat, and it reassured them of the efficacy of German military technology and strategy. Yet the period in which these authors were able to impress their readership was limited. Just a few months after the end of the war in Spain, the beginning of a much larger conflagration closer to home caused the achievements of the Condor Legion to drift into obscurity, as the triumphs of the early years of World War II were recorded and celebrated.

As for the many Germans who took a stand against Franco, whether with pen or sword or both, the outcome of the war in which they had invested so many hopes brought them little joy. The commitment that they brought to the war gave way to disillusionment and a bitter recognition that fighting the good fight did not guarantee victory. It was a disillusionment shared by writers from many national backgrounds, but it was particularly poignant for the Germans, who had to acknowledge that the long road to Berlin did not lead through Madrid after all. Many had to wait years until their work could be published, whether in the German Democratic Republic or the Federal Republic, and decades after the Spanish Civil War much of it is forgotten. Some, however, might argue that the example of the committed writer, who followed his or her conscience in placing literary talent and even life itself at the service of the Spanish republic, who acted out of the conviction that the act of writing could change the world for the better, remains valid.

Note

1. *Ein spanisches Testament* was originally published as *Spanish Testament* in 1937. *Dialogue with Death*, an abridged English translation of the German text, was published in 1942.

Carol Maier

Teaching the Literature of the Spanish Civil War in Spanish-to-English Translation

Preparing students to be informed readers of the literature of the Spanish Civil War in translation involves three integrally related responsibilities, of which the location and selection of materials is probably the one instructors think of first. Equally important are two responsibilities that distinguish teaching literature in translation from teaching literature in its original language. Instructors need to sensitize students to the fact that they are reading material in translation by introducing them, however briefly, to important principles of literary translation and the challenges that translation involves. Instructors must also ensure a discussion about not only the author of the work and the historical, political, and literary climate at the time the work was written but also the climate in which the translation was made, the translator, and the response to the translated work. This essay addresses those three responsibilities, first in general terms and then with a specific example, Mercè Rodoreda's *La plaça del Diamant*. The discussion of that novel offers suggestions for teaching literature in translation. Throughout, the guiding premise is that, as translation scholars have argued, monolingual students can be taught to read in translation, not just to read translations (Dingwaney and Maier; Maier, "Teaching"; Venuti, "Pedagogy"; and S. White). This objective requires informing students about the skills and inevitable mediation involved in translation and drawing them into the activity of searching for appropriate ways to convey unfamiliar concepts and situations.

The amount of literature related to the Spanish Civil War written in Spanish during the war and in the following decades might best be described as both abundant and limited. On the one hand, there is a wealth of material in many fine translations, and new translations continue to appear. In 2001, for example, Miguel Hernández's poetry was published in Ted Genoways's *Selected Poems of Miguel Hernández*, which includes translations by Genoways and ten other translators; 2002 brought the revised edition of Christopher Maurer's bilingual *Collected Poems*, by Federico García Lorca, with work by a dozen translators; 2003 saw translations of Javier Cercas's *Soldados de Salamina* (*Soldiers of Salamis*), two poems from Pablo Neruda's *España en el corazón* (*Spain in the Heart*, "What Spain Was Like" and "I Explain a Few Things [1937]"), and a selection from Nivaria Tejera's *El barranco* ("The Ravine"; "Children Can Wait"); and 2004 brought *Written in Water*, a translation of the prose poems of Luis Cernuda (*Ocnos* and *Variaciones sobre tema mexicano*). In addition, translated classics such as Arturo Barea's *The Forging of a Rebel* (*La forja de un rebelde*), Carmen Martín Gaite's *The Back Room* (*El cuarto de atrás*), Ana María Matute's *School of the Sun* and *Awakening* (translations of *Primera memoria*), and Ramón Sender's *Seven Red Sundays* (*Siete domingos rojos*) remain in print. On the other hand, much valuable material in translation is now out of print. This means that work such as José Gironella's *The Cypresses Believe in God* (*Los cipreses creen en Dios*), one of the few Nationalist novels to be translated into English; Sender's *Requiem for a Spanish Peasant* (*Réquiem por un campesino español*); and the anthologies of Valentine Cunningham (*Penguin Book*) and Alun Kenwood, both of which include Spanish material in English translation, are no longer available for classroom use. Some work that does remain in print, such as Carmen Laforet's *Nada*, or *Andrea* (*Nada*—a novel that cannot be considered a novel of the war in the strictest sense [G. Thomas 130] but affords much insight into the war and the years immediately after), is only available in such expensive editions that it is not appropriate for classroom use.

Other factors that limit abundance are the continued prominence of García Lorca, "a ubiquitous popular icon" (Maurer vii) and the Spanish writer that many readers and writers associate most with the war (if, indeed, they can think of others), and the infrequency with which peninsular literature is reviewed in the English-language press. About the enduring presence of García Lorca, Cary Nelson explains that after the war, elegies for the poet "were among the central and inescapable categories used to construct the war's intelligibility and its continuing power in the experience and memory of the Left" (*Wound* 37). Nelson's explanation, documented by many of the poems in the anthology *The Wound and the Dream*, is confirmed by the work of such diverse contemporary artists as the musician George Crumb and the poets Tom Andrews, Edward Hirsch, and Jack Spicer. Yet writers such as Cernuda, Hernández, and Matute, who have also made a strong impression on English-language writers and readers familiar with their work, continue to be less well known because translations of their work are not widely reviewed. Moreover, when their works in translation are reviewed, they are not always placed in an appropriate context. For instance, the translations of Hernández's work in *Selected Poems* were highly praised by the United States poet laureate Hirsch in a brief but informative and informed commentary that should prompt readers to look for the poems: "I don't know how anyone can come away unmoved by the work Hernández wrote when he was dying of tuberculosis in a Spanish prison" ("I Call"). But it is hard not to wonder what impression readers would derive from reading Hardie St. Martin's review of the *Selected Poems*, which was placed in a special feature, "Hispanic Poetry in the Americas." Like Hirsch, St. Martin praised Hernández, but St. Martin's review could easily lead readers to assume that Hernández was a writer from one of the Americas.

The lack of materials, however, and the predominance of García Lorca may actually offer an excellent way to introduce students to the literature of the Spanish Civil War in translation. An effective starting point might be a series of questions that concerned students' knowledge about Spain and Spanish history, their familiarity with Spanish (peninsular) literature, their knowledge of and opinions about war in general and civil war in particular, and their expectations for translated texts. The students' responses to those questions can provide the basis for lectures and discussions about not only the war and its literature but also the lack of material available in translation. Students can be asked to research the reasons that made it possible for Kenwood to write that the war has been "largely forgotten" by readers outside Spain (3), the disparity between the intense interest in Spain on the part of the English-speaking world during the 1930s and the relative lack of interest today, or the fact that there have not been more translations of literature from and about the war and that so many of the existing translations are no longer in print.

Asking students to work interrogatively as they begin to read a text has two advantages with respect to creating an awareness of translation. First, students are prompted to investigate a culture and a historical moment that is probably unfamiliar to them, a moment in their own culture that may also be unfamiliar, and any preconceptions they might have about either. Second, students are led to investigate the role and work of translators, their inevitable presence in the text, and the inextricable relation between translations and their contexts. This investigation can be guided by readings about translation theory and practice, the level of which can be determined by the students' preparation in literary and critical work.

Less advanced students can be asked to read essays such as those in Rainer Schulte and John Biguenet's *The Craft of Translation* or Rosanna Warren's *The Art of Translation*. They can also read the comments of practicing translators who probe beyond discussions of their personal solutions—Umberto Eco's "On Translating and Being Translated" or the exchanges between various translators in "Como Conversazione." For more advanced readers, the essays in Schulte and Biguenet's *Theories of Translation* and in Lawrence Venuti's *Translation Studies Reader* will be helpful, as will Venuti's introduction to his *Rethinking Translation*. Both *Theories* and *Translation Studies Reader* include José Ortega y Gasset's "The Misery and Splendor of Translation" and Walter Benjamin's "The Task of the Translator," although the latter may prove too difficult for most undergraduate students. *Theories* includes Friedrich Schleiermacher's classic "On the Different Methods of Translating," and *Translation Studies Reader* includes seminal pieces by Eugene Nida ("Principles of Correspondence"), Gideon Toury ("The Nature of Norms in Translation"), and Antoine Berman ("Translation and the Trials of the Foreign"). Ortega y Gasset's essay, like Octavio Paz's in *Theories* and Jorge Luis Borges's in *Translation Studies Reader*, was translated from the Spanish; all three essays might be of particular interest to students working with material originally written in Spanish.

Whichever of the essays students read, their reading, research, and discussion will engage them in some of the same activities in which translators are engaged as they translate. These activities enable students to approach translated texts as works of at least two writers that exist in more than one language and culture and at different moments in history (see also Valis ["Hemingway's War"] in this volume). They will recognize the importance of studying both moments and of learning about the translator and his or her background and approach to translation. They will also understand the value of knowing how a translation has fared in English and how the reception of the English text compares with that of the Spanish text. They will be prepared to read literature in translation knowledgeably and to discuss the translation critically. In short, they will come to understand the ways in which the mediation and re-presentation implicit in translation are definitely visible, as Venuti and other contemporary translation theorists have explained.

Rodoreda's *La plaça del Diamant* (1962) provides a rich example of a novel that can be successfully taught in English. The book offers a compelling story, a love story according to the author (*Plaça* 11), narrated in the first person by a young woman named Natàlia who speaks with a disarming, moving immediacy. In the opening chapter, Natàlia meets and falls in love with Quimet, the man who will soon become her husband. Their meeting takes place at a dance in the plaça del Diamant, a plaza or square located in the district of Barcelona known as the Barri de Gràcia. Quimet almost literally sweeps Natàlia off her feet, immediately claiming her as his future wife and renaming her Colometa, his little dove, or pigeon (*colom*). Both the plaza where they meet and Quimet's renaming of Natàlia are significant. Quimet redirects Natàlia's life, and doves, or pigeons, figure prominently throughout the novel, as does the plaza. When in 1982 Rodoreda reflected on the novel from Geneva, where she was living in exile, she stressed the importance to her of the plaza and the working-class neighborhood in which it is located. She expressed the wish that all the readers of the novel could share her affection for the Gràcia district and its inhabitants (*Plaça* 8). And, indeed, many of those readers, Catalonian or not, have responded to her strong sense of place, as if they realized that Colometa's words are "shaped [from what] is recognizably the stuff of collective existence" (Resina, "Link" 230). For Colometa speaks as an individual, a Catalonian woman whose life is irreversibly altered by the war, and as one of many ordinary working-class Catalonians. Her story focuses not on dates and well-known historical events but on the impact that those events had on her life and on the lives of the people who lived near the plaça del Diamant.

   The novel's engaging narrator, its strength as a work of literature, the esteem in which both the book and its author are held by critics and readers alike, and the fact that *La plaça del Diamant* enjoys a multifaceted existence

in English make it attractive for classroom use. Two English-language translations have been made: *The Pigeon Girl*, translated by Helen O'Shea and
published in the United Kingdom shortly after the novel appeared in Catalan, and *The Time of the Doves*, translated by David H. Rosenthal and published in the United States in 1980. *La plaça del Diamant*, a film version
made for Spanish television by Francesc Betriu in 1982, has been distributed
in the United States with English subtitles. The novel is also widely available
in a Spanish (Castilian) translation as *La plaza del Diamante*, and additional
work by Rodoreda is available in English translation (*A Broken Mirror*;
"That Wall, That Mimosa"). *Pigeon Girl* has long been out of print, but
copies are available through interlibrary loan, making it possible for an
instructor to introduce students to the work in two English versions and in
more than one medium and to show them the original in Catalan and its
Castilian translation.

To an instructor who teaches *The Time of the Doves*, I suggest that the
book's title and cover offer the best way to start sensitizing students to
translation. One glance at the titles in Catalan and English alerts even a
monolingual reader to the difference. The original Catalan title is the
name of a place, and on the front cover of my Catalan edition there is a
photograph of couples dancing in front of a bandstand and the Orquesta
Triunfal. Rosenthal's English title evokes not a space but a period of time
and the birds with which Colometa's life is closely identified. On the front
cover near the top there is a small photograph of two doves. The word
doves is written in capital letters and in a considerably larger font than the
rest of the title, and on most of the cover there are Colometa's words from
the text describing the calming effect the birds have on Quimet. O'Shea
also omits Rodoreda's reference to place from the title, and, like Rosenthal, she stresses Colometa's ties to the birds. But there are two important
differences: O'Shea's focus is not on time or space but on character and
gender; for her the birds are pigeons, not doves, and the effect they have
on Colometa is far from calming. On the dust jacket of *The Pigeon Girl*
there is a large, intensely violet-colored face of a young girl. The girl's gaze
is almost (but not quite) directed at the viewer, and superimposed on her
forehead are five rather garish orange birds that could be either doves or
pigeons. Both "dove" and "pigeon" are accurate translations of *colom*
(Andreu-Besó 151–52), and it has been argued that both English titles are
legitimate, since readers in English may not be drawn to a book named
after an unfamiliar place. Michael Ugarte refers to the change Rosenthal
made in Rodoreda's title as "elegant" and does not seem to mind that the

change "diminish[es]" the location's fundamental significance in the novel ("Mercè" 44).

Monolingual students will not be able to evaluate the translation decisions made by O'Shea and Rosenthal or the many differences between their versions. Even so, those differences can prompt them to think about the general issues involved in translating the novel and about the composition of the novel. A discussion of the changes in the title can lead to a discussion about the translator's possible reasons for making such changes and the effect they might have on a reader. Students can consider the comments in Rosenthal's introductory note and his evident desire to make Rodoreda's work known in English. They can think about why O'Shea might have wanted to stress the narrator and her gender. They can find reviews of, and comments about, the translations and the translators. Concerning the elimination of the plaça del Diamant from the title, they can be assigned Joan Ramon Resina's discussion of the novel as one whose "geopolitical and historical coordinates" ("Link" 226) are crucial and Enric Bou's comments about the constant presence of Barcelona and the events of the war in Colometa's life. They can be asked if they agree with Ugarte's assessment of Rosenthal's change and with Albert M. Forcadas's opinion that the change is helpful to the reader and makes the novel comprehensible, since "the new title tells more about the subject matter . . . than the original" (457). In this context, students can consider the introductory theoretical readings and the perpetual question of whether, in Schleiermacher's terms, a translator moves the reader toward the writer or the writer toward the reader.

A discussion of the title can also prompt a consideration of more specific translation challenges such as polysemy and narrative style. *Colom* and its two translations offer good examples of the challenges that can be presented by a single word. Although "dove" or "pigeon" can be used accurately with respect to Rodoreda's narrator, for an English-speaking reader there is a significant difference "at the symbolic level," as J. Vicente Andreu-Besó points out (151). What is more, the challenge for the translator is to make a choice based on his or her reading of the text or "point of view" (Andreu-Besó 152). That choice will not only eliminate the concise polysemy of *colom* but also introduce associations that may not be appropriate to Colometa's role in the novel or the role the birds play in her life, where they sometimes seem to be pigeons and other times doves. To discuss the polysemy throughout the novel (for instance, *contents*, Rodoreda's final word in the novel, could suggest that Natàlia and

Antoni are happy [Rosenthal] or content [O'Shea]), students will need to investigate the meanings of individual words and Rodoreda's use of language, and they will be encouraged to form their own readings of a text.

Even a passage as short as the one below could be used as the basis of a discussion about the choice of "dove" or "pigeon" and the constant association of the bird with both the war and Colometa's complex experience of it. The passage appears at the end of the chapter in which Colometa recounts the declaration of the Second Spanish Republic (14 Apr. 1931), a dramatic event that gave many people an enormous sense of relief and hope. But for Colometa it brought ever-increasing headaches and was linked with her ambivalent feelings about Quimet and her life with the birds that, like the Spanish people, were given a new freedom.

> It was Cintet's doing that the doves came out of the dovecote and we let them fly around, because he said doves had to fly, that they weren't made to live behind bars. . . . From then on I couldn't hang clothes on the roof because the doves would get them dirty. (*Time* 72–73)

> And it was all Cintet's fault that the pigeons came out of the dovecote and we let them fly around, because he said pigeons should fly around and not be spending their lives behind bars. . . . And from that day on I couldn't hang out my washing on the roof because the pigeons messed it up. (*Pigeon Girl* 69)

A discussion of the translation of register and of the indirect nature of Colometa's seemingly spoken narrative can also begin with a consideration of the title. As Andreu-Besó notes, North Americans tend to associate pigeons with "taking over squares and main streets in big cities" (151), whereas doves are associated with peace and reconciliation. By choosing "dove," Rosenthal evokes the more positive associations of *colom*. His choice seems to be consistent with his approach to the translation as a whole, which both Andreu-Besó and Helena Miguélez-Carballeira believe takes the edge off the raw, working-class reality of *La plaça del Diamant.* Rosenthal's translation also produces "a steadier and smoother transfer of expression" (Andreu-Besó 150) and "a neutralization of the original discourse's most distinctive features of cultural specificity and gendered language" (Miguélez-Carballeira 103). By choosing "pigeon," O'Shea evokes a grimmer world and Colometa's "internal war" against the birds, which are "a symbol of the political circumstances" (Andreu-Besó 151). O'Shea's choice seems consistent with the others made in her version, which Miguélez-Carballeira describes as a "highly localized text" that reflects a "manifest endeavour to preserve the numerous traces of Spanish and Catalan culture, as well as Barcelona's topography" (111).

An excellent example for discussion is the translation of Colometa's allusive narration of the outbreak of the war (17 July 1936). Here, as Miguélez-Carballeira explains, the two English-language versions differ significantly (119–20). Colometa's struggle is a "revolution" for Rosenthal and a "revolt" for O'Shea. Rosenthal's Colometa refers to the conflict directly, whereas O'Shea's (like the narrator in the Catalan) only alludes to the war as something implicitly inevitable.

> And I was working on the great revolution with the doves the day the war started and everyone thought it was going to be over quickly. (*Time* 113)

> And while I devoted my energies to the grand revolt against the pigeons, there took place what had to take place, and it seemed as if it would be over quickly. (*Pigeon Girl* 114)

For Andreu-Besó and Miguélez-Carballeira, neither English-language translation of *La plaça del Diamant* is completely satisfying. Miguélez-Carballeira in particular finds it impossible to accept either Rosenthal's suppression of Rodoreda's precise evocation of the Gràcia and its inhabitants or O'Shea's elevation of the narrator's speech—O'Shea's "lexical choices often raise the original text above its distinctly informal register" (103). Miguélez-Carballeira is also troubled by the "unforgivable howlers" (103), which she records in the two versions, and the lack of attention to the narrator's "pre-eminently gendered," "stereotypically female discourse," which she documents in Rosenthal's work in particular. This concern for issues of gender makes an important contribution to the discussion of *La plaça del Diamant* in English. It calls to mind Resina's related but different concern that an overattention to issues of gender on the part of North American feminist scholars was responsible for "displacing" Rodoreda's novel by studying it principally in the context of a "heterogenous cultural and social movement that poses as universal" (Miguélez-Carballeira 116). Together with Andreu-Besó's article, the comments by Miguélez-Carballeira suggest numerous avenues for discussion and examples of how much can be learned by studying the reception of work in translation and by reading multiple versions of the same text.

Since multiple versions and scholarly articles that discuss them are not always available, instructors can still alert students to translation even if only one version of a text is available. As Venuti has explained, students should be taught to "examine differences not only between the foreign text and the translation, but within the translation itself." To accomplish this task, he suggests "focusing on the remainder, [which are] . . . the domestic linguistic forms that are added to the foreign text in the translating process and run athwart the translator's effort to communicate that text" ("Pedagogy" 95). Students who have become familiarized with the historical and cultural context of both the original and the translation and have considered the preconceptions they bring to their readings will be prepared to think about the remainder, even if there is only one translation with which they can work. *La plaça del Diamant* and its various incarnations in English offer a model example, and the lack of multiple versions should not be seen as an insurmountable obstacle. There may not be many multiple English-language versions of literature of the Spanish Civil War, and the range of material in translation may be less wide than an instructor would like, but there is plenty of material at hand. There is also a wealth of material about the war available in English, and the amount of material in Spanish about the war is increasing rapidly.

Note

In writing this essay I greatly benefited from the roundtable discussion "Teaching Texts and Translations," sponsored by the MLA Publications Committee, at the 2000 MLA convention; from Kathleen Ross's collaboration in that session; and from Heather Fowler Salamini, with whom I had the privilege to teach the literature of the Spanish Civil War in translation.

Noël Valis

Hemingway's War

To teach or not to teach Hemingway in a course on the Spanish Civil War? He's been called chauvinistic and male-centered; his fiction has been seen as mired in stereotypes and phony romanticism. The first time I taught Hemingway in such a course I used the play *The Fifth Column* and four stories about the Spanish Civil War, with mixed results. My students and I found the play hopelessly dated, and the stories, while mildly interesting, seemed thin. The next time, with some trepidation, I chose *For Whom the Bell Tolls*. Surprisingly, class discussion was lively and stimulating. Students dwelled on Hemingway's use of Spanish words and phrases and his peculiar stylistic device of approximating English to Spanish by making English sound like a bad translation of Spanish. It became a game in class to figure out what kind of Spanish served as the linguistic base for some of Hemingway's English, and what words lay buried in his frequently mangled Spanish. Then it dawned on me that my students were dealing with *For Whom the Bell Tolls* as though it were a strange sort of translation itself.[1]

In our second class discussion, I proposed to my students that we look at Hemingway's novel as an unexpected contribution to the art of translation by examining his novel as an experiment in cross-cultural translation. For this approach, I found immensely helpful an essay by Anuradha Dingwaney and Carol Maier, "Translation as a Method for Cross-Cultural Teaching." They see

> translation as a cross-cultural activity in which the goal of immediacy or readability is tempered by a simultaneous willingness—even determination—to work in difference. Practicing within this definition, a translator does not strive to make possible rush of identification with an "other" unencumbered by foreignness. Rather, the goal is a more complex verbal "transculturation" in which two languages are held within a single expression. (48)

They propose a method of "cross-cultural reading based on this model of translation" (48). For Dingwaney and Maier a cross-cultural work is itself "an author's translation of a culture" (56). What we have, then, is a simultaneous double translating effort that sees a text as a particular kind of translation being produced and as a translation activity or process.

Is it possible to conceive *For Whom the Bell Tolls* as a cross-cultural text? While normally the term *cross-cultural* points to texts translated across cultures, I suggest that Hemingway crosses cultures within his novel. That is the sense in which I use *cross-cultural* here. Do we then run the risk of neutralizing or relativizing content and effect by translating one culture (the United States) into another (Spain)? Some critics would argue that this is exactly what Hemingway does: privilege and even superimpose American values over Spanish ones and stereotype his Spanish characters while allowing only one strongly delineated individual to emerge, his American protagonist, Robert Jordan. If that is what he does, is there any way we can save Hemingway from himself? Should we?

Hemingway once said of *For Whom the Bell Tolls*, "But it wasn't just the Civil War I put into it. It was everything I had learned about Spain for eighteen years" (qtd. in Valleau 44). The novelist's profound love for Spain is not in dispute, but the nature and extent of his cultural immersion are (see Capellán; Broer; Josephs, "Hemingway's Poor Spanish"; Barea, "Not Spain"; Stanton). To deal usefully with the question of Hemingway's cross-culturalism, students need some background material: first, the degree of Hemingway's commitment to the Spanish Republican cause, and then, the presence of an American ethos in *For Whom the Bell Tolls*. Both these contexts underline how complicated it is to position Hemingway in relation to the Spanish Civil War. Hemingway never faltered in his support of the Loyalists. He went to Spain four times in two years, to report and observe the war, writing thirty-one dispatches for the North

American Newspaper Alliance. He also collaborated in the making of the film documentary *The Spanish Earth* (for different perspectives on the film, see the essays by Shubert and Pingree in this volume) and devoted much time and effort to the Ambulance Corps Committee of the American Friends of Spanish Democracy. These are only a few of his activities—beyond the writing of his stories, play, and novel—during and after the war period. Throughout he remained a staunch antifascist.

But when *For Whom the Bell Tolls* appeared, in 1940, many American veterans of the Abraham Lincoln Brigade took exception to, among other things, Hemingway's critical portrayal of key Republican figures such as La Pasionaria and André Marty and to his extended (and powerful) account of a massacre of fascists by Republicans in a small village. Milton Wolff, the Lincoln Battalion's last commander, recalled his anger and feeling of betrayal many years later:

> I ripped off a letter to Hemingway, attacking the book. Somewhere in there I called him a tourist in Spain, saying that as such he could not know his ass from his elbow as to what the war was about, or words to that effect. ("'American Dead'" 13)

A few lines later Wolff admits "the choice of the word 'tourist' to describe what Hemingway did for our side in the war, and afterward, was way off the mark" (14). Perhaps not, however, judging from critical reevaluations of Hemingway's Spanish Civil War fiction as a form of cultural exoticism of the Spanish other (see B. Fleming; Werlock).

It is worth remembering that a sense of betrayal, occasioned by the Non-intervention Pact, the bitter splits among the left, and the increasing role of the Communists, is part of the Republican experience of the war. Hemingway was no exception. Cary Nelson's nuanced understanding of Hemingway's position is well taken:

> It seems likely that Hemingway used the writing of the novel [*For Whom the Bell Tolls*] to sort through his contradictory feelings about the very different sorts of Republican supporters he met in Spain. If he wrote about no devils on the fascist side, it may be because he took the demonic quality of fascist ideology as a given. ("Honor" 25)

Hemingway's conflicted sentiments come into play with the other context mentioned, the extent to which *For Whom the Bell Tolls* is infused with American values, especially the mythic appeal of the American West. Robert Jordan embodies the classic heroic westerner, the man who in the end stands alone, who probably always stood alone. It was no stretch to cast Hemingway's friend Gary Cooper in the lead role of the film version. It is helpful to show students a clip from the last scene, where Cooper, as Jordan, is alone and firing a machine gun in the "give 'em hell" tradition of war films and as a possible rewriting of Custer's last stand (Rehberger 177, 180). Cooper as the cool, steely marshal facing a slew of gunslingers in *High Noon* (1952) also visualizes for students the westerner as rugged individualist.

As a boy, Hemingway admired Teddy Roosevelt's ideal of the strenuous life, and he devoured dime novel westerns and nonfiction and fiction pieces on the American West from the monthly magazine *St. Nicholas*. His library contained western fiction by Luke Short, Max Brand, and, above all, Owen Wister, whose classic 1902 novel, *The Virginian*, starred Cooper in the 1929 film adaptation (see Reynolds; Rehberger). The western genre functioned as "one kind of anti-modernist response" to the increasing industrialization and urbanism of the United States (Rehberger 165). Hemingway's vision of Spain as possessing a kind of pure "primitivism" and a deep, unsullied connection with the land and nature recalls "the virgin land of the American past" (Guttmann 190). From 1936 to 1939 Spain and the Spanish, as a palimpsest of the American West and the westerner, make their last stand against what Hemingway called "mechanized doom" (87) in the novel, the weapons and technology of total war, as Allen Guttmann has aptly observed (167–95). This mythic version of Spain and the Spanish Civil War does not square well with the historical realities of ideological conflict and betrayal represented in the novel. Moreover, if Robert Jordan's mythic character functions in some ways in sympathetic synch with Hemingway's vision of Spanish values, in other, fundamental ways he clashes terribly with them as the quintessential outsider, recalling Wolff's tourist epithet for Hemingway (see also B. Fleming; Werlock).

It is here where the notion of a cross-cultural translation comes in. Hemingway's use of language (both English and Spanish) highlights a complex interplay between insider-outsider cultures, some, but not all, of which the novelist was acutely aware, as when Pablo asks Robert Jordan, "What right have you, a foreigner, to come to me and tell me what I must do?" (15). Or when Fernando criticizes Jordan, a college Spanish instructor back home, "But it is, in a way, presumptuous for a foreigner to teach Spanish" (209). Or when Jordan suddenly breaks into English because, as he says to Pablo,

> When I get very tired sometimes I speak English. Or when I get very disgusted. Or baffled, say. When I get highly baffled I just talk English

to hear the sound of it. It's a reassuring noise. You ought to try it
sometime. (180)

These lines reveal the stress to which the outsider, the nonnative, is subjected when the attempt to ventriloquize, to masquerade as the other, fails.
Similarly, T. E. Lawrence tried to blend into Arab culture, even though he
knew on at least one level he couldn't: "If I could not assume their character, I could at least conceal my own, and pass among them without evident
friction, neither a discord nor a critic but an unnoticed influence" (30).

Jordan's response to Pablo, "You ought to try it sometime," is self-
conscious and ironic. It isn't simply Jordan's English that makes him
different; it's his perceived feeling of superiority precisely because he is
an outsider that distinguishes him. Cultural and linguistic difference
is built into the character. In one key scene worth discussing in class, the
use of the word "Republican" comes up in conversation. Maria says her
father "was a Republican all his life. It was for that they shot him," to
which Jordan replies, "My father was also a Republican all his life. Also my
grandfather" (66). Later, Pilar asks him if his father is "still active in the
Republic":

"No. He is dead."
"Can one ask how he died?"
"He shot himself."
"To avoid being tortured?" the woman asked.
"Yes," Robert Jordan said. "To avoid being tortured." (66–67)

A moment later Maria says to him, "Then you and me we are the
same" (67). But they are not the same. They speak from different cultural,
historical, and semantic contexts, from two different kinds of republics
and Republicans, and from differing notions (and experience) of torture.[2]
What does Hemingway's sense of irony achieve here? The implied authorial presence hovering gently and even poignantly over this passage, it
seems to me, shuttlecocks unresolved between the ideal of universal
brotherhood and the reality of differences of all sorts (social, cultural, historical). That Jordan himself does not clarify the distinctions in usage of
the word "Republican" suggests discretion or unconscious superiority on
his part, or perhaps both. The Spanish characters, in turn, come across as
politically naive.

Hemingway's awareness of cultural and linguistic difference thus
works for and against him, in much the same way that Robert Jordan's linguistic and cultural masquerade—his presumed bilingual abilities, his one-

ness with shared ideals—ironically elevates him above and beyond the Spaniards he passionately admires. Jordan's speech, for example, is much less marked with the strange constructions and words attributed to Hemingway's Spanish characters (see B. Fleming 274). As Wolfgang Rudat observes, Jordan often "*thinks in English* and, uncritically, translates his thoughts into Spanish" ("Hemingway's Rabbit" 35).

Many critics, beginning with Arturo Barea and including notably Allen Josephs, have hated Hemingway's language experiment in *For Whom the Bell Tolls*.³ Barea writes:

> [H]e invents an artificial and pompous English, which contains many un-English words and constructions, most of which cannot even be admitted as literal translations of the original Spanish. ("Not Spain" 209)

Harry Levin notes that his characters "wander through the ruins of Babel, smattering many tongues and speaking a demotic version of their own" (151). Josephs says that "what Hemingway attempts to render, the effect of one language in another, is quite ambitious, but it requires wide knowledge of both languages, something Hemingway lacked" ("Hemingway's Poor Spanish" 218).

This linguistic rendering is also cultural, as expressed not only in the creation but also in the gendering of characters. Bruce Fleming notes that "the effect of such incorrect English is to make these people seem *strange*" (267). This strangeness (or foreignness), he argues, works against the sense of identification readers ordinarily feel with fictional characters. Like Robert Jordan himself, readers of *For Whom the Bell Tolls* remain outsiders, sightseers of a world that is exoticized, even folkloric at times (B. Fleming 274–75). But like Jordan, "the reader becomes bilingual in a sense," as Fleming observes (274). Of course, Jordan isn't really bilingual, but he behaves as if he were; he masquerades as the cultural (and linguistic) other, at the expense of his own self. Similarly, Lawrence writes that he "could not sincerely take on the Arab skin: it was an affectation only. . . . I had dropped one form and not taken on the other . . . , with a resultant feeling of intense loneliness in life" (31–32). This stressed sense of an assumed self, under linguistic and cultural strain, can prove useful in the classroom because it asks students to take on the bilingual mantle in which Hemingway envelops his novel.

By having students become active translators, the instructor can engage them more fully with the text, in some ways making them insiders as well as outsiders. For example, Hemingway makes use of the archaic "thee" and "thou" to render the intimate *tú* form in Spanish. Thus Jordan says to Anselmo, "Then it is thyself who will forgive thee for killing," in response to Anselmo's feeling of guilt in a godless universe (41). Anselmo, however, addresses Jordan as "you." Does this usage mean that Anselmo is speaking to Jordan with the equivalent of the more formal *usted*, indicating social distinctions? Or does the scene suggest the closeness Jordan experiences with Anselmo? A page later Anselmo uses "thou." This inconsistency is hard to read, but it does suggest a certain textual instability and narrative undecidability that should make us wonder where outside and inside are in this novel.

Other language experiments in *For Whom the Bell Tolls* seem awkward and contrived, as with Hemingway's attempts to get around the censorship of obscenities (see Gould). For example:

> "Where the hell are you going?" Agustín asked the grave little man as he came up.
>
> "To my duty," Fernando said with dignity.
>
> "Thy duty," said Agustín mockingly. "I besmirch the milk of thy duty." Then turning to the woman, "Where the unnameable is this vileness that I am to guard?"
>
> "In the cave," Pilar said. "In two sacks. And I am tired of thy obscenity."
>
> "I obscenity in the milk of thy tiredness," Agustín said. (92–93)

In passages like this one, Hemingway forces his reader to perform translation on the text. On the one hand, he does what a number of translation theorists now encourage: he foreignizes his novel, rather than naturalizing or domesticating the foreign (see Berman 284–85; Venuti, *Translation Studies* 341; Venuti, "Translation" 469).[4] On the other hand, he often falls into the trap of exoticizing the foreign. As Antoine Berman observes, "The traditional method of preserving vernaculars is to *exoticize* them," turning "the foreign from abroad into the foreign at home" (294).

If students only see the work of exoticization in Hemingway's novel, they may conclude that his translated civil war Spain, which represents a betrayal in the historical sense (as thematically portrayed), is also one in the cultural and linguistic senses. Like translation, this assumption would, as Maier observes,

> not only misrepresent but actually distort the activity of translation. . . . Translation . . . implies not so much (failed) exchange as (problematic) interchange that should not automatically be defined as loss. ("Toward a Theoretical Practice" 21)

This notion of interchange allows students to see texts like *For Whom the Bell Tolls* as poised somewhere between inside and outside two different cultures. In that sense, Hemingway's novel is a metaphor for the complicated and tangled, though clearly positive, relationship between American volunteers and Spaniards in the Spanish Civil War.

This in-betweenness is connected to the presence of both translation and masquerade in the text, modes of simultaneous insider-outsiderness. Jordan's imperfect cultural and linguistic masquerade, his problematic persona, is a form of translation itself. The effect of this translated mask is also at work in Hemingway's creation of Pilar and Maria; their gender seems at times overdetermined. Both are insistently linked to nature and the earth, both possess names symbolically tied to the Virgin Mary, and both are closely associated with the republic. Maria's father is a lifelong Republican and mayor of their town, and for that she is raped by National-ist soldiers. Pilar gives her unconditional support to blowing the bridge, part of the Republican offensive: "'I am for the Republic,' the woman of Pablo said happily. 'And the Republic is the bridge'" (53). It is worth remembering that the Spanish republic was symbolically figured as *la niña bonita*, "the pretty girl." Sex and gender are, in this historical context of the republic and the war, thus politicized through rape and allegiance.

Hemingway furthers the association between politics and gender in the most intense scene of the novel: Pilar's eyewitness account of the massacre of fascists by Republicans in a small village. In lending her voice to a violent, male-centered event, he accentuates her androgyny.[5] At one point, Pilar puts on one of the tricornered patent leather hats of the *guardia civil*, which she also does in the film version. I have found it helpful to screen in class the movie reenactment of the massacre, in which Pilar's voice-over not only narrates the events but also speaks the male characters' lines while their mouths move silently, thus producing the odd effect of ventrilo-quism.[6] Here the film makes explicit something that remains implicit in the novel: the sense that gender—like culture—has been ventriloquized in *For Whom the Bell Tolls*, voiced as feminine while pointing to something else that remains undefinable. The androgynous qualities attributed to Pilar and Maria (Maria's cropped hair, for example) suggest that the femi-nine, so closely associated with the republic and the war, must be read through this translated mask Hemingway often drops over his characters, a mask that he creates largely through the ambiguous veil of linguistic and cultural translation. As a cross-cultural text, *For Whom the Bell Tolls* may be a flawed yet fascinating reading experience, but, as Lawrence Venuti remarks on translation, such endeavors to communicate a foreign experience are always partial and utopian ("Translation" 473, 485). The foreign—here Spain and the Spanish Civil War—is always transmitted through the screen of the writer's (and reader's) culture. In that sense, the Spanish conflict can be conceived in *For Whom the Bell Tolls* as Hemingway's war.

Notes

1. Of course Hemingway's novel is not a literal translation. As Milton Azevedo points out, it is first of all an example of a literary dialect, in which the novelist "was trying to convey an impression rather than faithfully re-create the Spanish language in an English medium" (32). But I argue here that Hemingway's language experiment, whatever one chooses to call it, produces a "translation effect." My thanks to Carol Maier for her careful reading of my essay and for her calling my attention to Azevedo's thoughtful article. See also Maier in this volume.

2. In another comparative context, Jordan brings up the American Civil War (and the Indian wars): "Looking at Pablo, he wondered what sort of guerilla [sic] leader he would have been in the American Civil War." A moment later, Jordan says to himself, "There wasn't any Grant, nor any Sherman nor any Stonewall Jackson on either side so far in this war. No. Nor any Jeb Stuart either. Nor any Sheridan. It was overrun with McClellans though" (232–33).

3. But not all critics have hated it. V. S. Pritchett (1941) cited the "astonishingly real Spanish conversation" of the novel (348). I should point out that Josephs has since modified his views on Hemingway's use of Spanish (see *Hemingway's Undiscovered Country* 155).

4. In the 1920s and 1930s writers like Walter Benjamin and Ezra Pound returned to Friedrich Schleiermacher's notion of foreignizing translation. Others like Martin Buber and Franz Rosenzweig saw translation as part of a political and cultural agenda (see Venuti, *Translation Studies* 12–13). Was Hemingway aware of such discussions? It might be useful to read *For Whom the Bell Tolls* alongside Benjamin ("Task") or Pound ("Guido's Relations").

5. The study of gender, including androgyny in the writer's life and work, has produced more nuanced readings of Hemingway, de-emphasizing his male-centered side and reevaluating the presence of strong female characters like Pilar and even Maria (see Crozier; Spilka; and G. Sinclair).

6. The restored version of *For Whom the Bell Tolls*, available on videocassette and DVD, contains the massacre scene, as well as the political content of the movie, nearly all of which was cut in later releases of the film (see Deveny in this volume).

Part IV

The Arts and the War

Thomas Deveny

The Spanish Civil War in Films from the Franco Period

The Spanish Civil War is the first major conflict in which cinema plays so great a role in our understanding of it. It is the first war to take place after the shift from the silent screen to talkies, and technological improvements in the portability of the movie camera allowed the filming of battles, which resulted in newsreels that were shown internationally. Portrayal of the war in cinema demonstrates the power of the medium, since pro-Nationalist and pro-Republican factions in Spain and in other nations made both documentary and feature-length fiction films about the war to justify their cause (see both Pingree and Vernon in this volume). The sheer number of films on the war indicates the tremendous cinematic interest generated by the conflict: the *Catálogo general del cine de la guerra civil* (Amo García; "General Catalog of Civil War Films") lists 889 titles, but because hundreds of documentary films are listed under a few series titles, the actual number of films is much higher. For discussion in the classroom, there are limitations on the availability of films, and professors should keep in mind that special video equipment is needed to project foreign videos and DVDs. Presenting films of different political perspectives and of different nationalities to students will underscore the complex issues and the international interest in the conflict. It will allow students to grapple with the issue of representation of history on film (the official history by the regime in power versus other narratives that undermine it). I examine representative examples of Spanish films that show the Nationalist perspective, non-Spanish films about the war, and Spanish films that show the Republican point of view. In these movies, the relation between film text and society is crucial, and we should keep in mind Louis Montrose's contention, which applies to film as well as writing:

> Representations of the world in written discourse are engaged in constructing the world, in shaping the modalities of social reality, and in accommodating their writers, performers, readers, and audiences to multiple and shifting subject positions within the world they both constitute and inhabit. (16)

Raza ("Race"; 1941; available in DVD-Z0/PAL or video PAL format) and its cold-war version, *Espíritu de una raza* ("Spirit of a Race"; 1950; DVD/PAL format),[1] directed by José Luis Sáenz de Heredia, are two of the most important films about the Spanish Civil War from the Nationalist perspective. The script writer, whose pseudonym was Jaime de Andrade, was none other than Francisco Franco. The story of the Churrucas is a romanticized semiautobiographical story of his Galician family. The flashback narrative by Pedro Churruca of his ancestor's bravery in the battle of Trafalgar, as well as his own heroism while fighting in Cuba, gives a historical context to the proposition that a civil war demands extraordinary sacrifices.

One possible approach to *Raza* and *Espíritu* is to focus on how the films function as propaganda (for another perspective, see Moreiras-Menor in this volume). In *Espíritu* the propaganda begins with the word choice in the opening intertitles, which speak of a nation perishing in the catastrophes that Communism provokes. Both versions depict Republicans as materialistic, as opposed to the Nationalists, who espouse spiritual values. Marisol and Jaime most clearly exemplify this spirituality, but as Emilio García Fernández points out, Sáenz de Heredia manipulates the lighting for the "mystical" gazes of several characters (130). Indeed, the films show religion to be a key element of the Nationalist cause, and from the beginning (the words with which Don Pedro announces to Don Luis the death of his son), conflate patriotism and religion. *Raza* and *Espíritu* portray the Churruca family as very religious: Pedro and family stop by a church and pray, the widowed Isabel wears a cross, José's improbable survival of the firing-squad execution is attributed to divine intervention. The fate of Jaime particularly shows how religion is used to strike a chord with the audience. Close-ups of newspaper headlines emphasize the burning of convents, and the Republican militia's attack on Jaime's church includes sacrilegious activities. The role of children here (and throughout) provides an ingenuous point of view of the conflict, underscores the Manichaean nature of the films, and accentuates the empathy that the director wants the audience to feel toward the Nationalist victims.

Kathleen Vernon applies to *Raza* theories of historical film developed by José Enrique Monterde and Marta Selva, showing how the film overevaluates the hero, insists on Spain as a unified *patria*, selects "glorious moments" for inspiration, and condemns democratic politics ("Reviewing" 30–32). *Espíritu* constantly equates the Republican side with Russia and Communism, which is referred to in negative terms—an "abyss" and a "force that will cause Spain to perish." *Espíritu* equates Moscow to "terrorism and barbarism" and proclaims that Nationalists will finally win the battle against "barbarous and atheist Communism" and the "deaf materialists." When the firing squad shoots José, his final words, "Up with Spain," contrast with the graffiti on the wall seen in deep focus when he falls: "Long live Russia," with the *s* written backward, which further denigrates the Republican cause. The film likewise refers negatively to the International Brigades ("undesirables"). There is no mention of the aid provided to Franco by Hitler and Mussolini, but it is ironic that Moorish soldiers, who were so instrumental in Franco's victory, are prominent in the triumphant parades at the end of both films.

Both films capture the fratricidal conflict—the division of the Spanish family—by literally pitting brother against brother and establish Alfredo Mayo, who plays José, as the most important leading man of the decade. José's brother Pedro, a Republican politician, finally sees the light and risks his life for the Nationalist cause. Pedro represents the culmination of sacrifice in the films, which start with his ancestors and include the doctor and the dentist who risk helping José in Madrid; the fifty-eight-year-old Joaquín González, who enlists with the Nationalists after his two sons die for the cause; and the woman who becomes a Nationalist spy to offer her life for Spain.

The role of women in *Raza* and *Espíritu* is another important area to explore. The films portray Doña Isabel as an exemplary mother; in that portrayal, being Spanish is equated to self-sacrifice and being Christian. Marisol also represents faithfulness and devotion. The only Republican woman, the piano player in the bar, is seen as a sexual object. And in the final scene of *Espíritu*, it is Isabelita who tells her son that the triumph of the Nationalist cause, as represented by the parading troops, is "the spirit of a race" (and simply "race" in the original). Constant references to the "pure essences of Spanish tradition," "the great enterprise of returning Spain to its destiny," and so on reflect the strange titles of the films underlining Franco's ideal for Spain. The propagandistic rhetoric could not be stronger.

Juan de Orduña's *A mí la legión* ("The Legion for Me"; 1942; video in Spanish, PAL format) exalts the values of the fatherland and in particular military values espoused by the Spanish Foreign Legion: valor, honor, and reverence for the flag. Most of the film occurs in Morocco and deals with the incorporation into the legion of the newcomer Mauro, who refuses to give any information about himself. He befriends Grajo and Curro, whose Andalusian persona (heavy accent, constant joking, identity as a bullfighter, and cross-dressed cabaret performance of a flamenco singer) provides not only humor to the film but also the basis for Spanishness that the *patria*—and the film—represents. When Mauro suffers an injury while saving the wounded Grajo in a battle against Moors, he cements their brotherhood, another ideal espoused by the film. The plot takes an improbable twist when Mauro turns out to be the crown prince of the imaginary kingdom of Silonia, who must return to his homeland. However, a close-up of an invitation to a palace dance that is clearly dated 18 July 1936 sets the stage for the civil war theme. Grajo explains that "transcendental" events are occurring in Spain. The commander's words to the assembled troops capture the film's militaristic ideal that dying in battle is the greatest honor and that living as a coward is the worst thing one can do. His harangue ends with the patriotic admonitions, "Long live Spain!" and "Long live the legion!" The montage of war scenes then provides a background to the shot of the heroic pair of legionnaires as they march, sing, and carry the Nationalist flag. The sound track, which is filled with martial music, serves to raise the patriotic spirit of the audience.

Students should explore the Manichaean aspects of this film. It shows a certain anti-Semitism (for Franco, the triumvirate of evil consisted of Reds, Masons, and Jews), as the duplicitous murderer during a dance-room brawl is identified as Isaac Leví. Other bad guys, who are plotting to assassinate the crown prince, have a strong resemblance to Lenin. The final scene, in which the two legionnaires—the good guys—plant the Nationalist flag at the top of a hill, is filled with symbolism that an audience in 1942 would not miss.

The opening image of Pedro Lazaga's *La fiel infantería* ("The Loyal Infantry"; 1959; video in Spanish, PAL format), the sun rising behind a tall hill capped by a tower, implies a new beginning after obstacles are overcome. The film ends with a long shot of the same locale, which takes on new meaning after the heroic sacrifice of the Nationalist soldiers who fought and died to conquer Burned Hill. The shift from humor (Nationalist soldiers capture abandoned chickens) to pathos (Republican aviation kills one of the soldiers) draws a heightened emotional response from the audience. Humor is almost always an important component of these Nationalist films, and the soldiers tricking Don Blas while Miguel cheats on his history examination illustrates the recurring picaresque theme in Spanish culture. The film shifts to melodrama when Julia races after the departing troop train, waving good-bye and lowering her head. The sound track reflects this emotional gamut, with songs that are both humorous (the marching song accompanied by harmonica) and romantic (the solo sung with guitar around the campfire).

Most of the movie deals with the lives of the soldiers while on leave, and in particular it explores their romantic inclinations. The director Lazaga tantalizes the audience with sexual innuendo but idealizes these relationships to conform to the Catholic ideology of the Franco regime. Félix resists Elisa's charms before their wedding, and the honeymoon scenes are chaste. Dancing is allowed, if it is a traditional Spanish paso doble; more tropical rhythms are seen as strange. The model girlfriend is Paloma, an attractive blonde whose job working in the ticket office of the movie theater equates her with that glamour industry, and a close-up shot frames her with a poster of Jean Harlow, thus creating an ideal of feminine beauty that contrasts in great measure with Spanish reality.

The battle sequence shows losses on both sides, but the director obviously wants the audience to empathize with the death of the Nationalists Andrés and Félix. The newly married Félix, although both shot and stabbed with a bayonet, is able to give one final glance at the Nationalist flag triumphantly raised on the captured tower. The film is dedicated to all Spaniards, dead or alive, who fought, but the final words, "¡Larga paz!" ("Long peace!"), reflect the ideal of the Franco regime that was by then in its twentieth year of power.

Non-Spanish films often favor the Republican cause. *L'espoir / Sierra de Teruel* ("Man's Hope / The Sierra of Teruel"; 1938; NTSC video; released in 1945) was based on the director André Malraux's experiences as commander of a pro-Republican international air squadron and his novel of the same name. The film has Spanish dialogue with French subtitles and intertitles, as well as introductory comments in French (PAL format). The filming of *L'espoir* in Spain ended the day before Nationalist troops entered Barcelona, and the movie was completed in France but not publicly shown until 1945 (see also Boak in this volume for a discussion of Malraux's novel). Consequently, the film has the look of a documentary. A class on *L'espoir / Sierra de Teruel* could begin with a discussion of Marjorie Valleau's contention that it fits Joan Mellen's category of "fictional documentaries": films that are "rooted in a concrete historical context" and show the following qualities: a "search for a clarity about historical issues, the absence of a hero, and a director who is personally engaged and identifies with the protagonists"(81).

The diverse nationalities of the international combatants merit analysis. The fallen soldier whom the commandant eulogizes is Italian, and the mortally wounded pilot is German, thus showing the antifascist contribution from those countries, which contrasts with the official policy of their government; others are French and Arabic. Why does Malraux emphasize their involvement and not mention other international participation? On the other hand, the Republicans constantly refer to the *franquistes* in the Spanish dialogue as "Moors."

Another topic to explore is Valleau's observation that one of the main themes of the film, comradeship, is shown by groups of characters performing collective actions (82). Examples are the men who attack the cannon, José and Pío's reconnaissance, the men aboard the airplane, and the several shots of lines of civilians (who were mainly not professional actors). Peasants bring household receptacles to make bombs, men sit at tables in meetings, workers carry meat, and finally civilians carry the dead and wounded from the plane crash.

As in later films, the relative military poverty of the Republican side is a constant theme. The bag of pistols, lack of rifles, the need to use civilian vehicles to light the airfield, the six-month wait for airplane motors, and the complaint about using a gun from 1913 are examples. Valleau notes "the contrast between the vulnerability of the automobile and the power of the huge cannon" (84). The close temporal proximity to the conflict and the fictional documentary style make *L'espoir / Sierra de Teruel* a powerful film from the Republican perspective.

Instructors who choose to use *For Whom the Bell Tolls* (1943; in English, DVD NTSC format), Sam Wood's screen adaptation of the novel by Ernest Hemingway, should be sure to show the newly restored version of the film, since the shorter, edited version eliminated much of the political content of the movie. Classroom discussion might begin with the John Donne epigraph, and it could center on the meaning of those words with regard to Robert Jordan's specific involvement in the war and on the attitude of Americans in the 1930s to the events in Spain (official neutrality in contrast to the men who volunteered in the Abraham Lincoln Brigade) or in the early 1940s with regard to American foreign policy. Jordan's statement about why he is fighting in Spain should be examined in detail, especially since it was not in the novel. Why is it important that Jordan is a college instructor—indeed, a Spanish instructor? The ending, in which he fights alone against the forces of evil, is of particular note. As he shoots straight at us, do the words "They can't stop us, ever" implicate the audience? The cut to the tolling bell as the final image of the film brings us back to the epigraph. Is Jordan's choice to die as he does an embodiment of American, Spanish, or universal ideals? Marcel Oms notes that the film is articulated around the figure of Robert Jordan through the American myth of Gary Cooper (140; see also Valis ["Hemingway's War"] in this volume).

This film shows the clear military superiority of the Nationalist side. El Sordo and his men are defenseless against the Nationalist planes. But the Nationalist captain is made to be a *machista* fool, and Nationalist soldiers are portrayed as disobedient cowards (or perhaps as men with common sense!).

Students should consider various aspects of the portrayal of the Republicans in the film. They are a ragtag outfit beset with a good deal of infighting. Because Andrés is unable to reach General Golz on time, the film implies that the Russians are responsible for the military disaster, as Valleau indicates (39). To what extent does cultural stereotyping exist (esp. of the gypsy character, Rafael)? Discussion of gender roles in Spanish society of the time can center on Pilar: her leadership of the group culminates with her actions during the attack on the bridge. Pablo's betrayal and his lack of ethics (his murder of the three men who fight for the bridge) show how this film eschews a simplistic division between opposing sides.

Valleau contends that *For Whom the Bell Tolls* is "not a simple proRepublican and anti-Nationalist statement. Rather it is a film which questions the morality of war and violence" (44). References to violence toward civilians in the war occur on both sides. Joaquín cries when he recalls the death of family members at the hands of the Nationalists. Pilar's recounting of the violence toward the mayor and other fascists (in the tradition of *Fuenteovejuna*) occurs in flashback; Maria's narration, done without the flashback technique, is shot in close-up and is one of the culminating scenes between Robert and Maria. How does the love between them affect our response to the conflict and to the film?

Although the death of Franco in 1975 and the end of censorship allowed a striking change in perspective on the war, the deconstruction of the Franco regime's official version of the conflict began in the mid-1960s, as the once *dictadura*, or "hard" dictatorship, became a *dictablanda*, or "soft" dictatorship. Young Spanish filmmakers were interested in more than portraying the war; many of their films show its myriad effects. Indeed, Ignacio Sotelo believes that the Spanish Civil War only "ended with the death of Franco." As I have shown in *Cain on Screen: Contemporary Spanish Cinema*, which analyzes films from 1965 to the early 1990s, filmmakers portray the maquis (guerrilla fighters who continued the fight against the Franco regime); the misery and oppression of the postwar era; moles (Republicans living clandestine lives during the Franco era); a return to the past (the attempt to come to terms with the fratricidal conflict by evoking memories of that period or—for political exiles—returning to the homeland); the divisions in Spanish society that continued until the end of *franquismo*; and images of the war and its aftermath in new documentary films (some of which, such as *El caudillo*, were filmed in the early 1970s but not allowed to be released until Franco's death). For the classroom, excellent choices would include Carlos Saura's *La prima Angélica* and *La caza*, as well as Víctor Erice's *El espíritu de la colmena*.

From the mid 1960s to the early 1980s, Carlos Saura's films deal with historical memory revolving around the Spanish Civil War. The first of these is *La caza* ("The Hunt"; 1965; Spanish with English subtitles, NTSC video). This film marks the initial collaboration between Saura and the producer Elías Querejeta and establishes what John Hopewell terms the "Querejeta look" that will be significant in several films of the period (71). In *La caza*, three old friends, José, Paco, and Luis, go on a rabbit hunt. A young man, Enrique, accompanies them. Tension among the older men mounts throughout the film, and they end up killing one another. The film serves as an allegory of the Spanish Civil War and its aftermath. The allegorical nature of *La caza* is mainly due to the censorship still in force at the time. Saura notes his inability to tell the story directly (Gubern, *Cine* 19). The censors prohibited the words "civil war," so that the phrase "the war" "winds up taking on a strange meaning. By way of this indirection one gets the feeling that this is an oppressive environment, that there is a sense of violence, not only in the characters but in the setting itself" (qtd. in D'Lugo, *Films* 56). Dialogue in the film clearly implies that the older men are veterans of the Spanish Civil War. In addition, the choice of actors to portray the protagonists is crucial for this interpretation; Saura's use of stars of Francoist triumphalist films, Alfredo Mayo (*Raza, A mí la legión*) and Ismael Merlo (*La fiel infantería*), provides implicit intertextual references to the war.

The roles of Enrique and Juan are also important to the allegory. According to Marvin D'Lugo, "Enrique's constant presence works to remind the viewer of the insufficiency of what is presented and discussed. He is the opaque figure of inquiry into the habits of a false social normality" (*Films* 58). Students should note Enrique's use of field glasses and cameras, his gradual identification with the older generation, and the freeze-frame of this character at the end of the film (D'Lugo, *Films* 61–62, 64–66). García Fernández believes that the exploitation of Juan, the impoverished caretaker, by José, the landowner, also constitutes one of the key elements in a political reading of the film (254).

Students should pay particular attention to the construction of the film. Most important is the use of montage. For example, a close-up of Paco aiming his shotgun to the right juxtaposed with a close-up of José aiming his to the left creates the Kuleshov effect, giving the impression that they are about to shoot each other (Deveny 206). Hopewell notes the importance of the contrast between close-ups and long shots (73). Marsha Kinder believes that the dialectic montage functions on several levels, and she also considers that the final hunt sequence is divided into three acts (*Blood Cinema* 162).

The carnage of the rabbit hunt is one of many elements that foreshadow the violence at the end of the film (Deveny 206). Students should identify the many symbols and metaphors throughout the film. The setting is particularly significant, as several elements hark back to the civil war; also, characters repeatedly refer to the oppressive heat, which acquires the same existential weight as in Albert Camus's *The Stranger* (Deveny 206). The sound track, especially the percussive music, adds to the tone of violence and desperation (Kinder, *Blood Cinema* 161). The martial sound of a snare drum and Luis's whistling of "The Battle Hymn of the Republic" foreshadow the fratricidal bloodshed (Deveny 204, 205).

Hopewell believes that "the great quality of *La caza* is that complex associations are grounded in social and psychological observation" (74). Saura continued his acute observation and deconstruction of the Francoist victory and regime in films such as *El jardín de las delicias* (1970), *La prima Angélica* (1973), and *Dulces horas* (1982), which made him one of the most important directors of films during the transition to democracy in Spain.

La prima Angélica ("Cousin Angelica"; video in Spanish, PAL format), which explicitly presents the Republican perspective in a favorable light, was very controversial at the time. The protagonist, Luis (admirably played by José Luis López Vázquez), returns to Segovia, where he spent the war, and confronts memories of the past. He is conscious of his mental processes and their relation to literature, citing Marcel Proust when looking at old pictures in a photo album. His memories begin with what Kinder calls a "powerful germinal image," the opening shot of the film, "which is illuminated by strange overexposed lighting; the camera slowly glides through wreckage, observing signs of violence of some unknown disaster" ("Carlos Saura" 20). We fully understand the image only when it is taken in syntagmatic relation with later scenes: after a priest gives an emotional sermon about death and eternity, stressing that even young boys can be victims of "the red fury," the schoolboys hear the sound of airplanes and of bombs falling and exploding. The "germinal image" then is clear: it is an indelible memory from the civil war. Saura's use of the adult Luis, who appears in flashbacks when he evokes memories of 1936, raises many questions. How does memory function? How does the present impinge on the past? Is the past truly retrievable? D'Lugo points out that Luis's repositioning in the second roadside flashback allows him—and the audience—to analyze his experiences and "come to grips with his own misrecognized personal and collective history" ("Politics" 55).

Another key memory of the war occurs when we hear gunshots in the street—a symbol of the conflict to come—and the family anxiously listens to the radio for news. The announcement that the city has joined the "Movement of Salvation" of Franco's troops brings shouts of joy from the family. In jubilation, they sing the fascist hymn "Cara al sol" ("Facing the Sun"). The image of Luis apart from the group symbolizes that he is the black sheep of the family.

Religious iconography is also important in the film. Two paintings trigger flashbacks that show the role of the church during the war and the Franco regime. The priest's instructions to young Luis dressed as a Roman soldier, "Absolute immobility," must be taken in both a literal (physical) and figurative (spiritual) sense. The oneiric image of the nun is implicitly critical of the Catholic Church.

Luis relives seeing the film *Los ojos de Londres* ("The Eyes of London"), which priests showed their young students as a lesson on the horrors of eternal damnation. D'Lugo believes that this experience "equates the positioning effect of the cinematic apparatus with the larger cultural apparatus that has subjected Luis to a reimaging of lived experiences as well as imagining of experiences yet to be lived" (*Films* 122). He notes how the final image of Angélica and her daughter looking directly into the camera "effectively transposes Luis's troubled relation to a personal and collective past to the place of his spectator" and therefore triggers "a desire for a lucidity about the burden of . . . [Spanish] history as it continues to shape the present" (125).

That Saura has the same actor play the roles of Angélica's father and husband leads to a further questioning of the process of remembering. Although Luis "sees" his father executed because of Angélica's admonition, it is a false memory. The most controversial image of the film is Luis's memory of Angélica's father with his arm in a cast, frozen in what appears to be a fascist salute. This gesture contributed to an unprecedented emotional reaction to the film: rightist elements firebombed a movie theater in Barcelona and broke into the projection box at a theater in Madrid. Despite these attacks, the film became a great commercial success.

Erice's *El espíritu de la colmena* ("The Spirit of the Beehive"; 1973; Spanish with English subtitles, NTSC or DVD-Z2 PAL) is a seminal film in the history of Spanish cinema. Students will notice the deliberately slow pacing of the film. There are several reasons for it: the monotony of life in a Castilian village in the 1940s; the timelessness of the fairy-tale and mythic narratives with which the film is contextualized; and the oppressiveness of the Franco regime that led to a sense of stagnation in society. This oppressiveness is associated with the lack of communication between Fernando and his wife. Their political leanings are implied in Fernando's listening to clandestine radio broadcasts, in his relationship with Miguel de Unamuno (the photo of them together, their affinity for origami), and in Teresa's letter (addressed to a Red Cross station in Nice) and her rendition of "Zorongo gitano" (associated with the martyred Republican Federico García Lorca). The discordant notes point to the break between the happiness of their prewar existence and the current lack of harmony, on both a personal and political level.

The repression during the Franco regime is manifest at many levels. Ángel Camiña observes that at school the missing sexual organs on the mannequin represent the "absolute taboo" regarding sexual education in that period (121), and Hopewell notes that the recitation of verses by the Galician poet Rosalía de Castro is in Spanish, "the language of Franco's regime" (207). The portrait of Franco in the classroom and the drawing of the Virgin on the blackboard underscore the political and religious climate. The most important aspect of oppression in the film is the isolation that appears on many levels. D'Lugo indicates that "part of the film's complexity derives from the distinctive way each of the principal characters defines his or her relation to the outside world" (*Guide* 56).

Students can also explore the rich use of the Frankenstein myth in the film (see also Labanyi in this volume). E. C. Riley notes how the montage creates an association between the monster and Fernando (492). When Isabel instructs Ana to call the monster, we hear the father's footsteps. There is also a relation between the monster and the maquis. That the entire atmosphere of the film is filled with death applies, from an oppositional perspective, to life under the Franco regime. Marsha Kinder believes that the intertextual reference to Frankenstein is "the perfect myth" for those whom José Luis Borau calls "the children of Franco" ("Children" 61, 57), the generation of filmmakers opposed to Franco at the end of his regime. Likewise, she observes that "Erice's narrative appropriates the myth for a political discourse that was still suppressed from representation in Spain" (*Blood Cinema* 128).

Montrose notes that "the writing and reading of texts, as well as the processes by which they are circulated and categorized, analyzed and taught, are being construed as historically determined and determining modes of cultural work" (15). This observation applies to these filmic texts. *Raza, A mí la legión,* and *La fiel infantería* show how the Franco regime created and maintained over decades an official history of the Nationalist victory that promoted the fascist ideals of the regime. During Franco's final years, however, Spanish directors like Saura and Erice were able to subvert this history and show Spanish audiences the negative consequences of that victory. Students should analyze what these films tell us both about the civil war and about the end of Franco's regime. One aim of such non-Spanish films as *L'espoir / Sierra de Teruel* and *For Whom the Bell Tolls* was to create antifascist sentiment in France, the United States, and elsewhere. How successful were they? Given the power of the medium, it is important to analyze the relation between text and society with these films, both in the context in which they were created and in the context in which they were and are still received. From propagandistic to deconstructive, these films that portray the Spanish Civil War can teach us about the war itself and about how generations of Spaniards and non-Spaniards alike have reacted to it.

Note

1. PAL is Phase Alternating Line format; NTSC is National Television System Committee format.

Marvin D'Lugo

Representations of the Civil War
in Post-Franco Cinema

In the decades since the dismantlement of the Franco dictatorship, cinematic representations of the civil war have evolved, from cathartic evocations of the conflict in auteur films of the early years of political transition (Gubern, "Tendencies" 17) to a civil war genre stabilized around a relatively predictable set of anti-Franco themes and motives (Monterde 157) and finally to an aesthetic style only loosely related to historical discourses (Jordan and Morgan-Tamosunas, "Reconstructing" 16). In the post-Franco period, the attractiveness of the civil war as a cinematic trope has often been motivated more by commercial than by political interests, as producers discovered that it is a marketable commodity for the international distribution of Spanish films (D'Lugo, "Vicente Aranda's *Amantes*" 291).

As Esteve Riambau notes, in the immediate post-Franco period, part of that recuperative process of previously blocked history was to add a certain cultural prestige to the treatment of the war theme by adapting significant literary works about the war (422–24). Although this trend continued well beyond the transition years, the most imaginative of these adaptations was a film that came early in the process: Ricardo Franco's reformulation of the plot of Camilo José Cela's novel into *Pascual Duarte* (1975). The screen adaptation was directed by Franco under the aegis of

281

Elías Querejeta's production company, which had worked during the previous decade to support important oppositional filmmaking, including works by Carlos Saura, Víctor Erice, and Manuel Gutiérrez Aragón.

The film was conceived as two narratives that develop in parallel fashion. One is Pascual's linear biography, the violence woven into his life and actions; the other, his imprisonment and execution. Cela's fragmented first-person novel, *La familia de Pascual Duarte* (*The Family of Pascual Duarte*), does not in fact treat the civil war in any direct fashion (for an analysis of the novel, see López de Martínez in this volume). As Kathleen M. Vernon shows, however, a chain of opaque historical references in the work justifies the film's depiction of political events in the years before the civil war as a backstory to Pascual's narration (*"Politique"*). Political and social contexts of the years leading up to the war coincide with key moments in the life of Cela's protagonist. The most conspicuous moment is the dramatization of the radio proclamation of the republic by Alcalá Zamora on the second Sunday of April 1931, which coincides with Pascual's honeymoon in Trujillo, where he sees crowds congregating on the street to hear the announcement. Years later, when he returns from jail to his village, he sees from his train window graffiti proclaiming "Tierra y Libertad, C. N. T., F. A. I." ("Land and Freedom, C. N. T., F. A. I.").

Vernon contends:

> Cela's decision to present the events of Pascual's life, in effect, disconnected from the historical situation of the time is a political choice, just as surely as [is] Ricardo Franco's determination to make the interdependence of story and history essential to his film. (95n13)

As producer of the film, Querejeta worked with Franco and the script coauthor Emilio Martínez Lázaro to downplay the purely psychological motivations for the protagonist's action and to emphasize instead the political contexts from the novel, which is sparse on such historical details (Ángulo, Heredero, and Rebordinos 152). One possible approach to the film is to consider how Franco's script appropriates the Cela novel to capture the spirit of the period rather than simply dramatize the events of Pascual's story.

Taking obvious interpretive liberties, the film begins with the image of prisoners during the civil war being brought to their execution. This action serves as frame to flashbacks of Pascual's wretched life and horrible execution by garrote. The effect is what Eduardo Haro Tecglen has read as "an almost mathematical demonstration of the social pressures upon the Spanish rural population in the years leading up to the civil war" (qtd. in Martínez Lázaro, Querejeta, and Franco 28). Students may want to compare the similarity of narrative treatment of seemingly apolitical moments of the film's depicted violence (Pascual's killing of animals, his murder of Estirao and of his mother) with his shooting of Don Jesús, the local landowner, an action that is only alluded to in the novel but obviously has political resonance in the film's social setting.

One example of how Franco evokes the civil war is his use of auditory and visual elements to tell the political backstory. Vernon notes how a civil war siege in Pascual's village is staged:

> Pascual's return to his deserted home is presented in virtually total juxtaposition with the signs of the war, first perceived through the auditory channel of bombs and shots heard in the distance, then visually in the smoke and fire seen on the horizon. (94)

Students should consider how sounds and other nonverbal cues suggest social and political motivations for action. Scenes of Pascual's violent acts are never accompanied by explanatory dialogue. This structured absence leads audiences both to question the narrative motivation for them and to associate seemingly apolitical violence with the larger political backdrop of the film. The scenes chosen from the novel move toward a crescendo in Pascual's violent behavior that, as Marsha Kinder argues, "focuses exclusively on Spanish history (the repressive forces that intensify the violence in the Civil War) and makes the political reverberations far more explicit than in the novel" (*Blood Cinema* 184).

Violence, understood in both its individual and social context, is thus intimately related to the film's evocation of the civil war. *Pascual Duarte* differs from later literary adaptations in its ambitious repositioning of the Cela novel into political contexts. The questions that the film raises, however, go far beyond the politics surrounding the civil war and relate to the nature of violence and to the disempowerment of social classes that eventually leads to social upheaval. In this regard, the film seems a more ambitious conceptual project than many of the literary adaptations that followed it. Barry Jordan and Rikki Morgan-Tamosunas situate films dealing with the civil war during the prodigious "socialist decade" (1982–96) and beyond within the broader problematic persistence of historical cinema in Spain:

> Historical film, perhaps more than any other generic category, places the question of the relationship between reality, perception and

representation firmly in the spotlight. And since historical reality is itself an elusive concept, accessible only through the imperfections of memory and representation, the mediation of that reality (such as it is) inevitably interposes a series of lenses or filters which both facilitate and obfuscate its interpretation. ("Reconstructing" 16)

Indeed, many of the varied treatments of the war theme in Spanish films of the 1980s and 1990s need to be seen, in part, as an effort to emphasize the problematic nature of the relation of history to contemporary Spanish reality. One of the most original interrogations of representations of the war is Carlos Saura's *Dulces horas* (1982; "Sweet Hours"). The film appears to respond to Spanish variations on the international retro style common to the European and Hollywood "nostalgia films" of the 1980s (Jameson 137). As a critique of the Spanish version of this retro style, *Dulces horas* intertwines evocations of the war on the Republican home front with an overt parody of the ways those visual and aural evocations have been distorted in contemporary Spanish culture.

The story line of *Dulces horas* involves Juan Sahagún, a morose writer who finds that his present and future hold no attraction for him. What sparks his imagination are the "sweet hours" of the time he was a small boy and extremely close to his mother during the terrible days of the 1937 aerial bombings of Madrid. The adult Juan rents an apartment, which he decorates in the period style; hires actors to perform the roles of his family; and has them perform scenes from the past in which he assumes the role of himself as a ten-year-old. Through these reenactments he relives the past and is able to regain some of the sweetness of his oedipal desire. Inevitably, he falls in love with the actress who plays his mother.

Dulces horas self-referentially exposes the artifice of false memories of past experiences, of which the civil war is an instance. In this regard, Saura's film may work as an ideal companion text for Jaime Camino's 1978 documentary, *La vieja memoria* ("The Old Memory"), in which prominent participants in the war were filmed in the 1970s as they misremembered key moments in events that transpired a half century earlier. Unlike Camino's film, however, in which flawed memories are simply depicted, Saura underscores the social and personal mechanisms by which they are absorbed by individuals. Early in the film, for instance, Juan is speaking to his sister Marta about the suicide of their mother years ago. Marta's young daughters overhear the conversation and ask, "Did Grandma commit suicide?" The scene underscores the indirect influences of one generation on another. This information enters the children's consciousness not as an experienced event but as the result of hearing words: the contemporary generation's positioning is thus implicated and questioned.

Perhaps the most striking element of Saura's film is the dramatization of the ways sound becomes the conduit for aural memories that lead characters into the past. Juan recalls his childhood fear of the offscreen voices during air raids calling "apague esa luz" ("Turn off that light!") and the persistent strains of a period song by Imperio Argentina, "Recordar" ("Remember"), which contains the lyrics "las dulces horas de ayer" ("the sweet hours of yesterday"). The disembodied sounds of the past have remained and reinforced his nostalgic conception of the civil war and his mother's manipulation of him as alluring days. Saura, of course, comically overstates the seduction of these "sweet hours" for his protagonist. Yet implicit in the film's critique of evocations of the war is the cinematic stylization that by the mid-1980s, save in rare cases, was no longer tied to a political position but rather to a hollow retro style devoid of substantive content (Monterde 157–58).

Saura's film uses sounds and images in much the way that *Pascual Duarte* did—that is, to evoke the intangible memories of the past. Its importance lies in how it exposes the ideological apparatus of the family that has distorted the meaning of the war. Thus a theme to consider in relation to *Dulces horas* and the filmmaking tradition that gave rise to it is the way the family as the mechanism for beliefs and even identity has evolved from the symbolic Churruca family of the early Francoist epic *Raza* (1941; "Race") to films from the decade following Franco's death.

In general, by the 1990s, the civil war had ceased to be either a political or personal theme; it had become stabilized as a recognizable genre that recycled the visual icons of the war years into fairly predictable plots that imitated earlier treatments of the war. Two important exceptions are films by the gifted Basque filmmaker Julio Medem. *Vacas* (1991; "Cows"), Medem's first feature-length film, and *Los amantes del círculo polar* (1998; "Lovers of the Arctic Circle") are companion pieces (Rodríguez 75–76), similar in their emphasis on family genealogies that suggest the tensions between continuity and change in the Basque Country. Both contain sequences in which the civil war figures as a crucible of cultural and individual identity. Rooted in a highly personal and eccentric narrative style, each film leads its audience to question the presumed deterministic patterns in which history—and the civil war in particular—is linked to contemporary Basque identity.

Vacas traces violent feuds between the male members of two Basque families who live in adjacent hamlets separated by a forest in the Navarrese region of Elizondo. The action begins in 1875 in the midst of the second Carlist war, a pitched battle in which Manuel Irigibel and Karmelo Mendiluze are both fighting on the Carlist side. Manuel smears blood from the mortally wounded Karmelo on his own face and feigns death so he can avoid fighting. He will forever be branded a coward by his neighbors, and cowardice will follow his heirs. Two generations later, Peru, Manuel's grandson and the illegitimate scion of the union of the two clans, returns to Spain as a journalist for an American newspaper to report on the civil war. He arrives in the forest of his childhood and is captured by Nationalist troops. He is thrown before a firing squad along with members of his father's family but is saved when his maternal uncle tells the officer in charge that he is the grandson of Carlist soldiers. Like his grandfather Manuel, Peru has avoided death by denying his identity.

The amorous reencounter between Peru and his childhood sweetheart, Cristina, just before his capture by the Nationalists, seems to break the Manichaean pattern in which people of each clan are characterized as mad or cowardly. Medem inserts a fairy-tale happy ending that appears almost as a dream sequence. Cristina awakens from a deep sleep, unaware of the violence of the preceding scenes or of Peru's humiliation; she mounts a horse with him, and they ride off to France. In the final lines of dialogue Peru says, "You are what I most love in the world." She replies, "I've been waiting to love you all my life." With this exchange audiences are brought to consider that the personal narratives of love may have replaced the bellicose narratives of violence. Given the intertwining genealogies of the two families, where lineage is blurred by incest, students may want to explore the symbolic meaning of the film's conclusion, which suggests either a personal fantasy on Peru's part or, conversely, the triumph of a utopian rewriting of the community's history of violence.

By far the most striking feature of Medem's film is its unusual visual imagery related to animals, principally cows, which fill the canvases that old Manuel continually paints. Critics have suggested that the images of cows, especially in his painting *War*, are intertextual evocations of Picasso's famed painting *Guernica* (Rodríguez 88). The visual correspondences between Picasso's painting and the film's imagery should be explored both for how the painting may have inspired Medem's imagery and for the emphasis given to animals in the painting and film (see also Mendelson's essay on *Guernica* in this volume). The cows that give the title to the film appear prominently in each of the four main episodes, functioning as silent witnesses to the human folly of war. They create a unique narrative distance from events, as the camera often cuts from a dramatic scene to an image of a cow observing the action. Students might consider the function of cows in the material world of the rural Basque community portrayed and also their role in a narrative strategy that suggests continuities beyond those stated by the characters.

Vacas refigures the civil war as the culmination of nearly a half century of family and national struggles in the Basque Country, leading audiences to ponder what has shaped modern Basque identity. In *Lovers of the Arctic Circle*, Medem again evokes the war but this time from the perspective of a half century after the fateful conflict. The title suggests a love story connected to what is for Spaniards an unexpected and exotic geography.

Otto is the namesake of a German pilot who parachuted after participating in the bombing of Gernika (Guernica) during the civil war and was saved by the young Otto's grandfather. Years later, Otto's father leaves his German wife and goes to live with Olga, to whose daughter, Ana, Otto is attracted. After the suicide of Otto's mother, the young boy goes to live with his father's family but eventually abandons the house. Ana's mother soon leaves her husband for another man, a German whose father was the very pilot who years earlier had been befriended by Otto's grandfather, thereby closing one of the metaphoric circles of the plot. Ana goes off to the Arctic Circle where she hopes to be reunited with Otto but meets instead the original pilot. At the point of her reunion with the past and present Ottos, she is struck down by a bus and presumably dies.

This labyrinthine plot transforms the fixed moments in history into a series of chance encounters that lead to new permutations of identity. As in *Vacas, Lovers of the Arctic Circle* breaks with traditional uses of Spanish Civil War history by reframing the past in ways that diminish the importance of geographic borders, emphasizing instead the coincidences that have shaped the characters across those borders. Tellingly, the backstory of the civil war is reinscribed in the coincidence in which Olga becomes a television news anchor reporting the official apology of the German president for the Gernika bombing. Otto's identity as the child of a German woman and a Basque man is mirrored in Ana's new parentage: a Spanish mother now married to a German.

Discussion of the film might deal with how notions of family and national identity are reordered through the geographic movement of the protagonists, the various intermarriages, and even language. The bond between family and nation, so central in *Raza* and even in the anti-Franco films, has obviously undergone a radical transformation in contemporary Spanish cinema. Medem's film is a useful text through which to explore the changing mythologies of Spanish social identity as these involve reformulations of family and community affiliation. Part of the narrative project of both *Vacas* and *Lovers of the Arctic Circle* is a visual and narrative refiguration of the aerial bombing of Gernika—and by association a refiguration of the Spanish Civil War—in new genealogical contexts that relate to contemporary Basque regional identity. In *Vacas,* the war occurs in the final sequence and is presented as an ending, with Peru and Cristina departing for France. In *Lovers* the war and the bombing of Gernika, presented as a flashback, are really a beginning for the contemporary love story. Students may want to compare the meanings of the civil war and Gernika, as they constitute both an end and a beginning for characters in each film, and the elements of repetition in Medem's highly individualistic treatments of the civil war.

More than a half century since the end of the civil war, with Spain's realignment in European and global film culture, the war has become transformed into an aesthetic and commercial commodity barely recognizable from its earliest narrative depictions in the 1940s. Radically reduced in specific details of the conflict, the narrative of the civil war that emerges in recent Spanish film characteristically eschews the simplistic good-versus-evil versions of Spanish histories of the war in favor of narrative and cinematic strategies that lead audiences to question more objectively the meaning of the past for contemporary Spanish society.

Kathleen M. Vernon

Iconography of the Nationalist Cause

It is a paradox in the historical legacy and legend of the Spanish Civil War that the most memorable imagery of the conflict is associated with the Republican ranks, whereas the message of the Nationalists is probably best recalled through the spoken or printed word: Gonzalo Queipo de Llano's radio harangues, the charged language of Nationalist speeches denouncing the anti-Spain, and the military-inspired ritual chants of the National Movement's mass gatherings. And yet to understand fully the waging of the war as not only a military conflict but also a battle for hearts and minds, it is essential to reconstruct the corpus of images and icons that accompanied, complicated, and sometimes even undercut the bellicose rhetoric issuing from the Nationalist camp. How did the Nationalist forces understand the function of visual propaganda, primarily posters and films, in the war effort? Who was the intended audience for such works? While it is important to situate these posters and films in their moment of origin, we must also evaluate their impact on present-day viewers. The symbolic language of wartime propaganda, though shaped and directed by factors specific to a given conflict, offers certain recurring iconographic and discursive conventions that give us insight into the ideological and military confrontations of our own era. The antecedents of recent history's televised, living room wars—from Vietnam to Iraq—are found in the films and posters produced in Spain between 1936 and 1939.

The images of the Spanish Civil War are still with us, then, both in their influence on the visual representations of subsequent wars and, thanks to the expansion of video, digital, and Web-based technologies, through the growing availability of formal and informal archives of the war. An hour or two with a reliable Web search engine brings up numerous sites for locating films and downloading images of dozens of Spanish Civil War posters (see also "Resources" in this volume). With few exceptions, those images proceed from the Republicans and their supporters. Thus teaching the representations of the Nationalist cause must involve examining the reasons behind the near unavailability of Nationalist imagery outside specialized film archives and a handful of books devoted to the subject. Why have Nationalist representations of the war seemingly been forgotten? Is it because of ideological reasons, rooted in a repudiation of the Spanish right's ties to fascism, or, as many critics and historians have suggested, because the Nationalists simply produced fewer (and artistically less distinguished) posters and films? Finally, when viewed and studied today, in what possible contexts can Nationalist propaganda art be said to speak to the contemporary spectator?

My essay attempts to provide selected primary and secondary source materials for the study of Nationalist posters and documentary films while offering a broadly based critical framework for reading and analyzing these cultural artifacts as well as our responses to them. My concern is to identify the dominant imagery, rhetoric, and narrative tropes—the representational strategies—that shaped the Nationalist message. My intention is to question received ideas that have cast Nationalist propaganda art as the single-minded translation of a monolithic ideology and to reveal the complexity that informs the texts produced in support of the Nationalist cause.

In contrast to the importance accorded to the propaganda war by the republic and its varied constituencies, the Nationalist effort was initially characterized by an inability to recognize the potential importance of such tools of visual persuasion. The historical record shows that the Nationalist government, first in Salamanca and later in Burgos, was slow to centralize responsibilities for both print and visual media and thus to develop a coherent message for domestic public consumption, let alone for audiences beyond Spain's borders. The film historians Rosa Álvarez Berciano and Ramón Sala Noguer identify two stages in the Nationalist propaganda effort: the first, from 1936 to 1937, focused primarily on censorship, on controlling and filtering the flow of information and entertainment available in the Nationalist zone; the second, beginning in 1938 with the creation of the Dirección General de Prensa y Propaganda under the Falangist intellectual Dionisio Ridruejo, was devoted to the promotion and creation of a coherent Nationalist imagery and thematics (5–16). It is likely that a good part of this apparent failure to construct a functioning propaganda apparatus was the result of the geographical accidents of the military campaign as it took shape across the peninsula. Although the Nationalists were quickly able to consolidate their hold on the south and rural centers of the country, the technological infrastructure and human expertise for both the graphic arts and cinema production were centered in Madrid, Barcelona, and Valencia, major cities that remained in Republican hands until the end of the war. As a consequence, Nationalist film production was forced to depend on editing and sound synchronization facilities in Portugal, Italy, and Germany for the duration of the fighting, while poster production never reached the number or variety issued in the Republican zone.

This very inability, even under Ridruejo, to create anything resembling a unified and hierarchical command structure for the propaganda war, reveals a much more complex and heterogeneous industrial and ideological basis for Nationalist cultural production than is commonly supposed. Hence although the nascent Franco government moved to quash ideological differences among the Nationalists through the 1937 fusion of the major political groupings into the single party National Movement, a more fragmented and individualized approach to the graphic and cinema arts persisted throughout the war. This lack of systematic control allows us to examine the development of the Nationalist message as a work in progress, reflecting on the one hand a growing reliance on a series of central myths and symbols but on the other the persistence of unresolved contradictions.

Nationalist Poster Art

Despite differing ideological origins and intentions, Nationalist posters were heir to the same technical, stylistic, and thematic models that inspired their Republican counterparts. As the authors of a volume of war posters from the collection of the Hoover Institution observe, "the poster as we know it . . . was a creation of the nineteenth century, of its technological innovations and its social, economic and political transformations" (Paret, Lewis, and Paret viii). During World War I, the development of color lithography and techniques of mass reproduction made the poster available as a primary means of political communication and propaganda (Timmers 108). The subsequent growth and development of the political poster took place largely in the Soviet Union and Nazi Germany. By the 1930s, the propaganda poster had demonstrated its capacity to assimilate a range of diverse and even contradictory sources and styles. In the Soviet Union, poster designs based in the constructivist avant-garde vied with the purposeful (and presumably less ambiguous) imagery of so-called socialist realism and its cultivation of a muscular proletarian everyman or everywoman. Those Soviet sources were no barrier to the spread of similar images across the ideological divide to Nazi art and iconography or later to Republican and Nationalist posters (Carulla and Carulla 1:15; Timmers 120).

Although poster art played an important role in the arsenal of both German and Italian fascist propaganda, there is little evidence of direct Axis influence on Nationalist posters (Carulla and Carulla 1:15). Indeed critics and historians point to the relative neglect of the medium by the Nationalist camp in contrast to the privileged role of posters in other authoritarian regimes of the period. Carmen Grimau considers this alleged failure to develop a distinctive style of poster art a defining element for the Francoist political apparatus, symptomatic of its overall lack of an original political discourse ("Cartel" 273–74).

Grimau, the author of a well-known book on Republican posters, shares an overall tendency among scholars in Spain and elsewhere to identify and analyze Nationalist posters and their messages less on their own terms than as the negation and antithesis of Republican poster imagery and ideology. For Grimau, Nationalist posters are best defined as an absence ("no lugar") or lack: of dynamism, of content beyond a tautological reliance on preexisting Nationalist symbols, and of the reality of the war itself. In her view, the posters from the rebel side remain static, and the human figures portrayed are largely devoid of expression. We see no battles or soldiers at war, no terror, no fear or struggle, and no blood. Unlike the Republican posters, the Nationalist posters offer no sense of the evolution of the war (Vernon, "Gritos" 133). The goal of Nationalist posters is thus not to mobilize the masses but to manage and silence them (Grimau, "Cartel" 278). Furthermore, in the absence of contesting political ideologies in the Nationalist zone, there is little urgency to present a particular vision of the war, its goals, or its methods. Instead, Grimau concludes, "the global context of the posters exudes impeccable surfaces, asepsis, and dignity endured in silence" (281).

While I do not debate the validity of Grimau's arguments, I do question whether her position is not at least in part the product of a persistent dearth of documentation and serious analysis of a representative corpus of Nationalist posters. The posters Grimau cites, as well as many of those reproduced in the most accessible published sources, such as Jordi Carulla and Arnau Carulla's *La guerra civil en 2000 carteles*, tend to reinforce this vision of Nationalist graphic arts as "insignificant, mediocre, and grindingly repetitive" (Grimau, "Cartel" 273). What impact does this lack of information have on our understanding of Nationalist war imagery and our interpretation of individual posters? I cite a poster (fig. 1) identified by Carulla and Carulla as originating in right-wing electoral campaigns of 1933 (1: 133) but by the Hoover Institution as a Spanish Civil War era poster dating from 1937 (Paret, Lewis, and Paret 138).[1] "Comunismo destruye la familia" ("Communism destroys the family") runs the caption, in yellow cursive letters at the top of the image over a red and black background.[2] The scene depicted below the caption recalls the lurid imagery of a pulp novel: the hulking figure of a soldier, the peaks on his cap suggesting devilish horns, carries off the unclothed body of a lifeless woman, her bare breasts just visible in the stylized shadows. Two other figures occupy the lower left quadrant: the prone body of a perhaps would-be defender and a second, half-seated woman, her head and hair thrown back and her arms outstretched in supplication. The poster is striking for many reasons. Although its theme is entirely consistent with the right's pervasive identification of the Republican side with Soviet Communism, much in evidence in Nationalist speech making and in documentary films, the provocative style of the poster poses a challenge to Grimau's vision of the predominant Nationalist aesthetic as characterized by a static sobriety and lack of affect. Distant indeed are the controlled surfaces of official propaganda. In its aggressive demonizing of the left, the poster indulges a nightmare vision of sexualized violence run rampant against the innocent victims of Republican (Communist) savagery. Despite the poster's expressed subject, the defense of the family, no recognizable representation of the family appears. Instead, we find two highly eroticized female figures that evoke a threat of rape and the loss of nubile and desirable females to a sexually rapacious Republican soldier. In most Republican and Nationalist posters, women, when present at all, were contained within the desexualized roles of mother, wife, and daughter. It would take the melodramatic reimaginings of the war in the so-called crusade films of the early 1940s such as *Porque te vi llorar* (dir. Juan de Orduña, 1941; "Because I Saw You Cry") and

Figure 1. El comunismo destruye la familia. (Communism destroys the family.) SP12, Poster Collection, Hoover Institution Archives.

Boda en el infierno (dir. Antonio Román, 1942; "Wedding in Hell") to give free reign to the phantasm of Republican rape of Nationalist women.[3]

Another poster from the Hoover Institution collection (fig. 2) offers the opportunity to appreciate the execution and uses of a visually sophisticated design in the service of the Nationalist cause. Unlike Spanish scholars, the editors of the Hoover poster volume do not distinguish between Republican and Nationalist posters with respect to their relative aesthetic quality: "Posters from both sides of the Civil War are among the best political posters of the 1930s," they note (Paret, Lewis, and Paret 134). In this poster, the sculptural head of a helmeted soldier presides in the upper half over stylized images of the tip of a fountain pen, a plow, and a factory smokestack layered one on the other. The caption in black capital letters runs in slight diagonal across the bottom of the poster: "DISCIPLINA" ("discipline"). Like the soldier whose clenched fist holds the rifle barrel seen at the left edge of the image, those who wield the pen and plow or work in the factory—each group symbolized through the phallicly erect instruments of their chosen occupation—must unite under the banner of disciplined service to the cause. The editor Paul Paret's analysis calls attention to the function of the smallest details: "The soldier's neck and shoulders meet in architectonic right angles, making him one with the factory buildings" (Paret, Lewis, and Paret 138–39). The repeated images and graphic matches—the curve of the plow and the soldier's helmet, the factory chimney and the gun, the pointed tip of the pen and the bridge of the soldier's nose—"all indicate union and integration under military force" (137). Paret closes his commentary with reference to the poster's overall dynamism, produced by the positioning of the image on a slight diagonal.

More representative perhaps of the projection of Nationalist myth-making into the plastic arts are the images issued after 1938 by the Servicio Nacional de Propaganda, Departamento de Plástica, under the Dirección General de Prensa y Propaganda in Burgos. In a third poster, the war in its material reality is totally absent from the image, sublimated into the recurring Nationalist trope of the civil war as holy war (Carulla and Carulla 2: 542). Reading left to right, the viewer's gaze is drawn to a square pillar rising at an angle from the bottom left corner. Just before the pillar tapers at the top to form the number one, it is crossed by the word "CRUZADA" ("crusade"). The shadow created by the figure "1st crusade," given massive architectural form as a towering red cross, falls across a stylized representation of a smaller, blue earth with a much enlarged, red Iberian Peninsula at its center. On the lower edge of the abstracted earth,

Figure 2. Disciplina. (Discipline.) SP6, Poster Collection, Hoover Institution Archives.

three-dimensional red letters spell out a second caption: "ESPAÑA ORIENTADORA ESPIRITUAL DEL MUNDO" ("Spain, spiritual compass of the world"). This image of the earth suspended in a blue void encircled by red letters curiously recalls the Universal Pictures logo created in the 1920s and still used today, a three-dimensional earth transected by the word "UNIVERSAL."

Any study of Nationalist poster art or imagery must take into account the role of its most distinctive artist and illustrator, Carlos Sáenz de Tejada. In the years before the war Sáenz de Tejada enjoyed a flourishing career in cosmopolitan art circles, where his work absorbed and reflected influences ranging from the European avant-garde to art nouveau fashion magazines. During the Spanish Civil War he designed numerous illustrations for the magazine *Vértice*, a showcase for Falangist aesthetic theory and practice. After the Nationalist victory his role and visibility in the Francoist art establishment grew. He was named art director for the lavishly illustrated six-volume *Historia de la Cruzada Española*; he also designed calendars and an illustrated edition of the Falangist hymn "Cara al sol." Highly stylized and theatrical, baroquely eclectic in its sources, and always eccentric, Sáenz de Tejada's work is not easily confined within the ideological strictures it ostensibly served. As Gabriel Ureña Portero notes, the artist mixed European surrealism, cubism, and expressionism with such national strains as an El Greco–inspired spirituality and social realism in the style of his contemporary Ignacio Zuloaga (152).

Figure 3 shows an image produced by Sáenz de Tejada at the behest of Carmen Icaza, then director of the Falangist women's charitable organization, Auxilio Social. Like all the posters issued by the organization, it bears the violent logo whose spirit is seemingly contrary to the mission of the group. On the right-hand half of a circular emblem, a muscular forearm superimposed on a red background holds the pointed shaft of an arrow about to be plunged into the open jaws of a snarling black beast occupying the left side of the design.[4] On 10 December 1939 Icaza wrote Sáenz de Tejada the following instructions:

> The theme is to be a working-class family in the foreground, the man should appear optimistic, healthy, and young and should carry on his shoulders a young boy, with his arm raised on high; at his side his wife holding another child by the hand. (qtd. in Ureña Portero 128)

Although the text of Icaza's commission is cited by Ureña Portero as evidence of the lack of artistic liberty afforded even the best-known Nationalist

Figure 3. En nuestra justicia está nuestra fuerza. (In our justice is our strength.) Author's collection.

collaborators, we might look more closely at the potential responses generated by the resulting poster. For their part, the Hoover volume editors Peter Paret, Beth Irwin Lewis, and Paul Paret question the presumed semantic and rhetorical stability of the political propaganda poster, the assumption that meaning can be fixed without ambiguity and for all time. They argue that a poster cannot be presumed to speak with a single voice, especially when, as in this instance, we have evidence of a form of dual authorship. Furthermore, all readings rely on the viewer's own historical context as well as knowledge, or lack thereof, of the circumstances under which the poster was created (ix). When I showed a slide of this image recently in class, one student remarked on its similarity to a Norman Rockwell illustration. While I may question how a viewer can look past the characteristically dramatic, elongated figures and diagonal expressionist spatial configuration typical of Sáenz de Tejada's spiritualized army regulars and Carlist Requetés or of the idealized proletarian family pictured here to find the familiar American imagery of a Rockwell illustration, I certainly understood the gist of what my student meant. This image, unlike many Nationalist posters, seeks to establish an affective connection with the viewer in its evocation of the model family, complete with playful little dog, although typically, and again in contrast to Rockwell, this family portrait is abstracted from any recognizable setting, context, or specific milieu. Absent as well are the detailed backgrounds filled with the cherished objects of middle-American life characteristic of Rockwell's work. Nevertheless, as countless artists, novelists, and filmmakers have demonstrated, the iconography of the family is perhaps uniquely susceptible to multiple recontextualizations and ideological manipulations, especially in the relative absence of Rockwell-like contextual cues. Depictions of parent and child and appeals to family feeling pervade Republican posters as well as Nationalist ones and address viewers on a level apart from ideology. As such, the image of the family can be marshaled toward a variety of ends, supportive or subversive of dominant values.[5]

Nationalist Documentary Film

In a situation that belied their success on the battlefield, the Nationalists, limited by a near total lack of technical facilities and film personnel, were initially at a disadvantage in the war of images. It is telling that the first documentaries issued from the Nationalist zone were made with equipment left behind in Sevilla from a commercial shoot interrupted by the

Nationalist conquest of the city. The director, Fernando Delgado, and crew for that film, *El genio alegre* ("The Happy Temper"), an adaptation of a play by the brothers Serafín Álvarez Quintero and Joaquín Álvarez Quintero, went on to produce a series of short documentaries in 1937 charting the advance of the Nationalist armies: *Asturias para España* ("Asturias for Spain"), *Bilbao para España* ("Bilbao for Spain"), *Santander para España* ("Santander for Spain"), and *Sevilla rescatada* ("Seville Rescued"). Marcel Oms has identified the common narrative tropes and imagery underlying these films:

> The guiding theme is always the same: the city was prisoner of the evil enemy and its saviors have liberated it. . . . Death, ruins, fire, and blood are the cruel signs of a necessary expiation before the army of the crusaders may parade through the city streets. (qtd. in Gubern, *1936* 69)

This compulsion to identify contemporary actions, events, and personages with heroic models from Spain's imperial past was central to Nationalist self-representations, as we have already seen in the poster of the "1st crusade." Juan Antonio Ramírez finds the origins of this practice in the typological correspondences common in Christian religious iconography that cast the episodes and figures of the New Testament as the realization and culmination of Old Testament patterns and prophesies. This allegorical reading thus produced a kind of rhetorical template that would be used time and again to transform a war among Spaniards into the battle of an authentic and eternal Spain against a foreign usurper.

In *Bilbao para España*, it is Basque "separatists" who are scripted in the role of the anti-Spain and held responsible for the death, destruction, and ruin shown on-screen. While the narration celebrates the military prowess of the Nationalist army in its defeat of the vaunted Republican *cinturón de hierro* ("iron belt") protecting the city, the army is nevertheless seen as engaged in exclusively humanitarian tasks allegedly neglected by the fleeing Basques: tending to the wounded and even burying the enemy dead. Throughout the film the sound and visual tracks work on seemingly different levels. But if much of the imagery seems designed to appeal to sentiments beyond political identifications, the voice-over narration functions to anchor those images in partisan meaning.[6] Thus one sequence lingers over the faces of wounded Republican men, now cast by the narration as victims of separatist and Communist treachery. Another, longer scene takes us aboard a rickety boat where hungry women and children are said to wait in vain for their promised evacuation. On the heels of the Nationalist "liberation," soldiers and female volunteers are shown collaborating in the charitable duties of feeding the hungry people on board before escorting them off the boat, "restored forever to the New Spain."

From his headquarters in Burgos, Ridruejo also worked to consolidate Nationalist documentary film production under a single organism, the Departamento Nacional de Cinematografía. Although Franco had sought to temper Falangist influence with the unification decree, under Ridruejo the Falange and Falangist artists continued to exercise an important role in providing a coherent aesthetic vision and a central repertory of symbols and imagery. The work of Edgar Neville, a well-known diplomat, writer, and filmmaker who had worked in Hollywood, offers an example of the Falangist contribution to the cause. Neville's 1938 documentary *La ciudad universitaria* ("The University City") opens with an expressive if melodramatic epigraph: "To the youth of Spain, to the students, the peasants, and the workers, who have come to this university campus to earn doctorates in death." The film, with narration written and read by Neville, portrays the Nationalist occupation of the university campus, "five minutes from central Madrid's Puerta del Sol." As Álvarez Berciano and Sala Noguer observe, in the hands of Neville, roles are reversed between Spain's besieged capital and the Nationalist outpost in the university city (188). Taking a page from Republican portrayals of Madrid as the vulnerable human target of a technologically superior Nationalist war machine, the film depicts Madrid as a city of rubble, where a cross section of ordinary citizen-soldiers—those students, peasants, and workers evoked in the epigraph—go about their everyday routines (eating, sleeping, brushing their teeth) in the midst of war. Repeated pans over the remains of university buildings, evoked by name and with reference to their once distinguished architectural details, juxtapose the ordinariness of human activity with the solemn monumentality of ruins. Antonio Bonet Correa has analyzed this cultivation of ruins as a key feature of the National Movement's aesthetics in its attempt "to fix forever a temporality of war that denied the future as reality and exulted in the projection of the past over the present; ruins thus compose a permanent poem of violence" ("Espacios" 13).

If *La ciudad universitaria* provides an example of a keystone of the Nationalist aesthetic in the fixed monumentalism of the ruin, projecting a timeless empire in stone, *Ya viene el cortejo* (1939; "Here Comes the Procession") explores the opposite pole of Spanish fascist aesthetics, emphasizing the performative, the role of rituals and ceremonies. Presented as a "cinematic gloss on the poem 'Marcha triunfal,' by the immortal Rubén Darío," the film, directed by Carlos Arévalo, eschews the linear structure of chronological narrative for a poetic accumulation of images. *Cortejo* centers on the act that would become an essential ritual of the Francoist state, the Desfile de la Victoria ("Victory Parade"), which after its initial celebration in Madrid in 1939 was repeated annually on 1 April throughout the years of the dictatorship. Such choreographed mass public events clearly drew on Nazi and Mussolinian inspiration, and their potential political meaning for the Spanish state had been theorized as early as 1937 in the Falangist magazine *Vértice*, in an article devoted to "la estética de las muchedumbres" ("the aesthetic of crowds") (Álvarez Berciano and Sala Noguer 146–47).

The film opens with a series of images linked by lap dissolves that offers a vision of a timeless Spain in a fusion of iconic elements—varied natural landscapes, medieval pageantry, castles and churches, and women in traditional dress—all evoking Spain's different regions as a source of strength and unity rather than of division. Without transition, the scene shifts from rural and small town vistas to shots of one of Madrid's best-known boulevards, the Gran Vía, and back again to castle towers, flags, waves on the sea, and still more flags, including the Spanish national and Falangist emblems. In the absence of verbal narration, the filmic montage enacts the physical incorporation of Madrid into the reimagined geographical and spiritual body of the nation, cleansing and restoring the former Republican capital in preparation for its rededication as the site of the Victory Parade. The parade scenes that follow, set to the recitation of Darío's martial epic, are hardly a straightforward documentary representation of a pro-filmic event but rather a *summum* of Spanish history from the standpoint of an eternal present that defies temporal and geographical distance. Thus several examples of the latest technologies of modern warfare are juxtaposed with shots of medieval knights, Philip II's Escorial palace, and the national crest sculpted in stone—the simultaneous projection of a Spanish nation that is and always was, culminating in a superimposed portrait of Franco.

Cortejo thus codifies a series of visual tropes that later provided a repertory of rhetorical devices for official Francoist cinema, including the state-controlled NO-DO (Noticiarios y Documentales; "News and Documentaries") newsreel and *Raza* (1941; "Race"), the Spanish Civil War melodrama scripted by Franco, which closes with a similar Victory Parade montage (see also Moreiras-Menor in this volume). Also central to the film's performance of ritual is the reliance on recurring symbols—flags and banners, the cross, the imperial eagle, and the national crest—supplemented by Falangist emblems and slogans and the images of national heroes, Franco foremost among them. These religious and military motifs functioned as a kind of emphatic punctuation, straining to secure the ideological meaning of both posters and films in the absence of a radically distinctive imagery or narrative argument. Where many historians have questioned Francoism's lack of clear political identity or, like Grimau, have cast Francoism as a form of fascism manqué, this aspect of Nationalist propaganda is entirely consistent with Jeffrey Schnapp's characterization of fascist culture in Italy and elsewhere, which "required an aesthetic overproduction, a surfeit of fascist signs, images, slogans, books, and buildings in order to compensate for, fill in, or cover up its forever unstable ideological core" (qtd. in Golsan xi).

This instability pervades the visual arts created by the Nationalists during the Spanish Civil War, a result both of their particular circumstances of production and the inherent unpredictability of reception. The propaganda text, whatever its origin or intention, pursues an impossible goal, an unwinnable war to fix meaning against the entropic effects of time and multiple human subjectivities. For Nationalist posters and documentary films, recognition of this element of indeterminacy can aid the task of reconsidering Nationalist art on its own terms, rather than as the mere denial or antithesis of the Republican message and forms of expression.

Notes

1. Neither source indicates the poster's artist or issuing body, which would have helped to clarify its moment of origin.

2. All translations from the Spanish are my own.

3. See the chapter in Gubern, *1936* 81–103.

4. Auxilio Social ("Social Aid") was founded by Mercedes Sanz Bachiller, the widow of the Falangist leader Onésimo Redondo, in 1936. The original name of the organization Auxilio de Invierno ("Winter Aid") reflects its model in the Nazi German organization, Winter-Hilfe, which was also the source for Auxilio Social's emblem, or logo.

5. For reasons no doubt tied to the particular repertory of images that my own work entails, whenever I see this poster by Sáenz de Tejada I am invariably reminded of a scene in Pedro Almodóvar's film *Law of Desire*. On a warm midsummer night, three characters walk through the streets of Madrid: the transsexual

Tina; her homosexual film director brother Pablo; and ten-year-old Ada, the daughter of Tina's lesbian lover, played in the film by the real-life transsexual Bibi Anderson. Pablo carries Ada on his shoulders as Tina walks beside them; they are the very image of the ideal nuclear family.

6. Geoffrey Pingree's essay in this volume further explores the ideological instability of visual imagery in Spanish Civil War documentaries, showing how identical footage was often marshaled by both sides to make opposing points. Pingree alerts us to the recycling of material from Republican to Nationalist films and back again, following the trail of "the semiotically buoyant, floating bodies of the dying" whose identities and political meaning are ultimately conferred by context.

Geoffrey B. Pingree

The Documentary Dilemma and the Spanish Civil War

True or false? Fact or fiction? These are the questions that have sur-rounded *Falling Militiaman*—Robert Capa's compelling photograph of a Republican soldier falling backward, knees buckling, rifle slipping from his hand, at what is thought to be the moment of his death—since it appeared in 1937. What may be the Spanish Civil War's single most influential image, published widely around the world for decades, has also been one of its most disputed.[1] Yet whether the photograph was a result of luck, bravery, or deception, such two-sided queries do not initiate the most useful lines of examination, for Capa's image speaks about much more than the death, staged or real, of a Spanish Republican soldier.

Given the uncertainty of the photograph's circumstances and our instinct to believe that cameras do not lie, we might ask, What are the reliable truths in this image, and how might we best comprehend them? Every photograph documents something, and this photograph does offer a trustworthy mechanical record of a certain physical reality—of a body (whether performing or actually dying) falling on an Andalusian plain. What we can never trust with complete certainty is what that particular mechanical record means. The meaning of Capa's photograph is not intrinsic: every image documents some actuality but also supports a variety of possible meanings of that actuality. It is the contextualizing narrative frame, not the image itself, that carries meaning. Capa, like thousands of others who went to Spain to participate in or observe the war, fashioned himself a witness, and his photograph, exported to news outlets around the world, came to stand for a certain way of telling the story of that war. Capa's camera did not lie; the image it recorded was simply put to different uses in different contexts.

When studying an ambiguous image like this one, it is important for students to consider how process generates meaning. In the classroom this distinction is a crucial lesson and a good starting point for a discussion of the Spanish Civil War. Just as Capa's photograph is more complicated than it seems, so is the Spanish Civil War, and it is important to approach it with an eye to its inherent complexity, to its various contexts. But this approach requires focusing on representations of the war as representations, exploring how they work to shape our understanding. As a historical event, the war involves a vast amount of information that challenges students' understanding. Teaching students to interrogate the war's representations—whether historical accounts or artistic depictions—helps them organize the complexity of the war and understand its overlapping but conflicting contexts. Not just a battle for land, political power, or military supremacy, the Spanish Civil War was also a battle about narrative meaning—a struggle over Spain's national story, over who should tell it and how it should be told. Moving from factual summary to rhetorical analysis helps students move beyond simplistic and reductive views not only about what happened but also about what the war meant (and continues to mean).

The many possible meanings in Capa's photograph point to what I call the documentary dilemma: a recorded image provides evidence of what it depicts even as it shapes our perception of what it depicts. Capa's photograph does tell us something about the facts of the Spanish Civil War, but the image may reveal even more about the complex problem of reading: the tangled process of representation and the open-ended challenge of assessing that depiction. Historians, journalists, filmmakers—all those who emphasize the actual (actual things, actual persons, actual events)—face this dilemma. They must acknowledge, as Dominick LaCapra suggests, that "'documents' are themselves texts that 'process' or rework 'reality' and require a critical reading" (*History and Criticism* 19).

Two core purposes of using representations of the Spanish Civil War in the classroom are to teach students to identify the reworking processes in such representations and to read them critically. These objectives involve not only making students aware of political, economic, religious, and cultural contexts but also helping them think precisely about the power of particular rhetorical strategies and of specific media forms and modes.[2] Documentary images are susceptible to being physically reworked and have traditionally been granted unique authority in claiming the actual world. Rather than take such images as simply true or false, students can move between the abstract categories of documentary and propaganda and learn to read these representations with respect to both their claims to reality and their constructed properties.

Despite much artistic attention to the war, documentary flourished like no other form and played a uniquely powerful role. Indeed, no representational strategy surpassed documentary's ability to serve those who wished to bear witness to the civil war in Spain. The documentary emerged as the primary genre that artists worldwide used to gain narrative credibility, precisely because this mode provided a way not only to document the events they observed but also to authenticate those acts of observation. With its implicit promises of objectivity and verisimilitude, documentary could mobilize public opinion and resources; whoever could lay claim to telling the truth of this conflict would win the financial, military, and moral support of the world community.

Of the various documentary forms available to those seeking to bear witness to the war through artistic representation, film offered unmatched technological possibilities and emerged as a privileged medium of truth. To be sure, writing played a central role in political activism in the 1930s, and recent inventions had increased the role of many types of propaganda (presses with multicolor capabilities produced posters at an unprecedented rate, and photomontage, developed in Germany before Hitler's rise to power, came to maturity in time to be exploited widely in Spain), but film offered an even more persuasive mode of depiction (Cunningham, Introduction xxi). The camera's status as a mechanical instrument capable of precise visual reproduction conferred a superior sense of scientific authority on film's power to witness, convincing many that it was an antidote to the unreliability of print journalism. Moreover, cameras were now small and light enough to be transported easily into combat zones. The popular German Arriflex 35 mm camera, for example, whose compactness afforded cinematographers unprecedented mobility, first appeared in 1936 (Gubern, *1936* 11). And, perhaps most important, recorded sound finally emerged as a weapon; as Anthony Aldgate explains, "the hostilities in

Spain were the first of any magnitude to put to use the full might of sound and recording on film" (112).

From the very first footage of this conflict, documentary was a site of ideological struggle. According to the Spanish Civil War film catalog published by Spain's Ministry of Culture, 889 films made in response to the war still exist (Amo García 913–36). Most of these are nonfiction— actualities, newsreels, and feature documentaries. Exploited for political ends by virtually every one of the war's factions (from anarchist, Communist, Marxist, religious, and nationalist groups within Spain to foreign bodies such as the International Committee of the Red Cross, the Comintern, and the fascist governments in Germany and Italy), documentary became a place where words, sounds, and images struggled for narrative control of Spain. But because documentary functioned as a specially endowed vehicle of truth, it poses a troublesome paradox. In any discussion of the documentary cinema of the Spanish Civil War, it is important to bear in mind that despite its power as a technological medium and its authority as a conceptual mode, documentary, like all forms of representation, is a constructed way of seeing, a record of past choices that students must learn to decipher.

A good place to expand a discussion of documentary representation of the Spanish Civil War is with the first footage of the conflict. Shot entirely between 19 and 23 July 1936 by camera operators roaming the streets in the hours and days following the initial military uprising,[3] *Reportaje del movimiento revolucionario en Barcelona* (1936; "Report on the Revolutionary Movement in Barcelona") is a roughly chronological, loosely structured sequence of images that follows the public enthusiasm and celebration of the defeat of the military uprising, the new control of daily life in Barcelona, and the organization of the Durruti Column as it travels to the Zaragoza front. While this twenty-two-minute fragment documents some of the conflict's actual events, the visual information it offers can be read in various ways, in different contextual frames.

First, the film provides a clear frame through its voice-over narration, reflecting the director Mateo Santos's belief that film's primary function in the war in Spain was to be "the most active propaganda agent of the proletarian revolution, the most vivid reflection of the new society" (qtd. in Sala Noguer 47). Unlike many films made later during the war, *Reportaje*, the first documentary produced by the Office of Information and Propaganda of the Confederación Nacional de Trabajadores–Federación Anarquista

Ibérica (CNT-FAI), had little regard for the conflict's rapt international audience and wore its political stripes proudly. This focus is clearest in the film's depiction of the Catholic Church. In an early sequence, the camera pans across a row of nineteen exhumed nuns' bodies on display in the courtyard of the Iglesia de la Enseñanza. The exhumation and public display of the long-buried corpses of priests, nuns, and saints, a subversive ritual remarkable in its own right, is given a particularly sharp meaning by Santos's narration, recorded in the studio and added after the raw footage was edited:

> In this convent . . . nuns and monks were found martyred by the church leaders themselves. The sight of these twisted, tortured mummies has provoked the people's wrath and indignation. The Catholic Church, in this and other acts, has revealed its corrupt and withered soul; it has, in a matter of hours, revealed a lie that has lasted for twenty centuries. These petrified cadavers . . . constitute the most powerful indictment ever made against Catholicism.[4]

The images and words establish clearly the anarchist position: the clergy and military, loyal to the great enemy of the Spanish people, the Catholic Church, are traitors who have sought to thwart the heroic efforts of the anarchist freedom fighters. A shrill, partisan vision of what Spain has been (and what it should be) thus frames our understanding of these images. In them we recognize a straightforward political purpose and learn something of the war's political context.

But if we push beyond this immediate frame and consider other contexts, we can learn a great deal more about this particular document and about the war in general. Soon after the early months of the war, the memorable images of the exhumed cadavers on display, along with shots of churches burned and religious relics and icons paraded in the streets, ceased to appear in the left's films. This absence makes sense given the decline of the anarchists' power after the spring of 1937. But these sacrilegious images did not disappear altogether: they soon appeared in pro-Nationalist films. Whereas in *Reportaje*, the anarchists, who shared an uneasy alliance with the Republicans, displayed these images proudly, in later films, the Nationalists used the same footage, seized or stolen,[5] to prove the moral decay of the godless bolshevism that purportedly had propelled the Republican government's cause. Thus an original act of radical iconoclasm, once captured on film, suffered what Román Gubern has called the "boomerang" effect (*1936* 14), as the images of the nuns' bodies reappeared in opposed contexts.

In films as chronologically diverse as *España heroica* and *Background to Battle*—a joint German-Spanish production made in 1937 and a stridently anti-Soviet television documentary made in the United States in the 1950s—the nuns' bodies, once icons of particular religious significance, yielded their previous meaning to new and diverse political narratives. In Spain, where viewers were familiar with the church's powerful and often repressive social role, *Reportaje*'s anticlerical images might be understood in the larger context of a people's jubilant social revolution (exhumations and desecrations had figured in popular uprisings since the nineteenth century) as the citizens of Barcelona defeated the military uprising and began to see themselves as participants in the transformation of society. For those unacquainted with the roots of the Spanish Civil War, it is easy to imagine how these images might function as eyewitness proof for the Nationalist argument that Spain's Republican government was powerless against the Reds' assault on traditional values (see also Vincent in this volume). Indeed, such images were shocking and offensive even for outsiders sympathetic to the Loyalist cause (Sala Noguer 67). Foreign chroniclers like the Republican supporters Gabriel Jackson and Hugh Thomas seemed to regard these incidents with regret, and we can imagine that in the United States even non-Catholics found repellent the images of burning churches and exhumed nuns on display before large, jeering crowds. These images, only a sample of a vast number that suffered this boomerang effect, point beyond the factual to a rhetorical level of understanding. As Alfonso del Amo García, the head of the Filmoteca Española's Spanish Civil War film project, explains in an interview with *El país*, this rhetorical effect penetrated all levels of political discourse in the war:

> The aesthetic vehicle of the political message crosses interchangeably from one side to the other. In other words, one side will talk about "Fascist pigs" and the other about "Communist swine," but the rest of the discourse—the "horrendous crimes," the "savage killings"—remains the same. (qtd. in Palou 34)

Never intended for the international community, *Reportaje*, edited time and again, its images lifted from one context to another, was involuntarily enlisted to serve diverse political campaigns. By providing a store of potent images that could be reframed and disseminated anew, the film testifies to documentary's protean role in the Spanish Civil War.

Students exploring the documentary record of the war may begin to see how one film is a point of access to the larger network of the conflict's movies. The films share a distinctive formal discourse; they speak to one another. The semiotically buoyant, floating bodies of the dying militiaman and the exhumed nuns not only emphasize the contextual nature of their meaning but also reveal the often uniform strategies that characterized their deployment. The ideological differences of these films operated on a common foundation of binary rhetoric and stock images. In contrast to the political oppositions and alliances that are the focal point of much Spanish Civil War historiography, this formal collaboration among films with diverse political agendas can add a new and provocative area of study in the classroom. And while it is easy to wonder whether film — its narratives dramatically simple, its materials subject to manipulation, its evidence unreliable—is an adequate tool for depicting history, it is film's pliability that helps us better understand both the events themselves as well as how we think about the process of historical representation.

España heroica (1937; "Heroic Spain") and *España leal en armas* (1937; "Loyal Spain in Arms"), films that borrow images from *Reportaje*, further exemplify the rhetorical dynamics of documentary practice in the Spanish Civil War. Both films were made before the war's outcome was foreseeable, and, although they articulate opposed manifestos, both seek to create seamless national visions out of extreme diversity, offering strikingly similar nationalizing narratives of Spain past, present, and future. Each film lays claim to the nation by identifying its key components, from the public to the intimate, relying most heavily on the trope of the body—both national and individual.

The Nationalist *España heroica*, produced by Hispano-Film-Produktion, a corporation of Spaniards and Germans in Berlin,[6] featured ample Republican footage stolen from ships docking in Germany en route to Moscow (Gubern, *1936* 75). Both German- and Spanish-language versions were directed by Joaquín Reig, who worked as a film editor in Germany for the Francoists. The Republican *España leal en armas* was produced under the direction of Luis Buñuel in Paris at the request of the Republican government, which had sent him there as a special envoy to the Spanish embassy. Made in French, Spanish, and Italian versions, the film officially was directed by Jean-Paul Le Chanois, a member of the French Communist Party, though Buñuel seemed to have played at least a supervisory role.[7] The French version, entitled *Espagne 36*, featured prominently in Republican Spain's pavilion at the 1937 World's Fair held in Paris; as one of several documentary films selected by Buñuel to be screened there, it was part of a program designed to represent Spain to the outside world.[8]

España heroica and *España leal en armas* are typical of many transnational documentary films made during the Spanish Civil War (Joris Ivens's *The Spanish Earth* may be the best-known example). Such films frequently relied on community-building strategies that defined and legitimized the Spanish nation in relation to other countries. Both *España heroica* and *España leal* regularly exhibit maps, as well as images meant to illustrate the enemy's use of foreign aid in violation of the Non-intervention Pact. Both articulate the crisis of national identity in terms of cultural heritage and emphasize the importance of protecting the symbols of that heritage (*España heroica* features soldiers guarding artworks; *España leal* depicts the careful transfer of paintings from the recently air-bombed Prado). Both also extend their nationalizing tactics to include more intimate domains, imbuing the individual body itself with contrary but ideologically loaded meanings. And like Capa's photograph and *Reportaje*, both employ bodies for narrative and mythological purposes. As the lead character in each film's story, the individual body speaks for the national one, telling in graphic and visually accessible terms the tale of Spain's past and future. Sometimes physical bodies that have been destroyed in military battle are resurrected in the films. These bodies reappear in abstract form, as nameless martyrs or larger-than-life heroes: national identity is, in a sense, built at the expense of particular, individual identity.

By disregarding or actively subverting the usual questions that establish meaning (Whose body? How did he or she die?), these films strip the body of its individual identity and replace it with a carefully defined collective one. In *España heroica* a sequence of shots from Málaga, a southern port town, purportedly liberated by Franco's troops, demonstrates this narrative process forcefully. Following a scene of townspeople returning after this liberation, the film depicts visually what its voice-over narration alleges is the destruction caused by the invading Reds: damaged stores and offices, decimated homes, and countless dead bodies—victims of a bombing raid. The narrator somberly informs us, "The Reds' bombs murder women and children." This routine is familiar enough: films on both sides regularly used shots of dead bodies to accuse the enemy of murder. But what is arresting here is that the shots of dead women and children, the scenes of grieving, are not from Málaga; indeed, they are not from Nationalist territory. These shots are lifted from Republican footage, and they depict casualties in Madrid, portraying victims of the bombs dropped by Franco's own pilots.

In using stolen footage, *España heroica* was hardly unique. Most feature-length documentaries made during the war relied heavily on archival newsreel material that often changed hands. What stands out is just how personal the deception was: while this sequence leaves a graphic impression of particular bodies, it starkly diminishes the little individuality those subjects might have by removing the one or two things we supposed we knew about them—their apparent political affiliations or where they lived. Whatever moral claim to our sympathies the bombing victims might have had is destabilized, for we are not sure for whom or what they died. This may make them more sympathetic as victims, but it leaves us more suspicious and confused, less capable of attaching our feelings in any intimate way. In short, our naturally strong bodily identification is disrupted.[9]

This is just one more example of a rhetorical process of nation building illustrated by these, and other, documentary films of the war in Spain. It is reminiscent of a passage from George Orwell's *Nineteen Eighty-Four*, in which Big Brother exercises full control over history by creating "dead" heroes (50). Likewise, in this scene from *España heroica*, the images of dead bodies—emblems of real, complicated lives—are now anonymous heroes, literally bodies of evidence that can be shuffled around and ordered to serve a particular political message.

While these documentaries—politically interested, carefully composed representations that require contextual understanding—characterize the reductive, polarized views to which political partisans as well as artists subscribed during the Spanish Civil War, observations by Ivens and Orwell, documentarians intimately connected to the conflict, suggest a way of thinking about the documentary dilemma that can help students make sense of such representations as more than either simplistic truths or jaded political commentary.

When critics dismissed *The Spanish Earth* as mere propaganda, Ivens responded that he had not aimed for an "objective" film that would have taken into account the Nationalist interpretation of events, since "a documentary film maker has to have an opinion on such vital issues as fascism" (*Camera* 136–37). Ivens approached film from a point of view radically different from that of most in the American film industry; he believed it was the filmmaker's responsibility to become involved "directly in the world's most fundamental issues . . . if his work is to have any dramatic or emotional or art value" (*Camera* 136). In *The Spanish Earth* Ivens sought a convincing realism, but not a realism that depended on verisimilitude. The film, originally shot without audio, later featured a sound track fabricated to provide an authentic, warlike mood for the spectator.[10] Ivens saw *The Spanish Earth* as a subjective witnessing—a "testimony" in which he did not "hide" himself and in which the most important reality was the political message he conveyed (*Camera* 211). Like many of his comrades, Ivens laid special claim to the truth, presented the war in somewhat polarized terms, and, convinced of the moral correctness of his view, distorted his "truthful" images for the sake of his cause. As a filmmaker who believed that a documentary could be both truthful and political, Ivens offers a perspective useful for students navigating the relation between documentary and propaganda as they examine representations of the Spanish Civil War (for another view on this subject, see Shubert in this volume).

Orwell's belief that the purpose of art is to "push the world in a certain direction, to alter other people's idea of the kind of society that they should strive after" ("Why" 312–13), echoes Ivens's views. Orwell is often considered one of the most trustworthy witnesses to the war, and his credibility stems from his recognition of the documentary dilemma. Like Ivens, Orwell believed that there is an alternative to choosing between objective documentary representation and uselessly biased propaganda. Orwell spoke to this false dichotomy when, referring to the Spanish Civil War, he dramatically proclaimed that "history stopped in 1936" ("Looking" 197). With these words, Orwell was not declaring the end of history; rather, he was mourning the loss of a particular way of thinking about history, the loss of a certain perspective on the relation between the events of the real world and our narrative accounts of those events. Lost, in his view, was not the actual possibility of a totally objective history—he had always seen the folly in that—but a process of fashioning history that, through its regard for the ideal of objectivity, allowed for a diversity of meaningful if biased perspectives. What Orwell saw endangered in the Spanish Civil War was history as pluralistic dialogue, history as struggle for consensus.

Orwell, an admitted partisan who fought with and then became disillusioned by the left-supported republic, understood that in the Spanish Civil War conventional notions of history were under siege, that the history of this conflict had become indiscriminately unified in perspective, or totalized. Several years after the war, in *Nineteen Eighty-Four*, Orwell eloquently dramatized the process of totalization that he so deeply feared, describing how Big Brother and the Party exercised complete control over the public sense of past, present, and future: "All history was a palimpsest, scraped clean and re-inscribed exactly as often as was necessary" (43). Perhaps Orwell chose the palimpsest as a metaphor for history because it captured the seductive relation between totalitarianism (in any form) and the media of representation.

His selection of this image suited his darkly satirical purposes, for the palimpsest—a surface that can be wiped clean and written over—represented the pernicious techniques of information control that totalitarian regimes employed. But the figure of the palimpsest is especially useful for examining the documentary representation of this conflict, since it is a parchment that not only has been written on and erased repeatedly but also often bears the still-visible remnants of earlier writing. As Capa's photograph, *Reportaje*, *España heroica*, and *España leal en armas* illustrate, documentary representation in Spain was both a privileged window on reality and a pointed tool of propaganda; it functioned as a public palimpsest on which competing factions could authoritatively inscribe, erase, and reinscribe their images of the nation. By exploring the contexts, histories, and rhetorical dimensions of these images, students can learn to identify and use the traces that remain on this public palimpsest to deepen and enrich their own understanding of the war.

By glimpsing beyond the simple categories of documentary or propaganda, by refusing to read the conflict merely as a moral allegory, Ivens and Orwell, unlike many artists and writers of the time, provide pedagogically useful and intellectually satisfying models of inquiry about the role of documentary in the Spanish Civil War. Their work persuades us that the documentary film of the war was neither pure propaganda nor objective truth but rather a particular collection of representative codes and interpretive protocols that emerged in a context of extreme political crisis and ambitious artistic activity. Documentary can never fulfill its implied promises of neutral observation and depiction; yet, in contrast to other film traditions, it does make a distinct purchase on the real world—it poses and seeks to answer a different set of questions. Despite its cloak of neutrality, documentary film is, ironically, a medium especially subject to manipulation. By considering their frames and contexts, we can understand documentary representations as more than thin political assertions—they become rich sites for learning about the varied meanings of the events they depict. In such a course of study, students understand that as participants in class discussion, they too are framing what they study, helping shape the meanings of complex and resonant historical episodes such as the Spanish Civil War.

Notes

1. *Life* magazine's caption reads, "Robert Capa's camera catches a Spanish soldier the instant he is dropped by a bullet through the head in front of Córdoba" ("Death"). John Hersey wrote that Capa recalled taking the photograph by "timidly" raising his camera above a trench during heavy fighting and, "without looking, at the instant of the first machine gun burst, press[ing] the button"; only after sending "the film to Paris undeveloped" did Capa learn that his random snapshot had been published the world over (qtd. in Knightley 209–12; "Decisive Moment"; for another view, see Wasson, in this volume, whose essay on Spanish Civil War photography focuses in more detail on Capa's shot).

2. See Kathleen Vernon's essay in this volume, which examines this purpose with respect to Nationalist visual art.

3. There is some question about how many cinematographers were involved in shooting the footage used in *Reportaje*. For different accounts of the film's production, see Amo García 790–91; Gubern, *1936* 14; and Sala Noguer 66–70.

4. All translations are mine unless otherwise noted.

5. Such films generally passed to enemy hands in two ways: by being captured in conquered Republican territory or, more commonly, according to the Francoist film historian Carlos Fernández Cuenca, by being intercepted by German police at the Berlin airport, a key transition point for flights from Spain to Moscow (1: 467).

6. The Nationalists had little choice but to produce films internationally, since the republic held Madrid and Barcelona, the two centers of Spain's film industry. Fortunately for Franco, Germany, Italy, and (to a lesser degree) Portugal were willing to provide alternative means of production.

7. The extent of Buñuel's involvement in the film is disputed; despite his own comment to Max Aub that he merely supervised editing, some think Buñuel was more involved, and most agree that he helped write the commentary. For further discussion see Amo García 425–26; Aub, *Conversaciones* 93; Gubern, *1936* 25; and Sala Noguer 156–64.

8. The Vatican's pavilion provided space for Franco's Nationalist movement to exhibit itself as Spain's rightful government.

9. But even my belief—that it was Franco's Nationalists who stole these images of dead bodies from Republican footage—is essentially unverifiable. These images belong to the Republicans only in the sense that they appear and reappear in Republican films, where they signify victims of Franco's bombs. Ultimately, the sequence raises only questions about the ownership of images and about what kind of knowledge documentary film provides.

10. Ivens recalled that "we incorporated in our track . . . a piece of earthquake noise from [W. S. Van Dyke's 1936 film] *San Francisco*, which we ran backwards for our effect during a bombardment" (*Camera* 129–30). For further discussion of the sound track, see Ivens, *Camera* 128–30; Gubern, *1936* 44; and Sala Noguer 391.

Curtis Wasson

Photography and
the Spanish Civil War

Whenever I view a photograph from the period of the Spanish Civil War, I am tempted to take it for what it is: an extraordinary document of a pivotal moment in world history. My eyes tell me that I perceive in the photograph "what has been," and I am loath to disturb this understanding; I do not question what I am seeing (Barthes, *Camera* 85). Because I do not accord a photograph the same status as a literary text (which I would automatically question), I run the risk of not understanding the lessons that a photograph might teach.

I had this experience at the Metropolitan Museum of Art in New York. While visiting an exhibition of photography from the Gilman Paper Company Collection, I turned a corner to find Robert Capa's *Falling Militiaman*, taken near Cerro Muriano on or about 5 September 1936. Facing this marvelous photograph, I could only speculate what would have led Federico Borrell García, the dying soldier, to give his life. I felt more than a certain distance from the falling figure; this feeling was heightened by the historicizing gesture implied in a museum exhibition, as well as the heterogeneity of the collection I was viewing. The photograph was to me both archival and decontextualized; Borrell García's grand gesture, inconceivable (see C. Nelson, "Aura" 27).

Reflecting on this experience, I realized that what I felt may mirror what students feel when facing the immense body of photographs of the Spanish Civil War. Students are accustomed to seeing this kind of photography as a visual support to a news item. They lack an understanding of the ideological forces that led people not only to give their lives, as Borrell García did, but also to document the Spanish struggle, as did Capa, Henri Cartier-Bresson, Chim (David Seymour), Augustí Centelles, and others. In addition, students may not know how magazines and newspapers use imagery to advance a certain point of view; for, as Stuart Hall reminds us, the determination of what constitutes news "is a highly ideological procedure" (188). Though representation was often pictured as transparent in 1930s media (claims abounded that the photograph or the camera never lies), I would argue that both the substance of visual representation and its frame (caption, positioning, etc.) can skew the message that an image supposedly conveys unproblematically, to be understood by all: as Susan Sontag puts it, "[n]o 'we' should be taken for granted when the subject is looking at other people's pain" (*Regarding* 7).

In this essay I document social and technological changes that made Spanish Civil War photography possible. I then explore how these photographs came to be disseminated through print and other media and how the images were altered to suit ideological needs. Finally I subject a pair of photographs to the same kinds of alteration. I hope to suggest by this exercise not only a useful classroom activity but also a lesson that may be taught by such an activity, a lesson whose worth transcends the study of photographs from this particular conflict. The idea that "the objectivity of a picture is merely an illusion" is one that bears repeating (Freund 30–41).

Since the late 1800s, the photograph has been used increasingly in newspapers and magazines to communicate information, as publications came to rely on photographic images instead of lithographs or engravings for illustration. The first photograph to be published in a newspaper appeared in the New York *Daily Herald* on 4 March 1880, and the British *Daily Mirror* became the first newspaper in the world illustrated completely with photographs in 1904 (Balsells 190; Brothers, *War* 5). While the first photo journal was founded in 1890, the late 1920s and early 1930s mark the creation of the best-known examples of the genre, such as *Vu*, established in 1928 by Lucien Vogel; *Life*, inaugurated in 1936 by Henry Luce; and the British *Picture Post*, founded in 1938. The surge in the number of photo journals, as well as the increasing number of newspapers that used photographs as more than a simple supplement to the text, meant that the Spanish Civil War "was the first war to be extensively and freely photographed for a mass audience" (Brothers, *War* 2; see also Schneider 179; Lewinski 67–70, esp. 69). While many other conflicts have been photographed (most notably the American Civil War, by Matthew Brady and his team), the Spanish Civil War was perhaps the first that was best known worldwide through photographs, in large part because photographic technology was then coming into its own.

Photojournalism as we know it was made possible by developments in photographic technology. The most important of these developments was the portable camera. As Michael L. Carlebach noted in his study of American photojournalism, "[a] new generation of small, handheld cameras fitted with fast lenses . . . made indoor, available-light photography routine" in the 1920s and 1930s (173). Cameras such as the Ermanox with the Ernostar lens, which came out in 1924, and the Leica I, which was sold beginning in 1925, were of unquestionable value to photojournalists (Newhall 154; Denoyelle 104; Balsells 190). While the Ermanox took small glass plate negatives, the Leica used rolled 35 mm film negatives, a technical advance that permitted the photographer to take multiple shots rapidly without reloading.[1]

In an article on Centelles, the first journalistic photographer in Barcelona to own a 35 mm camera, Jerald R. Green explains that Centelles was in high demand as a press photographer because he could take pictures that other photographers could not. Technological advances decreased the size of the camera (which could be placed in his pocket and snuck in to courtrooms and prisons, places where cameras were normally not allowed) and allowed the photographer greater spontaneity and individuality ("Augustí Centelles" 149; see also Mellor 27–28).[2] It is this kind of individuality that gave rise to the profession of photojournalist and abetted the growing popularity of illustrated journals (Balsells 14).

Because photographers enjoyed a greater sense of freedom and engagement with their material than before, the photographs of the Spanish Civil War became expressions both of what really happened and of artistry, pulling photography in opposite directions. The blurred movements and diagonal perspectives of some photographs recall the fascination of futurism and other vanguard schools with line, speed, and movement as hallmarks of the modern age, though futurism's relation with photography was hardly uncomplicated (Lista). In addition, the ability to photograph events as they happen (the snapshot, or *instantané*) brings the camera closer to the ideal of automatic writing espoused by surrealism (André Breton called automatic writing "the photography of thought"[3]), though Olivier Lugon argued that surrealists only appreciated photography as a "docile source" of associative possibility (Walker 12; Breton 86; Lugon 27; also see Walker 168–87).

This tension between photography as art form and as document of the real is mirrored in the question of the photograph's objectivity. The photograph was more "objective," as Carlos Serrano puts it, "given that it came closer to the reality of cold, hard fact." It was in an important sense "more *engaged*" as well, "since the photo focused on the action from the point of view of the participant, . . . and thus it incited viewers to recognize and implicate themselves in certain events that they could contemplate up close" ("Pueblo" 20). This engagement opens the door to criticism of the photographer's impartiality, because the photographs seem to make clear that what is taking place is a process of selection of how war is represented: the spectator only views what the photographer wants him or her to see (Berrio 193; see also Whelan, *Robert Capa: A Biography* 119).

Though the selection process is most apparent at the level of the photographer, there are several other layers of editing that took place before photographic images of the Spanish Civil War made headlines. Military censors on both sides of the conflict were also responsible for what the public saw of the war. Although there was generally little censorship of those who covered the war from the Republican side (as compared with the extensive censorship of the photographers who accompanied the insurgents), it did occur.[4] Foreign journalists were required to submit their developed negatives to the Ministerio de Guerra (War Ministry) for review (Green, "Spanish Civil War"). Green also mentions that the Republicans censored photos of the bombardment of Madrid during the first year of the war, so as not to disseminate implicit "criticism of Loyalist anti-aircraft defenses"; it was only when the government realized in late 1937 that such pictures were effective propaganda that they encouraged their publication ("Spanish Civil War" 98; see also Cigognetti and Sorlin 20; Romeiser, "Spanish Civil War" 76).

More significant than the work of the military censors, perhaps, is that of the editors of the newspapers and photo journals that published the work of photographers at the front. Editors (at least, those in Britain and France) were often responsible for sanitizing the war, selecting images that showed bandaged soldiers rather than dying ones, thus making the conflict seem more anodyne and engaging in what could be called censorship by omission (Brothers, *War* 162). Certain magazines and newspapers in the United States employed violent and visceral imagery, although *Life* condemned such use, stating that some of the photographs released by Italy's Ministry of Press and Propaganda in support of the rebels were "too horrible to reproduce" ("Spanish Propaganda" 54).

A more drastic alteration of the truth is the cropping and captioning of photos to change their message.[5] The issue of tampering with photos was severe enough for *Life* to devote an article to Spanish propaganda that gave examples from both Nationalist and Loyalist campaigns. *Life* pretended to be an impartial witness ("*Life* neither believes nor disbelieves any of the captions attached by the Spanish antagonists to these pictures" ["Spanish Propaganda" 52]). However, as Aden Hayes notes, Luce, the founder of *Life*, was a supporter of fascism abroad and hated the inefficacy and messiness of the popularly elected governments in France and Spain (63). It is not coincidental that rebel photographs outnumber Loyalist pictures in the *Life* article, two to one. What is also interesting is the captioning of the photos: while aristocracy and piety are invoked to describe the rebels, the Loyalists are labeled "the newly liberated Spanish rabble" ("Spanish Propaganda" 53). The most fascinating caption brings to light the issue of the falsification of photographs. The caption reads:

> Rebel cruelty is the point of this obviously posed Loyalist picture of a Loyalist boy supposedly about to be shot by rebel captors. *Spaniards love to act out these tableaux.* The scene is near Huesca where Catalan armies have lately attacked after a year of loafing. (52; my emphasis)

The text reduces fealty to the government to playacting, trivializes the conflict, and, by folklorizing the behavior of Loyalist troops, paints the republic as primitive and traditional as opposed to contemporary and progressive.

The notion of tradition was, however, a multivalent sign in the propagandist's arsenal. Whereas in *Life* tradition could be invoked as a sign of the backward nature of the Spanish "rabble," other magazines (such as *Spain*, a clearly right-wing organ published in New York from 1937 to 1942) emphasized that the fascists were fighting to preserve Spanish tradition from Communist forces. According to the right-wing press, one of the clearest signs that the Loyalists disrespected tradition was the well-documented defacement and destruction of works of art and religious structures undertaken by leftists of differing political proclivities ("National Movement"; Edward Nash; Walters). Loyalists sought to counteract such imagery by accusing rebel troops of the same kinds of destruction, while vouchsafing, through photography, that government forces were interested in preserving even the treasures of the highest nobility ("Churches"; Capa, *Death*; "Spain").

Tied in with the notions of Spanishness and tradition utilized by both sides is the question of foreign participation in the war. Loyalists and fascists used photographs of foreign troops and weaponry as a clear sign of the participation of outsiders in the war, relying on the suasive power of photographic representation to make their case ("First Intervention"; "Foreign Commanders"; "Moral Support"; "Soviet Russia's Aid"). Of course, the question of the accuracy and truthfulness of these photographic representations was always raised ("How").

The *Life* caption discussed above was also subject to questioning, for embedded in it is the serious charge of using posed photographs as a tool of propaganda. *Life* should have known something about the practice, since Capa and Gerda Taro, like other photographers, occasionally staged battle scenes that they filmed and photographed for several photo journals, *Life* among them (Whelan, *Robert Capa: A Biography* 119). Capa's *Falling Militiaman*, perhaps the most famous war photograph ever, was until recently also one of the most hotly debated: at issue, its authenticity. O'Dowd Gallagher, a South African–born journalist, claimed to have been sharing a hotel room with Capa in a place far distant from Cerro Muriano on the day the photo was taken. He also stated that Capa used Franco's troops to stage the now famous photo at a later date, a somewhat absurd notion given Capa's political beliefs (Squiers 20). Richard Whelan dismisses the suggestion, claiming that Gallagher didn't even meet Capa until 1938 (*Robert Capa: A Biography* 97). It was only in 1995, when Mario Brotóns Jordà, a combatant from the village of Alcoy, self-published his memoir, *Retazos de una época de inquietudes* ("Fragments from an Era of Unrest"), that the name of the fallen soldier came to light (see Squiers 20; Whelan, "Robert Capa's *Falling Soldier*").

This evidence does not obviate the fact that some of the photographs from the Spanish Civil War were set pieces, staged or otherwise faked. I am not suggesting, however, that many of the tens of thousands of civil war photographs were posed or that photographers and editors were intent on capturing and displaying only images that favored their particular ideologies (see, as examples to the contrary, *Guerra civil espanyola* 61; Namuth and Reisner 43). Even if all the images of the conflict were created as simple propaganda, they would still capture a truth about the Spanish struggle: that many people fought, and died, for what they believed in. Students already understand this message before they step into the classroom; the more important message is that ideologies exist and that one must read—whether it be a photograph in a newspaper or this essay—with a critical eye.

To that end I propose the following exercise, inspired by an anecdote in Gisèle Freund's *The World in My Camera*. Freund, a colleague of Capa's at Magnum, recounts having seen a series of photos in *L'express* in December 1956, after the Hungarian revolution. She explains that the article showed how each photograph could have been used "to give absolutely contradictory but truthful versions of the events" (34). Thus I consider two photographs from the Spanish Civil War and use them to support both Loyalist and rebel positions. Something similar could be done in discussion sections as group work, could be assigned as the theme of a short essay, or could form part of a larger project that includes other representations of conflict, from either the Spanish Civil War or other modern wars.

I offer examples of what one might do with these photographs if one were a newspaper editor during the Spanish Civil War with a particular set of ideological beliefs or a propaganda officer on either side of the conflict. There is a problem with a caption to a photograph, as Sontag has noted:

> [T]he caption-glove slips on and off so easily. It cannot prevent any argument or moral plea which a photograph (or set of photographs) is intended to support from being undermined by the plurality of meanings that every photograph carries. (*On Photography* 109; also see Schneider 191–92)

The caption is the only way for the photograph to "speak," in Sontag's estimation; yet every caption is an interpretation of the photograph, and thus no caption can express the whole of an image (*On Photography* 108–09). There is always much about images that is unsaid, that resists articulation.

With that in mind, I would like to turn to a photograph that seems to speak for itself. *Propaganda* (fig. 1) was taken in Barcelona by Hans Namuth or Georg Reisner, probably in July or August 1936 (see also Namuth and Reisner 36). It depicts a young man in the street, wearing a sweater decorated with an insignia of the Communist Party. In his right hand he carries a trumpet or bugle, and his left hand holds a megaphone up to his mouth. Behind him are posters for the POUM (Partido Obrero de Unificación Marxista [Unified Marxist Workers' Party]) and the Alpinistas Jóvenes (Young Mountaineers).

Figure 1. *Propaganda.* Photograph by Hans Namuth or Georg Reisner. 1936.

If we were to look at this photo from a Republican perspective—somewhat of a chimera, given the composition of the Republican coalition—we might notice that the Loyalist militiaman is both a political agent and an agent of culture. He appears to be speaking to a group of some size (thus the need for the megaphone), preaching the virtues of the antifascist fight. This kind of photo is relatively common in Namuth and Reisner's work, and it suggests a popular protagonism and leadership among antifascist troops; it is not just the important figures of the day who deserve to be photographed. The Spanish Civil War, as Margarita Nelken asserts in an article published in *Regards,* is the scene of "the epic of the people" (also see Mellor 29; C. Nelson, "Aura" 33–34; Capa, *Death*; "War"). This anonymous quality is highlighted by the way the megaphone obscures the soldier's face.

This figure is not a traditional militiaman, though: there is little to suggest that he carries a gun. The strap crossing his chest is probably for an ammunition case, but that is not certain. Even if he carried a gun, he would still be an agent of culture; the rifle-brandishing soldier on the POUM poster exhorts the populace to read. Instead of arms, the militiaman uses a musical instrument (another sign of culture) and his megaphone. The presence of both the trumpet and the poster encouraging the populace to read counteracts a frequent claim made of both sides of the conflict (namely, of being destroyers of civilization); here the militiaman is seen as a preserver and transmitter of culture. In addition, because the megaphone is both translucent and clearly visible, its message is without duplicity. The notion that the message is reliable is redoubled by the visibility of the militiaman's mouth through the megaphone's mouthpiece, close to the center and the focal point of the picture.

Someone sympathetic to the rebels would start with the title of the photograph. The photograph seems too well composed, both in symbolic and photographic terms, to be an action shot. It is clearly designed as an exercise in propaganda; the title is nothing if not self-referential. Moreover, in entitling the picture *Propaganda*, the photographer has left room for the rebels to use this label to describe the message of the left: while the rebels speak true, the left uses Soviet propaganda to convert the populace to its point of view. Much could be made as well from the variety of propaganda on display in the picture: two different posters advocating two different left-wing organizations, with the hint of a possible third, on the canopy behind the soldier. The fascists were well aware of the fragmentation of the governmental coalition, though most of their propaganda simplified the ideological differences on the left ("Feuds"). Finally, the youth is an anonymous leader, a contradiction in terms for the rebels.

Rebel photography, in contrast, focused on the exemplary figure of the leader, the generals (and above all, Franco) being photographed to the point of excess. I am thinking here, for example, of Jalón Ángel (Ángel Hilario García de Jalón Hueto), whose *Forjadores de imperio* ("Forgers of Empire") is an album of majestic and regal photographs of Nationalist leaders (also see Meijer).

One Nationalist image that captured my attention is by Pascual Marín (fig. 2). Its caption, too lengthy to reprint in full here, is, much like the photograph, entirely focused on the figure of Franco. Of the caption's eight sentences or sentence fragments, Franco is mentioned in six and mentioned by name in four; in the others, he is called "Caudillo" and "General" (in *Guerra civil espanyola* 123). In the picture, Franco is in the foreground; no other element of the photograph is level with him. He is given a variety of salutes (the Falangist salute by the populace and some of the soldiers; a military salute by several other soldiers; two salutes with a sword) and is shown deference by those who are not saluting (the member of the *Guardia Civil* in the tricornered hat in the lower left-hand corner has his gaze downcast). Franco is directly in line with what appears to be a

Figure 2. Ejército victorioso. Franco, Caudillo del Ejército, Caudillo de España. (Victorious Army: Franco, Caudillo of the Army, Caudillo of Spain.) Photograph by Pascual Marín.

bullet hole in the center of the Nationalist banner, which marks the midpoint of the rooftop crowd as well. The bullet hole, which has left the banner intact, suggests that Franco's movement has been able to triumph over its opposition with relative ease. Franco's central position in the photograph emphasizes both his importance and the rightness (from a Falangist point of view) of his ideological approach. That he is below the civilian populace is significant; it could be read as a borrowing of Catholic ideology, wherein the pope is the servant of the church. Franco here is both the leader and a servant of the movement—a servant of those who believe in him: beneath them, but leading them as well.

A member of the Popular Front might see the photograph in another light. The photo makes it clear that Franco only serves a segment of the population: the soldiers, the middle and upper classes (the populace is nicely dressed), and the *Guardia Civil*. The bullet hole in the banner suggests, however, that the harmony and unity presented in the picture are illusory. The image highlights that Franco is nobody's servant: his central position ensures that he will dominate the spectator's eye and attention, just as he dominates the movement. While those surrounding Franco seem content with his victory, the margins (particularly the right-hand margin) contain unsmiling figures with eyes downcast. Their marginality seems to exclude them from the celebration, but it also highlights the impression that not all feel welcome within the confines of a movement that supposedly speaks for everybody.

A claim of objectivity is a claim to speak for the truth, to let the facts reveal themselves. We have seen how, in the Spanish Civil War photographs, each side of the conflict uses images to stake such a claim. My hope is that students may think critically about how news is presented once they see how this corpus of photographs has been—and can still be—manipulated.

Notes

My thanks to Noël Valis, Mario Feit, and Randy Main, whose comments on earlier versions of this article were most helpful.

1. Rolled film was not new in and of itself; George Eastman first sold Kodak cameras with rolled film in 1889 (Carlebach 18).

2. Indicative of this spontaneity is Cartier-Bresson's comment that he wanted to "preserve life in the act of living" and "to seize the whole essence . . . of some situation that was in the process of unrolling itself before my eyes" after discovering the Leica (Preface, n. pag.). The title of Capa's book of photographs from war-torn Spain, *Death in the Making*, also implies that photography's goal is to witness and capture process, not event, or, at a minimum, that the dialectic between process and event is greatly exaggerated.

3. All translations are mine unless otherwise noted.

4. Jorge Lewinski argues that censorship was widely prevalent on both sides of the conflict, but his viewpoint rests on a largely uncritical acceptance of H. Edward Knoblaugh's account (see Lewinski 86–87; Knoblaugh, *Correspondent* 130–46). The objectivity of Knoblaugh's version of events is called into question by its being excerpted in *Spain*, a notable fascist magazine ("How").

5. Caroline Brothers provides several examples in her *War and Photography* (see, e.g., 121–22). In his biography of Capa, Whelan gives a clearer example of the cropping of a photograph to suit ideological purposes, though the example is not related to the Spanish Civil War (*Robert Capa: A Biography* 101).

Jordana Mendelson

Learning from *Guernica*

In a cartoonlike series of drawings published in the New York newspaper *PM*,[1] the abstract artist Ad Reinhardt attempted to explain modern art to the American public. Popular in tone and aimed at a broad audience, Reinhardt's diagrammatic approach to art historical pedagogy was taken as a welcome exception to the highbrow rhetoric of art criticism. In his last "how to" lesson, dated 5 January 1947, Reinhardt took as his subject Picasso's *Guernica*. Reinhardt's visual analysis of the painting and accompanying commentary bring out fundamental issues raised by *Guernica*: the relation of propaganda to painting, the impact of photography on modern art, the relevance of history to the visual arts and of art to historical narration, and the difficulty of analyzing a work of art dense with overlapping and sometimes competing interpretive possibilities.

Reinhardt's diagram arrives at these complex and intersecting ideas quickly and provides a tool for teaching the Spanish Civil War because it pares down layers of meaning by sketching nuances in broad lines and easy-to-access fragments. His ideas about the painting and interpretations of its figures were not new and have been repeated since (see Spender, "Guernica"; Tuchman; and Held), but the manner of his presentation makes these ideas visible to the nonspecialist in a way that other academic studies

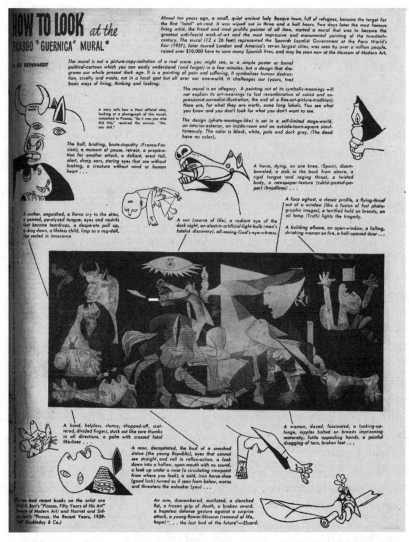

Ad Reinhardt, "How to Look at the Picasso *Guernica* Mural." *PM Sunday Feature*
5 Jan. 1947: 6. © Estate of Ad Reinhardt / Artists Rights Society (ARS) New York.
© Estate of Pablo Picasso / Artists Rights Society (ARS) New York.

may not. For scholars in disciplines outside art history, Reinhardt's illustration teaches a fundamental pictorial (and political) challenge: How does a painting do the work of propaganda without compromising its function as a work of art? Or, as Susan Suleiman asked in her review of the work's ability to function as a "committed painting": "apart from its immediate usefulness, how effective was *Guernica* as a political statement?" (939).

According to Reinhardt's display of the painting's elements, each contributed to a work whose political significance was inextricably wed to its form and whose form communicated immediately and almost transparently the violence and drama of war. Reinhardt claimed, "It is a painting of pain and suffering. It symbolizes human destruction, cruelty and waste, not in a local spot but all over our one-world. It challenges our (yours, too) basic ways of living, thinking and looking." As a politically committed person and an artist trained in the history of art, Reinhardt used the schematics of design and direct language to call readers' attention to the painting's continuing relevance to issues of social justice. It is also a painting that for others seemed to demand explanation; it is not a painting that is viewed simply but one that historians have demonstrated needs to be examined, meditated on, and activated through the addition of context and biography. Reinhardt also responded to this demand in his diagram.

Along the top left corner of Reinhardt's full-page entry his title directs, "How to Look at the Picasso *Guernica* Mural." At this time, the painting had already been hanging in New York's Museum of Modern Art (MoMA) for five years, after its tour through Europe and America to raise funds for the Spanish government and its display in several exhibitions on Picasso (Oppler 42).[2] The painting was almost continuously on exhibit at MoMA until its return to Spain in 1981. Thus it was no doubt well known to Reinhardt's readers. Nonetheless, his diagram takes it apart as if it were a recent acquisition to the public's consciousness. In the middle of the page, a photograph of the painting is reproduced with black lines pulling individual characters out from the rectangular composition and into the top and bottom quadrants: a bull bristling, a horse dying, a mother anguished, a sun, a face aghast, a building aflame, a woman dazed, an arm dismembered, a man decapitated, a hand helpless. Isolating iconographic elements to derive the painting's overall significance is a strategy that Reinhardt's diagram shares with a significant portion of *Guernica* scholarship, from the historically inaccurate if instructive video *Pablo Picasso's* Guernica (which incorrectly implies that the painting was done while General Francisco Franco was in power instead of during the Spanish Civil

War) to the most erudite and rigorous of art historical analyses, performed by Rudolf Arnheim, Meyer Schapiro, and Herschel Chipp.

Between the diagram's title and the identification of the painting's iconographic elements, Reinhardt provides a short historical note and a commentary that differentiates the painting from some forms of visual communication while comparing it with others:

> The mural is not a picture-copy-imitation of a real scene you might see, or a simple poster or banal political cartoon which you can easily understand (and forget) in a few minutes. . . . The design (photo-montage-like) is set in a self-limited stage-world, an interior-exterior. . . . The color is black, white, pale and dark gray. (The dead have no color.)

Here, Reinhardt signals a key comparison between *Guernica* and photomontage, while distancing the painting from other forms of political art, like posters or cartoons. One cannot help thinking of the thousands of posters published during the war, which hung throughout Spain and were sent abroad to places like New York (C. Nelson, *Shouts* 15). Surely, Reinhardt's readers were also familiar with these posters. Reinhardt argues that *Guernica* is different, its forms are denser and more complicated, its messages more transcendent, its impression far less ephemeral than the standard propaganda pamphlet; it requires more attention, more than a few minutes to register fully.

Reinhardt was not implying, however, that *Guernica* outlasted other political statements by abdicating its role as a historical record of what took place on 26 April 1937, when the Basque market town of Guernica (about twenty miles from Bilbao) and symbolic-historic cradle of the *fueros*, or medieval Basque privileges, was leveled by a massive air strike. The center of Guernica was left in smoldering ruins as hundreds of people (up to a thousand by some accounts) were killed, either from the bombs or the machine-gunning fighters who followed (H. Thomas, *Spanish Civil War* 606–07). Miles from the closest military action (the arms factory located nearby was left untouched), Guernica was filled with civilians and retreating soldiers. The bombing of Guernica became a touchstone for controversy in the press and for outrage by Spaniards and non-Spaniards alike throughout the war.

Reinhardt recognized the painting's function as witness to this specific event; he included in his comments the following: "A story tells how a Nazi official who, looking at a photograph of this mural, remarked to

Picasso, 'So it was you who did this,' received the answer, 'No, you did.'"
In replying as he did to the Nazi official, Picasso indicated verbally what he
had already represented pictorially in *Guernica*. Despite the conflicting
reports that emerged about the bombing in its immediate aftermath,
Picasso's painting drew on the account that was reproduced in *L'humanité* on 29 April 1937 (Chipp 38–43). The Nationalists denied involvement
in the destruction of Guernica; they blamed radical "Reds" for burning
the city during their retreat. Other reports linked the tragedy to the
German and Italian forces. It was George L. Steer's eyewitness report,
which appeared on 28 April in the London *Times* and was reproduced in
L'humanité, that has stood as the most accurate account of the bombing.
Steer identified unexploded German bombs and interviews with the inhabitants of Guernica as part of his evidence to demonstrate that it was the
Nationalists, supported by Hitler and Mussolini, who were behind the
town's destruction (Rankin 114–28).

For Picasso and viewers of *Guernica*, the painting has become witness
to, and proof of, the destruction brought on by the German Condor
Legion. This is the aspect of the painting that is immediate. What Reinhardt tries to explain is something else, not the role of *Guernica* in recording the tragedy of war, but how it makes that tragedy visible and lasting.
His assertion also raises the questions: What sets Picasso's representational
strategies apart from those of other artists? What makes *Guernica* something more than just propaganda (though it functioned as such)?[3]

At the time he published this commentary on Picasso's mural, Reinhardt had been experimenting with collages made from cutout papers, many
from newsprint, with photographic images visible (Lippard 30–31). Trained
in photography during his military service, he was aware of the differences
between the practice of photojournalism ("a picture-copy-imitation of a real
scene") and the creation of works of art ("photo-montage-like") (Lippard
42–43). In other words, Reinhardt clarified that Picasso did not simply copy
the photographs coming out of press accounts about *Guernica*; rather he
interpreted those events through a technique similar to montage, which
depends on appropriation, fragmentation, juxtaposition, and disjuncture.
Reinhardt scripts a narrative for Picasso that parallels his own vacillation
between the poles of realism and abstraction, between his collage activities
based on bits of newsprint and his large brightly colored abstract paintings.
Reinhardt forgets or oversimplifies, however, that photomontage was not
incompatible with propaganda: it was a key technique used by the avant-
garde and in propagandistic materials throughout the 1920s and 1930s.

For me, Reinhardt's diagram is a revelation because it helps explain a problem that has always shadowed my teaching and writing about *Guernica*. I cannot look at the painting without thinking of its original placement at the Spanish Pavilion in Paris for the 1937 Exposition Internationale des Arts et Techniques dans la Vie Moderne (see Mendelson). In the context of the pavilion, the relation between painting and photography, artistic creativity and propaganda, was staged continuously. The pavilion itself placed these media and expressive forms in dialogue. The architects who designed the building, Josep Lluís Sert and Luis Lacasa, built it to provide a stage for the exhibitions and to facilitate easy circulation through them (Alix 34–47). The use of standardized and prefabricated materials kept construction costs under control, and the building's clean lines and functional organization placed it squarely within the latest trend for modern architecture. Spain's leading artists contributed

View of exterior of Spanish Pavilion, 1937 Exposition Internationale des Arts et Techniques dans la Vie Moderne, Paris.

pieces that were either sent from Spain, already in Paris, or designed specifically for the pavilion, like Picasso's *Guernica* and Joan Miró's *The Reaper (Catalan Peasant in Revolt)*, which was painted directly on celotex panels that had already been installed in the pavilion's stairwell. Picasso, Miró, and Julio González were the most famous of the artists to appear in the pavilion, and their presence attracted international attention. They, however, like their compatriots, were also engaged in negotiating the balance between maintaining an independent artistic vision and contributing to the cause (Lubar 151–58).

In Spain, the press prominently featured debates on the political role of the artist, especially during the civil war. Heated exchanges appeared in which arguments were made for and against art in the service of politics. Alberto Sánchez, whose sculpture *The Spanish People Have a Path That Leads to a Star* was placed directly in front of the pavilion and served as a monumental declaration of the republic's resistance to the military insurgency, defended the use of abstract forms in political art in response to an editorial published by the Valencian artist Josep Renau, in his journal *Nueva Cultura*.[4] Renau also engaged in a polemical exchange with the painter Ramón Gaya that appeared in the literary magazine *Hora de España* in 1937.

Renau argued that artists should use the most advanced artistic strategies possible to create works that directly responded to the political requirements of the times. For Renau, who was a founding member of the Valencian Communist Party, this duty meant creating propaganda that drew on his knowledge of graphic design and his employment of photomontage. Gaya agreed that montage and its use in propaganda were effective for images sent abroad, where the principal task was to gain supporters for the government's defense. Yet he said that Spaniards needed art that would raise their spirits and show them that an artist's creativity offered hope for the future (Gamonal Torres 44–45, 174–79). Gaya argued for the independence of art. He saw the role of the artist as providing hopeful images grounded in artistic autonomy and expressive forms brought about by the artist's imagination. Renau disagreed. Throughout the war he continued to design posters and propaganda materials, and, in the same year as his polemic with Gaya, he published his writings on the "función social del cartel publicitario" ("the social function of the publicity poster") in *Nueva Cultura*.

Renau's commitment to outlining a strategy for producing graphically effective political designs that drew heavily on the montage practices of leftist artists in Germany and the Soviet Union is directly relevant to Reinhardt's observations about *Guernica*, even though the American artist most likely never made the connection. Renau occupied key positions in the Spanish government during the war, working as the director general of fine arts, which included heading efforts to protect the nation's artistic patrimony, and later as director of graphic propaganda when the government moved to Barcelona (Forment 144–48, 172–73). Renau also designed the exterior and interior photomurals that covered the pavilion. He knew Picasso, spoke with the artist about his honorary appointment as director of the Prado Museum, and later recounted suggesting to Picasso that, after the war, *Guernica* should be installed with Diego Velázquez's *Las Meninas* and Francisco Goya's *Execution on the 3rd May* (Held 36). It is Renau's photomurals that tug on my art historical consciousness every time I teach *Guernica*, perhaps because, for me, both artists' works operate in a shared aesthetic field, even when their fortunes in art history and their impact on viewers were quite different.

Before arriving at the pavilion, visitors were greeted by Renau's photomurals on the front and side corners of the building's exterior; posters were hung along the building's exit ramp, and it is possible that Renau's posters would have been among them. Picasso's mural was located on the bottom floor of the pavilion, which was an open area with a patio that was shaded by the pavilion's upper floors. After seeing *Guernica*, hung on a wall opposite Alexander Calder's mercury fountain, visitors ascended a ramp to the second floor. There and on the first floor, they again encountered Renau's photomurals, ranging in subject from regional scenery and traditions to the government's reforms in education and land ownership. Other photomurals dealt with the war's subjects, especially the protection of the nation's artistic patrimony. Thus *Guernica* was bracketed by Renau's photomurals. In such a context, how were visitors to understand Picasso's mural? It was similar in dimension to the photomurals. Painted in black, white, and gray, it also shared a palette with the photographs. The stippled marks of black lines on some of Picasso's figures even looked like abstracted newsprint.

Indeed, if we follow Reinhardt's logic, there might be little difference between the painted mural and the photomural (see also Tuchman 45). Both Picasso and Renau relied on a creative method that recycled images from the past and from their present-day media culture: Picasso's preparatory sketches have been exhibited often and published with *Guernica* to show the painting's genesis and transformation, and critics have pointed out the impact that photographs of the bombings must have had on the artist's ideas (Spender, "Guernica" 221). My own research has explored the ways in which Renau included appropriated photographs from the illustrated press, public archives, and his earlier design work in the 1937 photomurals. Had there been no qualitative difference between Picasso's "photo-montage-like" painting and Renau's mural-like photomontages, both works of art would be conserved and perhaps treated to the same reception in art history. Instead, Renau's murals have been erased almost completely from the scholarship about *Guernica* (except in those studies that mention the pavilion). Whereas *Guernica* is on display at the Museo Nacional Centro de Arte Reina Sofía in Madrid and has had a long post-pavilion history, Renau's photomurals were apparently destroyed after the International Exposition closed. The different legacies of these two artists and the work that they contributed to the pavilion tells as much about the history of art as it does about the extant differences between painting and photomontage, despite Reinhardt's allusion to their similarities.

Picasso's *Guernica* received wide acclaim, and some criticism, at the time of its production and later through its temporary exhibition world-wide and its permanent (or semipermanent) displays at MoMa, the Casón del Buen Retiro at the Prado, and now at the Museo Nacional Centro de Arte Reina Sofía. To review all the art historical literature on the painting far exceeds the limits of this essay; the painting's relevance to the greatest debates on the political function of art has given it a secure place in surveys of modern art. It has also had a significant afterlife in reproductions made of it and the uses to which it has been put for political causes in the present (just think of the controversy when the tapestry version of it hanging at the United Nations was covered up during a press conference by Colin Powell in February 2003).

Before launching complaints about the lowering of great art to the level of popular culture, we have to remember not only the remarks made by Reinhardt and others about *Guernica*'s relation to photography but also the original plans held for the painting by the Spanish government. From the start, the government intended to provide the public with the means to make *Guernica* and Picasso's other commission, a print series called *Sueño y Mentira de Franco* ("Dreams and Lies of Franco"), easily accessible and affordable: *Sueño* in postcards and *Guernica* in photographs (Read and Blunt 215). We should not be surprised that the pavilion included souvenirs that could be purchased to support the Republican government and that these were largely photographs, postcards, magazines, and prints. These are still the methods through which works of art circulate out of museums and into the hands of visitors; they were also the prime media chosen for propaganda during war. Concerning *Guernica*'s relation to its public (both historical and contemporary), a comment made by the art historian José López-Rey on the occasion of the painting's return to Spain is significant: "*Guernica* was, of course, widely known from reproductions that in Spain as elsewhere furthered the notion that it was an entirely monochrome painting" (144). No one confused the painting for a photograph, but it appeared to function like one for those who held a reproduction of it in their hands. *Guernica* represented a moment from history, it was prized as a work contiguous with the conditions of its production, and it circulated: it was a souvenir from the Spanish Civil War.

In the classroom, the painting can function as an illustration of war (for those who choose to read it as such), or it can open up discussion to questions both intrinsic and extrinsic to the Spanish Civil War. Whether in a class about European art between the world wars, a survey of Spanish art, or even a course dedicated to surrealism, I stop at Picasso's *Guernica* and ask students to think about how the violence of war has been rendered visually. What responsibility does an artist have? Are viewers, in turn, responsible for conjuring the correct response to the political urgency of the painting's depiction? What of the circulation of *Guernica*, transhistorically and transnationally during the twentieth century? These questions bring us at once to the historical specificity of the painting's production and always lead me into a discussion of the 1937 Spanish Pavilion in Paris. From there, our conversation often moves swiftly to related subjects and media, but we continually come back to Picasso's painting. Perhaps it is because, as Reinhardt predicted, we need more than a few minutes to think about the consequences of Picasso's and all artists' engagement with the world around them.

Notes

1. *PM* was begun in 1940 by Ralph McAllister Ingersoll as a different kind of newspaper, one that was filled with photographs, formatted for easy readability, and loudly pro-labor. It was pitched as the newspaper for the everyman and everywoman, who would appreciate information on a range of topics, from current events to the latest sales around town. Ingersoll supported the policies of Franklin Roosevelt, and his support was reflected in the paper's articles and in Eleanor Roosevelt's praise of *PM* in her column. Throughout its eight-year run the paper was accused by many of its critics of being too pro-Communist. The paper counted many women, Jews, and African Americans among its employees and published

articles against racism and anti-Semitism. Before *PM*, Ingersoll had worked for the *New Yorker*, *Fortune*, and Time Inc. When *PM* encountered dwindling subscriptions and financial losses, Marshall Field III financed the paper until 1948, when he sold it to Bartley Crum and Joseph Barnes, who published the last issue of *PM* on 22 June 1948 (see Margolick; Milkman).

2. In her book, Oppler reproduces Reinhardt's drawing with the title "How to Look at a Mural" (234–35).

3. In his interview with Jerome Seckler in 1945, Picasso indicated that he understood *Guernica* to function as propaganda: "'There is no deliberate sense of propaganda in my painting.' 'Except in Guernica,' I suggested. 'Yes,' he replied, 'except in the *Guernica*. In that there is a deliberate appeal to the people, a deliberate sense of propaganda'" (Oppler 151).

4. Sánchez's sculpture was remade on the occasion of his retrospective at the Museo Nacional Centro de Arte Reina Sofía in 2001. It was installed in front of the museum for the exhibition. In Barcelona, a reconstruction of the 1937 pavilion was built to coincide with the 1992 Olympics. Today, it houses the Biblioteca del Pavelló de la República, which specializes in research materials (primary and secondary) about the Spanish Civil War.

Part V

Memory, Displacement, and the War

Sebastiaan Faber

The Exile's Dilemma: Writing the Civil War from Elsewhere

A significant portion of the novels, short stories, poems, plays, and essays by Spanish authors about their civil war were written from exile. These texts were therefore most likely composed in circumstances of financial hardship, legal insecurity, and existential crisis; were probably written with a specific political agenda in mind, in response to other versions of the war by either the victors or fellow vanquished; were meant for a Spanish audience yet printed in small runs that hardly ever reached the peninsula (if they were printed at all); and even now, a quarter century after the transition to democracy, are barely known among the Spanish reading public and only marginally present in most Spanish cultural histories. There are exceptions, to be sure, such as the works of Francisco Ayala and of Ramón Sender; but these only serve to prove the sad general rule. Paulino Masip's outstanding civil war novel *El diario de Hamlet García* ("The Diary of Hamlet García"), for instance, was first printed in Mexico in 1944 but hardly distributed and not published in Spain until 1987. Arturo Barea's celebrated trilogy *La forja de un rebelde* (*The Forging of a Rebel*) was first brought out in English (1941–46) and then in Spanish in Buenos Aires (1951), while the first peninsular edition appeared twenty-six years later. Many other civil war works written in exile, such as Virgilio Botella

Pastor's *Porque callaron las campanas* (1953; "Because the Bells Were Silent"), Manuel Benavides's *Los nuevos profetas* (1942; "The New Prophets"), or Isabel de Palencia's *En mi hambre mando yo* (1959; "In My Hunger I Reign Supreme"), were never reissued at all. The war, in sum, caused an enormous cultural hemorrhage that will never be wholly remedied.

The bleeding started soon after July 1936; on 1 April 1939, when Franco declared victory, Spain had already lost most of its scholars, writers, teachers, and artists. Some had died, others had been imprisoned, but a great number had decided to leave their homeland, together with the almost five hundred thousand other refugees who had been crossing the Pyrenees since the outbreak of the war. In the years following, about half these refugees returned to Spain. The rest would settle in many different countries—most in France, Mexico, Argentina, and the Soviet Union.

From the moment these intellectual exiles left Spain, they found that they had an irresistible urge to write about their experiences. For intellectuals and nonintellectuals alike, writing became a way to deal with their multiple loss—losing the war, losing friends and families, but also losing a sense of identity and purpose in life. At the same time, it soon became clear that discourse—whether memoir or fiction—was, as Michael Ugarte puts it, a "shifting ground," far from the solid foundation they had hoped it to be (*Shifting Ground* 26). After all, how do you write about a life that has lost its coherence, having been radically split by exile? How do you describe a war that, while it lasted, drew the attention of the entire Western world but that was quickly forgotten and immediately distorted by the victors? What use is writing about Spain and the war, trying to make sense of it and especially to set the record straight, if you cannot ever hope to reach your readers? In other words, if leaving Spain provided a measure of intellectual and physical freedom unavailable to those who remained, that freedom was bought at an enormous price. "Exile," Edward Said rightly notes, "is one of the saddest fates" (*Representations* 47).

The problems facing writers in exile can be said to *constitute* their writing. If texts can never be seen separate from the social and political circumstances of their production and reception, this interconnection is even more obvious in the case of texts written in political exile. Spanish Civil War exile literature was largely driven by politics and the dilemmas of displacement but was also tragically thwarted, even crippled, by both. I suggest that a fruitful way to teach representations of the Spanish Civil War written from elsewhere is precisely to focus on these problems—to focus, that is, on the problems of life in exile; of writing from exile; and, more directly, of teaching exile literature, because if it is clear that exile has an impact on writing, it is not at all clear that it does so in any uniform or generalizable way. In this essay I briefly touch on these three aspects, where possible giving concrete references to texts that can be used in the classroom. For purposes of practicality I limit my examples to a small number of exile authors whose work is relatively accessible if not always well known.

Life in Exile

Apart from its many concrete, daily difficulties—finding a hospitable host country, making a living, sometimes learning a foreign language and customs or acquiring a new nationality—exile gives rise to loyalty conflicts of both a personal and political nature. For one, the act of leaving one's country is susceptible to radically opposing interpretations. It can be constructed as the supreme act of allegiance to one's nation—giving up what one loves most for the sake of its defense—or as a cowardly betrayal, an act of abandonment or desertion. Naturally, the Franco regime was eager to portray the Republican exiles in the latter fashion—they were, after all, the anti-Spain—while the exiles, turning the tables, represented the Francoists as traitors to the nation and themselves as absolute examples of national loyalty.

As Judith Shklar points out, for political exiles to continue to believe in their own patriotic loyalty—many times the raison d'être of their life abroad and, in the end, the only thing that keeps them going—they need to make a clear distinction between their legal obligations to the state that betrayed them and their loyalty to its people, who did not (40–41, 48). Masip, whose *Cartas a un español emigrado* (1939; "Letters to a Spanish Emigré") is largely concerned with fighting defeatism among his fellow exiles while boosting unity and morale, understood this well: for him, the Francoists were nothing but a bunch of isolated insurgents, "traitors twice over, for rebelling against a legitimate government and for selling themselves to foreign nations" (54).[1] If, however, a certain section of the larger population is classifiable as the exiles' enemy—as was evident for the German victims of the Nazis but also, despite Masip's assurances to the contrary, for the Spanish Republicans—the object of exiles' patriotic love becomes precarious. Shklar mentions the example of Willy Brandt, who, although persecuted by his own state and people, said on returning to

Germany after World War II that he had "kept faith with the real Germany, the true Germany." Shklar adds that "he cannot have meant the majority of his people, only their better possibilities, to which he remained loyal" (50). Similarly, Luis Cernuda saw himself compelled to distinguish between a Spain he loved, and that loved him, and another Spain defined by hate: "The hate and destruction that always live on / Dully, in the entrails, / Filled with eternal bile, of the terrible Spaniard" (*Poesía* 254). In the end, Cernuda's only lasting solution to the exile's dilemma of national loyalty was the conscious construction of an imaginary Spain, which he called "Sansueña." For Cernuda this "impossible fatherland, which is not of this world," was partly based on a nostalgic reading of Spain's heroic past (506; Faber, "Norte" 736–38).

The exile's allegiance to the host country is another potential source of problems. Political exiles are given refuge by foreign governments that tend to demand a certain loyalty in return for their hospitality; and this loyalty is not always wholly compatible with the exiles' existing allegiances (Shain 83; Shklar 51). For those Spaniards who ended up in the Dominican Republic ruled by Rafael Leónidas Trujillo, for example, it was all but impossible to square their own political position with that of their conservative, authoritarian host. But even for the more than ten thousand exiles who moved to the revolutionary Mexico of Lázaro Cárdenas, integration into the former colony was not easy. Cernuda, to be sure, fell in love with the country; after several years of cultural alienation in Great Britain and the United States, moving to Mexico in 1952 felt like coming home. But in reality Cernuda's Mexico was as idealized as his Sansueña. He himself realized that his postcolonial love for it was probably bound to remain unrequited: "what attracts you to it might not be more than a subtle, retrospective form of national pride," he remarks at the closing of *Variaciones sobre tema mexicano* ("Variations on a Mexican Theme"). "But this land is not one with yours anymore, nor are these people. Don't you realize that, for them, you can only be a stranger? More than a stranger: someone from a country that they perhaps still look upon with anger?" (657–58).

Indeed, even in Mexico the Spanish exiles ran into cultural and linguistic obstacles. The common colonial history proved to be a catalyst for integration as much as a source of friction, as Max Aub masterfully shows in his "La verdadera historia de la muerte de Francisco Franco" ("The True Story of the Death of Francisco Franco") (*Enero* 413). Politically, too, the Spaniards' position in Mexico was awkward. The regime of the Mexican ruling party claimed to be heir to the Mexican Revolution; but the Republicans arrived at the moment when Cárdenas's leftist populism was being abandoned in favor of capitalist development, later accompanied by anti-Communism and increasing corruption. The exiles, moreover, were constitutionally barred from participation in Mexican politics.

Initially, few refugees showed much interest in their host countries. They were too obsessed with Spain and the war (in fact the exiles' essayistic production on "the problem of Spain" rivals that of the turn of the century). The first years of exile were dominated by hopes of an imminent return, since it was generally expected that Franco would not survive the defeat of the Axis. By the late 1940s, when the perverse logic of the cold war compelled the West to leave Franco alone and even actively support him, for many exiles it was too late to start over and commit themselves fully to their new lives abroad. By then, too, a fatal anachronism had slipped into their patriotic love of Spain, however intensely and genuinely that love was felt. Like distant lovers, exiles and their homelands inevitably grow apart. While Spain continued to evolve after 1939, the exiles, in their isolation, were barred from witnessing that change, let alone from participating in it. Consequently, their image of Spain, already skewed by nostalgia, drifted further and further away from peninsular reality. When Aub returned to visit in 1969, he was shattered to realize that the Spain to which he believed he had been loyal for thirty years seemed to have disappeared into thin air (*Gallina* 413). He was also shocked to find out that, after three decades of Francoism, virtually all memory of his intellectual generation had been erased. As one of his characters puts it, "They have wiped us off the map" (*Enero* 466).

During the first years of displacement, the exiles' obsession with Spain, the frustration of defeat, and perhaps a certain degree of survivor's guilt gave rise to a feverish textual production and a strangely bombastic rhetoric with strong moralistic and nationalistic overtones. Such rhetoric is especially clear in early exile journals like *España Peregrina* (1940–41), the direct precursor of *Cuadernos Americanos*. Its founder and director, Juan Larrea, claimed among other things that the exiles represented the "seed of a deeper and more complex form of human organization launched by Spain, as a synthesis of the Western experience, to these fertile lands of Spanish America" ("Por un orden" 149). For him, the civil war had been tragic but necessary because it cleansed the popular spirit of Spain of all its hereditary defects and impurities, leaving the country in a state of pure spirituality that would eventually propel humanity into a higher form of existence. Ayala, in *Razón del mundo* (1944), similarly argued that the spiritual dimension of the Spanish national character could provide the basis for a new, universally valid way of life (113).

Later on, the exiles' discourse became more disenchanted and therefore more nuanced, low-key, and self-critical. Compared with the fiction and historiography on the Spanish Civil War published in Franco's Spain, especially, the exiles' production is notably less Manichaean and triumphalist (G. Thomas 121–22, 149, 227). Germán Gullón has argued that exile novels such as Masip's *Diario de Hamlet García* and Sender's *Réquiem por un campesino español* (*Requiem for a Spanish Peasant*) stand out for their dialogic qualities and their "lack of fear of the proliferation of meanings"—a consequence, very likely, of defeat and disillusionment but also of the exile experience itself, which tends to foster introspection, irony, and narrative self-awareness (230; Ugarte, *Shifting Ground* 19–20). At the same time, exile can lead to a certain quiet desperation brought about by a sense of aporia: the realization that there are no easy solutions to the Spanish problem, perhaps no solution at all. The anarchist, Republican, socialist, and Communist characters of Aub's civil war novels spend much of their time discussing politics and the war, but their differences of opinion almost always prove irreconcilable.

This kind of ideological polyphony is more characteristic of literary discourse than of the essay and pamphlet. As Yossi Shain points out, political exile also tends to breed ideological rigidity and infighting (43–44). Indeed, Spanish Civil War exiles spent much discursive energy on mutual accusations and petty personal conflicts. These were especially pronounced among different factions of the Socialist Party, which was split by the rivalry between Indalecio Prieto and Juan Negrín and between the Communists and the rest. The exiles' failure to present a united front also made it much harder to garner international support after 1945. Meanwhile, many major and minor players in the war filled the empty hours of exile writing memoirs to defend their past decisions and actions or to settle accounts with former brothers in arms. As Paul Preston writes, the republic's surviving political leaders spent much of their life in exile "locked in sterile polemic about the responsibility of their defeat" (*Spanish Civil War* 147). If the Trotskyist Víctor Alba used his novel *La vida provisional* (1950; "Provisional Life") to blame the defeat on the Communists, the Communist commander Enrique Líster wrote *Nuestra guerra* (1966; "Our War") to defend his party's role in the war. Sender, in turn, wrote in his prologue to *Los cinco libros de Ariadna* (1957; "The Five Books of Ariadna"), "We are all to blame for what happened in Spain. Some because of their stupidity and others because of their wickedness. The fact that we (the better side) were the stupid ones does not redeem us before history or before ourselves" (xii-xiii).

Writing from Exile

In 1949, Ayala, exiled in Argentina, published an essay in *Cuadernos Americanos* in which he reflected on the crucial question for the writer in exile: About what do I write and, more important, for whom? The civil war and the "problem of Spain," he argued, had obsessed the exiles for the past ten years; but now these topics were exhausted. "Our lives during this period," he wrote, "have been pure expectation, an absurd existence in parenthesis" (*Razón* 158). It was time to move on and start focusing on the host environment and the present. Ayala's advice was not generally heeded, however, and perhaps with good reason. Many exiles were not ready to put the war behind them. His friend Aub, for instance, would doggedly continue working on his *Laberinto mágico* ("Magic Labyrinth")—a collection of five novels, a film script, and some forty short stories about the war—publishing the last novel of his series, *Campo de los almendros* ("Field of Almond Trees"), as late as 1968. For Aub, not to write about the war was unthinkable. For one, it was the defining moment of his life and generation. But he also believed that, as long as Franco was in power, it was essential that there be a counterhegemonic voice to tell the true story of the struggle. "[W]hat matters," he wrote in *Campo de los almendros*, "is that what happened remain [recorded], even if it is for only one person in each generation" (363). It was a similar sense of obligation that motivated Aub's commitment to literary realism as an indispensable form of historical testimony: "For us novelists or playwrights the only thing left to do is to report on the times in more or less truthful chronicles" (*Hablo* 40).

But what use are truthful chronicles if there is no one to read them? "What matters to us is Spain, what we write about is Spain, and we write for Spaniards," Aub said in 1967. "The trouble is that we don't have Spanish readers" (qtd. in Embeita 1, 12). The problem of audience—that is, of Francoist censorship, which prohibited the circulation of any exile text until 1967 and even after that blocked most from entering Spain—was hard to overcome and constituted a major frustration for exile writers. Censorship had economic and emotional consequences. It forced them to take on jobs as translators, teachers, or scriptwriters to make a living (and to pay for publishing their books), and it sometimes led to depression and writer's block. Cernuda, with characteristic pessimism, resigned himself to being a readerless poet; his only hope was posthumous glory. In "A un poeta futuro" (1941; "To a Future Poet"), he writes the poetic equivalent of a message in a bottle, directing himself explicitly to a virtual future colleague:

> I won't be able to tell you how much I've been struggling
> To make sure that my words don't die,
> Silent, with me, and that they go, like an echo,
> To you . . .
>
> When, in future times, man will be free
> . . . let fate lead
> Your hand to the volume that holds
> My forgotten verses. . . .   (*Poesía* 342)

The protagonist of Aub's play *La vuelta: 1964* ("The Return: 1964"), a writer who goes back to Spain in 1964, meets a younger Spanish colleague who admits that he has not had a chance to read any of the writer's work published in exile but assures him he will do so as soon as he can. The writer, disheartened, answers that the young man can spare himself the trouble: "Books have their moment, like everything else: after that, they go to waste" (109). Another of Aub's returning exile writers points out in despair that his name is not mentioned in any history of literature, either Latin American or Spanish (*Enero* 470).

Exile literature, then, is not only readerless but stateless as well. It is not hard to see why exile writers would be overcome by a sense of alienation and futility. In 1964, Segundo Serrano Poncela writes that he is going through a "moment of strong depression and discouragement; thinking precisely how stupid it is to take literature seriously" (Montiel Rayo 196). Even where the Republicans were relatively well received, as in Mexico, they were never really able to participate fully in the host society. At the same time, they were well aware of their increasing estrangement from their homeland and of their lack of influence on the younger generations. Realizing that their memories became less and less reliable as they became colored by nostalgia and idealization, they also knew that those memories were, to a large extent, the only weapon against the oblivion and much more serious historical distortions imposed on Spain by Francoism.

There are two recurring concepts in the thousands of books, articles, and pamphlets on the civil war: tragedy and truth. The first is self-evident, the second maddeningly elusive. One can wonder whether the exiled intellectuals—fiction writers, poets, historians—succeeded in giving a more truthful representation of the war than their colleagues in Spain, who were writing either to please the regime or under the constrictions of censorship. On the other hand, it might be preferable to argue that the question, Who represents the truth?, is itself invalid because there is no truth about the Spanish Civil War. This notion, held by some civil war scholars, was one that the exiles were not ready to accept. They simply had too much invested in the notion that as victims of the Spanish tragedy they had access to that truth. This belief also helps explain the relative lack of sophistication of the theories of representation informing their literary practice. Despite the self-consciousness and aporetic nature of many of the exiles' representations of the civil war, the exiles were driven by the simple desire to write the war, in Leopold von Ranke's phrase, "wie es eigentlich gewesen" (vii; "how it really was"). Thus, for example, Aub's conscious commitment to a kind of nineteenth-century realism in effect sacrifices literary complexity for political expediency.

Teaching Exile Literature

Aub's *Laberinto mágico*, Sender's *Réquiem*, Barea's *La llama* ("The Flame"), or Mercè Rodoreda's *La plaça del Diamante* (*The Time of the Doves*) can be simply taught as representations of the civil war, but it also makes sense to teach them as exile literature. This approach, however, conjures up a series of problems of its own. Both exile and exile literature are slippery notions. As Shklar notes, "the more one thinks about them, the more numerous the forms of exile turn out to be" (38). It is one thing to state that exile affects writing, quite another to speak of exile literature as if it were a well-defined category, clearly distinguishable from nonexilic texts. Do exile texts have anything in common beyond the circumstances of their production?

Many critics have tried to answer this question in the affirmative. Paul Ilie speaks of an "exilic sensibility," which he defines as a "mental condition" determined by a "set of feelings or beliefs" that isolate an individual or group from the rest of society (2). Gareth Thomas perceives in the civil war novels written in exile certain "exilic symptoms," such as characters' "feeling cut off from others, failing to communicate with others, . . . not knowing where to go or what to do" (156). Ugarte argues that the experience of exile "leads the writer . . . into a dialogue with him or herself on the very nature of writing and on the problems that arise from an attempt to record reality" (*Shifting Ground* 19–20). I have argued that, for someone like Aub, the exile experience is manifested in a "realism of aporia"—that is, in an inability to move from the chaotic, all-inclusive war chronicle to a neatly composed historical novel (Faber, *Exile* 237–44). For Gullón, the civil war novel written in exile is characterized by a semantic and ideological openness or polyphony that the peninsular war novel generally lacks.

Still, these traits do not appear in all exile literature; more important, they are not exclusive to it. Ilie argues precisely that the "exilic sensibility" is more important than the actual geographic separation from the homeland and that this sensibility is in fact manifested in much of the literature written in Spain itself, by writers suffering a form of "inner exile" (2–4). While the notion of inner exile has proved quite useful, the fact that it turns exile, through metaphor, into a psychological or existential category is also confusing. From there it is a small step to concluding, as Ayala does, that "all writers live in exile" ("Para quién" 49). And why stop there— who isn't an exile of sorts? Said has stated that all true intellectuals, even if they are not exiles, should behave as if they were (52–53). On the one hand, all these notions are compelling, and they are useful insofar as they prevent us from establishing a too clear-cut separation between exile and nonexile writing. On the other hand, they can also be used as a subtle way of neutralizing the political nature of exile and thus trivializing the exiles' very real experience of geographic displacement. In the Spanish context, the concept of inner exile has been rejected by some critics as a euphemism for Francoist repression or, conversely, as a way for the conformist or collaborationist intelligentsia to acquire a form of undeserved heroic patina (Naharro-Calderón, "Des-lindes" 33).

Even though Spanish Civil War exile officially ended in 1977, its tragedy did not stop there. The particular dynamics of Spain's transition to democracy, which was based on a so-called pact of oblivion, prevented any genuine vindication of the exiles' forty-year legacy (Naharro-Calderón, "Y para qué" 63). There was, so to speak, no closure; accordingly, the recuperation of the Republican legacy is still scandalously unfinished. The Socialist Party (PSOE), whose history forms an important part of civil war exile, did hardly anything during its fourteen-year rule (1982–96) to recognize or recuperate Republican exile culture (Naharro-Calderón, "Des-lindes" 16). Only very recently have the socialists turned to the exilic past that is partly their own, when former Vice Prime Minister Alfonso Guerra, now president of the Fundación Pablo Iglesias, helped produce the documentary *El exilio republicano español* ("The Spanish Republican Exile") that was aired in 2002 on Spanish national television.

This broadcast, coordinated with an extremely well visited exhibit on the same topic in Madrid, can be seen as a belated response from the socialists to a renewed interest in the civil war and exile by the Spanish general public. This trend began some five years ago and has been salient since 2001. Civil war exile has even turned into something of a fashion, spurred by centenary celebrations of such prominent Republican intellectuals as Federico García Lorca (1998), Luis Buñuel (2000), Sender (2001), Rafael Alberti (2002), Cernuda (2002), Juan Rejano and Aub (2003), and María Zambrano (2004). Ironically, this fashion was enthusiastically backed by Spain's formerly ruling Partido Popular, a center-right party that has its roots in Francoism and that also stubbornly refused even to condemn the military rising that started the war. Not surprisingly, the party's appropriation of the exile legacy has not always been free of self-interest or, for that matter, respectful of historical and political reality (Naharro-Calderón, "Cuando" 25; Faber, *Exile* 270–73). Equally doubtful have been attempts by the left-wing critical establishment, notably the *El país* critic Miguel García-Posada, to normalize exile writers, minimizing the contingency of four decades of displacement and reinserting them into the Spanish literary canon as if nothing had happened.

Teaching representations of the Spanish Civil War as exile literature is a wonderful opportunity to discuss the politics of memory, particularly the conflicts between official history and the largely silenced—or only partially recuperated—memories of the marginalized.

Note

1. All translations are mine.

Francie Cate-Arries

Refugee Camp Warriors: Voices of Resistance from the Battleground of Exile

Quite a few years ago, I was asked to present a mock freshman seminar on the Spanish Civil War for prospective students at the College of William and Mary. I organized my remarks around issues of representation and point of view and ended my lecture and slide presentation with a magazine illustration published in Nationalist Spain in the winter of 1939. The stark black-and-white image juxtaposed the two faces of the nation that had emerged from the ravages of war. The top half, labeled in large white type-face "LOS VENCEDORES" ("The Winners"), depicted two Nationalist soldiers in close-up focus, their upturned faces bathed in light, their hands tightly wrapped around raised firearms. The bottom half, with its black-lettered caption "LOS DERROTADOS" ("The Losers") set against an empty expanse of sky, portrayed dozens of faceless Republican soldiers in distant retreat, their hunched backs to the camera, crossing the border into France. By choosing this particular photographic coda to my thumb-nail sketch of the war, I conveyed to the students two key messages about the victors and the vanquished. On the one hand, Franco's strong-armed winners would control not only the destinies of the losers—through sanctions, imprisonment, and firing squads—but they would manipulate the discourse about their defeated enemies as well. On the other hand, the

Republican fighters and supporters who fled that fate into exile in France, well, they simply disappeared from the scene in pitiable conditions of injury, illness, and despair.

Without intending to, I must have left the students with the same impression of the new exiles' passivity, anonymous victimhood, and silent suffering that was created by early postwar Francoist propagandists. José Esteban Vilaró, author of a scathing 1939 account of the "Red" emigration after the war, *El ocaso de los dioses rojos: Barcelona, Perthus, Argeles, París, Méjico* ("The Twilight of the Red Gods"), wrote scornfully of the "faceless, confused, broken mob" (8) that abandoned Spain in the winter of 1939:

> At this very moment begins the decline of their existence. They will wither away without glory in the most remote reaches of the globe. It is, when all is said and done, the history of all emigrants. Whoever believes that it is possible to live just anywhere, without any risks, should learn from their example. Here's the lesson about what familiar horizons and the routines of daily life really mean. Here's the proof that men, removed from the air they breathed as children, lose their joy in living and fade away like flowers deprived of sunlight. It becomes almost impossible to persevere in another land. (10)[1]

But tens of thousands of hapless Republican refugees did indeed persevere in France, even in the most extreme circumstances of exile, those of the brutally inhumane internment camps haphazardly constructed by the French government to contain the new arrivals. In this essay, I offer a closer look at those tiny retreating figures crossing the border that I had only superficially spotlighted in my teaching presentation years ago. I point out how instructors can more effectively utilize the refugees' own stories of their struggle of survival, as well as their continued ideological resistance to the forces of Franco—a resistance that took place in the most unlikely of locations during the earliest phase of the Spanish exile of 1939: the concentration camps of France.

To study how these refugee camps have been depicted in the chronicles of Spanish Civil War exile is to interrogate the profound connections among collective memory, historical trauma, and representations of the nation. In his 1990 volume *Nation and Narration*, Homi Bhabha includes Ernest Renan's 1882 essay "What Is a Nation?" Renan highlights the crucial role of sacrifice and its remembrance in the consolidation of the nation: "Suffering in common unifies more than joy does. Where national memories are concerned, griefs are of more value than triumphs, for they impose duties and require a common effort" (19). More recent theorists' work continues to develop the interrelation of crisis, memory, and national identity formation.

This line of inquiry has been particularly fruitful in the area of Holocaust studies. Dominick LaCapra, building on Pierre Nora's work on the "lieux de mémoire," claims in his *History and Memory after Auschwitz*, "A memory site is generally also a site of trauma" (10). I suggest that the earliest expressions of a shared exile identity begin to take root in the fertile imaginative terrain stimulated by the remembrance and representation of the French camps. The textualization of sites like Argelès-sur-Mer, Collioure, Saint-Cyprien, Vernet, or Barcarès in numerous versions penned by former inmates transforms the places of suffering, sacrifice, and trauma into powerful, enduring sites of memory, thereby creating a generative matrix for the cultural codes and values of a nascent nation in exile. Teachers of the exile period of the Spanish Civil War may productively use these narratives not only to retrieve the long-silenced voices of civil war history but also to foreground how the scenes of this history are staged through the representations of memory. This time the players are the war's *vencidos* ("vanquished"), not Franco's *vencedores* ("victors").

Before students are introduced to the unfamiliar terrain of the refugee camps as a site of cultural continuity and political opposition, it is useful to review with them how the end of the war and the beginning of exile have been inscribed in a national consciousness and memory. The dramatically contrastive visual images of Franco's victory and the Republicans' exodus depicted in 1939 have indeed become the most iconic representations of this moment of history. The pages published over the years by well-known civil war historians are filled with the recurring juxtapositions of the exultant victors' military triumph and weary refugees' utter defeat. Paul Preston's arrangement of the concluding illustrations for his 1986 *The Spanish Civil War, 1936–39* is typical. The same-page captions for two of the final photographs of the French-Spanish border identify two very different faces of the future. One header reads "Jubilant Nationalists salute French frontier police at Bourg-Madame at the western end of the Catalan Pyrenees"; the other succinctly labels the lamentable state of a Spanish refugee in France, "Exhausted and bewildered . . ." (163). The final destination of these vanquished, the internment camps, is featured in another photograph as a kind of endpoint to nowhere: "The camps set up for Republican refugees in France were little more than lines of huts in barbed wire compounds" (165).[2]

More recently, Rafael Torres inaugurated his study of political prisoners and forced labor battalions in Franco's post–civil war penal system, with a much-reproduced snapshot of the republic's other war victims; maimed and crippled children held by the hand by hollow-eyed adults, hobbling along the road to France (27). In a similar vein are two 2002 documents published in Spain that commemorate the civil war exile. The first is the publicity brochure that advertised the exhibition Exilio, organized by the Fundación Pablo Iglesias and the Museo Nacional Centro de Arte Reina Sofía and held at the Palacio de Cristal in Madrid's Retiro Park in the fall of 2002. Although the text of the brochure explains that the purpose of the exhibit is to pay homage to the productive, dynamic role of "thousands of Spaniards who, from the shores of exile, kept alive the ideal of a government and a legal system ruled by constitutional law" (Zapatero 17), its single photograph simply shows a small group of helpless refugees stumbling through the snow toward the border. The television documentary of the same year entitled *Exilio*, with equally poignant footage of both the border crossing and the refugee camps, contains interviews with several former camp internees. All the interview subjects, including the camp memoirist Eulalio Ferrer, offer testimony chronicling the ill-equipped camps as nothing more than infernal holes of disease, despair, and death. Ángel Gómez, for example, remembers his arrival at the camp of Saint-Cyprien as a passage into a barren, vacuous no-man's-land: "We didn't have huts, or bathrooms, or latrines, nothing. Really, there was nothing there."[3]

The reading that I propose of the camp literature produced in the early postwar years, when hopes for a Republican *reconquista* and a return to Spain ran high, certainly does not take issue with the harsh reality of suffering and hardship that the survivors of the camps recall so vividly today. I suggest instead that using texts written by former internees can help us present for our students a more complete postwar story, complementing the much more widely disseminated perspectives of the victors in the immediate period of the war's aftermath. I focus on how the defeated Republicans kept alive the legacy of the political cause they had defended in war, how they commemorated their own war dead far from the battlegrounds (and the Valley) of the fallen, and how they actively engaged in cultural activities designed to preserve their collective identity as fighters for social justice against the forces of tyranny.

In her excellent *Memory and Amnesia*, Paloma Aguilar Fernández laments the lack of early textual evidence of how the losers codified and remembered the civil war: "These discourses are much more difficult to trace, because a large number of the defeated were forced into exile" (133). By recovering the stories of camp refugees, we can address the omissions and gaps that Aguilar points to in the story of war and exile. Just as Michael Richards has documented the "small ways" (*Time* 150) in which the dispossessed *perdedores* in Spain expressed their dissent and defiance toward the regime, I propose to demonstrate that their imprisoned refugee counterparts similarly engaged in meaningful acts of resistance. Teachers can use these works to illustrate the Republican authors' efforts to inscribe a new national history in exile and reassemble (or at least represent) their political identity as warriors for the cause of freedom and equality.

The books I recommend here for classroom use are limited to those that were either composed or appeared in print during the first few years following the crisis scene of the border crossing into exile, between 1939 and 1944.[4] These works, unlike the spate of memoirs by camp inmates that were published in the mid-1970s, tend to share a common narrative pattern that is a function of their authors' sense that their uncertain future in political exile may be short-lived, depending on the outcome of World War II. These writings express the hope that their story of life in the camps may help shape international public opinion regarding the political legitimacy and viability, the moral authority, and the spiritual fortitude that still define the Spanish republic, even in exile. The refugee writers who in 1939–40 witness the European war take shape from their vantage point inside the concentration camps urgently make their case to a world audience who may yet rally to join their fight against fascist aggressors.

I organize my remarks around the recurring themes that I draw from a series of selected works about the camps. Professors could choose any one of these titles as a classroom text and successfully examine it in its entirety according to my discussion, since each tends to deploy a similar story-telling dynamic established between twin thematic poles. On the one hand, the authors underscore the dehumanized objectification to which the refugees are subjected in the camps; on the other, they concomitantly reject the refugees' role as passive, voiceless victims and shape their narrative as tales in which the refugees reclaim a position of political agency and autonomous action. The most significant manifestations that inform this discursive construct of the refugee as a resisting, speaking subject are acts of remembrance and commemoration, of resistance and defiance.

The Republican army units and the terrified civilian population that retreated toward the border as Nationalist aircraft bombed and strafed their slow-moving lines were virulently depicted in the right-wing French press at the time as hordes of low-life Reds. Worst of all, like swarming locusts, these filthy Reds were decimating the profits of the next tourist season. A 2 March 1939 article in the conservative *L'action française* lamented:

> Today the whole area stinks. . . . Our beach will be unusable this summer. . . . The Red invasion has killed tourism . . . since international clientele are not willing to deal with the filthy riff-raff that we have received in such record numbers. (qtd. in Rafaneau-Boj 113)

The British relief worker Francesca Wilson recalls in her memoir a conversation in the spring of 1939 with a Frenchwoman who similarly lamented the damage inflicted by the unwelcome refugees: "'The little towns in the Pyrenees were just preparing for their season,' she told me, 'now they are swamped with all these dirty refugees. Why didn't they stay at home?'" (221). While the conservative newspaper *Le roussillon* announced the border crossing of the Republicans with headlines like, "Ouvrez les yeux; c'est tout le marxisme qui passe" ("Open your eyes. It's all of Marxism passing by") (Grando, Queralt, and Febrés 46), local bystanders lined the streets as large groups of refugees were escorted under armed guard to the camps. Jaime Espinar writes of the townspeople's reception of the weary, haggard *vencidos*' passage through the streets as the very specter of war itself: "As we crossed through the picturesque villages, the residents lined up to watch the show: 'La guerre, la guerre! C'est finie la guerre d'Espagne!' ["The war! The war! The war in Spain is over!"] Others chatted and laughed" (24). Luis Suárez similarly describes how he and his companions marching through the town of Elne were seen by the French onlookers as a scary, albeit mesmerizing, parade of exotic foreigners in surrender: "The trucks, the cars, the carts, the people—those 'strange' people—on foot, looked like something straight out of one of their fairs" (38). The "peaceful neighbors," supposedly shielded by the pacts of nonintervention and of Munich, watch the freak show go by—including maimed and crippled soldiers, still wearing bloodied, dirty bandages and uniforms in rags—with something akin to horror. The fearful faces peering through the windows needn't have worried, as Suárez makes clear in his description of the "barbed-wire cages" (53) into which thousands of the refugees were immediately corralled. Here, he states wryly, is the optimum location for the dirty plague of Republican Spain that has spilled over the border (104).

Espinar describes swim meets that the bored inmates held, referring in particular to one internee who cups a makeshift speaker with his hand, imagining how the local reporters who swarmed the camps in the early days would record the spectacle of those crazy, fun-loving Reds:

> The reporters after a sensationalist story can bring their cameras and sing the praises of the delights of "country" living, of good "country" living. It's a story that'll go down easy with a meal, and the readers at home will say with a smile: "Those Spaniards! Those Spanish 'reds,' boy, they do hang in there. And always in such high spirits!" (99)

The self-consciousness of the Spaniard on the beach, his feeling that his presence provides an entertaining cultural spectacle to the curious gaze of the local population, was no figment of the imagination. The historian Marie Rafaneau-Boj reports that the French authorities who lamented the death of the tourist season in 1939 needn't have worried, since the camps themselves provided a popular new attraction. On 17 February, the paper *Le midi socialiste* reports on the incredibly long lines on Sunday afternoons that snake along the highway in view of the camp of Saint-Cyprien: "crowds like this have never been seen, not even during the most beautiful days of summer" (qtd. in Rafaneau-Boj 157). Some visitors, recalls Vicente Fillol, made primitive offerings through the barbed wire: "People from all over the country came to see us: we were the 'reds' . . . most of the people who came were happy to see us defeated and locked up; and, sometimes, they threw us crusts of bread, as if they were at the zoo" (89).

The inmates are abandoned to their abject otherness, a dehumanized status that is frequently figured in the literature in the form of an impotent, debased body. They are victimized even by their own bodily functions. Manuel García Gerpe recalls that he and his comrades are initially forced to relieve themselves in the same area where they eat and sleep, enduring the ignominy of having their physical misery literally thrown in their faces (15). The only other references to the human body that García Gerpe offers in the early pages of his book are those that describe in excruciating detail how death claims an alarming number of inmates before each new, icy dawn (14). He paints the portrait of a defenseless people at the mercy of the French, squirming under both the thumb of bureaucratic control and the stares of morbid curiosity from civilian onlookers. So begin most of the stories of the camps, with the common complaint of the paralyzing process of objectification and violent dehumanization. The refugee writers, however, tell their story of life behind barbed wire as a story of stubborn survival and expressive resistance. García Gerpe closes his introduction by describing his new home not as a place of capitulation or resignation but as the site of struggle, "because, even there, far from our Spain we continue to be united through the strong ties that bind us to an ideal, for which we are still prepared to die" (49).

On 3 April 1939, just two days after the official announcement that the war had ended, Franco's voice was heard across the airwaves of Radio Nacional, "Attention, Spaniards! Spain continues to wage war against all enemies from inside or outside her borders, forever faithful to her fallen" (qtd. in Torres 26). The Caudillo's uncompromising call to keep the war alive against the enemy in the name of the fallen was a rhetorical strategy shared as well by the exiles in France. One of the strongest commemorative impulses to honor the war dead, the camp veterans José Bartolí and Narcis Molins i Fàbrega's 1944 *Campos de concentración*, is a heavily illustrated volume of life in the camps that serves as an emotional call to arms. The elegiac function is the organizing principle that informs the book's thirty-one vignettes. This work, more than any other publication from the early post–civil war years, seeks to consecrate the place of the concentration camps in France as hallowed ground because it is the final resting place for so many exiled Republicans and the site of so much suffering.

The protagonist of *Campos* is introduced as a kind of divine prophet in the guise of a *pueblo* seeking refuge, the most humble of all messengers who first brings the news of fascism's fury to the world. The authors develop a fundamental narrative tension that obtains between this suffering messenger figure and the antagonistic, authoritative forces of power, wealth, and political self-interest that conspire to kill him. The Christlike allegory that the authors adopt as a vehicle to tell the story begins and ends in the same place: the tomb of the murdered messiahs. The first reference to the "asylum of the death shroud" that the refugees are offered in France describes the "grave sites of vast cemeteries" that masquerade as their sanctuary (16, 14). The narrator acknowledges the renowned practice in France of commemorative ceremonies, landmarks, and public monuments erected to its war dead; he bitterly contrasts this tradition with the ignoble treatment of Spanish exiles in France (see the illustration on 49). In the final vignette, Molins concludes his narrative at the site of the tomb, addressing his martyred hero, "You lie buried in oblivion. . . . In your tomb you feel forgotten by the world and its men" (155).

The authors construct a heartfelt memorial to commemorate the concentration camp victims and, more broadly, the war dead left behind in

Spain. Republican exiles abroad will be nurtured by the example of sacrifice of her fallen heroes not only on the battlefield of Spain but also in the camps of France. The final illustration depicts the one who leaves the camp and the one left behind. The small receding figure at the top of the frame has almost disappeared from view. The dominant image in the foreground is a single bony arm protruding from the sandy soil of the camp, clutching in its hand a piece of bowed barbed-wire sticking out of the earth like an unsteady cross (157). These Republicans—those who have died in the camps, those who have gone on to other places—are memorialized in the consciousness of a nation that dreams of resuming the fight to reclaim its sovereignty: "Bearing your cemetery's crown of thorns, you and they will one day soon march radiantly toward victory" (155).

Camp memoirists have documented the refugees' ritual performance of commemorative acts that paid tribute to the memory of the war dead. Ferrer chose the first anniversary of the Spanish republic observed on foreign soil, 14 April 1939, as an auspicious day to inaugurate the diary that he kept during the fifteen months of his confinement in camps and work crews in 1939–40. He frequently indicates that his sense of survival and hold on hope as a beleaguered camp inmate are strengthened by collective acts of commemoration and solidarity. Ferrer takes great care to document the camp community's observances in exile of national and international holidays, when the celebration of unifying political traditions and ideals creates a sense of optimism and purpose. In his diary, he weaves the threads of his own story into the larger fabric of national history. The inmates' public performance of patriotism and shared beliefs on an overcast 14 April, notes the young diarist, helps shake off the doldrums felt by so many:

> From early on, your ears tell you there's a party going on in the camp. Guitars and mandolins accompany voices that sing off-key and shout out the significance of today's date. The infectious, boisterous uproar spreads through the camp. The "streets"—the walkways between the huts—are swarming with people. Nobody is complaining like they were a few days before; there are shouts of *long live!* whoever and whatever you want, and everybody's talking to everybody else. Just when hope seemed to have disappeared from shared individual confessions, in a rush it is revived again in these collective demonstrations. . . . This cry of "long live the Republic!" is also a cry of "long live life!" (27)

The day of poetry recitals, boxing matches, sack races, and theatrical performances ends with a gathering of the elder Ferrer's friends, who sit and reminisce together about the events of 14 April 1931. Ferrer, ever the young idealist, pays tribute to the sustaining bonds of fraternity that tie him to his Republican brothers who from the sands of the concentration camp remember "the good fight":

> Today I've been acutely aware of how much our confinement has tightened the bonds of brotherhood around us. It's a brotherhood bound by the love of liberty, by the love for social justice. It's a love that will overcome defeat and is worth more than life itself! (28)

In a camp where public displays of the Republican flag are strictly forbidden, the tricolored banner makes only fleeting appearances (one stubborn inmate in the hut next door raises it religiously every Sunday—"I'd rather die than take it down!" [40]), but the emblem of the nation is always present in the mind's eye.

In his account of the gestures and expressions of dissent that took place in Franco's Spain, Richards has written:

> Resistance, or at least defiance, of authority, was also carried on in the perpetuation of certain rituals. To the consternation of Falangists, symbolic occasions, like 14 April . . . were, in many places, always marked in some manner by leftists. . . . May Day, the traditional "holiday of the proletariat," continued to be celebrated by bands of Republicans. (*Time* 157)

These Spanish leftists' counterparts imprisoned in camps in France enacted similarly prohibited performances of political speech. In his 1942 *St. Cyprien, plage* . . . ("Saint-Cyprien Beach"), Manuel Andújar refers to a familiar phenomenon during the early days of the camp. Gathered to watch as groups of inmates opt to return to Spain rather than endure any further the vicissitudes of the camps, a motley crew joins voices to protest the repatriation. The most marginalized among the Spaniards in exile stake out a position in the sands of Saint-Cyprien:

> The most vocal spectators were, for the most part, the war-injured, the infirm, and women. . . . And along the rows of deserters who hesitated, we shouted words of encouragement, of faith in the cause, of ardent patriotism, cries that broke through their ranks, and created two moral categories of campers. (24)

Andújar summarizes the pivotal instance of political protest as a foundational episode in the history of exile politics, still in its infancy: "Facing the Pyrenees, the Spanish antifascists demonstrated for the first time since beginning their emigration" (24).

The place of confrontation between those who turn back, resigned to their uncertain fate under Franco, and those who literally hold their ground is a recurring discursive site in the story of exile. The refusal to leave the horrific camps is generally inscribed as a moment of maximum defiance of French and Francoist authority and as an occasion for a display of loyalty to the ideals of the Spanish republic. Perhaps the most concerted effort to respond to the question of repatriation with an act of political resistance is reported by García Gerpe. He describes the summertime dissemination in the Septfonds camp of Franco's Political Responsibilities Act enacted in February 1939 against supporters of the republic. Reading out loud to his fellow inmates the full text, which he also reprints in his memoir, the author argues for a united response to the document. Not only should it incur outrage, but also it should be received by the internees as a catalyst to mobilize themselves in the struggle: "[a call] to all believers in democracy, to all humanists, to all those who love peace, to protest, to stop the executioners, to help the heroic Spanish people" (147). García Gerpe adds as an afterthought that he received five days of punishment for his political preaching against repatriation.

Andújar, like other camp authors, traces a time line of noteworthy political anniversaries as the months of internment drag by. He describes how the signs of Republican identity are rebelliously displayed in the camp. The flags of the republic mysteriously materialize, "From what truck's cadaver?" (51), and are brazenly raised in the face of official French control. Confronted with another repressive order against political expression on 1 May, the inmates share their subversive response to the official prohibition through covert communions and silent pantomimes of a fraternal conspiracy:

> On today's date, jubilation and anger run through the veins of the workers and laborers. Some commemorate the day by decorating a cake—obtained through scrimping and sacrifice—that leads to toasts in the main barrack, others march by twos along the main walkway as if they are just innocently strolling, winking knowingly at one another. (57–58)

Through furtive gestures and encoded body language, the Republicans publicly perform a private parade to celebrate the occasion. Andújar records the "snatches of conversation" that are later overheard as night falls in the camp. The text, which reads like a single cohesive call to action, begins like this: "May 1 demands that we Spanish antifascists affirm our unity and our fighting spirit. The struggle is not over. We are living in a new phase." The author connects the spirited commemoration to a new position of solidarity that gives the inmates a firmer foothold in exile: "It seems now, as you wrap up in an overcoat trying to get to sleep, that the sand isn't so hard on your hips, that the 'bedroom' is less squalid. There's something" (58).

The first anniversary in exile of 18 July, the Nationalists' uprising against the republic, is yet another opportunity for the internees to rally together and reaffirm their shared memories and ideals. Ferrer's diary entry from the Barcarès camp documents the day's observances. Miniature homemade flags reappear in the camp, dotting sand sculptures and pebble-and-stone decorations that memorialize the war dead. "Perhaps the most beautiful of all is the one we made; it shows a kind of tomb, with the effigy of a Spanish militiaman made out of clay, and a wreath of flowers with this inscription: *in memory of the fallen*" (112). A corps of shabbily dressed buglers travels throughout the camp, pausing to pay their respects in front of each commemorative exhibit. A minute of silence at noon, followed by the cry in unison of "¡Viva la República!" (113), a half dozen speeches, and an improbable orchestral concert of traditional Spanish tunes performed by camp musicians round out the festivities. Ferrer imagines the triumphant military pomp and circumstance that must have ushered in this day in Franco's Madrid and defends the humble display of patriotic spirit among the inmates as the authentic expression of the Spanish people's greatest ideal, freedom: "In Madrid there must be triumphant parades, headed by the Moors—the Senegalese of Spain—while here we honor our fallen and sing of freedom from captivity, which is preferable to captivity without freedom and with death" (112).

It will be useful for teachers to close this chapter of the French refugee camps by showing students that the rhetoric of the fight for freedom, so characteristic of the politicized discourse of the camp literature, formed part of the official exilic discourse long after the last camp was closed. The words were transformed into military action for many of the Republican inmates; their participation in the French resistance against Hitler during World War II and in the armed guerrilla movement of the Spanish maquis has been documented in numerous historical accounts (see Dreyfus-Armand; Pons Prades; S. Serrano). For the lucky few selected for immigration to America, their cultural and political activities in exile would be fueled by the memories of the war and the camps and by plans for an imminent *reconquista* of Spain. In May 1939 some sixteen hundred

Spanish refugees boarded the Mexico-bound ship *Sinaia*. Daily onboard newspaper installments published by several recently released camp internee writers (like Andújar and Juan Rejano) celebrated their newfound freedom ("The lack of barbed wire allows the imagination to flourish, and each person can plan for the future" [*Sinaia* 31]) and charted their hopes. Benjamín Jarnés, aware that the gaze of the world remains fixed on Franco's *vencidos*, reminds his fellow passengers that yes, they present quite a spectacle in exile, but theirs is an active, productive political role to play:

> We are making a scene [Estamos sirviendo de espectáculo]. *We represent Spain.* We should embrace the challenge with confidence. Our role is difficult; it is the role of Spain herself. Ours is not the role of an emigrant no longer needed in his country but that of a citizen who carries his country with him. . . . *We are not the problem, we are the solution.* (38)

The first stage of exile that began in the refugee camps is claimed, by the Republicans who once stumbled across the border, as a struggle for liberation rooted in the memory of those comrades left behind in Franco's Spain and rooted in the dream of going home again: "May the Spaniards who go to Mexico never forget that in Spain there remain hundreds of thousands of our brothers in jails, millions of oppressed Spaniards, and an entire country to reconquer!" (61).

Notes

1. All translations are mine.

2. For similar photographic depictions, see Purcell's juxtaposition of the joyous celebration of Nationalist troops' arrival in Barcelona ("A group of women give an enthusiastic reception for Franco's troops as they enter Barcelona") with that of the Republican retreat ("Thousands of Spanish refugees and Republican militia fled across the frontier" [105]). See also comparable contrastive images of these scenes in Pike, whose same-page photos are labeled "Les vainqueurs atteignent la frontière" ("the vanquishers reach the border") and "Le cheminement pitoyable" ("the pitiable journey" [320B]).

3. Ferrer's and Gómez's remarks are included in Martín Casas and Carvajal Urquijo's *El exilio español, 1936–1978*, in a chapter entitled "The Concentration Camps in France" (69–80). For commentary of additional concentration camp testimony, see related essays in the section entitled "Biografías y testimonios" in the 2003 volume edited by Alted Vigil and Llusia (39–74).

4. Sample texts include those written by Andújar (*St. Cyprien*); Aub (*Morir*); Bartolí and Molins i Fàbrega; Bartra; Benavides; Espinar; Ferrer; García Gerpe; and Suárez. For a detailed study of these and other authors of French concentration camp literature, see my *Spanish Culture behind Barbed Wire: Memory and Representation of the French Concentration Camps, 1939–1945.*

Margaret Van Epp Salazar

Personal Narrative: A Bridge in Time

I was speaking on the phone to a friend who had just returned from a visit to Madrid in the fall of 2002. A *madrileña* in her early seventies, she has lived most of her adult life in the United States, having left Spain as a child with her Republican parents toward the end of the Spanish Civil War. She spoke with enthusiasm about a documentary program on Spanish television, *Exilio*, she had seen during her visit and of an exhibit organized by the Fundación Pablo Iglesias in the Retiro Park's Palacio de Cristal, also on the exiles of the Spanish Civil War. "I saw the concentration camp where my uncle and father were held prisoner. . . . Many memories came to my mind." She observed that she had been surprised to see that the crowd of those attending the exhibit were almost exclusively elderly people her age or older. "It's as if, when the exiles left Spain, they had ceased to exist," she said sadly.

Despite the thirty years or so separating us from the death of Generalissimo Francisco Franco in 1975 and the nearly seventy years since the end of the Spanish Civil War, interest continues in publishing books and articles, in holding exhibits, and in making documentaries about this conflict. Those of us who teach courses related to the civil war period are often confronted, however, with an interesting dilemma: the contrast between this ferment of continued exploration, which brings to light formerly hidden or covered-up aspects of the war and postwar period, and our students' distance from that struggle and its complexities. As professors engaged with or fascinated by that period, we face in our classes the detachment our students typically feel toward a historical time they consider over and done with and long buried. The use of personal narrative, a genre that lies between the scholarly accounts of the Spanish Civil War narrated in historical studies and the imaginative re-creations of works of fiction and poetry, may help students develop a more personal connection with that period.

In Spain itself, the passion that the civil war and postwar periods hold for those generations who lived through the time of postwar silence is absent in a younger generation that views the war and the postwar period as old, over, and best forgotten—as forgotten as those exiles who left Spain, like my friend. Outside Spain, students today are far removed from the ideological battles that were behind much of the conflict, including the tremendous differences within the Republican cause itself. In the United States, words like *fascist, communist, anarchist,* and *socialist,* detached from their historical context, sometimes provoke an emotional reaction reminiscent of the McCarthy period. The Soviet Union is the failed and fallen enemy. It is easy for students to react just as a freshman did last spring to Ernest Hemingway's *For Whom the Bell Tolls,* writing that he was glad that the republic failed because otherwise it would have become another Communist enemy. The idealism that existed in the Second Republic may find little understanding or sympathy from our current students.

This ideological barrier is compounded by today's sense of insecurity, which lends itself to an idealization of law and order. Political agitation, revolutionary idealism, and even strikes, all of which form a significant part of the war's historical context, may appear to students as disruptive and therefore negative. Often students have little knowledge of the labor struggles of the United States (let alone of Spain) in the late nineteenth and early twentieth centuries, of the historical circumstances the working classes confronted, and therefore many of the political positions are totally foreign to them.

A critical challenge in teaching the civil war is to help students become engaged and break beyond the views and prejudices of their time, which are so deep-seated and innocently and unconsciously held. I would not try to make students adopt one point of view or another but would strive to create a more complex vision of what is otherwise a two-sided view of the world. I would attempt to awaken in them a passion for the civil war, so that they will continue to read, explore, and think about it for themselves. I want them to develop an abiding interest in the events of the first half of the twentieth century that have marked the history of the world up to today. I want my students to care about the fate of the Spanish people and to thrill to César Vallejo's lines, "If Mother Spain falls . . . / go out, children of the world; go find her!" (*Obra* 482; my trans.).

Personal narratives, which encompass oral histories, memoirs, and a wide range of anecdotal and testimonial accounts, provide a way to address the challenge. These works, which share with history the observation of events while, like fiction, constructing a narrative colored by memory and opinion, can provide insight into the civil war in a moving, relevant fashion that transports the reader more closely to the period than do other forms of narrative. One is left with this small window of experience, often containing vivid, unforgettable details—intimate details that a fictional account might lack and a historical study consider unimportant. The experiential nature of personal narratives creates a bond, or bridge in time, between reader and text that in turn allows for a sense of shared experience, even if full understanding remains elusive.

There is a vast amount of this literature, much of it published outside Spain in the years after the civil war, chronicling personal experience leading up to, during, and following the war. While all its authors were deeply affected by the conflict, their understanding of the political and social dimensions of the war vary tremendously. Some of the writers were actively engaged in the struggle, others were witnesses to events, and still others fell victim to unforeseen forces over which they had no control. Many wrote during the war itself to influence public opinion abroad in hopes of changing the policy of nonintervention. Others narrated their experiences as a form of exposé, to counter the distortion of events during the Franco dictatorship. More recently, others have recorded and transcribed the personal narratives of those whose voices were silenced over the forty years following the war. All these narratives help connect us with the past, allowing us to identify with the conflict and to share a point of view with someone who lived through it. This sharing can help break down the distance between students now and the period they are studying. Viewing the philosophical, political, and moral issues as their own, student will feel the tragedy as their own.

The documentary *¿Por qué perdimos la guerra?* ("Why Did We Lose the War?") begins with the words "In the political conflicts of Spanish history there were several winners . . . but only one loser: the Spanish people" (my trans.). This comment gives the impression of a unified force, *el pueblo*, facing multiple enemies. But if one considers the Spanish Civil War, in relation to the Spanish republic, the *pueblo* or "people" contained many diverse and often conflicting forces, leading to widely varying interpretations of the war, how it should have been fought, and why it was lost. A course designed to address the ideals and contradictions of the Republican cause that gives multiple perspectives might include the following personal narrative texts, which I have found useful in the classroom: Ronald Fraser's *In Hiding: The Life of Manuel Cortés*, George Orwell's *Homage to Catalonia*, James Yates's *Mississippi to Madrid: Memoir of a Black American in the Abraham Lincoln Brigade*, Gamel Woolsey's *Malaga Burning: An American Woman's Eyewitness Account of the Spanish Civil War*, and Patricio Escobal's *Death Row: Spain, 1936.*

Fraser interviewed a *topo* ("mole") when the *topo* came out of hiding after one of the amnesties Franco granted to former Republican survivors in the late 1960s. Manuel Cortés, a worker, a member of the trade union UGT (Unión General de Trabajadores), and during the republic the socialist mayor of the village of Mijas, near Málaga, before its fall to the Nationalist troops, spent thirty years (from the end of the war until 1969) in hiding in a secret room of his own house. Fraser's narrative contains transcriptions of testimony from both Cortés and his wife, giving two viewpoints to the events that unfolded during the war and the postwar period. Because Cortés was a politically conscious person, his narration is not only a story of danger, oppression, survival, and silence but also a lucid account of the war, including consideration of its deeper causes and the social vindication that the republic had hoped to redress.

Cortés felt that the anarcho-syndicalist trade union CNT (Confederación Nacional del Trabajo) had been exploited by the employers and landlords in his area to lessen the power the workers had with the socialist UGT. His unique experience of being a *topo*, coupled with his political position, permits students to observe, discuss, and question the reasons for his beliefs, the differences among these political organizations and their impact. As with all aspects of the war, a discussion of these differences and beliefs will bring up deep moral and ethical questions that may not have answers, or accessible answers, but that make the Spanish Civil War fascinating.

Orwell, in *Homage to Catalonia*, is one of the few writers sympathetic to the CNT, the POUM (Partido Obrero de Unificación Marxista), and the dynamic of the Barcelona revolution. His description of the takeover of the Telephone Exchange in May 1937 is telling for its complex interpretation of reasons behind the defeat of the republic. One way to approach the controversy in the Spanish republic is to discuss the war's revolutionary aspects. Orwell suggests that Republican suppression of the Spanish workers' revolutionary program that exploded in the early days of resistance damaged the Republican cause. The directors Diego Santillán and Francisco Galindo make a similar analysis in *¿Por qué perdimos la guerra?*, interviewing several men who had been active during the republic in different political parties, trade unions, and government positions. They are most critical, after pointing a finger at the Non-intervention Pact, of what they perceived as the Communist Party's conservative policy, which placed Stalin's interests over the survival of the republic. The film has extensive footage of major events of the civil war and uses the songs of the war as background.

Yates, in *Mississippi to Madrid*, begins his recollections with his family history, starting with his grandmother, who was alive when slavery was abolished during the American Civil War. His early years in Mississippi and the pre–civil rights situation of African Americans in the United States are in many ways similar to the condition of landless peasants in Spain in the early twentieth century. Yates's narrative is lively, heartbreaking, and filled with honest observations that break stereotypes. One difficulty today's students face when studying the Spanish Civil War is their general lack of knowledge of the historical period of the 1930s, with all its complexity. This book—with its descriptions of working conditions in the deep South, in Chicago, and in New York; of the Marcus Garvey back-to-Africa movement; of the Great Depression and the political activism that United States workers were engaged in, such as the labor protest march on Springfield—creates a useful bridge between the experiences of our students and the complex social and political arena of the Spanish Civil War era.

That Yates was a member of the American Communist Party colors his understanding of the war, and he does not question the strategies followed by the republic to win the war. The book is not a political account or analysis but rather a lively personal remembering of experiences and impressions. The care with which Yates names the people he encounters gives a sense of his personal tribute to members of the International Brigades and supporters of the Republican cause in general. He takes the role of witness, a recorder of what was heard and seen. He describes driving Hemingway, Herbert Matthews of the *New York Times*, and Sefton Delmer of the *London Daily Express* from Benicasim through war-ruined Teruel to Valencia, and riding in the back of a truck with Langston Hughes, who was covering the war for the Baltimore paper the *Afro-American*. Yates carefully records the names and any information he remembers about the African American members of the International Brigades, with a great sense of respect, affection, and honor, detailing the experiences of the captured, the killed, and the survivors.

His account does not end with the withdrawal of the International Brigades from Spain but continues with the stark contrast between being welcomed by New York crowds shouting, "No pasarán!" and then being denied a room in Greenwich Village because of his color. He provides details of a visit to Francoist Spain in 1971, after the resolution of the Paul Robeson case in 1958 allowed members of the Lincoln Brigade to recover their United States passports, and ends with the moving account of a meeting of one hundred twenty veterans of the Abraham Lincoln Brigade in Madrid, together with other members of the International Brigades, in 1986.

Woolsey, wife of the English writer Gerald Brenan, was living with her husband in a small town outside Málaga during the republic and the beginning of the Spanish Civil War. Her experiences are chronicled in *Malaga Burning*, originally published in 1939 under the title *Death's Other Kingdom*. Woolsey's title refers to the burning of the Calle Larios and other houses in wealthy areas of Málaga and describes the tensions and violence she witnessed during the period Málaga remained Republican after the uprising. The Brenans protected a landowner friend, hiding him in their house (an incident also described in Brenan's *The Face of Spain*).

Woolsey reflects in a very personal way both what she saw and her response to it. Her horror of all that was happening, of the escalation of violence, of the disturbance of the former state of affairs, aids us in understanding certain dynamics of the war. Precisely because she is not defending one particular side (she has perhaps more sympathy for the upper classes, with members of whom the Brenans were friendly), her narrative is valuable. She takes care to be impartial. For example, she describes the anarcho-syndicalist movement in Málaga, explaining the contradiction between the antimilitarism and nonviolence of the anarchists in general, which she observed in Churriana, with the town committee's maintaining order and respect for private property and protecting its townspeople as neighbors of a community, while bands of youth and "uncontrollables" (also anarchists) carried out assassinations (87).

Like many others who wrote during the war, Woolsey carefully sets the record straight about the information spread outside Spain. She describes conversations with English visitors leaving Spain and their delight in relating exaggerated or untrue stories of atrocities. She talks at length about what she terms the "pornography of violence": the claims that circulated (138). Defending the Spanish character against the stereotype of violence, she reminds her readers of violent reactions of civilians in Great Britain during World War I. Most of the atrocity stories she refutes were told by outsiders sympathetic to the military uprising and hostile to the republic. She also doubts those told about the Nationalists. She and Brenan initially enjoyed listening to the broadcasts of the Nationalist General Gonzalo Queipo de Llano on Radio Sevilla, although she did not know at the time that his terrifying threats were actually being carried out. It is clear she and Brenan thought they were hearing only absurd diatribes. (Brenan acknowledges this mistake in *Personal Record* [296–98]; Woolsey does not have the benefit of hindsight to correct her text. She only comments, "[b]ut unfortunately it was real" [53].)

Woolsey also explores the relation between fear and violence. She notes how, as the Nationalist bombings increased, the frenzy of nocturnal killings increased. Toward the end of the Brenans' stay in Spain, the fear begins to numb her as well. She explores her fastidious feelings of revulsion toward weeping women and children and describes with shame how her heart thawed when she saw a poor mother forget her own danger as she searched desperately for her child. Woolsey becomes so unnerved by the larger bombs, one of which falls in their very patio, she says that she could suffer either the bombings or the screams and crying but not both.

Escobal, a municipal engineer in Logroño and former Olympic soccer player, arrested and imprisoned at the outbreak of the Spanish Civil War, tells his experience in *Death Row: Spain, 1936*. His testimony is especially striking because of his moderate and humane view of life, even as he is witness to totalitarianism and extreme degradation. He describes in great detail the other Republican prisoners he encounters as well as the prison guards, execution squads, and military and church leaders. His reconstruction of conversations and of historical events, such as the jailing and death of the socialist leader Julián Besteiro at the end of the war, and his absolute fidelity to the belief that people are good not because of their beliefs but because of their actions give his narration integrity and power. Offering a firsthand view of the civil war as witnessed from behind the walls of prison camps, his memoir includes a summary of events leading up to the war. Acquitted and released with the help of an Italian general in June 1940, Escobal left Spain bound for exile in Cuba.

The year 1936 is far away for students who grew up at the turn of the millennium. The horrors of World War II overshadowed the Spanish tragedy. For our students, both wars are stories of their grandparents or great-grandparents, and those generations are quickly disappearing. A three-year war with at least a half million dead, the bombing of civilians, the targeting of civilian populations for reprisals as towns and cities fell—these occurrences that shocked the world are no longer extraordinary. Yet Spain's tragedy continues to fascinate us, for its ideals; for the loss of idealism that followed the Republican defeat, as if it had been one last chance for something unattainable; for the archetypal tragedy of a nation divided and fighting against itself. These personal narratives form a bridge in time between the present and the civil war. Just as our parents' and grandparents' stories connect us to an earlier era, eclipse the distance between decades and centuries, so these voices with their own particular vision and focus offer an unprecedented look at the Spanish Civil War.

Shirley Mangini

Teaching the Memory Texts of Spanish Women during the Civil War

Teaching a course on the Spanish Civil War presents us with a number of problems. Nearly seventy years have passed since the beginning of the war, yet many of the facts of the war are still subject to debate. Obviously, the Franco regime silenced any critical discussion of the war, and strict censorship during the dictatorship permitted only the publication of articles and books sympathetic to the victors. Even after the death of Franco in 1975, the government's campaign to forgive and forget left Spain in a continued state of historical somnolence. Through the 1980s, many still feared to give testimony and discuss the war after experiencing so many years of repression.

Silence on the theme of women who were activists in the war was even more pronounced; theirs was a dramatic story of buried history. Women were, after all, considered inferior by nature and fit only for housework and childbearing. Public life was off-limits to them, and those of the left who had been active politically were doubly condemned for their trangressions.[1] The activism of working-class women differed widely. There were the *milicianas* who responded to the call to arms in the first days of the war and a few months later were sent back to jobs away from the front lines. Many worked in factories, taking over men's jobs as they left for the front (only to be sent home at the end of the war). There were political activists who joined organizations such as Antifascist Women, Free Women, and the Socialist Youth group. Yet if we seek information on them before 1975 in mainstream texts published outside Spain, we find that women are barely mentioned and that, when they are, the comments are usually negative.

Since the 1980s, a great deal of historical information about female activists has come to light (see esp. M. Nash, *Defying, Mujeres en la guerra civil, Mujer*, and "*Mujeres Libres*"). Above all, the number of published life narratives and testimonies has assisted both historians and cultural critics in establishing a base from which it is now possible (and has frequently been done in recent years) to teach a course on the civil war that includes the analysis of female activists and their role in the war. Through the use of memory texts (see Mangini, *Memories* 53–66) and research on activist women during the last twenty years, we find that many of the activists felt empowered, useful, liberated, and proud of their contributions during those three years.

One would need to examine both the historical legacy of women in the war and what they perceived as their actual role. Of particular interest is how the women represented themselves in their texts—their truth about their role in the war—in contrast to how they were viewed during and after the war, the truth propagated by the books of mainstream history. I have found that life narratives or memory texts are excellent tools for analyzing how the women portray themselves in the context of the war and how they are portrayed by others who describe them in the light of their gender—that is to say, herstory versus history (Scott 20). I suggest utilizing the following texts: *They Shall Not Pass*, Dolores Ibárruri's impassioned apologetic work on her lifetime commitment to the Communist Party and her protagonism during the war; *In Place of Splendor*, Constancia de la Mora's equally fiery narrative of her odyssey from aristocrat to Communist; Juana Doña's novelized autobiography on prison life, *Desde la noche y la niebla* ("Into the Night and the Mist"); and Carlota O'Neill's tragic story of imprisonment in Morocco during the war entitled *Una mujer en la guerra de España* ("A Woman in Spain's War").[2] From the other side of the political spectrum, I recommend the memory text of the head of the Women's Section, Pilar Primo de Rivera, *Recuerdos de una vida* ("Memories of a Life"). I would also suggest making use of Paul Preston's book *Doves of War*, which consists of biographical studies of several women, Loyalists and Nationalists, who played varying roles during the war.

A very useful tool for understanding and analyzing the voices of these people is Abigail J. Stewart's essay "Toward a Feminist Strategy for Studying Women's Lives." In that essay—which focuses on Vera Brittain's *Testament of Youth*, where Brittain narrates her life in the framework of World War I—Stewart advances a set of prescriptions for how to look at women's memory texts. She identifies seven useful devices that are invaluable for classroom discussion of life narratives: search for what has been ignored in the text; recognize your own interpretive limitations; define the author's agency, that is, how she makes choices to avoid the repression she is experiencing; utilize gender as a means of understanding the text; understand how "gender defines power relationships" and how "power relationships are gendered"; examine race, class, and sexual orientation to understand the author's role; and finally, recognize that there are many selves in one person (13–30). I would add that the stated intention of the author is equally important to the understanding of who the "I" of the text is and how she views the magnitude of her role in the war. In a course taught in a literature department, analysis of style, form, and the literary quality of the text should also be considered. Joan W. Scott's *Gender and the Politics of History* convincingly explains the intrinsic relation between gender and political power (see also Higonnet et al. on this subject). Scott believes that "gender is a constitutive element of social relationships based on perceived differences between the sexes, and gender is a primary way of signifying relationships of power" (42). Like Stewart, she sees gender as a way of understanding the underpinnings of war and how female subordination is legitimized during war.

While interviewing women in the 1980s for my book *Memories of Resistance*, I was disarmed by the mental and physical fortitude of most of these women, then in their seventies and eighties. Of those I had interviewed, the majority said that their convictions from the 1930s remained intact—both those of the left and the right—which gave the impression that the war never really ended for them. Or perhaps their lives had been so completely shaped by the war that to justify the sacrifices they had to make and tragedies they had lived through, it was essential that they frame the war as a positive, fulfilling experience. This aspect, the memory text as apology, should also be discussed.

Class is an extremely important issue in analyzing these texts. Mora (1906–50), whose grandfather, Antonio Maura, had been one of Spain's major conservative statesmen,[3] was raised in a rarefied atmosphere of English nannies and boarding schools. She divorced her philandering husband and married a Communist aviator, who became a war hero. During the war, she began working for the republic as a press censor, at which time she was promptly ostracized by family and friends. She transgressed at every turn. Mora is at the center of her text, as in traditional autobiography.[4] *In Place of Splendor* traces her steps toward rebellion against her conservative milieu and outlines how and why she became a staunch supporter of the left during the war.

Ironically, class was the deciding factor that led another autobiographer, Ibárruri (1895-1989), in the same direction, though her social situation was diametrically opposed to that of Mora. Known as La Pasionaria, Ibárruri was born into an impoverished mining family in the Basque Country but managed to study until the age of fifteen (which was rare for poor children, especially females), when family obligations forced her to begin working full-time. She married a miner, and four of her six children died in infancy because of malnutrition and lack of medical attention. Aware of her tragic destiny and utilizing her agency[5] to change it, she began reading Marxist literature and quickly rose through the ranks of the Communist Party to become one of its most important leaders. She left her husband and began traveling to party meetings. By 1931 she was not only the party's most forceful orator but also one of the editors of the Communist newspaper *Mundo Obrero*. Like Mora's text, *They Shall Not Pass* is a somewhat traditional autobiography, in that it places Ibárruri at the center of the text and the self represented contextualizes the historical meaning of the civil war as she perceives it. As Jerome Bruner observes, "the constructed Self and its agentive powers become, as it were, the gravitational center of the world" (35).

Like Mora's book, Ibárruri's is an apology for her politics, and we view the war from her partisan perspective, which produces another challenge for a civil war course: the question of truth in testimonies and memory texts. Do Pasionaria and Mora tell the truth when they rationalize the decisions made by the Communist Party during the war and when they attack those made by the socialists and other groups? To analyze that question, students would have to be aware of the intrigues and underpinnings of the infighting among the left.[6] What we do know is that Pasionaria is telling her version of the truth when she talks about the poverty of her childhood and how she replaced Catholicism with Marxism in search of a more equitable society. Mora's turning point is more questionable, since she was raised in opulence, but she insists on the gender oppression she suffered and how that circumstance changed her politics. Ironically, despite their vast class difference, both Ibárruri and Mora were pushed into early marriages because, at all levels of Spanish society, girls were groomed for, and forced into, marriage and reproduction. Both women describe how they suffered because of societal pressure and because of their loutish husbands. Both utilized their sense of self-agency to change their lives through politics.

The visibility of Pasionaria and Mora and their political agenda clearly give them a reason to extol the virtues of their party and to condemn the evils of their opponents. The questions of intention and motivation are profoundly important when we analyze the texts, and those questions are intimately tied to when and where the texts were written. Pasionaria wrote her autobiography while living in the Soviet Union, and there is no doubt that her writing was scrutinized by her Russian colleagues. Mora denounces the socialists in her book, though her motives for writing *In Place of Splendor* differ from Ibárruri's. She is not simply setting the record straight, as Pasionaria purports to do in the 1960s. When she published the book in the United States in 1939, Mora was hoping that if she garnered sympathy for the republic and the hundreds of thousands of prisoners in Spain and exiles dispersed around the world, Franco might be removed from power. Both these authors had the intention of writing not an autobiography but a book of history that revolved around them. Or as Nelson Goodman describes it, they are "worldmaking" (qtd. in Bruner 35).

The significant passage of time since war's end vastly changes how many of the narrators represent themselves in texts about prison life, which in general do not place the author at the center of the narration. Doña's novelized autobiography *Desde la noche y la niebla* reveals somewhat feminist leanings. Doña (1918–2003), who was from a working-class family, became a Communist at age fourteen and was very active in party activities until she was imprisoned after the war. She was given the death sentence, but it was commuted to thirty years. In all, she spent some twenty years in Franco's prisons. In the 1930s, very few working-class women had any feminist consciousness; in fact only a handful of educated Spanish women were feminists at that time. But Doña wrote her book after she had been in exile in France observing the feminist movement there, and she describes herself and her cell mates as victims of both the Franco regime and misogyny. She speaks for all her cell mates with what I call "the urgent solitary voice of collective testimony" (Mangini, *Memories* 57); like other women who wrote or transcribed testimonies about life in prison many years after the Franco regime ended, she denounces the tragedies that were inflicted on her and her fellow sufferers.

At the other end of the political spectrum is Pilar Primo de Rivera (1907–91), who clearly accepted the subservient role that the state-church monolith had assigned women in Spain since the formation of the Spanish nation in the fifteenth century. Pilar was the daughter of General Miguel Primo de Rivera, whose dictatorship lasted from 1923 to 1930, and the sister of José Antonio, the founder of the violent Falange movement in 1933, which played a key role in the mobilization of the right and in the destabilization of the republic from 1933 to 1936. José Antonio also founded the female organization called the Women's Section,[7] naming Pilar head of the group. In her text, Pilar explains why she never married (single women were often considered aberrant creatures), insinuating that she was considered a candidate to be Hitler's wife by those hoping to create a fascist dynasty. She clarifies her position on this possibility by saying, "I never felt that I could be the trustee of such an important mission—and besides, my private life was my own" (210).[8] Whether this remark reflects any serious attempt to unite Spain and Germany is doubtful; what it does reflect is Pilar's commitment to politics, while still expressing her humility as a woman.

At that time both in Spain and Germany (see Koonz), fascist women staunchly defended the right of the patriarchy to suppress women, given their inferiority and given the need to maintain male dominance in the home. Pilar was highly influenced by the Nazi women's group Winterhilfe when she organized the Women's Section. Unlike the women of the left, she espoused abnegation for women and completely embraced the subservience of women to men. Yet as Preston points out, she was very controlling and jealous of her position (*Doves* 246). When she sensed that Mercedes Sanz Bachiller, who was leading the successful Auxilio de Invierno (Winter Aid) group[9] during the war, was undermining her leadership as the head of the Women's Section, Primo de Rivera worked assiduously to discredit Sanz Bachiller so that she would be relieved of her duties. In her text, Primo de Rivera never mentions the vicious battle she fought against the more charismatic Sanz Bachiller, only referring to the rivalry as "that problem" (103), but when she describes her rival, as Preston says, one can "read between the lines" (246). Clearly, as Stewart cautions, it is necessary to look for what the author chooses not to tell in this text. Primo de Rivera did not want to diminish how she represents herself in the book—as the selfless female who espoused abnegation and humility for all women in the Women's Section—by confessing to her jealousy of Sanz Bachiller and her overpowering need to be the uncontested leader of the Women's Section.

The importance of analyzing how and why the women tell their stories the way they do, what they choose to emphasize and what they choose to avoid, should be stressed. Why, for instance, does Pasionaria discuss at length the animosity between her party and the Socialist Party and ignore many of the issues of her private life? An icon, a myth among Communists around the world, she could not afford to reveal that she violated the sanctity of holy marriage by leaving her husband and taking a lover much younger than she. These exceptional women who were protagonists of history do not include what they think would be perceived as female flaws. Pasionaria occasionally mentions her children and comments on how she could not care for them properly because of her political commitment, but she minimizes the issue to stress her dedication to the party and to the republic. In addition, undoubtedly she was advised by her Soviet superiors to adhere to the official story of her political role. Primo de Rivera wrote as Pasionaria did, to justify her sympathies and, in her case, to provide an apology for her support of the overthrow of the legitimate government. Therefore, though gender is the key factor here, we cannot dismiss the importance of political allegiance among more prominent women and how it affects what they choose to discuss.

Questions of style and the quality of the written memory texts present us with another topic of discussion. Mora's and O'Neill's writing is far superior to some of the transcribed testimonies or memory texts written by imprisoned women with little education. Mora was relatively well educated; she may also have had some help in the editing of her book from American journalists she befriended in Madrid. O'Neill was a journalist, and her writing reveals her professional skills. But how do we approach a book like Doña's novelized memory text *Desde la noche y la niebla*? Do we treat it as we do those that purport to be a true rendering of life? Perhaps we can, if we take into consideration one of Doña's reasons for using the novelized form: the need to protect her friends who were still in prison (Mangini, *Memories* 109). Yet some aspects of her account have been altered, so this text cannot be considered truly self-representative.

A subject worth exploring is how the Spanish women of the left differ from resistance women in Italy, Germany, and France. I have often used the theme of fascism to underscore the differences between Spanish women and their European counterparts in World War II. The double repression for women ended in 1945 in the rest of Europe, but in Spain those who survived were not liberated until 1975. When we read memory texts of women such as Lucie Aubrac—one of the great heroines of the French resistance during World War II, who escaped to London shortly before the war ended—it becomes clear that the fate of Spanish women was radically different. Spanish women endured thirty more years of fascist domination. War, prison, and loss had been assimilated into their individual and collective memories. For this reason, the trauma of war never ended for most of the vanquished—and it especially endured for the women who remained in Spain, were persecuted, and labeled Red whores over nearly forty years (see Mangini, *Memories* 144). Many who went into exile suffered the alienation of displacement throughout their lives. Most were never celebrated as heroines of the Spanish republic but rather systematically humiliated and persecuted; for that reason, even in the 1980s, many of the activists I interviewed were still afraid to tell their stories. For the same reason, prison texts do not display the tone of triumph that we find in a text like Aubrac's *Outwitting the Gestapo*; instead they reflect indignation and deep sadness.

Students should be reminded not to let their own situations and sympathies limit their power of analysis. Inevitably, the sinister relationship of the Spanish Nationalists with Hitler and Mussolini and the subsequent systematic liquidation of Franco's enemies after the war will color their thinking. Yet if we are to grasp how power and gender affect the lives of women, we must seek to understand these women in all their plurivalent dimensions and on their own terms. As Stewart points out, they are not one voice; rather, there are many contradictory voices in one person. O'Neill, in her gripping memory text, narrates the fateful vacation that she embarked on with her two small children in Morocco in the summer of 1936, to be near her husband, an air force captain stationed there. When the war broke out, Captain Leret was shot by a firing squad when he refused to join the insurgents. O'Neill was apprehended and imprisoned in the first days of the war because of her Republican affiliation, and her children were taken away to be raised by relatives sympathetic to the insurgents. She reveals that after she received the news of her husband's assassination, she lost all desire to live and hoped for death. Yet she persevered for the sake of her children and for another compelling reason: as a writer, she felt she had the responsibility of recounting the stories of her innocent cell mates.[10] She wrote the first two versions while in Spain, risking imprisonment after her release in 1939; she destroyed both at the insistence of her family. Only in exile in Mexico did she dare to publish her final version of the text, which was followed by a sequel, *Segunda parte de una mexicana en la guerra de España* ("The Second Part of a Mexican Woman in the Spanish War"). O'Neill dedicated many years of her life to narrating her experiences and those of her cell mates and to denouncing the ferocious Franco regime. Her initial weakness, the desire to die, had turned into—by her account—indomitable strength during and after the war.

The texts and transcribed testimonies of these victims of long-term trauma have other dimensions to be dealt with in the classroom. Useful when confronting texts that deal with loss, mental and physical torture, illness, and humiliation is Shoshana Felman and Dori Laub's *Testimony: Crises of Witnessing in Literature, Psychoanalysis, and History*, especially chapter 1, in which Felman discusses the "vicissitudes of teaching" the traumatic effects of war and how they can provoke emotion in the classroom. Contemplating the punishment that the Franco regime meted out to those who had defended the republic often upsets students. Felman specifically addresses testimonial events, but I find that the impact of reading about women in prison is equally disquieting to many students and prompts them to go through a process that is "performative, and not just cognitive" (Felman and Laub 53).

Identifying with some of the women, students often begin to share fragments of their own lives and to note how repressive societal rules for women have affected them or female members of their families. They also assume the responsibility for transcribing their families' witnessing and their trauma. Such students may go through a cathartic process of their own. As Laub says of those who are exposed to testimonies of trauma, "By extension, the listener . . . comes to be a participant and a co-owner of the traumatic event" (57). O'Neill lived for the day she would be reunited with her children. Yet by the time she was released, she had assimilated the prison experience to such an extent that she feared leaving. She was no longer the person who entered prison in 1936, and when she looked in a mirror for the first time, she did not recognize herself, "that woman with a tremendous expression of anguish" (199). Having a knowledge of long-term suffering—her own and that of her prison mates—had completely changed her. Once digested, this knowledge leaves students with the need to do something, perhaps to tell another story of suffering that has been shared with them.

The tragedy of mothers and their children is a theme of the prison texts more disturbing than that of the constant threat of torture or firing squads. Doña focuses on the plight of women with small children in prison, who often perished there because of malnutrition and disease. The trauma of watching their babies die caused many women to become mentally ill. Older children were taken from the mothers, and many were never heard of again. Part of the "positive eugenics" enforced by Vallejo Nágera, chief psychiatrist of Franco's army, was to take children from their "racially decadent" and "mentally inferior and dangerous" mothers so that they would not be contaminated. Thus, "the country could be liberated from such a fearsome plague" (qtd. in Sòria, "Inquisidor").

For many the Spanish Civil War did not end until Franco's death. Even then the mind-set of the victors did not significantly change, and there was an attempt to erase all vestiges of the crimes against humanity committed during and after the war, which is why so many of those crimes are still surfacing. As Ricard Vinyes, author of *Irrendentas: Las presas políticas y sus hijos en las cárceles de Franco* ("Unredeemed: Female Political Prisoners and Their Children in Franco's Prisons"), discussed in a symposium on the subject in October 2002, there was an attempt to "existentially transform" political prisoners into common criminals (qtd. in Sòria, "Anatomía"). By separating female prisoners from their families, especially their children, the regime hoped to destroy their identities, though—as is visible in these texts and as Vinyes proves—it was unsuccessful in many cases. One of the few uplifting themes of the prison texts is precisely the solidarity that the women demonstrated in their desire to maintain their integrity and uphold their ideals against all odds.

Perhaps the most serious challenge in teaching these texts is to understand philosophically how a civilized country full of an intense zest for life and a rich and sophisticated cultural heritage could turn into a land of killing fields and human misery and how, after the war, Spain reverted to a system reminiscent of the Inquisition, in which every available building was converted into a prison. Through these texts we find some answers, though much of the horror can only be imagined and remains unanswered and unanswerable. As the journalists Elaine Sciolino and Emma Daly remarked in November 2002, when it became obvious that the vanquished had begun to clamor for the recuperation of historical memory, "Suddenly, if episodically, Spain is waking from the collective amnesia that has paralyzed it for more than a quarter of a century." Teaching texts of this kind is therefore a work in progress as well as one of profound psychological and existential dimensions.

Notes

1. To understand how the female activists were viewed, it is worthwhile to quote from the findings of Antonio Vallejo Nágera, chief psychiatrist of Franco's army, who directed a psychological research team to study the personality of concentration camp prisoners in 1938 and 1939: "In order to understand such active participation of the female sex in Marxist revolution, do remember their characteristic psychic instability, the weakness of their mental equilibrium, their lower resistance to environmental influences, their insecurity of personality control, and their tendency to be impulsive, all psychological qualities which in special circumstances lead to abnormalities in social behavior and which drag the individual into psychopathological states. . . . If women usually have a gentle, sweet and kindhearted character, it is due to the brakes which socially restrain [them]; however, as the female psyche has many points in common with that of the infant and the animal, when the brakes that socially hold them back disappear and they are released from the inhibitions on their instinctive impulses, then there awakes in the female sex the cruelty instinct, surpassing all possibilities imaginable, precisely because they lack the inhibitions of intelligence and logic. It is often observed that women who go into politics do not do so motivated by their ideas, but rather by their feelings, which attain immoderate or even pathological proportions, due to the very irritability of the female personality" (Vallejo Nágera and Martínez, qtd. in Bandrés and Llavona 7).

2. *Una mujer* was first published as *Una mexicana en la guerra de España* ("A Mexican Woman in Spain's War") in 1964. O'Neill was born in Madrid of Mexican parents, and when she was released from prison, she went into exile in Mexico.

3. Maura was president of Spain from 1903 to 1904, from 1907 to 1909, and then again briefly in both 1918 and 1919.

4. Autobiography was traditionally a genre practiced by the colonial white male who wrote to impart lessons to his subjects. As Brodzki and Schenk say, the autobiographer "placed himself at the center of his own cosmology" (4). It should be noted that new research suggests that Mora did not write *In Place of Splendor* but rather told her story to the writer Ruth McKenney, who then wrote the book (Fox).

5. Expressing an idea not unlike Stewart's concept of agency, Jerome Bruner describes the events in an autobiographer's life that motivate the author to move in a new direction as "turning points," which "represent a way in which people free themselves in their self-consciousness from their history, their banal destiny, their conventionality" (32).

6. Obviously students should have a working knowledge of the main causes and events of the war. Useful for this is Gabriel Jackson's *A Concise History of the Spanish Civil War*. Also of interest are several films that portray activist women. In the documentary *De toda la vida* (*All Our Lives*), several anarchist women living in exile in France in the 1980s tell of their lives during and after the war. Two feature

films that romanticize the role of the *milicianas* in the war are Vicente Aranda's *Libertarias* and Ken Loach's *Land and Freedom*.

7. José Antonio Primo de Rivera was killed at the beginning of the war and became the most important martyr of the civil war on the Francoist side.

8. All translations are mine unless otherwise noted.

9. Winter Aid was an affiliate of the Women's Section that supplied food and clothing and offered child care to war victims.

10. Many of the women were imprisoned simply because their fathers, brothers, husbands, or other family members had fought against the insurgents.

Gina Herrmann

The Witness in the Classroom: Survivor Oral Histories of the Spanish Civil War

> *War is the ground where* history *and* story, *two directly related words, overlap and coalesce. War as event and oral history as discourse, therefore, share the fact of being the grounds of encounters between personal experience and history, the spaces where the individual narrative of biography meets the collective narrative of history.*
>
> –Alessandro Portelli, *The Battle of Valle Giulia*

I write this piece while mourning the death of George Cullinen, the Abraham Lincoln Brigade veteran I invited to speak to a packed auditorium at Colby College in 1999. His passing stands as a reminder that there is little time left to speak with those people who lived through the Spanish Civil War. Although the general aim of this essay is to discuss the classroom use of video and print oral histories, it is with a sense of urgency and enthusiasm that I also offer strategies and resources for the organization of campus and classroom visits of Spanish Civil War survivors. I believe that the live presence of veterans and witnesses provides an intersubjective encounter with a human being who traveled a crossroads in Western political and social history that no other format can offer. While the logistics of

386 Witness in the Classroom

bringing a veteran or eyewitness to the classroom can be daunting, every effort should be made to do so before it is too late. The appendix to this essay lists the contact information for various veteran and survivor organizations in the United States and Spain that may be of use in contacting speakers. However, since the funding needed to bring Spanish Civil War witnesses to the classroom and auditorium may be prohibitive, the pedagogical strategies and their attendant theoretical rationales I describe serve all the genres of eyewitness testimony—namely, tape-recorded testimonies, audiovideo interviews in documentary film, and transcribed and edited oral histories found in many collections of the personal narratives of witnesses to the Spanish Civil War. Fortunately, survivors of the war have been interviewed for many decades now, and dozens of documentary films and printed testimonial collections are readily available for use by teachers and their students. Some of these videos and book collections are also listed in the appendix.

Oral or video witness testimonies are particularly good objects for teaching how history is subjective, contextualized, contingent, and partial. By comparing varied individual experiences of war, we can elucidate the representational quality of discourses that are too easily ascribed truth-value. At the same time, first-person witness accounts summon us to think about the history of war through the filter of individual and collective affective, ideological, and moral experience. Oral history, then, is a unique genre, for it moves us away from a concern with veracity and toward questions of human situatedness in the contexts of extreme political and social circumstances. The continuing critical and theoretical interest in the subject of experience and its epistemological relations to the categories of identity and experience additionally justify the inclusion of oral sources in a Spanish Civil War course, particularly at the graduate level. Interviews with witnesses or survivors serve as excellent critical objects that advanced students can use to work through the experiential and existential dimensions of evidence, trauma, agency, and memory (LaCapra, *History in Transit*; Moya and Hames-García). What are the uses (or abuses) of Spanish Civil War memory as symbolic capital in the present—in the service, for example, of the structuring of the memory of the 11 March bombings and the victory of the PSOE (Spanish Socialist Party) in 2004?

Witness testimonies also offer a window onto the process by which particular national myths about the Spanish Civil War have been formed. In the United States, the memory of the war has been dominated by the legendary status of the Abraham Lincoln Brigade to the exclusion, for the most part, of contradictory versions of the conflict. When it comes to the presentation of survivor testimony, too often United States student audiences do not move beyond (the indeed wonderful) *The Good Fight* documentary about the Lincolns. But to juxtapose that film's representation of the war with, for example, Spanish Falangist and anarchist testimonies read side by side, reveals the extent to which narratives are translations of lived events that in turn circulate to make meanings about political history, cultural values, and national identity. This comparative approach with oral history sources invites broad questions, including why certain witness-narrators represent the war as they do. Because oral histories are representational, crafted objects, they hold aesthetic value and thus promote aesthetic analysis. We can engage our students in discussions about the narrative and rhetorical quality of testimonial discourse to address the idea of storytelling as it relates to the tellability of history. Whose stories get told? How are they told? Why are they memorable? What work do they do?

Finally, the presence of a live witness allows listeners to become interlocutors who can ask questions about an endless number of themes, especially regarding the degree of continuity or rupture between the present and the past. In this essay, I first describe the theoretical material assigned to students to prepare them for a unit of study based on oral sources. I then give concrete strategies for working oral testimonies into lesson plans as well as the theoretical bases and ideological goals of the inclusion of these exercises. Finally, I offer a pragmatic guide for the organization of a survivor's campus visit, drawing on my experience with Cullinen. Overall, I attempt to provide at least partial answers to questions about how students might be led to think about the relations among memory, subjectivity, and history (or what Jo Labanyi, in this collection, calls "teaching history through memory work").

In the following discussion of pedagogical strategies, I have literally taken a page from the lesson book of teachers of Holocaust studies who, for many years, have been drawing up networks, protocols, and lesson plans regarding the use of survivor testimony in the classroom. From Claude Lanzmann's *Shoah*, Steven Spielberg's Survivors of the Holocaust Visual Shoah Foundation, and educational initiatives such as Facing Our History and Ourselves, oral histories or testimonial interviews are the *materia prima* of the cross-generational transmission of the Holocaust. So too for the Spanish Civil War. An eyewitness interview or the viewing of video-based oral sources supplement written historical accounts. This pedagogical approach allows a human face to emerge from an anonymous collective, and it inspires ethical reflection on how the individual story might be linked to students in the present. Oral sources, then, connect the past with the present moment of narration as no other genre can. For the sake of getting our students to respond both intellectually and affectively to history, testimonial accounts should stand at the core of the Spanish Civil War curriculum.

Student Preparation for the Study of Oral Sources

When teaching the Spanish Civil War,[1] I have set up my lesson plans so that oral histories form the centerpiece of the course. In anticipation of Cullinen's visit in 1999, students were asked to prepare for the entire oral history unit by reading both practical and theoretical texts about oral history. To understand the difference between the practice and the analysis of oral history, the students began by exploring Linda Shopes's valuable Web site *Making Sense of Oral History* (historymatters.gmu.edu/mse/oral). This site describes, at an introductory level, how to do oral history and explains the methods for its interpretation. The students enjoyed working in groups in a computer lab perusing the site and going to the links of "exemplary oral history sites" so that they could see how visual-media-based oral history projects look and sound. After this, they read two ground-breaking articles by the oral historian Alessandro Portelli, whose works are among the most creative, literary-minded, and ideologically nuanced in the field. These articles, "What Makes Oral History Different?" and "There's Always Gonna Be a Line: History-Telling as a Multivocal Art," accomplish various pedagogical goals. The first article teaches students how to think about oral history as a different genre of historiography— different for its orality, narrative structure, subjectivity, the special credibility of memory, and the intersubjective nature of the interview encounter between narrator and interviewer. Even more significant for the purposes of the course, the article argues for the embeddedness of subjectivity in history as a function of a critical method, as the "study of the cultural forms and processes by which individuals express their sense of themselves in history" (Introduction ix). The second article, "There's Always Gonna Be a Line," again addresses the issue of intersubjectivity by reminding the student that an oral history is an encounter before it becomes an artifact, or as Portelli puts it, "an *experience* before it becomes a *text*" (xiii). He reminds us that oral histories are available for narrative analysis, but they also "impact one's own subjectivity" (xiii). Reading these two articles, the students become aware that oral history demands both their intellectual and their emotional activity. The second article also presents what I have found to be an invaluable method for encountering and interpreting not just oral history texts but cultural artifacts of all sorts, from novels to architecture. Always reaching for the broadest possible understanding of oral history, Portelli exposes how

> oral personal narrative can achieve levels of structural complexity comparable to those of literary texts, and can therefore stand the close individual analysis we usually devote to written literature, while retaining its cultural and generic difference. ("There's" 25)

He defines three

> modes of history-telling, that is, three ways of organizing historical narrative in terms of point of view, social, and spatial referents:
>
> 1. Institutional
> Social referents: politics and ideology; government, parties, unions, elections, and so on. Spatial referent: the nation, the state, [the "war machine"]. Point of view: third-person, impersonal.
>
> 2. Communal
> Social referent: the community, the neighborhood, the job; strikes, natural catastrophes, rituals; collective participation at the institutional level, [the battalion, the guerrilla group, the French resistance, the División Azul, etc.]. Spatial referent: the town, the neighborhood, the workplace, [the prison, the concentration camp, cultural centers, youth group meeting places, etc.]. Point of view: first-person plural.
>
> 3. Personal
> Social referent: private and family life; the life cycle: births, marriages, jobs, children, deaths; personal involvement in the two other levels. Spatial referent: the home, [communal spaces taking on the quality of home, particularly as the result of war, as familial relations are forged among unrelated persons]. Point of view: first-person singular.
>
> These modes are never totally and explicitly separate . . . in fact, history-telling is precisely the art of combining the modes into meaningful patterns. . . . We may, however, use these categories as a map to orient ourselves in the analysis. (27; my additions given in brackets)

While the applicability of this model for the study of oral sources in general is obvious, it may be especially useful for the student of war. What makes Portelli's work relevant and appealing is his hypothesis about the special place of war in memory texts:

> War keeps coming back in narratives and memories as the most dramatic point of encounter between the personal and the public, between biography and history. . . . The child's question—"Daddy, what did you do in the war?"—is an embryonic way of phrasing the larger question: What is our place in history, and what is the place of history in our lives? . . . (Introduction ix)

War brings to the fore questions about the essence of what is human and signals "the difference between the time of the events and the time of the telling, the time of history and the time of discourse, highlighting through memory and storytelling the changing historical and narrative subject" (x). This convincing and moving statement makes the case for the inclusion—indeed, even the primacy—of oral testimonies in the Spanish Civil War classroom.

Returning to Portelli's modes of history telling, we can see how war is so integral an experience that it is inevitably narrated in all three categories: the personal, the communal, and the institutional ("There's" 34). We can ask students to listen for statements that address each of the modes (personal: "My best friend died"; institutional: "At the ministry they didn't know what they were doing"; communal: "We organized a literacy campaign") and then for the moments where these modes overlap. This type of exercise hones the students' ability to listen and read both critically and affectively, working to capture the complexities of experience beyond the vagaries of the past and the merely personal. It is a practice in understanding the political and ideological dimensions of subjectivity.

The last two preparatory readings I assign when teaching this course are the introductions to two collections of oral histories of the Spanish Civil War: Ronald Fraser's *Blood of Spain: An Oral History of the Spanish Civil War* and Mary Giles's translated edition of Tomasa Cuevas's *Prison of Women*. In these short selections the interviewer's perspective receives the attention. The students are reminded not only that the interview itself is the context of the finished oral history product but that the situatedness of the interviewer affects the story told by the narrator. While Fraser comes to his subjects from a position of national, linguistic, and generational difference, Cuevas spent decades interviewing her own cohort, women who were her prison mates during the Franco regime. At this point, I encourage students to reflect on the differences between insider and outsider interviewing. Since the interviewer usually disappears in both documentary film and printed collections of testimonies, these two readings provide some insight into the intersubjective aspect of oral history. Finally, in those cases where a class has the opportunity to conduct a small-scale oral history with a survivor who comes to campus, these introductions attune students to their role as interviewers.

Approaches for Working with Video Interviews and Print Testimonies

If the testimonial portion of the course forms a unit, two preparatory series of exercises help students consider the historical context of the narratives they will hear or read as well as heighten their sensitivity to the subjectivity of the narrator. Both these lesson approaches are modified from *Survivors: Testimonies of the Holocaust*, the Shoah Foundation's video and CD-ROM educational module developed with Facing History and Ourselves, a tolerance education organization. The first exercises have students identify the core historical concepts of the Spanish Civil War through introductory readings and lectures during the first few weeks of class. Then students devise a compendium to those concepts or themes. One tactic is to end each class session by isolating one main historical issue on which students write a short response paper for the next class meeting. These core topics, which should be very broad, might include "Factors That Led to Disunity among the Republicans," "How the Nationalists Coalesced," "International Responses to the Non-intervention Pact," "Military Strategy," "Fascism versus Francoism," "The Struggles of the Republican Government," "Terror," and "Madrid as Symbol." A list of themes, once established, translates into learning objectives for the duration of the course and serves as the broad outline for student analysis of the different testimonial texts. Afterward, the class divides into groups; each group is responsible for developing one or two educational objectives associated with the larger theme assigned to it. Over the course of the academic term, each group refines the objectives in such a way that they can be incorporated into the analysis of the oral testimonies, serve as the basis for group presentations or final research papers, and help formulate questions the students will ask if they are able to interview a survivor in person.

For example, after reading and discussing the nature of the Francoist project, students come up with the core theme "Fascism versus Franco-ism." Then a group of three to four students, with teacher guidance, elaborates an educational objective, which might be to understand the hybrid ideology of *franquismo*. This theme is particularly good for drawing out the ideological beliefs and biases of the testimonial narrators the students will be hearing and reading. While it may not prove relevant for every testimonial text, a survivor's vision of who Franco and the Nationalists were and what they stood for appears in some form, however briefly, in most eyewitness accounts.

Before this work begins, I assign the class the introduction and first chapter to Michael Richards's *A Time of Silence: Civil War and the Culture of Repression in Franco's Spain, 1936–45*. A solid understanding of the complexities of the Nationalist project allows students to be better interviewers if the class is able to set up a visit with a veteran or survivor. In the specific case of Cullinen's visit to Colby College, it was fascinating to observe how, on one hand, Cullinen did not draw distinctions between Spain's Nationalists and the fascists and, on the other, how he used "antifascist" and "Communist" as interchangeable, self-descriptive labels. When my students carried out small-group interviews with him, I reminded them that their job was not to disabuse him of his beliefs but merely to ask questions that might later help us analyze positions of ideology and subjectivity in his personal history. The questions they asked, related to this educational objective about Francoism, included ones that required him to think about the differences between Nazis and Nationalists in his own history as a veteran of the Spanish Civil War and witness to World War II. Comparing Cullinen's testimony with others they read and saw in videos, the students were able to situate his story in a wider frame of reference about how people of disparate political beliefs and social experience understood fascism in the context of the Spanish Civil War.

It is satisfying, in this series of exercises, to see students determine what big historical questions are at play, isolate an objective with the purpose of interrogating historical assumptions, and then finally have the opportunity to situate a concrete historical theme in the framework of an individual's historically bound experience. Challenging the macronarratives of history, they become active, empathic listeners and learn to analyze connections among personal protagonism, myth, and the affective aspects of history. The lesson of oral history is that it teaches us to attend to meaning beyond events.

Another teaching strategy I have adapted from *Survivors* is the use of an identity chart. At the center of a page, students write the name of the person whose identity they are charting. From the name, various lines are drawn out in a circle, forming a constellation, each line pointing to some characteristic of the subject's life or selfhood. For example, in a student's own chart, lines might point to the words "Spanish major," "born in New York," "volunteer firefighter," "my best friend," "brother fought in Gulf War," "doesn't watch TV," and so on. This identity chart serves various functions. First, when students chart themselves, it alerts them in a highly personal way to the role of subjectivity in history. The work with the charts is made that much richer when combined with Portelli's schema for the modes of history telling. By attending to the personal, communal, and institutional phenomena that make up their own identity, students are poised to engage with the oral testimonies with greater sophistication and sensitivity.

The identity chart, as it is filled out for each testimony read, viewed, or heard, acts as a new object for comparative work. Students can take the charts of persons from the same or different political, social, geographic sphere and, connecting this strategy with the thematic work described above, compare eyewitness accounts as they relate to one of the historical issues defined by the class. In my course, students developed identity charts for two loosely defined Nationalist participants in the Spanish Civil War whose testimonies appear in Fraser's *Blood of Spain: An Oral History of the Spanish Civil War,* a Falangist farmer and a Carlist peasant. I urged them to think about how the oral accounts confirmed or contested Richards's description of Francoist ideology as a composition of "Catholicism, specifically Spanish myths, exacerbated nationalism and European fascism" (16). We were then able to discuss how Nationalism expressed itself through belief systems that did not necessarily appear to have much to do with Francoism.

Through the comparison of the charts of the Falangist and the Carlist, the students not only discovered places of contact and divergence between the two men but also were able to capture the subtleties of the right wing that would have been utterly lost on them had they considered only Cullinen's perspective on the fascists. The same kind of exercise can be applied to an analysis—within a party or across party lines—of videotaped testimonies with members of the International Brigades and the División Azul in Javier Rioyo and José Luis López Linares's film *Extranjeros de sí mismos.* Applying the identity chart to the testimonies is extremely challenging, because most of the oral accounts in, for instance, Fraser's book and *La vieja memoria*, Jaime Camino's documentary interviews with protagonists of the civil war, tend to describe the peripatetics of war and not the subjective response to it. The speakers demonstrate a narrative preference for communally lived events as opposed to anecdotes from the personal sphere. Therefore, just like oral historians, students must carry out very subtle analyses of history beyond the events.

Oral History Live

In 1999 I taught a senior seminar on the Spanish Civil War at Colby College in Waterville, Maine. That year I also became involved with the Veterans of the Abraham Lincoln Brigade (VALB) and the Abraham Lincoln Brigade Archives (ALBA). I wanted my students to have the opportunity to meet and interview a Spanish Civil War survivor. I knew there were still some Lincoln vets who traveled to colleges and high schools, giving talks and participating in class activities. Since travel to rural Maine in April (which is usually still winter) presents certain challenges, I tried to locate a vet who lived in the Northeast. I contacted ALBA, and they put me in touch with Cullinen, a Vermont resident, who happily agreed to a public lecture and classroom discussion at Colby. Because I wanted him to have an impressive turnout for his public talk, I invited my students to think about how we might cultivate the interest of other departments on campus. During class time we brainstormed about thematic and temporal points of intersection between our course and other topics being taught at Colby that semester. We came up with a surprisingly long list. The students realized that we could draw an audience from courses such as US Literature between the Wars, US Foreign Policy, Stalin and Stalinism, Theories of Marxism, Twentieth-Century Russian History, Holocaust Studies, The Vietnam War, and classes that included the study of *testimonio*. I contacted the professors for each of these courses and asked if they would be interested in attending Cullinen's lecture. The response was so overwhelmingly positive that I put together a small study packet about the Spanish Civil War for each of these groups. In anticipation of the veteran's visit, these professors assigned a twenty-five-minute video about the Spanish Civil War and had their students locate and read a synopsis of the war either online or in an encyclopedia. Most of the professors made attendance at the talk mandatory!

The next task we faced as a class was how best to advertise the events of Cullinen's visit to the wider college community. We discussed the problem of focusing exclusively on the Spanish Civil War in our propaganda campaign, since many people do not know the difference between Spain's fratricidal conflict and the Spanish-American War. I asked the students to think about what made Cullinen's history transgressive in the context of United States history and culture, and they came up with, "He is a Communist!" So using the striking photographic portrait of him taken by the Spanish photojournalist Sofía Moro, I enlisted the aid of the graphic design department at Colby to put together a poster that read, above the veteran's picture, "Abraham Lincoln Brigade Veteran, George Cullinen," and below, "Why I became a Communist and fought in the Spanish Civil War." We posted it all over campus one week and then again the day before the visit.

Cullinen's visit to Waterville comprised three events: a public lecture about his life, focusing on the Spanish Civil War; a luncheon with any student who wanted to attend; and a series of group interviews or discussions with my students. I want to emphasize once again the educational and moral value of an in-the-flesh encounter with an eyewitness testimonial narrator. Two things happened during the talk that brought this point home to me. First, the talk was far longer and less focused on the war than I would have liked. There were moments where Cullinen clearly lost his audience. But during the question-and-answer session, one of my best students asked him to describe what it was like to be on the battlefield. The response was chilling. In a somewhat flustered and perhaps even angry tone, Cullinen painted a picture of carnage and trauma in the context of his helplessness to save dying comrades. The audience sat in silence, captivated by this exposition. We were reminded of the physical and psychological costs of war as Cullinen described the post-traumatic stress that left him unable to fight after only a few days on the front lines.

The second involved a colleague's reaction to the talk and the students' witnessing, in turn, her interaction with Cullinen. While some students shed tears during the evening, this young woman professor, also a teacher of contemporary Spanish culture, wept openly. After the talk, and while students were still waiting to speak to Cullinen, she went to introduce herself and through her sobs thanked him for "what he did for Spain." It was extremely powerful for the students to watch a thirty-something American teacher being embraced in the weathered arms of an American veteran of the Spanish Civil War. Students witnessed the transgenerational inheritance of the memory of the war as it literally passed through these two bodies. At the same time, the embrace and tears suggested to them that the aura of the Spanish Republican cause still retains its political and emotional relevance outside Spain, in the present.

Note

1. The course was an advanced undergraduate seminar on the Spanish Civil War in which most of the students were Spanish majors.

Appendix

Resources for Survivor Visits

Abraham Lincoln Brigade Veterans' Association and Archive. www.alba-valb.org

AGE (Asociación Archivo Guerra Civil). Maintains databases of Spanish Civil War survivors and exiles. www.nodo50.org/age

Amigos de las brigadas internacionales. www.fut.es~aabi/aab-info.htm

Asociación para la recuperación de la memoria histórica. Organization dedicated to the uncovering of human remains of Republican victims of Franco, primarily in rural mass graves. www.memoriahistorica.org

Foro por la memoria. Partido comunista español. Spanish Communist Party Web site. Clearinghouse for cultural, historical, and legislative issues related to historical memory of the civil war and the Franco dictatorship. Also undertaking the recovery and identification of remains in mass graves. www.pce.es/foroporlamemoria

Fundación Andreu Nin (POUM). www.fundanin.org

Fundación Anselmo Lorenzo. Anarchist. www.cnt.es/fal/home/php

International Brigades. www.brigadasinternacionales.org

Documentary Films Based on Oral Sources and Interviews

De toda la vida. Dir. Carol Mazer and Lisa Berger. Interviews with anarchist women.

Extranjeros de sí mismos. Dir. Javier Rioyo and José Luis López Linares. Interviews with members of the International Brigades and the División Azul.

Forever Activists: Stories from the Veterans of the Abraham Lincoln Brigade. Dir. Judith Montell. About the continuing political activism of the Lincoln veterans. Nominated for an Oscar.

The Good Fight. Dir. Noel Buckner, Mary Dore, and Sam Sills. Interviews with veterans of the Abraham Lincoln Brigade.

La guerra cotidiana. Dir. Daniel Serra and Jaume Serra. On daily lives of women from both sides of the conflict during the Spanish Civil War.

La guerrilla de la memoria. Dir. Javier Corcuera. Testimonies of maquis.

Into the Fire. Dir. Julia Newman. On American nurses in the Spanish Civil War.

Mujeres del 36. Dir. Llum Quiñones. Interviews with Republican women.

Els nens perduts del franquisme (*Los niños perdidos del franquismo*). Dir. Montserrat Armengou and Ricard Belis. Interviews with and about children of Republican women taken from their families during and after the war.

The Spanish Civil War. Contains excerpts of interviews by Ronald Fraser in his *Blood of Spain: An Oral History of the Spanish Civil War.*

La vieja memoria. Dir. Jaime Camino. Interviews with twenty-one protagonists of the civil war from all sides of the conflict.

Collections of Testimonies

Bullón de Mendoza, Alfonso, and Álvaro de Diego. *Historias orales de la guerra civil.*

Cuevas, Tomasa. *Prison of Women: Testimonies of War and Resistance in Spain, 1939–1975.*

Elordi, Carlos, ed. *Los años difíciles: El testimonio de los protagonistas anónimos de la guerra civil y la posguerra.*

Fraser, Ronald. *Blood of Spain: An Oral History of the Spanish Civil War.*

Leguineche, Manuel, and Jesús Torbado. *Los topos: El testimonio estremecedor de quienes pasaron su vida escondidos en la España de la posguerra.*

Reverte, Jorge M., and Socorro Thomás. *Hijos de la guerra: Testimonios y recuerdos.*

Rodrigo, Antonina. *Mujer y exilio, 1939.*

Romeu Alfaro, Fernanda. *El silencio roto: Mujeres contra el franquismo.*

Randolph D. Pope

Fighting the Long Battle of Memory: Autobiographical Writing about the Spanish Civil War

The time framed by 18 July 1936, the military uprising, and 28 March 1939, the Nationalists' entry into Madrid, is usually accepted as the duration of the Spanish Civil War, and, as far as external chronology is concerned, students must learn these dates. Such deceptively clear mileposts are a good place to begin questioning how the past is structured for collective remembrance. Under the labels of "causes" and "consequences," this period must be extended into its past and future, for inevitably the narrative of a civil conflict overflows its official boundaries. This excess responds to four persistent questions: How did we get into such a terrible conflict, what actually happened, how could it have been different, and how did my own life change? On a ship returning to New York after the war, John Tisa, a volunteer in the International Brigades, could not join the other passengers in their games. Instead he repeatedly asked himself, "What went wrong? Why did we lose to the fascist juggernaut? How was it possible for evil to have triumphed over what I was idealistically certain had been a lofty and rightful cause? Answers did not come easily" (*Recalling* 4). Answers have not come later to innumerable persons who have also asked them, as any class would again ask them today. While battles cease, the exploration of these and similar issues proliferates endlessly. The standard versions of the history of the conflict do address them, but in a general way; these versions are decanted by reflection; aided by extensive documentation; and pared, as much as possible, of willful misrepresentation. Yet, if we wish to convey to our students how these events were actually and individually experienced, passionately felt, willfully misrepresented, and endlessly revisited in scarred memories, we do well to approach the war through autobiographical writing.

The greatest difficulty for teachers is to allow their students to understand that for a civil conflict to become violent, there must be people on both sides convinced of their truth and that those people should be allowed to make their case in their own words. Since there have been literally thousands of autobiographical texts written about the Spanish Civil War, opening up to the many stories they tell is not to approach conclusions or judgment but to allow oneself to be immersed in the feeling of everyday life. The first caution, then, is to select texts from a representative variety of political positions, geographic regions, genders, and social classes. While *The Chances of Death*, a selection from the diaries of Priscilla Scott-Ellis, a twenty-year-old British woman who served as a nurse for the Franco forces and was a friend of the royal family, may not seem politically correct—she drove a fancy car, despised the Republicans, loved the good life—her vivid descriptions of the hospitals in which she served and of life on the Nationalist side are startling for their immediacy and their understated heroism. She merits a hearing next to more-established texts such as George Orwell's *Homage to Catalonia* or Franz Borkenau's *The Spanish Cockpit*.

From the Republican side, Ángel Merino Galán, in *Mi guerra empezó antes* ("My Own War Started Before"), a text completed in 1974, doubts the wisdom of adding one more text to the over thirty thousand he calculates exist on the topic, but he finds his justification in the need to tell about *his* war. Yet a common experience of autobiographers is that any exploration of the self reveals that it is situated in the context of numerous institutions, among them the family, the city, and the nation. Therefore there is only a tenuous claim to the possessive, and the rift between *my* and *our* or even *their* is traced with a certain anxiety. The text cannot exist in a private enclosure; it is returned to the social field where the arguments and counterarguments that originated the conflict still remain unresolved. I have found it useful to engage students in an exercise in which they try to delimit what in their lives is unique and private to them. Unless they understand how the presentation of the self is always made up of common elements, they will not completely grasp how Spaniards and the foreigners who joined them saw their individual projects interrupted and their private hopes and expectations hijacked by history.

When did the war begin for each person who participated in it? Merino Galán affirms that it surely began "much before the historical date" (10),[1] but then he hesitates among several moments of his life that seem, retrospectively, turning points: school experiences of rebellion against authority, loss of faith during adolescence, the encounter in the university with politics, and his witnessing the repression of the opposition to the government. One can clearly see here that the educational system, religious institutions, the state, and political parties were engaged in a struggle to gain people's minds long before the war.

This competition for students, model citizens, members, and so on is part of all societies; what was unusual in Spain was its intensity, variety, and lack of tolerance for other points of view. During the war, the Republican side especially made many efforts to win over people to its cause—among them were traveling theater groups and a creative collection of posters. But, as Sandie Holguín describes it in *Creating Spaniards*, this campaign was not an easy task, since "some who sided with the Republic in general opposed the ideas and methods of the Republican leaders to impose cultural unification" (75). As the memoirs of Dionisio Ridruejo show (*Casi*), the Nationalist side also experienced a falling apart of the different positions that composed it. Gonzalo Santonja in *De un ayer no tan lejano* ("From Almost Yesterday") provides a detailed presentation of the propaganda efforts of the Franco regime during the war and its aftermath. This battle for the mind, begun much earlier than the actual conflict, continued through it and after it. Much of autobiographical writing is part of this contest for making a point of view dominant or exclusive, and readers should therefore exert great caution in accepting any version as definitive. Autobiographical writing is always mired in the difficulties of conscious or unconscious self-occultation and construction, but the texts we examine here—originating from the civil war—are frequently aligned with one of the many sides of the conflict, and they contain a need to convince us of the rightfulness of their own cause and the misguided ideas and behavior of their opponents. Reading them today provides an excellent opportunity to examine with students how texts seek to convince and how we tend to grant greater credibility to those with whose ideology we are sympathetic.

Women had even more reason to see the origins of the war as impossible to determine, since they were not direct participants in the decisions that would lead to it. Mary Nash's *Defying Male Civilization: Women in the Spanish Civil War* provides abundant evidence of the persistence of patriarchal images that hampered the active role of women in the war. Shirley Mangini describes their situation in terms that resonate to us as truthful today but that at the time would have been seen as only one of several competing rhetorical positions:

> We are listening to white European women who were colonized, economically and politically, by their own white European countrymen [;] . . . their colonization was brought about by systematic church-state repression through the centuries, without respite. Until the 1930's and again after the war, they had a mentality so infused with a multilayered colonizing patriarchy that it is miraculous that they have spoken at all. They were women, therefore less important than men; they were generally without personal financial recourse, therefore less worthy than the rich. And they were Catholic and Spanish, therefore doubly or triply subjugated—to men (husband, father, brothers)/god (priest)/civil authority (after the war, Franco's "Gestapo-like" police). (*Memories* 55)

When the novelist Dolores Medio writes in her engaging memoirs of the war, *Atrapados en la ratonera* ("Caught in the Mousetrap"), "who knows when the uprising began that would lead us to the most painful and cruel of our Spanish civil wars" (28), she is expressing this general feeling—glossed over by the authoritative conclusions of historical discourse—of being plunged into a life-transforming event not of her own doing. I would argue that teaching the Spanish Civil War as it was experienced by its participants must convey this confusion and uncertainty about its origins, not to clarify that confusion and uncertainty with our own opinions but to expose our students to one of the basic drives of autobiographical writing: the difficult exploration of the self. Given the great number of books on autobiography as a genre, I would strongly recommend Paul John Eakin's *How Our Lives Become Stories: Making Selves*, because it contains a chapter most appropriate for our topic: "Relational Selves, Relational Lives: Autobiography and the Myth of Autonomy" (43–98).

One of the most attractive aspects of these testimonies is the great variety that they show in their response to societal pressures. Pilar Jaraiz Franco, Francisco Franco's niece, in *Historia de una disidencia* ("History of a Rebellion"), sees her story as an evolution from the dutiful offspring of a conservative family in the northern port of El Ferrol, later to be known as El Ferrol del Caudillo, to a liberal professor of law and dissident from her uncle's regime. She presents that evolution as gradual (11), not prepared by the models she saw in her childhood, a time when, according to her,

> women lived strongly conditioned by certain taboos. . . . What could a young woman do who belonged to the clan of privileged navy officers, in a city such as Ferrol, other than take care of her house, dream of a prince charming in the shape of a midshipman and pray for the salvation of a frail child king who could give us hope and save the country from all dangers? (25)

As Jaraiz Franco looks back, she wonders how it was possible that in such conditions everyone did not become a fool (18). The gap between the narrator and the person she was is a bewildering evidence of history, of the disconnection to the past from a much-changed present. She was incarcerated during the war for over two years for no other reason than that she was Franco's relative; yet she emerged decades later more sympathetic to the republic than to the dictatorship. Movingly, under a photograph of herself dressed up in a white first Communion dress, she writes, "The woman I have become feels a sort of tenderness and some anguish for that little girl who she was" (19).

While the experience of a changed self through conversion is not an unusual topic of autobiographical writing, the experience of war produced an interruption of individual life projects, especially for the many Spaniards who had to immigrate abroad after the conflict. María Teresa León, for example, in *Memoria de la melancolía* ("A Memory of Melancholy")—a masterful text—refers to herself as a child and young adolescent in the third person. The daughter of a military man and married early to a person she did not care about, she saw the civil war as her chance for liberation and for the attainment of a self she could embrace. As a political activist, writer, and lover of the poet Rafael Alberti, she created allegiances that gave her a chosen, not imposed, new continuity. Merino Galán in *Mi guerra empezó antes* formulates this break brilliantly:

> Much on the backburner, not yet past, could not be forgotten, but it was necessary to relegate it to the furthest and less illuminated corner of our conscience. That earlier time was not only the days before the war, the projects of our personal life, our illusions and affections—none of this had ended, because it all still lived in us, waiting for the parenthesis of the war to close—because in our heart of hearts the war appeared as a parenthesis, a brief interruption of the anticipated development of our personality and our goals. (165)

Most of the foreign volunteers have described how participating in the civil war changed their lives. The testimony of Tisa in *Recalling the Good Fight: An Autobiography of the Spanish Civil War* is an example among many: "When on a cold 5 January 1937 I walked up the gangway of the *SS Champlain*, a French passenger liner, with passport number 359 499, issued a few days earlier, little did I suspect how completely my life was going to change" (3). More dramatically, Pedro de Répide writes in *Memorias de un aparecido* ("Memoirs of a Ghost"), "I am like Orpheus who returns from hell. I did not descend there for my own pleasure, nor had I lost a Euridice, unless we consider Spain and my own good fortune to be such" (15).

Many of our students may not be old enough to have experienced the forceful substitution of cherished personal hopes for societal obligations, the crushing of the individual story by history, and yet some surely have lived it, or they have observed this process in someone else. This is why in teaching any course involving autobiography I require students to write their own autobiographical texts. Perhaps then they will have a real, sympathetic insight into the brutal experience of the Spanish Civil War as seen by those who were protagonists not of great events but simply of adaptation and survival. Students should spend some time contemplating a photograph of themselves as young children and ask about their own continuity. Then they will be prepared to understand why the memoirs and novels of Jorge Semprún, for example, are heroic not just for his defense of the republic, both during the war and later in the underground fighting from France; for his survival of the German concentration camp; and for his overcoming the internal political infighting of the Communist Party but also for managing against all odds to produce a coherent narrative. Once one has understood how devastating the war was for the continuity of the self, one can also see why there were so many narratives stemming from it and how autobiography became a healing genre to deal with a disaster never quite overcome in the mind.

The issue of the truthfulness of these accounts is sure to come up in any class. I believe that to reduce all writing to fiction is possible only if we understand fiction as a form of doing, of creating in words an image that may or may not correspond to real life—or we may chose to think that there is in fact no real life at all, since it is filtered by a mind already colonized by culture. But if we take a more limited definition—fiction is a narrative that is free of any constraint from the rules of other forms of discourse, such as the historical or judicial—then autobiographical writing is not fiction, since it is an attempt to give an account that can stand the scrutiny of a judge or a historian. That there is a desire to be believed, even a need, is manifested in innumerable instances of declarations such as these:

> We have a duty to present the facts rid of the accretions of propaganda or of the trappings of tendentious versions. Simply put, one must be able to see and know how to reach, as far as possible, the core of the matter. . . . For me it was not easy. (Jaraiz Franco 13)

> In this account there is not one single imaginative detail. Literary fantasy has no place where reality offers a living drama, throbbing and bleeding. A simple narration is enough for days in which daily life becomes monstrous and the abnormal normal. (Répide 13)

> There aren't in *Facts* any products of the imagination. I assure you of their authenticity. I have lived them. Frequently I have been not only an immediate witness, but, even more, the main protagonist. (Moral i Querol 7)

Such affirmations serve as good starting points for a discussion of our belief systems. Needless to say, in examining a conflict in which different versions of reality resulted in war, the consideration of the epistemological difficulties of any narrative is fundamental. A seminar that cannot come to a unified conclusion about who is telling the truth, how the truth is being told, and what the truth is provides a perfect example of this issue. War offers many cases in which the narrators themselves doubt their senses, such as when Harry Fisher in *Comrades* is stunned when one of his friends is asked to execute a soldier of their own army: "Neither of us could believe that this was happening" (141). Belief, then, must replace certainty when dealing with autobiographical texts.

Ultimately these narratives offer the sort of details that allow us to imagine we can remember along with the authors from a period long gone. Medio recalls how she and her sister burned their chairs to keep warm (114), a desperate domestic decision that stands out in her mind almost as much as the process of learning how to deal with death:

> The news of our friends' deaths and of some other acquaintances at first made us shout, "But, it is not possible!," as if, because they were our friends nothing could happen to them, but then we grew accustomed until we were not surprised when we heard such news. Do you know a stray bullet killed Laína Pondal? Not so stray that it did not aim directly at her heart when she was in the kitchen of her house preparing dinner for her children. (54)

Finally, using autobiographical texts to evoke the Spanish Civil War also allows us to explore some aspects of war usually relegated to footnotes of history, such as the experience of those who were caught on the wrong ideological side. The testimony of Manuel González Fresco, written mostly in Spanish but partly in Galician, *Memoria dun fuxido* ("Memoirs of One Who Got Away"), is a splendid example. A defender of Republican ideas, a sharpshooter opposed to violence, he is forced to flee and hide in the mountains of Galicia for several months until he is hunted down and killed. This brief narrative of 1936 is as engaging as a 2001 best-selling novel by Javier Cercas, *Soldados de Salamina* (*Soldiers of Salamis*), in which the author equivocates with autobiographical writing and historical events—the moment in which the Falangist leader Sánchez Mazas is not shot by a Republican soldier—reminding us in this way that the most compelling approach to the past is to make ourselves seekers of a human face to history, to recover history, as far as possible, as it was experienced in its time.

Note

1. All translations from the Spanish are mine.

Joan Ramon Resina

Window of Opportunity: The Television Documentary as "After-Image" of the War

Traumatic experiences are events that resist being articulated as memories; instead they emerge in the present through their aftereffects. For the Spanish Civil War, and especially the long postwar period and dictatorship, official history and social memory have failed to articulate a convincing representation of those traumatic decades. In the absence of a thick description that brings to consciousness the magnitude of the events, the depth and nature of the trauma must be inferred from social symptoms that distort the past and thus facilitate a return of the repressed. The dissipation of the liberal and libertarian traditions, the ingrained intimidation of several generations of losers, the massive conformism and scapegoating mechanisms, and the low public awareness of the historical facts are some of those symptoms. Although dealing with social processes and not strictly with the subjective dimension of repression and distortion, I avail myself of three psychoanalytic notions: trauma, resistance, and substitute formations as ways of acting out. Specifically, I analyze the television documentary as a means of working through the resistance to memory. The choice of television relates to this medium's popularity, intimacy, and loose conditions of reception, which may include a certain degree of interaction between viewers and programmers. These features, combined with the low level of attention demanded from the viewer, make the television screen a projective surface onto which psychic formations are transferred on a large scale. While it would be far-fetched to compare the viewer's couch with the psychoanalyst's, television can nonetheless help objectify inarticulate emotions and reflexes.

Simmering emotion keeps the memories of the civil war and the dictatorship from becoming merely historical knowledge. I do not mean that historians are unable to establish the facts or weigh their implications. What I mean is that the melancholic attachment to that past (confirmed by the recent spate of novels and films revisiting the war) is consistent with the failure to engage in collective mourning during the democratic transition. Had mourning taken place, the transition would have become a conscious exercise of recognition as a prelude to letting go of the past. The difficulty of historicizing this particular past relates to the emotional side of intelligence, to passionate attachments that keep an ethical conflict unresolved and alive. In these conditions it is very difficult to engage in pure recollection, as the recent history wars demonstrate.[1]

Political changes have much to do, of course, with the ways history is coded and recoded and with the territories opened to memory or sunk into oblivion. There is an ozone layer affecting the past that, like the one in the atmosphere, is caused by human activity below. The world political climate has changed dramatically since 1989 and therewith the local perspectives on the Spanish Civil War. With the cold-war paradigm gone, the "two sides" of the Spanish Civil War could begin to be disentangled from the old Manichaean readings and considered in their complexity. This softening of the frame of reference made it possible to refloat some images of the past. However, a more limber ideological frame also encourages revisionism. Once more, the Franco era is being officially cleansed of its barbarous aspects and rationalized. A gray area develops, blurring the distinction between victim and perpetrator, with incalculable consequences not only for Spanish democracy but also for coexistence among Spaniards.

Traumatic experiences overpower an individual's rational defenses and are absorbed without benefit of cognition or understanding. Of these experiences there is no available memory, although, as Sigmund Freud emphasized, often there are retrospective explanations and interpretations. The unavailability of the memory to consciousness does not imply that the memory does not exist or that it is inactive. As Freud explained in his fundamental study "Erinnern, Wiederholen und Durcharbeiten"

(1914), although patients do not remember the traumatic events, they act them out, unwittingly repeating the repressed scene. The past is rehearsed through symptoms that may appear inconsistent with the new context in which they surface but are fully intelligible in reference to the repression (520). A traumatic event is reproduced, then, not as memory (i.e., not in the sphere of representation) but as deed. Although, strictly speaking, it is always the individual psyche that somatizes a trauma, some collective dramas seem to mimic this psychic mechanism, multiplying its effects and incorporating them into the culture. From this analogy it seems possible to infer the existence of a collective unconscious as a working hypothesis. By "collective unconscious" I mean the reverse of "collective memory," a term borrowed from the sociology of Maurice Halbwachs and used here in the sense of a pattern of intersubjective memory shared by a group and maintained through the ordinary exchanges of its members in their social milieu. The collective unconscious would stand, then, for the darkened area of the public memory where the causes of social dispositions and reflexes have fallen out of view for reasons that are also social in nature.

The full experience of the war and the repression is irretrievable. No representation can express the horror of the first experiments in carpet bombing on a market day in Guernica, General Juan Yagüe's machine-gunning of the prisoners massed in the bullfighting ring in Badajoz, or the thousands of nightly executions in Mallorca wrenchingly denounced by Georges Bernanos, who anticipated the incredulity of his conservative French readers even as he wrote, "Evidently, you find that hard to read. It is also hard for me to write it. It was harder to see, to hear" (132).[2] Because of the difficulty in seeing and hearing, any account of the war and the ideological cleansing must remain inadequately abstract. How could a witness transmit in symbolic language the impression produced by the routine shootings without trial, the slave labor of Republican POWs, the terror of being rounded up by Nazis in occupied France at the behest of Francoist authorities, the months and years in prison fearing the nightly executions, the macabre intimidation of entire populations? A witness is someone whose eyes are full and whose mouth jams as he or she tries to articulate the private images in common language.

Although novels and films about the war and the postwar period never transcend their fictional status, they perform an important social function by structuring the garbled grammar of the emotions and introducing sense into the erratic logic of experience. But that sense is made ambiguous by the fact that these cultural products often replace, and so displace, the historical actors' direct encounter with the public sphere and the reader's or viewer's experience of being summoned to that encounter. Witnessing is more than acting as a medium; the witness must consciously recollect the origin of present reflexes and dispositions,[3] laying bare the impulse to repeat the archaic scenario of victimization either symbolically or in fact.

What feeds the debates about historical memory in post-Franco Spain is not the absence of knowledge about the past but the unwillingness to face up to that knowledge and to draw practical consequences for the public sphere. If we admit the social origin of statistically significant human behavior, then we will have to admit that the diffuse violence in contemporary Spain originates at least in part in the sadism unleashed during the war and postwar period. Having seeped into the ground of collective life, that violence reemerges through a transformation neurosis not only in the reactive violence of terrorism and the counterreactive persistence of torture and the readiness to countenance torture[4] but also in violence with a clear scapegoating component, ranging from the symbolic and discriminatory violence against minorities to neofascist violence against immigrants and paupers and to the spectacular incidence of domestic violence, mostly against women. Freud remarked that the stronger the resistance to confront the past is, the more thoroughly will remembrance be substituted through action that repeats the aim of the repressed memory ("Erinnern" 521). Exactly in the same way, the transition's refusal to objectify the past in the public consciousness sustains the symbolic violence directed against the victims of the fascist uprising and sustains the victims' entrapment into their resigned humiliation, timidity, and even self-hatred. Symptoms of this state of affairs are the refusal to compensate individuals and groups for violations of their physical integrity and for property impounded during or after the war; the ongoing plunder of the "enemy" regions; the refusal to return private documentation considered war booty;[5] the rehabilitation of doctrines associated with the dictatorship; and, after only twelve years, the redeployment of the Francoist clans at the summit of political, media, and economic power.

To some extent the victims share the responsibility for the veil of silence thrown over the crimes. Traumatic events produce discontinuous memories. That events fester in the background while new memories intervene makes it difficult to retrieve experiences of utmost importance to the traumatized person.[6] Although the Franco regime continued to kill, torture, and abuse until its last day, intense and deliberate intimidation hindered the naming of the terror. Shortly after democracy was reestablished, a failed coup d'état in February 1981 quelled the transition's dynamic, burdening the political process with a stark reminiscence of its real origins. The storming of the Cortes by the *guardia civil* and the occupation of the streets of Valencia by the tanks of rebellious generals were compulsive repetitions of the events that had haunted the social unconscious of Spaniards for forty years.

At the time, the suppression of facts and the eradication of memories were rationalized as necessary for the consolidation of a democratic regime. Calling for reconciliation, politicians turned to the task of refashioning the truth of the nation, a task that involved refashioning the truth of Francoism as well. If, as Jane Jacobs claims, "Reconciliation is an official entry into the process of disclosing previously repressed aspects of the nation's history and setting these 'secrets' into a national framework of 'truth'" ("Resisting" 207–08), the Spanish transition offers a casebook example of deceitful reconciliation, with the consequence that the resulting national truth is rife with tensions. It is true, as Jacobs warns, that "what can and cannot be said in the emerging truth of the reconciled nation will not of course transcend existing power relations" (208). Precisely for this reason, the continued repression of certain voices, the impossibility of saying and even of excavating the full truth about the past, exposes the power relations that presided over the transition, set its limits, established its course, and coordinated its objectives. Construed as the demise of Francoism, the transition was, at heart, a timely sloughing off of the outer tissues without loss to the vital organs. A face-lift.[7]

One obstacle to the objective determination of the truth was the continued censorship under the form of barred access to the archives that contained the official documents of the repression. But if those sources were for the most part inaccessible, there was a wealth of memory waiting to be tapped: that of the survivors of the war and the repression whose voices had been silenced for decades. Their accounts could have furnished later generations with a sense of immediacy by filling in the sensory gaps in the official or academic accounts and laying bare the emotional folds where memories were buried. But this source was rarely mined.[8] Recently, however, there has been a surge of interest in oral history. The new proliferation of testimonies partakes of the worldwide fascination with traumatic memory, a fascination that was heightened, if not inspired, by Claude Lanzmann's *Shoah* (1985). It is difficult to ascertain if *Shoah* directly influenced the vogue of testimonial documentaries in Spain, since that film could not be watched there until 2002.[9] Lanzmann's obtrusive intervention and his strong transferential drive are absent from the Spanish documentaries, which studiously avoid his aggressive pressure on witnesses and his obdurate stance against "understanding" (see LaCapra, *History and Memory*).

In line with the tenets of oral history, Dolors Genovès produced the documentary *In Memoriam* for Televisió de Catalunya (TVC), the Catalan public television channel, in 1986. In a novel approach, instead of focusing on well-known political personalities, she interviewed ordinary working-class informants in their familial setting. Aiming to reconstruct the experience of the war for an ordinary working-class family, her interviews helped socialize memories that had remained private. In the course of the interviews, the deterioration of the public memory of the conflict became evident in the gap between the family transmission of the past to the younger generations and in the formal teaching of history at school. Six years later Genovès produced another documentary on the war, *Operació Nikolai* (1992; "Operation Nikolai"). Making use of hitherto inaccessible Soviet files, she traced the abduction and assassination of the POUM (Partido Obrero de Unificación Marxista) leader Andreu Nin in 1937 all the way back to Stalin. Then, in 1994, she struck closer to home with *Sumaríssim 477* ("Trial 477"), probing the memory of a Francoist crime in which Catalan fascists were implicated. Again making use of previously classified materials, Genovès reconstructed the court-martial and execution of Manuel Carrasco i Formiguera, a member of the Catalan government, in Burgos in 1938.

Genovès was not the first to break the taboo on fascist crimes. In 1989 Francesc Escribano had produced, also for TVC, a documentary on the final hours of Salvador Puig Antich, a young Catalan libertarian who was court-martialed for allegedly slaying one policeman, condemned without evidence, and executed in 1974 after the sentence was confirmed by the Council of Ministers presided over by General Franco. But *Sumaríssim 477* disturbed a tacit compact between the media and the powerful. The transition had put a premium on the perpetrators' self-protection. When Genovès was permitted to consult the files on Carrasco's trial, all those implicated were beyond their earthly reputations. Even so, the pact of silence on which the transition rested was so strong that the socialist vice president of the government forbade TVC to reveal the names of the witnesses for the prosecution. Genovès, however, insisted on full disclosure. After some hesitation, TVC let her have her way.

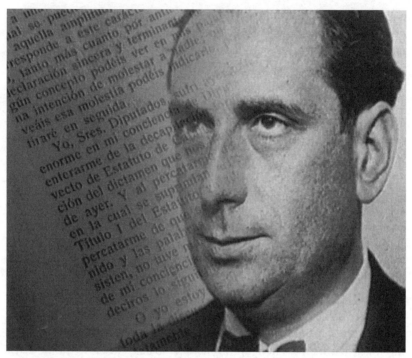

Portrait of Manuel Carrasco i Formiguera overlapped with the text of his intervention in support of Catalonia's Statute of Autonomy in the Republican Spanish
Cortes in 1932. His democratic defense of Catalonia's bill of rights constituted the
decisive argument for the death penalty passed on him by a court-martial six years
later. From Dolors Genovès's 1994 documentary *Sumaríssim 477.* Televisió de
Catalunya.

As might have been expected, the program rankled in a society that
put a premium on the dissembling of responsibilities. The perpetrators
were all dead, but they had left families behind, and some of the offspring
were well-placed. *Sumaríssim 477* ended with the statement that Carrasco
had been condemned exclusively on the testimony of the eight witnesses
for the prosecution. This statement became the centerpiece of a lawsuit
brought by the family of one of the witnesses, Carlos Trías Bertran, against
Genovès and TVC for slurring the honor of this former Francoist. The
controversy was byzantine, because there is no question that the court-
martial, however predetermined its outcome, drew its spurious legitimacy
from the formalities, and the protocol required the connivance of the witnesses. This same conclusion, in different words, was reached by the

Supreme Court when it overturned two previous sentences by lower courts that had ruled in favor of the plaintiff. In its sentence 216/1999, the Supreme Court stated, "The truthfulness [of the facts] is indisputable," refining its criterion of truthfulness to distinguish between documented facts and acceptable inferences: "The documentary narrates truthful facts and value judgments befitting a historian's [use of] scientific freedom."[10] The value judgments referred to the documentary's assumption that the witnesses volunteered their attestations, to the description of their testimony as "pitiless," to the use of the word "exclusively" in assessing the significance of the witnesses' depositions for the trial's outcome, and to the arguably implied suggestion of a link between the witnesses' conduct and the official privileges they enjoyed under the dictatorship.

Genovès was also criticized for dramatizing the court-martial.[11] But the main objection was to Carrasco's dignified last words to the court, denouncing its vindictiveness. Not only are those words not in the proceedings, but the record suggests that at the last moment the defendant pledged his allegiance to the National Movement in an effort to save his life.[12] Had Genovès falsified the record in order to show an unbroken martyr who goes down accusing his judges? To the charge that she had forged the evidence, she retorted that she had merely reproduced a statement from the defense counsel's allegation, whose author, she believes, was the lawyer Carrasco himself. Her decision raises a delicate question concerning the status of historical truth. Is this truth enshrined in literalism? Or does it call for judgment and thus for an ethical choice in the use of available documents?

The question is relevant not only with regard to the historian's sense of the priorities in the face of conflicting data but also with regard to her sense of the facts in dealing with documentary ambiguity or downright mendacity. Was she right or wrong to represent Carrasco uttering words, which, although extracted literally from the defense's allegation, may not have been voiced by the defendant in court? Were those words actually written by Carrasco, and did the judges replace the victim's statement with a cowardly adherence in extremis? Carrasco's plea for clemency in the name of his ad hoc adherence to the National Movement is formulaic and appears to have been used habitually by the defense in courts-martial. Should it be given more credibility than the defense's carefully prepared allegation, which doubtlessly reflects Carrasco's position? Which is historically truer: the statement Carrasco deliberately prepared either by himself or with the aid of his counsel, or the ritual words he might have pronounced when all was lost and the murderous nature of the process stared him in the face? These are all valid questions with no objectively verifiable answers. The audience must decide, and it can do so only through a transferential working out of the material, considering the facts and their internal relation against the background of what it, the audience, already knows.

There is no doubt that Genovès aimed for an effect. However, the presence of rhetorical features in the retrieval of the past is hardly remarkable (see H. White, *Metahistory* and *Tropics*). Her dramatized reconstruction of the court-martial may be compared with the docudrama, a film form that helps audiences come to terms with a difficult past through mimetic dramatizations. Apropos of the docudrama, Marita Sturken observes, "In the cultural reenactment of the original drama, coherence and narrative structure emerge, and fragments of memory are made whole" (85). This observation applies to Genovès's retrospection of Carrasco's life to the moment of his execution, but whereas docudramas constitute "a site for healing and redemption" (Sturken 89), *Sumaríssim 477* created a situation in which, ironically, the perpetrators could be portrayed as the victims of a vendetta. The general director of TVC, Joan Granados, apologized to the witnesses' families, faulting Genovès for her obsession to "get to the bottom of things."[13]

To criticize the dramatization of a trial is to miss the point about the nature of the documentary in the absence of historical footage. It is not just that Carrasco's plight was inherently dramatic; drama is inherent to television. Even in a direct situation such as an interview, says Martin Esslin, the main interest falls not on the facts but on the emotional impact (27). TV makes us witnesses by proxy and therefore contemporaneous with the emotions of the "in real time" witnesses. In a sense, viewers occasion the emotion. It is for their sake that the witness struggles with the failure of language, the loss of composure, and irrepressible pain and anguish.

Orality is the interview's inner law, and plausibility the touchstone of the interview's evidential value. This value is contingent on the interviewing techniques and the interviewer's emphases. When an interview is incorporated into a visual medium like television, new factors come into play that can affect the status of the evidence. The problem is compounded when the televised interview is interspersed with a different visual sequence, as happens often in the testimonial documentary. Under these conditions, the verbal message loses its linearity, increasing in symbolic value with the help of the visuals. TV makes the verbal messages more ambiguous than a purely verbal medium would. The images themselves are more ambiguous than in other media. Whereas cinema establishes regular conditions of viewing for limited audiences, TV establishes communication with an indeterminate audience in indefinable, pragmatic settings. The variability in interplay between the image and its conditions of reception gives TV messages a somewhat random or haphazard meaning (Wolton 66). But TV also brings forth an immediacy unavailable to verbal media. For example, it can contextualize interviews by furnishing the informants' physical environment (Thompson 235), although it does not always do so.

In *Sumaríssim 477*, Genovès used a mixed technique to great effect. The interviews were conducted in a nearly abstract manner, framing the informants to isolate them from their ordinary surroundings so that their voices might carry the full weight of the past. In that way the past that the interspersed visuals evoke can be grasped as the witnesses' relevant environment, indeed as the moral environment that the documentary seeks to capture and foreground as a bane secretly afflicting the present. It is the covert past that entices Genovès and focuses her attention on the assassination of an innocent man on whom a fascist court laid an inordinate, symbolic onus. "Carrasco is everything: he is Catalonia and he is the Republic," says the voice-over interpreting the sentence. That is why she reserves the conveyance of immediacy for the historical visuals and, to some extent, for the reenacted court-martial, inviting the emotional transference through the viewer's mediated proximity to the victim.

Techniques like editing and framing can smooth out the tension between the visuals and the discourse. One instance of this editing was Llum Quiñonero's *Mujeres del 36* ("Women of 1936"), produced for TV2,[14] a government channel, in 1999. Republican women from various parties and political associations were invited to reminisce about their wartime experiences. While some of them described harsh social conditions before the war, they were surprisingly silent about the fate of politicized women in the postwar period. Furthermore, their memories were strikingly free from any traces of trauma. Concha Liano, a member of the anarchist organization Mujeres Libres, described her participation in the revolution in the eager tone of a schoolboy recounting a field day. The desire to underscore female agency may account for the fact that Liano's more jovial presence intensified at the end of the program, outweighing the other testimonies, especially through the sense of closure given to her elated remark, "The things one can say now in Spain!" Ending on this note, the documentary unwittingly deactivated memory's potential for indictment, sublimating the pain that wells up from the past in the freedom that legitimates the posttransition state through the self-celebration of its media.

After *Sumaríssim 477*, TVC continued to produce documentaries about the civil war, but it was some time before it returned to the Francoist repression. In November 2000 it broadcast *Els últims morts de Franco* ("Franco's Last Killings"), a documentary about the last executions of the regime. In September 1975, five ETA (Euskadi Ta Askatasuna) militants had been court-martialed without procedural guarantees, without witnesses, and at one point without defense. A terminally ill General Franco confirmed their death sentences. Then, in March 2002, TVC launched a series of three documentaries under the title *Oblidar o recordar?* ("Forget or Remember?"). These programs deserve special attention, because, with the framing rhetorical question, TVC was laying bare the dilemma bequeathed by the transition.

The first installment was *Veus ofegades: Cartes d'un exili a França* ("Smothered Voices: Letters of an Exile in France"). This film, directed by Montserrat Besses, focused on the fate of the five hundred thousand Republican exiles (about half of whom were Catalan) who crossed the Pyrenees between February and March 1939. The film grips the viewer as it relates the conditions of internment in the camps of Argelès-sur-Mer, Saint Cyprien, Ribes Altes, and Agde. Confined without shelter, sanitary conditions, or adequate food supplies, internees huddled together or buried themselves in the sand to retain body heat during the cold winter nights. Their detention was aggravated by arbitrary family separations, isolation, and forced labor for the men. Some, considered dangerous elements on account of their political militancy, were incarcerated. After the German occupation, many men were handed over to the Germans and dispatched to Mauthausen, while women and children were sent to Franco's Spain. In unoccupied France, the Vichy government also "repatriated" Republican women and children and drafted the men into the infamous foreign labor corps. There, conditions were so bad that the men missed the concentration camps and some even escaped to occupied France, preferring to work for the Germans, who, needing to build their Atlantic defenses, paid the refugees for their work. Vichy, in the meantime, shipped unwilling Spanish workers to Germany as part of *la relève*, a prisoners-for-workers trade between the two governments.

The documentary centers on the letters written by refugees: letters describing the situation in the camps, begging political or, most often, economic assistance, and also letters from the families left behind in Catalonia, where hungry relatives deprived themselves in order to send some ounces of flour, a handful of worm-eaten beans, or a few eggs to their loved ones in wealthier France. But the letters that provide both the title and the pathos of this documentary are three hundred letters written between February and August 1939 and intercepted by the prefect of the district. Letters bespeaking affection and nostalgia, a wife's longed-for intimacy, the desperate pain of a mother who reports the death of a young daughter to an unsuspecting father, the unbearable hardship in the camp. Unread by their addressees, the letters were kept in the archives of the *département* of Haute-Garonne until 1998, when they were casually discovered. Smothered for sixty years, these spectral voices from the past sound in this documentary for the first time.

Next in the series was a documentary about the armed resistance to Franco during the 1940s. Inspired by Ferran Sànchez Agustí's book *Maquis a Catalunya,* Enric Calpena produced this two-part documentary, *Els maquis: La guerra silenciada,* balancing the testimonies of former resistance fighters, *guardia civil* officers, and villagers who had been accidental spectators of the skirmishes. But despite the neutral tone, the emotional dissonance inherent in the subject matter occasionally breaks through the civil, unimpassioned reporting, as when a former resistance fighter, after relating his interrogation by the army, explains that his now disfigured face was smashed on that occasion. Such moments bear out Dai Vaughan's definition of the documentary as "the attempt at a materialist reading of film" (108). The documentary is materialist in the sense that the resistance fighter's composed signaling to his broken face anchors the viewer's response in a past that cannot be reduced to fancy. The body underwrites the emotion that the image elicits from viewers. Thus, although the interviews synthesize a historical memory for reflection, the memory's overwhelming power stems from the transference of an emotional undercurrent that the witnesses' composed words can hardly conceal. This transference exists as much for the pain of the broken and defeated as for the resentment of the Francoist veteran who sixty years later still remembers the unpaid meat and bread requisitioned by the *maquis* during their failed incursion in Franco territory. Transference, as Dominick LaCapra observes, is inevitable as long as trauma is not inert. To the extent that the past is still with us, it implicates us in events we would rather inspect as impartial bystanders (*History and Memory* 40).

The third and last program in the series was *Els nens perduts del franquisme* ("Francoism's Lost Children"). In this documentary Montse Armengou and Ricard Belis tackled one of the least-known episodes of the dictatorship: the fate of imprisoned children. The film begins with the origins of fascist social experimentation, recalling the establishment, during the war, of the Gabinete de Investigaciones Psicológicas (Psychological Research Unit) on direct orders from General Franco. In this center, Dr. Antonio Vallejo Nágera, an apologist for the doctrine of racial purification,[15] experimented with POWs, hoping to prove that Marxism was a disease to which mentally retarded individuals were particularly vulnerable. Women, being intellectually feeble, were especially responsible for the revolutionary excesses on the Republican side. These were the "scientific" origins of a policy of preemptive education of Republican children about which few Spaniards knew or remembered the details.

Next, women are given the floor in front of the camera. Several recall their capture and transportation to prison. Suffocating in closed wagons, in the stench of excrement and the decaying bodies of dead children, they slowly made their way across Spain to their appointed places of captivity. Many of these women and children were arrested when the fascists failed to capture the men. Some of them lost their lives in place of their husbands and fathers. Others were refugee children who had been living in foreign countries until they were repatriated against their parents' wishes or the host countries' consent. The Gestapo aided Franco in the abduction of children residing in countries occupied by the Germans. Back in Spain, the children were renamed to prevent reclamation by their families, confined to special asylums, and raised in stern disciplinary conditions. The purpose was to preclude the emergence of a new generation of Republican-minded individuals, but punishing Franco's enemies was clearly part of the endeavor.

In the documentary, mothers describe how, in the appalling conditions of the prison, they tried to keep their infected children from being taken to the infirmary, from which none ever returned. One informant was a captive at the age of four. She remembers a child suckling from a breast on which the bow and arrows, the fascist symbol, had been branded. Another witness remembers a prisoner calling her child Lenin; the guards, infuriated by the name, smashed the child's head against a wall. One priest recalls the women's despair at being separated from their children moments before their execution and begging their butchers to kill the children with them. Nuns serving as prison wardens ate the children's rations. They did not succor dying children but praised God because the children went to heaven.

In 1936, shortly after the onset of the war, the Franco government created the Auxilio de Invierno (Winter Aid), a copy of Nazi Germany's Winterhilfe. Renamed Auxilio Social (Social Aid), it was placed under the direction of Mercedes Sanz Bachiller, widow of Onésimo Redondo, one of the earliest fascist leaders and a Nazi admirer. After 1943, through Auxilio Social twelve thousand children were placed in state or religious institutions. Asked about this mandatory state tutelage, Sanz denies having any knowledge of it. She also denies that mothers or children were abused in these institutions. By means of skillful editing, her statements are interlaced with the counterstatements of witnesses, former wards of the Auxilio Social who tell a chilling tale of inhumanity. By collating the witnesses' testimony with the perpetrators' denial, the documentary brings both parties face-to-face in a virtual courtroom for the viewer's ethical verdict. Furthermore, testifying against the deniers, the witnesses raise grave objections to the character of the democracy that supervened. Teresa Martín, who was incarcerated as a child, denounces society's culpable obliviousness:

> After forty years of dictatorship and twenty-five of democracy, people still don't know anything about what happened. . . . Not one of us has been given a voice; not in the TV channels, not in the radio or the press; not one of us. A couple of books, two dozen books. Much has disappeared, but when someone wants memory to endure, memory is there. All that person needs to do is ask, and I am speaking. We have not been given a voice. I am sixty-two, and it's the first time that I have spoken out. It's the first time someone asked me. (*Els nens*)

To denounce the perpetrators after a shameful pact of silence requires courage and the willingness to compromise a professional aloofness that may be disgraceful under certain circumstances. In *Sumaríssim 477*, Genovès relinquished the position of onlooker, a safe position that LaCapra considers "particularly questionable in the case of the Holocaust and other extreme or limit-events" (*History and Memory* 41). The real question, of course, is how extreme Spanish fascism was, how brutal and inexorable its sadism against the class enemy, the national minorities, and other resisters. The answers to this question fall along a spectrum of projective positions, some of which are anchored in compulsory forgetting. Genovès's attempt to crack the silence that protects the perpetrators had been impugned through censure of her professional ethics. But no one could refuse an incarnate victim the right to turn memory to account. In *Els nens perduts del franquisme*, Soledad Real, a frail old woman, proclaims with considered ardor, "I want to talk about this because I want people to know that something must be done. We may not weep. We must do, we must do something." Who could take exception to her exhortation?

Immediately after *Els nens perduts del franquisme*, TVC staged a two-tier debate, one in the television studio, featuring intellectuals and politicians, and the other in a bar, where young people born after the death of Franco gathered to speak about the convenience of forgetting or remembering. Although the debate among the seniors was undistinguished, the young people's discussion was memorable. Half of them expressed their impatience with a past that, in the words of the German historian Ernst Nolte, "does not want to go away." That past seemed too discontinuous with their lives to have any real claim on them. They argued in favor of letting the civil war dwindle into an academic subject. They also felt that fascination with the past paralyzes and attention to past injustices deflects attention from present issues. Although conventional, these arguments stated the case for turning the page and letting the older generation bury its dead.

The other youngsters retorted that the world is not a virginal place or Francoism something one can skip and move on. Without knowledge of the dictatorship, said twenty-one-year-old Montse Dalmau, much of what is happening today is incomprehensible—the return of neo-Francoists to power, for instance. "You just have to look at the present government. . . . They are all the legacy of new generations [of Francoists] and some old ones who stayed on." Marta Vallejo, nineteen years old, understood that information is not enough and that the intergenerational transmission of traumatic memory is crucial to historical evolution. Grief and anguish, the inevitable by-products of mourning, must be accepted to apprehend the—in her words—"hallucinated historical moment" lived by previous generations. That moment is hallucinated for the young, who must confront its ghosts in the twilight of the historical imaginary, but it is, or was, real enough for the witnesses—real in the psychoanalytic sense of something that shatters the ego's defenses. There is nothing surprising in young people's refusal to allow the real in memory to shatter the defenses that still protect them.

Joan Rota, a young man of twenty-four, also understood the intersubjective transmission of the scars of the past:

> We must be fully aware of our situation and [of the fact] that it has inherited this entire process. They [the previous generation] were educated in fear, and we ought to consider if our parents did not somehow educate us with the consciousness of all they have lived through.

Rota raises the important question whether it is possible, or even desirable, to approach the past without analyzing one's own relation to it. The fear of the vanquished and of the victims is loose on the historical scene, as are the arrogance of the victors and the impunity of the perpetrators.

If grief and anguish, or even anger, are the unpalatable affections experienced by those who try to cope with the past, anxiety may well be the emotion lurking behind the refusal to probe the past. Rota suggests as much when he asks, "Does the lack of mobilization among the young play any role in the subject we are discussing?" In other words, what is the relation between conformity and forgetting? Replying to Juan Reguera, a twenty-six-year-old who had earlier derided the notion of trying to distinguish among old people those who were victims from those who were perpetrators, he goes on to say, "We cannot afford to have people walking around who were directly implicated in death penalties, in executing whomever they found annoying at that time." Rota understands that only if memory is hitched to action can the compulsion to repeat be finally curbed. Freud had pointed out that a traumatic disorder cannot be healed by treating it as a historical matter; it must be viewed as an actual power in the present ("Erinnern" 521). For the young man it is urgent that people discern that the traumatic experience of the past lives on in the social forces that oppress us in the present. In this light, the transition's pact of silence appears as a countertherapeutic procedure leading to the return of the repressed.

Freud believed that the way to control the drive to repeat was to transform it into a source of memory. But to accomplish this transformation, first the anxieties must be displaced to a safer ground where they can unfold without harm. Only then can the drives working at the root of trauma be recognized for what they are. I suggest that, in the social sphere, television is such a symbolic outlet for the processing of traumatic memory. By staging the anxiety that goes unacknowledged in everyday life, television creates an opportunity to scrutinize the traumatic past. Coupling the medium's intimacy with the detachment brought by the intervening screen, TV provides a transferential space where the drives can unfold as on a playground. The viewers who discharge their emotions through the phone line during the program's intermissions bring home this potential. Released from liability, their faceless voices move freely over the range of subject positions, from the neofascist who provocatively asserts that Franco raised Spain to its historical zenith to the outraged caller who, with a quivering voice, denounces the flaunting of portraits of Franco and José Antonio Primo de Rivera in certain homes in Barcelona.

The TVC memory documentaries do not attempt to suture the past. They do not resolve the viewers' anxieties by means of a structured narrative or other reassuring devices. On the contrary, the montage of historical photographs and film bonded by reconstructive sequences points to the elusive nature of a memory in ruins. Each image proclaims its merely symptomatic value and calls for exegetic action on the part of the viewer. Thus, the images' instability foregrounds their semantic displacement. They are inevitably objects of interpretation. Their truth depends not only on their anchorage in something that was actually there but also on a retina that can no longer behold that something except by means of transference and in the illumination of the pale light that comes from another time somewhere beyond the screen. Images, seen in this way, are "after-images,"[16] windows of opportunity to trace the passage of the real over the surface of the eye.

Notes

1. For a concise discussion of the government's decree on secondary education and the Real Academia de la Historia's report on history textbooks, see Resina, "Short of Memory" 114–17.

2. All translations are mine, unless otherwise indicated.

3. This is one reason why survivors are rarely pleased with films allegedly made in their honor. Vicente Aranda's *Libertarias*, for example, met with the disapproval of the real militia women.

4. Eric Sottas, director of the World Organization against Torture, is alarmed at the growing approval of torture as an antiterrorist method among Spanish and Basque citizens (Arbós).

5. I refer to the affair of the Salamanca papers, the archives of the Generalitat de Catalunya and of various Catalan cities, organizations, and individuals impounded by the fascists. Filed in the Archivo de la Causa General contra el Marxismo, el Separatismo y la Masonería, which was renamed the Archivo Histórico

Nacional, Sección Guerra Civil, shortly after the transition, these papers were used by Franco's Brigada Social to persecute, torture, and execute individuals. The scandal surrounding these "blood papers" lies not only in the government's refusal to return them to their rightful owners—in defiance of The Hague International Agreement on the Protection of Cultural Property in Case of Armed Conflict—but also in the inclusion of these stolen materials in an exhibition on the occasion of Salamanca's turn as 2002 European City of Culture. The significance of this issue in connection with the topic of memory and the persistence of the traces of the war into the posttransitional society can be gauged by the fact that people in Salamanca are terrified of speaking out against the government's position. Some, including the archive staff, have done so on condition of anonymity, and the only local journalist who spoke in favor of returning the documents was fired from his newspaper. In February 2006, thirty years after the documents' reclamation by the Catalan government, the first truckload of files was delivered to the legitimate owners, not without extraordinary resistance and delaying tactics on the part of the neo-Francoist mayor of Salamanca and the regional government of Castilla-Léon.

6. In July 2002, as I was writing this essay, a mass grave was excavated in the province of León, at the site where thirty-seven Republican militiamen were shot on the night of 5 November 1937. The existence of the grave was known to villagers all along, but no one had dared speak about it. Other mass graves have been found, and others are sure to turn up as people start "remembering" crimes from more than half a century ago. It has taken that long to establish the number of people killed by the fascist repression, which historians now set at 150,000.

7. Many political analysts deny the continuity between the two regimes. Paloma Aguilar Fernández, for example, asserts, "Today, it is evident that in the end there was a break with the past, since the current Spanish democracy is, without doubt, consolidated and the [political] balance is comparable to that of many other European countries" (13). Significantly, Aguilar grounds her opinion in the fact that the new democracy did not assign political or juridical responsibilities for the fascist crimes (14). Thus, she indirectly confirms the links among impunity, continued repression of the facts, and the less than immaculate nature of the political pact and of the regime that evolved in its wake.

8. Ronald Fraser was the first to apply the principles of oral history to the Spanish Civil War (*Blood of Spain: An Oral History of the Spanish Civil War*).

9. When *Shoah* opened in Madrid, a group of Castilian neo-Nazis distributed negational propaganda under the protective gaze of the police. During the projection of the second part, a bomb warning caused the police to evacuate the theater, and the projection was never resumed. Thus the film's running in Barcelona in 2002 constituted its true premiere in Spain.

10. The daily *El país* reported the sentence on 18 March 1999 ("El Tribunal").

11. Arcadi Espada called it "a cheap stylistic exercise" (189).

12. According to the proceedings, Carrasco, when asked by the president of the court if he had something to declare, appealed to the court for leniency on the grounds of being Catholic, being married and the father of eight children, and being "today a supporter of Spain's Salvation Movement or desiring its triumph."

13. A narrative of this episode is given by one of its instigators, the journalist Arcadi Espada.

14. I thank Alonso Carnicer and Judith Aranich, of TVC, for kindly supplying the visual materials discussed in this essay.

15. In *Eugenesia de la hispanidad*, a book on racial eugenics, he pathologized the poor and working classes and laid out the politics of segregation, sexual control, and indoctrination later implemented by the Franco regime.

16. For a discussion of the concept of "after-image," see Resina, "Concept."

Noël Valis

Civil War Ghosts Entombed: Lessons of the Valley of the Fallen

On 1 April 1959, Generalissimo Francisco Franco ended his speech inaugurating the civil war monument the Valley of the Fallen (El Valle de los Caídos) with these words: "The dead demand of us . . . that we keep alive for all the generations the lessons of History, thus making the blood they so generously spilt fecund, . . . that their blood be the last shed in wars among Spaniards" (qtd. in Sueiro 243).[1] In a similar vein, the chief architect of the monument complex saw it as a "tangible remembrance of a tragedy that must not be repeated. Perennial lesson of our history" (D. Méndez 11). For Franco and his architect, the lessons of history were as clear and bright as the blood image of the civil war dead. But what were those lessons, and does the Valley of the Fallen transmit the same message to us now? Does this monument indeed teach us anything? If what remains of historical events are more often than not merely images, or representations of history, what do we do with more tangible reminders like monuments? How can we infuse the breath of history into dense stone for our students? Is it true that the substance and actions of history vanish when we try to talk about such things? Can history mean so little?

In 1970 when I first went to Spain, I could not make myself enter the Valley of the Fallen.[2] This monument, after all, represented Franco's dead;

the Republican dead were there only as ghosts. By April 2001, however, I had changed my mind. As we passed through the series of antechambers leading to the heart of the underground basilica, where Franco and the Falangist leader José Antonio Primo de Rivera are entombed, my companion and I felt at once appalled and fascinated. The monumental proportions of the complex dwarf the human presence. The nave is bigger than Saint Peter's in Rome and Saint Paul's in London! While many fascist buildings, sculptures, and monuments have disappeared or been transformed into something else, this one perseveres, despite periodic demands for its destruction or conversion. Spanish travel agencies now call it a tourist horror ("espanta-turistas"), claiming it a "politically incorrect" place to visit in these democratic times ("Todavía").

But such sites as the Valley of the Fallen should be preserved, no matter how embarrassing they prove to current governments, to remind us of the terrible cost in human lives, freedom, and dignity that these monuments represent. One of the difficulties in communicating the significance of this monument to students has to do with its physical and ideological impact, the immediacy of seeing it firsthand. Most students won't have that opportunity. So teachers need to find other ways of making this material real. There is an even more fundamental question that monuments like this one pose: how to retrieve the memory of history itself. As James Young remarks, "It is as if once we assign monumental form to memory, we have to some degree divested ourselves of the obligation to remember" (94).

With the Valley of the Fallen, however, there is more than collective and individual amnesia at stake. History itself has been airbrushed out of the picture. The way that the Franco regime presented the monument to its visitors constitutes in itself a significant part of that history. Appropriately, Young contends that historical inquiry, particularly with regard to commemorative forms, should include "the combined study of both *what happened* and *how it is passed down* to us" (11). To uncover the specific history and significance encased in the Valley of the Fallen gives us insight into the ways the Spanish Civil War continues to haunt history at both the local and international levels.

I see two interconnected approaches as especially useful to students' understanding of the subject. First, the monument complex needs to be contextualized locally, which means our situating it within Franco's obsession with resurrecting Spain's past imperial and Catholic greatness while obliterating modern history, especially the Republican era. Two kinds of cultural-historical texts can help penetrate the intimidating facade of the Valley of the Fallen. First are speeches by Franco and regime spokesmen and other forms of discourse, such as recorded testimony of those who built the memorial; and architecture itself—namely, the relation between the Escorial of Philip II and Franco's monument. Second, it helps us understand the concrete circumstances and significance of the monument as fascist architecture when we compare it with the aims of contemporary architecture in fascist Germany and Italy. At both levels, the Spanish Civil War turns out to be what distinguishes Franco's monument not only from the Escorial but also from such sites as Hitler's new Reich Chancellery or Mussolini's Sacrarium of the Martyrs.

Before we enter more fully into the differences (and similarities), some background to the creation of the monument complex is necessary. The decree authorizing the Valley of the Fallen was promulgated 1 April 1940, precisely one year after the war's end. From the beginning, this was the generalissimo's personal project. "It drove me crazy with impatience," he said, "trying to identify and locate an image [of the site] that I had been carrying inside my head for quite some time" (Pérez de Urbel 6). The Cuelgamuros Valley, situated only a short distance from Philip II's palace-necropolis, El Escorial, seemed "predestined" as the sacred site for the memorial Franco planned, according to the abbot of the Benedictine monastery that is part of the complex (10). The Valley of the Fallen, which took nearly twenty years to complete, was meant to serve as the final resting place for those who had died fighting for the Nationalist crusade. But it was also a monument to Franco himself and to the power of his regime. Thus the presumed sacredness of the site is irremediably politicized from the start.

To appreciate the dramatic impact of this memorial, imagine a long, winding drive into an extraordinary landscape of craggy masses, reforested pines, oaks, and black poplars. From a distance you see the 410-foot-high cross that dominates the valley (fig. 1). Surrounding the cross are monumental sculptures of the four evangelists and the four cardinal virtues. The first thing you come to are the four "Juanelos," sixteenth-century stone monoliths created by Juanelo Turriano (fig. 2). These massive, cylindrical objects seem oddly modern in their abstract plainness and vaguely menacing. A flight of ten steps (a repeated Decalogue motif of the complex) gains you access to an imposing esplanade; another ten steps take you to the underground basilica built into the rock (fig. 3). An enormous pietà rests on the cornice of the principal facade. You move through a series of

Figure 1. 410-foot-high Cross, Valley of the Fallen. Archivo Fotográfico Oronoz.

Figure 2. The four "Juanelos," sixteenth-century stone monoliths, Valley of the Fallen. Archivo Fotográfico Oronoz.

Figure 3. Esplanade, with Decalogue of ten steps, Valley of the Fallen. Archivo Fotográfico Oronoz.

antechambers (a vestibule, an atrium, and an intermediate space) and a traditional iron gate decorated with warriors and martyr saints, before coming to the nave itself. This drawn-out passage into the basilica at once suggests a staged form of spiritual preparation and a depersonalizing message of immense political power. Indirect lighting contributes to the theatrically hushed atmosphere. In the intermediate space, two bronze archangels in niches, Saints Gabriel and Michael, stand guard, striking an attitude that is "meditative and vigilant," in Justo Pérez de Urbel's words (26). It is difficult, however, to see these sculptures as meditative, given their massive size looming over us and their physical stance, hands firmly clasped on long swords. Traditional subjects of religious art, they incorporate both spiritual and secular motifs, seeming more warriors than saints. The wings look artificially attached to soldiers' bodies. Inside the nave, Franco's burial site is situated at the foot of the altar.

Students at this point may be tempted to dismiss the monument as "at once absurdly kitsch and cruelly frightening," as Elizabeth Nash remarks (182). The excessive proportions of the complex, along with the incongruities of spiritual ornamentation subjected to secular aims, certainly induce such a view of hollow grandiosity. More significant, the Valley of the Fallen has been emptied of much of its historical context. This historical void is both intentional and accidental, in the way that the history of the monument has been passed down to us. Tourism has contributed its share toward neutralizing the effect and meaning of the memorial. The 1998 *Michelin Green Guide to Spain* sums up the site as a "striking monument to the dead of the Civil War" (336). A current guidebook says that it "was the express desire of its founder [Franco] to construct a final resting-place for the fallen of both sides during the civil war of 1936–1939" (Tornero 5).[3] But neither the 1940 decree nor Franco's 1959 inaugural speech nor any other official government document suggests that the Valley of the Fallen was intended for both sides of the conflict. Only belatedly did the regime make awkward overtures to the families of the Republican dead, stipulating, however, that they had to be Spanish and Catholic.

By juxtaposing texts of the regime with the content-neutral words of guidebooks, students can begin to understand not only how ideology works but also how to interpret and question what texts cover up: in this case, the exclusion or silencing of one side of a bloody conflict. Roland Barthes's notion of myth as "a type of speech chosen by history," in which history has been banalized or emptied of its meaning, is a useful tool in this regard (*Mythologies* 110, 142). Take, for example, the preamble to the 1940 decree authorizing the construction of the Valley of the Fallen:

> The dimensions of our Crusade, the heroic sacrifices entailed in victory and the transcendence that this epic has had for the future of Spain, cannot be perpetuated by the simple monuments with which the salient events of our History and the glorious episodes of our people have generally been commemorated in towns and cities. The stones that will be erected must have the grandeur of ancient monuments, they must defy time and forgetting, and they must constitute a place of meditation and repose in which future generations will render admiring tribute to those who bequeathed to them a better Spain. It is to these ends that the choice of a secluded place responds, where the grandiose temple of our dead will be raised that, for all eternity, prays for those fallen on the path of God and Country. A perennial place of pilgrimage, in which the grandeur of nature will make a worthy frame to the land in which the heroes and martyrs of the Crusade repose. (qtd. in D. Méndez 314)

Three images in Franco's rhetoric stand out here: "our Crusade," "the stones that will be erected," and "the grandeur of nature" as "a worthy frame." As many historians have noted, the crusade is a fundamental trope of the regime. The war itself was conceived in similar terms, as an epic struggle for national salvation against the demonized, "red" Spain of the republic. "Spain had been reconquered as sacred space," as Michael Richards remarks (*Time* 71). Such rhetoric reminds us that in many ways the Spanish Civil War was also a religious war, a "struggle between traditional triumphalist Catholicism and liberal-proletarian secularism," in the words of one historian (Payne, Preface xi; see also Vincent in this volume).

The Valley of the Fallen provides a concrete example to students of how the rhetoric of the war, from the Nationalist side, becomes literally materialized in stone. To make those stones speak, however, the teacher needs to return to the words of Franco and those of other apologists of the regime such as Abbot Pérez de Urbel and the architect Diego Méndez. The monument speaks, in effect, of a holy war. Over and over Francoists justified their rebellion against the legitimate Republican government as a holy war and thus a just one. But is a holy war the same as a just war? Is a holy war possible, or is it a contradiction in terms? The Valley of the Fallen, like the war it invokes, offers students and teachers a platform of discussion on a subject that is equally compelling now, after the events of 9/11. Particularly apposite are Jacques Maritain's eloquent words:

> Just or unjust, war against a foreign power or war against fellow-citizens remains . . . , of necessity, what it really is by its own nature, something profane and secular, not sacred. . . . And if sacred values are in question, defended by one side and attacked by the other, this does not make the profane complex either holy or sacred; on the contrary, the sacred values are secularised by this profane complex and dragged down to its temporal ends. (31; see also J. Sánchez, *Spanish Civil War* 155)

A just war is not a holy war. It can also be argued, as moral theologians have traditionally upheld, that a war that causes greater evils than those it opposes may not be considered a just war.

The second image—"the stones that will be erected"—speaks to us not only of how those stones were raised but what they signify. The language of the decree suggests a passive agency bereft of human contact that will assemble these stones. Moreover, they will "defy time and forgetting." How can students get past such dehistoricizing clichés? By juxtaposing these words with those of some of the men who actually built the Valley of the Fallen, namely Republican prisoners whose numbers were overflowing Franco's jails, detention centers, and concentration camps in the early 1940s. Their testimony, which can be found in Daniel Sueiro's taped interviews (*El Valle*) and in Rafael Torres's *Los esclavos de Franco*, speaks volumes of forced labor conditions, by which Republican prisoners were able to reduce their sentences (see also Juliá). That Franco criminalized those who had supported the Republic was an example of his "politics of revenge" (Preston, *Politics*; see also Richards in this volume). Many political prisoners died building the monument, either through accidents or silicosis; others were maimed for life. We have no reliable statistics for these deaths and accidents, which is another way that history has been passed down to us by omission or silence. Forgetting has, in truth, been built into the Valley of the Fallen, despite the decree's rhetoric (see Aguilar Fernández, *Memoria* 116–30).

The stones of this memorial speak in yet another way. That "grandeur of ancient monuments" alludes to the past splendor of imperial, Catholic Spain and, more pointedly, to the nearby sixteenth-century Escorial of

Philip II, which served as an ideological touchstone for the regime, its Herreran neoclassical style inspiring much Francoist architecture, including the Valley of the Fallen (Coad 224). The Escorial not only stood for the symbolic power of kingship but also served as the burial place for the Hapsburg dynasty, establishing a deep "connection between death and the sacred character of the Spanish monarchy," as Carlos Eire points out (366). It was also the repository of several thousand holy relics, which Philip II obsessively collected. Franco's relics in the Valley of the Fallen are the dead themselves. Like the Escorial, the monument has death at its center. Unlike the Escorial, it was also built on a foundation of death, the deaths of Republican prisoners. These are the ghosts of the Spanish Civil War, forever entombed in the stones of this memorial. Franco's obsession with past imperial greatness led him to emulate Philip II in the building of his own mausoleum as a second Escorial (see Preston, *Politics* 42, 45; Elizabeth Nash 185).

Finally, we come to the third image-cliché in the preamble, nature as a frame for the Valley of the Fallen. The trope of nature performs two functions. It effectively dehistoricizes and thus naturalizes the monument site. But it also sacralizes it. From the very beginning, the Cuelgamuros Valley was conceived as sacred space. The mental image Franco projected of the place already situates it in the realm of the sacred, by making it the singular object of a quest. Both processes of sacralization and naturalization erase the monument's historical specificity. Thus a recent guidebook can continue to say that the giant cross "seems like a prolongation of the rock itself" (Tornero 10) or, as in Diego Méndez's book, that the valley itself was a "great basilica of nature" (173). By comparing official documents like the 1940 decree with guidebooks, students should be able to see how both kinds of texts effect an erasure of history (see Aguilar Fernández 125–26 for more guidebook examples). The 1940 decree is, strictly speaking, historical for us now; in the Barthian sense, it is also myth. By grasping this distinction, students are on the way to understanding as well how the Spanish Civil War has been at once present and absent in the history of Spain since 1939.

Like the civil war, the Valley of the Fallen has an international context. This architecture is, after all, fascist, with its counterparts in Germany and Italy. In both the social and the artistic realms, the Franco regime claimed to have returned to what was authentically Spanish. "The principal potentiality of our Crusade of Liberation," Franco said in his 1959 speech, "resided in having returned us to our essential being, Spain having found itself once more" (qtd. in Sueiro 241). Pérez de Urbel wrote that "all the work here [in the Valley of the Fallen] is Spanish" (35). For Méndez, the monument had been built "to honor and glorify racial virtues" (12). The Republican prisoners in Cuelgamuros, on the other hand, represented an anti-Spain. This construction of Spanishness bears some resemblance to the cult of Romanness in fascist Italy and of Aryan purity in Hitler's Germany (Coad 223; Affron and Antliff 15–16). Like much Nazi art, the Valley of the Fallen architecturally looks to the past as authenticating its national character. In contrast, Italian fascist art, with its origins in futurism, was more often decidedly modernist in vision.

German fascist architecture and Franco's monument both demonstrate a palpable "loss of any sense of scale" (Adam 227). Everything is excessive. The monumentality of the Valley of the Fallen had the same aims as Nazi architecture: "to impress and to intimidate" as well as "to unite the people" (227). To reach Hitler's inner sanctum in the new Reich Chancellery, one had to walk 720 feet through a series of rooms, recalling the staging of antechambers and long passageway to the basilica nave in the Valley of the Fallen. Monumentality was achieved through stone. And stone, in both Nazi and Francoist architecture, held deep symbolic meaning, as we have seen in Franco's monument (227).

Unsurprisingly, all three regimes drew on the notion of empire and Greco-Roman classicism as symbols of power and authority. But the Valley of the Fallen differs in a fundamental way, for underlying the neoclassical style is catastrophe, the sense of building on ruins, the ruins of civil war. Catholicism also distinguishes Franco's monument from fascist architecture in Germany and Italy, where religion did not play a dominant ideological role. Comparing the Valley of the Fallen with other national forms of fascist architecture should enable students to see more clearly how fundamental the memory of the Spanish Civil War is and how it is inscribed into this contested site in ways that are both visible and invisible. In 1959 Franco wrote that "Anti-Spain has been defeated and crushed, but it isn't dead" (qtd. in Sueiro 241). For Franco, symbol and stone fuse in this monument, and the lesson is obvious—yet, for us today, still invisible, like the civil war ghosts entombed in the walls.

Notes

1. All translations from the Spanish are mine.

2. After I finished this piece, I ran across Carolyn Kizer's poem "The Valley of the Fallen," in which she speaks of a similar reaction to the monument: "My hus-

band and I shudder a bit and smile—/ He's an architect, has seen photographs / Of Franco's grandiose memorial, / The Valley of the Fallen. / At first the thought appalled, but we've decided / It's part of architecture, part of history too, / So we drive the road from the Escorial. / Climb tiers and tiers of stairs, / Take in the view" (252).

3. The only video on the Valley of the Fallen that I know of is presented as an innocuous filmed guidebook, in which practically all history has been eradicated (see *El Valle de los Caídos*). As classical music swells in the background, the narrator describes the monument as a heroic, Franco-inspired enterprise dedicated to "the fallen." Still, pedagogically the film is useful as an ideological exercise. I am grateful to Eva Teba Fernández and Andrés Fuentes for locating this video for me. Newsreels following the progress of construction of the monument were standard movie fare (and propaganda) during the regime (see Lafuente, *Esclavos* 130–31). My thanks go to Michael Ugarte for pointing out this reference.

Jo Labanyi

Teaching History through Memory Work: Issues of Memorialization in Representations of the Spanish Civil War

I write this piece at the end of a new course to final-year undergraduates on how the Spanish Civil War has (or has not) been memorialized.[1] The aim of the course was not so much to provide information about what happened in the past as to make students reflect on the importance of, and factors conditioning, transgenerational transmission. My hypothesis was that, for twenty-two-year-olds to engage with the past, they must first understand why they should. The course proved hugely rewarding, for two reasons. First was the enthusiasm with which the students embraced the idea that they, as young people (some of Spanish origin but mostly not), had an ethical responsibility to be the bearers of the past for generations after them. I attribute this enthusiasm to various factors: the inclusion in the course materials of documents—photographs, printed and audiovisual testimonies—that gave direct (if mediated) access to the past as lived by individuals; the framing of the course with discussion of key theoretical texts on memory, mourning, and trauma, which provided a way of understanding the cultural issues, public and private, at stake in the memorialization process; and, most important, the placing of the students at the center of the transmission process, by engaging with the past from the vantage point of its reception at later moments—the dates of publication or exhibition of the cultural representations studied and the present time of the students in exploring this material. I return to these issues.

The second reason was something very special that happened. At the end of the first seminar, after a discussion of what promotes, allows, or blocks memorialization, a student came up to me (I recount this with her permission) to say she could now appreciate why her grandmother—the daughter of the Nationalist colonel who surrendered Teruel to the Republicans and was later shot by a Republican firing squad—had never spoken openly in the family about her father's death. The student (Natalia) was aware of certain objects in her grandmother's home that were connected with her great-grandfather: some on public display in the sitting room, most kept in her grandmother's bedroom closet. But her communication with her grandmother about this personal loss had been limited to two indirect forms of expression. First, Natalia had learned since childhood never to mention in her grandmother's presence the fact that it was snowing, because (as her mother explained to her) it was snowing when her great-grandfather was taken to his execution. Second, one day Natalia's grandmother came to her bedroom and gave her a photograph of the bishop of Teruel (Obispo Polanco, recently beatified), saying that she wanted Natalia to have it since he had died with her great-grandfather. Natalia could now appreciate that the sight of snow triggered a traumatic reenactment of the past for her grandmother and that the gift of the photograph was, effectively, her grandmother's gift to her of the past that she could not tell. Natalia wrote her project on how her great-grandfather's death had been memorialized (or not) in the family. She conducted a series of in-depth interviews with her grandmother that allowed her grandmother to tell her story in full for the first time.

This case brought home to all of us in the class a key point: the past cannot be transmitted unless there is an interlocutor willing to receive it. It also made us sensitive to the use of the word *trauma*, since, while Natalia's grandmother suffered from traumatic reenactments of the past, she was not a classic trauma victim in that every detail of the past remained engraved in her mind. She suffered not from a blocking of memory but from lack of a receptive audience. When studying the various testimonial texts required for the course, we kept finding that trauma theory was an inappropriate framework since, even though the effects of trauma were often apparent, the past had been registered perfectly clearly in the mind of the victims; the problem was the blocking not of memory but of the possibility of its telling (for another perspective on trauma and civil war memory, see Resina in this volume). This blocking, caused first by the Franco dictatorship, had been perpetuated by the *pacto del olvido* of the transition period, which facilitated the return to democracy through a collective agreement to consign past wounds to oblivion (Aguilar Fernández). Another lesson I learned from the story of Natalia's grandmother was that I had been mistaken in assuming that the obsessively repeated public rituals of mourning staged by the early Franco regime enabled the Nationalist bereaved to work through the mourning process. There were complex factors at play in this instance, since Natalia's great-grandfather had been repudiated as a traitor by the Nationalists for surrendering Teruel to save lives. Her grandmother was given permission to claim and rebury the body only in 1972, on condition that the press not be informed. But the triumphalist tone of the Nationalist public expressions of mourning did not allow private grief to be acknowleged. Natalia's interview with her grandmother taught me that the bereaved on the winning side also needed willing interlocutors, particularly since most scholars have been interested only in the story of the Republican losers. We should ask ourselves why we are so seduced by the stories of history's losers. I am not here advocating political neutralism but the need to listen also to the uncomfortable stories of those whose politics one deplores.

A major aim of this course, in focusing on issues of memorialization, was to go beyond empiricist concepts of historiography. The premise was that the historian cannot recover the past but can only chart a series of disappearances (Klein 1–23). That is, the historian's task is to track the traces of a past that has been lost forever but that makes itself felt in the present through its emotional and material residues. Sigmund Freud's classic essay "Mourning and Melancholia" is crucial here in its analysis of how people suffering loss introject the lost object: temporarily in the mourning process, indefinitely and pathologically in melancholia. Also crucial is the work on trauma that has been conducted particularly in relation to the Holocaust. Ernst Van Alphen stresses how trauma is not just "failed memory" but "failed experience," since our modern Western belief that the human subject is defined by its capacity for individual autonomy supposes that if we are denied any agency, we cease to be human. Van Alphen notes how Holocaust survivors often recount their concentration camp experiences in the third person, as if they had not experienced them personally for their complete lack of agency had made them things and not persons (28–29). In the circumstances of war and political repression with which we are concerned in this volume, people frequently found themselves reduced to the status of a thing. We can learn from Van Alphen's reminder that what can be remembered depends on the narratives that are sanctioned both politically and philosophically in any given culture.

There seems to be an absence in Spanish culture of representations of the civil war that set out to reproduce the fissured, nonnarrative structures of trauma. Instead of recollection, with trauma there is compulsive repetition in the form of reenactment. This replacement of narration with performance effectively involves a break with representation itself. One can draw a contrast with the work of the Chilean neo-avant-garde grouped around Nelly Richard's *Revista de Crítica Cultural*, whose break with representation and narrative in favor of an aesthetics of trauma has provided a major critique of the hegemonic narratives of Chile's transition to democracy.[2] The contrast is significant, because the consensual politics of the Chilean transition were based on an official rhetoric of mourning, whose goal was to bring rapid closure by laying the past to rest. The *pacto del olvido* of the Spanish transition, on the other hand, opted for oblivion without any prior phase of working through the past. A striking example of this failure to engage with the aesthetic implications of trauma is Carlos Saura's *¡Ay, Carmela!* (1990), whose realist aesthetics is at odds with its depiction of historical trauma (at the end the traumatized Gustavete recovers his voice). This disconnect is surprising since Saura's earlier *Cría cuervos* (1975; "Raise Ravens"), made as General Franco lay dying, is a superb example of a film whose structures echo those of traumatic antinarrative. Kathleen Vernon notes ("War") that the experimental films produced at the end of the Franco regime, when censorship required indirect statement, engage with the consequences of the civil war more successfully than do the plethora of recent films that represent the war in hyperrealist mode—for example, Vicente Aranda's *Libertarias* (1995; "Libertarians"), José Luis Cuerda's *La lengua de las mariposas* (1999; "Butterfly"), and Montxo Armendáriz's *Silencio roto* (2000; "Broken Silence"). The earlier films circumvent censorship by focusing not on the past but on the memory processes whereby an unspeakable past is recovered by later generations (hence the predilection for child protagonists).

The realist aesthetics adopted by most recent Spanish films about the Spanish Civil War suggest not only a concern to show off high production values (Vernon, "War") but also a lack of concern with the question of how the past is transmitted. This lack helps explain why intellectuals continue to accuse democratic Spain of collective amnesia, despite the existence of a nostalgia industry re-presenting the war and its aftermath in the form of heritage-style movies and facsimile editions of early Francoist school textbooks (Harvey). Fiction has been more concerned with exploring memory processes (Llamazares) and the need for transgenerational transmission (Muñoz Molina, *Beatus ille* and *El jinete polaco*; Cercas).[3] While one applauds the recent flood of historical works documenting the resistance fighters who waged war on the Francoist state until 1951 (S. Serrano, Marín Silvestre, among many others), it is noticeable that few Spanish historians have engaged with memory work, continuing to prefer an empiricist approach. A notable exception is Ángela Cenarro, whose oral history interviews with first- and second-generation survivors of reprisals in Aragón (on both political sides) have brought to the fore psychological factors—such as the internalization of guilt—that have made the memory of past violence hard to assimilate.

There is in fact a recent boom in testimonies related to the civil war and its aftermath, but it has been conducted not by historians but by newspaper and radio journalists (Leguineche and Torbado; Lafuente, *Tiempos*; Reverte and Thomás; Elordi) as well as by documentary filmmakers (see Camino's *Niños de Rusia*; Corcuera's *Guerrilla de la memoria*). The intellectual rigor of these works is problematic—there is an infuriating lack of information about the circumstances and editing of the interviews (as in the British historian Ronald Fraser's pioneering *Blood of Spain: The Experience of Civil War, 1936–1939*). Nevertheless they succeed in engaging the reader with the affective dimensions of the past, bringing it alive through this memory work in a way that no empiricist historian is able to achieve. We should also note here the recent efforts of the Asociación para la Recuperación de la Memoria Histórica (Association for the Recovery of Historical Memory) in digging up mass graves from the war, in order to identify the bodies. What is striking here is not that the bodies have been found—relatives mostly knew they were there—but that the identification of these remains finally allows the mourning process, and a proper burial, to take place, after a hiatus of over sixty years.

The question of what happens to a society that has not been allowed to mourn the victims of political violence for over sixty years is an important one. One should here interrogate the notion—encouraged by psychoanalysis—that remembering is always good and forgetting always bad. It depends on who forgets; on whether the forgetting is enforced or chosen; and on the reasons why it is chosen. The key point for those who have suffered atrocities is that past events must be recognized and transmitted. This process requires willing interlocutors who permit the passing of their stories to future generations. Frequently the transmission of knowledge about the civil war leapfrogs a generation (as with Natalia). Such leapfrogging raises the issue of postmemory, Marianne Hirsch's term for the memories by later generations of atrocities suffered by their parents and transmitted to them—by words, objects, or silences—through family life (*Family Frames*). The question of how later generations remember a past that they did not experience themselves is crucial to any concept of collective identity.

The other theoretical framework that was central to the course is Walter Benjamin's messianic concept of history, which gives the historian the redemptive role of scavenger among the debris of the past, concerned to rescue from oblivion the traces of history's losers (*Illuminations*). While I would argue that we should resist Benjamin's sole focus on the losers, his point that the providentialist vision of modern Western historiography edits out the multiple potential of the past that, through defeat, did not translate into subsequent events, is an important one, for it calls into question our notion of history as teleological, linear narrative. Benjamin's Angel of History—blown backward into the future by the storm of progress, with its face trained on the mounting wreckage of the past (249)—evokes a multidirectional notion of history that requires a rethinking of narrative. Eduardo Cadava argues that Benjamin's view of history is a photographic one, since Benjamin wants to arrest the forward march of time, detaching from their context the objects salvaged from the ruins of the past, in the process investing them with new meaning through their irruption into the here and now.

The course started by considering the photographs of the Spanish Civil War by the Hungarian anarchist photographer Kati Horna, donated by her to the Spanish Ministry of Culture after Franco's death.[4] These photographs are notable for the way they capture a moment in midflow, making us aware of the past through what is absent from the photograph: the invisible space outside the frame at which the figures are looking; the stories encapsulated in their material traces—photographs in the photograph; furniture piled in the street after a bombing raid; the evocation of the absent (dead?) occupant of a bed in a field hospital, present through the material memories of his suitcase, the cutouts of film stars on the wall, and the imprint of a body on the bedclothes (Labanyi, "Politics" 99–101).

The Benjaminian photographic reading of history permitted by Horna's photographs provided a way of reading the reliance on image rather than on narrative in Víctor Erice's *El espíritu de la colmena* (1973; "The Spirit of the Beehive") and the 2001 Spanish-Mexican coproduction by the Mexican director Guillermo del Toro, *El espinazo del diablo* ("The Devil's Backbone"). Both films use photographs to evoke a past that is not narrated: in the first, the family album that Ana leafs through provides the only information she—and we—have about her parents' prewar past; in the second, the family photographs that the film's villain, Jacinto, finds in the safe instead of the Republican gold he is looking for forces him to confront a past that he has attempted to annihilate. As Jacinto drowns at the film's end, these photographs float to the surface, as reminders of an unspoken past that insists on surfacing.

In keeping with this insistence on evoking a past that remains beyond narration, both films, in addition to dealing with children as the inheritors of an unspeakable past, adopt the horror movie format. In *Espíritu*, the unspeakable past is embodied materially by Frankenstein's monster (see also Deveny in this volume); in *Espinazo*, by the double ghosts of the murdered child Santi and of the Republican schoolteacher Dr. Casares, killed toward the end of the film. These films are graphic evocations of the concept of history as a haunting proposed by Jacques Derrida in *Specters of Marx*. Derrida elaborates the ethical imperative to acknowledge the ghosts of the past who summon us with their unwelcome gaze. As I discuss elsewhere ("History"), Derrida proposes hauntology as a replacement for an essentialist ontology, to develop a nonempiricist notion of history based on recognition of the traces in the present of a past irretrievably lost. His reading of ghosts is a materialist one, for ghosts are embodied, material traces that return to demand reparation: here Derrida is close to Benjamin's messianic concept of history.

In both Erice's and Del Toro's films, history is an absence evoked by its material traces: note the footprint in *Espíritu* into which Ana inserts her tiny foot; in *Espinazo*, the unexploded bomb embedded in the school courtyard, animated by its "heartbeat," which directs Carlos to Santi's ghost, whose demand for reparation he will meet. Del Toro's use of digital special effects constructs a very embodied ghost, for his ghost story has nothing to do with the supernatural but is, like Derrida's, a materialist reading of history. Erice depicts Frankenstein's monster first through Ana's subjective point-of-view shots, then moves to an objective vantage point that holds both the monster and Ana in the frame, implying that the monster is really there (Labanyi, "History" 78). Del Toro goes further, showing us Santi's ghost from an objective point of view before Carlos sees it, even filming several shots from the ghost's (and the unexploded bomb's) point of view. It is possible to read Del Toro's film as entirely narrated by the film's second ghost—that of Dr. Casares, so materially embodied that it is indistinguishable from the living figure—whose voice-over, reflecting on the question, "What is a ghost?," starts and ends the film.

Del Toro's training in the horror genre allows his film to evoke the civil war more successfully than recent realist films made by Spanish directors, because it does not attempt to represent historical events, instead dramatizing a ghost story that conveys their horror. The film's period realism is another special effect, reproducing the past in the form of its material residues rather than of events: we are close here to the Lacanian concept of the real as that which lies beyond representation. Erice made his film at a time when censorship prohibited unauthorized representations of history; Del Toro, filming in 2001, adopts a similar aesthetics of haunting that co-opts the postmodern stress on virtual reality (his use of digital effects) to make a statement about our duty to acknowledge the presence of an absent past. As the surviving boys limp off into an unknown future at the film's end, Dr. Casares's ghost stands guard over the school's ruins.

The use of the werewolf motif in Julio Llamazares's 1985 novel *Luna de lobos* ("Moon of the Wolves") about the Republican maquis (resistance fighters) in northwestern Spain similarly co-opts the horror genre. The novel's subject is not historical events but the memory process that keeps them alive. The last surviving resistance fighter, Ángel, is forced into exile when his village and family expel him from their memories. In a community no longer willing to keep his memory alive, he is already dead. His first-person narrative frequently describes the maquis as the living dead: an image found in the interviews Manuel Leguineche and Jesús Torbado conducted with people who went underground after the civil war, in many instances until the amnesty of 1969 if not later. Leguineche and Torbado collected these testimonies with *topos* ("moles") from 1969 to 1974 and published their research in 1977; *Los topos* anticipated by two decades the flood of printed and audiovisual testimonies that has appeared since the mid-1990s (the book was reissued in 1999). What emerges from Leguineche and Torbado's interviews with these ghosts of the past (several hid in makeshift underground graves) is a form of oral narrative whose temporality is not linear but discontinuous and repetitive—not because the speakers are marked by trauma (all seem to have perfect recall) but because popular memory constructs history as a discontinuous series of catastrophes (Samuel 6).

The temporality of *topo* testimonies is also constructed around family cycles, in this case signaling disaster instead of celebration. One *topo* recounts graphically how, when his wife became pregnant, she had to say that she had been sleeping around to avoid betraying her husband's presence in the attic. When her father died, leaving no other males in the household, the *topo* dressed in women's clothes so that the washing hanging out to dry would not give him away (Leguineche and Torbado 71, 83). These men—and their families—embodied an experience of history in which what could be seen was a mask for an unspeakable reality that revealed itself only through betrayal. These testimonies also operate according to a process of displacement whereby the impossibility of narrating the experience of being confined to immobility and invisibility for sometimes thirty years deflects the narrative into an account of what the speakers did in the civil war before they went into hiding. We get an overwhelming sense of people who, while skilled in the art of survival, were often caught up in history instead of being its agents. Again, we are reminded that we need forms of historical narrative that are not based on the assumption that its subjects are defined—at least, not all the time—by their capacity for individual autonomy.

This short account does not allow me to do justice to all the texts studied in the course I have described. The selection of texts—always contingent[5]—sometimes produced unexpected connections. For example, when we studied Juan Goytisolo's 1955 novel *Duelo en el Paraíso* (*Children of Chaos*) immediately after the 1941 film *Raza* ("Race"), based on a script written under a pseudonym by General Franco, it was curious to see how the sacrificial ethos elaborated in the film is repeated in Goytisolo's novel, albeit for personal motives and not out of service to the state—a sign, no doubt, of the difficulty experienced by the children of the victors in thinking outside the narratives sanctioned by their elders. The two versions of *Raza*—the original 1941 version having been destroyed after the 1950 remake, which excised the fascist salute and derogatory references to liberal democracy and the United States (Alberich)[6] –brought home the importance of viewing historical representations in the context of the moment of their reception.

The imbrication of the past in the present was also forcefully conveyed in the two film documentaries we studied, *Los niños de Rusia* and *La guerrilla de la memoria*. The start of *Guerrilla*, filming the former leader of the Agrupación Guerrillera de Sierra Morena, Comandante Ríos, on his way to work, makes the point that the ordinary-looking elderly people we see around us on the bus may carry quite extraordinary stories. Especially moving is the footage (included in the DVD extras) of the Gijón Film Festival, at which this film was shown in the presence of the former resistance fighters interviewed. As these men and women climb onto the stage to receive the audience's applause, we are made aware of the importance of giving recognition to those whose story remained untold—or perhaps we should say unheard—for so long.

Los niños de Rusia brilliantly combines interviews with former children evacuated to the Soviet Union during the civil war with Spanish and Soviet newsreel footage: this editing gives objective support to the first-person accounts but also shows (by zooming in on individuals) that behind every person in the archival footage lies a different story. The superimposition onto the faces of the interviewees of photographs of themselves as children produces a sense of the haunting of the present by the past. The film is notable for its juxtaposition of very different accounts of the same events; it ends with its subjects reunited over dinner, quarreling about the interpretation of the past. Several of its personal narratives also make us aware of how material objects can become carriers of memory: one evacuee, describing his departure from Spain, speaks of the blisters produced by his first pair of leather shoes—the pain of separation becomes condensed in a material hurt. Similarly, one woman fingers the ring on her hand, telling us that it is her mother's wedding ring; her mother gave it to her at the moment of departure. Later in the film we hear this same woman's story of how, on the day of her arrival back in Spain with the first returnees in the mid-1950s, she failed to establish any relationship with her mother, whom she never saw again. The ring remains on her hand as a replacement for an impossible connection to her origins. The one thing on which all the interviewees agree is the failure to bond with parents on their return to Spain; many went back to the Soviet Union.

By a fortunate coincidence, I was able to have present in the class a former child evacuee to the Soviet Union (the mother of a colleague). Benita's matter-of-fact account of her experiences growing up in the Soviet Union contrasted strikingly with the tone of high tragedy constructed by Camino's film (reinforced by the musical sound track). This contrast again made us aware of the importance of the intended audience: *Los niños de Rusia* supposes that its Spanish audience wants to hear a tragic story of loss of Spanish origins. Benita, happy to be what she called a citizen of the world, felt no attachment to Spain. If her oral account focused on her everyday life, Camino's film presents a narrative in which everyday life is interrupted and eclipsed by historical disasters (the Spanish Civil War, the German invasion of the Soviet Union). As noted above, we need to reflect on the dangers of being seduced by the story of tragic victims; to acknowledge the untold stories of atrocities does not mean that we should blind ourselves to the everyday stuff of which the past is made.

I conclude with an image from Manuel Rivas's novel (written originally in Galician), *El lápiz del carpintero* (1998; *The Carpenter's Pencil*). Its account of the journey through various Francoist prisons to exile of a leading figure of Galician nationalism, fictionalized as Doctor Da Barca, is dictated to the narrator (a former Francoist thug) by the pencil inherited by him from the Republican carpenter whom he shot, whose ghost whispers constantly in his ear. At the end of the novel the narrator gives the pencil to his interlocutor: a Lusophone African prostitute who, as another displaced migrant, is an appropriate inheritor of Da Barca's story. In a key chapter, Da Barca, treating a fellow prisoner plagued by the pain of his amputated foot, explains that he is suffering from "el dolor fantasma" ("phantom pain"): "They say it's the worst kind of pain. A pain that becomes unbearable. The memory of pain" (119). This image provides an eloquent gloss on the concept of history I have tried to elaborate in this essay. My concern has been to show how the exploration of the past through its memorialization can open up forms of historical understanding that connect the past to the present. Such forms accept that the past can be known to us only as a haunting, through the emotional and material traces of what is lost. This approach to the past places us at the center of the historical process, for without a chain of transgenerational transmission there can be no history.

Notes

1. The course was taught at the University of Southampton. Since 2006 I teach a revised version of the course to graduate students at New York University.

2. I acknowledge here my debt to my student Marcela Pizarro, whose PhD thesis examines the aesthetics of the *Revista de Crítica Cultural*.

3. A welcome exception to my criticism of recent films for their lack of concern with issues of memory and transmission is David Trueba's 2003 adaptation of Cercas's *Soldados de Salamina*.

4. A limited selection of Horna's photographs can be accessed on the following Web sites: www.barranque.com/guerracivil/horna.htm, www.mcu.es/lab/archivos/kati/menuindex.htm, www.uv.es/republica/kati/, and www.guerracivil.org/Diaris/981127pais.htm (last accessed Oct. 2003).

5. My choice of texts was inevitably constrained by what books and video versions of films were in print at the time. This constraint ruled out Aranda's *Libertarias*, which, while hugely disturbing in its representation of gender and especially

race, nevertheless allows discussion of how the role of women in the civil war has been memorialized. In future years, I expect to include Dulce Chacón's recent *La voz dormida* (2002; *The Sleeping Voice*). Based on extensive research and interviews, this novel gives voice to a range of women characters incarcerated after the civil war in Madrid's Ventas prison or involved in the resistance. Dedicated "a los que se vieron obligados a guardar silencio" ("to those who were forced to keep silent"), the novel is driven by an ethical impulse to transmit a forgotten past to younger generations. Its main female figure brings up the daughter of a female prisoner executed after giving birth in prison; the daughter will in turn take up her dead mother's political mantle.

6. Both versions have now been made available on video and DVD by Filmoteca Española; the DVD has invaluable extras.

Part VI

Resources

María Crocetti and Noël Valis

with the assistance of Isabel Jaén-Portillo, Regina Sloan, and Eleonora Crocetti

Introduction

There are an enormous number of primary and secondary materials pertaining to the Spanish Civil War. "Resources" is intended as a representative selection and guide to this wealth. We have divided this section of the volume into cinematography, music, photography, posters, poetry, prose, and secondary sources.

Asterisks in the cinematography entries indicate that we were unable to view the documentary or feature film listed but felt we should include it, in the hope that readers might be more successful than we were in finding it. To locate films, we searched the Net and consulted catalogs (e.g., that of Films for the Humanities, which unfortunately has terribly overpriced items) and bibliographies. The Instituto Cervantes has a large collection of films listed online, which it lends to its members. We also recommend that readers check out some of the Web sites in "Resources," particularly that of ALBA (the Abraham Lincoln Brigade Archives), from which some documentaries are available, and new Internet services like Netflix.com. We note the available formats of films, keeping in mind that many departments now have cassette and DVD players that will play both PAL (Phase Alternating Line) and NTSC (National Television System Committee) formats.

We briefly annotated entries in cinematography, music, photography, posters, poetry, novels, short stories, plays, and dialogues. Publication details for entries under "Photography," "Posters," "Poetry," "Prose," and "Secondary Sources" are in Works Cited. Whenever possible, English translations have been included.

There are probably thousands of novels on the war. For more information, see Maryse Bertrand de Muñoz's *La guerra civil española en la novela: Bibliografía comentada* and *La novela europea y americana y la guerra civil española*, both of which annotate civil war fiction produced in several different languages; Bertrand de Muñoz's *Literatura sobre la guerra civil* references novels, short stories, plays, memoirs and testimonies, film, iconography of the war, and secondary sources.

Cinematography

Documentaries

Art in the Struggle for Freedom. Dir. Abe Osheroff. United States: A. Osheroff, 2000. 28 mins. Videocassette, NTSC.

On the role and significance of posters, poetry, and music for the Republican side.

Bilbao para España. Dir. Fernando Delgado. Spain: CIFESA, 1937. 26 mins.
Nationalist film focusing on Basque separatists as the "anti-Spain."

The Canadians / Los Canadienses. Dir. Laszlo Gefin and Albert Kish. Canada: Natl. Film Board of Canada, 1975. 60 mins. Videocassette.
On the MacKenzie-Papineau Battalion of the International Brigades.

Canciones para después de una guerra. Dir. Basilio Martín Patino. Spain: Turner, 1971, 1976. Distributor: José Esteban Alenda. 100 mins. Videocassette, PAL and NTSC.
Evokes through songs popular cultural memory of the postwar period.

Casas Viejas. Dir. José L. López del Río. Spain: Andalusí-Cine, 1983. 137 mins. Videocassette, PAL.
A dramatic reconstruction of the anarchist uprising at Casas Viejas.

El caudillo. Dir. Basilio Martín Patino. Spain: Fotofilm, 1977. Madrid: Metrovideo–Imagen 35. Films for the Humanities. 130 mins. Videocassette, NTSC.
A biography of Francisco Franco from his birth to the end of the Spanish Civil War. Viewpoints from the Republican and Falangist sides. Includes poems of Rafael Alberti, Pablo Neruda, Luis Fernández Ardavín, and Antonio Machado and songs from the civil war.

La ciudad universitaria. Dir. Edgar Neville. Spain: Departamento Nacional de Cinematografía, 1938. 13 mins.
Falangist director Neville depicts the Nationalist occupation of the University of Madrid campus.

El comboi dels 927. Dir. Montse Armengou and Ricard Belis. Spain: Televisió de Catalunya, 2004. 53 mins.
Focuses on a train filled with 927 Republican refugees, from which the men ended up in the Mauthausen concentration camp in 1940.

Death in El Valle. Dir. C. M. Hardt. United Kingdom: CM, Channel Four Television, 1996. 50 mins. DVD, NTSC, PAL.
C. M. Hardt goes back to El Valle to investigate the death of her Republican grandfather after the war. First shown in Spain in 2005.

De toda la vida / All Our Lives. Dir. Carol Mazer and Lisa Berger. Spain and United States: Point of View, 1986. 52 mins. Videocassette, NTSC. With English subtitles.
Interviews with anarchist women.

Dreams and Nightmares. Dir. Abe Osheroff. United States: A. Osheroff, 1974. 54 mins. Videocassette, NTSC.

Osheroff, an Abraham Lincoln Brigade veteran, returned secretly to Spain to film this footage. Personal reminiscences of the war.

Durruti en la revolución española. Dir. Paco Ríos. Spain: Fundación Anselmo Lorenzo de Madrid, 1998. 55 mins. Videocassette, PAL.
On Buenaventura Durruti, libertarian Communist militant leader.

España heroica. Dir. Joaquín Reig, with Paul Laven and Fritz C. Mauch. Spain and Germany: Falange Española Tradicionalista y de las Jons, Hispano Filmproduktion, 1937. 71 mins. German version, 1938. 86 mins. Also known as *Helden in Spanien.*
Newsreel archive footage, pro-Franco.

España leal en armas. Dir. Jean-Paul Le Chanois. Spain and France: Susecretaría de Propaganda del Gobierno de la República, 1937. 35 mins. Also known as *España 36.* French (*Espagne 36*) and Italian versions. Prod. Luis Buñuel.
Featured in the Spanish Pavilion at the 1937 World's Fair in Paris.

L'espoir / Sierra de Teruel. Dir. André Malraux and Boris Peskin. Spanish dialogues by Max Aub. France: Édouard Corniglion-Moliner, 1945. Argentina: Kinema. 106 mins. Videocassette, PAL.
Based on Malraux's novel *L'espoir* (1937). A lyrical cinematographic text on the human condition when people are faced with military force, depicts heroic acts in everyday life. Filmed in 1938 in Spain, completed in France, but not released until 1945.

Exilio: El exilio republicano español, 1939–1970. Dir. Pedro Carvajal. Spain: Planeta D, Televisión Española, Fundación Pablo Iglesias, Educo, Mediapark, 2002. 120 mins. Videocassette, PAL. *Exile: Spanish Civil War Refugees Remember.* Disk 1: *Escaping Franco: From Danger into Danger* (59 mins.); disk 2: *Holding on, Fighting Back: The Long Road Home to Spain* (60 mins.). Films for the Humanities and Sciences, 2004. DVD, NTSC. With English subtitles.
Poignant, revealing interviews with men and women, who as children were forced to leave Spain after the Republican defeat.

Extranjeros de sí mismos. Dir. Javier Rioyo and José Luis López Linares. Spain: Cero en Conducta, 2000. 81 mins. Videocassette, PAL.
Interviews with members of the International Brigades and the Francoist División Azul.

Forever Activists: Stories from the Veterans of the Abraham Lincoln Brigade. Dir. Judith Montell. United States: Kino Intl., 1990. 60 mins. Videocassette, NTSC.
In October 1986 surviving brigade veterans return to Spain for the fiftieth anniversary of the war. Academy Award nominee.

Les fosses del silenci. Dir. Montse Armengou and Ricard Belis. Spain: Televisió de Catalunya, 2003. 60 mins.
  Prize-winning documentary on Francoist postwar repression, with footage on the recent exhumation of mass graves.

*Gernika en flames. Dir. Francesc Ribera Raichs. Spain: Gamma, 1979. 10 mins.
  On the bombing of Guernica by the German Condor Legion.

*Gernika Lives. Dir. Begonya Plaza. Spain: Izar, 1989. 45 mins. Videocassette, PAL, 2003.
  Interviews with survivors of the bombing of Guernica.

The Good Fight: The Abraham Lincoln Brigade in the Spanish Civil War. Dir. Noel Buckner, Mary Dore, and Sam Sills. United States: ALBA Film Project, 1984. 98 mins. Videocassette, NTSC.
  Includes interviews with members of the Abraham Lincoln Brigade. Narrated by Studs Terkel.

*Guernica. Dir. Alain Resnais and Robert Hessens. France: Panthéon, 1950. 13 mins. Videocassette, NTSC.
  On Picasso and his painting *Guernica*, with footage of the Guernica bombing.

*La guerra cotidiana. Dir. Daniel Serra and Jaume Serra. Spain: Sagrera TV, Planeta D, 2001. 71 mins. Videocassette, PAL.
  On the daily wartime lives of women from both sides of the conflict.

*La guerrilla de la memoria. Dir. Javier Corcuera. Spain: Alta, Oria, 2002. 67 mins. Videocassette, PAL. Alternate title: *Maquis, el exilio interior*.
  On the 1940s resistance movement of the maquis and their families.

*In Memoriam. Dir. Dolors Genovès and Llorenç Soler. Spain: Televisió de Catalunya, 1986. 60 mins.
  Interviews with Republican working-class families.

Into the Fire: American Women in the Spanish Civil War. Dir. Julia Newman. United States: Exemplary, 2002. 60 mins. Videocassette, NTSC.
  Sixteen stories of American women volunteers (nurses, writers, and journalists). This film was a finalist for best documentary at the Seattle Film Festival.

*Els maquis: La guerra silenciada. Dir. Enric Calpena. Spain: Televisió de Catalunya, 2001. 118 mins.
  On the Republican armed resistance to Franco after 1939.

Mourir à Madrid / To Die in Madrid. Dir. Frédéric Rossif. France: Nicole Stéphane, 1962. Spanish title: *Morir en Madrid*. Buenos Aires: Ancinex. Distributors: Altura, S. L., 1965; Renacimiento–Vídeo del Este, 1992. Music: Maurice Jarre. 87 mins. Videocassette, PAL.

Juxtaposes the image of the Republican militiamen and partisans to the Nationalist or *franquista* soldiers. This creative production gathers astonishing images of public demonstrations, desperation, massacres, and executions. Includes flashes of the 1931 Spanish situation, the abdication of Alfonso XIII, the 1934 upheavals, hunger in Andalucía, Federico García Lorca's execution, the Popular Front against the Falangists in the streets of Madrid, and an interesting portrayal of the Nationalist bourgeoisie with its counterpart of peasants, women, and children lacking the most basic human needs.

Mujeres del 36. Dir. Ana Martínez. Spain: ARTE-TVE, 1999. 86 mins.
Interviews with Republican women, emphasizing their daily lives.

Els nens perduts del franquisme. Dir. Montse Armengou and Ricard Belis. Spain: Televisió de Catalunya, 2002. 60 mins.
Prize-winning documentary on the fascist treatment of the children of Republican parents.

Los niños de Rusia. Dir. Jaime Camino. Spain: Nirvana, Wanda Vision, 2002. 93 mins. Videocassette, PAL.
On the children of Republicans evacuated to the Soviet Union during the war.

Operació Nikolai. Dir. Dolors Genovès and Ricard Belis. Spain: Televisió de Catalunya, 1992. 60 mins.
On POUM leader Andreu Nin's assassination in 1937.

Pablo Picasso's Guernica. United States: Kultur Video, DOM Multimedia, 1999. 36 mins. Videocassette, NTSC.
Part of Discovery of Art series. An attempt to outline the context, structure, and codes of the painting; contains historical inaccuracies.

¿Por qué perdimos la guerra? Dir. Diego Santillán and Francisco Galindo. Spain: Francisco Galindo Cine, 1978. 90 mins. Videocassette, PAL.
A series of interviews with sympathizers of the anarchist trade union, the CNT.

Reportaje del movimiento revolucionario en Barcelona. Dir. Mateo Santos. Spain: CNT-FAI (Oficina de Información y Propaganda), 1936. 22 mins.
Footage on the defense and daily life of Barcelona, and on the Durruti Column.

The Spanish Civil War. United Kingdom: Granada Television Intl., 1983. Distributor: MPI Home Video. Approx. 6 hours. 2 videocassettes, NTSC. Spanish title: *La guerra civil española*. Distributor: Vídeo Saber. 1993. 320 mins. 3 videocassettes.
Based, in part, on Hugh Thomas's book. John Blake directed parts 1, 2, and 3; David Hart parts 4, 5, and 6. A collection of photographic and film

images with interviews of protagonists of the Spanish Civil War. Part 1: "Prelude to Tragedy"; part 2: "Revolution, Counter-revolution, and Terror"; part 3: "Battleground for Idealists"; part 4: "Franco and the Nationalists"; part 5: "The Revolution"; part 6: "Victory and Defeat."

The Spanish Civil War: Blood and Ink. Spain: Tranquilo Producciones, 2002. Distributor: Films for the Humanities. 50 mins. Videocassette, NTSC. Interviews and dramatic readings from Machado's "Muerte de un niño herido," Pemán's "De ellos es el mundo," Hernández's *Viento del pueblo*, and works of other writers.

The Spanish Civil War: The Story of a Country at War. Dir. Mike Leighton. United Kingdom: Cromwell, 1998. History of Warfare series. Alternate title: *Brother against Brother: The Spanish Civil War*. Kultur Video, 2001. Distributor: Kalender Video Argentina, 55 mins. Videocassette, NTSC.
Interviews with British International Brigades veterans and archival footage, including the bombing of Guernica. Includes poems of John Cornford, Antonio Machado, and Miguel Hernández.

The Spanish Earth. Dir. Joris Ivens. Commentary by Ernest Hemingway. United States and Holland: Contemporary Historians Inc., 1937. Spanish title: *Tierra española*. Buenos Aires: Época Vídeo Ediciones. 54 mins. Videocassette, NTSC. With Ivens's *The 400 Million*. Slingshot, 2000. DVD, NTSC. Includes Orson Welles's original narration.
Pictures the defense of Madrid and the struggle of the citizens of the small town of Fuentedueña to irrigate their land to produce food for themselves and the Republican soldiers. Buenos Aires version, with Spanish subtitles.

Spanish Writers in Exile. Spain: Tranquilo Producciones, 2002. Distributor: Films for the Humanities. 50 mins. Videocassette, NTSC.
Interviews and dramatic readings from Alberti's "A través de la niebla," Cernuda's "Un español habla de su tierra," Rosa Chacel's "Cultura y pueblo," and works of other writers.

Sumaríssim 477. Dir. Dolors Genovès and Lluís Montserrat. Spain: Televisió de Catalunya, 1994. 66 mins.
On Francoist crimes committed by Catalan fascists.

El Valle de los Caídos. Spain: Video Affin, Atrio, 2000. 30 mins. Videocassette, PAL.
A filmed guidebook of the civil war monument, with most of the history edited out.

Veus ofegades: Cartes d'un exili a França. Dir. Montserrat Besses. Spain: Televisió de Catalunya, 2002. 63 mins.
On the fate of the 500,000 Republican exiles, especially those in the French concentration camps.

La vieja memoria. Dir. Jaime Camino. Spain: Profilmes, 1978. 161 mins.
Interviews with participants from both sides of the conflict (Abad Santillán,
José María Gil Robles, Dolores Ibárruri, among others).

Ya viene el cortejo. Dir. Carlos Arévalo. Spain: CIFESA; Juan de Orduña,
1939. 11 mins.
Nationalist film centering on Franco's Victory Parade.

"*You Are History, You Are Legend*": *The Legacy of the International Brigades*.
Dir. Judith Montell. United States: Kino Intl., 1997. 20 mins. Videocassette, NTSC.
On the sixtieth anniversary of the Abraham Lincoln Brigade, surviving
members return to Spain to receive honorary citizenship. A sequel to *Forever Activists*.

Feature Films

Los amantes del círculo polar / Lovers of the Arctic Circle. Dir. Julio Medem.
Spain: Sogetel, Le Studio Canal, 1998. 110 mins. New Line Home
Video, 2001. Videocassette and DVD, NTSC. With English subtitles.
A love story, in which the memory of the civil war plays a role in determin-
ing the fate of a pair of lovers.

A mí la legión. Dir. Juan de Orduña. Spain: CIFESA, UPCE, 1942. 82 mins.
Videocassette, PAL.
Set in Morocco, the film centers on the pro-Franco Spanish Foreign
Legion.

The Angel Wore Red. Dir. Nunnally Johnson. United States and Italy: MGM,
1960. 99 mins.
A clergyman comes to Spain and joins the Republicans.

L'arbre de Guernica / L'albero di Guernica / The Tree of Guernica. Dir. Fer-
nando Arrabal. France and Italy: Babylone, Ci-Le, Les Productions
Jacques Roitfeld, Luso, 1975. Distributor: New Line Cinema, 1976.
With English subtitles. 110 mins.
A surrealist vision of the war.

¡Ay, Carmela! Dir. Carlos Saura. Spain: Iberoamericana Films Internacional;
Italy: Ellepi, 1990. Distributor: HBO Video. 105 mins. Videocassette,
NTSC. Based on the play by José Sanchis Sinisterra. With English
subtitles.
The film features the tragic journey of a Republican theater troupe trapped
behind enemy lines in 1938. Wonderful performance by Carmen Maura.

Behold a Pale Horse. Dir. Fred Zinnemann. United States: Columbia, Tristar
Studios, 1964. 118 mins. Videocassette and DVD, NTSC.

The ideological battles of the war continue in the postwar period. Some footage from *Mourir à Madrid* is incorporated into the film.

Belle Epoque. Dir. Fernando Trueba. Spain: Lola, 1992. Distributor: Columbia Tristar Home Video. 109 mins. Videocassette and DVD, NTSC. With English subtitles.
An imaginative take on the prewar period.

Las bicicletas son para el verano. Dir. Jaime Chávarri. Spain: In-cine, Jet, 1983. 103 mins. Videocassette, PAL. Based on the play by Fernando Fernán Gómez.
The film depicts the effects of the Spanish Civil War on the daily life of a middle-class family in Madrid.

Blockade. Dir. William Dieterle. United States: United Artists, 1938. 85 mins. 2002. Image Entertainment: DVD, NTSC.
Romance drama, with Henry Fonda as a Spanish peasant. Screenplay by John Howard Lawson (later one of the "Hollywood Ten").

La caza / The Hunt. Dir. Carlos Saura. Spain: Elías Quejereta, 1965. Distributor: Film Forum. 93 mins. Videocassette, PAL and NTSC; DVD, PAL. With English subtitles.
Four friends (three Nationalist ex-combatants and a young man) meet on a summer Sunday to hunt. A violent fight provoked by repressed civil war trauma ensues. A Saura classic.

Confidential Agent. Dir. Herman Shumlin. United States: Warner Brothers, 1945. 113 mins.
Based on the Graham Greene novel about an antifascist secret agent.

The Disappearance of García Lorca. Dir. Marcos Zurinaga. United States: Miramar, Enrique Cerezo Producciones, Antena 3 Televisión, Esparza, Katz, Le Studio Canal, 1997. 114 mins. United States: Columbia, Tristar Home Video, 1999. Videocassette, NTSC. Also known as *Death in Granada.*
During the Franco regime, an expatriate writer investigates Lorca's 1936 murder by fascists, in this factually loose version of events.

Dragón rapide. Dir. Jaime Camino. Spain and Italy: Tibidabo, 1986. 105 mins. Videocassette, PAL and NTSC.
Features the preparation of the rebel coup and the role of Franco in the uprising.

*Dulces horas. Dir. Carlos Saura. Spain and France: Elías Querejeta Producciones, Les Productions Jacques Roitfeld, 1982. 106 mins.
A critique of the Spanish nostalgia film, focusing on false memories of the war.

En el balcón vacío. Dir. José Miguel (Jomi) García Ascot. Mexico: Ascot, Torre, 1962. 70 mins. Videocassette, NTSC.

A poetic, haunting re-creation of exile.

España, otra vez. Dir. Jaime Camino. Spain: Pandora Filmproduktion, 1969. 108 mins. Vanguard Intl. Cinema, 2003. Videocassette and DVD, NTSC. With English subtitles.
An American volunteer returns to Spain thirty years after the war. A film of homecoming and loss. Alvah Bessie collaborated on the screenplay.

El espinazo del diablo / The Devil's Backbone. Dir. Guillermo del Toro. Spain and Mexico: El Deseo, Tequila Gang and Anhelo Producciones, 2002. 110 mins. Sony Pictures. DVD, NTSC. Subtitles in English.
The war metamorphoses into an imaginative ghost story.

El espíritu de la colmena / The Spirit of the Beehive. Dir. Víctor Erice. Spain: Elías Querejeta, 1973. Distributor: Public Media Home Vision Entertainment, 1993. 93 mins. Videocassette and DVD, NTSC. Distributor: Optimum Home Entertainment, 2003. DVD, PAL. With English subtitles.
A haunting allegorical reading of the civil war.

The Fallen Sparrow. Dir. Richard Wallace. United States: RKO, 1943. 94 mins. Based on the novel by Dorothy B. Hughes.
A suspense film, whose hero (John Garfield) was tortured by Spanish fascists.

*La fiel infantería. Dir. Pedro Lazaga. Spain: Ágata, 1959. 113 mins. Videocassette, PAL.
Based on the Nationalist novel by Rafael García Serrano.

*Five Cartridges / Fünf Patronenhülsen. Dir. Frank Beyer. Germany: Icestorm Intl., LLC, 1960. 88 mins. Videocassette, PAL and NTSC. With English subtitles.
Five International Brigades members on a mission.

For Whom the Bell Tolls. Dir. Sam Wood. United States: Paramount, 1943. MCA Universal Home Video, 1995. 2 hrs. 46 mins. 2 videocassettes, NTSC. Universal, 1998. DVD, NTSC.
Based on the novel by Ernest Hemingway. Restored version, with footage that was cut immediately after theatrical premiere.

La guerre est finie. Dir. Alain Resnais. France and Sweden: Sofracima, Europa, 1966. 116 mins. Videocassette, NTSC. MM Image Entertainment, 2001. DVD, NTSC. With English subtitles.
Script by Jorge Semprún. A Spanish Communist in exile must make one more trip to Spain to further the anti-Franco movement, which is seen as a continuation of the war.

*El hermano bastardo de Dios. Dir. Benito Rabal. Spain: Almadraba Producciones, S. A.–Televisión Española, 1986. 102 mins. Videocassette, PAL and NTSC.

Based on the novel by José Luis Coll. Childhood memories of the war in Cuenca.

El jardín de las delicias. Dir. Carlos Saura. Spain: Elías Querejeta, 1970. 95 mins. Altura, 1971. Videocassette, PAL and NTSC. With English subtitles.

The war and Franco's victory are evoked through a complex play of memory in the main character, Antonio Cano, inspired by the notorious industrialist and Franco supporter Juan March.

Land and Freedom: A Story from the Spanish Revolution. Dir. Ken Loach. United Kingdom, Spain, and Germany: Parallax, Messidor, Road Movies Dritte Produktionen, 1995. New York: Polygram Video Distributor. 109 mins. Spanish title: *Tierra y libertad.* Buenos Aires: RKV Distributor, 2000. Cinematográficas S. A. 107 mins. Videocassette, NTSC.

Portrays internal fights on the Republican side as seen by a young English volunteer. Based in part on George Orwell's *Homage to Catalonia.*

*El lápiz del carpintero. Dir. Antón Reixa. Spain: Sogecine, Morena, 2003. 106 mins.

Based on Manuel Rivas's novel.

Las largas vacaciones del 36. Dir. Jaime Camino. Spain: J[osé] F[rade] Producciones Cinematográficas, 1976. Buenos Aires: RKV Distributor, 2000. 107 mins. Videocassette, PAL.

Portrays a group of bourgeois families who, dismayed by Barcelona's resistance to the Nationalist army, decide to prolong for the next two years their summer vacation in the mountains.

The Last Train from Madrid. Dir. James Hogan. United States: Paramount, 1937. 85 mins.

Set in 1936 besieged Madrid, focusing on nine characters trying to get to Valencia.

La lengua de las mariposas / Butterfly. Dir. José Luis Cuerda. Spain: Sogetel, Las Producciones del Escorpión, Canal + Spain, TVE and TVG, Miramax, 1999. 95 mins. Videocassette and DVD, NTSC. With English subtitles.

Shows the fatal effects of the civil war on the sensibility of a child and the destruction of his relationship with the village teacher, a freethinking antifascist. Based on a story by Manuel Rivas.

*Libertarias. Dir. Vicente Aranda. Spain: Academy, Canal + España, Era, Sogetel; Lola, TVE, 1996. 115 mins. Videocassette, PAL.

Story of a drafted nun and several women who fight for the republic.

*Luna de lobos. Dir. Julio Sánchez Valdés. Spain: Brezal P. C., Julio Sánchez Valdés P. C., 1987. 110 mins. Videocassette, PAL.

Focuses on a small group of 1940s resistance fighters (the maquis). Based on Julio Llamazares's novel.

Mambrú se fue a la guerra. Dir. Fernando Fernán Gómez. Spain: Altair Producciones Filmográficas, 1986. 100 mins. Videocassette, PAL and NTSC. With English subtitles.
Centers on the life of a *topo*, or mole, a Republican who went into hiding after the war.

La niña de tus ojos. Dir. Fernando Trueba. Spain: Lola, 1998. 121 mins. Videocassette, PAL.
In 1938 Spanish filmmakers are invited to Nazi Germany to make two versions (German and Spanish) of a musical drama.

Pascual Duarte. Dir. Ricardo Franco. Spain: Elías Querejeta, 1975. 94 mins. Videocassette and DVD, PAL.
Unlike its source, Camilo José Cela's novel, the film version foregrounds the civil war.

La plaza del Diamante. Dir. Francesc Betriu. Spain: Figaró, 1982. 117 mins. Videocassette, PAL and NTSC. With English subtitles.
Based on Mercè Rodoreda's classic novel.

La prima Angélica. Dir. Carlos Saura. Spain: Elías Querejeta, 1973. 100 mins. New Yorker, 1977. Videocassette, PAL and NTSC; DVD, PAL.
The trauma of the civil war remembered by a child of Republican parents.

Raza. Dir. José Luis Sáenz de Heredia. Spain: Cancillería del Consejo de la Hispanidad Production, 1941. 105 mins. Videocassette, PAL. Divisa Ediciones, 2002. DVD, PAL.
Based on a script by Jaime de Andrade (pseud. of Francisco Franco). Franco's Nationalist drama of family sacrifice and patriotic-religious ideals. The DVD also contains the 1950 version, *Espíritu de una raza* (96 mins.). Iconic Nationalist film.

Réquiem por un campesino español. Dir. Francesc Betriu. Spain: Nemo, Venus Producción, 1985. 95 mins. Videocassette, PAL.
Based on the celebrated novel by Ramón Sender.

El rey y la reina. Dir. José Antonio Páramo. Spain, Italy, and United Kingdom: TVE, 1985. 125 mins. Videocassette, PAL and NTSC. With English subtitles.
Based on the Ramón Sender novel.

Les routes du sud / Roads to the South. Dir. Joseph Losey. France and Spain: Tinacra, Pro Filmes, 1978. 100 mins. Videocassette, NTSC. In French with English subtitles.
A continuation of *La guerre est finie*. Script by Jorge Semprún.

Silencio roto. Dir. Montxo Armendáriz. Spain: Oria, 2001. 115 mins. Videocassette, PAL.
Focuses on the women who participated in the anti-Francoist guerrillas
during the 1940s.

Soldados de Salamina. Dir. David Trueba. Spain: Lola, Fernando Trueba P. C.,
TVE, Vía Digital, 2003. 115 mins. DVD, PAL.
Based on the novel by Javier Cercas, which explores through fact and fiction why the Nationalist writer Rafael Sánchez Mazas was not executed
during the war.

Vacas. Dir. Julio Medem. Spain: Sogetel, 1991. 92 mins. Videocassette, PAL.
Vanguard International Cinema, 2002. DVD, NTSC. With English
subtitles.
Refigures the war as a harrowing generational conflict in the Basque Country.

La vaquilla. Dir. Luis García Berlanga. Spain: In-cine, Jet, 1985. 122 mins.
Videocassette, PAL.
Set in 1938. Republican soldiers attempt to steal a young bull from the
Nationalist side.

El viaje de Carol / Carol's Journey. Dir. Imanol Uribe. Spain: Aiete, Ariane,
Sogecine, 2002. 100 mins. Film Movement, 2004. DVD, NTSC. With
English subtitles.
A coming-of-age film, focusing on a young Spanish American girl
brought to Spain in 1938. Loosely based on García Roldán's novel *A boca
de noche.*

Music

*Cantos de la guerra de España / Chants de la guerre d'Espagne / Songs of the
Spanish Civil War.* Cobla de Barcelona. Dir. Gustavo Pittaluga and
Rodolfo Halffter. France: Le Chant du Monde, 1963, 1996. 37 mins.
Audio CD.
Fourteen songs, including "Himno de Riego," "Els Segadors," and
"Somos los soldados vascos."

Pasiones: Songs of the Spanish Civil War, 1936–39. Perf. Jamie O'Reilly and
Michael Smith, with Katrina O'Reilly. Executive Prod. Stuart Rosen-
berg. Chicago: WFMT Studios, 1997. 62 mins. Audio CD.
Twenty songs, including "Quinto Regimiento," "Los cuatro generales,"
"Asturias," and "Song of the International Brigade." Musical sources:
España: 1936–1938: 25 himnos y canciones de la guerra civil española and
Songs from a Franco Prison, by Max Parker, 1982. A multilingual produc-
tion in Spanish, English, French, and German.

Songs of the Spanish Civil War. Perf. Ramón López Quartet. Leo Records, 2001. Audio CD.
Eleven songs, including "Els Segadors," "El tren blindado," and "El paso del Ebro."

See also *Canciones para después de una guerra*, under "Cinematography: Documentaries."

Photography

Capa, Robert. *Death in the Making*.
Photographs by Capa and Gerda Taro. Taro died, aged twenty-six, at the front.

———. *Fotógrafo de guerra: España, 1936–1939*.
The collection concentrates on these categories: "Hombres y mujeres," "Niños," and "Propaganda."

———. *Heart of Spain: Capa's Photographs of the Spanish Civil War*.
Documents battles, air raids, and Republican soldiers' intimate, quiet moments of silent camaraderie. Includes Capa's celebrated *Falling Militiaman*. Desolate images of pain—stricken women, lonely female figures dressed in black and wandering among the rubble, the solitude captured in children's eyes—depict a world of fear and violence.

La guerra civil espanyola: Fotògrafs per a la història.
Wonderful collection of an international array of photographers (Capa, Namuth, Centelles, Marín, Chim, and others), with essays, short biographies, and bibliography.

Horna, Kati. *Fotografías de la guerra civil española, 1937–1938*.
Of Hungarian origin, Horna presents 272 photographs that reflect a kind of complicity between author and subject. She portrays strategic sites of Republican Spain. Women breast-feeding their babies, a stroll through the market, smiles on young girls' faces projecting simultaneously sadness and hope, and shelled buildings are captured in this series.

Imágenes inéditas de la guerra civil, 1936–1939.
An arresting series of previously unpublished photographs, representing both sides of the war.

Namuth, Hans, and Georg Reisner. *Spanisches Tagebuch, 1936: Fotografien und Texte aus den ersten Monaten des Bürgerkriegs*.
With an introductory essay by Diethart Kerbs. Extraordinary photos of civilians and soldiers, from the first months of the war.

Nelson, Cary. *The Aura of the Cause: A Photo Album for North American Volunteers in the Spanish Civil War*.

A superb visual record of the North American volunteers in the war, with additional materials by Nelson, Rafael Alberti, Edwin Rolfe, Ernest Hemingway, and Dolores Ibárruri (La Pasionaria). This book is the catalog that accompanies the exhibit.

―――. *Shouts from the Wall: Posters and Photographs Brought Home from the Spanish Civil War by American Volunteers.*
Includes a chronology; an essay on Spanish Civil War posters; artist biographies; and an annotated guide to the exhibit, for which this book is the catalog.

Whelan, Richard, ed. *Robert Capa: The Definitive Collection.*
Comprehensive collection that includes a selection of pictures of young people going about everyday chores, despairing children and families, wrecked buildings, and soldiers.

See also "Secondary Sources: Web Sites."

Posters

Carulla, Jordi, and Arnau Carulla. *La guerra civil en 2000 carteles: República, guerra civil, posguerra.*
Extraordinary collection from the Republican and Nationalist sides.

Ferré, Facundo Tomás. *Los carteles valencianos en la guerra civil española.*
An excellent account of the historical and artistic development of the poster artists, their work, and the activist role they played on the Republican side.

Grimau, Carmen. *El cartel republicano en la guerra civil.*
A study of Republican posters as art and political propaganda, with illustrations.

Paret, Peter, Beth Irwin Lewis, and Paul Paret. *Persuasive Images: Posters of War and Revolution from the Hoover Institution Archives.*
The Spanish Civil War is included in part 2, with illustrations from both sides.

Tisa, John. *The Palette and the Flame: Posters of the Spanish Civil War.*
Great reproductions of the Republican posters.

See also C. Nelson, *Shouts from the Wall*, under "Photography."

Poetry

Alberti, Rafael. *De un momento a otro: Poesía e historia.*
Includes such poems as "La revolución y la guerra," "Los soldados se duermen," and "Quinto Cuerpo del Ejército: A Modesto, su Jefe."

————. *Entre el clavel y la espada, 1939–1940.*
On the role of the poet during wartime. Dedicated to Pablo Neruda.

————. *The Owl's Insomnia: Poems.*
Bilingual edition. Includes such poems as "The Coming Back of an Assassinated Poet," "Ballad of the Lost Andalusian," and "The Bad Moment."

————. *Poesía civil con un poema de Pablo Neruda.*
Includes poems such as "Madrid-Otoño," "A las Brigadas Internacionales," "Abril 1938," and "Vosotros no caísteis."

————. *El poeta en la calle: Poesía civil, 1931–1965.*
Includes "S.O.S.," "Vosotros no caísteis," and a poem by Neruda.

————, ed. *Romancero general de la guerra española.*
Includes poems such as "Romance fronterizo de la guerra civil," by Antonio Oliver, a militiaman; "José Colom," by Manuel Altolaguirre; burlesque poems; and other lyric texts.

————. *Selected Poems.*
Includes "They Fell and Did Not Fall," "The Soldiers Sleep," "And after the War," and "Nocturne." With words and ink, the poet tries to convey the outer and inner struggle and the interweaving of suffering, disorder, and bullets.

Altolaguirre, Manuel. *Poesías completas.*
Includes "¡Alerta, los madrileños!," "La toma de Caspe," "José Colom," and "La torre de El Carpio."

Auden, W. H. *The English Auden: Poems, Essays, and Dramatic Writings, 1927–1939.*
Includes the drastically revised "Spain 1937" (the original, titled "Spain," was restored in *Selected Poems*).

Bauer, Carlos, ed. *Cries from a Wounded Madrid: Poetry of the Spanish Civil War.*
Bilingual edition. Sections include "Romancero de la Guerra Civil," "Poetas en la España leal," and "Homenaje de Despedida a las Brigadas Internacionales."

Baútista de la Torre, Sebastián. *Revivir: Poemas de la liberación.*
Compilation of thirty-five poems of fascist orientation. Dedicated to Nationalist prisoners in the Republican zone.

Bernardete, M. J., and Rolfe Humphries, eds. *. . . and Spain Sings: Fifty Loyalist Ballads Adapted by American Poets.*
Introduced by the poet Lorenzo Varela (who is also featured). Poems by Rafael Alberti, José Moreno Villa, Vicente Aleixandre, Emilio Prados, Rosa Chacel, José Bergamín, and Antonio Machado. Translations by Rolfe Humphries, Stanley Kunitz, Maxwell Singer, Katherine Garrison Chapin, and others.

Calle Iturrino, Esteban. *Romancero de la guerra.*
Calle Iturrino is also the author of *Cantos de guerra y de imperio* and *Don Quijote, Fausto y el fascismo.* He says he was inspired by the most glorious episodes of the Crusades.

Campbell, Roy. *Flowering Rifle: A Poem from the Battlefield of Spain.*
A vitriolic, frequently offensive pro-Nationalist long poem, with flashes of brilliance.

Cancionero de las Brigadas Internacionales.
Features texts in fifteen languages, accompanied by musical scores.

Caudet, Francisco, ed. *Romancero de la guerra civil.*
Introduction and notes by the editor. Includes poems by José Herrera Petere, Juan Gil-Albert, Pedro Garfias, Emilio Prados, and Arturo Serrano Plaja.

Cernuda, Luis. *Las nubes, 1937–1938.*
Includes "A un poeta muerto [F. G. L.]," "Elegía española," and "Niño muerto."

———. *Selected Poems.*
Bilingual edition. Includes a selection from *Las nubes / Clouds,* such as "To a Dead Poet (F. G. L.)," "A Spaniard Speaks of His Land," and "Lamentation and Hope."

Chacel, Rosa. *Poesía, 1931–1991.*
Chacel's more accessible poetry from the war period moves away from her earlier neo-Gongorist, experimental verses.

Champourcín, Ernestina de. *Primer exilio.*
Reflective poetry written nearly four decades after the war.

Claudel, Paul. *Poèmes et paroles durant la guerre de trente ans.*
Includes "Aux martyrs espagnols."

Conde, Carmen. *Obra poética, 1929–1966.*
Includes the collection of pacifist-inspired prose poems *Mientras los hombres mueren.*

Corona de sonetos en honor de José Antonio Primo de Rivera.
Poems by Manuel Machado, Eduardo Marquina, Eugenio D'Ors, Leopoldo Panero, José María Pemán, Luis Rosales, and other Nationalist poets.

Cunningham, Valentine, ed. *The Penguin Book of Spanish Civil War Verse.*
The editor says this is the first "comprehensive assembly of British poems" about the Spanish Civil War. Includes Auden, Spender, Sylvia Townsend Warner, John Cornford, Herbert Read, C. Day-Lewis, as well as Neruda, Alberti, and others in English translation.

Díaz-Plaja, Fernando, ed. *La guerra civil y los poetas españoles.*

A selection of poems from both sides, in an attempt at neutrality. Thematic division of chapters, with commentaries in which the editor uses the poems to create an argument.

Dietz, Bernd, ed. and trans. *Un país donde lucía el sol: Poesía inglesa de la guerra civil española.*
Bilingual edition. Poems by Edgar Foxall, George Barker, and others.

Felipe, León. *Obra poética escogida.*
In the section "Español del éxodo y del llanto: Doctrinas de un poeta español en 1939" is included *El hacha*, composed of two poems: "Elegía española" and "¿Qué quieren esos hombres?"

Guillén, Nicolás. *España: Poema en cuatro angustias y una esperanza.*
Establishes a historical correlation between Spain and pre-Columbian Latin America. "Angustia Cuarta" is a lyrical search for Federico García Lorca. This text is a gem.

———. *Obra poética.*
Volume 1 includes "España: Poema en cuatro angustias y una esperanza," written in Mexico, 1937, before Guillén left for Spain to participate in the II Congreso Internacional de Escritores para la Defensa de la Cultura. Volume 2 contains "Madrid," on a dead militiaman and included in a larger poem, "Ciudades."

Hernández, Miguel. *Obra completa.*
Volume 1 includes *Viento del pueblo, El hombre acecha*, and poems such as "Memoria del Quinto Regimiento," "Canción de la ametralladora," and "Las puertas de Madrid."

———. *The Selected Poems.*
Bilingual edition. Contains a generous selection of war and prison poems (1936–42).

Homenaje a las Brigadas Internacionales.
Includes poems by Alberti, Altolaguirre, Gil-Albert, and Hernández.

López Aranda, A. Esteban. *Romances de Madrid.*
A fascist collection dedicated to Franco.

Machado, Antonio. *Antología comentada.*
See "Poesías de la guerra," which includes "A Líster," "El crimen fue en Granada," and "Voz de España."

———. *Times Alone: Selected Poems.*
Bilingual edition. Includes a selection of civil war poems, among them "The Death of the Wounded Child."

Machado, Manuel. *Poesía de guerra y posguerra.*
Pro-Nationalist. Includes "¡Emilio Mola! ¡Presente!," "Saludo a Franco," and "¡Presentes!"

MacNeice, Louis. *Collected Poems, 1925–1948.*
Includes "And I Remember Spain."

Méndez, Concha. *Lluvias enlazadas.*
Poems of anguish, despair, and pain, reflecting the horrors of war.

Millán Astray, Pilar. *Cautivas: 32 meses en las prisiones rojas.*
Poems by a Franco supporter, composed during imprisonment. Illustrated.

Nelson, Cary, ed. *The Wound and the Dream: Sixty Years of American Poems about the Spanish Civil War.*
An anthology of American poems about the war written between 1936 and 1999. With a useful introduction, "The International Context for American Poetry about the Spanish Civil War."

Neruda, Pablo. *Five Decades: Poems: 1925–1970.*
Bilingual edition. Includes poems from the civil war period, among them "Explico algunas cosas" and "Cómo era España."

———. *The Poetry of Pablo Neruda.*
Contains two versions of "Ode to Federico García Lorca" and the Spanish original, also *Spain in Our Heart*. With various translators. Not fully bilingual: some poems are given in both Spanish and English, others only in English.

———. *Spain in the Heart: Hymn to the Glories of the People at War.*
Bilingual edition. Poems from 1936 and 1937, including "Invocation," "Bombardment," "Landscape after a Battle," and the powerful "Madrid, 1937."

———. *Tercera residencia.*
Includes "España en el corazón" and "Canto en la muerte y resurrección de Luis Companys."

Neruda, Pablo, and Nancy Cunard, eds. *Los poetas del mundo defienden al pueblo español (París 1937).*
With insert "Recuerdo de la inefable Nancy Cunard," by Ramón J. Sender. Poems by Alberti, Auden, Cunard, Langston Hughes, Tristan Tzara, Lorca, and others.

Pemán, José María. *Poema de guerra, 1936–38: Poema de la bestia y el ángel.*
Epic Nationalist poem, invoking Isabella and Ferdinand's united Spain.

Pereda Valdés, Ildefonso, ed. *Cancionero de la guerra civil española.*
Divided thematically; includes authors such as Lorca, Neruda, Antonio Machado, Emilio Prados, Huidobro, and Altolaguirre.

Pillement, Georges, ed. *Le romancero de la guerre civile.*
Poems by Altolaguirre, Varela, Aleixandre, and Bergamín; translated by Pillement, Parrot, and others.

Poetas en la España leal.
Comprehensive anthology of the most prolific Republican poets who wrote during and on the Spanish Civil War: Alberti, Altolaguirre, Cernuda, A. Machado, Gil-Albert, L. Felipe, and others.

Prados, Emilio. *Poesía extrema: Antología.*
Includes *Destino fiel: 1936–1939*, with such poems as "Presente oficio," "Al camarada Antonio Coll," "Ciudad sitiada," "A Hans Beimler," and "Estancia en la muerte con Federico García Lorca."

Pujals, Esteban, ed. *Plumas y fusiles: Los poetas ingleses y la guerra de España.*
A compilation of ten English poets with an introduction.

Ramos-Gascón, Antonio, ed. *Romancero del ejército popular.*
Offers poems of anonymous soldiers, sergeants, militiamen, and International Brigaders.

Salaün, Serge, ed. *La poesía de la guerra de España.*
With a study of the poetics of the civil war, exploring the theoretical relation between form and ideology.

———, ed. *Romancero de la guerra de España.*
Contents: *Romancero libertario, Romancero de la defensa de Madrid, Romancero de la tierra, Romancero de los héroes, Romancero de los poetas, Romancero del aire y del mar*, and an untitled volume.

Sánchez Saornil, Lucía. *Poesía.*
Poetry from a feminist anarchist of the war period. See the section "Romancero de Mujeres Libres."

Santonja, Gonzalo, ed. *Todo en el aire: Versos sin enemigo: Antología insólita de la poesía durante la guerra incivil española.*
The editor sees this poetry as witness to the voices and sufferings of ordinary people. Poems by Antonio Machado, Alberti, Altolaguirre, Chacel, and others.

Spender, Stephen. *The Still Centre.*
Part 3 is "Poems on Spain."

Spender, Stephen, and John Lehmann, eds. *Poems for Spain.*
Features British authors and translations of Hernández, Altolaguirre, Neruda, and others. Organized in the categories "Action," "Death," "The Map," "Satire," "Romances," and "Lorca."

Teweleit, Horst Lothar, ed. *No pasarán! Romanzen aus dem Spanienkrieg.*
Bilingual edition. With an introduction on the *Romancero de la guerra civil*, glossary, and notes.

Vallejo, César. "Battles in Spain: Five Unpublished Poems."
Contains "Trilce," "(Untitled)," "XXX," "Battles in Spain," and "Funereal Hymn for the Ruins of Durango."

————. *España, aparta de mí este cáliz.*
Bilingual edition. Includes such poems as "Cortejo tras la toma de Bilbao" and "Pequeño responso a un héroe de la República."

Vicente Hernando, César de, ed. *Poesía de la guerra civil española.*
Comprehensive anthology with historical introduction. Poems from the Nationalist and Republican points of view, by Rafael Alberti, Miguel Hernández, Inés Montero, Herminia Fariña, and others.

Vulpe, Nicola, and Maha Albari, eds. *Sealed in Struggle: Canadian Poetry and the Spanish Civil War: An Anthology.*
Poems written from 1936 to the present.

See also A. Bessie, *Heart*; Mainer; Rodríguez-Puértolas, under "Prose."

Prose

Novels, Short Stories, Plays, and Dialogues

Alberti, Rafael. *Noche de guerra en el Museo del Prado.*
Play, in which Goya paintings in the Prado come to life and construct a barricade during the siege of Madrid.

Aldecoa, Josefina R., ed. *Los niños de la guerra.*
Anthology of stories and excerpts of novels by Carmen Martín-Gaite, Ana María Matute, Jesús Fernández Santos, and others; contains biographical sketches and commentaries.

Amat, Núria. *El país del alma.*
Novel, focusing on Catalonia after the civil war. An English extract "The Wedding" appears in Bush and Dillman.

Anderson, Maxwell. *Key Largo.*
Play, in which the Spanish Civil War figures significantly as the ideological and moral context for the main character's actions.

Andújar, Manuel. *Historias de una historia.*
First unabridged edition. Novel, from the cycle *Lares y penares.* Focuses on the Barcelona militias.

————. *La voz y la sangre.*
Novel, from the cycle *Lares y penares.* Centers on the life of an exile.

Aparicio, Juan Pedro. *La forma de la noche.*
Novel, which weaves together myth, reality, and switched identities in wartime Asturias.

Arana, José Ramón. *El cura de Almuniaced.*
Novel. Focuses on a priest in a small Aragonese town. Worth reading alongside Sender's *Réquiem por un campesino español.*

Arrabal, Fernando. *Fando y Lis [and] Guernica [and] La bicicleta del condenado.* In French: *Guernica.* In English: Guernica *and Other Plays.*
Guernica is an experimental, surreal play on the war.

Aub, Max. *Campo abierto.*
Novel. Takes place between 18 July and 7 November 1936, in Valencia,
Burgos, and Madrid.

———. *Campo cerrado.*
Opens the series of novels called *El laberinto mágico* and is centered on the
prewar period, ending with the early days of the war.

———. *Campo del moro.*
Novel on the defense of Madrid (from 5 to 13 Mar. 1939).

———. *Campo de los almendros.*
One of the best-known works about the civil war and the sixth book of *El
laberinto mágico,* from 1968. Deals with the end of the war and the
Republican defeat.

———. *Campo de sangre.*
Set in Barcelona and Teruel between 31 December 1937 and 19 March
1938. Book 3 of *El laberinto mágico.*

———. *Campo francés.*
On the experience of Republican prisoners in the French concentration
camps.

———. *No son cuentos.*
Includes the short story "El cojo."

Ayala, Francisco. *La cabeza del cordero.*
Includes the stories "El mensaje," "El Tajo," "El regreso," "La cabeza del
cordero," and "La vida por la opinión."

Azaña, Manuel. *La velada en Benicarló: Diálogo sobre la guerra de España.* In
English: *Vigil in Benicarló.*
President of the republic, Azaña composed this melancholy dialogue of
conflictive voices echoing the many ideological splits in Spain.

Azúa, Félix de. *Cambio de bandera.*
Novel, focusing on a Basque nationalist and the period of the republic to
June 1937.

Barea, Arturo. *The Forging of a Rebel.*
Hybrid novel-autobiography in three parts: "The Forge," "The Track,"
and "The Clash."

Bartra, Agustí. *Cristo de 200.000 brazos: Campo de Argelès.*
Novel, first titled *Xabola* (Mexico, 1943); the second version is in Catalan
(Barcelona, 1968). The story of four Republican companions in the
Argelès concentration camp.

Benet, Juan. *Volverás a Región.* In English: *Return to Region.*
Novel. Allegorical vision of history and the war.

Bessie, Alvah, ed. *The Heart of Spain: Anthology of Fiction, Non-fiction, and Poetry.*
Writings by Lillian Hellman, Martha Gellhorn, Langston Hughes, Lorca, and others.

Borrás, Tomás. *Checas de Madrid: Epopeya de los caídos.*
Novel, filled with raw details, on the Soviet-style kangaroo courts, or *checas.* Pro-Nationalist.

Brecht, Bertolt. *Brechts Gewehre der Frau Carrar.* In English: *Señora Carrar's Rifles.*
One-act play, in which the merits of neutrality are debated; neutrality is ultimately rejected.

Candel, Francisco. *El santo de la madre Margarita.*
Novel in which a group of nuns is saved by a Republican atheist in wartime Barcelona.

Castillo-Puche, José Luis. *Conocerás el poso de la nada.*
Novel. Last volume of Castillo-Puche's *Trilogía de la liberación,* reflecting on death, the effects of war, and memory.

Castresana, Luis de. *El otro árbol de Guernica.*
Testimonial novel on the Basque children of Republican parents sent abroad during the war. Premio Nacional de Literatura Miguel de Cervantes, 1967.

Castroviejo, Concha. *Los que se fueron.*
Novel. On the experiences of Republican exiles.

———. *Víspera del odio.*
Winner of the 1958 Elisenda de Moncada Prize, this novel is about an unhappy marriage, the war, and revenge.

Cela, Camilo José. *La familia de Pascual Duarte.* In English: *The Family of Pascual Duarte.*
In this classic 1942 novel, the war is only suggested.

———. *Vísperas, festividad y octava de San Camilo del año 1936 en Madrid.* In English: *San Camilo, 1936.*
Experimental novel, narrated in the second person mostly, on events in Madrid during the week before the Nationalist uprising.

Cercas, Javier. *Soldados de Salamina.* In English: *Soldiers of Salamis.*
A young reporter investigates the circumstances surrounding the Falangist writer Rafael Sánchez Mazas's near execution during the war, in this immensely popular novel.

Chacón, Dulce. *Cielos de barro.* English extract: "Black Oaks."
Novel, with parallel stories of servants and masters, winners and losers, set in the backdrop of the war and its aftermath.

———. *La voz dormida.* In English: *The Sleeping Voice.*
About Republican women in Franco's prisons and the guerrilla movement. Based on real testimony.

Chirbes, Rafael. *La caída de Madrid.* Barcelona: Anagrama, 2000.
Novel on the memory of the war in November 1975, when Franco dies.

Coll, José Luis. *El hermano bastardo de Dios.*
Novel. The author is part of the comedy team Tip y Coll.

Delibes, Miguel. *Cinco horas con Mario.* In English: *Five Hours with Mario.*
Brilliant, stylistically complex novel, in which the civil war is a constant motif.

———. *377A, madera de héroe.* In English: *The Stuff of Heroes.*
Novel. A chronicle of postwar suffering.

Díaz Garrido, María del Carmen. *Los años únicos: Andanzas de una niña en el Madrid rojo.*
Semiautobiographical novel, organized in four parts corresponding to each year of the war.

Drieu la Rochelle, Pierre. *Gilles.*
The epilogue of this novel centers on the main character's experience as a volunteer on the Nationalist side.

Enzensberger, Hans Magnus. *Der kurze Sommer der Anarchie: Buenaventura Durrutis Leben und Tod.*
Novel, on the anarchist leader Durruti's life and death.

Eslava Galán, Juan. *La mula.*
Novel that centers on a peasant from Jaén and his mule.

Espina, Concha. *Luna roja: Novelas de la revolución.*
Dedicated to the Nationalist soldiers, this volume includes the short novels *El Dios de los niños*, *Tragedia rural*, *El hombre y el mastín*, and *La carpeta gris.*

———. *Retaguardia: Imágenes de vivos y de muertos.*
Pro-Nationalist novel, in which the conflict is seen along class lines.

Fernán Gómez, Fernando. *Las bicicletas son para el verano.*
Play, on which the film is based.

Ferrero, Jesús. *Las trece rosas.*
Novel, based on the story of thirteen young women, nearly all minors, belonging to a leftist political group, who were executed by the Nationalists in August 1939.

Foxá, Agustín de. *Madrid de corte a checa.*
Pro-Nationalist novel (1938), written in a grotesque, sometimes brilliant, *esperpento* style, dwelling on Republican excesses.

Franco, Francisco (pseud. Jaime de Andrade). *Raza: Anecdotario para el guión de una película.*
Quasi-novelized script for the film *Raza.*

Gabantxo, Amaia. "Your Gernika."
Short story, focusing on an Alzheimer-afflicted grandmother's memory of the bombing of Guernica. Written in English.

Gallego, Gregorio. *Asalto a la ciudad.*
Novel. Describes the battle for Madrid. Gallego was an officer in the Republican army and a member of the first Junta de Defensa de Madrid. He was imprisoned in numerous jails and concentration camps.

García Roldán, Ángel. *A boca de noche.*
Allegorical rendering of the war, about an unnamed conflict and country, in a town called Pueblo, where the mystery of two violent deaths is explored.

García Serrano, Rafael. *Eugenio o la proclamación de la primavera.*
Falangist novel, expounding the "pedagogy of the pistol."

———. *La fiel infantería.*
This novel won the José Antonio Primo de Rivera Prize in 1943. Depicts life in the Nationalist trenches. The author founded the Falangist student union SEU (Sindicato Español Universitario).

Gironella, José María. *Los cipreses creen en Dios.* In English: *The Cypresses Believe in God.*
Novel. Narrates events in Gerona leading up to the war.

———. *Un millón de muertos.* In English: *One Million Dead.*
Controversial sequel to *Los cipreses creen en Dios* (Nationalist Spain did not consider it appropriate to mourn *all* the dead).

Goytisolo, Juan. *Duelo en el Paraíso.* In English: *Children of Chaos.*
Novel. Reflects on the horror of war and the destruction of innocence.

———. *Señas de identidad.* In English: *Marks of Identity.*
Experimental novel that deconstructs history, focusing on the life of a Spanish exile.

Greene, Graham. *The Confidential Agent.*
Thriller, featuring an antifascist secret agent and with the civil war as background.

Hemingway, Ernest. The Fifth Column *and Four Stories of the Spanish Civil War.*
Hemingway's only full-length play (*The Fifth Column*) and four stories: "The Denunciation," "The Butterfly and the Tank," "Night before Battle," and "Under the Ridge."

———. *For Whom the Bell Tolls.*

Novel, about brotherhood and betrayal. A bridge is blown up as part of the Republican offensive.

Herrera Petere, José. *Cumbres de Extremadura: Novela de guerrilleros.*
Novel. First published in 1938. A band of Republican *guerrilleros* fights in the Nationalist rear guard.

Herrick, William. *¡Hermanos!*
Novel, on volunteers in the International Brigades. Based on personal experience.

Hughes, Dorothy B. *The Fallen Sparrow.*
Thriller, about a character who returns to the States after having been tortured by Spanish fascists.

Iráizoz, Carmen. *Belzunegui: El ocaso de una familia.*
First novel of a trilogy titled *Cuesta arriba, cuesta abajo*, depicting the devastating impact of the war on a family.

Iturralde, Juan. *Días de llamas.*
Novel. The story of Tomás Labayen, a Republican lawyer, who is accused of conspiracy and executed.

Jarnés, Benjamín. *Su línea de fuego.*
Novel, written between 1937 and 1940 but unpublished until 1980. Set in a hospital, a meditation on the war and the impossibility of dialogue.

Laforet, Carmen. *Nada.* In English: *Andrea* and *Nada.*
Novel, written in 1944, winner of the Nadal Prize in 1945. The life of a young girl during the grim post–civil war period in Barcelona.

León, María Teresa. *Juego limpio.*
Novel. Explores the Spanish Civil War through the eyes of a theater company bringing entertainment to the frontline Republican troops.

Lera, Ángel María de. *Las últimas banderas.*
Novel. Won the Planeta Prize of 1967. Describes the fall of Madrid, the anguish and expectations of Republican soldiers, and the ambivalent reaction of people to Franco's victory.

Llamazares, Julio. *Luna de lobos.*
In this lyrical, intense novel, a resistance group of maquis struggles to survive after Franco's victory.

López Mozo, Jerónimo. *Guernica.*
Experimental play, with characters created from Picasso's painting.

López Salinas, Armando. *Año tras año.*
Novel, on the reprisals and harsh postwar living conditions for the defeated Republicans.

Luca de Tena, Torcuato. *La brújula loca.*
Novel. Curious chapter organization by alphabet, *a* to *z*. Psychological profile of a child during the civil war.

Mainer, José Carlos, ed. *Falange y literatura: Antología.*
Writings by García Serrano, Foxá, Ridruejo, Torrente Ballester, and others.

Malraux, André. *L'espoir.* In English: *Man's Hope.*
Brilliant novel based on Malraux's experiences as commander of an air squadron for the republic.

March, Susana. *Algo muere cada día.*
Novel. Portrayal of the personal dissatisfactions, desires, and contradictions of a woman. The Spanish Civil War serves as background and context.

Marsé, Juan. *Si te dicen que caí.* In English: *The Fallen.*
Anti-Franco resistance and corruption share the stage in postwar Barcelona in this well-written, intense novel.

Martín Gaite, Carmen. *El cuarto de atrás.* In English: *The Back Room.*
Blends history (the war and postwar years) and fantasy beautifully in this now classic text.

Masip, Paulino. *El diario de Hamlet García.*
Metaphysical-social novel about a modest citizen who feels trapped in the conflict and obliged to act to survive.

Matute, Ana María. *Luciérnagas.* In English: *Fireflies.*
Novel. First published in a censored version as *En esta tierra* (Barcelona: Éxito, 1955). About a young girl and her sense of loss and alienation arising from the war.

———. *Primera memoria.* In English: *School of the Sun* and *Awakening.*
Psychological, poetic novel of adolescence and the war.

Maulvault, Lucien. *El requete.*
Novel, about an idealistic Carlist volunteer on the Nationalist side.

McGratty, A[rthur] R. *Face to the Sun.*
Pro-Franco, Catholic novel, in which the Nationalist defense of the Alcázar in Toledo is part of the story.

Medio, Dolores. *Diario de una maestra.*
The war as seen in the misfortunes and suffering of a Republican schoolteacher.

Montero, Rosa. *La hija del caníbal.*
Novel. Two narratives, one contemporary and the other about an anarchist's experiences before, during, and after the civil war.

Muñoz Molina, Antonio. *Beatus ille.*

The war haunts this beautifully written novel as memory and allegory.

———. *El jinete polaco.*

Novel. Received the 1991 Planeta Prize. Complex interweaving of history and fable, in which the civil war plays a significant role.

Olaizola, José Luis. *La guerra del general Escobar.*

Novel. Based on the real story of a Republican general who was accused of treason, imprisoned, and executed in the Montjuich castle in 1940.

Palencia, Isabel de. *En mi hambre mando yo.*

Novel. Interweaves a love story with social issues of the Spanish peasantry.

Pawel, Rebecca C. *Death of a Nationalist.*

Mystery novel set in 1939 Madrid, with a member of the *guardia civil* as protagonist.

———. *Law of Return.*

Pawel's second mystery novel centers again on the Nationalist Carlos Tejada, now a lieutenant in the *guardia civil*, and on political difficulties in postwar Salamanca.

———. *The Watcher in the Pine.*

In this third mystery, Tejada deals with Republican guerrillas in the Liébana region.

Pressburger, Emeric. *Killing a Mouse on Sunday.*

Novel, showing the postwar consequences of the conflict in the figure of a Republican exile still fighting Franco's forces. Film adaptation: *Behold a Pale Horse.*

Regler, Gustav. *Das große Beispiel.* In English: *The Great Crusade.*

Semiautobiographical novel of Regler's experiences as a political commissar in the International Brigades. First published in English.

Riera, Carme. *Senyora, ha vist els meus fills? / Ma'am, Have You Seen My Sons? Moveable Margins: The Narrative Art of Carme Riera.*

A one-act play with three women characters, about the war, class, and sexuality. The original Catalan is followed by the English translation.

Rivas, Manuel. *O lapis do carpinteiro.* In Spanish: *El lápiz del carpintero.* In English: *The Carpenter's Pencil.*

The destiny of an imprisoned, antifascist doctor is linked to that of several characters during the civil war.

Rodoreda, Mercè. *La plaça del Diamant.* In Spanish: *La plaza del Diamante.* In English: *The Time of the Doves* and *The Pigeon Girl.*

Lyrical and powerful novel about the destiny of an ordinary Catalan woman before, during, and after the war.

Rodríguez-Puértolas, Julio, ed. *Literatura fascista española: Antología.* Vol. 2.

Narrative, theater, essay, and poetry by Gonzalo Torrente Ballester, Eugenio D'Ors, Luis Rosales, Concha Espina, Rafael García Serrano, Gerardo Diego, and others.

Salom, Jaime. *La casa de las Chivas.*
Play. Nine people gather in one house during the war.

Sanchis Sinisterra, José. *¡Ay, Carmela! [and] Ñaque o, de piojos y actores.*
Play, on which the Saura film is based.

Sartre, Jean-Paul. "Le mur." In English: *"The Wall" and Other Stories.*
Powerful exploration of terror and guilt. Pablo, a Republican prisoner, is interrogated by fascists during the Spanish Civil War.

Sender, Ramón J. *Réquiem por un campesino español.* In English: *Requiem for a Spanish Peasant.*
First published in 1953 as *Mosén Millán.* Classic novel that blends poetry and politics, sacrifice and betrayal, with an explosive ending.

———. *El rey y la reina.* In English: *The King and the Queen.*
Novel. Sender weaves Eros and Thanatos into a symbolic account of fascism and war.

———. *Siete domingos rojos.* In English: *Seven Red Sundays.*
Novel. Explores labor unrest, the anarcho-syndicalist movement, and circumstances leading to the civil war.

Serrano Poncela, Segundo. *La viña de Nabot.*
First published in 1979, this well-written novel depicts the growing disillusionment of a Republican intellectual during the war.

Sinclair, Upton. *No Pasarán! (They Shall Not Pass).*
The subtitle of this tendentious novel is "A Story of the Battle of Madrid."

Soler, Bartolomé. *Los muertos no se cuentan.*
Novel. Set in Llano del Vallés, Catalonia; focuses on the pain, terror, and hatred experienced during the war.

Tejera, Nivaria. *El barranco.* English extract: "Children Can Wait."
Novel, narrated by an unnamed child and situated in the Canary Islands during the war.

Torrente Ballester, Gonzalo. *Javier Mariño: Historia de una conversión.*
The 1985 edition contains the author's "Nota breve" contextualizing the novel.

Umbral, Francisco. *Leyenda del César visionario.*
Excellent, compact novel on Franco's quest for power and his marginalization of the Falangist intelligentsia, interwoven with the story of a Republican trapped in the Nationalist zone.

Wolff, Milton. *Another Hill: An Autobiographical Novel.*

On the experiences of the American volunteers in the Abraham Lincoln Brigade, covering such issues as the desertion of some Americans, the execution of fascist prisoners, and black market activities. By the last commander of the Lincoln Brigade.

Biography, Memoirs, and Testimonies

Acier, Marcel, ed. *From Spanish Trenches: Recent Letters from Spain.*

Aguirre y Lecube, José Antonio de. *De Guernica a Nueva York, pasando por Berlín.* In English: *Escape via Berlin: Eluding Franco in Hitler's Europe.*

Álvarez del Vayo, Julio. *Freedom's Battle.*

Andújar, Manuel. *St. Cyprien, plage . . . campo de concentración.*

Armengou, Montse, and Ricard Belis. *Las fosas del silencio: ¿Hay un Holocausto español?*

Bartolí, José, and Narcis Molins i Fàbrega. *Campos de concentración, 1939–194 . . .*

Bernanos, Georges. *Les grands cimetières sous la lune.* In English: *A Diary of My Times.*

Bessie, Alvah. *Men in Battle.*

Bessie, Alvah, and Albert Prago, eds. *Our Fight: Writings by Veterans of the Abraham Lincoln Brigade, Spain, 1936–1939.*

Bessie, Dan, ed. *Alvah Bessie's Spanish Civil War Notebooks.*

Borkenau, Franz. *The Spanish Cockpit.*

Bowers, Claude G. *My Mission to Spain: Watching the Rehearsal for World War II.*

Bullón de Mendoza, Alfonso, and Álvaro de Diego. *Historias orales de la guerra civil.*

Carretero, José María [El Caballero Audaz]. *La revolución de los patibularios.*

Cuevas, Tomasa. *Prison of Women: Testimonies of War and Resistance in Spain, 1939–1975.* Trans. of both *Cárcel de mujeres* and *Mujeres de la resistencia.*

Davis, Frances. *My Shadow in the Sun.*

Doña, Juana. *Desde la noche y la niebla: Mujeres en las cárceles franquistas.*

Dwinger, Edwin Erich. *Spanische Silhouetten: Tagebuch einer Frontreise.*

Elordi, Carlos, ed. *Los años difíciles: El testimonio de los protagonistas anónimos de la guerra civil y la posguerra.*

Escobal, Patricio P. *Death Row: Spain, 1936.*

Everard, Conrad. *Luftkampf über Spanien: Kriegserlebnisse eines freiwilligen englischen Kampffliegers bei der nationalen Armee.*

Felsen, Milt. *The Anti-warrior: A Memoir.*

Ferrer, Eulalio. *Entre alambradas.*

Fisher, Harry. *Comrades: Tales of a Brigadista in the Spanish Civil War.*

Fraser, Ronald. *Blood of Spain: An Oral History of the Spanish Civil War.*

———. *In Hiding. The Life of Manuel Cortés.*

García Gerpe, Manuel. *Alambradas: Mis nueve meses por los campos de concentración de Francia.*

Gates, John. *The Story of an American Communist.*

Gellhorn, Martha. *The Face of War.*

González Fresco, Manuel. *Memoria dun fuxido, 1936.*

Hermanos, Juan. *El fin de la esperanza: Testimonio.*

Ibárruri, Dolores. *Pasionaria [and] Memorias [and] La lucha y la vida.*

———. *They Shall Not Pass: The Autobiography of La Pasionaria.*

Jaraiz Franco, Pilar. *Historia de una disidencia.*

Kee, Salaria. *A Negro Nurse in Republican Spain.*

Kent, Victoria. *Cuatro años en París, 1940–1944.*

Koestler, Arthur. *Spanish Testament.*

Lee, Laurie. *A Moment of War: A Memoir of the Spanish Civil War.*

Leguineche, Manuel, and Jesús Torbado. *Los topos: El testimonio estremecedor de quienes pasaron su vida escondidos en la España de la posguerra.*

León, María Teresa. *Memoria de la melancolía.*

McNair, John. *Spanish Diary.*

Medio, Dolores. *Atrapados en la ratonera: Memorias de una novelista.*

Merino Galán, Ángel. *Mi guerra empezó antes.*

Mora, Constancia de la. *In Place of Splendor: The Autobiography of a Spanish Woman.* Spanish version: *Doble esplendor: Autobiografía de una mujer española.*

Moral i Querol, Ramon. *Diari d'un exiliat, 1939–1945.*

Nelson, Cary, and Jefferson Hendricks, eds. *Madrid, 1937: Letters of the Abraham Lincoln Brigade from the Spanish Civil War.*

Nelson, Steve. *The Volunteers: A Personal Narrative of the Fight against Fascism in Spain.*

O'Neill, Carlota. *Una mujer en la guerra de España.*

Orwell, George. *Homage to Catalonia.*

Palencia, Isabel de. *I Must Have Liberty.*

Primo de Rivera, Pilar. *Recuerdos de una vida.*

Répide, Pedro de. *Memorias de un aparecido.*

Reverte, Jorge M., and Socorro Thomás. *Hijos de la guerra: Testimonios y recuerdos.*

Rodrigo, Antonina. *Mujer y exilio, 1939.*

Romeu Alfaro, Fernanda. *El silencio roto: Mujeres contra el franquismo.*

Rubin, Hank. *Spain's Cause Was Mine: A Memoir of an American Medic in the Spanish Civil War.*

Salazar, Margaret Van Epp. *Si yo te dijera . . . : Una historia oral de la sierra de Huelva.*

Scott-Ellis, Priscilla. *The Chances of Death: A Diary of the Spanish Civil War.*

Sender, Ramón J. *Contraataque.* In English: *Counter-attack in Spain* and *The War in Spain.*

Sender Barayón, Ramón. *A Death in Zamora.*

Silva, Emilio, and Santiago Macías. *Las fosas de Franco.*

Souchy, Agustín. *The Tragic Week in May.*

Strobl, Ingrid. *Partisanas.*

Strong, Anna Louise. *Spain in Arms, 1937.*

Tisa, John. *Recalling the Good Fight: An Autobiography of the Spanish Civil War.*

Trautloft, Hannes. *Als Jagdflieger in Spanien: Aus dem Tagebuch eines deutschen Legionärs.*

Vinyes, Ricard, Montse Armengou, and Ricard Belis. *Los niños perdidos del franquismo.*

Woolsey, Gamel. *Malaga Burning: An American Woman's Eyewitness Account of the Spanish Civil War.* Also known as *Death's Other Kingdom.*

Yates, James. *Mississippi to Madrid: Memoir of a Black American in the Abraham Lincoln Brigade.*

Secondary Sources

History

Aguilar Fernández, Paloma. *Memoria y olvido de la guerra civil española.* In English: *Memory and Amnesia: The Role of the Spanish Civil War in the Transition to Democracy.*

Alted Vigil, Alicia, Encarna Nicolás Marín, and Roger González Martell. *Los niños de la guerra de España en la Unión Soviética: De la evacuación al retorno, 1937–1999.*

Armengou, Montse, and Ricard Belis. *El convoy de los 927.*

Beevor, Antony. *The Spanish Civil War.*

Bolloten, Burnett. *The Grand Camouflage.*

———. *The Spanish Civil War: Revolution and Counter-revolution.*

Brenan, Gerald. *The Spanish Labyrinth.*

Broué, Pierre, and Émile Témime. *The Revolution and the Civil War in Spain.*

Cárcel Ortí, Vicente. *Mártires españoles del siglo XX.*

———. *La persecución religiosa en España durante la Segunda República, 1931–1939.*

Carr, Raymond. *The Civil War in Spain, 1936–39.*

———. Introduction. *The Spanish Civil War: A History in Pictures.*

Carroll, Peter N. *The Odyssey of the Abraham Lincoln Brigade: Americans in the Spanish Civil War.*

Castro Albarrán, Aniceto de. *La gran víctima.*

Cate-Arries, Francie. *Spanish Culture behind Barbed Wire: Memory and Representation of the French Concentration Camps, 1939–1945.*

Caudet, Francisco. *Hipótesis sobre el exilio republicano de 1939.*

Cortada, James W., ed. *A City in War: American Views on Barcelona and the Spanish Civil War.*

———, ed. *Historical Dictionary of the Spanish Civil War, 1936–1939.*

Coverdale, John F. *Italian Intervention in the Spanish Civil War.*

Devillard, María José, Álvaro Pazos, Susana Castillo, and Nuria Medina. *Los niños españoles en la URSS, 1937–1997: Narración y memoria.*

Dreyfus-Armand, Geneviève. *El exilio de los republicanos españoles en Francia: De la guerra civil a la muerte de Franco.*

Eby, Cecil. *Between the Bullet and the Lie: American Volunteers in the Spanish Civil War.*

Elordi, Carlos, ed. *Los años difíciles: El testimonio de los protagonistas anónimos de la guerra civil y la posguerra.*

Esenwein, George, and Adrian Shubert. *Spain at War: The Spanish Civil War in Context, 1931–1939.*

Eslava Galán, Juan. *Una historia de la guerra civil que no va a gustar a nadie.*

Esperabé de Arteaga, Enrique. *La guerra de reconquista española y el criminal comunismo: El glorioso ejército nacional.*

Estes, Kenneth W., and Daniel Kowalsky, eds. *The Spanish Civil War.*

Faber, Sebastiaan. *Exile and Cultural Hegemony: Spanish Intellectuals in Mexico, 1939–1975.*

Fagen, Patricia W. *Exiles and Citizens: Spanish Republicans in Mexico.*

Foss, William, and Cecil Gerahty. *The Spanish Arena.*

Fyrth, Jim, and Sally Alexander, eds. *Women's Voices from the Spanish Civil War.*

García Durán, Juan. *Bibliography of the Spanish Civil War / Bibliografía de la guerra civil española, 1936–1939.*

———. *La guerra civil española: Fuentes: Archivos, bibliografía y filmografía.*

Gerassi, John, ed. *The Premature Antifascists: North American Volunteers in the Spanish Civil War, 1936–39: An Oral History.*

Graham, Helen. *The Spanish Civil War: A Very Short Introduction.*

———. *The Spanish Republic at War, 1936–1939.*

Guttmann, Allen. *The Wound in the Heart: America and the Spanish Civil War.*

Holguín, Sandie. *Creating Spaniards: Culture and National Identity in Republican Spain.*

Howson, Gerald. *Arms for Spain: The Untold Story of the Spanish Civil War.*

Jackson, Angela. *British Women and the Spanish Civil War.*

Jackson, Gabriel. *A Concise History of the Spanish Civil War.*

———. *The Spanish Civil War: Domestic Crisis or International Conspiracy?*

———. *The Spanish Republic and the Civil War, 1931–1939.*

Keene, Judith. *Fighting for Franco: International Volunteers in Nationalist Spain during the Spanish Civil War, 1936–39.*

Lannon, Frances. *The Spanish Civil War, 1936–1939.*

Leguineche, Manuel, and Jesús Torbado. *Los topos: El testimonio estremecedor de quienes pasaron su vida escondidos en la España de la postguerra.*

Loureiro, Ángel G., ed. *Estelas, laberintos, nuevas sendas: Unamuno [and] Valle-Inclán [and] García Lorca [and] La guerra civil.*

Madariaga, María Rosa de. *Los moros que trajo Franco: La intervención de tropas coloniales en la guerra civil.*

Mangini, Shirley. *Memories of Resistance: Women's Voices from the Spanish Civil War.* In Spanish: *Recuerdos de la resistencia: La voz de las mujeres de la guerra civil.*

Marín Silvestre, Dolors. *Clandestinos: El maquis contra el franquismo, 1934–1975.*

Méndez, Diego. *El Valle de los Caídos: Idea, proyecto y construcción.*

Mendizábal, Alfred. *The Martyrdom of Spain: Origins of a Civil War.*

Moa, Pío. *Los mitos de la guerra civil.*

Las mujeres y la guerra civil española: III Jornadas de Estudios Monográficos.

Nash, Mary. *Defying Male Civilization: Women in the Spanish Civil War.*

Nelson, Cary, ed. *Remembering Spain: Hemingway's Civil War Eulogy and the Veterans of the Abraham Lincoln Brigade.*

Payne, Stanley. *Falange: A History of Spanish Fascism.*

Pons Prades, Eduardo. *Realidades de la guerra civil.*

Preston, Paul. *The Coming of the Spanish Civil War.*

———. *Doves of War: Four Women of Spain.*

———. *The Politics of Revenge.*

———, ed. *Revolution and War in Spain, 1931–39.*

———. *The Spanish Civil War, 1936–39.*

Radosh, Ronald, Mary R. Habeck, and Grigory Sevostianov, eds. *Spain Betrayed: The Soviet Union in the Spanish Civil War.*

Raguer, Hilari. *La pólvora y el incienso: La iglesia y la guerra civil española, 1936–1939.*

Ranzato, Gabriele. *The Spanish Civil War.*

Reig Tapia, Alberto. *Memoria de la guerra civil: Los mitos de la tribu.*

Rein, Raanan, ed. *Spanish Memories: Images of a Contested Past.*

Richards, Michael. *A Time of Silence: Civil War and the Culture of Repression in Franco's Spain, 1936–1945.*

Rosenstone, Robert A. *Crusade of the Left: The Lincoln Battalion in the Spanish Civil War.*

Sánchez, Isidro, Manuel Ortiz, and David Ruiz, eds. *España franquista: Causa General y actitudes sociales ante la dictadura.*

Sánchez, José M. *The Spanish Civil War as a Religious Tragedy.*

Schwartz, Fernando. *La internacionalización de la guerra civil española: Julio de 1936–marzo de 1937.*

Serrano, Secundino. *Maquis: Historia de la guerrilla antifranquista.*

Skoutelsky, Rémi. *L'espoir guidait leurs pas: Les volontaires français dans les Brigades Internationales, 1936–1939.*

Southworth, Herbert. *Guernica! Guernica!*

———. *El mito de la cruzada de Franco.*

The Spanish Civil War Collection. A Guide to the Microfilm Collection.

Stein, Louis. *Beyond Death and Exile: The Spanish Republicans in France, 1939–1955.*

Stradling, Robert. *History and Legend: Writing the International Brigades.*

Sueiro, Daniel. *El Valle de los Caídos: Los secretos de la cripta franquista.*

Thomas, Hugh. *The Spanish Civil War.*

Torres, Rafael. *Los esclavos de Franco.*

Trotsky, Leon. *The Spanish Revolution, 1931–39.*

Tuñón de Lara, Manuel, et al. *La guerra civil española 50 años después.*

Usandizaga, Aránzazu, ed. *Ve y cuenta lo que pasó en España: Mujeres extranjeras en la guerra civil: Una antología.*

Vinyes, Ricard. *Irredentas: Las presas políticas y sus hijos en las cárceles de Franco.*

Whealey, Robert H. *Hitler and Spain: The Nazi Role in the Spanish Civil War, 1936–1939.*

Literature and the Arts

Arte protegido: Memoria de la Junta del Tesoro Artístico durante la guerra civil.

Bannasch, Bettina, and Christiane Holm (with Carl Freytag), eds. *Erinnern und Erzählen: Der Spanische Bürgerkrieg in der deutschen und spanischen Literatur und in den Bildmedien.*

Benson, Frederick. *Writers in Arms: The Literary Impact of the Spanish Civil War.*

Bertrand de Muñoz, Maryse. *La guerra civil española en la novela: Bibliografía comentada.*

———. *Guerra y novela: La guerra española de 1936–1939.*

———. *La guerre civile espagnole et la littérature française.*

———, ed. *Literatura sobre la guerra civil: Poesía, narrativa, teatro, documentación: La expresión estética de una ideología antagonista.*

———. *La novela europea y americana y la guerra civil española.*

Bessie, Alvah, ed. *The Heart of Spain.*

Binns, Niall. *La llamada de España: Escritores extranjeros en la guerra civil.*

Boak, Denis. *Malraux: L'espoir.*

Brown, Frieda S., et al., eds. *Rewriting the Good Fight: Critical Essays on the Literature of the Spanish Civil War.*

Calamai, Natalia. *El compromiso en la poesía de la guerra civil española.*

Chipp, Herschel B. *Picasso's Guernica.*

Cirici, Alexandre. *La estética del franquismo.*

Collado, Fernando del. *El teatro bajo las bombas en la guerra civil.*

Coma, Javier. *La brigada Hollywood: Guerra española y cine americano.*

Cunningham, Valentine, ed. *Spanish Front: Writers on the Civil War.*

Devine, Kathleen, ed. *Modern Irish Writers and the Wars.*

Escolar, Hipólito. *La cultura durante la guerra civil.*

Fernández Cuenca, Carlos. *La guerra de España y el cine.*

Ford, Hugh D. *A Poet's War: British Poets and the Spanish Civil War.*

Geist, Anthony L., and Peter N. Carroll. *They Still Draw Pictures: Children's Art in Wartime from the Spanish Civil War to Kosovo.*

Gibson, Ian. *The Assassination of Federico García Lorca.*

Gubern, Román. *1936–1939: La guerra de España en la pantalla.*

"Guerra civil y producción cultural: Teatro, poesía, narrativa."

Hanrez, Marc, ed. *Les écrivains et la guerre d'Espagne.*

Hart, Stephen M., ed. *"¡No pasarán!": Art, Literature, and the Spanish Civil War.*

Hoskins, Catherine Bail. *Today the Struggle: Literature and Politics in England during the Spanish Civil War.*

Huxley, Aldous. Introduction. *They Still Draw Pictures! A Collection of Sixty Drawings Made by Spanish Children during the War.*

Kenwood, Alun, ed. *The Spanish Civil War: A Cultural and Historical Reader.*

Leeds Papers on Lorca and on Spanish Civil War Verse.

Luengo, Ana. *La encrucijada de la memoria: La memoria colectiva de la guerra civil española en la novela contemporánea.*

Martin, Rupert, and Frances Morris, eds. *No pasarán! Photographs and Posters of the Spanish Civil War.*

Martin, Russell. *Picasso's War: The Destruction of Guernica and the Masterpiece That Changed the World.*

Miller, John, ed. *Voices against Tyranny.*

Monleón, José. *El mono azul: Teatro de urgencia y romancero de la guerra civil.*

Monteath, Peter. *The Spanish Civil War in Literature, Film, and Art.*

———. *Writing the Good Fight: Political Commitment in the International Literature of the Spanish Civil War.*

Muste, John. *Say That We Saw Spain Die: Literary Consequences of the Spanish Civil War.*

Naharro-Calderón, José María, ed. *El exilio de las Españas de 1939 en las Américas: "¿Adónde fue la canción?"*

Oms, Marcel. *La guerre d'Espagne au cinéma.*

Oppler, Ellen C., ed. *Picasso's* Guernica.

Pabellón Español. *Exposición Internacional de París, 1937.*

Pérez, Janet, ed. "Voces poéticas femeninas de la guerra civil española."

Pérez, Janet, and Wendell Aycock, eds. *The Spanish Civil War in Literature.*

Ponce de León, José Luis S. *La novela española de la guerra civil, 1936–1939.*

Quintanilla, Luis. *All the Brave: Drawings of the Spanish War.*

———. *Franco's Black Spain: Drawings.*

Las Republicanas: Antología de textos e imágenes de la República y la guerra civil.

Ripoll-Freixes, Enric. *Cien películas sobre la guerra civil española.*

Rodríguez-Puértolas, Julio, ed. *Literatura fascista española.*

Romeiser, John, ed. *Red Flags, Black Flags: Critical Essays on the Literature of the Spanish Civil War.*

Rosenthal, Marilyn. *Poetry of the Spanish Civil War.*

Sanderson, Rena, ed. *Blowing the Bridge: Essays on Hemingway and* For Whom the Bell Tolls.

Sim [José Luis Rey Vila]. *Estampas de la revolución española 19 julio de 1936.*

Sperber, Murray A., ed. *And I Remember Spain: A Spanish Civil War Anthology.*

Thomas, Gareth. *The Novel of the Spanish Civil War.*

Trapiello, Andrés. *Las armas y las letras: Literatura y guerra civil, 1936–1939.*

Valis, Noël. "Nostalgia and Exile."

Valleau, Marjorie A. *The Spanish Civil War in American and European Films.*

Vernon, Kathleen, ed. *The Spanish Civil War and the Visual Arts.*

"Voces y textos de la Guerra Civil Española / Voices and Texts of the Spanish Civil War."

Vulpe, Nicola. "This Issue Is Not Ended: Canadian Poetry and the Spanish Civil War."

Weintraub, Stanley. *The Last Great Cause: The Intellectuals and the Spanish Civil War.*

Whelan, Richard. *Robert Capa: A Biography.*

Whiston, James. *Antonio Machado's Writings and the Spanish Civil War.*

See also "Secondary Sources: History," García Durán, *Bibliography* and *La guerra civil*; Spanish Civil War Collection.

Web Sites

These sites were last accessed 15 November 2005.

About the Spanish Civil War.

<http://www.english.uiuc.edu/maps/scw/scw.htm>.

Organized by Cary Nelson, the site contains Modern American poetry on the Spanish Civil War, a generous selection of other texts, and images.

Abraham Lincoln Brigade Archives.

<http://www.alba-valb.org>.

This site lists ALBA's ongoing projects, including the traveling exhibitions: a poster-collection section, *Shouts from the Wall,* and a photographic exhibit, *The Aura of the Cause,* with information about each show. Under "Education" are a high school curriculum and information about an annual essay contest. There are contact information for representatives of ALBA around the country and a bibliography of the organization's most recent articles. Along with an extensive selection of links to Web sites on the Spanish Civil War, ALBA offers a learning module of the Jewish men and women who participated as international volunteers in the Spanish Civil War. Its Web-based educational program For Your Liberty and Ours contains "Tools for Teachers and Educators," which provides resources and practical teaching tools on the war. Issues of the magazine of ALBA, *The Volunteer,* from 1938 to the present, are accessible. The archives are housed at New York University's Tamiment Library.

Alta Voz del Frente.

<http://www.altavozdelfrente.tk>.

Republican songs of the war. The site is in Spanish.

Anarchy Archives: The Spanish Civil War.

<dwardmac.pitzer.edu/Anarchist_Archives/spancivwar/Spanishcivilwar.html>.

This anarchist site includes various articles on the Spanish Civil War, pamphlets, information on the participation of women, links to collections of pictures and posters, and a list of online books. There is also a lengthy article by Eddie Conlon, "The Spanish Civil War: Anarchism in Action."

Archivo Guerra y Exilio.

<http://www.galeon.com/agenoticias>.

This Web site gives priority to the search for missing persons. It allows users to post information about missing relatives from the Spanish Civil War. Also included are articles, editorials, and current events.

Asociación de Amigos de las Brigadas Internacionales.

<http://www.brigadasinternacionales.org>.

Dedicated to preserving the memory of the International Brigades. Includes maps, photographs, a traveling exhibit, and other texts.

Asociación para la Recuperación de la Memoria Histórica.
<http://www.memoriahistorica.org>.
This site focuses on the recovery of historical memory, to aid in finding missing victims of the war and to increase public awareness of the lasting effects of the war.

British Pathé Film Archive.
<http://www.britishpathe.com>.
British Pathé has remastered and fully digitalized footage from its archives. More than seventy items on the Spanish Civil War can be accessed, at no charge.

La Cucaracha: The Spanish Civil War, 1936–1939.
<http://lacucaracha.info/>.
Includes music of the Spanish Civil War.

La guerra de Nuestros Abuelos. Ed. Aurelio Mena Hornero.
<http://platea.pntic.mec.es/~anilo/abuelos/portada.htm >.
A site that makes available oral histories of the war and postwar period.

IBMT: The International Brigade Memorial Trust.
<http://www.international-brigades.org.uk>.
The trust is meant to "educate the public in the history of the men and women who fought in the International Brigades . . . by preserving and cataloguing valuable historical material . . . [and] by making such material available to the public." It has a comprehensive list of both published and unpublished accounts of working-class volunteers.

Legion Condor. Axis History Factbook. Ed. Marcus Wendel.
<http://www.axishistory.com/index.php?id=235>.
On the German Condor Legion, which supported Franco.

Marx Memorial Library.
<http://www.marxlibrary.net>.
The library contains what is "arguably, the most comprehensive collection in the world on the Spanish Civil War."

Southworth Spanish Civil War Collection. Mandeville Special Collections Lib., U of California, San Diego.
<http://orpheus.ucsd.edu/speccoll/southwcoll.html>.
The collection contains six hundred drawings by Spanish schoolchildren and an impressive poster collection.

The Spanish Civil War, Dreams and Nightmares. Imperial War Museum.
<http://www.iwm.org.uk/upload/package/5/spanish/index.htm>.
The site has multiple components: a wonderful sound archive with extracts of interviews with participants in the Spanish Civil War, a summary of events, a catalog of publications, a list of printed books, and a section on Spanish cinema and the civil war.

The Spanish Civil War: Obscure Wars Series, Axis and Allies Variant.
<http://www.guildofblades.com/empires/spanish.html>.
This Web site sells board games relating to historic events, in this case the
Spanish Civil War. It has obituaries, important meeting dates, letters, and
announcements for various conferences on the Spanish Civil War.

La Web del Barranque.
<http://www.barranque.com/guerracivil>.
This well-organized site aims to present a nonpartisan view of the war. It
contains an extensive collection of photographs and images of the war.

Working Class Movement Library.
<http://www.wcml.org.uk>.
This collection in Salford, England, offers particularly good holdings of
unpublished memoirs from local (northwest of England) volunteers.

Part VII

Course Syllabi

Jo Labanyi

Memory, History, Representation: The Spanish Civil War and Its Aftermath

Course Description

The course, taught to final-year undergraduates, aims to explore the ways in which the Spanish Civil War and its aftermath of repression and deprivation have been memorialized, through study of a number of written and visual texts ranging from the time of the war to 2002. Particular attention is paid to recent texts. Key issues are the importance of transgenerational transmission, the context of the moment in which these memorializations were read and viewed, and the context in which they were produced. A central hypothesis is that memorialization is blocked not only by censorship and repression but also by a lack of receptive interlocutors (which may result from both political and individual factors). The texts studied are photographs of the Spanish Civil War, written and audiovisual testimonies, feature films produced under the early Franco regime (the 1941 and 1950 versions of the film *Raza* scripted under a pseudonym by General Franco) and after the return to democracy, novels written during the dictatorship by writers who were children at the time of the war, and novels written after its end by younger writers. These texts not only provide historical information about the civil war and the early Franco dictatorship but also encourage reflection on how violent and traumatic events are remembered (or not). Ethical questions about memory and forgetting are raised throughout. Students are introduced to theoretical writing on memory and trauma and to historical writing on the political uses of memory and forgetting. All the texts studied invite reflection on how historical knowledge is mediated by cultural representations and, conversely, on the importance of grounding cultural representations in a concrete historical context.

Evaluation

Students are evaluated on two written tasks and a class presentation. The first written task is an analysis (approximately 2,000 words) of a theoretical or historical text on the list of further reading, as specified below, counting for 30% of the course grade. The second written task is a substantial essay on one or more of the prescribed primary texts, exploring a research question formulated by students in consultation with the course instructor (approximately 3,500 words) and counting for 60% of the course grade. The aim of this task is to encourage students to produce a high-level argument, backed by evidence, that provides a transition to postgraduate work. All students give a short class presentation (approximately 10 minutes) in the seminars. A choice of topics for each week is listed in the schedule of class sessions below.

For the analysis of a theoretical or historical text, choose one of the following:

Evaluate the arguments presented in one of the theoretical articles or chapters on memory listed below and consider their usefulness for thinking about how difficult periods of history are—or are not, or might be—remembered.

Evaluate the strategies used by one of the historical texts on Spain listed below to present a story of the Spanish Civil War or of its aftermath.

Reading and Viewing Materials

Aguilar Fernández, Paloma. *Memoria y olvido de la guerra civil española.*
Alberich, Fernán. "*Raza.*"

Alted Vigil, Alicia, Encarna Nicolás Marín, and Roger González Martell. *Los niños de la guerra de España en la Unión Soviética.*

¡Ay Carmela! Dir. Carlos Saura.

Barthes, Roland. *Camera Lucida.*

Benjamin, Walter. "A Small History of Photography."

———. "Theses on the Philosophy of History."

Cadava, Eduardo. *Words of Light.*

Chun, Kimberly. "What Is a Ghost?"

Connerton, Paul. *How Societies Remember* (esp. the chapter "Social Memory").

Devillard, María José, Álvaro Pazos, Susana Castillo, and Nuria Medina. *Los niños españoles en la URSS, 1937–1997.*

D'Lugo, Marvin. *The Films of Carlos Saura.*

Elordi, Carlos, ed. *Los años difíciles.*

El espinazo del diablo. Dir. Guillermo del Toro.

El espíritu de la colmena. Dir. Víctor Erice.

Espíritu de una raza. Dir. José Luis Sáenz de Heredia. Revised version of his *Raza.*

Felman, Shoshana, and Dori Laub. *Testimony.*

Franco, Francisco (pseud. Jaime de Andrade). *Raza* (original script for the film).

Fraser, Ronald. *Blood of Spain: The Experience of Civil War, 1936–1939.* Spanish translation: *Recuérdalo tú y recuérdalo a otros.*

Freud, Sigmund. "Mourning and Melancholia."

Goytisolo, Juan. *Duelo en el Paraíso.*

Graham, Helen, and Jo Labanyi, eds. *Spanish Cultural Studies* (esp. part 2 and section 1 of part 3).

La guerrilla de la memoria. Dir. Javier Corcuera. Documentary film.

Gugelberger, Georg M., ed. *The Real Thing.*

Hirsch, Marianne. "Mourning and Postmemory."

Horna, Kati. *Fotografías de la guerra civil española, 1936–1937.* Exhibition catalog.

Jordan, Barry, and Rikki Morgan-Tamosunas. "Reconstructing the Past."

Labanyi, Jo. "The Ambiguous Implications of the Mythical References in Juan Goytisolo's *Duelo en el Paraíso.*"

———. "History and Hauntology; or, What Does One Do with the Ghosts of the Past?"

———. "The Politics of the Everyday and the Eternity of Ruins."

Lafuente, Isaías. *Tiempos de hambre.*

Leguineche, Manuel, and Jesús Torbado. *Los topos.* Testimonies.

Llamazares, Julio. *Luna de lobos.*

Moreiras-Menor, Cristina. "Sombras de una dictadura."

Los niños de Rusia. Dir. Jaime Camino. Documentary film.

Radstone, Susannah, ed. *Memory and Methodology.*

Raza. Dir. José Luis Sáenz de Heredia.

Reig Tapia, Alberto. *Memoria de la guerra civil.*

Rein, Raanan, ed. *Spanish Memories.* (See esp. Cenarro; Richards, "From War"; Aguilar Fernández and Humlebaek; Narotsky and Smith).

Resina, Joan Ramon, ed. *Disremembering the Dictatorship.*

Richards, Michael. *A Time of Silence.*

Rivas, Manuel. *El lápiz del carpintero.* Translated into Castilian from the original Galician.

Sánchez Biosca, Vicente, ed. *Materiales para una iconografía de Francisco Franco.*

Serrano, Secundino. *Maquis.*

Smith, Paul Julian. "Between Metaphysics and Scientism."

Van Alphen, Ernst. "Symptoms of Discursivity."

Zafra, Enrique, Rosalía Crego, and Carmen Heredia. *Los niños españoles evacuados a la URSS.*

Week   Topic, Student Presentations, Readings

1   Thinking about memory, history, and representation: introduction to issues involved in memory and memorialization, with a brief outline of the history of remembering and forgetting under the Franco dictatorship and the return to democracy. The lecture stresses the importance of getting beyond empiricist ("factual") forms of historiography to capture the emotional residues of the past. Student presentations: Discussion of Van Alphen's "Symptoms of Discursivity"; Freud's "Mourning and Melancholia"; Benjamin's "A Small History of Photography."

2   The civil war photographs of Kati Horna: discussion of ways of reading photographs and of their value as historical documents (what exactly are they documenting?), with references to specific photographs by Horna. Student presentations: three students will each analyze one photograph by Horna, allocated in advance. Readings: Cadava 7–13,

59–66; Benjamin, "Small History" and "Theses"; "Politics."

3   *Raza*: explanation of the political and historical background to u.. and its two versions. The film is set in the context of Spanish cinema in the years immediately following the civil war. We discuss the issue of official memorializations of the past and of how one responds to this film as a version of history given by the instigators and victors of the civil war (the Nationalist coalition of fascists, monarchists, Carlists, Catholics, and the right-wing in general). Student presentations: the significance for the film's representation of national history of the sacrificial ethos on which the film is built; the film's depiction of gender roles; how the film encourages spectator identification with certain characters to legitimize the civil war through the use of camera work, acting style, costume, etc. Reading: Alberich.

4   *Duelo en el Paraíso*: The novel is set in the context of the emergence in the mid-1950s of an intellectual opposition, mostly drawn from the sons of the Nationalist victors, who experienced the civil war as children. We discuss the novel's use of biblical allegory (the fall from paradise) as an indirect form of statement in order to get around the censorship and how allegory trains readers to decode a hidden message. We ask how interpretation of the novel might have been circumscribed at the time of its publication in 1955, given prevailing political ideologies. Student presentations: the effects created by the construction of the novel around a series of flashbacks (in particular, think about how this device affects the novel's representation of historical time); the novel's ambivalent attitude to violence; how class affects the novel's depiction of history. Reading: Labanyi, "Ambiguous Implications."

5   *El espíritu de la colmena*: the film's relation to the notion of history as a haunting (the traces or wound left by a past that cannot be recovered) that demands reparation. We discuss the film in the context of the notion of trauma. We think particularly about how the historical moment when the film appeared (1973) may have affected viewers' responses and about its meanings when viewed today. In particular we emphasize the importance of the film's treatment of transgenerational transmission and ask whether its use of indirect forms of representation (required at the time by censorship) may not remain more effective than realist treatment (which has characterized many films about the civil war since the return to democracy). Student presentations: the role of silence in the film; the role of photographs in the film; how the mise-en-scène makes indirect statements in the film. Readings: Labanyi, "History and Hauntology"; Smith.

6   *Los topos*: We discuss *testimonio* as a genre, bearing in mind this volume's pioneering role as one of the first of its kind in Spain. We consider the significance of its reissue in 1999 (sixty years after the civil war's end, at a time of a boom in memory work around the civil war

and its aftermath). We ask what is the status of such first-person accounts and what is the role of the editors. We also ask what kind of therapeutic value the accounts may have had for the speakers, the interviewers and editors, and readers (both in 1977 and in 1999). Student presentations: three students each to discuss one *testimonio* from *Los topos*, allocated in advance, paying particular attention to how these first-person accounts differ from the historical accounts given by historians, both in what they talk about and in the way they organize their material. Readings: Felman and Laub; Gugelberger.

7   *Luna de lobos*: We set this novel (Llamazares's first) in the context of his fictional production, all of it concerned with the recovery of historical memory through attachment to place. We discuss the concept of place memory and its relation to collective memory. We also relate the novel to Corcuera's 2002 documentary *La guerrilla de la memoria*, stressing the importance of the existence of an interlocutor for a story to be told. With reference to both texts, we discuss the emphasis on community. Student presentations: the significance of the first-person narration of the novel; how the novel uses landscape description as a way of saying something about history; the kind of picture of the anti-Francoist guerrilla fighters that emerges from *La guerrilla de la memoria* and the narrative and cinematic strategies used to convey it. (Watch the DVD extras as well as the film, especially the scene from the Gijón Film Festival.) Viewing and readings: *La guerrilla de la memoria*; Paul Preston, "The Urban and Rural *Guerrilla* of the 1940s," in Graham and Labanyi 229–37; Serrano.

8   *¡Ay, Carmela!*: We set the film in the context of Saura's shift toward increasingly self-reflexive (postmodern?) forms of representation, asking what is the function of performance in the film. We also ask how this stress on performance might relate to the film's realist cinematography and whether realism is sufficient to convey a sense of history. Student presentations: the extent to which Saura's film reduces history to performance; the success of the film's mix of comedy and tragedy as a means of depicting the civil war; the function of Gustavete in the film. Reading: Jordan and Tamosunas-Morgan.

9   *El lápiz del carpintero*: We discuss the significance of the novel's Galician perspective, set in a wider national and international scenario. In particular we ask why Rivas chose a former Francoist thug as his narrator and a Lusophone African prostitute as the recipient of his story. We ask how this novel interpellates the Galician (and Spanish) reader of its time of publication (1998). Student presentations: how Rivas's novel might be seen as an attempt to heal old divisions among the different factions in the civil war; the effects created by making the protagonist's death the trigger that generates the whole story; the image of Republican Spain that the novel conveys to readers in 1998 through its protagonist Doctor Da Barca.

10   *El espinazo del diablo*: The film is compared with *El espíritu de la col-mena* for its use of haunting as a central metaphor. We argue that the film is successful precisely because it avoids a realistic depiction of the events of the civil war. We consider how the ghost story format functions as an allegory of the ethical duty to transmit the horror of the past to future generations. We ask how the film's appeal to the horror genre fits with its realistic re-creation of period settings. We also discuss the very embodied nature of the ghosts in the film. Student presentations: the relation of the ghost of Santi to the ghost of the teacher Casares and why the film has two ghosts; the film's use of visual images to say something about the horror of war; what the film is trying to say about history through its representation of the character Jacinto. Readings: Benjamin, "Theses"; Cadava; Chun; Labanyi, "History and Hauntology."

11   *Los niños de Rusia*: We take further the discussion of *testimonio* begun with the classes on *Los topos*, looking at what is specific to the use of film, rather than print, as the medium of diffusion. Student presentations: the effects produced by the way Camino has organized the material from the oral history interviews; the added value provided by the visual image and musical sound track (as opposed to what is said) in Camino's documentary; how our reception of these *testimonios* is affected by our knowledge of the historical fact of the demise of Soviet Communism in 1989. Readings: Alted Vigil, Nicolás Marín, and González Martell; Devillard, Pazos, Castillo, and Medina; Felman and Laub; Gugelberger; Zafra, Crego, and Heredia.

Note: Publication details for all works mentioned in this syllabus are provided in the list of works cited at the end of this book.

Tabea Alexa Linhard

To the Barricades: Civil War, Cultural Production, and Gender in Spain

Course Description

I introduced this seminar, taught in the spring semester of 2000 at Duke University, to an audience of first- and second-year undergraduates, by describing the motivation behind my engagement with this particular teaching and research area. At the risk of sounding too romantic, I referred to the death of the *Trece Rosas*, thirteen young women, nearly all minors, who had belonged to the Unified Socialist Youth and who were executed in August of 1939. Their story is narrated in a small group of texts: poems written by the women's fellow prisoners; scattered testimonies and memoirs; as well as the letters that Julia Conesa, one of the minors, wrote to her mother from prison. These letters end with the words, "Do not let my name be erased from history."

It would be preposterous to assume that this course actually succeeded in rescuing Conesa's name from the murky amnesia of Spanish history. However, this anecdote still represents the origins from which most of the issues covered in the course emerged and the juncture where at the end of the semester all the topics we addressed came together.

The Spanish Civil War can be and has been taught from a variety of perspectives. Issues ranging from the representation of iconic gendered images in wartime posters to the cultural production of memory, among a long list of others, can be covered in courses addressing the conflict, its origins, and its aftermath. Since it is impossible to discuss every single aspect of the Spanish Civil War in a one-semester seminar, I structured my class so that students would learn the ways in which a major historical event not only signifies a paradigm shift but also fosters a number of myths, symbols, and icons as well as a mainstream narrative. The focus on gender gave the students the necessary tools to recognize the contradictions, conflicts, and limits of this mainstream narrative. Such an approach called for the inclusion of a variety of genres that alternated between well-known, canonical texts on the Spanish Civil War and other, more marginal texts that allowed the students to question how major historical events are narrated, who narrates them, and who remains excluded from them.

The seminar was organized around eight questions that moved from a general perspective of the war, to the role of cultural production on both sides, to women's participation at the front and at the home front, to coming of age in times of war, and finally to the question of memory. These questions delineated a progression of literary, historical, and theoretical issues that helped the students develop critical positions in relation to the discussed texts. Even though gender, cultural production, and memory were underlying themes throughout the course, our discussions in class (as well as the students' papers and presentations) did not exclusively revolve around these topics. Ramón J. Sender's novel *Réquiem por un campesino español* sparked discussions on the role of (institutionalized) religion during the war; Ken Loach's film *Land and Freedom* addressed conflicts among the Republican left. Students' presentations also covered, among others, Ernest Hemingway's *For Whom the Bell Tolls*, Picasso's *Guernica*, and civil war testimonies from British and American women.

Though tackling every aspect of the war in one semester is impossible, we did accomplish a number of pedagogical goals that came together in the final discussion of the death of the *Trece Rosas*. By the time we engaged with the poems, testimonies, and letters dedicated to the thirteen young women, the students were able to understand and discuss the cultural construction of myths and icons that permeate discourses of gender and war—not only in the Spanish context. They were also familiar with the historical and cultural context that led to the execution of thirteen young women whose only crime had been their membership in a leftist political party. Finally, they addressed questions of history and memory in contemporary Spain.

Judging from students' evaluations, the interdisciplinary approach that framed the course was very productive and succeeded in providing a variety of perspectives of the Spanish Civil War. Some students found that reading and studying different genres were challenging at times, but this interdisciplinarity gave them the chance to question cultural representations—not only of women in war—they might otherwise have taken for granted.

Even though I was generally satisfied with the course, I will make a number of changes in the syllabus next time I teach the Spanish Civil War. With two brief exceptions, Antonio R. Guardiola's poem "La mano de Franco," and the essay "La tierra roja," all primary texts were exclusively written by supporters of the republic (I do not mention this text in the syllabus but included it later in the course. It can be found in Eutimio Martín's article "La mujer en la poesía de la Guerra Civil Española."). Including at least a number of texts stemming from the other side would, I believe, have allowed the students a more complicated understanding of women's roles in relation not just to Francoism but also to fascism. More-over, focusing solely on women on the Republican side might have perpet-uated, at least to a degree, a binary thinking that associated women in Republican Spain with emancipatory possibilities, while exclusively ascrib-ing domesticating gestures to the women of Francoist Spain.

The materials used in this course represent a very specific cross-section of the large amount of available texts that center on the intersections of gender and war during the conflict in Spain. If we consider the civil war as a whole, the resources used here are but a minimal and very consciously chosen selection. I believe, however, that a careful engagement with apparently very particular, even ephemeral, issues like the death of the *Trece Rosas* might be one of the most productive ways to approach an enormously complex topic like the Spanish Civil War in the classroom.

This course has two main objectives: first, to examine the cultural pro-duction of the Spanish Civil War; second, to discuss the contradictions and ambiguities that arise when women participate in revolutions and wars. Literary texts, poems, films, photographs, and posters of the war are ana-lyzed in their relation to more theoretical questions dealing with revolu-tion, literature, and gender. We discuss the myths and stereotypes that are part of narratives of war and revolution, the role of literature and cultural production in times of war and revolution, the relation between art and political propaganda, and the motives for the participation of foreigners in the war and the effects of the conflict in the international arena. Besides offering a panoramic view of the cultural and historical period of the Spanish Civil War, the course raises the fundamental question, Who has the right and responsibility to narrate and represent revolutions and wars?

Evaluation

In this course we read two novels, war poetry, stories, excerpts from memoirs, and political pamphlets. Brief readings on the historical circumstances in Spain are also assigned; they include both canonical and little-known texts directly related to the participation of women in the war. Films and documentaries are shown. The course is divided into seven sections, which permits students to develop their own critical positions. At the end of each of the first six sections, they hand in an essay of one to two pages. The final essay is a little longer (4–5 pp.) and covers at least two of the texts discussed in class or in student presentations. Of their grade for the essays, 66% is based on content, 33% on grammar. Attendance and class participation are required.

Each student is required to make an oral presentation of twenty minutes on a theme related to the course. This theme can be on a Spanish Civil War text not discussed in class (e.g., Hemingway's *For Whom the Bell Tolls* or Orwell's *Homage to Catalonia*) or a text on other revolutions or wars in the Spanish-speaking world that deals with the themes discussed in the course (e.g., Margaret Randall's *Sandino's Daughters* or Cristina García's *Dreaming in Cuban*). Presentations can be made individually or in tandem.

Grades are based on participation (30%), the six essays (40%), presentations (15%), and the final essay (15%).

Reading and Viewing Materials

Aldecoa, Josefina, ed. *Los niños de la guerra.*
Alted Vigil, Alicia. "The Republican and National Wartime Apparatus."
Las bicicletas son para el verano. Dir. Jaime Chávarri.
Caudet, Francisco, ed. *Romancero de la guerra civil.*
El caudillo. Dir. Basilio Martín Patino.
Di Febo, Giuliana. *Resistencia y movimiento de mujeres en España, 1936–1976.*
Graham, Helen. "Gender and the State."
———. "Women and Social Change."
Graham, Helen, and Jo Labanyi, eds. *Spanish Cultural Studies.*

Hernández, Miguel. *Viento del pueblo.*

Ibárruri, Dolores. *A las mujeres madrileñas.*

Labanyi, Jo. "Propaganda Art."

Land and Freedom. Dir. Ken Loach.

León, María Teresa. "Una estrella roja."

Libertarias. Dir. Vicente Aranda.

Lina Odena.

Linhard, Tabea Alexa. "The Death Story of the 'Trece Rosas.'"

El Mono Azul.

Montero, Rosa. "Las Trece Rosas."

"Mujeres libres."

Neruda, Pablo. *España en el corazón.*

Ramos-Gascón, Antonio, ed. *Romancero del ejército popular.*

Ramos-Gascón, Antonio, and Manuel Moreno, eds. *Lina Odena.*

Las Republicanas.

Rivas, Manuel. "La lengua de las mariposas."

Rodoreda, Mercè. *La plaza del Diamante.*

Rodrigo, Antonina. *Mujeres para la historia.*

———. *Mujer y exilio, 1939.*

Romeu Alfaro, Fernanda. *El silencio roto.*

Sender, Ramón J. *Réquiem por un campesino español.*

The Spanish Civil War. Granada Television.

Strobl, Ingrid. *Partisanas.*

Vicente Hernando, César de, ed. *Poesía de la guerra civil española.*

Class	Topic, Assignments
	The Front
1	Introduction. Web sites related to the civil war.
2	Republicans and Nationalists, posters of the Spanish Civil War. Neruda, "Explico algunas cosas," in *España en el corazón.*
3	Ideologies; documentary. Handout; *The Spanish Civil War*, part 1.
4	The importance of cultural production on both sides. Alted, Labanyi.
5	*El Mono Azul* (handout).
	Civil War Poetry
6	The death of Federico García Lorca. Antonio Machado, "El crimen fue en Granada," in Vicente Hernando 343.

| 7 | *El romancero general de la guerra* and *El romancero del ejército popular.* Miguel Hernández, "Vientos del pueblo me llevan," in Vicente Hernando; Antonio R. Guardiola, "La mano de Franco," in Vicente Hernando. |
| 8 | Félix Paredes, "Encarnación Jiménez," in Vicente Hernando; Nicolasa Giménez, "Madrileñas ¡A las armas!," in Ramos-Gascón. |

Fiction about the Front

| 9–11 | *Réquiem por un campesino español.* |
| 12–13 | *Land and Freedom.* |

Why Did Women Want to Participate?

14	Political parties and the participation of women in the war. Graham, "Women and Social Change."
15	Female anarchists. "Mujeres libres."
16	Female Communists. Rodrigo, "Pasionaria," in her *Mujeres para la historia*; Ibárruri.
17	Militiawomen. Testimony of Fifi and Chico, in Strobl.
18	The case of Lina Odena. *Lina Odena*; Pla y Beltrán, "A Lina Odena, muerta entre Guadix y Granada," and Lorenzo Varela, "Lina Odena," in Ramos-Gascón and Moreno.
19	The case of Rosario Sánchez Mora, *dinamitera*. Rodrigo, "Rosario Sánchez Mora, Dinamitera," in her *Mujer y exilio*; "Rosario, Dinamitera," in Hernández.
20–21	*Libertarias.*
22–23	Presentations and songs.

The Rearguard

| 24–25 | Where does the front end and where does the rearguard begin? *Las bicicletas son para el verano.* |
| 26–30 | Rodoreda. |

The Children of the War

31	Aldecoa; León.
32	Rivas.
33–37	Presentations and songs.

The End of the War, Memory, and Amnesia

38	What happens when the war is lost? Graham, "Gender."
39–40	*Trece Rosas*, a counternarrative? The letters of Julia Conesa, in Romeu Alfaro; Montero.
41	Poems on the deaths of the *Trece Rosas*, in *Las Republicanas*, Romeu Alfaro, and Di Febo, "La última noche de las Trece Rosas," in Linhard.
42	Review.

Note: Publication details for all works mentioned in this syllabus are provided in the list of works cited at the end of this book.

James Mandrell

Representations of, and Reactions to, the Spanish Civil War

Course Description

The undergraduate course on the Spanish Civil War that I taught at Brandeis University was developed in response to a distinct need and a genuine opportunity. The need was relatively simple: to teach a course on the Spanish Civil War in English translation that would appeal to diverse constituencies throughout the university. This was not as easy as it might at first appear. Given the vagaries of publishing in the late-twentieth and early-twenty-first centuries, the possibility of finding Spanish texts translated to English and readily available semester after semester, year after year, cannot be taken for granted. Texts move in and out of print so rapidly that even a few months can change what is possible to offer students. And with the increasing legal limitations on photocopying, what was once a fallback position is no longer an option.

The opportunity that I wanted to explore was to send students into the Abraham Lincoln Brigade Archives (ALBA), which were housed until recently in Farber Library at Brandeis.[1] I thought that the opportunity for students to work with primary sources relating to the Spanish Civil War and its aftermath was too extraordinary to pass up. I therefore decided to focus not on the Spanish Civil War per se but on representations of, and reactions to, the war, as a means of rendering more complex the notion of history with which many students seem to have become comfortable.

I began the course with brief lectures on modern Spanish history leading up to the civil war so that students would better be able to understand some of the competing factions and interests. We followed this by reading and discussing those sections from Raymond Carr's *Spain, 1808–1975* pertaining to the years before and during the Spanish Civil War (esp. 640–94) and then moved into a consideration of history and representation by reading Hayden White's "The Historical Text as Literary Artifact," as well as selections from David Hackett Fischer's *Historians' Fallacies* alongside the schemata on "telling" and "understanding" in Claude Lévi-Strauss's "The Structural Study of Myth."[2] My purpose in juxtaposing material on the historical backdrop to events in Spain with essays on the rhetorical aspects of historical—indeed, all—narratives was to open up the possibility of reading different depictions of the Spanish Civil War and its effects without continual recourse to what was "real" or "true."

At this point, we started reading various accounts of the Spanish Civil War, principally by writers who were not themselves Spanish. These texts included journalistic perspectives as well as autobiographical accounts and poetic responses. The sheer range of genres and outlooks guaranteed fruitful discussions and set the stage for visual reactions to the war: the beautiful posters used to further the Republican cause and Pablo Picasso's *Guernica*.[3] Although Picasso's painting is notoriously difficult to interpret, the context provided by documentary footage of the bombing of Guernica as well as the Paris World's Fair of 1937 made possible a rich mix of commentary that set the stage for the novels by Mercè Rodoreda and Juan Goytisolo.

In addition to the readings for the course, students were encouraged to attend films shown outside class. These films were a mix of documentaries from both before and after the war—for example, Luis Buñuel's *Las Hurdes: Land without Bread*, Lisa Berger and Carol Mazer's remarkable *De toda la vida (For All Our Lives)*—as well as commercial Spanish releases that addressed the dynamics of the period or the war either implicitly, as in Fernando Trueba's *Belle Epoque*, or explicitly, as in Carlos Saura's *¡Ay, Carmela!* Again, with the emphasis on representation, especially the selection of and ordering of events, the movies provided yet another avenue for a consideration of the historical dimensions of the Spanish Civil War.

Yet the most meaningful aspect of this course by far was the archival project, which was extraordinarily time-consuming. Students were required to identify early in the semester materials found in the Abraham Lincoln Brigade Archives with which they would work over the course of the semester. The first step in the project was to produce a catalog of a set of materials from the archives—for example, documents from the Spanish Refugee Archives (mostly in Spanish and French), a specific set of photographs, background for the film *The Good Fight*, and videos in the Harriman Collection. The second step was designed to give students a sense of how work with primary sources can be expanded into a larger project. At this stage, students were asked to compile a selected bibliography of materials related to the archival work and to annotate each entry. Finally they were encouraged to write a paper for the course using documents from their archival research.

Student response to the course was positive, but by far the most exciting part of the class was the archival project. For students the distinction between primary and secondary sources was real, not abstract, as they came into contact with, say, handwritten letters sent home from somewhere in Spain. Creased and stained, these original documents spoke with an immediacy that could not be found in a collection of different kinds of texts; they embodied the people who wrote and then received them and brought some of the human dimensions of the Spanish Civil War into the students' present.

Virtually any course on the Spanish Civil War would appeal to students. But the possibility of studying the texts in question in the context of doing archival research on an event now so remote to people born in the late twentieth century makes the material much more compelling. Although the Abraham Lincoln Brigade Archives are no longer housed at Brandeis, it is my hope that with the advent of the WWW pertinent primary sources will soon be available to students and scholars around the world.

In this course we study the various ways in which the events of the Spanish Civil War are portrayed or represented. We begin with a brief historical overview of the history of Spain of the nineteenth and twentieth centuries in general and of the civil war in particular. In the first half of the course, we continue with a consideration of foreign interpretations of the war. During the second half of the course, we turn to Spanish considerations, including artistic works and literary texts. Because this was a library-intensive course, students were required to work with the holdings of the Spanish Civil War Archives in Goldfarb Library.

Several films relating to the war are shown. Although attendance at the films is optional, they provide a review of pertinent information on the war, a sample of different perspectives and commentaries on the war and its participants, and a sense of how the war continues to have an impact on and in Spain.

Notes

1. The Archives are now located at New York University's Tamiment Library.

2. The selection from Fischer has to do with "fallacies of narration" (131–44). See Lévi-Strauss 213–15.

3. I find Chipp's study of *Guernica* to be particularly useful and ask students to read the eighth chapter, "Guernica in Paris, July-October 1937" (137–55). Also of interest are the essays collected in Oppler's *Picasso's* Guernica; and Russell Martin's 2002 book.

Evaluation

The final course grade is based on participation (20%), the archival research project (30%), a midterm exam (15%), a six-to-eight-page paper (15%), and a final exam (20%).

Reading and Viewing Materials

An asterisk indicates that the work or a selection of it is contained in the course pack.

¡Ay, Carmela! Dir. Carlos Saura.

Belle Epoque. Dir. Fernando Trueba.

The Canadians. Dir. Laszlo Gefin and Albert Kish.

*Carr, Raymond. *Spain, 1808–1975.*

*Cunningham, Valentine, ed. *The Penguin Book of Spanish Civil War Verse.*
   Poems by Rafael Alberti, Manuel Altolaguirre, Francis Fuentes, Antonio García Luque, Pedro Garfias, Raúl González Tuñón, Julio D. Guillén, Miguel Hernández, José Herrera Petere, José Moreno Villa, Félix Paredes, Pascual Pla y Beltrán, Stephen Spender, Luis de Tapia, and Lorenzo Varela.

*———, ed. *Spanish Front.*

De toda la vida (*For All Our Lives*). Dir. Carol Mazer and Lisa Berger.

Dreams and Nightmares. Dir. Abe Osheroff.

The Good Fight. Dir. Noel Buckner, Mary Dore, and Sam Sills.

Goytisolo, Juan. *Señas de identidad* (*Marks of Identity*).

Guernica. Dir. Alain Resnais and Robert Hessens.

Hemingway, Ernest. The Fifth Column *and Four Stories of the Spanish Civil War*.

Las Hurdes: Land without Bread. Dir. Luis Buñuel.

Mourir à Madrid (*To Die in Madrid*). Dir. Frédéric Rossif.

*Neruda, Pablo. *España en el corazón* (*Spain in the Heart*).

Orwell, George. *Homage to Catalonia*.

Picasso, Pablo. *Guernica*.

Rodoreda, Mercè. *La plaza del Diamante* (*The Time of the Doves*).

Spain 1936: Prelude to Tragedy. Dir. Jean-Claude Dassier and Gilles Delannoy.

The Spanish Civil War. Granada Television.

*Vallejo, César. *España, aparta de mí este cáliz* (*Spain, Take This Cup from Me*).

*White, Hayden. "The Historical Text as Literary Artifact."

Yates, James. *Mississippi to Madrid*.

Class   Topic, Readings, Films

1   Introduction to course.

2–3   History of Spain in the nineteenth and twentieth centuries.

4   The Civil War. Carr xiv–xxx, 640–92. *Las Hurdes: Land without Bread* ("Las Hurdes: Tierra sin pan"): In English. 27 mins. Documentary-style exposé of life in a remote part of Spain in the early 1930s. Although obviously not objective, the depiction is horrifying and helps give a sense of the conditions giving rise to social unrest in Spain. *To Die in Madrid (Mourir à Madrid)*: In English. 90 mins. Documentary-style treatment of the Spanish Civil War, including events in Spain leading up to the conflict.

5–6   Library orientation.

7   History and representation. White. *The Good Fight*: Documentary on the Abraham Lincoln Battalion and the International Brigades. *Guernica*: In English. 13 mins. A peculiar documentary on Picasso and the painting *Guernica*. Particularly interesting for the opening footage on the bombing of the town Guernica.

8   In Cunningham, *Spanish Front*: Stephen Spender, "Spain Invites the World's Writers"; Sylvia Townsend Warner, "What the Soldier Said"; Jef Last, "Noble Pages in History's Book"; V. S. Pritchett, "Last's Disillusionment"; Gustav Regler, "Straying Buffalo." In Hemingway: "The Denunciation."

9   In Hemingway: "The Butterfly and the Tank," "Night Before Battle," "Under the Ridge."

10   In Hemingway: *The Fifth Column*.

11   Breathing space 1.
12–14   Yates, *Mississippi to Madrid. Dreams and Nightmares*. 63 mins. A personal
              look at and reminiscence on the Spanish Civil War and its subsequent
              importance by a member of the Abraham Lincoln Battalion. *The Cana-
              dians (Los Canadienses)*. 60 mins. The National Film Board of Canada.
              On the MacKenzie-Papineau Battalion, the Canadian members of the
              International Brigades. Good on the social and political climate in
              Canada.
15   Breathing space 2.
16–19   Orwell, *Homage to Catalonia*. *Spain 1936: Prelude to Tragedy*: In En-
              glish (with some French). 79 mins. A highly ideological presentation
              of the events leading up to the Spanish Civil War. Informative and
              curious. *De toda la vida (For All Our Lives)*: In Spanish (more or
              less) with English subtitles. 54 mins. A remarkable video-documen-
              tary on the lives of several women, all of them members of the anar-
              chist trade union CNT and participants in the social revolution in
              Spain during the civil war.
20   Posters of the Spanish Civil War.
21   In Cunningham, *Spanish Front*: Spender, "Poems for Spain," "Ultima
              Ratio Regum," "Port Bou," "Fall of a City"; W. H. Auden, "Spain";
              Roy Campbell, "Hard Lines, Azaña!"; John Cornford, "A Letter
              from Aragon," "Poem,"; Louis MacNeice, "And I Remember
              Spain."
22   Neruda, "I Explain a Few Things," "The Way Spain Was," "Battle of
              the Jarama River."
23   Breathing space 3.
24–25   Vallejo. *The Spanish Civil War*: In English. 104 mins. A Granada Tele-
              vision production in six parts, the program charts slowly and carefully
              the events leading up to the Spanish Civil War as well as various
              aspects of the war itself and the distinct factions and participants.
              Parts 1 (Prelude to Tragedy 1931–1936) and 2 (Revolution,
              Counter-Revolution, and Terror).
26   In Cunningham, *Penguin Book*, Spanish *romanceros*.
27   Picasso, *Guernica*.
28   Breathing space 4. *The Spanish Civil War*, parts 3 (Battleground for
              Idealists) and 4 (Franco and the Nationalists).
29   Picasso, *Guernica*.
30   In Cunningham, *Spanish Front*: Virginia Woolf, "The Educated Man's
              Sister," "Remembering Julian," "Women Take Sides on the Spanish
              War"; Rosamond Lehmann, "Books for Spain"; Nan Green, "Death
              on the Ebro"; Sylvia Townsend Warner, "The Drought Breaks";
              Ethel Mannin, "Spanish Struggles"; Simone Weil, "Letter to
              Georges Bernanos."
31–34   Rodoreda. *The Spanish Civil War*, parts 5 (The Revolution) and 6 (Vic-
              tory and Defeat). *¡Ay, Carmela!*: In Spanish with English subtitles.
              105 mins. Perhaps not a great film, but certainly interesting for the
              mixing of ideological perspectives on the social and political roles of

the artist as well as Italian involvement in the Nationalist cause. Carmen Maura is particularly fine as Carmela. The shots of the posters in
the opening scene are worth the price of admission (after all, it's
free).

35–38   Goytisolo. *Belle Epoque*: In Spanish with English subtitles. 109 mins.
Quite a different take on the period leading up to the Spanish Civil
War, almost elegiac. Political allegory is somewhat oddly grafted
onto surprisingly modern sexual dynamics and a rather conventional
love story. Certainly in a different key when compared with Saura's
¡Ay, Carmela!

39   Last things.

Note: Publication details for all works mentioned in this syllabus are provided in the list of works cited at the end of this book.

Cristina Moreiras-Menor

The Spanish Civil War: A Cultural History

Course Description

The main purpose of an undergraduate class dealing with the Spanish Civil War and its cultural representation is, in my opinion, to examine the war as the foundational trauma (or episode) on which Spanish modernity and its cultural production are based. Teaching the war exposes students to its direct influence on literature and film and examines how the profoundly ideological discourses of both the left and the right were embodied in the cultural field of the time and after the victory of Franco. This examination allows the class to study, analyze, and reflect on the cultural production of a society divided into two ideologically oppositional groupings not only during the period 1936–39 but until the death of Franco. Thus some important themes to include in the class are the literature of exile; the construction of memory-history; *falangista* literature and its vision of the nation; the role of women during the war; the social, cultural, and national consequences of the war; *tremendismo* and the creation of the future; and realism, representation, testimonialism, and existentialism. The course should also include the filmic reconstruction of the conflict, as well as articles dealing with the sociopolitical, cultural, and epistemological consequences of genocide. The Spanish Civil War is one of the most challenging classes in our field, since both the teacher and the students have to be (or become) familiar with fictional texts (literary and filmic), historical documents, and artistic objects (posters, paintings, etc.) and be able to think across fields.

The Spanish Civil War as a historical event has given rise to a great number of cultural works (narrative, theater, poetry, film, propaganda posters, comics) whose principal interest lies both in portraying daily life in Spain during this period and in discursively constructing the ideologies that dominated those writers and intellectuals who participated in the war or who experienced it in less immediate but always real terms. In this class we analyze texts written shortly after the war or during the postdictatorship and consider how Spaniards represent in writing or on the screen a reality marked by trauma and radicalism, both of which work toward defining, at times in extreme ways, national identity. The course is given in Spanish.

Evaluation

First paper, 25%; final research paper, 35%; oral presentation, 10%; short commentaries on readings and films, 20%; class participation 10%.

Reading and Viewing Materials

An asterisk indicates that the work or a selection of it is contained in the course pack.

*Alberti, Rafael, ed. *Romancero general de la guerra española.*

*Aub, Max. *La verdadera historia de la muerte de Francisco Franco.*

¡Ay, Carmela! Dir. Carlos Saura.

Ayala, Francisco. *La cabeza del cordero.*

Las bicicletas son para el verano. Dir. Jaime Chávarri.

*Castro, Américo. "Sobre la guerra civil."

La caza. Dir. Carlos Saura.

Corazón del bosque. Dir. Manuel Gutiérrez Aragón.

Fernán Gómez, Fernando. *Las bicicletas son para el verano.*

Jackson, Gabriel. *A Concise History of the Spanish Civil War.*

Laforet, Carmen. *Nada.*

Land and Freedom. Dir. Ken Loach.

Libertarias. Dir. Vicente Aranda.

Llamazares, Julio. *Luna de lobos.*

*Mainer, José-Carlos, ed. *Falange y literatura.* Contains Rafael García
   Serrano, "La fiel infantería"; Víctor de la Serna, "Elogio de la
   alegre retaguardia"; Dionisio Ridruejo, "Umbral de la
   madurez."

*Marichal, Juan. "De algunas consecuencias intelectuales de la guerra civil
   española."

Nash, Mary. *Defying Male Civilization.*

Payne, Stanley. *The Spanish Revolution.*

Preston, Paul. *The Spanish Civil War, 1936–39.*

Rodoreda, Mercè. *La plaza del Diamante.*

*Sánchez Albornoz, Claudio. "Las dos Españas."

Sender, Ramón J. *Réquiem por un campesino español.*

Thomas, Hugh. *The Spanish Civil War.*

Class	Topic, Readings, Films
1	Introduction to the course
2	Origins of the war
3	The war: Nationalists and Republicans
4	The war: Franco, the Falange, and the construction of the nation
5–6	*Land and Freedom*
7	Brief Nationalist accounts of the war. In Mainer: García Serrano; de la Serna; Ridruejo
8–9	Sender
10–11	Llamazares
12–13	*Corazón del bosque*
14	Aub
15–16	Ayala
17	First paper due. Poetry on the war. In Alberti: Alberti, Machado, Hernández, Altolaguirre
18	Poetry; participation and significance of the International Brigades
19	*¡Ay, Carmela!*
20–21	Fernán Gómez
22	*Las bicicletas son para el verano*
23–24	Rodoreda
25	Women in the war: *milicianas* and *falangistas*
26	*Libertarias*
27	Intellectuals and the war: Américo Castro, Sánchez Albornoz, Marichal

516 A Cultural History

28–29 Consequences of the civil war: literary production of the postwar.

516 A Cultural History

516 A Cultural History

516 A Cultural History

28–29   Consequences of the civil war: literary production of the postwar. Laforet.

30–31   Symbolic approach to the war: censorship. *La caza*

32   Conclusions

Note: Publication details for all works mentioned in this syllabus are provided in the list of works cited at the end of this book.

Stephanie Sieburth

The Spanish Civil War: Literature, History, and Culture

Course Description

I developed this class as a lower-level undergraduate course that a student might take as a second, or sometimes even first, course in literature. My challenge was to find texts that were not too long or difficult for lower-level students. But the abundance of poems, pamphlets, and other short texts on or from the war in some ways encourages teaching at this level.

I am passionate about teaching this course, because I want to introduce American students, who are exposed to such a narrow range of ideologies, to a fuller range of ideological beliefs and movements, from anarchism to Carlism. I want them to understand that the various factions on both sides of the conflict were trying to put into practice a specific worldview and set of values, not just after the war but during the war itself. I want students to reflect on what the volunteers on both sides of the conflict were willing to die for and what their own deeply held values might be. I want students to read texts written by, not just about, members of all the political parties and movements that came together in the war. I hope students will emerge with an understanding of what it means to be a socialist, a Communist, an anarchist; I want them to see that values can change according to time and place and that no ideology should be

517

dismissed out of hand. I want them to reflect on the role of gender in the conflict and on the contradictions that women on the left faced in their struggle against oppression. Finally, I want students to understand the complicity of the Western democracies in the downfall of the Spanish republic and to link the case of Spain to other, more recent cases in which intervention and nonintervention on the part of the United States have led to authoritarian rule.

When I first taught the war, I taught mainly literary texts from the Republican side of the conflict, because I found them artistically superior. I soon realized that some of my students were curious about fascism. I decided not only to include poetry from the Nationalist side but also to adopt a broader, cultural studies approach to the whole course, making use of the microfilmed copy of the Herbert Southworth collection in Duke's library. Accordingly, the course studies not only poetry, prose, drama, and essays but also songs, posters, political speeches, propaganda pamphlets, and of course art and film in addition to histories of the war. (It is fascinating to watch the conservative students discover the banality of fascism through its own propaganda.) I supplement the books on the syllabus with a course pack that contains such items as maps, Francoist propaganda on the Alcázar in Toledo, a manifesto of Mujeres Libres, a pamphlet on the creation of libraries during the Spanish Civil War, poetry, Alberti's wonderful "Mi última visita al Museo del Prado," and selections from postwar speeches by Franco in which he explains the meaning of the war.

It has been some years since I last taught the course; I am now beginning to revamp it to teach it again with the new materials that have appeared in recent years, so some texts and films will no doubt change the next time I teach the course. The basic structure of the course, however, remains the same. I begin with a concise introduction to ideologies, then start filling in the historical causes of the war, using Ramón Sender's *Mosén Millán* (*Réquiem por un campesino español*) as a fictionalized account of many of these causes. This part of the course is the most challenging for me, and I would love to know what others do. The problem is to get across both the long-standing historical problems of Spain and the complexity of the history of the Second Republic without overwhelming the students. Once they can identify the names and ideologies of political parties and movements, they are off and running, but the going can be tough before that.

Looking at the war itself, we view films that give overviews of the first months of the conflict. Then we proceed to consider politics and everyday life behind the lines in each zone, in terms of ideologies, social revolution, gender roles, the Communist-anarchist conflict, and more, using a course pack of short texts from the time. The primary role of culture as a tool against fascism on the Republican side and the differences between Republican and Nationalist poetry deepen students' understanding. Finally, we consider the decisive role that international intervention and nonintervention played in the outcome of the war. At this point students are ready to start their own research projects.

They choose one of four topics on which to work in groups: fascism, anarchism, Communism, and international volunteers. (I chose these groups so that students would have to do in-depth work on ideas and ways of being that they had not encountered before.) Each group member selects a primary document from the Southworth collection, and the group collectively plans a presentation that puts the document in a broader ideological context for the rest of the class. A document might be the program for a Falangist summer camp, or a poster, or an account by an Irish volunteer who fought for Franco, or a speech by La Pasionaria, or a poem by W. H. Auden. Students circulate a short selection from their document to the class in advance of the presentation, so that the class is prepared with questions, and we simulate a conference panel in the class. After the presentations, students continue working individually on their major research paper. They compile a bibliography to help them answer questions arising from their primary document. They meet individually with me to receive guidance as they structure the paper. This work is challenging for them in a lower-level course, but they stretch, rise to the occasion, and gain confidence in their reading and speaking abilities in Spanish.

Meanwhile, the course continues with songs and posters, the conflicting initial accounts of the bombing of Guernica, and the Fernán Gómez play. Although I love Fernán Gómez's *Las bicicletas son para el verano*, students find that it moves too slowly, and I will replace it with another play in the next incarnation of the course. The documentary film *The Good Fight* teaches students about the remarkable American volunteers who fought in the war and shows them how the international Communist propaganda sanitized and simplified the war as a battle between liberal democracy and fascism.

Finally, we discuss the end of the war and the repressive apparatus that Franco put into motion afterward. I would like to spend a little more time on this section in the future, using the wealth of recently reprinted editions of Francoist schoolbooks and other propaganda materials.

To me, this course plays an important larger role in the Spanish major. Because the civil war is the final result of long-standing economic and cultural problems, some of them originating in the Middle Ages, students have a way to look backward at earlier Spanish history. They also have an important way to look forward in time. Many of our majors spend a semester in Madrid as juniors or seniors. They will arrive aware of the war and dictatorship in a way that will help them fill out and question the versions they hear from their host families or in the speeches of tourist guides in Spain.

Evaluation

Class participation, 30%; midterm exam, 20%; group participation, 25%; final term paper, 25%.

Reading and Viewing Materials

An asterisk indicates that the work or a selection of it is contained in the course pack.

*Abella, Rafael. "Una patria, un estado, un caudillo."

*Ackelsberg, Martha A. "Creación y desarrollo de la organización 'Mujeres Libres,' 1936–39."

———. "Captación y capacitación."

*———. *Free Women of Spain.*

*Alberti, Rafael. "Defensa de Madrid, defensa de Cataluña."

*———. "Mi última visita al Museo del Prado."

*Brenan, Gerald. *The Spanish Labyrinth.*

*Calvo, Blanca. "La memoria de la modernidad."

El caudillo. Dir. Basilio Martín Patino.

*Di Febo, Giuliana. "El monje guerrero."

Fernán Gómez, Fernando. *Las bicicletas son para el verano.*

*García Lorca, Federico. *Poema del cante jondo* [and] *Romancero gitano.* Contains "La guitarra," "Sorpresa," "Romance sonámbulo."

The Good Fight. Dir. Noel Buckner, Mary Dore, and Sam Sills.

*Hernández, Miguel. *Obra poética completa.* Contains "Nanas de la cebolla," "Vientos del pueblo me llevan."

*Jackson, Gabriel. *Breve historia de la guerra civil española.*

*Kenwood, Alun, ed. *The Spanish Civil War.*

Land and Freedom. Dir. Ken Loach.

*Machado, Antonio. "El crimen fue en Granada."

*Machado, Manuel. *Horas de oro.* Contains "La litera de Carlos V," "Francisco Franco," "Tradición," "¡España!"

*Martín Abril, Francisco Javier. *Antología poética del Alzamiento, 1936–39.* Contains "Niños y mujeres."

*Monforte Gútiez, María Inmaculada. "La labor cultural de María Teresa León."

* *Las mujeres y la guerra civil española.*

*Nash, Mary. *Defying Male Civilization.*

*Neruda, Pablo. *Five Decades.* Contains "Explico algunas cosas."

Orwell, George. *Homage to Catalonia.* 1966.

*Pastor i Homs, María Inmaculada. "El modelo de mujer que se quiere imponer."

*Payne, Stanley G. *A History of Spain and Portugal.*

*Preston, Paul. *La guerra civil española, 1936–1939.*

*Primo de Rivera, José Antonio. *El pensamiento político hispánico.* 112–21, 368–71.

Sender, Ramón J. *Mosén Millán.*

The Spanish Civil War. Granada Television.

Spanish Civil War Collection.

Class	Topic, Readings, Films
1	Introduction to the course.

The Prewar Period

2	Ideologies: socialism, anarchism, Communism, fascism.
3–7	History of Spain up to the Republic; history of institutions: church, military, political parties. Sender; Brenan; Nash; Ackelsberg.

The War

8	Panoramic view of the war. Payne; Jackson 46–63. *Spanish Civil War*, part 1, as a review before class. The first months of the conflict, fifth-columnist war, international posture.
9	The Nationalist zone. Jackson 75–80; Kenwood. Siege of Alcázar in Toledo. In *The Spanish Civil War Collection*, speeches of Primo de Rivera; the twenty-six points of the Falange; *Spanish Civil War*, part 4, before class.

10	The Nationalist zone; the Republican zone. Jackson 65–75; Kenwood; photographs; Ackelsberg, "Captación y capacitación" and "Creación y desarrollo"; Nash, ch. 3; *Spanish Civil War*, part 5, before class.
11	*Land and Freedom.*
12	The Republican zone. Orwell.
13	Review. Pick up midterm exam.
14	Culture: Republican zone. Monforte Gútiez; Alberti, "Mi última visita"; Lorca; A. Machado.
15	Hand in midterm exam.
16	Calvo; poetry by Miguel Hernández.
17	Culture: Nationalist zone. Di Febo; M. Machado; Martín Abril. Form work groups.
18–19	Group work. Songs of the war.
20–21	The siege of Madrid. Jackson; Preston; poems by Neruda and Alberti. *Spanish Civil War*, part 3; selections of *Caudillo*. Work in groups.
22	Guernica. In *Spanish Civil War Collection*, "The Crime of Guernica" and "La tragedia de Guernica."
23–25	Group work. Fernán Gómez; war posters. Presentations.

The Postwar Period

26–28	Presentations. Fernán Gómez. Discussion. Abella.
29	See me in my office to talk about final paper.
30	*The Good Fight.*
31	The end of the war. Pastor.
32	Recapitulation.
33	Hand in final paper.

Note: Publication details for all works mentioned in this syllabus are provided in the list of works cited at the end of this book.

Enric Ucelay-Da Cal

A Clear-Cut Case: The Imaginings of the Spanish Civil War

Course Description

The Spanish Civil War remains the outstanding example of a highly ideol-ogized and symbolic conflict in modern Europe. All the leading ideologies of the twentieth century—socialism, anarchism, Communism (Stalinist and anti-Stalinist), liberal democracy, fascism, Catholic traditionalism, Christian democracy, and minority nationalism—played significant roles, proffering their respective formulas for utopia. The Spanish war seemed to sum up, from numerous and discordant perspectives, the contradictions of the interwar period in Europe if not in the world. It has been evaluated as such by both international and Spanish historians. As research and recent scholarship accumulate, however, the standard perceptions of Spanish events and their international implications can be seen in radically different ways. Equally, the experience of later civil wars in the Mediterranean area can be used to reinterpret the Spanish revolution and counterrevolution in a less grandiose and less Eurocentric manner, one less subject to the ideo-logical preconceptions of left, right, and center.

Topics to be covered are the significance of the war, the political and social background of Spanish events, Mediterranean diplomacy, the chal-lenge to "collective security" and the major powers, Spanish society through the prism of the Popular Front, religious traditions and the external evaluation of events, the selling of the respective causes as a function of cultural and religious perspectives, the conflict as seen by Spaniards (including Catalan, Basque, and Moroccan nationalists), Italian and French ambitions in the war and their respective antecedents, British and Russian perspectives, the importance of Chinese events, the Spanish war seen within World War II, the continuation of the war as a frozen political example during the cold war, the democratization of Spain after 1975, and the maintenance of a rigid historical understanding. The course attempts to attain a critical balance and some tentative conclusions.

The course was taught in English on the undergraduate level at Venice International University from 12 February to 9 May 2002.

Evaluation

Grading is based on a final paper (10–15 pp.), course reading, an exam essay, and class participation.

Reading Materials

Álvarez Junco, José, and Adrian Shubert, eds. *Spanish History since 1808.*

Beevor, Antony. *The Spanish Civil War.*

Bolloten, Burnett. *The Spanish Civil War.*

Brenan, Gerald. *The Spanish Labyrinth.*

Carr, Edward Hallett. *International Relations between the Two World Wars, 1919–1939.*

Coverdale, John F. *Italian Intervention in the Spanish Civil War.*

Díaz, Elías. "The Left and the Legacy of Francoism."

Ealham, Christopher. "Anarchism and Illegality in Barcelona, 1931–37."

Fischer, Louis. *Men and Politics.*

Fusi, Juan Pablo. "Centre and Periphery, 1900–1936."

Gannes, Harry, and Theodore Repard. *Spain in Revolt.*

Gorkin, Julian. "Spain: First Test of a People's Democracy."

Graham, Helen. "'Against the State.'"

Guttmann, Allen. *The Wound in the Heart.*

Herr, Richard. *Spain.*

Hochman, Jiri. *The Soviet Union and the Failure of Collective Security, 1934–1938.*

Jackson, Gabriel. *The Spanish Republic and the Civil War, 1931–1939.*

Latourette, Kenneth Scott. *A Short History of the Far East.*

Madariaga, Salvador de. *Spain: A Modern History.*

Morrow, Felix. *Revolution and Counterrevolution in Spain, 1938.*

Powell, Charles T. "Spain's External Relations, 1898–1975."

Preston, Paul. "Decay, Division, and the Defence of Dictatorship."

Puzzo, Dante A. *Spain and the Great Powers, 1936–1941.*

Sánchez, José M. *Reform and Reaction.*

———. *The Spanish Civil War as a Religious Tragedy.*

Schapiro, J. Salwyn. *Anticlericalism.*

Story, Jonathan. "Spain's External Relations Redefined, 1975–89."

Taylor, A. J. P. "Spain and the Axis."

Thomas, Hugh. *The Spanish Civil War.*

Ucelay-Da Cal, Enric. "The Nationalisms of the Periphery."

Watkins, K. W. *Britain Divided.*

Weber, Eugen. *The Hollow Years.*

Weintraub, Stanley. *The Last Great Cause.*

Whealey, Robert H. *Hitler and Spain.*

Willmott, Hedley Paul. *The Great Crusade.*

Class Topic, Readings

1 Introduction to the Spanish Civil War: Which revolution? An isolated local conflict or a dress rehearsal for World War II? The power of symbols in internal and international politics.

2 The political and social background: Spanish revolution and counter-revolution in the nineteenth century. Herr 77–112.

3 The Spanish liberal system and its failure, 1875–1923. In Álvarez Junco and Shubert: Jacobson and Luzón, Moradiellos, Ucelay-Da Cal, Radcliff.

4 The Spanish dictatorship and its failure, 1923–1930. Brenan 57–86; Herr 133–53.

5 The Second Spanish Republic and its failure, 1931–1936. Madariaga 400–20; Herr 154–87.

6 The chronology of the civil war: phases and interpretations. Herr 188–210; Jackson 478–98.

7   Left-wing idealizations: Spanish society through the prism of the Popular Front. Hochman 78–94; Gannes and Repard 201–34; Morrow 8–16.

8   Spontaneous social revolution up to the May revolt in 1937? Bolloten 191–215; Graham; Ealham; Beevor 117–28.

9   Stalinist dictatorship or popular democracy in 1937–39? Bolloten 490–531, 600–10; Gorkin.

10   Internal opportunities: the conflict as seen by Catalan, Basque, and Moroccan nationalists. Ucelay-Da Cal; Fusi.

11   Religious traditions and the external evaluation of Spanish events: the selling of the respective causes as a function of cultural and religious perspectives and the epic mythologization of the war. Schapiro 86–101, 184–87; Sánchez, *Reform and Reaction* 214–18 and *The Spanish Civil War as a Religious Tragedy* 145–71.

12   External logic: Mediterranean diplomacy and the challenge to "collective security" in the 1930s. Carr 215–31; Powell.

13   French politics and Italian ambitions in the Spanish war. Puzzo 75–103; Weber 163–69; Coverdale 31–65, 384–410.

14   British and Russian perspectives; the preeminence of Chinese events. Latourette 566–611; Willmott 1–42; Fischer 444–52.

15   The source of transcendence: emotional conflict in British and North American politics. Guttmann 167–95; Weintraub 301–13.

16   The indifferent interloper and the unforeseen consequence: Germany in Spanish events and Franco's pariah status. Taylor; Whealey 135–42; Herr 211–36.

17   The open controversy: the Spanish circumstance in World War II. Watkins 196–233.

18   A frozen political example: the cold war and the memory of the Spanish conflict. Herr 237–61; Díaz; Preston.

19   The Spanish transition from dictatorship to democracy after 1975. In Álvarez Junco and Shubert: Aguilar; Story.

20   The maintenance of a rigid historical understanding: a critical balance, comparisons with the Greek Civil War and the Bosnian war in ex-Yugoslavia and some tentative conclusions.

Note: Publication details for all works mentioned in this syllabus are provided in the list of works cited at the end of this book.

Noël Valis

The Spanish Civil War:
Words and Images

Course Description

Why does the Spanish Civil War continue to fascinate us? Although it was primarily a local conflict of national significance, this war has also been seen as both the military and ideological testing ground and precursor of World War II. Fascists and Communists, liberals and conservatives fought bitterly over the future of the Spanish territory. Many in Europe and the Americas saw the war as the "last great cause," as the "good war," which was worth fighting, which had to be fought, because the alternative— fascism or, for others, Communism—was unthinkable. The Second Republic (1931–36) and the war played out against the growing polarization between the extreme right and left occurring elsewhere in Germany, Italy, and the Soviet Union. But, as we explore in this course, during the civil war what Spain meant to non-Spaniards was not necessarily what it meant to Spaniards. We also look at how the war was represented—that is, interpreted and experienced—through literature and the arts. Here, we distinguish between what happened during (and after) the war and how what happened was represented in words and images. Finally, we examine some of the consequences of the war, especially its impact on Spain: almost four decades of Franco's dictatorship.

Evaluation

Class participation, 10%; three commentaries (2–3 pp. each), 30%; final paper (10 pp.), 30%; final exam, 30%.

Reading and Viewing Materials

An asterisk indicates that the work or a selection of it is contained in the course pack. Films are shown outside class.

¡Ay, Carmela! Dir. Carlos Saura.

*Beevor, Antony. *The Spanish Civil War.* 79–96.

*Campbell, Roy. *Flowering Rifle.* 13–28.

La caza. Dir. Carlos Saura.

Cercas, Javier. *Soldados de Salamina.* Trans. as *Soldiers of Salamis.*

The Civil War: Traditional American Songs and Instrumental Music Featured in the Film by Ken Burns: Original Soundtrack Recording.

*Cunningham, Valentine, ed. *The Penguin Book of Spanish Civil War Verse.*

*———, ed. *Spanish Front.* 51–72.

*Esenwein, George, and Adrian Shubert. *Spain at War.* 37–48, 78–99.

For Whom the Bell Tolls. Dir. Sam Wood.

*Foxá, Agustín de. *Madrid, de corte a checa.* 234–41, 256–63.

*Franco, Francisco. "Decreto del 1 de abril de 1940."

*———. "Discurso en la inauguración del Valle de los Caídos, el 1 de abril de 1959."

*Goebbels, Joseph. *The Truth about Spain.*

The Good Fight. Dir. Noel Buckner, Mary Dore, and Sam Sills.

*Graham, Helen, and Jo Labanyi, eds. *Spanish Cultural Studies.*

Hemingway, Ernest. *For Whom the Bell Tolls.*

*———. "On the American Dead in Spain."

*Hernández, Miguel. "Rosario, dinamitera." *Obra completa,* vol. 1.

*Holguín, Sandie. *Creating Spaniards.* 168–94.

Land and Freedom. Dir. Ken Loach.

Llamazares, Julio. *Luna de lobos.*

*Machado, Antonio. "El crimen fue en Granada."

*Machado, Manuel. "Francisco Franco."

*Nash, Mary. *Defying Male Civilization.* 43–61.

*Nelson, Cary, and Jefferson Hendricks, eds. *Madrid, 1937.*

Orwell, George. *Homage to Catalonia.*

*Pla y Beltrán, Pascual. "A Lina Odena, muerta entre Guadix y Granada."

*Preston, Paul. *The Spanish Civil War, 1936–39.* 3–31.

Raza. Dir. José Luis Sáenz de Heredia.

Rodoreda, Mercè. *La plaza del Diamante.* Trans. as *The Time of the Doves.*

*Sánchez, José M. "The Anticlerical Fury."

Sender, Ramón J. *Réquiem por un campesino español.* Trans. as *Requiem for a Spanish Peasant.*

The Spanish Civil War. Granada Television.

The Spanish Earth. Dir. Joris Ivens.

El Valle de los Caídos.

Class — Topic, Readings, Films

1 Introduction. Europe and America in the 1930s, significance of the Spanish Civil War, the war as both national and international, Spaniards and the International Brigades. Realities and myths. Capa, *Falling Militiaman*, Hemingway, "On the American Dead in Spain"; in Cunningham, *Spanish Front*: "There's a Valley in Spain Called Jarama" (2 versions), 43–44. Contrast with the American Civil War. In Burns, Sullivan Ballou's letter to his wife.

2 Prelude to war: "La Niña Bonita"; The Second Spanish Republic. Preston 3–31; *The Spanish Civil War*, part I.

3 Causes and issues of the war: land, the church, social conflicts, regionalisms. Esenwein and Shubert; in Graham and Labanyi, Ucelay-Da Cal, "Catalan Nationalism"; Sánchez.

4 Taking sides: the Republican zone and the Nationalist zone. Beevor; in Cunningham, *Spanish Front*, *Authors Take Sides on the Spanish War.* The International Brigades: in Nelson and Hendricks, letters from the Abraham Lincoln Brigade; in Cunningham, *Penguin Book*, Spender, "Ultima Ratio Regum." The policy of nonintervention.

5–6 Orwell; in Cunningham, *Penguin Book*, Auden, "Spain."

7 *The Good Fight*

8 Orwell. Discussion of *The Good Fight.*

9–11 Hemingway, *For Whom the Bell Tolls*, excerpt from film.

12 Foxá; Campbell; Goebbels.

13–15 Sender; excerpt from *Raza.*

16 *The Spanish Earth.* Discussion of film.

17 *Land and Freedom*

18 Discussion of *Land and Freedom*; Culture and the war. Holguín; in Graham and Labanyi, Alicia Alted, "The Republican and Nationalist

Note: Publication details for all works mentioned in this syllabus are provided in the list of works cited at the end of this book.

Glossary

africanomilitaristas   Officers from the colonial army, characterized by their militaristic and antidemocratic ideology, also known as *africanistas*.

ALBA   Abraham Lincoln Brigade Archives, with materials and publications on the American pro-Republican volunteers. The archives are housed at New York University's Tamiment Library.

Anti-Spain / *Anti-España*   Nationalist blanket term for supporters of the republic.

Asturian Revolt   Miners' insurrection and attempted social revolution in October 1934, in the northern province of Asturias, followed by massive repression carried out by the colonial army under orders from the center-right government.

Carlism / *carlismo*   Political group that espoused a traditionalist, ultra-Catholic monarchy. Also called the Traditionalist Communion (Comunión Tradicionalista), especially strong in Navarra and Álava.

CEDA   Confederación Española de Derechas Autónomas, the largest prewar conservative Catholic political party, led by Gil Robles.

checas   Soviet-style kangaroo courts that began operating in the summer of 1936; also refers to Communist-run private prisons.

CNT   Confederación Nacional del Trabajo, anarcho-syndicalist trade union founded in 1910.

Condor Legion   Pro-Nationalist German military force composed mostly of bomber and fighter units, under General von Sperrle.

ERC   Esquerra Republicana de Catalunya, nationalist Catalonian Left Republican Party, led by Lluís Companys.

FAI   Federación Anarquista Ibérica, elite insurrectionary anarchist group within the CNT.

Falange Española   Spanish Fascist-style party founded by José Antonio Primo de Rivera in 1933; it merged with the pro-Nazi Juntas de Ofensiva Nacional-Sindicalista (JONS) in 1934. In April 1937 Franco forced it to merge with the Carlists, thus creating the Falange Española Tradicionalista y de las JONS.

fascistas   "Fascists," Republican blanket term applied to Nationalists.

First Spanish Republic   Short-lived, failed attempt at Republican governance in 1873–74.

Francoists / *franquistas*   Supporters of General Francisco Franco's revolt against the republic; also called Nationalists.

Guernica   Basque market town and cradle of the *fueros*, or medieval Basque privileges, bombed by the German Condor Legion on 26 April 1937; the bombing was the inspiration for Picasso's painting.

International Brigades   Foreign volunteers, largely recruited by Comintern agencies in Paris and numbering 35,000, who fought for the republic.

Law of Political Responsibilities   Francoist law proclaimed on 13 February 1939 making Republican supporters retroactively guilty of a crime or subversive activity committed since October 1934.

Lliga Regionalista   Catalan conservative regionalist party, whose goal was home rule in Spain.

Loyalists   Republicans loyal to the Second Republic.

Maquis   Republican resistance fighters in the postwar period.

milicianas   Militiawomen, belonging to the popular militia. See also *milicianos.*

milicianos   Militiamen, members of popular militia, largely working-class armed resistance to Franco's forces; they were organized by labor unions, anarchist and Communist groups.

moros   "Moors," Moroccan troops serving under Franco.

National Movement / Movimiento Nacional   Mass political movement that merged all rightist political parties into one, the FET de las JONS, in 1937, under General Francisco Franco's leadership; also refers generally to the Nationalist revolt of July 1936; often just referred to as the Movement.

Nationalists / *nacionalistas* (also Nationals)   Supporters of Franco's right-wing rebellion against the Second Republic. Also called Francoists, *franquistas*, and rebels.

Non-intervention Pact   Agreement among the great powers and other countries not to intervene or supply arms to either side of the conflict.

paseos   Politically motivated assassinations, roughly corresponding to "being taken for a ride."

PCE   Partido Comunista de España, the Moscow-oriented Spanish Communist Party.

PNV   Partido Nacionalista Vasco, conservative nationalist Basque Party.

Popular Front / Frente Popular   Coalition of leftist Republicans, socialists, and Communists that won the 16 February 1936 elections in Spain.

POUM Partido Obrero de Unificación Marxista, an anti-Stalinist party, based mainly in western Catalonia and led by Andreu Nin and Joaquín Maurín.

pronunciamiento Military coup d'état, prevalent in nineteenth- and early-twentieth-century Spain.

rebels Nationalists who supported the right-wing uprising against the Republican government.

Republicans / *republicanos* Supporters of the Second Republic. Also known as Loyalists.

Requetés / *requetés* Carlist militias.

romance Traditional epicolyric narrative ballad composed of eight-syllable lines, revived for wartime use. Modern ballad collections called *romanceros* were especially popular on the Republican side.

rojos "Reds," Communists, anarchists, leftists in general; Nationalist blanket term applied to supporters of the republic.

Sección Femenina Women's Section, Falangist organization created in 1934 and directed by Pilar Primo de Rivera, which became a Francoist instrument of indoctrination and social control.

Second Spanish Republic Republican democratic political system (1931–39), established after municipal elections in April 1931 and Alfonso XIII's abdication.

topos "Moles," Republicans in hiding after the war.

Tragic Week Antimilitarist, anticlerical violence in Barcelona beginning on 26 July 1909, provoked by reservists' refusal to be sent to the Moroccan War. It was followed with government repression.

transition Political period of democratization following the death of Franco in November 1975.

UGT Unión General de Trabajadores, trade union strongly linked to the Spanish Socialist Party (PSOE), founded in 1882.

VALB Veterans of the Abraham Lincoln Brigade, American volunteers who fought for the republic.

Notes on Contributors

Denis Boak has held teaching posts at the Universities of Hong Kong, Hull, Calgary, and Western Australia, where he is now emeritus professor and honorary senior research fellow. From 1975 to 2000 he was the editor of the journal *Essays in French Literature*. He has published books on Roger Martin du Gard, Jules Romains, André Malraux, and Sartre, as well as many chapters and articles on aspects of modern literature. His most recent book is *Malraux:* L'espoir (2003).

Francie Cate-Arries, professor of Hispanic studies at the College of William and Mary, is the author of *Spanish Culture behind Barbed Wire: Memory and Representation of the French Concentration Camps, 1939–1945* (2004). She has published articles on a variety of topics, including the Spanish exile of 1939 in Mexico, the detective novel, and the art of Remedios Varo. Her current project deals with Madrid, community, and the commemorative cultures of 11 March 2004.

Antonio Cazorla-Sánchez teaches European history at Trent University (Canada). He has published three books in Spanish on the Francoist regime policies and several articles in international journals. He is currently working on a social history of Franco's Spain based on ordinary people's experiences. He is doing research on the impact of political violence on people's attitudes and values during the dictatorship.

Robert S. Coale is maître de conférences (associate professor) in Hispanic studies at the Université de Vincennes–Paris 8. He is a regular contributor to *The Volunteer: Bulletin of the Veterans of the Abraham Lincoln Brigade* and the author of "Las Brigadas Internacionales: Apoteosis de la fraternidad," in *Realidades de la guerra civil* (ed. Eduardo Pons Prades, 2005). His research interests include the Spanish Civil War, the International Brigades, the contemporary Spanish novel, literary awards, and cultural history. He is currently at work on the participation of Spanish Republican exiles in the Free French Army during World War II.

María Crocetti was born in Italy and raised in Argentina. She was the director of the Spanish Language Program at Yale University, where she directed a number of Lorca's plays and Cervantes's *entremeses* as part of her course Theater and Poetry. Her first book of poetry, *Las últimas baldosas del patio*, was published in 1995, and she is presently working on her second book of poetry. Other publications include "*La dama duende*: Spatial and Hymeneal Dialectics" and poetry in *Antigone* and elsewhere. She has also been a member of the Yale Poetry Group.

Thomas Deveny is professor of Spanish and comparative literature at McDaniel College. He is the author of numerous articles on Spanish literature and film. His books include *Cain on Screen: Contemporary Spanish Cinema* (1993, 1999) and *Contemporary Spanish Film from Fiction* (1999, 2003), as well as a translation of Adelaida García Morales's *The South / Bene* (1999). His current projects include research on the cinema of Spain and Latin America and on *Don Quixote*.

Marvin D'Lugo teaches Spanish and Latin American cinema at Clark University, Worcester. He is the author of *The Films of Carlos Saura: The Practice of Seeing* (1991), *Guide to the Cinema of Spain* (1997), and *Pedro Almodóvar* (2006). He has written widely on questions of national cinema and authorship in Latin America (Buñuel, Tomás Gutiérrez Alea, Eliseo Subiela). He is currently preparing a book-length study of transnational Hispanic star discourse.

George Esenwein is associate professor of history at the University of Florida. His writings on modern Spain and Europe have appeared in scholarly reference works, journals, and books. He is the author of *Anarchist Ideology and the Working-Class Movement in Spain* (1989), *Spain at War: The Spanish Civil War in Context, 1931–1939* (with Adrian Shubert, 1995), and *The Spanish Civil War: A Modern Tragedy* (2005). He is currently working on projects relating to the Spanish Civil War and European intellectual history.

Sebastiaan Faber is associate professor of Hispanic studies at Oberlin College. His book, *Exile and Cultural Hegemony: Spanish Intellectuals in Mexico, 1939–1975* (2002), studies the ideological evolution of Spanish Civil War exiles in Mexico. He has published on Spanish Civil War exile, Spanish and Latin American literature, Pan-Americanism, panhispanism, and ideology. Currently he is working on a book about the impact of the Spanish Civil War on hispanism in the United States, the United Kingdom, and the Netherlands.

Kevin Foster teaches in the School of English, Communications, and Performance Studies at Monash University. He was a contributor to *The Spanish Civil War: A Cultural and Historical Reader* (1993). He is the author of *Fighting Fictions: War, Narrative, and National Identity* (1999) and a study of British literary constructions of Latin America, *Imaginary Continent* (forthcoming). His current project is a critical study of Ken Loach.

Gina Herrmann teaches peninsular literature and culture at the University of Oregon, where she is completing a book about Spanish Communists. In addition to her work on autobiography and political culture in Spain, she conducts oral histories with leftist women who lived during the Spanish Civil War. She is a member of the board of directors of the Abraham Lincoln Brigade Archive and its publication, *The Volunteer*.

David K. Herzberger is professor of Spanish and chair of the Department of Hispanic Studies at the University of California, Riverside. He is the author of books on Juan Benet and Jesús Fernández Santos and of *Narrating the Past: Fiction and Historiography in Postwar Spain* (1995). He has coedited two books on modern Spanish literature. His major fields of research are the modern Spanish novel and contemporary Spanish theater.

Sandie Holguín is associate professor of history and women's studies at the University of Oklahoma. She has written *Creating Spaniards: Culture and National Identity in Republican Spain* (2003), which was translated into Spanish as *República de ciudadanos: Cultura e identidad nacional en la España republicana.* She works on the cultural history of Spain and its relation to that of Western Europe and is beginning research in the cultural history of flamenco.

Michael Iarocci is associate professor of Spanish at the University of California, Berkeley. He writes on the literatures and cultures of modern Spain (eighteenth to twentieth centuries) and has published articles on Cadalso, Larra, Bécquer, Galdós, and Lorca. He is the author of *Enrique Gil y la genealogía de la lírica moderna* (1999) and *Properties of Modernity: Romantic Spain, Modern Europe, and the Legacies of Empire* (2006). His recent research has focused on the intersections among history, ideology, aesthetics, and theory in nineteenth-century Spanish studies.

Jo Labanyi is professor of Spanish at New York University. Recent books include *Gender and Modernization in the Spanish Realist Novel* (2000) and *Constructing Identity in Contemporary Spain* (ed., 2002). She is director of the collaborative projects *An Oral History of Cinema-Going in 1940s and 1950s Spain* and *Film Magazines, Photography, and Fashion in 1940s and 1950s Spain.* Of special interest are memory and the Spanish Civil War.

Tabea Alexa Linhard is assistant professor of Spanish at Washington University in Saint Louis. She has published articles focusing on the intersections among gender, violence, and revolution in the 1930s. Her book, *Fearless Women in the Mexican Revolution and the Spanish Civil War*, was published in 2005. Current projects include a book-length project that examines Jewish exile in Spain between 1931 and 1945.

Adelaida López de Martínez, professor of Spanish and women's studies at the University of Nebraska, Lincoln, is the author of *Sor Juana Inés de la Cruz* (1985) and *Dynamics of Change in Latin American Literature* (1996) and the coeditor of the *Cambridge Companion to the Modern Spanish Novel* (with Harriet Turner, 2003). She received the 1981 Southern Council on Latin American Studies Award for her essay "Las babas del diablo: Teoría y práctica del cuento en Julio Cortázar." In progress is a book, "Literatura y globalización: La progresiva desaparición del territorio nacional en la actual narrativa española."

Carol Maier is professor of Spanish at Kent State University, where she is affiliated with the Institute for Applied Linguistics. Among her publications are translations of Rosa Chacel's *Memoirs of Leticia Valle* (1994) and María Zambrano's *Delirium and Destiny* (1999). She has published widely on translation pedagogy and theory, Spanish peninsular literature, and Hispanic women writers. Current projects include translations of work by Rosa Chacel and Severo Sarduy, an edited collection of essays in homage to the late Helen Lane, and a coedited collection of essays about teaching literature in translation.

James Mandrell is the author of *Don Juan and the Point of Honor* (1992), as well as articles on the broad sweep of Spanish literature. He teaches at Brandeis University and is currently working on a comparative study of Canadian, United States, and Mexican film in the post-NAFTA period.

Shirley Mangini is professor emerita of Spanish at California State University, Long Beach. She has taught at Yale, Middlebury, and Stanford. Her main focus is on intellectual figures from the Franco regime and prewar period. A Spanish version of *Memories of Resistance: Women's Voices from the Spanish Civil War* appeared in 1997; *Las modernas de Madrid*, on female intellectuals in Madrid during the 1920s and 1930s, appeared in 2001. She is currently at work on a book on the painter Maruja Mallo and the Spanish avant-garde. The recipient of an NEH and two Fulbright grants, she serves on the board of the Abraham Lincoln Brigade Archives.

Jordana Mendelson is associate professor of art history at the University of Illinois, Urbana-Champaign. Her essays on Spanish modern art and the history of photography have appeared in *Journal of Spanish Cultural Studies*, *Modernism/Modernity*, *Art Journal*, and numerous anthologies and exhibition catalogs. She was cocurator and coauthor of *Margaret Michaelis: Fotografía, vanguardia y política en la Barcelona de la República* (1998), and she coedited *Lipchitz and the Avant-Garde: From Paris to New York* (2001). Her book *Documenting Spain: Artists, Exhibition Culture, and the Modern Nation, 1929–39* appeared in 2005.

Peter Monteath lectures in European history at Flinders University, Adelaide. He is the author of *Zur Spanienkriegsliteratur: Die Literatur des Dritten Reiches zum Spanischen Bürgerkrieg* (1986) and *Writing the Good Fight: Political Commitment in the International Literature of the Spanish Civil War* (1994). He compiled *The Spanish Civil War in Literature, Film, and Art: An International Bibliography of Secondary Literature* (1994). His current research interests are primarily modern and contemporary German history.

Cristina Moreiras-Menor is associate professor of Spanish literature and culture and women's studies at the University of Michigan, Ann Arbor. She has

published extensively on nineteenth- and twentieth-century Spanish literature and film, Spanish women writers, and Galician literature. She is the
author of *Cultura herida: Literatura y cine en la España democrática*
(2002), and she edited a special issue of *Journal of Spanish Cultural Studies*,
entitled *Critical Interventions on Violence*. She is currently working on a
book on the cultural history of Galicia and the notion of (national) borders,
entitled "Galicia y sus fronteras."

Cary Nelson is Jubilee Professor of liberal arts and sciences at the Univer-
sity of Illinois, Urbana-Champaign. His books include *Repression and
Recovery* (1989), *Manifesto of a Tenured Radical* (1997), *Revolutionary
Memory* (2001), and *Office Hours: Activism and Change in the Academy*
(with Stephen Watt, 2004). His edited books include *Cultural Studies*
(1992), *Higher Education under Fire* (1994), *Madrid 1937: Letters of the
Abraham Lincoln Brigade from the Spanish Civil War* (1996), and *The
Wound and the Dream: Sixty Years of American Poetry about the Spanish
Civil War* (2002).

Janet Pérez is Paul Whitfield Horn Professor of Romance languages and
Qualia Chair of Spanish at Texas Tech University. She is the author of *Ana
María Matute* (1971), *Gonzalo Torrente Ballester* (1984), *Women Writers of
Contemporary Spain* (1988), *Modern and Contemporary Spanish Women
Poets* (1996), *Camilo José Cela Revisited* (2000); the coeditor of the *Dictio-
nary of Literature of the Iberian Peninsula* (1993); and editor, with Maureen
Ihrie, of the *Feminist Encyclopedia of Spanish Literature* (2002); as well as
the author of over two hundred thirty articles and chapters in books, prima-
rily on nineteenth- and twentieth-century Spanish literature.

Geoffrey B. Pingree is associate professor of cinema studies and English at
Oberlin College and an independent writer, photographer, and documentary
filmmaker who works in Spain. Currently finishing *Voices over Spain: Documentary and Cinema, 1931–1981*, he is coeditor of *New Media, 1740–1914* (2003).
He writes regularly about Spanish politics and culture for the *New York Times*,
the *Christian Science Monitor*, *Time*, the *Nation*, the *American Prospect*, the
Economist, and *Cineaste*, among others; his photographs have appeared in publications such as the *New York Times*, the *Washington Post*, the *Los Angeles
Times*, the *Christian Science Monitor*, and the *Boston Herald*; and at present
he is editing a feature-length documentary about his years in Guatemala.

Randolph D. Pope is Commonwealth Professor of Spanish and Comparative
Literature and chair of the Department of Spanish, Italian, and Portuguese
at the University of Virginia. He has published books on Spanish autobiography, the Spanish novel, and Juan Goytisolo, as well as over one hundred
articles on Spanish and Latin American literature. His research and teaching
interests include the Spanish and Latin American novel, autobiography,

literature and music, philosophy, and literature. His current project is a book-length study of Spanish realism.

Joan Ramon Resina is professor of Spanish at Stanford University. The author of five books, including *La búsqueda del Grial* (1988), *El cadáver en la cocina: La novela policíaca en la cultura del desencanto* (1997), and *El postnacionalisme en el mapa global* (2004), he has edited six volumes, among them *Mythopoesis* (1992), *Disremembering the Dictatorship* (2000), and *Iberian Cities* (2001). The editor of *Diacritics* (1998–2004), for which he coedited a special issue, *New Coordinates: Spatial Mappings, National Trajectories*, he is preparing a book on literary images of modern Barcelona.

Michael Richards lectures in contemporary European history at the University of the West of England. The author of *A Time of Silence: Civil War and the Culture of Repression in Franco's Spain, 1936–1945* (1998) and coeditor of *The Splintering of Spain: Cultural History and the Spanish Civil War, 1936–1939* (2005), he publishes widely on cultural representations of the Spanish Civil War in relation to memory, ritual and mourning, and psychiatry and identity. Current projects include work on Spanish public health and epidemics, modern European memory and migration, and a broad social history of the period 1936–92 in Spain.

Margaret Van Epp Salazar is associate professor of Spanish at the University of Idaho. She is the author of *"Si yo te dijera": Una historia oral de la sierra de Huelva* (1998), as well as articles on oral narrative in *Demófilo*, *West Virginia University Philological Papers*, and *Romance Quarterly*. She is currently conducting research in Spain for a book of second-hand stories on the Spanish Civil War, told by the generation brought up by those who had lived during and been traumatized by the war.

Adrian Shubert is professor of history and associate vice president international at York University in Toronto. He is the author of a number of books on nineteenth- and twentieth-century Spain, including *The Road to Revolution in Spain: The Coal Miners of Asturias, 1860–1934* (1984), *A Social History of Modern Spain* (1990), *Death and Money in the Afternoon: A Social History of Spanish Bullfighting* (1999), and coeditor, with José Álvarez Junco, of *Spanish History since 1808* (2000). His most recent major publication is *The West and the World since 1500: Contacts, Conflicts, Connections* (with Arthur Haberman; 2002).

Stephanie Sieburth is associate professor at Duke University. The author of *Reading "La Regenta"* (1990) and *Inventing High and Low* (1994), she works on the realist novel; literature and popular culture; gender studies; mysticism and its modern legacy; and war, dictatorship, and memory. Her current project is a book entitled "Popular Culture and Survival: The Psychological Uses of Movies and Songs in Postwar Spain."

Enric Ucelay-Da Cal is professor of contemporary history at the Universitat Autònoma de Barcelona. Among his books are *La Catalunya populista: Imatge, cultura i política en l'etapa republicana, 1931–1939* (1982) and a biography of Francesc Macià (1984). The director of the pioneering compilation *La Joventut a Catalunya al segle XX: Materials per a una Història* (1987), he wrote, with Francisco Veiga, *El fin del segundo milenio* (1994). *El imperialismo catalán* appeared in 2003.

Michael Ugarte, professor of Spanish literature at the University of Missouri, Columbia, has written on Juan Goytisolo (*Trilogy of Treason*, 1982), Spanish Civil War exile literature (*Shifting Ground*, 1989), and the literary representations of Madrid (*Madrid 1900*, 1996). He is currently working on the cultural relations between Africa and Spain in the twentieth and twenty-first centuries, particularly on the history and literature of Equatorial Guinea.

Noël Valis is professor of Spanish at Yale University. She is the author of nineteen books, including *The Decadent Vision in Leopoldo Alas* (1981), *The Novels of Jacinto Octavio Picón* (1986), *My House Remembers Me* (poetry, 2003), and *Reading the Nineteenth-Century Spanish Novel* (2005), and the coeditor, with Carol Maier, of *In the Feminine Mode: Essays on Hispanic Women Writers* (1990). Her book *The Culture of Cursilería: Bad Taste, Kitsch, and Class in Modern Spain* (2002) won the MLA's Katherine Singer Kovacs Prize in 2003. Her current project is a book titled "Body Sacraments: Catholicism and the Imagination in Modern Spanish Narrative."

Kathleen M. Vernon is associate professor of Hispanic languages and literature at the State University of New York, Stony Brook. She is the editor of *The Spanish Civil War and the Visual Arts* (1990) and the author of numerous essays on twentieth-century Spanish cinema, literature, and culture. She is currently completing a book entitled "The Rhythms of History: Cinema, Music, and Cultural Memory in Contemporary Spain."

Mary Vincent is senior lecturer in history at the University of Sheffield, United Kingdom. Among her publications are *Catholicism in the Second Spanish Republic: Religion and Politics in Salamanca, 1930–1936* (1996) and numerous articles on religion, gender, and right-wing politics in twentieth-century Spain. Her *Modern Spain 1833–2002: The Problem of the State* will be published in 2007. She edits the Cambridge University Press journal *Contemporary European History* and is currently beginning work on a monographic study of Franco's crusade.

Curtis Wasson is assistant professor of Spanish at Reed College. He has published book reviews in *MLN, Romance Quarterly*, and *Rocky Mountain Review*. Current projects include articles on Benito Pérez Galdós, Leopoldo Alas, and Ernestina de Champourcín. He is working on a book-length manuscript, tentatively titled "Romanticism's Progeny," on the persistence of Romanticism in peninsular literature.

James Whiston is professor of Spanish at Trinity College, Dublin. His main work has been on the novels of Pérez Galdós. He has also published books on the Spanish Civil War writings of Antonio Machado (1996) and on Valera's *Pepita Jiménez* (1977). An edition of Galdós's *Fortunata y Jacinta* is in press, and a book on the poetry of Antonio Machado is at the early project stage. He is the general editor of the *Bulletin of Spanish Studies*.

Works Cited

Books and Articles

Abella, Rafael. "Una patria, un estado, un caudillo." *La vida cotidiana en España bajo el régimen de Franco*. Barcelona: Argos Vergara, 1985. 15–25.

Acier, Marcel, ed. *From Spanish Trenches: Recent Letters from Spain*. New York: Modern Age, 1937.

Ackelsberg, Martha A. "Captación y capacitación: El problema de la autonomía en las relaciones de 'Mujeres Libres' con el movimiento libertario." *Mujeres* 35–40.

———. "Creación y desarrollo de la organización 'Mujeres Libres,' 1936–39." *Mujeres* 31–34.

———. *Free Women of Spain: Anarchism and the Struggle for the Emancipation of Women*. Bloomington: Indiana UP, 1991.

Adam, Peter. *Art of the Third Reich*. New York: Abrams, 1992.

Affron, Matthew, and Mark Antliff. "Art and Fascist Ideology in France and Italy: An Introduction." *Fascist Visions: Art and Ideology in France and Italy*. Ed. Affron and Antliff. Princeton: Princeton UP, 1997. 3–24.

Aguilar, Miguel Ángel. "Los Nacionales." *El país digital* 2 Feb. 1999. 16 Nov. 2006 <http://www.elpais.es>.

Aguilar, Pilar. *Justicia, política y memoria: Los legados del franquismo en la Transición española*. Estudio / Working Paper 2001/163. Madrid: Instituto Juan March de Estudios e Investigaciones, 2001.

Aguilar Fernández, Paloma, and Carsten Humlebaek. "Collective Memory and National Identity in the Spanish Democracy: The Legacies of Francoism and the Spanish Civil War." Rein 121–64.

Aguirre y Lecube, José Antonio de. *De Guernica a Nueva York, pasando por Berlín*. Buenos Aires: Vasca Ekin, 1944. Trans. as *Escape via Berlin: Eluding Franco in Hitler's Europe*. Introd. and ed. Robert P. Clark. Reno: U of Nevada P, 1991.

Alba, Víctor. *La vida provisional. Novela de malas costumbres*. Mexico City: Compañía Importadora y Distribuidora de Ediciones, 1950.

Alberich, Fernán. "*Raza*: Cine y propaganda en la inmediata posguerra." *Archivos de la Filmoteca* 27 (1997): 50–61.

Alberti, Rafael. "Defensa de Madrid, defensa de Cataluña." Santonja, *Romancero* 71–74.

———. *De un momento a otro: Poesía e historia*. Madrid: Europa América, 1938. Ed. José María Balcells. Barcelona: PPU, 1993.

———. *Entre el clavel y la espada, 1939–1940*. Barcelona: Seix Barral, 1978.

———. "Mi última visita al Museo del Prado." *La historia tiene la palabra*. Ed. María Teresa León. Madrid: Hispamérica, 1977. 63–68.

———. *Noche de guerra en el Museo del Prado*. Buenos Aires: Losange, 1956.

———. *The Owl's Insomnia: Poems*. Trans. Mark Strand. New York: Atheneum, 1973.

————. *Poesía civil con un poema de Pablo Neruda*. Ed. Aitana Alberti. Madrid: Aguilar, 1978.

————. *El poeta en la calle: Poesía civil, 1931–1965*. Paris: Globe, 1966.

————, ed. *Romancero general de la guerra española*. Buenos Aires: Patronato Hispano Argentino de Cultura, 1944.

————. *Selected Poems*. Trans. Lloyd Mallan. New York: New Directions, 1944.

Aldecoa, Josefina R., ed. *Los niños de la guerra*. Madrid: Anaya, 1983.

Aldgate, Anthony. *Cinema and History: British Newsreels and the Spanish Civil War*. London: Scolar, 1979.

Alexander, Bill. *British Volunteers for Liberty*. London: Lawrence, 1982.

Alix, Josefina. *Pabellón Español: Exposición Internacional de París 1937*. Madrid: Ministerio de Cultura; Museo Nacional Centro de Arte Reina Sofía, 1987.

Allen, Jay. Preface. Capa, *Death* [1–4].

Almond, Gabriel A., and Sidney Verba. *The Civic Culture*. Princeton: Princeton UP, 1963.

Alonso Baño, Antonio. "El gobierno de conciliación, 18 julio 1936." *Homenaje a Diego Martínez Barrio*. Paris: Ruche Ouvrière, 1978. 63–124.

Alpert, Michael. *A New International History of the Spanish Civil War*. New York: Macmillan, 1994.

Alted Vigil, Alicia. "The Republican and National Wartime Cultural Apparatus." Graham and Labanyi 152–61.

Alted Vigil, Alicia, and Manuel Llusia, eds. *La cultura del exilio republicano español de 1939*. Vol. 1. Madrid: U Nacional de Educación a Distancia, 2003.

Alted Vigil, Alicia, Encarna Nicolás Marín, and Roger González Martell. *Los niños de la guerra de España en la Unión Soviética: De la evacuación al retorno, 1937–1999*. Madrid: Fundación Francisco Largo Caballero, 1999.

Altolaguirre, Manuel. *Poesías completas*. Ed. Margarita Smerdou Altolaguirre and Milagros Arizmendi. Madrid: Cátedra, 1982.

Álvarez Berciano, Rosa, and Ramón Sala Noguer. *El cine en la zona nacional, 1936–1939*. Bilbao: Mensajero, 2000.

Álvarez del Vayo, Julio. *Freedom's Battle*. Trans. Eileen E. Brooke. New York: Knopf, 1940.

Álvarez Junco, José. "El anticlericalismo en el movimiento obrero." *Octubre 1934: Cincuenta años para la reflexión*. Ed. Germán Ojeda et al. Madrid: Siglo XXI, 1985. 283–300.

Álvarez Junco, José, and Adrian Shubert, eds. *Spanish History since 1808*. London: Arnold, 2000.

Álvarez Oblanca, Wenceslao. *La represión de postguerra en León: Depuración de la enseñanza, 1936–1943*. Madrid: n.p., 1986.

Amat, Núria. *El país del alma*. Barcelona: Seix Barral, 1999.

————. "The Wedding." Trans. Peter Bush. Bush and Dillman 7–19.

Amo García, Alfonso del, with María Luisa Ibáñez. *Catálogo general del cine de la guerra civil*. Madrid: Filmoteca Nacional, 1996.

Anderson, Benedict. *Imagined Communities: Reflections on the Origin and Spread of Nationalism*. London: Verso, 1983.

Anderson, Maxwell. *Key Largo*. Washington: Anderson House, 1939.

Andreu-Besó, J. Vicente. "Rodoreda's *La plaça del Diamant.*" *Voices and Visions: The Words and Works of Mercè Rodoreda.* Ed. Kathleen McNerny. Selinsgrove: Susquehanna UP, 1999. 148–55.

Andrews, Tom. "Script for Home Video and Flashlight after García Lorca." *Hotel America* 1.1 (2002): 6.

Andújar, Manuel. *Historias de una historia.* Barcelona: Anthropos, 1986.

———. *St. Cyprien, plage . . . campo de concentración.* 1942. Huelva: Diputación Provincial de Huelva, 1990.

———. *La voz y la sangre.* Madrid: Ibérico Europea de Ediciones, 1984.

Ángulo, Jesús, Carlos F. Heredero, and José Luis Rebordinos. *Elías Querejeta: La producción como discurso.* Donostia-San Sebastián: Filmoteca Vasca, 1996.

Aparicio, Juan Pedro. *La forma de la noche.* Madrid: Alfaguara Hispánica, 1994.

Arana, José Ramón. *El cura de Almuniaced.* Pref. Manuel Andújar. Madrid: Turner, 1979.

Arbós, Montserrat. "Entrevista: Eric Sottas, Director de l'Organització Mundial Contra la Tortura (OMCT)." *Avui Digital* 2 Nov. 2002.

Armengou, Montse, and Ricard Belis. *Las fosas del silencio: ¿Hay un Holocausto español?* Pref. Santiago Carrillo. Barcelona: Televisió de Catalunya, 2004.

Arnheim, Rudolf. *The Genesis of a Painting: Picasso's* Guernica. Berkeley: U of California P, 1973.

Arrabal, Fernando. *Fando y Lis [and] Guernica [and] La bicicleta del condenado.* Ed. Francisco Torres Monreal. Madrid: Alianza, 1986.

———. *Guernica.* Trans. Luce Arrabal. Paris: Jullard, 1961.

———. Guernica *and Other Plays.* Trans. Barbara Wright. 1969. New York: Grove, 1986.

Arte protegido: Memoria de la Junta del Tesoro Artístico durante la guerra civil. Ed. Isabel Argerich and Judith Ara. Museo Nacional del Prado, 27 June–14 Sept. 2003. Madrid: Ministerio de Educación, Cultura y Deporte, 2003.

Aub, Max. *Campo abierto.* Mexico City: Tezontle, 1951.

———. *Campo cerrado.* Mexico City: Tezontle, 1943.

———. *Campo del moro.* Mexico City: Mortiz, 1963.

———. *Campo de los almendros.* Mexico City: Mortiz, 1968. Ed. Francisco Caudet. Madrid: Castalia, 2000.

———. *Campo de sangre.* Mexico City: Tezontle, 1945.

———. *Campo francés.* Paris: Ruedo Ibérico, 1965.

———. *Conversaciones con Buñuel.* Madrid: Aguilar, 1985.

———. *Enero sin nombre: Los cuentos del Laberinto mágico.* Presentation Francisco Ayala. Ed. Javier Quiñones. Barcelona: Alba, 1994.

———. *La gallina ciega: Diario español.* Ed. Manuel Aznar Soler. Barcelona: Alba, 1995.

———. *Hablo como hombre.* Mexico City: Mortiz, 1967.

———. *Laberinto mágico.* Ed. Joan Oleza Simó. 2 vols. Valencia: Generalitat Valenciana, 2002.

———. *Morir por cerrar los ojos.* Mexico City: Tezontle, 1944.

———. *No son cuentos.* Mexico City: Tezontle, 1944.

———. *La verdadera historia de la muerte de Francisco Franco.* Segorbe: Fundación Max Aub; Ministerio de Educación, Cultura y Deporte, 2001.

──────. *Las vueltas.* Mexico City: Mortiz, 1965.

Aubrac, Lucie. *Outwitting the Gestapo.* Lincoln: U of Nebraska P, 1983.

Auden, W. H. *Collected Poems.* Ed. Edward Mendelson. London: Faber, 1977.

──────. *The English Auden: Poems, Essays, and Dramatic Writings, 1927–1939.* Ed. Edward Mendelson. New York: Random, 1977.

──────. *Selected Poems.* Ed. Edward Mendelson. New York: Vintage, 1989.

Authors Take Sides on the Spanish War. London: Left Review, 1937.

Ayala, Francisco. *La cabeza del cordero.* Buenos Aires: Losada, 1949. Ed. Rosario Hiriart. Madrid: Cátedra, 1978.

──────. "La excentricidad hispana." *Los ensayos: Teoría y crítica literaria.* Madrid: Aguilar, 1972. 1181–86.

──────. "Para quién escribimos nosotros." *Cuadernos Americanos* 43.1 (1949): 36–58.

──────. *Razón del mundo: La preocupación de España.* 2nd ed. Xalapa: U Veracruzana, 1962.

──────. "El Tajo." Ayala, *Cabeza* 103–34.

──────. *Los usurpadores.* Buenos Aires: Sudamericana, 1949.

Azaña, Manuel. *Obras completas.* Ed. Juan Marichal. 4 vols. Mexico City: Oasis, 1966.

──────. *La velada en Benicarló: Diálogo sobre la guerra de España.* Buenos Aires: Losada, 1939. Trans. as *Vigil in Benicarló.* Trans. Josephine Stewart and Paul Stewart. Rutherford: Fairleigh Dickinson UP, 1982.

Azevedo, Milton M. "Shadows of a Literary Dialect: *For Whom the Bell Tolls* in Five Romance Languages." *Hemingway Review* 20.1 (2000): 30–48.

Azúa, Félix de. *Cambio de bandera.* Barcelona: Anagrama, 1991.

──────. "¿Será suficiente el perdón?" *El país digital* 10 Nov. 2004. 16 Nov. 2006 <http://www.elpais.es>.

Baker, Carlos. *Ernest Hemingway.* New York: Scribner, 1969.

Bakhtin, Mikhail. *La poétique de Dostoieski.* Paris: Seuil, 1970.

Bakker, Kees, ed. *Joris Ivens and the Documentary Context.* Amsterdam: Amsterdam UP, 1999.

Balibar, Étienne. "Is There a 'Neo-Racism'?" *Race, Nation, and Class: Ambiguous Identities.* Ed. Balibar and Immanuel Wallerstein. London: Verso, 1988. 17–28.

Balsells, David. "Fotógrafos para la historia." *Guerra* 189–92.

Bandrés, Javier, and Rafael Llavona. "Psychology in Franco's Prisons." *Psychology in Spain* 1.1 (1997): 3–9.

Bannasch, Bettina, and Christiane Holm (with Carl Freytag), eds. *Erinnern und Erzählen: Der Spanische Bürgerkrieg in der deutschen und spanischen Literatur und in den Bildmedien.* Tübingen: Narr, 2005.

Barea, Arturo. *The Clash.* 1946. London: Fontana, 1984.

──────. *The Forging of a Rebel.* Trans. Ilsa Barea. New York: Reynal, 1946. London: Granta, 2001. Trans. of *La forja de un rebelde.* Madrid: Turner, 1977.

──────. *La llama.* Buenos Aires: Losada, 1951.

──────. "Not Spain but Hemingway." *Hemingway and His Critics: An International Anthology.* Ed. Carlos Baker. New York: Hill, 1961. 202–12.

Barrès, Maurice. *Du sang, de la volupté et de la mort.* Paris: Plon-Nourrit, 1909.

Barsam, Richard Meran. *Nonfiction Film: A Critical History.* New York: Dutton, 1973.

Barthes, Roland. *Camera Lucida: Reflections on Photography.* Trans. Richard Howard. New York: Hill, 1981.

———. *Mythologies.* Trans. Annette Lavers. New York: Hill, 1972.

Bartolí, José, and Narcis Molins i Fàbrega. *Campos de concentración, 1939–194 . . .* Mexico City: Iberia, 1944.

Bartra, Agustí. *Cristo de 200.000 brazos: Campo de Argelès.* 1943. Mexico City: Novaro, 1958. Barcelona: Plaza y Janés, 1970. First titled *Xabola.*

Bauer, Carlos, ed. *Cries from a Wounded Madrid: Poetry of the Spanish Civil War.* Athens: Swallow, 1984.

Bautista de la Torre, Sebastián. *Revivir: Poemas de la liberación.* Jaén: n.p., 1939.

Beevor, Antony. *The Spanish Civil War.* New York: Penguin, 1982.

Benavides, Manuel. *Los nuevos profetas.* Mexico City: Colección Luz Sobre España, 1942.

Benet, Juan. *Volverás a Región.* Barcelona: Destino, 1967. Trans. as *Return to Region.* Trans. Gregory Rabassa. New York: Columbia UP, 1985.

Beneyto, José María. *Tragedia y razón: Europa en el pensamiento español del siglo XX.* Madrid: Taurus, 1999.

Benjamin, Walter. *Illuminations.* Ed. Hannah Arendt. Trans. Harry Zohn. London: Fontana, 1992.

———. "A Small History of Photography." *One-Way Street.* London: Verso, 1979. 240–47.

———. "The Task of the Translator." Venuti, *Translation Studies* 15–23.

———. "Theses on the Philosophy of History." Benjamin, *Illuminations* 245–55.

Benson, Frederick. *Writers in Arms: The Literary Impact of the Spanish Civil War.* New York: New York UP, 1967.

Berman, Antoine. "Translation and the Trials of the Foreign." Trans. Lawrence Venuti. Venuti, *Translation Studies* 284–97.

Bernanos, Georges. *Les grands cimetières sous la lune.* Paris: Plon, 1938. Trans. as *A Diary of My Times.* Trans. Pamela Morris. London: Boriswood, 1938.

Bernardete, M. J., and Rolfe Humphries, eds. *. . . and Spain Sings: Fifty Loyalist Ballads Adapted by American Poets.* New York: Vanguard, 1937.

Berrio, Jordi. "El fotoperiodismo en la guerra civil española: El documento humano y social de una tragedia." *Guerra* 192–97.

Bertrand de Muñoz, Maryse. *La guerra civil española en la novela: Bibliografía comentada.* 2 vols. Madrid: José Porrúa Turanzas, 1982.

———. *Guerra y novela: La guerra española de 1936–1939.* Sevilla: Alfar, 2001.

———. *La guerre civile espagnole et la littérature française.* Quebec: Didier, 1972.

———, ed. *Literatura sobre la guerra civil: Poesía, narrativa, teatro, documentación: La expresión estética de una ideología antagonista.* Spec. issue of *Anthropos* 39 (1993).

———. *La novela europea y americana y la guerra civil española.* Madrid: Júcar, 1994.

Bessie, Alvah, ed. *The Heart of Spain: Anthology of Fiction, Non-fiction, and Poetry.* New York: Veterans of the Abraham Lincoln Brigade, 1952.

————. *Men in Battle*. New York: Pinnacle, 1977.

Bessie, Alvah, and Albert Prago, eds. 1939. *Our Fight: Writings by Veterans of the Abraham Lincoln Brigade, Spain, 1936–1939*. Introd. Ring Lardner, Jr. New York: Monthly Review; Veterans of the Abraham Lincoln Brigade, 1987.

Bessie, Dan, ed. *Alvah Bessie's Spanish Civil War Notebooks*. Lexington: UP of Kentucky, 2002.

Betjeman, John. *John Betjeman's Collected Poems*. London: Murray, 1979.

Binns, Niall. *La llamada de España: Escritores extranjeros en la guerra civil*. Mataró: Montesinos, 2004.

Blasco Herranz, Inmaculada. *Armas femeninas para la contrarrevolución: La Sección Femenina en Aragón, 1936–1950*. Málaga: U de Málaga, 1999.

Bley, Wulf. *Das Buch der Spanienflieger: Die Feuertaufe der neuen deutschen Luftwaffe*. Leipzig: Von Hase, 1939.

Boak, Denis. *Malraux:* L'espoir. London: Grant, 2003.

Bolloten, Burnett. *The Grand Camouflage*. London: Hollis, 1961.

————. *The Spanish Civil War: Revolution and Counter-revolution*. Chapel Hill: U of North Carolina P, 1991.

Bonet Correa, Antonio, ed. *Arte del franquismo*. Madrid: Cátedra, 1981.

————. "Espacios arquitectónicos para un nuevo orden." Bonet Correa, *Arte* 11–46.

Borkenau, Franz. *The Spanish Cockpit: An Eyewitness Account of the Political and Social Conflicts of the Spanish Civil War*. London: Faber, 1937. Liberation Classics. London: Pluto, 1986.

Borrás, Tomás. *Checas de Madrid: Epopeya de los caídos*. Madrid: Escelicer, 1940.

Borràs Betriu, Rafael. *Los que no hicimos la guerra*. Barcelona: Nauta, 1971.

Bosch, Aurora. "Agrociutats i anticlericalisme a la II República." *L'avenç* June 1996: 6–11.

Botella Pastor, Virgilio. *Porque callaron las campanas*. Mexico City: Libertad, 1953.

Bou, Enric. "Exile in the City: Mercè Rodoreda's *La plaça del Diamant*." *The Garden across the Border: Mercè Rodoreda's Fiction*. Ed. Kathleen McNerny and Nancy Vosburg. Selingsgrove: Susquehanna UP, 1994. 31–41.

Bouley, Alan, ed. *Catholic Rites Today*. Collegeville: Liturgical, 1992.

Bowers, Claude G. *My Mission to Spain: Watching the Rehearsal for World War II*. New York: Simon, 1954.

Boyd, Carolyn. *Historia Patria: Politics, History, and National Identity in Spain, 1875–1975*. Princeton: Princeton UP, 1997.

Bradbury, Malcolm, and James McFarlane, eds. *Modernism, 1890–1930*. Harmondsworth: Penguin, 1976.

Brecht, Bertolt. *Brechts Gewehre der Frau Carrar*. 1937. Ed. Klaus Bohnen. Frankfurt: Suhrkamp, 1982. Trans. as *Señora Carrar's Rifles*. Ed. Tom Kuhn and John Willett. Trans. Willett. London: Methuen, 2001.

Bredel, Willi. *Begegnung am Ebro: Aufzeichnungen eines Kriegskommissars*. Paris: du 10 Mai, 1939.

Brenan, Gerald. *The Face of Spain*. 1951. London: Penguin, 1987.

————. *Personal Record, 1920–1975*. 1933. New York: Knopf, 1975.

————. *The Spanish Labyrinth*. 1943. Cambridge: Cambridge UP, 1971.

Breton, André. *Les pas perdus*. 1924. Paris: Gallimard, 1979.

Brittain, Vera. *Testament of Youth*. 1933. New York: Wideview, 1970.

Brodzki, Bella, and Celeste Schenk. *Life/Lines: Theorizing Women's Autobiography*. Ithaca: Cornell UP, 1988.

Broer, Lawrence R. *Hemingway's Spanish Tragedy*. Tuscaloosa: U of Alabama P, 1973.

Brothers, Caroline. *War and Photography: A Cultural History*. London: Routledge, 1997.

————. "Women at Arms." Brothers 76–98.

Brotóns Jordà, Mario. *Retazos de una época de inquietudes*. Alcoy: Brotóns Jordà, 1995.

Broué, Pierre, and Émile Témime. *The Revolution and the Civil War in Spain*. Trans. Tony White. London: Faber, 1970.

Brown, Frieda S., et al., eds. *Rewriting the Good Fight: Critical Essays on the Literature of the Spanish Civil War*. East Lansing: Michigan State UP, 1989.

Brugarola, Martín. *La recristianización de la cultura española*. Madrid: Magisterio Español, 1949.

Bruner, Jerome. "Self-Making and World-Making." *Narrative and Identity: Studies in Autobiography, Self, and Culture*. Ed. Jens Brockmeier and Donal Carbaugh. Amsterdam: Benjamins, 2001. 25–37.

Bruzzichezi, Ave. Letters. Nelson and Hendricks 362–68, 433–34, 458–59, 466–72.

Bullón de Mendoza, Alfonso, and Álvaro de Diego. *Historias orales de la guerra civil*. Barcelona: Ariel, 2000.

Bush, Peter, and Lisa Dillman, eds. *Spain: A Traveler's Literary Companion*. Berkeley: Whereabouts, 2003.

Cadava, Eduardo. *Words of Light: Theses on the Photography of History*. Princeton: Princeton UP, 1997.

Calamai, Natalia. *El compromiso en la poesía de la guerra civil española*. Barcelona: Laia, 1979.

Calle Iturrino, Esteban. *Romancero de la guerra*. Bilbao: Escuelas Gráficas Santa Casa de Misericordia, 1938.

Calvo, Blanca. "La memoria de la modernidad." *La lectura pública en España durante la II república*. Madrid: Biblioteca Nacional, 1991. 9–12.

Calvo Serer, Rafael. "España, sin problema." *Arbor* 14.45–46 (1949): 160–73.

Cámara Villar, Gregorio. *Nacional-catolicismo y escuela: La socialización política del franquismo, 1936–1951*. Madrid: Hesperia, 1984.

Camiña, Ángel. "*El espíritu de la colmena* de Víctor Erice." *Cine para leer, 1973*. Bilbao: Mensajero, 1974. 120–23.

Campbell, Roy. *Flowering Rifle: A Poem from the Battlefield of Spain*. New York: Longmans, 1939.

————. *Mithraic Emblems*. London: Boriswood, 1936.

Camus, Albert. *L'état de siege*. Paris: Gallimard, 1948.

Camus, Albert, et al. *Révolte dans les Asturies*. Algiers: Charlot, 1936.

Cancionero de las Brigadas Internacionales. Introd. Arthur London. Madrid: Nuestra Cultura, 1978.

Candel, Francisco. *El santo de la madre Margarita.* Barcelona: Ronsel, 2004.

Cano Ballesta, Juan, ed. *La poesía española entre pureza y revolución, 1930–1936.* Madrid: Gredos, 1972.

Capa, Robert. *Death in the Making.* Photographs by Capa and Gerda Taro. Trans. and pref. Jay Allen. New York: Covici-Friede, 1938.

———. *Fotógrafo de guerra: España, 1936–1939.* Ed. Lolo Rico. Hondarribia: Argitelexte Hiru, 2000.

———. *Heart of Spain: Robert Capa's Photographs of the Spanish Civil War.* Vincenzo, It.: Aperture, 1999.

Capellán, Ángel. *Hemingway and the Hispanic World.* Ann Arbor: UMI Research, 1985.

Cárcel Ortí, Vicente. *Mártires españoles del siglo XX.* Madrid: Autores Cristianos, 1995.

———. *La persecución religiosa en España durante la Segunda República, 1931–1939.* Madrid: Rialp, 1990.

Carlebach, Michael L. *American Photojournalism Comes of Age.* Washington: Smithsonian, 1997.

Carr, Edward Hallett. *International Relations between the Two World Wars, 1919–1939.* New York: Harper, 1966.

Carr, Raymond. *The Civil War in Spain, 1936–39.* London: Weidenfeld, 1986.

———. Introduction. *The Spanish Civil War: A History in Pictures.* New York: Norton, 1986. 7–23.

———. *Spain, 1808–1975.* 2nd ed. Oxford: Clarendon, 1982.

———. "Spain and the Communists." *New York Review of Books* 10 Apr. 2003: 62–67.

Carretero, José María [El Caballero Audaz]. *La revolución de los patibularios.* 6 vols. Madrid: Caballero Audaz, 1940.

Carroll, Peter N. *The Odyssey of the Abraham Lincoln Brigade: Americans in the Spanish Civil War.* Stanford: Stanford UP, 1994.

Cartier-Bresson, Henri. *The Decisive Moment: Photography by Henri Cartier-Bresson.* New York: Simon; Verve, 1958.

Carulla, Jordi, and Arnau Carulla. *La guerra civil en 2000 carteles: República, guerra civil, posguerra.* 2 vols. Barcelona: Postermil, 1997.

Castells Peig, Andreu. *Las Brigadas Internacionales.* Barcelona: Ariel, 1974.

Castillo-Puche, José Luis. *Conocerás el poso de la nada.* Barcelona: Destino, 1982.

Castresana, Luis de. *El otro árbol de Guernica.* Madrid: Prensa Española, 1967.

Castro, Américo. *España en su historia: Cristianos, moros y judíos.* Buenos Aires: Losada, 1948.

———. "Sobre la guerra civil." *De la España que aún no conocía.* Vol. 1. Barcelona: PPU, 1990. 42–60.

Castro Albarrán, Aniceto de. *La gran víctima.* 4th ed. Salamanca: n.p., 1940.

Castroviejo, Concha. *Los que se fueron.* Barcelona: Planeta, 1957.

———. *Víspera del odio.* Barcelona: Garbo, 1959.

Cate-Arries, Francie. *Spanish Culture behind Barbed Wire: Memory and Representation of the French Concentration Camps, 1939–1945.* Lewisburg: Bucknell UP, 2004.

Caudet, Francisco, ed. *Hipótesis sobre el exilio republicano de 1939.* Madrid: Fundación Universitaria Española, 1997.

——, ed. *Romancero de la guerra civil.* Madrid: Torre, 1978.

Cela, Camilo José. *La familia de Pascual Duarte.* 1942. Barcelona: Destino, 1995. Trans. as *The Family of Pascual Duarte.* Trans. Anthony Kerrigan. Boston: Little, 1964.

——. *Vísperas, festividad y octava de San Camilo del año 1936 en Madrid.* Madrid: Alfaguara, 1970. Trans. as *San Camilo, 1936.* Trans. J. H. R. Polt. Durham: Duke UP, 1991.

Cenarro, Ángela. "Memory beyond the Public Sphere: The Francoist Repression Remembered in Aragón." Rein 165–88.

Cercas, Javier. *Soldados de Salamina.* Barcelona: Tusquets, 2001. Trans. as *Soldiers of Salamis.* Trans. Anne McClean. London: Bloomsbury, 2003.

Cernuda, Luis. *Las nubes, 1937–1938.* Madrid: Visor Libros, 2002.

——. Ocnos *seguida de* Variaciones sobre tema mexicano. Madrid: Taurus, 1977.

——. *Poesía completa.* Ed. Derek Harris and Luis Maristany. Madrid: Siruela, 1993.

——. *Selected Poems.* Trans. Reginald Gibbons. Riverside-on-Hudson: Sheep Meadow, 1999.

——. *Variaciones sobre tema mexicano.* Mexico City: Porrúa y Obregón, 1952.

——. *Written in Water.* Trans. Stephen Kessler. San Francisco: City Lights, 2004.

Chacel, Rosa. *Poesía, 1931–1991.* Barcelona: Tusquets, 1992.

Chacón, Dulce. "Black Oaks." Trans. Barbara D. Riess. Bush and Dillman 195–99.

——. *Cielos de barro.* Barcelona: Planeta, 2000.

——. *La voz dormida.* Madrid: Alfaguara, 2002. Trans. as *The Sleeping Voice.* Trans. Nick Caistor. New York: Harvill, 2006.

Champourcín, Ernestina de. *Primer exilio.* Madrid: Rialp, 1978.

Chipp, Herschel B. *Picasso's* Guernica: History, Transformations, Meanings. Berkeley: U of California P, 1988.

Chirbes, Rafael. *La caída de Madrid.* Barcelona: Anagrama, 2000.

Chomsky, Noam. *American Power and the New Mandarins.* New York: Pantheon, 1969.

Chun, Kimberly. "What Is a Ghost? An Interview with Guillermo del Toro." *Cineaste* 27.2 (2002): 28–32.

"Churches Wrecked by Fascism." *Spain at War* 4 (1938): 122–23.

Cierva, Ricardo de la. *Historia esencial de la guerra civil española: Todos los problemas resueltos, sesenta años después.* Madridejos (Toledo): Fénix, 1996.

Cigognetti, Luisa, and Pierre Sorlin. "Quando si parla della guerra civile spagnola: Immagine e rappresentazione, 1936–1939." *Immagini nemiche: La guerra civile spagnola e le sue rappresentazioni, 1936–1939.* Ed. Luca Alessandrini. Bologna: Compositori, 1999. 14–26.

Cirici, Alexandre. *La estética del franquismo.* Barcelona: Gili, 1977.

The Civil War: Traditional American Songs and Instrumental Music Featured in the Film by Ken Burns: Original Soundtrack Recording. Nonesuch, 1990.

Clark, Manning. *A Short History of Australia*. New York: Mentor, 1987.

Claudel, Paul. "Aux martyrs espagnols." *Œuvres complètes*. Vol. 10. Paris: Gallimard, 1952. 240–46.

———. *Poèmes et paroles durant la guerre de trente ans*. Paris: Gallimard, 1945.

Cleminson, Richard. "Beyond Tradition and 'Modernity': The Cultural and Sexual Politics of Spanish Anarchism." Graham and Labanyi 116–23.

Coad, Emma Dent. "Constructing the Nation: Francoist Architecture." Graham and Labanyi 223–25.

Coll, José Luis. *El hermano bastardo de Dios*. Pref. Gonzalo Torrente Ballester. Barcelona: Planeta, 1984.

Collado, Fernando del. *El teatro bajo las bombas en la guerra civil*. Madrid: Kaydeda, 1989.

Coma, Javier. *La brigada Hollywood: Guerra española y cine americano*. Barcelona: Flor del Viento, 2002.

"Como Conversazione: On Translation." *Paris Review* 155 (2000): 255–312.

Conde, Carmen. *Mientras los hombres mueren*. Milan: Cisalpino, 1952.

———. *Obra poética, 1929–1966*. Madrid: Biblioteca Nueva, 1967.

Connerton, Paul. *How Societies Remember*. Cambridge: Cambridge UP, 1989.

Corona de sonetos en honor de José Antonio Primo de Rivera. Barcelona: Jerarquía, 1939.

Cortada, James W., ed. *A City in War: American Views on Barcelona and the Spanish Civil War*. Wilmington: Scholarly Resources, 1985.

———, ed. *Historical Dictionary of the Spanish Civil War, 1936–1939*. Westport: Greenwood, 1982.

Courtois, Stéphane, and Jean-Louis Panné. "The Shadow of the NKVD in Spain." Courtois et al. 333–52.

Courtois, Stéphane, et al., eds. *The Black Book of Communism*. Cambridge: Harvard UP, 1999.

Coverdale, John F. *Italian Intervention in the Spanish Civil War*. Princeton: Princeton UP, 1975.

Cronin, Mike. *The Blueshirts and Irish Politics*. Dublin: Four Courts, 1997.

Cronin, Sean. *Frank Ryan: The Search for the Republic*. Dublin: Repsol, 1980.

Crozier, Robert D. "The Mask of Death, the Face of Life: Hemingway's Féminique." *Hemingway Review* 4.1 (1984): 2–13.

Crumb, George. *Ancient Voices of Children: A Cycle of Songs on Texts by Federico García Lorca*. Perf. Gilbert Kalish, James Freeman, Raymond Des Roches, Richard Fitz. Elektra; Asylum; Nonesuch, 1975.

———. *Federico's Little Songs for Children. Quest*. Perf. Susan Naruki, Susan Palma Nidel, Stacey Shames. Bridge Records, 1996.

———. *Songs, Drones, and Refrains of Death: A Cycle of Poems by Federico García Lorca*. By Roger Sessions. KEM Enterprises, 1998.

Crusells, Magí. *Las Brigadas Internacionales en la pantalla*. Ciudad Real: U de Castilla–La Mancha, 2001.

Cruz, Rafael. *Pasionaria: Dolores Ibárruri, historia y símbolo*. Madrid: Biblioteca Nueva, 1999.

Cueva Merino, Julio de la. "Religious Persecution, Anticlerical Tradition and Revolution: On Atrocities against the Clergy during the Spanish Civil War." *Journal of Contemporary History* 33 (1998): 355–69.

———. " 'Si los curas y frailes supieran . . .': La violencia anticlerical." *Violencia política en la España del siglo XX*. Ed. Santos Juliá. Madrid: Taurus, 2000. 191–233.

Cuevas, Tomasa. *Cárcel de mujeres*. 2 vols. Barcelona: Sirocco, 1985.

———. *Mujeres de la resistencia*. Barcelona: Sirocco, 1986.

———. *Prison of Women: Testimonies of War and Resistance in Spain, 1939–1975*. Ed. and trans. Mary E. Giles. Albany: State U of New York P, 1998.

Cullingford, Elizabeth. *Yeats, Ireland, and Fascism*. Dublin: Gill, 1981.

Cunningham, Valentine. *British Writers of the Thirties*. Oxford: Oxford UP, 1989.

———. Introduction. Cunningham, *Spanish Front* xix–xxxiii.

———, ed. *The Penguin Book of Spanish Civil War Verse*. Harmondsworth: Penguin, 1980.

———, ed. *Spanish Front: Writers on the Civil War*. Oxford: Oxford UP, 1986.

Davis, Frances. *My Shadow in the Sun*. New York: Carrick, 1940.

Day-Lewis, C. *Collected Poems*. London: Cape, 1954.

"Death in Spain: The Civil War Has Taken 500,000 Lives in One Year." *Life* 12 July 1937: 19.

Debicki, Andrew. *Spanish Poetry of the Twentieth Century: Modernity and Beyond*. Lexington: UP of Kentucky, 1994.

"The Decisive Moment." *New York Times* 1 Sept. 1996, sec. 4: 2.

Delgado Ruiz, Manuel. "Anticlericalismo, espacio y poder: La destrucción de los rituales católicos." *El anticlericalismo. Ayer* 27. Ed. Rafael Cruz. Madrid: Marcial Pons, 1997. 149–80.

Delibes, Miguel. *Cinco horas con Mario*. Barcelona: Destino, 1966. Trans. as *Five Hours with Mario*. Trans. Frances M. López-Morillas. New York: Columbia UP, 1988.

———. *377A, madera de héroe*. 1987. Barcelona: Destino, 1995. Trans. as *The Stuff of Heroes*. Trans. Frances M. López-Morillas. New York: Pantheon, 1990.

Delperrié de Bayac, Jacques. *Les Brigades Internationales*. Paris: Fayard, 1968.

Denoyelle, Françoise. "Paris, capitale mondiale de la photographie, 1919–1939." *Guerres mondiales et conflits contemporains* 169 (1993): 101–16.

Derrida, Jacques. *Specters of Marx: The State of the Debt, the Work of Mourning, and the New International*. Trans. Peggy Kamuf. New York: Routledge, 1994.

Deveny, Thomas. *Cain on Screen: Contemporary Spanish Cinema*. Metuchen: Scarecrow, 1999.

Devillard, María José, Álvaro Pazos, Susana Castillo, and Nuria Medina. *Los niños españoles en la URSS, 1937–1997: Narración y memoria*. Barcelona: Ariel, 2001.

Devine, Kathleen, ed. *Modern Irish Writers and the Wars*. Gerrards Cross, Eng.: Smythe, 1999.

Díaz, Elías. "The Left and the Legacy of Francoism: Political Culture in Opposition and Transition." Graham and Labanyi 283–91.

Díaz Garrido, María del Carmen. *Los años únicos: Andanzas de una niña en el Madrid rojo*. Pref. Rafael García Serrano. Madrid: Prensa Española, 1972.

Díaz-Plaja, Fernando, ed. *La guerra civil y los poetas españoles*. Madrid: San Martín, 1981.

———. *La guerra de España en sus documentos*. Madrid: Sarpe, 1986.

————. *Los poetas en la guerra civil española*. Barcelona: Plaza y Janés, 1975.

Dietz, Bernd, ed. and trans. *Un país donde lucía el sol: Poesía inglesa de la guerra civil española*. Bilingual ed. Madrid: Hiperión, 1981.

Di Febo, Giuliana. "El monje guerrero: Identidad de género en los modelos fran- quistas durante la guerra civil." *Mujeres* 202–10.

————. *Resistencia y movimiento de mujeres en España, 1936–1976*. Barcelona: Icaria, 1979.

Dingwaney, Anuradha, and Carol Maier, eds. *Between Languages and Cultures: Translation and Cross-Cultural Texts*. Pittsburgh: U of Pittsburgh P, 1995.

————. "Translation as a Method for Cross-Cultural Teaching." Dingwaney and Maier 303–19. *Understanding Others: Cultural and Cross-Cultural Studies and the Teaching of Literature*. Ed. Joseph Trimmer and Tilly Warnock. Urbana: Natl. Council of Teachers of English, 1992. 47–62.

D'Lugo, Marvin. "Carlos Saura: Constructive Imagination in Post-Franco Cin- ema." *Quarterly Review of Film Studies* 8 (1983): 35–47.

————. *The Films of Carlos Saura: The Practice of Seeing*. Princeton: Princeton UP, 1991.

————. *Guide to the Cinema of Spain*. Westport: Greenwood, 1997.

————. "The Politics of Memory: Saura and the Civil War on Screen." Vernon, *Spanish Civil War* 46–61.

————. "Vicente Aranda's *Amantes*: History as Cultural Style in Spanish Cin- ema." *Modes of Representation in Spanish Cinema*. Ed. Jenaro Talens and San- tos Zunzunegui. Minneapolis: U of Minnesota P, 1998. 289–300.

Doña, Juana. *Desde la noche y la niebla: Mujeres en las cárceles franquistas*. Madrid: Torre, 1978.

Dreyfus-Armand, Geneviève. *El exilio de los republicanos españoles en Francia: De la guerra civil a la muerte de Franco*. Trans. Dolors Poch. Barcelona: Crítica, 2000.

Drieu la Rochelle, Pierre. *Gilles*. Paris: Gallimard, 1939.

Durgan, Andy. Rev. of *Land and Freedom*, dir. Ken Loach. *Socialist Review* July 1996: 18–19.

Dwinger, Edwin Erich. *Spanische Silhouetten: Tagebuch einer Frontreise*. Jena: Dietrichs, 1937.

Eakin, Paul John. *How Our Lives Become Stories: Making Selves*. Ithaca: Cornell UP, 1999.

Ealham, Christopher. "Anarchism and Illegality in Barcelona, 1931–37." *Contem- porary European History* 4.2 (1995): 133–51.

Eby, Cecil. *Between the Bullet and the Lie: American Volunteers in the Spanish Civil War*. New York: Holt, Rinehart, 1969.

Eco, Umberto. "On Translating and Being Translated." *Experiences in Transla- tion*. Trans. Alastair McEwen. Toronto: U of Toronto P, 2001. 3–63.

Edmonds, Robert. *About Documentary*. Dayton: Pflaum, 1974.

"La Educación Femenina II." *La Escuela en Canal Nostalgia*. 2000–04. ¿Te Acuerdas? 13 Oct. 2005 <http://www.teacuerdas.com/nostalgia-escuela- mujer2.htm>.

Eire, Carlos M. N. *From Madrid to Purgatory: The Art and Craft of Dying in Six- teenth-Century Spain*. Cambridge: Cambridge UP, 1995.

Elordi, Carlos, ed. *Los años difíciles: El testimonio de los protagonistas anónimos de la guerra civil y la posguerra*. Madrid: Aguilar, 2002.

Elorza, Antonio, and Marta Bizcarrondo. *Queridos camaradas*. Barcelona: Planeta, 1999.

Embeita, María. "Max Aub y su generación." *Ínsula* 253 (1967): 1, 12.

Enzensberger, Hans Magnus. *Der kurze Sommer der Anarchie: Buenaventura Durrutis Leben und Tod*. Frankfurt am Main: Suhrkamp, 1972.

Escobal, Patricio P. *Death Row: Spain, 1936*. Trans. Tana de Gámez. Indianapolis: Bobbs-Merrill, 1968.

Escolar, Hipólito. *La cultura durante la guerra civil*. Madrid: Alhambra, 1987.

Esenwein, George, and Adrian Shubert. *Spain at War: The Spanish Civil War in Context, 1931–1939*. London: Longman, 1995.

Eslava Galán, Juan. *La mula*. Barcelona: Planeta, 2003.

Espada, Arcadi. *Contra Catalunya*. Trans. Jaume Boix Angelats. Barcelona: Flor del Viento, 1997.

Esperabé de Arteaga, Enrique. *La guerra de reconquista española y el criminal comunismo: El glorioso ejército nacional: Mártires y héroes*. Madrid: San Martín, 1940.

Espina, Concha. *Luna roja: Novelas de la revolución*. Valladolid: Librería Santarén, 1939.

———. *Retaguardia: Imágenes de vivos y de muertos*. Pref. Víctor de la Serna. Madrid: Nueva España, 1937.

Espinar, Jaime. *Argelès-sur-Mer: Campo de concentración para españoles*. Caracas: Elite, 1940.

Esslin, Martin. *The Age of Television*. San Francisco: Freeman, 1982.

Esteban Vilaró, José. *El ocaso de los dioses rojos: Barcelona, Perthus, Argeles, París, Méjico . . .* Barcelona: Destino, 1939.

Estes, Kenneth W., and Daniel Kowalsky, eds. *The Spanish Civil War*. Vol. 18 of *History in Dispute*. Detroit: St. James, 2004.

Everard, Conrad. *Luftkampf über Spanien: Kriegserlebnisse eines freiwilligen englischen Kampffliegers bei der nationalen Armee*. Berlin: Scherl, 1937.

Faber, Sebastiaan. *Exile and Cultural Hegemony: Spanish Intellectuals in Mexico, 1939–1975*. Nashville: Vanderbilt UP, 2002.

———. " 'El norte nos devora': La construcción de un espacio hispánico en el exilio anglosajón de Luis Cernuda." *Hispania* 83 (2000): 733–44.

Fagen, Patricia W. *Exiles and Citizens: Spanish Republicans in Mexico*. Austin: U of Texas P, 1973.

Felipe, León. *Obra poética escogida*. Ed. Gerardo Diego. Madrid: Espasa-Calpe, 1975.

Felman, Shoshana, and Dori Laub. *Testimony: Crises of Witnessing in Literature, Psychoanalysis, and History*. New York: Routledge, 1992.

Felsen, Milt. *The Anti-warrior: A Memoir*. Introd. Albert E. Stone. Iowa City: U of Iowa P, 1989.

Ferguson, Niall. *The Pity of War*. London: Lane, 1998.

Fernández, Carlos. *La guerra civil en Galicia*. La Coruña: Voz de Galicia, 1988.

Fernández Cuenca, Carlos. *La guerra de España y el cine*. 2 vols. Madrid: Nacional, 1972.

Fernán Gómez, Fernando. *Las bicicletas son para el verano.* Introd. Eduardo Haro Tecglen. Madrid: Espasa-Calpe, 1984.

Feros, Antonio. "Civil War Still Haunts Spanish Politics." *New York Times* 20 Mar. 2004. <www.nytimes.com/2004/03/20/arts/20SPAN.html?th>.

Ferré, Facundo Tomás. *Los carteles valencianos en la guerra civil española.* Valencia: Ayuntamiento de Valencia, Delegación Municipal de Cultura, 1986.

Ferrer, Eulalio. *Entre alambradas.* Barcelona: Grijalbo, 1988.

Ferrero, Jesús. *Las trece rosas.* Madrid: Siruela, 2003.

"Feuds in Red Spain." *Spain* 1 Mar. 1938: 4.

Fillol, Vicente. *Los perdedores: Memorias de un exiliado español.* Madrid: Gaceta Ilustrada, 1973.

"First Intervention." *Spain at War* 3 (1938): 108.

Fischer, David Hackett. *Historians' Fallacies: Toward a Logic of Historical Thought.* New York: Harper, 1970.

Fischer, Louis. *Men and Politics: Europe between Two World Wars.* New York: Harper, 1966.

Fisher, Harry. *Comrades: Tales of a Brigadista in the Spanish Civil War.* Fwd. Pete Seeger. Lincoln: U of Nebraska P, 1997.

Fleming, Bruce. "Writing in Pidgin: Language in *For Whom the Bell Tolls.*" *Dutch Quarterly Review* 15.4 (1985): 265–77.

Fleming, Robert. "Communism vs. Community in *For Whom the Bell Tolls.*" *North Dakota Quarterly* 60.2 (1992): 144–50.

Fletcher, Angus. *Allegory: The Theory of a Symbolic Mode.* 1964. Ithaca: Cornell UP, 1975.

Forcadas, Albert M. Rev. of *The Time of the Doves,* by Mercè Rodoreda, trans. David H. Rosenthal. *World Literature Today* 37.1–2 (1981): 457–58.

Ford, Hugh D. *A Poet's War: British Poets and the Spanish Civil War.* Philadelphia: U of Pennsylvania P, 1965.

"The Foreign Commanders of the Red Army." *Spain* 15 Oct. 1938: 10+.

Forment, Albert. *Josep Renau: Història d'un fotomuntador.* Catarrosa: Afers, 1997.

Foss, William, and Cecil Gerahty. *The Spanish Arena.* Fwd. Duke of Alba and Berwick. London: Right Book Club, [1938].

Foster, Kevin. "Silent Homage: Orwell in Catalonia." *Southern Review* 29.1 (1996): 9–32.

Fox, Soledad. *Constancia de la Mora in War and Exile: International Spokesperson for the Spanish Republic.* Brighton: Sussex Academic, 2006.

Foxá, Agustín de. *Madrid de corte a checa.* 1938. 3rd ed. Madrid: Prensa Española, 1962.

Fox-Genovese, Elizabeth. "Literary Criticism and the Politics of the New Historicism." Veeser 213–24.

Franco, Francisco. "Decreto del 1 de abril de 1940." D. Méndez 314.

———. "Discurso en la inauguración del Valle de los Caídos, el 1 de abril de 1959." Sueiro 239–43.

———. *Franco ha dicho.* Madrid: Voz, 1949.

——— (pseud. Jaime de Andrade). *Raza: Anecdotario para el guión de una película.* Madrid: Fundación Nacional Francisco Franco, 1981.

Fraser, Ronald. *Blood of Spain: An Oral History of the Spanish Civil War.* New York: Pantheon, 1979.

———. *Blood of Spain: The Experience of Civil War, 1936–1939.* London: Lane, 1979.

———. *In Hiding: The Life of Manuel Cortés.* New York: Pantheon, 1972.

Freud, Sigmund. "Erinnern, Wiederholen und Durcharbeiten." *Werkausgabe in zwei bänden.* Vol. 1. Ed. Anna Freud and Ilse Grubrich-Simitis. Frankfurt am Main: Fischer, 1978. 518–25.

———. "Mourning and Melancholia." *On Metapsychology.* Penguin Freud Lib. 11. London: Penguin, 1984. 251–67.

Freund, Gisèle. *The World in My Camera.* Trans. June Guicharnaud. New York: Dial, 1974.

Furet, François. *The Passing of an Illusion: The Idea of Communism in the Twentieth Century.* Trans. Deborah Furet. Chicago: U of Chicago P, 1999.

Fusi, Juan Pablo. "Centre and Periphery, 1900–1936: National Integration and Regional Nationalisms Reconsidered." Lannon and Preston 33–44.

———. *El País Vasco, 1931–1937: Autonomía, revolución, guerra civil.* Madrid: Biblioteca Nueva, 2002.

Fussell, Paul. *The Great War and Modern Memory.* Oxford: Oxford UP, 1975.

Fyrth, Jim, and Sally Alexander, eds. *Women's Voices from the Spanish Civil War.* London: Lawrence, 1991.

Gabantxo, Amaia. "Your Gernika." Bush and Dillman 47–53.

Galland, Adolf. *Die Ersten und die Letzten.* 1953. 9th ed. Munich: Heyne, 1979.

Gallego, Gregorio. *Asalto a la ciudad.* Barcelona: Argos Vergara, 1984.

Galloway, Joseph L. "A Soldier's Story." *U.S. News and World Report* 31 May 1999: 43–47.

Gamonal Torres, Miguel A., ed. *Arte y política en la guerra civil española: El caso republicano.* Granada: Diputación Provincial, 1987.

Ganivet, Ángel. *Idearium español.* Ed. E. Inman Fox. Madrid: Espasa-Calpe, 1999.

Gannes, Harry, and Theodore Repard. *Spain in Revolt.* London: Gollancz, 1936.

García de Cortázar, Fernando, and Juan Pablo Fusi. *Política, nacionalidad e iglesia en el País Vasco.* San Sebastián: Txertoa, 1988.

García de Jalón Hueto, Ángel Hilario [Ángel Jalón]. *Forjadores de imperio.* Introd. José María Peman and Federico García Sánchez. Zaragoza: Vitor, 1939.

García de la Concha, Víctor. *De la preguerra a los años oscuros.* Madrid: Cátedra, 1987. Vol. 1 of *Poesía española de 1935 a 1975.*

García de Prieto, Manuel, Marqués de Alhucemas. "Carta—Prologo." Esperabé de Arteaga ix–xi.

García Durán, Juan. *Bibliography of the Spanish Civil War / Bibliografía de la guerra civil española, 1936–1939.* Montevideo: Siglo Ilustrado, 1964.

———. *La guerra civil española: Fuentes: Archivos, bibliografía y filmografía.* Barcelona: Crítica, 1985.

García Fernández, Emilio C. *Historia ilustrada del cine español.* Madrid: Planeta, 1985.

García Gerpe, Manuel. *Alambradas: Mis nueve meses por los campos de concentración de Francia.* Buenos Aires: Celta, 1941.

García Lorca, Federico. *Collected Poems.* Rev. ed. Introd. and ed. Christopher Maurer. New York: Farrar, 2002.

———. *Poema del cante jondo* [and] *Romancero gitano.* Ed. Allen Josephs and Juan Caballero. Madrid: Cátedra, 1984.

García-Nieto, María Carmen, and Javier M. Donézar, eds. *La España de Franco, 1939–1973.* Madrid: Guadiana, 1975.

García-Posada, Miguel de. "Max Aub y el exilio." *El país digital* 31 Mar. 2001 <http://www.elpais.es>.

García Roldán, Ángel. *A boca de noche.* Barcelona: Plaza y Janés, 1988.

García Serrano, Rafael. *Eugenio o la proclamación de la primavera.* Burgos: n.p., 1938. Rodríguez-Puértolas 2:268–72.

———. *La fiel infantería.* Madrid: Nacional, 1943. Madrid: Eskúa, 1958. Mainer 126–44.

Gates, John. *The Story of an American Communist.* New York: Nelson, 1958.

Geiser, Carl. *Prisoners of the Good Fight: The Spanish Civil War, 1936–1939.* Westport: Hill, 1986.

Geist, Anthony L., and Peter N. Carroll. *They Still Draw Pictures: Children's Art in Wartime from the Spanish Civil War to Kosovo.* Fwd. Robert Coles. Urbana: U of Illinois P, 2002.

Gellhorn, Martha. *The Face of War.* 1959. London: Virago, 1986.

———. Rev. of *Land and Freedom,* dir. Ken Loach. *Evening Standard* 5 Oct. 1995, sec. D: 21.

Gerassi, John, ed. *The Premature Antifascists: North American Volunteers in the Spanish Civil War, 1936–39: An Oral History.* New York: Praeger, 1986.

Gibson, Ian. *The Assassination of Federico García Lorca.* London: Penguin, 1983.

Gide, André. *Journal, 1889–1939.* Paris: Gallimard, 1951.

———. *Retour de l'U.R.S.S.* Paris: Gallimard, 1936. Trans. as *Return from the U.S.S.R.* New York: Knopf, 1937.

Gikandi, Simon. "Theory as Translation: Teaching 'Foreign' Concepts." *Teaching Contemporary Theory to Undergraduates.* Ed. Dianne F. Sadoff and William E. Cain. New York: MLA, 1994. 233–44.

Gillespie, Richard, Fernando Rodrigo, and Jonathan Story, eds. *Democratic Spain: Reshaping External Relations in a Changing World.* London: Routledge, 1995.

Gilmore, David D. *Aggression and Community: Paradoxes of Andalusian Culture.* New Haven: Yale UP, 1987.

Giménez Caballero, Ernesto. *Exaltaciones sobre Madrid.* N.p.: Jerarquía, 1937.

Girard, René. *The Scapegoat.* Trans. Yvonne Freccero. Baltimore: Johns Hopkins UP, 1986.

Girón de Velasco, José Antonio. *Si la memoria no me falla.* Barcelona: Planeta, 1994.

Gironella, José María. *Los cipreses creen en Dios.* Barcelona: Planeta, 1955. Trans. as *The Cypresses Believe in God.* 2 vols. Trans. Harriet de Onís. New York: Knopf, 1955.

———. *Un millón de muertos.* Barcelona: Planeta, 1961. Trans. as *One Million Dead.* Trans. Joan MacLean. Garden City: Doubleday, 1963.

Goebbels, Joseph. *The Truth about Spain.* Berlin: Müller, 1937.

Golsan, Richard J., ed. *Fascism, Aesthetics, and Culture.* Hanover: UP of New England, 1992.

Gomá y Tomás, Isidro. "Apología de la Hispanidad." *Acción Española* 11 (1934): 193–238.

———. *La familia según el derecho natural y cristiano.* Barcelona: Librería Litúrgica, 1931.

González Cuevas, Pedro. *Acción Española: Teología política y nacionalismo autoritario en España, 1913–1936.* Madrid: Tecnos, 1998.

González Fresco, Manuel. *Memoria dun fuxido, 1936.* Ed. Víctor F. Freixanes. Vigo: Xerais de Galicia, 1979.

Goodman, Al. "Spanish Poetry Icon to Be Exhumed." *CNN.com/world* 4 Sept. 2003. <www.edition.cnn.com/2003/WORLD/europe/09/04/spain>.

Gorkin, Julian. "Spain: First Test of a People's Democracy." *The Strategy of Deception: A Study of World-wide Communist Tactics.* Ed. Jeane J. Kirkpatrick. New York: Farrar, 1963. 195–226.

Gould, Thomas E. "'A Tiny Operation with Great Effect': Authorial Revision and Editorial Emasculation in the Manuscript of Hemingway's *For Whom the Bell Tolls.*" Sanderson 67–81.

Goytisolo, Juan. *Duelo en el Paraíso.* Barcelona: Planeta, 1955. Trans. as *Children of Chaos.* Trans. Christine Brooke-Rose. London: MacGibbon, 1958.

———. *Señas de identidad.* 1966. Madrid: Mondadori, 1991. Trans. as *Marks of Identity.* Trans. Gregory Rabassa. London: Serpent's Tail, 1990.

Graham, Helen. "'Against the State': A Genealogy of the Barcelona May Days, 1937." *European History Quarterly* 29.4 (1999): 485–542.

———. "The Barcelona May Days and Their Consequences." Graham, *Spanish Republic* 254–315.

———. "Gender and the State: Women in the 1940s." Graham and Labanyi 182–95.

———. *The Spanish Civil War: A Very Short Introduction.* Oxford: Oxford UP, 2005.

———. *The Spanish Republic at War, 1936–1939.* Cambridge: Cambridge UP, 2002.

———. "Women and Social Change." Graham and Labanyi 99–116.

Graham, Helen, and Jo Labanyi, eds. *Spanish Cultural Studies: An Introduction: The Struggle for Modernity.* Oxford: Oxford UP, 1995.

Grando, René, Jacques Queralt, and Xavier Febrés. *Vous avez la mémoire courte . . . 1939: 500.000 républicains venus du Sud "indésirables" en Roussillon.* Perpignan: Chiendent, 1981.

Green, Jerald R. "Augustí Centelles: Spanish Civil War Photographer." *History of Photography* 12.2 (1988): 147–59.

———. "Spanish Civil War Photography: A Bibliographical and Source Study." Vernon, *Spanish Civil War* 97–103.

Greene, Graham. *The Confidential Agent.* London: Heinemann, 1939. New York: Viking, 1943.

Grimau, Carmen. "Cartel político y publicidad comercial." Bonet Correa, *Arte* 273–90.

———. *El cartel republicano en la guerra civil.* Madrid: Cátedra, 1979.

Guardiola, Antonio R. "La mano de Franco." Vicente Hernando 221.

Gubern, Román. *Cine contemporáneo.* Barcelona: Salvat, 1973.

———. *1936–1939: La guerra de España en la pantalla*. Madrid: Filmoteca Española, 1986.

———. "Tendencies, Genres, and Problems of Spanish Cinema in the Post-Franco Period." *Quarterly Review of Film Studies* 8.2 (1983): 15–26.

La guerra civil espanyola: Fotògrafs per a la història. Barcelona: Museu Nacional d'Art de Catalunya; Arxiu Nacional de Catalunya, 2001.

Guerra civil y producción cultural: Teatro, poesía, narrativa. Issue of *Anthropos* 148 (1993).

Gugelberger, Georg M., ed. *The Real Thing: Testimonial Discourse and Latin America*. Durham: Duke UP, 1996.

A Guide to "Survivors: Testimonies of the Holocaust." Survivors of the Shoah Visual History Foundation and Facing History and Ourselves National Foundation. 1998. <www.vhf.org>; <www.facing.org>.

Guillén, Nicolás. *España: Poema en cuatro angustias y una esperanza*. Mexico City: México Nuevo, 1937.

———. *Obra poética*. 2 vols. La Habana: Letras Cubanas, 1995.

Gullón, Germán. "El discurso literario: Entre el monólogo y el diálogo (Cela, Massip, Delibes)." *Serta Philologica F. Lázaro Carreter*. Vol 2. Madrid: Cátedra, 1983. 223–34.

Guttmann, Allen. *The Wound in the Heart: America and the Spanish Civil War*. New York: Free Press of Glencoe, 1962.

Halbwachs, Maurice. *The Collective Memory*. Trans. Francis J. Ditter, Jr., and Vida Yazdi Ditter. New York: Harper, 1980.

Hall, Stuart. "The Determination of News Photographs." *The Manufacture of News: A Reader*. Ed. Stanley Cohen and Jock Young. Beverly Hills: Sage, 1973. 176–90.

Hannington, Wal. *Unemployed Struggles, 1919–1936*. London: Lawrence, 1977.

Hanrez, Marc, ed. *Les écrivains et la guerre d'Espagne*. Paris: Panthéon, 1974.

Hart, Stephen M., ed. *"¡No pasarán!": Art, Literature, and the Spanish Civil War*. London: Tamesis, 1988.

Harvey, Jessamy. "The Value of Nostalgia: Reviving Memories of National-Catholic Childhoods." *Journal of Spanish Cultural Studies* 2.1 (2001): 109–18.

Hayes, Aden. "The Spanish Civil War in *Life* Magazine." Vernon, *Spanish Civil War* 62–70.

Held, Jutta. "How Do the Political Effects of Pictures Come About? The Case of Picasso's *Guernica*." *Oxford Art Journal* 11.1 (1988): 33–39.

Hemingway, Ernest. The Fifth Column *and Four Stories of the Spanish Civil War*. New York: Scribner's, 1969.

———. *For Whom the Bell Tolls*. New York: Scribner's, 1940. 1995.

———. "On the American Dead in Spain." C. Nelson, *Remembering* 36–37.

———. *The Sun Also Rises*. New York: Scribner's, 1926.

Herce Vales, Fernando, and Manuel Sanz Nogués. *Franco, el reconquistador*. Madrid: Sanz Nogués, 1939.

Hermanos, Juan. *El fin de la esperanza: Testimonio*. Introd. Francisco Caudet. Pref. Jean-Paul Sartre. Madrid: Tecnos, 1998.

Hernández, Miguel. *Obra completa.* 2 vols. Ed. Agustín Sánchez Vidal and José Carlos Rovira. Madrid: Espasa-Calpe, 1992.

———. *Obra poética completa.* Ed. Leopoldo de Luis and Jorge Urrutia. Madrid: Zero, 1979.

———. *The Selected Poems of Miguel Hernández: A Bilingual Edition.* Ed. Ted Genoways. Trans. Genoways et al. Fwd. Robert Bly. Chicago: U of Chicago P, 2001.

———. *Viento del pueblo.* Madrid: Socorro Rojo, 1937.

Herr, Richard. *Spain.* Englewood Cliffs: Prentice, 1971.

Herrera Petere, José. *Cumbres de Extremadura: Novela de guerrilleros.* 1938. Introd. María Zambrano. Barcelona: Anthropos, 1986.

Herrero, Javier. *Los orígenes del pensamiento reaccionario español.* Madrid: Alianza U, 1994.

Herrick, William. *¡Hermanos!* New York: Simon, 1969.

Higonnet, Margaret R., et al. *Behind the Lines: Gender and the Two World Wars.* New Haven: Yale UP, 1987.

Hirsch, Edward. *The Demon and the Angel: Searching for the Source of Artistic Inspiration.* New York: Harcourt, 2002.

———. "I Call Myself Clay though Miguel Is My Name." *Washington Post* 27 Jan. 2002: 12T.

Hirsch, Marianne. *Family Frames: Photography, Narrative, and Postmemory.* Cambridge: Harvard UP, 1997.

———. "Mourning and Postmemory." M. Hirsch, *Family Frames* 17–40.

Hochman, Jiri. *The Soviet Union and the Failure of Collective Security, 1934–1938.* Ithaca: Cornell UP, 1984.

Holguín, Sandie. *Creating Spaniards: Culture and National Identity in Republican Spain.* Madison: U of Wisconsin P, 2002.

Homenaje a las Brigadas Internacionales. Madrid: Hispamérica, 1978.

Hopewell, John. *Out of the Past: Spanish Cinema after Franco.* London: British Film Inst., 1986.

Horna, Kati. *Fotografías de la guerra civil española, 1937–1938.* Salamanca: Ministerio de Cultura, 1992.

Hoskins, Catherine Bail. *Today the Struggle: Literature and Politics in England during the Spanish Civil War.* Austin: U of Texas P, 1969.

Howson, Gerald. *Arms for Spain: The Untold Story of the Spanish Civil War.* New York: St. Martin's, 1998.

"How the Red Newspapers Inform Their Readers." *Spain* 15 May 1938: 15.

Hughes, Dorothy B. *The Fallen Sparrow.* New York: Duell, 1942.

Huxley, Aldous. Introduction. *They Still Draw Pictures! A Collection of Sixty Drawings Made by Spanish Children during the War.* New York: Spanish Child Welfare Assn. of Amer. for the Amer. Friends Service Committee, 1938. 4–8.

Ibárruri, Dolores (Pasionaria). *A las mujeres madrileñas.* Madrid: Partido Comunista Comité Provincial de Madrid, 193[8].

———. *En la lucha: Palabras y hechos, 1936–1939.* Moscow: Progreso, 1968.

———. *Pasionaria [and] Memorias [and] La lucha y la vida.* Barcelona: Planeta, 1985.

———. *They Shall Not Pass: The Autobiography of La Pasionaria*. New York: Intl., 1966.

———. *El único camino*. Moscow: Progreso, 1976.

Ilie, Paul. *Literature and Inner Exile: Authoritarian Spain, 1939–1975*. Baltimore: Johns Hopkins UP, 1980.

Imágenes inéditas de la guerra civil, 1936–1939. Introd. Stanley G. Payne. Madrid: Agencia EFE, 2002.

The International Brigade Memorial Trust. 22 Nov. 2005 <www.international-brigades.org.uk>.

Iráizoz, Carmen. *Belzunegui: El ocaso de una familia*. Pamplona: Gómez, 1969.

Iturralde, Juan. *Días de llamas*. Madrid: Debate, 2000.

Ivens, Joris. *The Camera and I*. Berlin: Seven Seas, 1969. New York: Intl., 1969.

———. "Documentary: Subjectivity and Montage." Bakker 250–58.

Jackson, Angela. "The Aftermath: Women and the Memory of War." *British Women and the Spanish Civil War*. London: Routledge, 2002. 160–207.

Jackson, Gabriel. *Breve historia de la guerra civil española*. Barcelona: Grijalbo, 1986.

———. *A Concise History of the Spanish Civil War*. New York: Thames, 1974.

———. *The Spanish Civil War: Domestic Crisis or International Conspiracy?* Lexington: Heath, 1967.

———. *The Spanish Republic and the Civil War, 1931–1939*. Princeton: Princeton UP, 1971.

Jacobs, Jane M. *Cities and the Wealth of Nations*. New York: Vintage, 1985.

———. *Quebec and the Struggle over Sovereignty: The Question of Separatism*. New York: Random, 1980.

———. "Resisting Reconciliation: The Secret Geographies of (Post)colonial Australia." *Geographies of Resistance*. Ed. Steve Pile and Michael Keith. London: Routledge, 1997. 203–18.

Jameson, Fredric. *Signatures of the Visible*. New York: Routledge, 1992.

Jaraiz Franco, Pilar. *Historia de una disidencia*. Barcelona: Planeta, 1981.

Jarnés, Benjamín. *Su línea de fuego*. Ed. Pascual Hernández del Moral and Juan Ramón Torregosa. Zaragoza: Guara, 1980.

Jerrold, Douglas. *Georgian Adventure*. London: Right Book Club, 1938.

Johnstone, Verle B. *Legions of Babel: The International Brigades in the Spanish Civil War*. University Park: Pennsylvania State UP, 1968.

Jordan, Barry, and Rikki Morgan-Tamosunas. "Reconstructing the Past: Historical Cinema in Post-Franco Spain." *Contemporary Spanish Cinema*. Manchester: Manchester UP, 1998. 15–60.

Josephs, Allen. For Whom the Bell Tolls: *Hemingway's Undiscovered Country*. New York: Twayne, 1994.

———. "Hemingway's Poor Spanish: Chauvinism and Loss of Credibility in *For Whom the Bell Tolls*." *Hemingway: A Revaluation*. Ed. Donald R. Noble. Troy: Whitston, 1983. 205–23.

Juliá, Santos, ed. *Víctimas de la guerra civil*. Madrid: Temas de Hoy, 1999.

Kallis, Aristotle A., ed. *The Fascism Reader*. London: Routledge, 2003.

Kee, Salaria. *A Negro Nurse in Republican Spain*. New York: Negro Committee to Aid Spain; Medical Bureau; North Amer. Committee to Aid Spanish Democracy, 1938.

Keene, Judith. *Fighting for Franco: International Volunteers in Nationalist Spain during the Spanish Civil War, 1936–39.* London: Leicester UP, 2001.

Kemp, Peter. *Mine Were of Trouble.* London: Cassell, 1957.

Kent, Victoria. *Cuatro años en París, 1940–1944.* Buenos Aires: Sur, 1947.

Kenwood, Alun, ed. *The Spanish Civil War: A Cultural and Historical Reader.* Providence: Berg, 1993.

Kinder, Marsha. *Blood Cinema: The Reconstruction of National Identity in Spain.* Berkeley: U of California P, 1993.

———. "Carlos Saura: The Political Development of Individual Consciousness." *Film Quarterly* 32 (1979): 14–25.

———. "The Children of Franco." *Quarterly Review of Film Studies* 8 (1983): 57–76.

Kizer, Carolyn. "The Valley of the Fallen." C. Nelson, *Wound* 251–53.

Klehr, Harvey, et al. "Fighting Deviationists and Bad Elements in the Spanish Civil War." *The Secret World of American Communism.* New Haven: Yale UP, 1995. 158–87.

Klein, Norman M. *The History of Forgetting: Los Angeles and the Erasure of Memory.* London: Verso, 1997.

Knightley, Phillip. *The First Casualty.* New York: Harvest, 1975.

Knoblaugh, H. Edward. *Correspondent in Spain.* London: Sheed, 1937.

———. "How the Loyalist Propaganda Machine Operates." *Spain* 15 Dec. 1937: 18+.

Knox, Bernard. "Premature Anti-fascist." First Annual Abraham Lincoln Brigade Archives-Bill Susman Lecture. King Juan Carlos I of Spain Center, New York U, New York. 1998.

Koestler, Arthur. *Spanish Testament.* London: Gollancz, 1937. *Ein spanisches Testament: Aufzeichnungen aus dem Bürgerkrieg.* Zurich: Europa, 1938. Trans. as *Dialogue with Death.* Trans. Trevor Blewitt and Phyllis Blewitt. New York: Macmillan, 1942.

Kolbert, Elizabeth. "Looking for Lorca." *New Yorker* 22–29 Dec. 2003: 64–75.

Koonz, Claudia. *Mothers in the Fatherland: Women, the Family, and Nazi Politics.* New York: St. Martin's, 1987.

Kowalsky, Daniel. *La Unión Soviética y la guerra civil española: Una revisión crítica.* Barcelona: Crítica, 2004.

Kreuzer, Helmut. "Zum Spanienkrieg: Prosa deutscher Exilautoren." *LiLi: Zeitschrift für deutsche Literaturwissenschaft und Linguistik* 15.60 (1985): 10–43.

Krivitsky, W. G. *I Was Stalin's Agent.* London: Hamilton, 1939.

Kühn, Dieter. *Luftkrieg als Abenteuer: Kampfschrift.* Munich: Hanser, 1975.

Labanyi, Jo. "The Ambiguous Implications of the Mythical References in Juan Goytisolo's *Duelo en el Paraíso.*" *Modern Language Review* 80 (1985): 845–57.

———. "History and Hauntology; or, What Does One Do with the Ghosts of the Past? Reflections on Spanish Film and Fiction of the Post-Franco Period." Resina, *Disremembering* 65–82.

———. "The Politics of the Everyday and the Eternity of Ruins: Two Women Photographers in Republican Spain (Margaret Michaelis 1933–37, Kati Horna

1937–38).” *Cultural Encounters: European Travel Writing in the 1930s*. Ed. Charles Burdett and Derek Duncan. Oxford: Berghahn, 2002. 85–103.

———. “Propaganda Art: Culture by the People or for the People.” Graham and Labanyi 161–66.

LaCapra, Dominick. *History and Criticism*. Ithaca: Cornell UP, 1985.

———. *History and Memory after Auschwitz*. Ithaca: Cornell UP, 1998.

———. *History in Transit: Experience, Identity, Critical Theory*. Ithaca: Cornell UP, 2004.

Laforet, Carmen. *Andrea*. Trans. Charles F. Payne. New York: Vantage, 1964. Trans. of *Nada*.

———. *Nada*. 1945. Ed. Domingo Ródenas de Moya. Barcelona: Crítica, 2001.

———. *Nada*. Trans. Glafrya Ennis. Catalan Studies 8. New York: Lang, 1993.

———. *Nada*. Trans. Edith Grossman. New York: Modern Lib.–Random; London: Harvill–Random, 2007.

Lafuente, Isaías. *Esclavos por la patria: La explotación de los presos bajo el franquismo*. Madrid: Temas de Hoy, 2002.

———. *Tiempos de hambre*. Madrid: Temas de Hoy, 1999.

Rev. of *Land and Freedom*, dir. Ken Loach. World Socialist Web Site. 23 Oct. 1995. <http://www.wsws.org/arts/1998/aug1998/land-96.shtml>.

Landis, Arthur. *The Abraham Lincoln Brigade*. New York: Citadel, 1967.

Lannon, Frances. “The Church's Crusade against the Republic.” Preston, *Revolution* 35–58.

———. *The Spanish Civil War, 1936–1939*. London: Osprey, 2002.

———. “Women.” Lannon, *Spanish Civil War* 70–72.

———. “Women and War: Two Memoirs.” Lannon, *Spanish Civil War* 80–83.

Lannon, Frances, and Paul Preston, eds. *Elites and Power in Twentieth-Century Spain*. Oxford: Oxford UP, 1990.

Last, Jef. *The Spanish Tragedy*. Trans. David Hallett. London: Routledge, 1939.

Latourette, Kenneth Scott. *A Short History of the Far East*. New York: Macmillan, 1957.

Lawrence, T. E. *Seven Pillars of Wisdom: A Triumph*. 1926. Garden City: Doubleday, 1935.

Leavis, F. R. *Mass Civilisation and Minority Culture*. Cambridge: Minority, 1930.

Lechner, Johannes. *El compromiso en la poesía española del siglo XX*. Leiden: U Pers Leiden, 1968.

Lee, Laurie. *A Moment of War: A Memoir of the Spanish Civil War*. 1991. New York: New, 1993.

Leeds Papers on Lorca and on Spanish Civil War Verse. Ed. Margaret A. Reese. Leeds: Trinity and All Saints' College, 1988.

Lefebvre, Michel, and Rémi Skoutelsky. *Las Brigadas Internacionales: Imágenes recuperadas*. Madrid: Ludwerg, 2003.

Leguineche, Manuel, and Jesús Torbado. *Los topos: El testimonio estremecedor de quienes pasaron su vida escondidos en la España de la postguerra*. 2nd ed. Madrid: El País; Aguilar, 1999.

León, María Teresa. “Una estrella roja.” *Cuentos de la España actual*. Mexico City: Dialéctica, 1938. 38–43.

———. *Juego limpio*. Buenos Aires: Goyanarte, 1959.

———. *Memoria de la melancolía*. 2nd ed. Barcelona: Laia, 1977. Ed. Gregorio Torres Nebrera. Madrid: Castalia, 1998.

Lera, Ángel María de. *Las últimas banderas*. Barcelona: Planeta, 1967.

Lerner, Daniel. *The Passing of Traditional Society: Modernizing the Middle East*. Glencoe: Free, 1958.

Levenson, Leonard. "U.S. Communists in Spain: A Profile." *Political Affairs* 65.8 (1986): 22–28.

Levin, Harry. "Observations on the Style of Ernest Hemingway." *Contexts of Criticism*. New York: Atheneum, 1963. 140–67.

Levine, Linda Gould. "Carmen Martín Gaite's *El cuarto de atrás*: A Portrait of the Artist as Woman." *From Fiction to Metafiction: Essays in Honor of Carmen Martín Gaite*. Ed. Mirella Servodidio and Marcia L. Welles. Lincoln: Soc. of Spanish and Spanish-American Studies, 1983. 161–72.

Lévi-Strauss, Claude. *The Savage Mind*. Trans. G. Weidenfield. Chicago: U of Chicago P, 1966.

———. "The Structural Study of Myth." *Structural Anthropology*. Trans. Claire Jacobson and Brooke Grundfest Schoepf. Vol. 1. New York: Basic, 1963. 206–31.

Lewinski, Jorge. *The Camera at War: A History of War Photography from 1848 to the Present Day*. London: Allen, 1978.

Lina Odena: Heroína del pueblo. Madrid: Europa América, 1937.

Lincoln, Bruce. "Revolutionary Exhumations in Spain, July 1936." *Comparative Studies in Society and History* 27 (1985): 241–60.

Lindqvist, Sven. *Historia de los bombardeos*. Madrid: Turner, 2002.

Linhard, Tabea Alexa. "The Death Story of the 'Trece Rosas.'" *Journal of Spanish Cultural Studies* 3.2 (2002): 187–202.

Linz, Juan J. "Fascism as 'Latecomer': An Ideal Type with Negations." Kallis 64–70.

Lippard, Lucy. *Ad Reinhardt*. New York: Abrams, 1981.

Lista, Giovanni. *Futurism and Photography*. London: Merrell; Estorick Collection of Modern Italian Art, 2001.

Líster, Enrique. *Nuestra guerra. Aportaciones para una historia de la guerra nacional revolucionaria del pueblo español, 1936–1939*. Paris: Librairie du Globe, 1966.

Llamazares, Julio. *Luna de lobos*. Barcelona: Seix Barral, 1985.

López Aranda, A. Esteban. *Romances de Madrid*. Valencia: Arte Tipográfico, 1939.

López Mozo, Jerónimo. "Guernica." *Cuatro Happenings*. Murcia: U de Murcia, 1986. 81–104.

López-Rey, José. "*La guerre est finie*: Picasso and Spain." *Art News* 81.9 (1982): 142–45.

López Salinas, Armando. *Año tras año*. Paris: Ruedo Ibérico, 1962.

Loureiro, Ángel G., ed. *Estelas, laberintos, nuevas sendas: Unamuno [and] Valle-Inclán [and] García Lorca [and] La guerra civil*. Barcelona: Anthropos, 1988.

Lubar, Robert. "Painting and Politics: Miró's *Still Life with Old Shoe* and the Spanish Republic." *Surrealism, Politics, and Culture*. Ed. Raymond Spiteri and Donald LaCoss. Aldershot: Ashgate, 2003. 127–60.

Luca de Tena, Torcuato. *La brújula loca*. Barcelona: Planeta, 1964.

Lucas, Scott. *The Betrayal of Dissent: Beyond Orwell, Hitchens, and the New American Century*. London: Pluto, 2004.

Luengo, Ana. *La encrucijada de la memoria: La memoria colectiva de la guerra civil española en la novela contemporánea*. Berlin: Frey, 2004.

Lugon, Olivier. *Le style documentaire: D'August Sander à Walker Evans, 1920–1945*. Paris: Macula, 2001.

Lunn, Arnold. *Spanish Rehearsal: An Eyewitness in Spain during the Civil War, 1936–1939*. 1937. Old Greenwich: Adair, 1974.

Lynn, Kenneth S. *Hemingway*. New York: Simon, 1987.

Machado, Antonio. *Antología comentada: I: Poesía*. Ed. Francisco Caudet. Madrid: Torre, 1999.

———. "El crimen fue en Granada." *The Generation of 1898 and After*. Ed. Beatrice P. Patt and Martin Nozick. New York: Harper, 1960. 170–71.

———. "El crimen fue en Granada." Machado, *Antología* 331–33.

———. *Poesía y prosa*. Ed. Oreste Macrì. 4 vols. Madrid: Espasa Calpe; Fundación Antonio Machado, 1988.

———. *Times Alone: Selected Poems*. Trans. Robert Bly. Middletown: Wesleyan UP, 1983.

Machado, Manuel. "Francisco Franco." M. Machado, *Poesía* 171.

———. *Horas de oro: Devocionario poético*. Valladolid: Reconquista, 1938.

———. *Poesía de guerra y posguerra*. Ed. Miguel D'Ors. Granada: U de Granada, 1992.

MacNeice, Louis. *Collected Poems, 1925–1948*. London: Faber, 1949.

Madariaga, María Rosa de. *Los moros que trajo Franco: La intervención de tropas coloniales en la guerra civil*. Barcelona: Martínez Roca, 2002.

Madariaga, Salvador de. *Spain: A Modern History*. New York: Praeger, 1958.

Maeztu, Ramiro de. *Defensa de la Hispanidad*. Madrid: n.p., 1934.

Maier, Carol. "Teaching Monolingual Students to Read in Translation (as Translators)." *ADFL Bulletin* 33.1 (2001): 44–46.

———. "Toward a Theoretical Practice for Cross-Cultural Translation." Dingwaney and Maier 21–38.

Mainer, José Carlos, ed. *Falange y literatura: Antología*. Barcelona: Labor, 1971.

Malraux, André. *Antimémoires*. Paris: Gallimard, 1967.

———. *La condition humaine*. Paris: Gallimard, 1933.

———. *Les conquérants*. Paris: Grasset, 1928.

———. *L'espoir*. Paris: Gallimard, 1937.

———. *Man's Hope*. Trans. Stuart Gilbert and Alastair MacDonald. New York: Random, 1938. Trans. of *L'espoir*.

Manfredi, Domingo. *Juan, el negro*. Barcelona: Caralt, 1977.

Mangini, Shirley. *Memories of Resistance: Women's Voices from the Spanish Civil War*. New Haven: Yale UP, 1995.

———. *Recuerdos de la resistencia: La voz de las mujeres de la guerra civil*. Barcelona: Península, 1997.

Manning, Maurice. *The Blueshirts*. Dublin: Gill, 1970.

"Manuales Escolares." Museo del Niño. 2001–05. Museo del Niño y Centro de Documentación Histórica de la Escuela. 13 Oct. 2005 <http://www.Museodelnino.es/sala1/manuales/manuales.htm>.

March, Susana. *Algo muere cada día*. Barcelona: Planeta, 1955.

Margolick, David. "*PM*'s Impossible Dream." *Vanity Fair* Jan. 1999: 116–32.

Marichal, Juan. "De algunas consecuencias intelectuales de la guerra civil española." *El nuevo pensamiento político español*. Mexico City: Finisterre, 1966. 65–77.

Marín Silvestre, Dolors. *Clandestinos: El maquis contra el franquismo, 1934–1975*. Barcelona: Plaza y Janés, 2002.

Maritain, Jacques. Introduction. Mendizábal 1–48.

Marsé, Juan. *Si te dicen que caí*. Barcelona: Seix Barral, 1976. Trans. as *The Fallen*. Trans. Helen R. Lane. Boston: Little, 1979.

Martín, Eutemio. "La mujer en la poesía de la Guerra Civil Española." *Cahiers d'Études Romanes* 5 (1978): 19–31.

Martin, Rupert, and Frances Morris, eds. *No pasarán! Photographs and Posters of the Spanish Civil War*. Bristol: Arnolfini Gallery, 1986.

Martin, Russell. *Picasso's War: The Destruction of Guernica, and the Masterpiece That Changed the World*. New York: Dutton, 2002.

Martín Abril, Francisco Javier. "Niños y mujeres." *Antología poética del Alzamiento, 1936–39*. Ed. Jorge Villén. Cádiz: Establecimientos Cerón y Librería Cervantes, 1939. 24–28.

Martín Casas, Julio, and Pedro Carvajal Urquijo. *El exilio español, 1936–1978*. Barcelona: Planeta, 2002.

Martínez Cachero, José María. *La novela española entre 1939 y 1969*. Madrid: Castalia, 1975.

Martínez Lázaro, Emilio, Elías Querejeta, and Ricardo Franco. *Pascual Duarte*. Madrid: Querejeta, 1976.

Martínez Tórtola, Esther. *La enseñanza de la historia en el primer bachillerato franquista, 1938–1953*. Madrid: Tecnos, 1996.

Martín Gaite, Carmen. *El cuarto de atrás*. Barcelona: Destino, 1978. Trans. as *The Back Room*. Trans. Helen R. Lane. New York: Columbia UP, 1983. San Francisco: City Lights, 2000.

The Marx Memorial Library. 16 Nov. 2005. 22 Nov. 2005 <http://www.marxlibrary. net>.

Masip, Paulino. *Cartas a un español emigrado*. San Miguel de Allende, Guanajato: Cuadernos de Nigromante, 1989.

———. *El diario de Hamlet García*. Pref. Pablo Corbalán. Mexico City: Manuel León Sánchez, 1944. Barcelona: Anthropos, 1987.

Matthews, Herbert L. *Two Wars and More to Come*. New York: Carrick, 1938.

Matute, Ana María. *Awakening*. Trans. James Holman Mason. London: Hutchinson, 1963. Trans. of *Primera memoria*.

———. *En esta tierra*. Barcelona: Éxito, 1955.

———. *Luciérnagas*. Barcelona: Destino, 1993. Trans. as *Fireflies*. Trans. Glafyra Ennis. Catalan Studies 21. New York: Lang, 1998.

———. *Primera memoria*. Barcelona: Destino, 1960.

———. *School of the Sun*. Trans. Elaine Kerrigan. 1963. New York: Columbia UP, 1989. Trans. of *Primera memoria*.

Maulvault, Lucien. *El requete*. Paris: Fayard, 1937.

Maurer, Christopher. Introduction. García Lorca, *Collected Poems* xi–lxiv.

McGarry, Fearghal. *Irish Politics and the Spanish Civil War*. Cork: Cork UP, 1999.

McGratty, Arthur R. *Face to the Sun*. Milwaukee: Bruce, 1942.

McNair, John. *Spanish Diary*. 1937. Ed. Don Bateman. Stockport: Greater Manchester Branch of Independence Labour, 1976.

Medio, Dolores. *Atrapados en la ratonera: Memorias de una novelista*. Madrid: Alce, 1980.

———. *Diario de una maestra*. Barcelona: Destino, 1961.

Meijer, Arnold. "To Speak of Nationalist Spain Is to Speak of Franco." *Spain* 15 Jan. 1938: 4.

Mellor, David. "Death in the Making: Representing the Spanish Civil War." Martin and Morris 25–31.

Mendelson, Jordana. *Documenting Spain: Artists, Exhibition Culture, and the Modern Nation, 1929–1939*. University Park: Pennsylvania State UP, 2005.

Méndez, Concha. *Lluvias enlazadas*. La Habana: La Verónica de Manuel Altolaguirre, 1940.

Méndez, Diego. *El Valle de los Caídos: Idea, proyecto y construcción*. Madrid: Fundación de la Santa Cruz del Valle de los Caídos, 1982.

Mendizábal, Alfred. *The Martyrdom of Spain: Origins of a Civil War*. Introd. Jacques Maritain. London: Bles; Centenary, 1938.

Menéndez Pelayo, Marcelino. *Historia de los heterodoxos españoles*. 3 vols. Madrid: Librería Católica de San José, 1880–82.

Merino Galán, Ángel. *Mi guerra empezó antes*. Madrid: Índice, 1976.

Merriman, Marion, and Warren Lerude. *American Commander in Spain: Robert Hale Merriman and the Abraham Lincoln Brigade*. Reno: U of Nevada P, 1986.

Michelin Green Guide to Spain. Clermont-Ferrand, Fr.: Michelin, 1998.

Miguel, Jesús M. de. *Estructura y cambio social en España*. Madrid: Alianza, 1998.

Miguélez-Carballeira, Helena. "Language and Characterization in Mercè Rodoreda's *La Plaça del Diamant*: Towards a Third Translation into English." *Translator* 9.1 (2003): 101–24.

Milkman, Paul. PM: *A New Deal in Journalism, 1940–1948*. New Brunswick: Rutgers UP, 1997.

Millán Astray, Pilar. *Cautivas: 32 meses en las prisiones rojas*. Valencia: Saturnino Calleja, [1940].

Miller, John, ed. *Voices against Tyranny*. Signature ed. New York: Scribner's, 1986.

Millet, Martha. "Women of Spain" C. Nelson, *Wound* 63.

Miranda Calvo, José. *La reconquista de Toledo por Alfonso VI*. Toledo: Instituto de Estudios Visigótico-Mozárabes de San Eugenio, 1980.

Miravitlles, Jaume, et al. *Carteles de la república y de la guerra civil*. Barcelona: Centre d'Estudis d'Història Contemporània, 1978.

Miró, Emilio, ed. *Antología de poetisas del 27*. Madrid: Castalia, 1999.

Mistral, Gabriela. *Tala*. Buenos Aires: Losada, 2003.

Mitchell, Timothy. *Violence and Piety in Spanish Folklore*. Philadelphia: U of Pennsylvania P, 1988.

Mitchell, W. J. T. "Representation." *Critical Terms for Literary Study*. Ed. Frank Lentricchia and Thomas McLaughlin. Chicago: U of Chicago P, 1990. 11–22.

Moa, Pío. *Los mitos de la guerra civil*. Madrid: Esfera, 2003.

Mola, Emilio. *Obras completas*. Valladolid: Santarén, 1940.

Monforte Gútiez, María Inmaculada. "La labor cultural de María Teresa León." *Mujeres* 148–51.

Monleón, José. *El mono azul: Teatro de urgencia y romancero de la guerra civil.* Madrid: Ayuso, 1979.

El Mono Azul: Hoja Semanal de la Alianza de Intelectuales Antifascistas para la Defensa de la Cultura. Aug. 1936–Feb. 1939. Rpt. Glashütten im Taunus: Auvermann–Kraus Reprint, 1975.

Monteath, Peter. "Anarchist Poetry." Monteath, *Writing* 174–85.

———. "Hitler and the Spanish Civil War: A Case Study of Nazi Foreign Policy." *Australian Journal of Politics and History* 32. 3 (1986): 428–42.

———. "Literature and the Popular Front." Monteath, *Writing* 67–87.

———. *The Spanish Civil War in Literature, Film, and Art.* Intl. Bibliography of Secondary Lit. Westport: Greenwood, 1994.

———. *Writing the Good Fight: Political Commitment in the International Literature of the Spanish Civil War.* Westport: Greenwood, 1994.

Monterde, José Enrique. *Veinte años de cine español: Un cine bajo la paradoja, 1973–1992.* Barcelona: Paidós, 1993.

Monterde, José Enrique, and Marta Selva. "Le film historique franquiste." *Cahiers de la cinématèque* 38–39 (1984): 65–82.

Montero, Rosa. *La hija del caníbal.* Madrid: Espasa, 1998.

———. "Las Trece Rosas." *El país semanal* 4 Aug. 1994: 4.

Montero Moreno, Antonio. *Historia de la persecución religiosa en España.* Madrid: Autores Cristianos, 1961.

Montherlant, Henry de. *Les bestiaires.* Paris: Grasset, 1926.

———. "Le comble de l'art d'écrire." *Essais.* Paris: Gallimard, 1963. 1245.

Montiel Rayo, Francisca. "Escribir fuera de España: La correspondencia entre Max Aub y Segundo Serrano Poncela." *Actas del Congreso Internacional "Max Aub y el laberinto español."* Ed. Cecilio Alonso. Vol 1. Valencia: Ayuntamiento de Valencia, 1996. 185–201.

Montrose, Louis. "Professing the Renaissance: The Poetics and Politics of Culture." Veeser 15–36.

Mora, Constancia de la. *Doble esplendor: Autobiografía de una mujer española.* Mexico City: Atlante, 1944. Barcelona: Crítica, 1977.

———. *In Place of Splendor: The Autobiography of a Spanish Woman.* New York: Harcourt, 1939.

Morales, Andrés, ed. *España reunida: Antología poética de la guerra civil española.* Santiago: Ril, 1999.

Moral i Querol, Ramon. *Diari d'un exiliat, 1939–1945.* Barcelona: Serrador; L'Abadia de Montserrat, 1979.

"Moral Support or Intervention? The Camera Decides." *Spain* 1 Dec. 1937: 17.

Morán, Gregorio. *Los españoles que dejaron de serlo: Euzkadi 1937–1982.* Barcelona: Planeta, 1982.

Moreiras-Menor, Cristina. "Sombras de una dictadura." King Juan Carlos I Center, New York U. 23 Sept. 2002.

Morgan, Kevin. Rev. of *Land and Freedom,* dir. Ken Loach. *New Times* 30 Sept. 1995: 8.

Morrow, Felix. *Revolution and Counterrevolution in Spain, 1938.* New York: Pathfinder, 1974.

Moya, Paula, and Michael Hames-García. *Reclaiming Identity: Realist Theory and the Predicament of Postmodernism.* Berkeley: U of California P, 2000.

"Mujeres Libres." M. Nash, *"Mujeres Libres"* 169–71.

Las mujeres y la guerra civil española: III Jornadas de Estudios Monográficos. Serie Debate 11. Salamanca, Oct. 1989. Madrid: Ministerio de Cultura; Instituto de la Mujer, 1991.

Mullen, Edward J. *Langston Hughes in the Hispanic World and Haiti.* Hamden: Archon, 1977.

Muñoz Molina, Antonio. *Beatus ille.* Barcelona: Seix Barral, 1986.

———. *El jinete polaco.* Barcelona: Planeta, 1991.

Mussolini, Benito. *The Doctrine of Fascism.* Rome: Ardita, 1935.

Muste, John. *Say That We Saw Spain Die: Literary Consequences of the Spanish Civil War.* Seattle: U of Washington P, 1966.

Naharro-Calderón, José María. "Cuando España iba mal: Aviso para 'navegantes' desmemoriados." *Ínsula* 627 (1999): 25–28.

———. "Des-lindes de exilio." Naharro-Calderón, *Exilio* 11–39.

———, ed. *El exilio de las Españas de 1939 en las Américas: "¿Adónde fue la canción?"* Barcelona: Anthropos, 1991.

———. "¿Y para qué la literatura del exilio en tiempo destituido?" *El exilio literario español de 1939: Actas del Primer Congreso Internacional.* Ed. Manuel Aznar Soler. Vol. 1. Barcelona: Gexel, 1998. 63–83.

Namuth, Hans, and Georg Reisner. *Spanisches Tagebuch, 1936: Fotografien und Texte aus den ersten Monaten des Bürgerkriegs.* Ed. Diethart Kerbs. Berlin: Nishen, 1986.

Narotsky, Susana, and Gavin Smith. "'Being *político*' in Spain: An Ethnographic Account of Memories, Silences and Public Politics." Rein 189–228.

Nash, Edward. "The Destruction of the National Artistic Treasure by the Marxist Revolutionaries." *Spain* 1 June 1938: 8–9.

Nash, Elizabeth. *Madrid: A Cultural and Literary Companion.* New York: Interlink, 2001.

Nash, Mary. "The Battle Lost." M. Nash, *Defying* 177–85.

———. *Defying Male Civilization: Women in the Spanish Civil War.* Denver: Arden, 1995.

———. "Heroines, Combative Mothers, and Mythmakers: The Changing Images of Women." M. Nash, *Defying* 48–61.

———. "Liberate the Prostitutes." M. Nash, *Defying* 163–65.

———. "'Milicianas' or Homefront Heroines: Women's Place in the War." M. Nash, *Defying* 101–39.

———. *Las mujeres en la guerra civil.* Madrid: Ministerio de Cultura, 1989.

———. *"Mujeres Libres": España, 1936–1939.* Barcelona: Tusquets, 1975.

———. *Mujer y movimiento obrero en España, 1931–1939.* Barcelona: Fontamara, 1981.

"National Movement: Spain and Her Art." *Spain* 15 Nov. 1937: 5.

Nelken, Marguerite (Margarita). "L'épopée des paysans d'Espagne." *Regards* 3 Sept. 1936: 4–5.

Nelson, Cary. *The Aura of the Cause: A Photo Album for North American Volunteers in the Spanish Civil War*. Waltham: Abraham Lincoln Brigade Archives, 1997.

———. "The Aura of the Cause: Photographs from the Spanish Civil War." C. Nelson, *Aura* 19–44.

———. "Honor and Trauma: Hemingway and the Lincoln Vets." C. Nelson, *Remembering* 19–40.

———, ed. *Remembering Spain: Hemingway's Civil War Eulogy and the Veterans of the Abraham Lincoln Brigade*. Urbana: U of Illinois P, 1994.

———. *Revolutionary Memory: Recovering the Poetry of the American Left*. New York: Routledge, 2001.

———. *Shouts from the Wall: Posters and Photographs Brought Home from the Spanish Civil War by American Volunteers*. Waltham: Abraham Lincoln Brigade Archives, 1996.

———, ed. *The Wound and the Dream: Sixty Years of American Poems about the Spanish Civil War*. Urbana: U of Illinois P, 2002.

Nelson, Cary, and Jefferson Hendricks, eds. *Madrid, 1937: Letters of the Abraham Lincoln Brigade from the Spanish Civil War*. New York: Routledge, 2001.

Nelson, Steve. *The Volunteers: A Personal Narrative of the Fight against Fascism in Spain*. New York: Masses, 1953.

Neocleous, Mark. *Fascism*. Minneapolis: U of Minnesota P, 1997.

Neruda, Pablo. *Antología poética*. Ed. Rafael Alberti. Madrid: Austral, 1985.

———. *España en el corazón: Himno a las glorias del pueblo en la guerra, 1936–1937*. Santiago: Ercilla, 1937. Santiago: Literatura América Reunida, 1988.

———. "Explico algunas cosas." Neruda, *Five Decades* 52–56.

———. *Five Decades: Poems, 1925–1970*. Trans. and ed. Ben Belitt. New York: Grove, 1974.

———. *The Poetry of Pablo Neruda*. Ed. Ilan Stavans. New York: Farrar, 2003.

———. *Spain in the Heart: Hymn to the Glories of the People at War*. Trans. Richard Schaaf. Introd. Leonard Lamb. Washington: Azul, 1993.

———. *Tercera residencia*. Buenos Aires: Losada, 1961.

———. "What Spain Was Like" and "I Explain a Few Things (1937)." Trans. John Felstiner. *American Poetry Review* 32.4 (2003): 4–5.

Neruda, Pablo, and Nancy Cunard, eds. *Los poetas del mundo defienden al pueblo español (París 1937)*. Pref. Roberto González Echevarría. Seville: Renacimiento, Facsímiles de Revistas Literarias, 2002.

Newhall, Beaumont. *The History of Photography from 1839 to the Present Day*. Rev. ed. New York: Museum of Modern Art; Eastman, 1964.

Nolte, Ernst. "Vergangenheit, die nicht vergehen will." *"Historiker-Streit."* München: Piper, 1987. 39–47.

Norris, Christopher, ed. *Inside the Myth: Orwell, Views from the Left*. London: Lawrence, 1984.

Olaizola, José Luis. *La guerra del general Escobar*. Barcelona: Planeta, 1983.

Oms, Marcel. *La guerre d'Espagne au cinéma: Mythes et réalités*. Paris: Cerf, 1985.

O'Neill, Carlota. *Una mujer en la guerra de España*. Madrid: Turner, 1979.

————. *Segunda parte de una mexicana en la guerra de España.* Mexico City: Periódicos SCL, 1973.

Oppler, Ellen C., ed. *Picasso's* Guernica. Norton Critical Studies in Art History. New York: Norton, 1988.

Orlov, Alexander. *The Secret History of Stalin's Crimes.* New York: Random, 1953.

Ortega y Gasset, José. *España invertebrada.* 1921. Madrid: Revista de Occidente, 1963. Madrid: Alianza, 1998. Trans. as *Invertebrate Spain.* New York: Norton, 1937.

Orwell, George. *The Collected Essays, Journalism, and Letters.* Vol. 1. Ed. Sonia Orwell and Ian Angus. London: Secker, 1968.

————. *A Collection of Essays.* New York: Harcourt, 1946.

————. *Homage to Catalonia.* London: Secker, 1938. Introd. Lionel Trilling. Boston: Beacon, 1966. San Diego: Harcourt, 1980.

————. "Looking Back on the Spanish War." Orwell, *Collection* 188–210.

————. *Nineteen Eighty-Four.* London: Harcourt, 1949.

————. *The Penguin Essays of George Orwell.* London: Penguin, 1984.

————. *The Road to Wigan Pier.* London: Penguin, 1937.

————. "Spilling the Spanish Beans." *Orwell in Spain.* Ed. Peter Davison. London: Penguin, 2001. 215–23.

————. "Why I Write." Orwell, *Collection* 309–16.

Pabellón Español. *Exposición Internacional de París, 1937.* Madrid: Ministerio de Cultura; Museo Nacional Centro de Arte Reina Sofía, 1987.

Palencia, Isabel de. *En mi hambre mando yo.* Mexico City: Libro Mex, 1959.

————. *I Must Have Liberty.* New York: Longmans, 1940.

Palou, Josep. "Cerdos fascistas y cochinos rojos: La Filmoteca Española cataloga todo el material fílmico existente en el mundo sobre la guerra civil." *El país* 7 Apr. 1994: 34.

Paret, Peter, Beth Irwin Lewis, and Paul Paret. *Persuasive Images: Posters of War and Revolution from the Hoover Institution Archives.* Princeton: Princeton UP, 1992.

Parsons, I[an] M[acnaghten], ed. *Men Who March Away: Poems of the First World War.* London: Chatto, 1965.

Pasamar Alzuria, Gonzalo. *Historiografía e ideología en la postguerra española: La ruptura de la tradición liberal.* Zaragoza: U de Zaragoza, 1991.

Pastor i Homs, María Inmaculada. "El modelo de mujer que se quiere imponer." *La educación femenina en la postguerra, 1939–45: El caso de Mallorca.* Madrid: Ministerio de Cultura; Instituto de la Mujer, 1984. 31–38.

Pawel, Rebecca C. *Death of a Nationalist.* New York: Soho, 2003.

————. *Law of Return.* New York: Soho, 2004.

————. *The Watcher in the Pine.* New York: Soho, 2005.

Payne, Stanley. *Falange: A History of Spanish Fascism.* Stanford: Stanford UP, 1961.

————. "Fascism as a 'Generic' Concept." Kallis 82–100.

————. *Fascism in Spain, 1923–1977.* Madison: U of Wisconsin P, 1999.

————. *The Franco Regime, 1936–1975.* London: Phoenix, 2000.

————. *A History of Spain and Portugal.* Madison: U of Wisconsin P, 1973.

————. Preface. Sánchez, *Spanish Civil War* ix–xi.

————. *The Spanish Revolution*. New York: Norton, 1970.

Paz, Octavio. "The Barricades and Beyond." *New Republic* 9 Nov. 1987: 26–30.

Pemán, José María. *Poema de guerra, 1936–38: Poema de la bestia y el ángel*. Zaragoza: Jerarquía, 1938.

Pemartín, José. *Qué es "lo nuevo": Consideraciones sobre el momento español presente*. 2nd ed. Santander: Aldus, 1938.

Pereda Valdés, Ildefonso, ed. *Cancionero de la guerra civil española*. Montevideo: Claudio García, 1937.

Pérez, Janet. "Fascist Models and Literary Subversion." *South Central Review* 6.2 (1989): 73–87. Golsan 128–42.

————, ed. "Voces poéticas femeninas de la guerra civil española." *Letras Peninsulares* 11.1 (1998): 263–79.

Pérez, Janet, and Wendell Aycock, eds. *The Spanish Civil War in Literature*. Lubbock: Texas Tech UP, 1990.

Pérez de Urbel, Justo. *El monumento de Santa Cruz del Valle de los Caídos*. Madrid: Instituto de Estudios Madrileños, 1959.

Pérez Infante, Luis. "Volunteers for Liberty." Trans. Hans Kahle and Leslie Phillips. *Kingdom Come* 3.9 (1941): 20–21.

Pérez Ledesma, Manuel. "Studies on Anticlericalism in Contemporary Spain." *International Review of Social History* 46 (2001): 227–55.

Picasso, Pablo. *Guernica*. Museo Nacional Centro de Arte Reina Sofía, Madrid.

Pike, David Wingeate. *Les français et la guerre d'Espagne, 1936–1939*. Paris: PUF, 1975.

Pillement, Georges, ed. *Le romancero de la guerre civile*. Pref. Jean Cassou. Paris: Commune, 1937.

Pla y Beltrán, Pascual. "Girl Fighter of Spain." C. Nelson, *Revolutionary Memory* 199.

————. "A Lina Odena, muerta entre Guadix y Granada." *Antología poética, 1930–1961*. Ed. Manuel Aznar Soler. Valencia: Ayuntamiento de Valencia, 1985. 173–74.

Poetas en la España leal. Madrid: Ediciones Españolas, 1937; Madrid: Hispamérica, 1976.

Ponce de León, José Luis S. *La novela española de la guerra civil, 1936–1939*. Madrid: Ínsula, 1971.

Pons Prades, Eduardo. *Realidades de la guerra civil: ¡Mitos no, hechos!* Madrid: Esfera de los Libros, 2005.

————. *Republicanos españoles en la 2a guerra mundial*. Barcelona: Planeta, 1975.

Portelli, Alessandro. *The Battle of Valle Giulia: Oral History and the Art of Dialogue*. Madison: U of Wisconsin P, 1997.

————. Introduction. Portelli, *Battle* vii–xx.

————. "There's Always Gonna Be a Line: History-Telling as a Multivocal Art." Portelli, *Battle* 24–39.

————. "What Makes Oral History Different?" *"The Death of Luigi Trastulli" and Other Stories: Form and Meaning in Oral History*. New York: State U of New York P, 1991. 45–58.

Porton, Richard. Rev. of *Land and Freedom*, dir. Ken Loach. *Cineaste* 22.1 (1996): 32–34.

"Por un orden consciente." *España Peregrina* 1.4 (1940): 147–49.

Pound, Ezra. "Guido's Relations." Venuti, *Translation Studies* 26–33.

Powell, Charles T. "Spain's External Relations, 1898–1975." Gillespie, Rodrigo, and Story 11–29.

Prados, Emilio. "El moro engañado." Santonja, *Romancero* 53–55.

———. *Poesía extrema: Antología*. Ed. Francisco Chica. Sevilla: Andaluzas Unidas; Biblioteca de la Cultura Andaluza, 1991.

Pressburger, Emeric. *Killing a Mouse on Sunday*. New York: Harcourt, 1961.

Preston, Paul. *The Coming of the Spanish Civil War*. London: Methuen, 1983.

———. *A Concise History of the Spanish Civil War*. London: Fontana, 1996.

———. "Decay, Division, and the Defence of Dictatorship: The Military and Politics, 1939–1975." Lannon and Preston 203–28.

———. *Doves of War: Four Women of Spain*. London: Harper, 2002.

———. *La guerra civil española, 1936–1939*. Barcelona: Plaza y Janés, 1987.

———. Introduction. Preston, *Revolution* 1–13.

———. Rev. of *Land and Freedom*, dir. Ken Loach. *New Times* 30 Sept. 1995: 9.

———. "Nan Green." Preston, *Doves* 121–201.

———. "La Pasionaria." *¡Comrades! Portraits from the Spanish Civil War*. London: Harper, 1999. 277–318.

———. *The Politics of Revenge: Fascism and the Military in Twentieth-Century Spain*. 1990. London: Routledge, 1995.

———, ed. *Revolution and War in Spain, 1931–1939*. London: Methuen, 1984.

———. *The Spanish Civil War, 1936–39*. Chicago: Dorsey, 1986.

———. "The Urban and Rural *Guerrilla* of the 1940s." Graham and Labanyi 229–37.

Preston, Paul, and Ann L. Mackenzie, eds. *The Republic Besieged: Civil War in Spain, 1936–1939*. Edinburgh: Edinburgh UP, 1996.

Primo de Rivera, José Antonio. "Discurso fundacional de Falange Española (1933)." Rodríguez-Puértolas 2:103–08.

———. "España y la barbarie: Conferencia (1935)." Rodríguez-Puértolas 2:112–15.

———. *El pensamiento político hispánico*. Buenos Aires: Depalma, 1968.

Primo de Rivera, Pilar. *Recuerdos de una vida*. Madrid: DYRSA, l983.

Pritchett, V. S. Rev. of *For Whom the Bell Tolls*, by Ernest Hemingway. 1941. *Hemingway: The Critical Heritage*. Ed. Jeffrey Meyers. London: Routledge, 1982. 344–50.

"Propósito." *Hora de España* 1 (1937): 5.

Puccini, Darío. *Romancero della resistenza spagnola, 1936–1939*. Bari: La Terza, 1970.

Pujals, Esteban, ed. *Plumas y fusiles: Los poetas ingleses y la guerra de España*. Madrid: U Complutense, 1989.

Purcell, Hugh. *The Spanish Civil War*. London: Wayland, 1973.

Puzzo, Dante A. *Spain and the Great Powers, 1936–1941*. New York: Columbia UP, 1962.

Qualter, Terence. *Opinion Control in the Democracies*. New York: St. Martin's, 1985.

Quickenden, Roy. Rev. of *Land and Freedom*, dir. Ken Loach. *Abanderado* 16 (1996): n.p.

Quintanilla, Luis. *All the Brave: Drawings of the Spanish War*. Text by Elliot Paul and Jay Allen. Pref. Ernest Hemingway. New York: Modern Age, 1939.

———. *Franco's Black Spain: Drawings*. Commentary by Richard Watts, Jr. New York: Reynal, 1946.

Radcliffe, Pamela. *From Mobilization to Civil War: The Politics of Polarization in the Spanish City of Gijón, 1900–1937*. Cambridge: Cambridge UP, 1996.

Radosh, Ronald, Mary R. Habeck, and Grigory Sevostianov, eds. *Spain Betrayed: The Soviet Union in the Spanish Civil War*. New Haven: Yale UP, 2001.

Radstone, Susannah, ed. *Memory and Methodology*. Oxford: Berg, 2000.

Rafaneau-Boj, Marie-Claude. *Los campos de concentración de los refugiados españoles en Francia, 1939–1945*. Barcelona: Omega, 1995.

Raguer, Hilari. *La pólvora y el incienso: La iglesia y la guerra civil española, 1936–1939*. Barcelona: Península, 2001.

Ramírez, Juan Antonio. "Imágenes para un pueblo." Bonet Correa, *Arte* 225–260.

Ramos-Gascón, Antonio, ed. *Romancero del ejército popular*. Madrid: Nuestra Cultura, 1978.

Ramos-Gascón, Antonio, and Manuel Moreno, eds. *Lina Odena: Una mujer*. Barcelona: Comisió d'Alliberament de la Dona Lina Odena, 1999.

Rampersad, Arnold. *The Life of Langston Hughes*. 2 vols. New York: Oxford UP, 1986.

Ranke, Leopold von. *Geschichte der romanischen und germanischen Völker von 1494 bis 1514: Zur Kritik neuerer Geschichtschreiber*. Leipzig: Duncker, 1885.

Rankin, Nicholas. *Telegram from Guernica: The Extraordinary Life of George Steer, War Correspondent*. London: Faber, 2003.

Ranzato, Gabriele. *The Spanish Civil War*. Trans. Janet Sethre Paxia. New York: Interlink, 1999.

Read, Herbert, and Anthony Blunt. Editorials on *Guernica*. 1937. Cunningham, *Spanish Front* 213–20.

Regler, Gustav. *Das große Beispiel: Roman aus dem Spanischen Bürgerkrieg*. Frankfurt am Main: Suhrkamp, 1978. Trans. as *The Great Crusade*. Trans. Whittaker Chambers and Barrows Mussey. New York: Longman's Green, 1940.

———. *Das Ohr des Malchus: Eine Lebensgeschichte*. Cologne: Kiepenheuer, 1958.

Rehberger, Dean. "'I Don't Know Buffalo Bill'; or, Hemingway and the Rhetoric of the Western." Sanderson 159–84.

Reig Tapia, Alberto. *Memoria de la guerra civil: Los mitos de la tribu*. Madrid: Alianza, 1999.

Rein, Raanan, ed. *Spanish Memories: Images of a Contested Past*. Spec. issue of *History and Memory* 14.1–2 (2002).

Reinhardt, Ad. "How to Look at the Picasso *Guernica* Mural." *PM Sunday Feature* 5 Jan. 1947: 6.

Remarque, Erich Maria. *Im Westen nichts Neues*. Berlin: Propyläen, 1929. Trans. as *All Quiet on the Western Front*. Trans. A. W. Wheen. Boston: Little, 1929. London: Putnam, 1929.

Renan, Ernest. "What Is a Nation?" Trans. Martin Thom. *Nation and Narration.* Ed. Homi K. Bhabha. London: Routledge, 1990. 8–22.

Renau, Josep. *Función social del cartel.* 1937. Valencia: Torres, 1976.

Renn, Ludwig. *Im Spanischen Krieg.* Berlin: Aufbau, 1955.

Répide, Pedro de. *Memorias de un aparecido.* Madrid: Vassallo de Mumbert, 1977.

Las Republicanas: Antología de textos e imágenes de la República y la guerra civil. Madrid: Librería Mujeres, 1996.

Resina, Joan Ramon. "The Concept of After-image and the Scopic Apprehension of the City." *After-images of the City.* Ed. Resina and Dieter Ingenschay. Ithaca: Cornell UP, 2003. 1–22.

——, ed. *Disremembering the Dictatorship: The Politics of Memory in the Spanish Transition to Democracy.* Amsterdam: Rodopi, 2002.

——. "The Link in Consciousness: Time and Continuity in Rodoreda's *La plaça del Diamant.*" *Catalan Review* 11.2 (1987): 225–46.

——. "Short of Memory: The Reclamation of the Past since the Spanish Transition to Democracy." Resina, *Disremembering* 83–125.

Reverte, Jorge M., and Socorro Thomás. *Hijos de la guerra: Testimonios y recuerdos.* Madrid: Temas de Hoy, 2001.

Reynolds, Michael. "Hemingway's West: Another Country of the Heart." Sanderson 27–35.

Riambau, Esteve. "La década 'socialista,' 1982–1992." *Historia del cine español.* Ed. Román Gubern, José Enrique Monterde, Julio Pérez Perucha, Riambau, and Casimiro Torreiro. Madrid: Cátedra, 1995. 399–447.

Richards, Michael. "Civil War, Violence, and the Construction of Francoism." Preston and MacKenzie 197–239.

——. "Constructing the Nationalist State: Self-Sufficiency and Regeneration in the Early Franco Years." *Nationalism and the Nation in the Iberian Peninsula.* Ed. Clare Mar-Molinero and Angel Smith. Oxford: Berg, 1996. 149–67.

——. "From War Culture to Civil Society: Francoism, Social Change and Memories of the Spanish Civil War." Rein 93–120.

——. *A Time of Silence: Civil War and the Culture of Repression in Franco's Spain, 1936–1945.* Cambridge: Cambridge UP, 1998. Trans. as *Un tiempo de silencio: La guerra civil y la cultura de la represión en la España de Franco, 1936–1945.* Barcelona: Crítica, 1999.

Richmond, Kathleen. *Women and Spanish Fascism: The Women's Section of the Falange, 1934–1959.* London: Routledge, 2003.

Ridruejo, Dionisio. *Casi unas memorias: Con fuego y con raíces.* Barcelona: Planeta, 1976.

——. *Primer libro de amor, Poesía en armas, Sonetos.* Ed. Ridruejo. Madrid: Castalia, 1976.

——. "Umbral de la madurez." Mainer 184–91.

Riera, Carme. *Senyora, ha vist els meus fills? / Ma'am, Have You Seen My Sons? Moveable Margins: The Narrative Art of Carme Riera.* Ed. Kathleen M. Glenn, Mirella Servodidio, and Mary S. Vásquez. Lewisburg: Bucknell UP, 1999. 291–312.

Riera, Ignasi. *Los catalanes de Franco.* Barcelona: Plaza y Janés, 1998.

Rieuneau, Maurice. *Guerre et révolution dans le roman français de 1919 à 1939.* Paris: Klincksieck, 1974.

Riley, E. C. "The Story of Ana in 'El espíritu de la colmena.'" *Bulletin of Hispanic Studies* 61 (1984): 491–97.

Ripoll-Freixes, Enric. *Cien películas sobre la guerra civil española.* Barcelona: Centro de Investigaciones Literarias Españolas e Hispanoamericanas, 1992.

Rivas, Manuel. *O lapis do carpinteiro.* Vigo: Xerais de Galicia, 1998. Trans. as *The Carpenter's Pencil.* Trans. Jonathan Dunne. Woodstock: Overlook, 2001.

———. *El lápiz del carpintero.* Madrid: Alfaguara, 1998.

———. "La lengua de las mariposas". *¿Qué me quieres, amor?* Madrid: Alfaguara, 1995. 23–41.

Rivière, Aurora. "Envejecimiento del presente y dramatización del pasado." *La gestión de la memoria: La historia de España al servicio del poder.* Ed. Sisinio Pérez Garzón. Barcelona: Crítica, 2000. 161–219.

Rivière, Margarita. *El problema: Madrid-Barcelona.* Madrid: Temas de Hoy, 1996.

Rodoreda, Mercè. *A Broken Mirror.* Trans. and introd. Josep Miguel Sobrer. Lincoln: U of Nebraska P, 2006.

———. *The Pigeon Girl.* Trans. Edna O'Shea. London: Deitsch, 1967. Trans. of *La plaça del Diamant.*

———. *La plaça del Diamant.* 1962. Barcelona: Club Editor Jove, 1996.

———. *La plaza del Diamante.* Trans. Enrique Sordo. Barcelona: Edhasa, 1979.

———. "That Wall, That Mimosa." *Catalonia: A Self-Portrait.* Trans. Josep Miquel Sobrer. Bloomington: Indiana UP, 1992. 76–80. *"My Christina" and Other Stories.* Trans. David H. Rosenthal. Saint Paul: Gray Wolf, 1984. 26–31.

———. *The Time of the Doves.* Trans. David H. Rosenthal. New York: Taplinger, 1980. Trans. of *La plaça del Diamant.*

Rodrigo, Antonina. *Mujeres para la historia: La España silenciada del siglo XX.* Madrid: Compañía Literaria, 1996.

———. *Mujer y exilio, 1939.* Madrid: Compañía Literaria, 1999.

Rodríguez, María Pilar. *Mundos en conflicto: Aproximaciones al cine vasco de los noventa.* San Sebastián: U de Deusto; Filmoteca Vasca, 2002.

Rodríguez-Puértolas, Julio, ed. *Literatura fascista española: Antología.* 2 vols. Madrid: Akal, 1986–87.

Rolfe, Edwin. *The Lincoln Battalion: The Story of the Americans Who Fought in Spain in the International Brigades.* New York: Veterans of the Abraham Lincoln Brigade, 1939.

Romeiser, John Beals, ed. *Red Flags, Black Flags: Critical Essays on the Literature of the Spanish Civil War.* Fwd. Frederick R. Benson. Madrid: Porrúa Turanzas, 1982.

———. "The Spanish Civil War and Fox Movietonews, 1936–1939." Vernon, *Spanish Civil War* 71–77.

Romeu Alfaro, Fernanda. *El silencio roto: Mujeres contra el franquismo.* Madrid: Intervención Cultural, 1994.

Rosenstone, Robert A. *Crusade of the Left: The Lincoln Battalion in the Spanish Civil War.* New York: Pegasus, 1969.

Rosenthal, Marilyn. *Poetry of the Spanish Civil War*. New York: New York UP, 1975.

Rous, Jean. "Spain 1936–39: The Murdered Revolution." *Revolutionary History (The Spanish Civil War: The View from the Left)* 4.1–2 (1992).

Rubin, Hank. *Spain's Cause Was Mine: A Memoir of an American Medic in the Spanish Civil War*. Fwd. Peter N. Carroll. Carbondale: Southern Illinois UP, 1997.

Rudat, Wolfgang E. H. "Hamlet in Spain: Oedipal Dilemmas in *For Whom the Bell Tolls*." *North Dakota Quarterly* 60.2 (1992): 83–101.

———. "Hemingway's Rabbit: Slips of the Tongue and Other Linguistic Games in *For Whom the Bell Tolls*." *Hemingway Review* 10.1 (1990): 34–51.

Russell, Frank D. Epilogue. Oppler 309–12.

Sáez Marín, Juan. *El Frente de Juventudes: Política de juventud en la España de la postguerra, 1937–1960*. Madrid: Siglo XXI, 1988.

Said, Edward W. *Orientalism*. Harmondsworth: Penguin, 1978.

———. *Representations of the Intellectual*. New York: Vintage, 1996.

Sala Noguer, Ramón. *El cine en la España republicana durante la guerra civil, 1936–1939*. Bilbao: Mensajero, 1993.

Salaün, Serge. "La poesía escrita en la zona republicana." *Historia y crítica de la literatura española*. Vol. 7. Ed. Víctor García de la Concha. Madrid: Crítica, 1984. 804–09.

———, ed. *La poesía de la guerra de España*. Madrid: Castalia, 1985.

———. "Poetas 'de oficio' y vocaciones incipientes durante la guerra de España." *Creación y público en la literatura española*. Madrid: Castalia, 1974. 181–211.

———, ed. *Romancero de la guerra de España*. 7 vols. Barcelona: Ruedo Ibérico, 1982.

———, ed. *Romancero libertario*. Alençon, Fr.: Ruedo Ibérico, 1971.

Salazar, Margaret Van Epp. "*Si yo te dijera . . .* ": Una historia oral de la sierra de Huelva*. Sevilla: Fundación Machado; Diputación de Huelva, 1998.

Salcedo, Juan. *Madrid culpable: Sobre el espacio y la población en las ciencias sociales*. Madrid: Tecnos, 1977.

Salom, Jaime. *La casa de las Chivas*. Madrid: Escelicer, 1969.

Samuel, Raphael. *Theatres of Memory*. London: Verso, 1994.

Sánchez, Isidro, Manuel Ortiz, and David Ruiz, eds. *España franquista: Causa General y actitudes sociales ante la dictadura*. Albacete: U de Castilla la Mancha, 1993.

Sánchez, José M. "The Anticlerical Fury." Sánchez, *Spanish Civil War* 1–18.

———. *Reform and Reaction: The Politico-Religious Background of the Spanish Civil War*. Chapel Hill: U of North Carolina P, 1964.

———. *The Spanish Civil War as a Religious Tragedy*. Notre Dame: U of Notre Dame P, 1987.

Sánchez Agustí, Ferran. *Maquis a Catalunya: De la invasió de la Vall d'Aran a la mort de Caracremada*. Lleida: Pagès, 1999.

Sánchez Albornoz, Claudio. "Las dos Españas." Sánchez Albornoz, *España* 2:661–74.

———. *España, un enigma histórico*. 2 vols. Buenos Aires: Sudamericana, 1956. Barcelona: Edhasa, 2000.

Sánchez Biosca, Vicente, ed. *Materiales para una iconografía de Francisco Franco.* 2 vols. Spec. issue of *Archivos de la Filmoteca* 42–43 (2002–03).

Sánchez Recio, Glicerio. *De las dos ciudades a la resurrección de España: Magisterio pastoral y pensamiento político de Enrique Pla y Deniel.* Valladolid: Ámbito; Instituto Juan Gil-Albert, 1994.

Sánchez Saornil, Lucía. *Poesía.* Introd. Rosa María Martín Casamitjana. Valencia: Pre-Textos, 1996.

———, ed. *Romancero de Mujeres Libres.* Barcelona: Mujeres Libres, 1938.

Sanchis Sinisterra, José. *¡Ay, Carmela! [and] Ñaque o, de piojos y actores.* Ed. Manuel Aznar Soler. Madrid: Cátedra, 1991.

Sanderson, Rena, ed. *Blowing the Bridge: Essays on Hemingway and* For Whom the Bell Tolls. New York: Greenwood, 1992.

San Juan, E., Jr. "Ideological Form, Symbolic Exchange, Textual Production: A Symptomatic Reading of *For Whom the Bell Tolls.*" *North Dakota Quarterly* 60.2 (1992): 119–43.

Santonja, Gonzalo. *De un ayer no tan lejano: Cultura y propaganda en la España de Franco durante la guerra y los primeros años del Nuevo Estado.* Madrid: Noesis, 1996.

———, ed. *Romancero de la guerra civil.* Serie 1. Madrid: Visor, 1984.

———. *Todo en el aire: Versos sin enemigo: Antología insólita de la poesía durante la guerra incivil española.* Barcelona: Galaxia Gutenberg; Círculo de Lectores, 1997.

Sartre, Jean-Paul. "Le mur." *Le mur.* Paris: Gallimard, 1939. 11–34. Trans. as *"The Wall" and Other Stories.* 3rd ed. Trans. Lloyd Alexander. New York: New Directions, 1988.

Schapiro, J. Salwyn. *Anticlericalism: Conflict between Church and State in France, Italy, and Spain.* Princeton: Van Nostrand, 1967.

Schapiro, Meyer. "Guernica: Sources, Changes (1966)." *The Unity of Picasso's Art.* Ed. Lillian Milgram Schapiro. New York: Braziller, 2000. 151–85.

Schneider, Sigrid. "Manipulating Images: Photojournalism from the Spanish Civil War." *German and International Perspectives on the Spanish Civil War: The Aesthetics of Partisanship.* Ed. Luis Costa, Richard Critchfield, Richard Golsan, and Wulf Koepke. Columbia: Camden, 1992. 179–98.

Schulte, Rainer, and John Biguenet, eds. *The Craft of Translation.* Chicago: U of Chicago P, 1999.

———. *Theories of Translation: An Anthology of Essays from Dryden to Derrida.* Chicago: U of Chicago P, 1992.

Schwartz, Fernando. *La internacionalización de la guerra civil española: Julio de 1936–marzo de 1937.* Epilogue by Edward Malefakis. Barcelona: Planeta, 1999.

Sciolino, Elaine, and Emma Daly. "Spaniards at Last Confront the Ghost of Franco." *New York Times* 11 Nov. 2002, late ed.: A3.

Scott, Joan Wallach. *Gender and the Politics of History.* New York: Columbia UP, 1988.

Scott-Ellis, Priscilla. *The Chances of Death: A Diary of the Spanish Civil War.* Ed. Raymond Carr. Wilby: Russell, 1995.

Sección Femenina de FET y de las JONS. *Formación familiar y social.* Madrid: FET, 1943.

Seidman, Michael. *Republic of Egos: A Social History of the Spanish Civil War.* Madison: U of Wisconsin P, 2002.

Sender, Ramón J. *Los cinco libros de Ariadna.* New York: Ibérica, 1957.

———. *Contraataque.* Salamanca: Almar, 1978. Trans. as *Counter-attack in Spain.* Trans. Peter Chalmers Mitchell. Boston: Houghton, 1937. Trans. as *The War in Spain.* Trans. Mitchell. London: Faber, 1937.

———. *Mosén Millán.* Ed. Robert M. Duncan. Lexington: Heath, 1964.

———. *Réquiem por un campesino español.* Buenos Aires: Proyección, 1961. Barcelona: Destino, 1974. Trans. as *Requiem for a Spanish Peasant.* Trans. Elinor Randall. New York: Las Américas; Cypress, 1960. Orig. *Mosén Millán* (1953).

———. *El rey y la reina.* Buenos Aires: Jackson, 1948. Trans. as *The King and the Queen.* Trans. Mary Low. New York: Grosset, 1968.

———. *Siete domingos rojos.* 1932. Rev. ed. Buenos Aires: Proyección, 1970. Trans. as *Seven Red Sundays.* Trans. Peter Chalmers Mitchell. Chicago: Dee, 1990.

Sender Barayón, Ramón. *A Death in Zamora.* Albuquerque: U of New Mexico P, 1989.

Serna, Víctor de la. "Elogio de la alegre retaguardia." Mainer 153–56.

Serrano, Carlos. *L'enjeu espagnol: Le PCF et la guerre d'Espagne.* Paris: Messidor, 1987.

———. "El pueblo en armas: Robert Capa y la guerra de España." *Fotografías de Robert Capa sobre la guerra civil española: Colección del Ministerio de Asuntos Exteriores.* Madrid: El Viso, 1990. 15–23.

Serrano, Secundino. *Maquis: Historia de la guerrilla antifranquista.* Madrid: Temas de Hoy, 2001.

Serrano Poncela, Segundo. *La viña de Nabot.* 1979. Barcelona: Plaza y Janés, 1984.

Shain, Yossi. *The Frontier of Loyalty: Political Exiles in the Age of the Nation-State.* Middletown: Wesleyan UP, 1989.

Sheenan, Vincent. *Not Peace but Sword.* New York: Doubleday, 1939.

Sheridan, Alan. *André Gide: A Life in the Present.* London: Hamish Hamilton, 1998.

Shklar, Judith N. *Political Thought and Political Thinkers.* Ed. Stanley Hoffmann. Chicago: U of Chicago P, 1998.

Shubert, Adrian. *A Social History of Modern Spain.* London: Routledge, 1992.

Silkin, Jon, ed. *The Penguin Book of First World War Poetry.* 2nd ed. Harmondsworth: Penguin, 1981.

Silva, Emilio, and Santiago Macías. *Las fosas de Franco: Los republicanos que el dictador dejó en la cuneta.* Barcelona: Círculo de Lectores, 2003.

Sim [José Luis Rey Vila]. *Estampas de la revolución española 19 julio de 1936.* Barcelona: CNT/FAI, 1936.

Sinaia: Diario de la primera expedición de republicanos españoles a México. 1939. Facsim. ed. Alcalá: U de Alcalá, 1999.

Sinclair, Gail D. "Revisiting the Code: Female Foundations and 'The Undiscovered Country' in *For Whom the Bell Tolls.*" *Hemingway and Women: Female Critics and the Female Voice.* Ed. Lawrence R. Broer and Gloria Holland. Tuscaloosa: U of Alabama P, 2002. 93–108.

Sinclair, Upton. *No Pasarán! (They Shall Not Pass): A Story of the Battle of Madrid.* Pasadena, 1937. Pub. by the author.

Skelton, Robin, ed. *Poetry of the Thirties.* Harmondsworth: Penguin, 1964.

Skoutelsky, Rémi. *L'espoir guidait leurs pas: Les volontaires français dans les Brigades Internationales, 1936–1939.* Paris: Grasset, 1998.

———. *Novedad en el frente: Las brigadas internacionales en la guerra civil.* Madrid: Temas de Hoy, 2006.

Smith, Paul Julian. "Between Metaphysics and Scientism: Rehistoricizing Víctor Erice." *Spanish Cinema: The Auteurist Tradition.* Ed. Peter W. Evans. Oxford: Oxford UP, 1999. 93–114. Rpt. in *The Moderns: Time, Space, and Subjectivity in Contemporary Spanish Culture.* Oxford: Oxford UP, 2000. 23–41.

Sobejano, Gonzalo. "The Testimonial Novel and the Novel of Memory." *The Cambridge Companion to the Spanish Novel.* Ed. Harriet Turner and Adelaida López de Martínez. Cambridge: Cambridge UP, 2003. 172–92.

Soler, Bartolomé. *Los muertos no se cuentan.* Barcelona: Juventud, 1960.

Sontag, Susan. *On Photography.* New York: Farrar, 1977.

———. *Regarding the Pain of Others.* New York: Farrar, 2003.

Sopeña Monsalve, Andrés. *El florido pensil: Memoria de la escuela nacionalcatólica.* Barcelona: Crítica, 1997.

Sòria, Josep Maria. "Anatomía del 'gulag' franquista." *La Vanguardia Digital* 23 Oct. 2002. <http://www.lavanguardia.es/web/20021023/5544093.html>.

———. "Un inquisidor para el siglo XX." *Vanguardia Digital* 27 Oct. 2002. <http://www.lavanguardia.es/Vanguardia/Publica?COMPID=59773528and ID_PAGINA=788andID_ FORMATO=1andPARTICION=91>.

Sotelo, Ignacio. "Fascismo y memoria histórica." *El país* 12 Feb. 1986: 11.

Souchy, Agustín. *The Tragic Week in May.* Barcelona: Oficina de Información Exterior de la CNT y FAI, 1937.

Southworth, Herbert. *Guernica! Guernica! A Study of Journalism, Diplomacy, Propaganda, and History.* Berkeley: U of California P, 1977.

———. *El mito de la cruzada de Franco.* Paris: Ruedo Ibérico, 1963.

"Soviet Russia's Aid to Red Spain." *Spain* 1 May 1938: 7.

Spain in My Heart: Songs of the Spanish Civil War. Appleseed, 2003.

The Spanish Civil War Collection: A Guide to the Microfilm Collection. Woodbridge: Research, 1987. 57 reels.

"Spanish Propaganda Pictures Appeal to the World to Take Sides in the Conflict." *Life* 25 Oct. 1937: 51–54.

"Spain Protects Her Heritage." *Spain at War* 3 (1938): 98–105.

Spender, Stephen. *Collected Poems, 1928–53.* London: Faber, 1955.

———. "Guernica." *New Statesman and Nation* 15 Oct. 1938: n.p. Cunningham, *Spanish Front* 220–22.

———. *The Still Centre.* London: Faber, 1939.

Spender, Stephen, and John Lehmann, eds. *Poems for Spain.* London: Hogarth, 1939.

Sperber, Murray A., ed. *And I Remember Spain: A Spanish Civil War Anthology.* London: Hart Davis, 1974; New York: Collier, 1974.

Spicer, Jack. *After Lorca: The Collected Books of Jack Spicer.* Ed. Robin Blaser. Los Angeles: Black Sparrow, 1975.

Spilka, Mark. *Hemingway's Quarrel with Androgyny.* Lincoln: U of Nebraska P, 1990.

Squiers, Carol. "Capa Is Cleared: A Famed Photo Is Proven Authentic." *American Photo* May-June 1998: 18–20.

Stallworthy, Jon. *Wilfred Owen: A Biography.* Oxford: Oxford UP, 1974.

Stanton, Edward F. *Hemingway and Spain: A Pursuit.* Seattle: U of Washington P, 1989.

Steele, Jonathan. Rev. of *Land and Freedom,* dir. Ken Loach. *Guardian* 30 Sept. 1995, sec. C2.

Stein, Louis. *Beyond Death and Exile: The Spanish Republicans in France, 1939–1955.* Cambridge: Harvard UP, 1979.

Stewart, Abigail J. "Toward a Feminist Strategy for Studying Women's Lives." *Women Creating Lives: Identities, Resilience, and Resistance.* Ed. Carol E. Franz and Stewart. Boulder: Westview, 1994. 11–35.

St. Martin, Hardie. "Goat Songs: The European Roots." Rev. of *The Selected Poems of Miguel Hernández,* by Miguel Hernández and trans. Ted Genoways. *American Book Review* Nov.-Dec. 2002: 1, 4.

Story, Jonathan. "Spain's External Relations Redefined, 1975–89." Gillespie, Rodrigo, and Story 30–50.

Stradling, Robert A. *History and Legend: Writing the International Brigades.* Cardiff: U of Wales P, 2003.

———. *The Irish and the Spanish Civil War, 1936–39.* Manchester: Mandolin, 1999.

Strobl, Ingrid. *Partisanas.* Barcelona: Virus, 1996.

Strong, Anna Louise. *Spain in Arms, 1937.* New York: Holt, 1937.

Sturken, Marita. *Tangled Memories: The Vietnam War, the AIDS Epidemic, and the Politics of Remembering.* Berkeley: U of California P, 1997.

Suárez, Luis. *España comienza en los Pirineos.* Mexico City: ICD, 1944.

Sueiro, Daniel. *El Valle de los Caídos: Los secretos de la cripta franquista.* 2nd rev. ed. Barcelona: Argos Vergara, 1983.

Suleiman, Susan Rubin. "Committed Painting." *A New History of French Literature.* Ed. Denis Hollier. Cambridge: Harvard UP, 1989. 935–42.

Taylor, A. J. P. "Spain and the Axis." *Europe: Grandeur and Decline.* Harmondsworth: Penguin, 1967. 224–28.

"Teacher-Training Manual." *Survivors: Testimonies of the Holocaust.* Survivors of the Shoah Visual History Foundation. 2001.

Tejera, Nivaria. *El barranco.* [Santa Clara]: U Central de Las Villas, Departamento de Relaciones Culturales, 1959.

———. "Children Can Wait." Trans. Carol Maier. Bush and Dillman 219–35.

Teweleit, Horst Lothar, ed. *No pasarán! Romanzen aus dem Spanienkrieg.* Berlin: Rütten, 1986.

Thibaud, Cécile. "L'Espagne exhume son passé." *L'express international* 20–26 Nov. 2003: 24–25.

Thomas, Frank. *Brother against Brother: Experiences of a British Volunteer in the Spanish Civil War.* Ed. Robert Stradling. Phoenix Mill: Sutton, 1998.

Thomas, Gareth. *The Novel of the Spanish Civil War, 1936–1975.* Cambridge: Cambridge UP, 1990.

Thomas, Hugh. Rev. of *Land and Freedom*, dir. Ken Loach. *Daily Telegraph* 29 Sept. 1995, sec. C3.

———. *The Spanish Civil War*. 3rd ed. Harmondsworth: Penguin, 1986. New York: Modern Lib., 2001. London: Penguin, 2003. Trans. as *La guerra civil española*. Paris: Ruedo Ibérico, 1961.

Thomas, Joan Maria. *Lo que fue la Falange*. Barcelona: Plaza y Janés, 1999.

Thompson, Paul. *The Voice of the Past: Oral History*. 2nd ed. Oxford: Oxford UP, 1988.

Timmers, Margaret. *The Power of the Poster*. London: V and A, 1998.

Tisa, John, ed. *The Palette and the Flame: Posters of the Spanish Civil War*. New York: Intl., 1979.

———. *Recalling the Good Fight: An Autobiography of the Spanish Civil War*. South Hadley: Bergin, 1985.

"Todavía tendremos 'Valle de los Caídos' para este verano." <http://www.geocities.com/SoHo/Café/3627/caidos.htm-6k->.

Tornero, José Manuel. *Santa Cruz del Valle de los Caídos*. 3rd ed. León: Everest, 2000.

Torrente Ballester, Gonzalo. "Gerineldo." Torrente Ballester, Ifigenia *y otros cuentos* 152–73.

———. *El golpe de estado de Guadalupe Limón*. Madrid: Nueva Época, 1946.

———. *Ifigenia*. Madrid: Alfonso Aguado, 1949. Torrente Ballester, Ifigenia *y otros cuentos* 11–117.

———. Ifigenia *y otros cuentos*. Barcelona: Destino, 1987.

———. *Javier Mariño: Historia de una conversión*. Madrid: Nacional, 1943. Barcelona: Seix Barral, 1985.

———. *La princesa durmiente va a la escuela*. Barcelona: Plaza y Janés, 1983.

———. *El retorno de Ulises*. Madrid: Nacional, 1946.

———. *La Saga / fuga de J. B.* Barcelona: Destino, 1972.

Torres, Rafael. *Los esclavos de Franco*. Pref. Mirta Núñez Díaz-Balart. Madrid: Oberón, 2000.

Trapiello, Andrés. *Las armas y las letras: Literatura y guerra civil, 1936–1939*. Barcelona: Península, 2002.

Trautloft, Hannes. *Als Jagdflieger in Spanien: Aus dem Tagebuch eines deutschen Legionärs*. Berlin: Pauck, 1940.

"El Tribunal Supremo dicta que TV-3 no atentó contra el honor en 'Sumaríssim.' " *El país* 18 Mar. 1999: 15.

Trotsky, Leon. *The Spanish Revolution, 1931–39*. New York: Pathfinder, 1973.

Tuchman, Phyllis. "Guernica and *Guernica*." *Artforum* Apr. 1983: 44–51.

Tuñón de Lara, Manuel, et al. *La guerra civil española 50 años después*. Barcelona: Labor, 1986.

Tusell, Javier. *Las elecciones del Frente Popular*. 2 vols. Madrid: Cuadernos para el Diálogo, Edicusa, 1971.

Ucelay-Da Cal, Enric. "Catalan Nationalism." Graham and Labanyi 144–51.

———. "Ideas preconcebidas y estereotipos en las interpretaciones de la Guerra Civil española: El dorso de la solidaridad." *Historia Social* 6 (1990): 23–43.

———. "Llegar a capital: Rango urbano, rivalidades interurbanas y la imaginación nacionalista en la España del siglo XX." *Ideologías y movimientos políticos*. Ed.

Antonio Morales Moya. Madrid: España Nuevo Milenio, 2001. 221–63. <http://www.fundaciocampalans.com>.

———. "Lost Causes as a Historical Typology of Reaction: A Spanish Perspective, from Jacobites to Neofascists and Spanish Republicans." *Journal of Spanish Cultural Studies* 5.2 (2004): 145–64.

———. "The Nationalisms of the Periphery: Culture and Politics in the Construction of National Identity." Graham and Labanyi 32–39.

———. "Prefigurazione e storia: La guerra civile spagnola del 1936–39 come riassunto del passato." *Guerre fratricida: Le guerre civili in età contemporanea*. Ed. Gabriele Ranzato. Torino: Bollati Boringhieri, 1994. 193–220.

Ugarte, Michael. "Mercè the Great: *La plaça del Diamant* and the Canon." *ADFL Bulletin* 33.1 (2001): 42–44.

———. *Shifting Ground: Spanish Civil War Exile Literature*. Durham: Duke UP, 1989.

Ugarte Tellería, Javier. *La nueva Covadonga insurgente: Orígenes sociales de la sublevación de 1936 en Navarra y el País Vasco*. Madrid: Biblioteca Nueva, 1998.

Uhse, Bodo. *Leutnant Bertram*. Mexico City: El Libro Libre, 1943.

Umbral, Francisco. *Leyenda del César visionario*. Barcelona: Seix Barral, 1991.

Ureña Portero, Gabriel. "La pintura mural y la ilustración como panacea de la nueva sociedad y sus mitos." Bonet Correa, *Arte* 113–57.

Usandizaga, Aránzazu, ed. *Ve y cuenta lo que pasó en España: Mujeres extranjeras en la guerra civil: Una antología*. Barcelona: Planeta, 2000.

Valis, Noël. "Nostalgia and Exile." *Journal of Spanish Cultural Studies* 1.2 (2000): 117–33.

Valleau, Marjorie A. *The Spanish Civil War in American and European Films*. Ann Arbor: UMI Research, 1982.

Vallejo, César. *Battles in Spain: Five Unpublished Poems by César Vallejo: Sparrow 65*. Trans. Clayton Eshleman and José Rubia Barcia. Santa Barbara: Black Sparrow, 1978.

———. *España, aparta de mí este cáliz*. Mexico City: Séneca, 1940. Ed. Felipe D. Obarrio. Madrid: De la Torre, 1992. Trans. as *Spain, Take This Cup from Me*. Trans. Clayton Eshleman and José Rubia Barcia. New York: Grove, 1974.

———. *Obra poética*. Madrid: Colección Archivos, 1996.

Vallejo Nágera, Antonio. *Eugenesia de la hispanidad y regeneración de la raza*. Burgos: Española, 1937.

Vallejo Nágera, Antonio, and Eduardo Martínez. "Psiquismo del fanatismo marxista: Investigaciones psicológicas en marxistas femeninas delincuentes." *Revista española de la medicina y cirugía de guerra* 9 (1939): 398–413.

Van Alphen, Ernst. "Symptoms of Discursivity: Experience, Memory, and Trauma." *Acts of Memory: Cultural Recall in the Present*. Ed. Mieke Bal, Jonathan Crewe, and Leo Spitzer. Hanover: UP of New England, 1999. 24–38.

Vaughan, Dai. *For Documentary*. Berkeley: U of California P, 1999.

Veeser, H. Aram, ed. *The New Historicism*. New York: Routledge, 1989.

Venuti, Lawrence. "The Pedagogy of Literature." *The Scandals of Translation*. New York: Routledge, 1998. 88–105.

————, ed. *Rethinking Translation: Discourse, Subjectivity, Ideology*. New York: Routledge, 1992.

————. "Translation, Community, Utopia." Venuti, *Translation Studies* 468–88.

————, ed. *The Translation Studies Reader*. London: Routledge, 2000.

Vernon, Kathleen M. "Gritos de la pared / Shouts from the Wall." Vernon, *Spanish Civil War* 132–47.

————. "*La politique des auteurs*: Narrative Point of View in *Pascual Duarte*, Novel, and Film." *Hispania* 72.1 (1989): 87–96.

————. "Re-viewing the Spanish Civil War: Franco's Film '*Raza*.'" *Film and History* 16.2 (1986): 26–34.

————, ed. *The Spanish Civil War and the Visual Arts*. Ithaca: Center for Intl. Studies; Cornell UP, 1990.

————. "War and Historical Memory." King Juan Carlos I Center, New York U. 18 Nov. 2002.

Vicente Hernando, César de, ed. *Poesía de la guerra civil española, 1936–1939*. Madrid: Akal, 1994.

Vidal, Martine. Rev. of *Land and Freedom*, dir. Ken Loach. *New Politics* 6.1 (1996): 4–6.

Villén, Jorge, ed. *Antología poética del alzamiento, 1936–1939*. Cádiz: Establecimientos Cerón y Librería Cervantes, 1939.

Vincent, Mary. *Catholicism in the Second Spanish Republic: Religion and Politics in Salamanca, 1930–1936*. Oxford: Oxford UP, 1996.

————. "The Martyrs and the Saints: Masculinity and the Construction of the Francoist Crusade." *History Workshop Journal* 47 (1999): 68–98. <www.broadartfoundation.org/collection/salle.html>.

Vinyes, Ricard. *Irredentas: Las presas políticas y sus hijos en las cárceles de Franco*. Madrid: Temas de Hoy, 2002.

Vinyes, Ricard, Montse Armengou, and Ricard Belis. *Los niños perdidos del franquismo*. Barcelona: Plaza y Janés; Televisió de Catalunya, 2002.

Vitzthum, Carlta, and John Carreyrou. "Among Spaniards, Al Qaeda Attacks Awaken Old Feuds." *Wall Street Journal* 26 Mar. 2004: A1+.

Voces y textos de la Guerra Civil Española / Voices and Texts of the Spanish Civil War. Issue of *Letras Peninsulares* 11.1 (1998).

Voros, Sandor. *American Commissar*. Philadelphia: Chilton, 1961.

Vulpe, Nicola. "This Issue Is Not Ended: Canadian Poetry and the Spanish Civil War." *Canadian Literature* 142–43 (1994): 157–81.

Vulpe, Nicola, and Maha Albari, eds. *Sealed in Struggle: Canadian Poetry and the Spanish Civil War: An Anthology*. Tenerife: Center for Canadian Studies, U de La Laguna, 1995.

Walker, Ian. *City Gorged with Dreams: Surrealism and Documentary Photography in Interwar Paris*. Manchester: Manchester UP, 2002.

Walters, Walter. "The Hammer and the Sickle at Work: Notes on the Masterpieces Destroyed by the Reds." *Spain* 15 Nov. 1937: 12–13.

"The War and the People." *Spain at War* 1 (1938): 4–7.

Warren, Rosanna, ed. *The Art of Translation: Voices from the Field*. Boston: Northeastern UP, 1989.

Watkins, K. W. *Britain Divided: The Effect of the Spanish Civil War on British Political Opinion.* London: Nelson, 1963.

Watson, William Branch. "Hemingway's Attacks on the Soviets and the Communists in *For Whom the Bell Tolls.*" *North Dakota Quarterly* 60.2 (1992): 103–18.

Weber, Eugen. *The Hollow Years: France in the 1930s.* New York: Norton, 1994.

Weintraub, Stanley. *The Last Great Cause: The Intellectuals and the Spanish Civil War.* London: Allen, 1968.

Werlock, Abby H. P. "'With a Man There Is a Difference': The Rejection of Female Mentoring in Hemingway's *For Whom the Bell Tolls.*" *The Erotics of Instruction.* Ed. Regina Barreca and Deborah Denenholz Morse. Hanover: UP of New England, 1997. 127–46.

Whealey, Robert H. *Hitler and Spain: The Nazi Role in the Spanish Civil War, 1936–1939.* Lexington: UP of Kentucky, 1989.

Whelan, Richard. *Robert Capa: A Biography.* New York: Knopf, 1985.

———, ed. *Robert Capa: The Definitive Collection.* London: Phaidon, 2001.

———. "Robert Capa's *Falling Soldier*: A Detective Story." *Aperture* 166 (2002): 48–55.

Whiston, James. *Antonio Machado's Writings and the Spanish Civil War.* Liverpool: Liverpool UP, 1996.

White, Hayden. "The Historical Text as Literary Artifact." *Tropics* 81–99.

———. *Metahistory: The Historical Imagination in Nineteenth-Century Europe.* Baltimore: Johns Hopkins UP, 1973.

———. *Tropics of Discourse: Essays in Cultural Criticism.* Baltimore: Johns Hopkins UP, 1978.

White, Steven. "Translation and Teaching: The Dangers of Representing Latin America for Students in the United States." *Voice-Overs: Translation and Latin American Literature.* Ed. Daniel Balderston and Marcy Schwartz. Albany: State U of New York P, 2002. 235–44.

Wilkinson, James D. "Truth and Delusion: European Intellectuals in Search of the Spanish Civil War." *Salmagundi* 76–77 (1987–88): 3–52.

Williams, Raymond. *Keywords.* Rev. ed. New York: Oxford UP, 1983.

Willmott, Hedley Paul. *The Great Crusade: A New Complete History of the Second World War.* London: Joseph, 1989.

Wilson, Francesca. *In the Margins of Chaos: Recollections of Relief Work in and between Three Wars.* London: Murray, 1944.

Wolff, Milton. *Another Hill: An Autobiographical Novel.* Introd. Cary Nelson. Urbana: U of Illinois P, 1994.

———. "Hemingway's 'On the American Dead in Spain.'" C. Nelson, *Remembering* 7–17.

Wolton, Dominique. *Éloge du grand public: Une théorie critique de la télévision.* Paris: Flammarion, 1990.

Woolman, David S. *Rebels in the Rif: Abd el Krim and the Rif Rebellion.* Stanford: Stanford UP, 1968.

Woolsey, Gamel. *Malaga Burning: An American Woman's Eyewitness Account of the Spanish Civil War.* Introd. Zalin Grant. Paris: Pythia, 1998. Also known as *Death's Other Kingdom.* London: Longman's, 1939.

The Working Class Movement Library. Sept. 2005. 22 Nov. 2005 <www.wcml. org.uk>.

Wright, Patrick. *On Living in an Old Country: The National Past in Contemporary Britain*. London: Verso, 1985.

Yates, James. *Mississippi to Madrid: Memoir of a Black American in the Abraham Lincoln Brigade*. Seattle: Open Hand, 1989.

Young, James E. *At Memory's Edge: After-images of the Holocaust in Contemporary Art and Architecture*. New Haven: Yale UP, 2000.

Zafra, Enrique, Rosalía Crego, and Carmen Heredia. *Los niños españoles evacuados a la URSS*. Madrid: Torre, 1989.

Zapatero, Virgilio. "El legado." *Exilio*. Madrid: Fundación Pablo Iglesias, 2002.

Films, TV, Videos

Los amantes del círculo polar / Lovers of the Arctic Circle. Dir. Julio Medem. Spain: Sogetel; Le Studio Canal, 1998.

A mí la legión. Dir. Juan de Orduña. Spain: CIFESA, 1942.

The Angel Wore Red. Dir. Nunnally Johnson. United States and Italy: MGM, 1960.

L'arbre de Guernica / L'albero di Guernica / The Tree of Guernica. Dir. Fernando Arrabal. France and Italy: Babylone, 1975.

Art in the Struggle for Freedom: The Posters, Poetry, and Music of the Spanish Civil War. Dir. Abe Osheroff. United States: A. Osheroff, 2000.

¡Ay, Carmela! Dir. Carlos Saura. Spain: Iberoamericana Films Intl.; Italy: Ellepi, 1990.

Behold a Pale Horse. Dir. Fred Zinnemann. United States: Columbia, Tristar, 1964.

Belle Epoque. Dir. Fernando Trueba. Spain: Lola, 1992.

Las bicicletas son para el verano. Dir. Jaime Chávarri. Spain: In-cine, Jet, 1983.

Bilbao para España. Dir. Fernando Delgado. Spain: CIFESA, 1937.

Blockade. Dir. William Dieterle. United States: United Artists, 1938.

The Canadians / Los Canadienses. Dir. Laszlo Gefin and Albert Kish. Canada: Natl. Film Board of Canada, 1975.

Canciones para después de una guerra. Dir. Basilio Martín Patino. Spain: Turner, 1971, 1976.

Casablanca. Dir. Michael Curtis. United States: Warner Brothers, 1942.

Casas Viejas. Dir. José L. López del Río. Spain: Andalusí-Cine, 1983.

El caudillo. Dir. Basilio Martín Patino. Spain: Fotofilm, 1977.

La caza / The Hunt. Dir. Carlos Saura. Spain: Elías Quejereta, 1965.

La ciudad universitaria. Dir. Edgar Neville. Spain: Departamento Nacional de Cinematografía, 1938.

El comboi dels 927. Dir. Montse Armengou and Ricard Belis. Spain: Televisió de Catalunya, 2004.

Confidential Agent. Dir. Herman Shumlin. United States: Warner Brothers, 1945.

Corazón del bosque. Dir. Manuel Gutiérrez Aragón. Spain: Arandano, 1979.

Cría cuervos. Dir. Carlos Saura. Spain: Elías Quejereta, 1975.

Death in El Valle. Dir. C. M. Hardt. United Kingdom: CM, Channel Four Television, 1996.

De toda la vida / All Our Lives. Dir. Carol Mazer and Lisa Berger. Spain and United States: Point of View, 1986.

The Disappearance of García Lorca. Dir. Marcos Zurinaga. United States: Miramar, 1997. Also known as *Death in Granada*.

Dragón rapide. Dir. Jaime Camino. Spain and Italy: Tibidabo, 1986.

Dreams and Nightmares. Dir. Abe Osheroff. United States: A. Osheroff, 1974.

Dulces horas. Dir. Carlos Saura. Spain: Elías Quejereta, 1982.

Durruti en la revolución española. Dir. Paco Ríos. Spain: Fundación Anselmo Lorenzo de Madrid, 1998.

En el balcón vacío. Dir. José Miguel (Jomi) García Ascot. Mexico: Ascot, Torre, 1962.

España, otra vez. Dir. Jaime Camino. Spain: Pandora Filmproduktion, 1969.

España heroica. Dir. Joaquín Reig, Paul Laven, and Fritz C. Mauch. Spain and Germany: Falange Española Tradicionalista y de las Jons, Hispano Filmproduktion, 1937. German title: *Helden in Spanien*.

España leal en armas. Dir. Jean-Paul Le Chanois. Prod. Luis Buñuel. Spain and France: Susecretaría de Propaganda del Gobierno de la República, 1937. Also known as *España 36*. French title: *Espagne 36*.

El espinazo del diablo / The Devil's Backbone. Dir. Guillermo del Toro. Spain and Mexico: El Deseo, Tequila Gang and Anhelo Producciones, 2002.

El espíritu de la colmena / The Spirit of the Beehive. Dir. Víctor Erice. Spain: Elías Querejeta, 1973.

Espíritu de una raza. Dir. José Luis Sáenz de Heredia. Spain: Cancillería del Consejo de la Hispanidad Production, 1950.

L'espoir / Sierra de Teruel. Dir. André Malraux. France: Édouard Corniglion-Moliner, 1938.

Exilio: El exilio republicano español, 1939–1978. Dir. Pedro Carvajal. Spain: Planeta D, 2002.

Extranjeros de sí mismos. Dir. Javier Rioyo and José Luis López Linares. Spain: Cero en Conducta, 2000.

The Fallen Sparrow. Dir. Richard Wallace. United States: RKO, 1943.

La fiel infantería. Dir. Pedro Lazaga. Spain: Ágata, 1959.

Five Cartridges / Fünf Patronenhülsen. Dir. Frank Beyer. Germany: Icestorm Intl., 1960.

Forever Activists: Stories from the Veterans of the Abraham Lincoln Brigade. Dir. Judith Montell. United States: Kino Intl., 1990.

For Whom the Bell Tolls. Dir. Sam Wood. United States: Paramount, 1943.

Les fosses del silenci. Dir. Montse Armengou and Ricard Belis. Spain: Televisió de Catalunya, 2003.

Gernika en flames. Dir. Francesc Ribera Raichs. Spain: Gamma, 1979.

Gernika Lives. Dir. Begonya Plaza. Spain: Izar, 1989.

The Good Fight: The Abraham Lincoln Brigade in the Spanish Civil War. Dir. Noel Buckner, Mary Dore, and Sam Sills. United States: ALBA Film Project, 1984.

Guernica. Dir. Alain Resnais and Robert Hessens. France: Panthéon, 1950.

La guerra cotidiana. Dir. Daniel Serra and Jaume Serra. Spain: Sagrera TV, 2001.

La guerre est finie. Dir. Alain Resnais. France and Sweden: Sofracima, 1966.

La guerrilla de la memoria. Dir. Javier Corcuera. Spain: Oria, 2002.

El hermano bastardo de Dios. Dir. Benito Rabal. Spain: Almadraba Producciones, 1986.

Las Hurdes: Land without Bread. Dir. Luis Buñuel. Spain: Ramón Acín, 1932.

In Memoriam. Dir. Dolors Genovès and Llorenç Soler. Spain: Televisió de Catalunya, 1986.

Into the Fire: American Women in the Spanish Civil War. Dir. Julia Newman. United States: Exemplary, 2002.

El jardín de las delicias. Dir. Carlos Saura. Spain: Elías Querejeta, 1970.

Land and Freedom: A Story from the Spanish Revolution. Dir. Ken Loach. United Kingdom and Spain: Parallax, Messidor, 1995.

El lápiz del carpintero. Dir. Antón Reixa. Spain: Sogecine, Morena, 2003.

Las largas vacaciones del 36. Dir. Jaime Camino. Spain: J. F. Producciones Cinematográficas, 1976.

The Last Train from Madrid. Dir. James Hogan. United States: Paramount, 1937.

La lengua de las mariposas. Dir. José Luis Cuerda. Spain: Sogetel, 1999.

Libertarias. Dir. Vicente Aranda. Spain: Academy, 1995.

Luna de lobos. Dir. Julio Sánchez Valdés. Spain: Brezal, 1987.

Mambrú se fue a la guerra. Dir. Fernando Fernán Gómez. Spain: Altair Producciones Filmográficas, 1986.

Els maquis: La guerra silenciada. Dir. Enric Calpena. Spain: Televisió de Catalunya and Mercuri SGP, 2001.

Mourir à Madrid / To Die in Madrid. Dir. Frédéric Rossif. France: Nicole Stéphane, 1962. Spanish title: *Morir en Madrid.*

Mujeres del 36. Dir. Ana Martínez. Spain: ARTE-TVE, 1999.

Els nens perduts del franquisme. Dir. Monserrat Armengou and Ricard Belis. Spain: Televisió de Catalunya, 2002. In Spanish: *Los niños perdidos del franquismo.*

La niña de tus ojos. Dir. Fernando Trueba. Spain: Lola, 1998.

Los niños de Rusia. Dir. Jaime Camino. Spain: Nirvana, Wanda Vision, 2002.

Operació Nikolai. Dir. Dolors Genovès and Ricard Belis. Spain: Televisió de Catalunya, 1992.

Pablo Picasso's Guernica. Discovery of Art Ser. United States: Kultur Video, DOM Multimedia, 1999.

Pascual Duarte. Dir. Ricardo Franco. Spain: Elías Querejeta, 1975.

La plaza del Diamante. Dir. Francesc Betriu. Spain: Figaró, 1982.

¿Por qué perdimos la guerra? Dir. Diego Santillán and Francisco Galindo. Spain: Francisco Galindo Cine, 1978.

La prima Angélica. Dir. Carlos Saura. Spain: Elías Querejeta, 1974.

Puig Antich: Les últimes hores. Dir. Francesc Escribano. Spain: Televisió de Catalunya, 1989.

Raza. Dir. José Luis Sáenz de Heredia. Spain: Cancillería del Consejo de la Hispanidad Production, 1941.

Reportaje del movimiento revolucionario en Barcelona. Dir. Mateo Santos. Spain: CNT-FAI (Oficina de Información y Propaganda), 1936.

Réquiem por un campesino español. Dir. Francesc Betriu. Spain: Nemo, 1985.

El rey y la reina. Dir. José Antonio Páramo. Spain and Italy: TVE, 1985.

Les routes du sud / Roads to the South. Dir. Joseph Losey. France and Spain: Tinacra, 1978.

Silencio roto. Dir. Montxo Armendáriz. Spain: Oria, 2001.

Soldados de Salamina. Dir. David Trueba. Spain: Lola, 2003.

Spain 1936: Prelude to Tragedy. Dir. Jean-Claude Dassier and Gilles Delannoy. France: Jean-Paul Thomas, 1986.

The Spanish Civil War. United Kingdom: Granada Television Intl., 1987. Spanish title: *La guerra civil española*.

The Spanish Civil War: Blood and Ink. Spain: Tranquilo Producciones, 2002.

The Spanish Civil War: The Story of a Country at War. Dir. Mike Leighton. United Kingdom: Cromwell, 1998. Also known as *Brother against Brother: The Spanish Civil War*.

The Spanish Earth. Dir. Joris Ivens. Commentary by Ernest Hemingway. United States and the Netherlands: Contemporary Historians Inc., 1937. Spanish title: *Tierra española*.

Spanish Writers in Exile. Spain: Tranquilo Producciones, 2002.

Sumaríssim 477. Dir. Dolors Genovès and Lluís Montserrat. Spain: Televisió de Catalunya, 1994.

Els últims morts de Franco. Dir. Joan Salvat and Lluís Montserrat. Spain: Televisió de Catalunya, 2000.

Vacas. Dir. Julio Medem. Spain: Sogetel, 1991.

El Valle de los Caídos. Spain: Video Affín, Atrio, 2000.

La vaquilla. Dir. Luis García Berlanga. Spain: In-cine, Jet, 1985.

Veus ofegades: Cartes d'un exili a França. Dir. Montserrat Besses. Spain: Televisió de Catalunya, 2002.

El viaje de Carol / Carol's Journey. Dir. Imanol Uribe. Spain: Aiete, Ariane, 2002.

La vieja memoria. Dir. Jaime Camino. Spain: Profilmes, 1978.

Ya viene el cortejo. Dir. Carlos Arévalo. Spain: CIFESA, Juan de Orduña, 1939.

"You Are History, You Are Legend": The Legacy of the International Brigades. Dir. Judith Montell. United States: Kino Intl., 1997.

Index

Modern Language Association of America
Options for Teaching
Joseph Gibaldi, series editor

Teaching Representations of the Spanish Civil War. Ed. Noël Valis. 2007.

Teaching the Representation of the Holocaust. Ed. Marianne Hirsch and Irene Kacandes. 2004.

Teaching Tudor and Stuart Women Writers. Ed. Susanne Woods and Margaret P. Hannay. 2000.

Teaching Literature and Medicine. Ed. Anne Hunsaker Hawkins and Marilyn Chandler McEntyre. 1999.

Teaching Shakespeare through Performance. Ed. Milla Cozart Riggio. 1999.

Teaching the Literatures of Early America. Ed. Carla Mulford. 1999.

Teaching Oral Traditions. Ed. John Miles Foley. 1998.

Teaching Contemporary Theory to Undergraduates. Ed. Dianne F. Sadoff and William E. Cain. 1994.

Teaching Children's Literature: Issues, Pedagogy, Resources. Ed. Glenn Edward Sadler. 1992.

Teaching Literature and Other Arts. Ed. Jean-Pierre Barricelli, Joseph Gibaldi, and Estella Lauter. 1990.

New Methods in College Writing Programs: Theories in Practice. Ed. Paul Connolly and Teresa Vilardi. 1986.

School-College Collaborative Programs in English. Ed. Ron Fortune. 1986.

Teaching Environmental Literature: Materials, Methods, Resources. Ed. Frederick O. Waage. 1985.

Part-Time Academic Employment in the Humanities: A Sourcebook for Just Policy. Ed. Elizabeth M. Wallace. 1984.

Film Study in the Undergraduate Curriculum. Ed. Barry K. Grant. 1983.

The Teaching Apprentice Program in Language and Literature. Ed. Joseph Gibaldi and James V. Mirollo. 1981.

Options for Undergraduate Language Programs: Four-Year and Two-Year Colleges. Ed. Renate A. Schulz. 1979.

Options for the Teaching of English: Freshman Composition. Ed. Jasper P. Neel. 1978.

Options for the Teaching of English: The Undergraduate Curriculum. Ed. Elizabeth Wooten Cowan. 1975.